THE
PLANT
WORLD

THE
PLANT
WORLD

Fifth Edition

Harry J. Fuller

Zane B. Carothers

Willard W. Payne

Margaret K. Balbach

New York   Chicago   San Francisco
Atlanta   Dallas   Montreal
Toronto   London   Sydney

Holt, Rinehart
and Winston, Inc.

Cover reproduction from the painting,
Leaf Variations #2 (Begonias) by ANTON VAN DALEN 1970.
Courtesy Graham Gallery

Library of Congress Catalog Card Number:
72–150106

ISBN: 0-03-077395-4

Printed in the United States of America

4 5   071   9 8 7 6 5

Dedicated to Professor Chester A. Arnold upon his official retirement as Professor of Botany at the University of Michigan, and in honor of his distinguished service to the fields of morphology and paleobotany.

PREFACE

Never in the history of Man has the study of plants appeared to be so necessary for his survival. In this time of concern for the preservation of natural resources, plants alone have the potential for renewal into the unlimited future. In this critical period of burgeoning human populations, the food production capacity of the Earth's cultivated and pasturage species ultimately will establish the unsurpassable limits. In this era of concern for the quality of the human condition, the beauty of plants in contrived and natural settings affords us pleasure. In what has appropriately been dubbed the Age of Ecology, we are coming truly to comprehend that the survival of the plant-dependent world ecosystem which supports man and of which he is an integral component will be possible only if we are able to forestall overwhelming and irreversible damage to it. Beyond these all but irresistible pragmatic concerns, the study of plants is, in and of itself, a satisfying and inexhaustible exercise for the human intellect.

This fifth edition has been prepared with the above issues in mind. It is intended that this book will guide the introductory study of plant science for college or advanced high school students of all botanical aspirations, from those for whom botany is simply seen as one more important area of everyday concern with which the educated person must be familiar, to those who hope to proceed further in theoretical and applied fields. However, we have attempted to focus our efforts upon the requirements of those students for whom a single botany course will comprise the totality of formal exposure to the subject. Thus, as with earlier editions, the approach is broad—emphasizing biological principles and the relationships between plants and man.

In the present edition, several chapters have been completely reorganized, and all have been extensively revised and updated. We would point out particularly the inclusion of much new material in the areas of cell ultrastructure, photosynthesis, and water relationships, and the use of a scheme of classification that we believe better reflects current theories of relationship and appropriate categorization. The line illustrations have been redone throughout, most with the use of color. Many new photographs have been added, and we are pleased to acknowledge our gratitude to those persons and organizations who generously contributed them. Individual picture credits have been included with the captions.

To all of our colleagues who gave advice and assistance during preparation of this edition, we extend our sincere thanks. We are especially grateful to Dr. John S. Boyer for his many valuable contributions in all areas of plant physiology, and to Dr. John R. Laughnan for his helpful suggestions concerning the genetics chapter. The responsibility for selection and final treatment of all the material presented here, including possible errors of omission or commission, rests solely with the authors.

Z. B. C.

Urbana, Illinois W. W. P.
October 1971 M. K. B.

CONTENTS

THE
PLANT
WORLD

1

THE NATURE OF PLANT SCIENCE

Botany, the study of plants, is one of the most interesting and important of scientific endeavors. Much of the interest in botany can be attributed to the value this science has for our understanding of life properties, to the intriguing beauty and appeal of plants, and to man's intimate association with them. The great importance of plant study lies in the facts that plants are the sole producers of food and oxygen, and that if we are to maintain a world biological system that can continue to support man comfortably we must understand the essential plants well enough to avoid irreparable damage to the system. It is also important because plants provide thousands of products, in addition to foods, upon which societies and civilizations have been based and upon which we still depend.

HISTORICAL BACKGROUND

With the dawn of human intelligence, man must have learned to use plants, and he must have begun to accumulate information about them. We cannot assess the contribution of prehistoric man to our present wealth of cultivated plants, of plant lore, and of botanical fact, but we can sense its extent from studies of prehistoric plant domestication, from indications of plant uses found in archaeological investigation, and by study of plant significance in contemporary aboriginal societies. Plants suitable for food, weapons, and shelter must have been recognized and named quite early. Later, tribal chieftains and witch doctors preserved and augmented information regarding use of plants as medicinals, as sources of mystical power, and as objects of reverence.

Civilization became possible with the domestication of plants, particularly of certain types of grasses, including rice, wheat, and maize. Crop plant cultivation permitted settled populations to remain within defined regional areas. Agriculture was a more certain and efficient way of obtaining adequate food supplies than was simple foraging; it allowed one man to accumulate more food than he could himself eat, releasing others to serve as leaders, warriors, and priests. The latter, in particular, could devote time to developing symbolic language, to record keeping, to teaching, and to philosophical thought. Fragments of information about plants known to early civilized man have been preserved in ancient manuscripts, in pictures painted on walls of tombs, in plant remains found in burial sites, and in stone carvings preserved through the ages. Studies of such material indicate, for example, that the early Assyrians, Chinese, Egyptians, Greeks, Romans, and Aztecs possessed extensive knowledge of plant cultivation, of edible plant crops, of the medicinal and hallucinatory properties of plants, of irrigation of agricultural lands, and of production of useful fibers, beverages, spices, and other plant derivatives. Most of this knowledge was practical, but as civilization advanced and philosophical thought became a valuable and desirable pursuit, as in the Golden Age of Greece, philosophers such as Aristotle and Theophrastus made a number of scientific discoveries concerning the intrinsic nature of plant life. Indeed, in Western civilization, the works of the Greek and Roman philos-

FIG. 1-1. Medieval herbal illustration showing a tree, the leaves of which transform themselves into birds and fishes after falling on land or into water. (Courtesy of Missouri Botanical Garden.)

ophers provided the early foundation of the science of botany. Of particular importance were the herbals, compendia of information about medicinal plants wherein plants were described, figured, and named and their putative healing properties enumerated.

The degeneration of plant study during the Dark Ages is intriguing. The art of scientific observation declined; ancient works were sanctioned as ultimate sources of knowledge, and they were copied, corrupted, and augmented by attempts at extrapolation that today we find both pathetic and amusing. Strange superstitions arose regarding the magical properties of plants, the influence of planets and physical forces upon

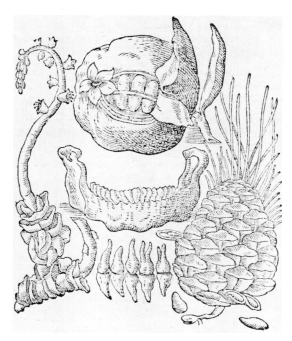

FIG. 1-2. Herbal illustration of Doctrine of Signatures, a medieval belief that certain plant parts resembled human structures and constituted a remedy for diseases of the latter. Note the resemblance of pomegranate seeds and pine cone scales to human teeth. (Courtesy of Missouri Botanical Garden.)

plant growth, and the relationships between the plant and animal kingdoms. For example, some of the herbals from this period illustrate the transformation of plant parts into butterflies, fish, and birds (Fig. 1–1). Progress in the healing arts was retarded by such concepts as the Doctrine of Signatures, which held that useful plants possessed signs bestowed by the Creator to indicate their curative properties (Fig. 1–2).

The renaissance of creative thought following the Dark Ages led to reexamination of knowledge accepted in earlier times and to renewed enthusiasm for objective study of real plants. The herbals produced after the fifteenth century were gradually purged of old superstitions and inaccuracies. Active world exploration provided an explosion of information about newly discovered plants, and the herbals and other plant works produced in the seventeenth and eighteenth centuries provided the expanded foundation for the plant science fields of today.

Botany was formally established as a pure science in the eighteenth century, and various of its disciplines began to develop immediately. The first branches of botany to expand were the largely descriptive ones that were essential for later work. These were **taxonomy,** the study of plant identification, nomenclature, and classification, and **morphology,** the study of plant structure and form. These fields developed first because they satisfied a primary need to organize the growing body of information about plant kinds and occurrences, because they could be accurately pursued with minimal supporting information from other phases of plant investigation, and because they required little technical apparatus. The chief prerequisites for the investigator in these fields, then as now, are the ability and patience to observe carefully and to describe observations accurately. With the background and terminologies thus provided, and with the development of the compound microscope, the way was prepared for **plant anatomy,** the study of fine details of internal plant structure. Thereafter, the growth of botanical information and the concurrent development of the basic principles of physics and chemistry led to the emergence of **plant physiology,** the study of plant functions and processes; **plant pathology,** the study of plant diseases; and **plant ecology,** the study of relationships between plants and their environments. At the same time, sister disciplines developed in zoology, and discoveries in both major fields augmented and supported further growth. The most recent fields are **paleobotany,** the study of plant life from past ages; **plant evolution,** the continuous genetic adaptation of species to the environment; **cytology,** the microscopic study of cell structure and cell behavior; and **genetics,** the study of inheritance. Significant advances in all these fields have occurred during the present century, which has witnessed both a growing awareness of the contribution of bio-

logical science to the welfare of man and the development of sophisticated research techniques and refined apparatus.

All these botanical fields are highly interrelated and interdependent. They constitute the core of "pure" botany, from which discoveries and information are supplied to derivative or supportive disciplines to be translated into experiments, practices, and products that enrich our daily lives. There is no sharp line of separation, however, between botany as a pure science and such applied sciences as agronomy and horticulture, for the practical, economically valuable discoveries made in these applied sciences may commonly be traced back to the pure-science discoveries made by botanists, as will be indicated in various chapters of this book.

PLANTS AS LIVING ORGANISMS

Plants constitute one of the two great kingdoms of living organisms; the other is the animal kingdom. All living things, both plant and animal, demonstrate certain attributes that, in their totality, provide them with the dynamic qualities of "aliveness." Some of these characteristics, such as irritability, are virtually restricted to living things, while others, such as growth and movement, are found in nonliving systems as well. For example, a crystal of ice may grow and a bit of camphor on the surface of water may move swiftly back and forth, but neither is alive. Attributes that must be present concurrently to indicate life as we know it are (1) cellular structure; (2) the ability to carry out the intricately correlated chemical reactions that permit the organism to remain alive, to grow, and to react to stimuli; and (3) the power to reproduce.

Life is a flexible, plastic phenomenon, involving numerous processes of cellular and organismic growth, irritability, and reproduction, all main-

FIG. 1–3. (Above). Thallophyta: an alga, *Polysiphonia.*
FIG. 1–4. (Below). Thallophyta: an alga, *Agardhiella.*
(Courtesy Photo Researchers, Inc.)

tained by metabolic activities. The substances of which living organisms are made are developed from elemental chemicals common on earth. However, one is unable to explain life on the basis of the physical and chemical properties of these elements; rather, the secret of life lies in the ways in which these materials are organized in cellular components, in organisms, and in populations. Many of these organizational secrets are being revealed by modern research, but many remain tantalizingly obscure.

Many of the simplest forms of extant life possess a mixture of plant and animal characteristics, and scientists believe that both the plant and animal kingdoms developed from such organisms. Although we have no difficulty in classifying a rosebush or a pet as plant or animal, the task becomes increasingly difficult as we extend our investigation to other, simpler forms. If we disregard those exceptional, and possibly intermediate "plantimals," as one biologist has called them, we may list a few criteria that serve to distinguish *most* kinds of plants from *most* kinds of animals:

1. Most plants are able to manufacture foods from simple chemicals of the air and soil by means of photosynthesis. Such plants are termed **autotrophic,** or self-nourishing. Photosynthesis requires a special green pigment, **chlorophyll,** by means of which light energy is absorbed and used to synthesize foods and to accomplish other purposes. Autotrophic plants are typically green; however, a number of plants, such as molds, mushrooms, and Indian pipes, lack chlorophyll and are not green and thus cannot manufacture their own food. Such plants resemble animals in their nutritional requirements. Animals are unable to manufacture food and are completely dependent for foods upon plants, either directly (herbivorous animals) or indirectly (carnivorous animals).

2. Most plants possess a structural framework of **cell walls,** the most abundant chemical constituent of which is the carbohydrate **cellulose.** Animals, with the exception of a small group called tunicates, lack cellulose.

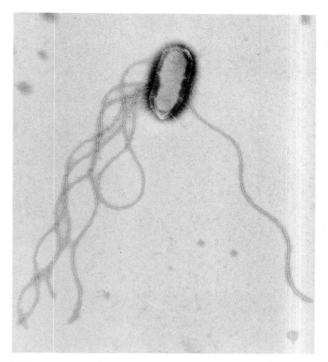

FIG. 1–5. Bacillus cell with flagella. (Courtesy of Dr. Judith Hoeniger.)

3. The majority of the plants with which we are most familiar lack the power of **locomotion;** they are firmly anchored in one place, whereas most animals can move from place to place. Unlike animals, plants need not seek shelter, and they have the ability to adapt themselves structurally and physiologically to normal environmental conditions. Unlike animals, plants have no need to catch food, for they either make their own or depend upon available food supplies in their immediate vicinities. Similarly, they usually have no need to seek mates because water, wind, insects, and other agencies transport their sex cells. However, there are some exceptions to this generalization; just as some animals pass their adult lives in an immobile condition, some rather primitive plants are able to swim from place to place in water. Further, the members of most major plant groups produce motile sperms or

FIG. 1–6.   Thallophyta: a mushroom fungus, *Cortinarius*. (Courtesy of Dr. Alexander H. Smith.)

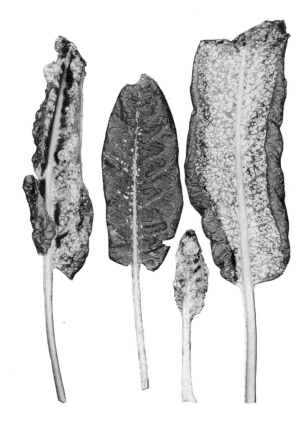

FIG. 1–7.   (Above). Thallophyta: a fungus, earthstar, or *Geaster*. (Copyright, General Biological Supply House, Chicago.) FIG. 1–8.   (Right). Thallophyta: white rust fungus, *Albugo,* on horseradish leaves. (Courtesy of H. W. Anderson.)

FIG. 1–9. Embryophyta: a liverwort, *Marchantia.* (Copyright, General Biological Supply House, Chicago.)

FIG. 1–10. (Above). Embryophyta: a moss, *Polytrichum.* (Courtesy of Dr. Paul L. Redfearn, Jr.) FIG. 1–11. (Right). Embryophyta: a horsetail, *Equisetum.* (Copyright, General Biological Supply House, Chicago.)

FIG. 1–12. Embryophyta: Clubmoss, *Lycopodium*. (Courtesy of Dr. R. T. Wilce, U. of Massachusetts.)

other cells that can swim in water, as do similar cells of animals.

4. Nearly all of the more advanced plants have an **open system of growth** that may be characterized by continued (and theoretically unlimited) development of certain organs. Such indeterminate growth results from the activity of small masses of perpetually juvenile tissue called **meristems.** Animals generally possess a closed system of growth in which the individual achieves a characteristic form and size at maturity; as an adult the animal changes relatively little.

A study of these differences indicates that no single difference separates all plants from all animals. It is relatively easy to distinguish, on the basis of these four criteria, the higher types of plants from the higher animals, but distinction becomes difficult, often impossible, with lower

forms. The inevitable conclusion is that plants and animals are similar in many ways, and that they ultimately reach back to common ancestors.

THE KINDS OF PLANTS

Plants display nearly infinite variety of size, form, and behavior. They vary in size from structurally simple, microscopic organisms, such as bacteria, some of which are only ½ micron long by ⅕ micron wide (about 1/50,000 inch by 1/125,000 inch), to large, structurally complex plants, such as the California redwood trees, which may attain heights of more than 350 feet and diameters of more than 40 feet. Such plants as bacteria and redwoods represent the extremes of size in the plant kingdom; between these limits are all other kinds of plants, such as mosses, ferns, mush-

FIG. 1–13. *Left:* Spikemoss, *Selaginella.* (Courtesy Dr. A. S. Heilman, U. of Tennessee, Knoxville.) *Right:* Marginal shield fern, *Dryopteris marginalis.* (Courtesy Mr. Charles Neidorf.)

rooms, oak trees, corn plants, and hundreds of thousands more.

The forms of plants are also remarkably varied, and it is chiefly on the basis of differences in form and structure of parts that we learn to distinguish different kinds or **species** of plants. At present approximately 350,000 species are known, each with its own characteristic habit of growth, method of reproduction, structure, and other peculiarities. Some plants lack true roots, stems, and leaves; others possess these parts. Some have flowers and seeds; some do not. Some species are trees, others are shrubs, some are vines, still others are herbs of low stature, and some are too simple in structure to qualify as any of these.

Plant species differ in many of their physiological qualities, as well as in size and structure. For example, some species store foods chiefly as sugars or starches; others store them as fatty substances. Some species require abundant supplies of water for their survival and growth; others thrive in desert regions. Many plant species inhabit only the hot, humid forests of equatorial regions; others are found growing in regions of hot summers and cold winters; and still others thrive only where temperatures are always quite low or quite high. Some plant species live submerged in water; others inhabit the land. Yellow pigments accumulate in the petals of some species, red ones in others, and so on.

FIG. 1-14. (Above). Embryophyta: a cycad, *Cycas.* (Copyright, General Biological Supply House, Chicago.)

FIG. 1-15. (Right). Embryophyta: Lodgepole pine, *Pinus,* Yellowstone National Park. (Courtesy of U.S. Dpt. of the Interior, National Park Service.)

One of the most striking differences among plants is found in their diverse methods of reproduction and in the varying nature of their reproductive parts. These reproductive differences, together with differences in structure, are the major criteria used by botanists to group plants into various assemblages. Botanists have classified plants into two major groups, both to facilitate their identification and to indicate something about their relationships. These groups, or subkingdoms, are the **Thallophyta** and **Embryophyta.** The Thallophyta comprise such primitive, structurally simple plants as bacteria, seaweeds, molds, mushrooms, and many others. The Embryophyta include mosses, ferns, club mosses, pines and other cone-bearing trees, and the thousands of species of flowering plants. Members of this subkingdom produce many-celled young plants, or **embryos,** which for at least a brief period are enclosed by some many-celled protective structure. Thallophyta do not produce embryos.

FIG. 1-16. Embryophyta: columbine, *Aquilegia*, a flowering plant. (Photo by Bodger Seed Co., El Monte, California.)

Each of these two subkingdoms consists of a number of smaller groups or **divisions,** some of which are illustrated in Figs. 1-3 through 1-16. Several divisions from each of the subkingdoms are treated in the later chapters of this book, but a few that include only extinct plants or rare plants of no special significance have been omitted. The most advanced or highly developed plant division in the subkingdom Embryophyta is the division **Anthophyta,** or **angiosperms,** the flowering plants, which number more than 200,000 species. Less specialized than the Anthophyta are the nonflowering, seed-bearing **Coniferophyta,** or **gymnosperms,** which include the pines, spruces, firs, cypresses, and others. Because these two divisions constitute the most conspicuous and most numerous plants inhabiting the land areas of the earth, and because they are the most important of all plants to human life, the flowering plants, and, to a lesser extent, the gymnosperms, will be studied in greater detail than other groups. The first half of this book will deal chiefly with angiosperms.

SUMMARY

1. The study of plants is of interest and importance because of the vital roles plants play in science and in man's life.

2. Early man possessed considerable information about crop and medicinal plants; the development of cultivated plants and agriculture, particularly of certain grasses, permitted the concurrent development of civilization.

3. The science of botany has its origins in the observations of the early Greek and Roman philosophers; it has expanded enormously since the nineteenth century.

4. The basic fields of botany are areas in which information about the nature and diversity of plant life is sought. They include:

    a. taxonomy, the study of identification, nomenclature, and classification

    b. morphology, the study of structure and form

    c. anatomy, the study of functions and processes

    e. pathology, the study of diseases

    f. ecology, the study of plants and their environments

    g. paleobotany, the study of plants of past ages

    h. evolution, the study of plant relationships

    i. genetics, the study of inheritance

    j. cytology, the microscopic study of cell structure and behavior.

5. Plants constitute one of the two great kingdoms of living things.

6. Living organisms usually display the following attributes:

    a. cellular structure

    b. the ability to carry on metabolism, including respiration, digestion, assimilation, and photosynthesis

    c. the ability to receive and react to external stimuli

    d. growth, including both (1) enlargement and cell production and (2) cellular organization to produce multicellular organisms

    e. reproduction, the ability to produce offspring.

7. The dynamic condition called life requires organization of the chemical elements of protoplasm into cellular components, organisms, and populations.

8. Plants and animals can usually be distinguished on the following bases:

    a. Many plants are autotrophic, i.e., food-producing, while animals cannot produce food.

    b. Plants possess walls of cellulose; animals do not.

    c. Most plants are incapable of movement.

    d. Plants have an open system of growth that usually permits enlargement throughout life.

9. Plants are extremely variable in form, structure, size, and physiology: we presently recognize more than 350,000 species or kinds of plants.

10. The plant kingdom is divided into two subkingdoms, the simple Thallophyta and the more complex, embryo-producing Embryophyta.

11. The subkingdoms contain numerous divisions; two of the best known Embryophyta are the flowering plants, or angiosperms, in the division Anthophyta, and the pines and their relatives, or gymnosperms, in the division Coniferophyta.

SUGGESTED READINGS FOR INTERESTED STUDENTS

1. Anderson, Edgar, *Plants, Man and Life,* Little, Brown and Co., Boston, 1952.

2. Arber, Agnes, *Herbals,* Cambridge University Press, Cambridge, England, 1938.

3. Peattie, Donald C., *Flowering Earth.* Viking Press, New York, 1961.

4. Reed, H. S., *A Short History of the Plant Sciences.* Ronald Press, New York, 1942.

TOPICS AND QUESTIONS FOR STUDY

1. How do you think primitive man may have discovered the medicinal properties of certain plants?

2. Why have primitive and civilized men frequently used plants as designs in their paintings, architecture, and sculpture?

3. Have you used any plants or plant products in the past three hours? Make a list of as many as you can remember, but not more than fifty.

4. Plants are sometimes harmful or disadvantageous to human life. List several examples.

5. Name and define the major branches of modern botany. Which of these developed first?

6. What are the major properties of living things?

7. What are the major distinctions between plants and animals?

8. Are plants and animals similar in some ways? Explain.

9. Distinguish between thallophytes and embryophytes.

10. What are the Anthophyta?

2

SEED STRUCTURE AND GERMINATION

The study of the flowering plants (Anthophyta or angiosperms) may logically begin with a study of seeds. Seeds are familiar objects; they constitute an early stage in the development of flowering plants, and their production is a distinct phase in the life cycle of such plants. Seeds of angiosperms are formed within structures called fruits (the word "angiosperm" means "covered seed," in reference to the development of seeds within the tissues of a fruit); a fruit is generally produced by the ovary portion of a flower. Thus, flowers produce fruits and fruits contain seeds. When a

fruit is mature, it commonly splits open or disintegrates, releasing the mature seeds. The reproductive processes that lead to the production of seeds will be described in detail in Chapter 17.

SEED STRUCTURE

A typical angiospermous seed consists of an immature plant **(embryo),** accompanied by a quantity of stored food **(endosperm)** available for its early nourishment, and a protective **seed coat.** All mature seeds capable of **germination** (sprout-

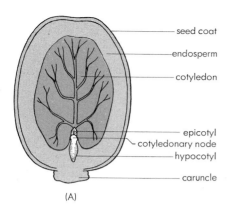

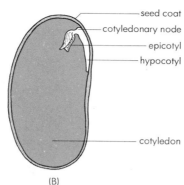

FIG. 2-1. A. Longitudinal section of a castor bean seed. B. Longitudinal section of a garden bean seed. In each of the drawings, only one of the two cotyledons is shown.

ing) have embryos and seed coats (Fig. 2–1). Although endosperm is present in every young, developing seed, this storage tissue may not be present in later stages of seed maturation. In the seeds of beans, peas, peanuts, pumpkins, and other species of plants, the embryo absorbs the food in the endosperm tissue before the seeds are fully formed. When these seeds are mature they, therefore, consist only of embryos and seed coats. In many other species, such as corn, castor bean, and wheat, the embryo does not use the endosperm until after the seeds are planted and begin to absorb water. In this second kind of seed, then, there are present at maturity an embryo, a seed coat, and endosperm. Seeds of this type generally germinate slowly, for their embryos must remove food from the endosperm before they can begin vigorous growth. Beans, peas, and other seeds, whose embryos absorb the foods stored in the endosperm tissues before the seeds are mature, generally germinate more quickly, for the preliminary step of food transfer from endosperm to embryo is completed before the seeds are planted.

Considerable variation in structure may be found among the seed coats in angiospermous species. For example, some seeds have a thick, resistant outer layer and a thin, delicate inner one, while others consist of a single layer only. In some species of plants (peas, orchid, peanut) the seed coats are thin and papery; in others

(clover, cotton, lotus) the coats are tough and hard. Seed coats in most species are partially waterproof and thus retard evaporation of water from internal tissues. Seed coats also afford protection against the entry of parasites, against mechanical injury, and in some species with thick seed coats, possibly against unfavorably high and low temperatures. A common feature found on the outer surface of the seed coat is the **hilum,** a small scar that marks the point of the seed's former attachment to the short stalk or **funiculus,** which connects the seed with the inside of the fruit. Also apparent on the coats of many kinds of seeds is the **micropyle,** the pore through which the sperm-carrying pollen tube entered the undeveloped seed, or **ovule,** prior to fertilization. In some species, such as the garden bean, the micropyle is distinctly visible at seed maturity, whereas in other species, it is obscured by postfertilization growth of the coat. Seed coats of some plants (for example, castor bean) bear a ridge **(raphe)** formed by the fusion of the funiculus with the seed coat. Castor bean seeds also bear a spongy structure, the **caruncle,** which aids in water absorption when the seeds are planted (Fig. 2–1,A). Each castor seed has a micropyle, but its presence is often hidden by the caruncle.

The embryo of an angiosperm consists of a short axis on which are borne one or two **cotyledons,** or **seed leaves.** The point of attachment of the cotyledons to the axis — referred to as the cotyledonary node — divides the axis into two regions. The lower of these, appropriately called the **hypocotyl,** terminates in an embryonic root, or **radicle.** After the seed has germinated, the radicle develops into the first or **primary root** of the seedling. The upper axial region, or **epicotyl,** is more variable in appearance. In plants such as castor bean, the epicotyl is somewhat slow to develop and usually is represented in the seed by a small, conical mass of cells. In contrast, the epicotyl of a garden bean embryo resembles a diminutive cluster of small but recognizable leaves borne close to the cotyledonary node (Fig. 2–1, B). Regardless of its degree of development in the seed, the epicotyl is interpreted morphologically as an immature **shoot,** or leaf-bearing stem. Structurally the cotyledons are leaves that function primarily in the digestion, absorption, and storage of food from the endosperm. Because of their specialized functions, cotyledons rarely resemble the mature leaves of the plants whose seeds they belong to. In many species, such as the castor bean, the flat, broad cotyledons persist for several weeks after germination, become green, and manufacture food. On the other hand, the fleshy cotyledons in garden beans and other species wither within a few days after germination following depletion of their stored food.

The endosperm tissue contains in its cells large amounts of usually insoluble stored food, which the embryo withdraws before or during seed germination, as described earlier. Carbohydrates are stored in large quantities in the seeds of many plants, usually as starches (corn, wheat, rice, beans), less frequently as sugars, and occasionally as more complex foods called hemicelluloses (date seeds, nasturtium seeds). Carbohydrates serve chiefly as sources of energy for growth and partly for the structural material of cell walls. Proteins are stored in all seeds and are used mainly in the formation of new protoplasm as germination begins and continues. Fats and oils are reserve foods used primarily for energy. The endosperm of the seeds of some plants, such as

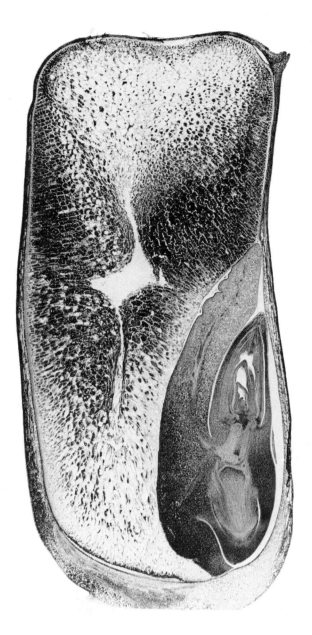

FIG. 2–2.   Longitudinal section of a corn grain. (Courtesy Iowa State College Press, Ames, Iowa.)

lilies and tulips, contains no starch whatsoever; the chief energy foods in the seeds of these species are fats and oils. In most kinds of seeds, all three major groups of foods — carbohydrates, fats, and proteins — are represented in the storage tissues. In all seeds, **digestion** (the conversion of water-insoluble foods to water-soluble foods) is a preliminary phase of germination, for growing embryos can utilize only water-soluble foods.

The seeds of garden beans and of castor beans contain embryos with two cotyledons (Fig. 2–1); those of corn have embryos with one cotyledon (Fig. 2–2). The angiosperms are divided into two subgroups on the basis of this difference: **monocotyledons** have one cotyledon in their embryos and include grasses, lilies, irises, sedges, palms, and orchids; and **dicotyledons** have embryos with two cotyledons and include such plants as beans, peas, geraniums, oaks, and sunflowers.

SEED GERMINATION

The first sign of germination is the absorption by the seed of large quantities of water. This is followed by enzyme activation, the beginning of rapid increase in respiration rate, and the beginning of protoplasm synthesis. The amount of stored food decreases as digestion and respiration continue; sprouted seeds usually have smaller dry weights than ungerminated seeds, largely because of the utilization of some of the stored foods in respiration. The energy released by respiration is used chiefly in cell duplication and other phases of growth; some of this energy is radiated as heat from germinating seeds and can be measured by suitable thermometers. With the absorption of water, the release of energy, and the inception of growth processes, the embryo becomes too large for the seed coat. Splits appear in the coat and the tip of the radicle emerges (Fig. 2–4). The emergence of the young root before other parts of the embryo is a distinct advantage, for a root system that anchors the seedling and absorbs water and nutrients is thus established

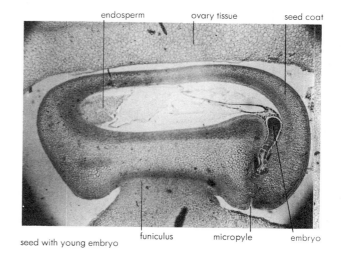

seed with young embryo

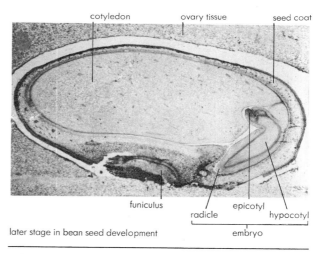

later stage in bean seed development

FIG. 2–3. Development of seeds of garden bean.

before the epicotyl begins to develop into the shoot system. When the epicotyl commences its activities, the primary root and, usually, a few secondary roots or adventitous roots are supplying the embryo with the large amounts of water needed for its subsequent growth.

In some species of plants, such as garden peas and corn, the hypocotyl and cotyledons remain in the soil; only the shoot, formed by the growth of the epicotyl, appears above the soil surface.

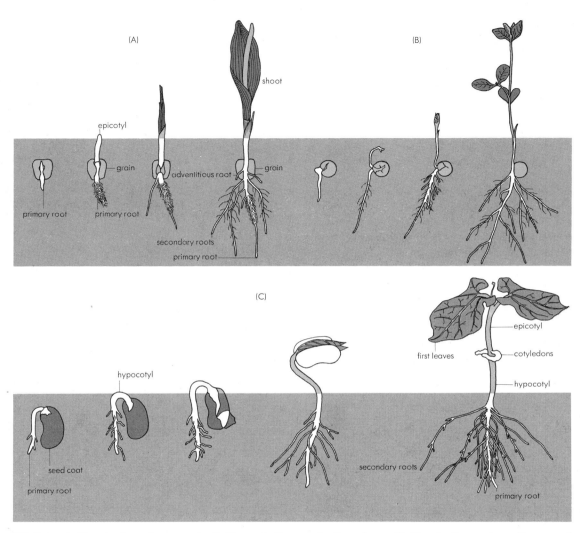

FIG. 2-4. A. Germination of corn grain. B. Stages in the germination of pea. C. Germination and seedling growth of garden bean.

In other species, such as garden beans and castor beans, the root primordium of the embryo forms the primary root, as it does in peas and corn; but the upper part of the hypocotyl, instead of remaining below ground as it does in pea and corn seedlings grows above ground for several inches, carrying the cotyledons up with it (see Fig. 2-5). The upper part of the hypocotyl is frequently arched during its growth upward through the soil, but it straightens out after it has emerged into the air. The arch of the hypocotyl forces a path through the soil, as a result of which the epicotyl and cotyledons are protected against injury by soil particles, for they are literally pulled up by the growing crook-shaped hypocotyl. They do not push their own way upward through the soil. Thus, in beans and castor beans, the lowermost part of the aerial axis is hypocotyl,

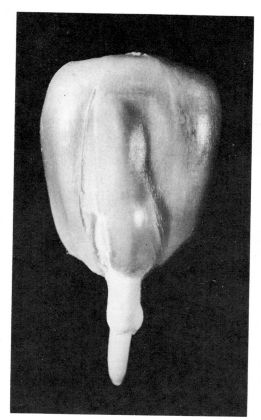

FIG. 2-5. - Germinating grains. *Left:* Corn grain in early stage of germination. The primary root has penetrated the sheath and is emerging from the grain. *Middle:* A later stage in the germination of a corn grain. The primary root has numerous root hairs, and the plump epicotyl has emerged. Slender adventitious roots are seen emerging from behind the epicotyl. *Right:* A germinating wheat grain, showing the primary root with root hairs, the short, blunt epicotyl, and several young adventitious roots. (Courtesy of O. T. Bonnet.)

whereas in peas and corn the aerial axis develops entirely from epicotyl, the hypocotyl remaining in the soil.

When the shoots have appeared above the soil, they continue to grow and develop, producing the mature organs of the plants. These organs will be studied in later chapters.

Seeds are able to sprout and grow, often for several weeks, in darkness. The resulting seedlings have an unnatural pale yellowish appearance, a condition termed **etiolation.** Growth in darkness continues only so long as stored food is available within the seedling for further growth and respiration. When all the food reserves are exhausted, seedlings in darkness die. Continued growth can occur only if the seedlings are illuminated, since light is essential for food manufacture in leaves.

FACTORS REQUIRED FOR GERMINATION

Many factors of the external environment exert marked effects upon the sprouting and early growth of seeds. Most important of these external influences are **moisture, temperature,** and **oxygen.** Also important but less well understood are the roles played by carbon dioxide and light. Abundant water must be available for seed germination to begin; the early stages of the process result in a tremendous increase in seed volume, (from

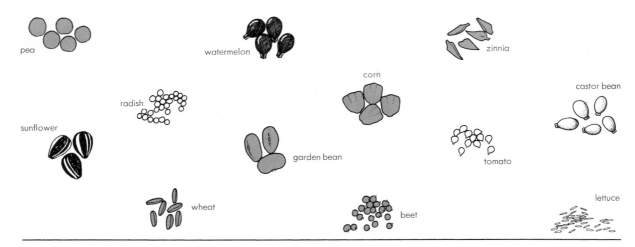

FIG. 2–6. Seeds of some familiar plants. (Some of these structures are really one-seeded fruits, for example, sunflower and zinnia.)

approximately 25 to 200 percent), an increase attributable largely to water intake. Water is important in the germination of seeds in that it softens seed coats, enabling the radicle and epicotyl to break through them more easily and promoting the entrance of oxygen, for gases pass more readily through moist cell walls. The uptake of water enables enzymes to activate physiological processes, such as digestion, movement of foods among tissues within the seed, respiration, and growth. The protoplasm of dry seeds contains so little water (5 to 10 percent in most cases) that physiological activities are able to proceed at only very slow rates. Water also provides the internal pressure necessary for cell enlargement and growth.

An adequate supply of atmospheric oxygen is ordinarily required to support the high respiration rate at the time of germination. Since oxygen content decreases with increasing soil depth, many kinds of seeds will die from lack of oxygen if planted too deeply. If water is present in such large quantities in the soil that oxygen is reduced or excluded, seeds frequently rot, for they are usually unable to germinate without some atmospheric oxygen. In addition, they are often attacked by bacteria that thrive in low concen-

trations of oxygen. Thus, seeds often die in water-logged soils, particularly clay soils, which hold water tenaciously. However, seeds of such plants as water lilies and cattails, which live in water or swampy soils, germinate more rapidly under water or in water-soaked soils than they do under conditions of moderate moisture in the substratum.

It is known that high carbon dioxide levels within the seed will retard certain enzymatically controlled reactions and thus adversely affect germination. The respiration rate of seeds stored under cool, dry conditions is typically very low; hence, little carbon dioxide is liberated by the respiratory process. Conversely, excessive amounts of carbon dioxide are commonly encountered in seeds that have been improperly dried and stored. Poor storage conditions — for example, warm, moist atmosphere and inadequate ventilation — often facilitate rapid growth of fungi and other heterotrophic organisms, and thereby permit rapid accumulation of CO_2 and a concomitant increase in temperature.

Temperature requirements for seed germination usually coincide with temperature requirements for the growth of active plant organs. Seeds of different species vary widely in their optimum temperature requirements for germination and in their tolerance to extremes of temperature. Seeds of tropical plants ordinarily germinate at higher minimum temperatures than do seeds of plants from temperate and subarctic regions. Thus, barley grains are able to germinate at a soil temperature near the freezing point of water, while corn grains and pumpkin seeds ordinarily germinate well only if soil temperatures exceed 50°F. It is reasonable to generalize that few seeds are able to germinate at soil temperatures below 40°F, that seeds of most species germinate best between 65°F to 85°F, and that temperatures above 100°F often are harmful to germinating seeds.

It has been known for at least a century that some seeds will not germinate until they have been exposed to light, but only in recent years have botanists made significant progress toward understanding the physiological basis of this fact. Investigators have shown that such seeds contain minute amounts of a light-sensitive protein pigment, **phytochrome,** that permits germination after brief exposure to red light but that inhibits germination after exposure to light in the far-red portion of the spectrum. This physiological mechanism may explain why some seeds will germinate in a forest clearing exposed to full sunlight but not on the forest floor where the sunlight has been filtered by the foliage overhead. Most seeds contain sufficient quantities of stored food within their tissues to promote germination and to support the growth of seedlings until they produce their own food-synthesizing organs, the leaves. Thus, most seeds do not need soil nutrients for germination, although if seedlings are to continue their growth and develop into normal, mature plants, they must begin to absorb soil nutrients at an early stage; however, soil nutrients are not necessary for germination itself, as shown by the fact that most seeds can be germinated in distilled water.

Dormancy In many species of plants, the newly formed seeds are dormant and cannot germinate until some time after they are liberated from the fruit. This period of dormancy is advantageous, particularly in temperate zones, for dormant seeds remain in a condition of low physiological activity during the winter, when low temperatures might kill seeds in an active state of germination or postgermination growth. Seeds may thus be regarded, in some degree at least, as structures that are able to carry a species safely through a period of unfavorable environmental conditions that might be fatal to actively growing plant tissues.

A distinction must be made between dormancy, which is the result of one or more internal conditions of a seed, and **quiescence,** which is a rest period caused by external conditions unfavorable to germination. A seed may pass through its dormant period and may be capable of sprouting, yet fail to germinate because of insufficient soil moisture, subfreezing temperatures, or other external factors that retard or prevent germination.

The causes of seed dormancy in different species of plants are varied, frequently complex, and by no means well understood. Some seed coats are thick and impermeable to water or oxygen. In such seeds, germination cannot occur until the seed coats have been cracked or rendered permeable by natural forces such as bacterial action, by freezing and thawing, or by artificial scratching of the seed coats **(scarification).** Many agriculturally important seeds (for example, sweet clovers and other members of the legume family) must be scarified prior to planting. In some species of plants, the seeds contain water-soluble inhibitory compounds that prevent germination. Only after these inhibitors have been leached out can germination take place. In other species, the embryos are not fully developed when the seeds are shed from the fruits; in such seeds a period of dormancy occurs during which embryo maturation is completed. In many seeds, complex chemical changes must be completed before germination is possible. These reactions are initiated in some seeds by such factors as exposure to light or low temperatures. Hawthorn seeds must experience a slowly increasing acidity of internal tis-

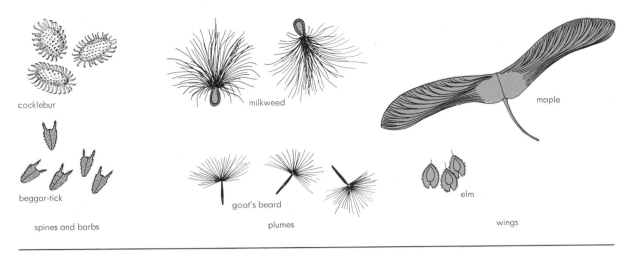

cocklebur

milkweed

maple

beggar-tick

goat's beard

elm

spines and barbs

plumes

wings

FIG. 2–7. Dispersal mechanisms in some seeds and fruits.

sues before they can sprout. Not uncommonly, a seed will require more than one external stimulus in order to remove the block or blocks that prevent germination; for example, seeds of garden cress must receive both light and temperature stimuli before they can sprout.

Seed Viability   Different kinds of seeds retain their **viability,** or ability to germinate, for varying periods of time. The seeds of certain orchids and willows remain viable for only a few hours or days, while those of many weeds may remain viable under proper conditions for nearly a century. During recent years a few reliable cases of extreme longevity of seeds have been reported. The most remarkable example is probably that involving seeds of the arctic lupine (*Lupinus arcticus*) that were discovered in ancient, dry lemming burrows, several feet beneath the surface of permanently frozen soil in Alaska. These lupine seeds were approximately 10,000 years old, but several were germinated under laboratory conditions and have since grown into healthy, normal plants. Such cases, however, are highly exceptional, and seed viability for most species under usual conditions seldom exceeds a few years. Although each species of plant has a char-

acteristic viable period, the length of this period is affected by storage conditions. Seeds stored in cool, dry places generally retain their viability longer than those exposed to warm, humid air. If seeds are stored in a poorly ventilated bin, the heat generated by respiration during incipient germination may become great enough to damage the embryos and even to cause fire in the stored seeds. Poor ventilation in a warm, moist seed bin also encourages the growth of fungi that rob seeds of food and injure or kill their embryos.

The causes of loss of seed viability are not fully known. As seeds grow old, proteins in the protoplasm slowly coagulate, regulatory substances involved in respiration often lose their activity, and cells lose their ability to divide. Exhaustion of food reserves is not the cause of loss of viability in most seeds, for long after they have lost their ability to sprout, seeds usually still contain appreciable quantities of starch, fats, and other storage foods.

FRUIT AND SEED DISPERSAL

Many kinds of plants have fruits or seeds that are equipped with special structures or peculiarities of behavior that increase the effectiveness of their spread, or **dispersal,** over wide areas. Among the common dispersal mechanisms of seeds and fruits are:

1. *Wings* — such as those of elm, maple, and ash fruits and catalpa seeds. These structures facilitate dispersal by wind.

2. *Plumes* — such as those of dandelion fruits and milkweed seeds, which are also dispersed by wind.

3. *Spines* and *barbs* — such as those of the fruits of needle grass, beggar's tick, and wild carrot. These fruits are fastened by their spines to the fur of animals and the clothes of human beings and are thus carried as "hitch-hikers" (see Fig. 2–7).

Many other methods of seed dispersal occur in plants. Brightly colored, sweet, pulpy fruits, such as raspberries, cherries, and currants, are eaten by birds and other animals who pass the seeds through their systems without damaging them, drop them in their feces, and thus disperse them. Some kinds of fruits and seeds are buoyant and can float in water for long periods of time; such structures often travel great distances in the currents of rivers and oceans and are thus dispersed. One of the most interesting examples of the effectiveness of water dispersal is the frequent appearance of seeds and fruits from the Orinoco river valley of South America upon the beaches of the Scandinavian peninsula. Some species of plants have fruits that explode as they mature, scattering their seeds widely. Explosion sometimes occurs as the result of unequal drying of fruit tissues, as, for example, in wood sorrel and jewelweed, the fruits of which suddenly split as they mature, shedding their seeds in the process. In other types of explosive fruits (for example, those of the squirting cucumber), the cause of the explosion is the development of water pressure within the fruits; when the pressure becomes great enough, a segment of the fruit bursts forth, followed by a stream of internal tissues and seeds, which may be shot out for a distance of several feet. Some kinds of seeds are readily dispersed by virtue of their small size and light weight; thus the minute seeds of orchids, several dozen of which just cover the head of a small pin, are carried considerable distances by winds.

Man is one of the most important agents of seed dispersal. In his migrations he has carried with him to all parts of the world valuable crop plants and, inadvertently, some of the most obnoxious weeds. Thus, rice, a native of southeastern Asia, is now grown in tropical and subtropical regions of both eastern and western hemispheres; corn, a native of tropical America, is extensively grown in both the Old and the New World; and some of our most troublesome weeds, such as thistles and dandelions, are truly cosmopolitan in their distribution.

ECONOMIC IMPORTANCE OF SEEDS

Seeds are of fundamental importance to man because they constitute the chief method of propagation of the seed plants. Many seeds provide man's most important foods—for example, corn, wheat, rice, barley, rye, oats, beans, peas, soybeans, peanuts, walnuts, pecans, almonds, and coconuts. Some furnish oils; the oils from coconuts, soybeans, flax seeds, tung, cotton, and corn are used as foods and in the manufacture of paints, varnishes, linoleum, lubricants, soaps, and other products. Many seeds are used for the flavors they impart to foods: anise, dill, caraway, nutmeg, mustard, and others. Some seeds furnish medicines—for example, castor beans, chaulmoogra (used in the treatment of leprosy), and psyllium. Seeds of coffee and cacao (or cocoa) furnish important beverages. Hard hemicellulose material of the seeds of the ivory-nut palm furnishes the "vegetable ivory" used in the manufacture of buttons and as a substitute for ivory in inlays, chessmen, toilet articles, etc.

SUMMARY

1. Seeds (matured ovules) are reproductive structures of seed plants.

2. A seed consists of a seed coat, an immature plant or embryo, and food storage tissue. In many angiospermous seeds, the endosperm tissue is absorbed by the embryo before the seeds leave their parent plants; such seeds contain no endosperm at the time of their maturity.

3. Seed coats are protective structures that reduce evaporation of water from seed tissues, protect the inner structures of seeds from attacks of certain insects and fungi, and often render seeds resistant to unfavorable external temperatures and mechanical forces.

4. The embryo of a flowering plant consists of one or two (sometimes more) cotyledons, an epicotyl, and a hypocotyl. Cotyledons digest and absorb foods stored in endosperm tissues; the epicotyl grows into the shoot of a seedling; and a portion of the hypocotyl produces the primary root.

5. Starch, fats and oils, and proteins are stored in the endosperm and cotyledons of seeds.

6. Seed germination begins with water absorption, which is followed by food digestion, energy release in respiration, cell duplication, and other growth processes.

7. In germination, the embryo swells and the seed coat ruptures. The radicle at the hypocotyl tip is the first part of the embryo to emerge from the seed coat; it forms the primary root. As this root becomes established in the soil, the epicotyl emerges and begins to develop into the young shoot of the plant. The cotyledons may remain in the soil, or they may be carried into the air by the upward growth of the upper part of the hypocotyl.

8. Cotyledons may persist on the seedling for several weeks and sometimes become green, leaflike, food-making organs, or they may wither and fall shortly after germination when their food reserves are depleted.

9. The principal external factors influencing seed germination are temperature, water supply, and availability of free oxygen. Seeds of different species vary greatly in their requirements of these three conditions. Most seeds do not require soil nutrients for germination.

10. Seeds are able to germinate in darkness, and seedlings similarly are able to develop in the absence of light, until all their food reserves are exhausted. Unless they receive the light necessary for food manufacture, they die.

11. Dormancy is a resting condition of seeds that results from certain internal conditions. It may be the result of embryo immaturity, impermeability of seed coats to oxygen or water, or the incompleteness of certain chemical changes. Dormancy is ended under natural conditions by such factors as freezing and thawing, the action of certain bacteria upon seed coats, and aging. It may also be terminated by seed scarification.

12. Quiescence is a resting condition of seeds resulting from environmental conditions, such as low temperatures and insufficient supply of moisture, which retard or prevent seed germination.

13. Seed germination is affected by various internal factors: completion of the dormant period, seed age, amount of growth-regulating substances present, amount of stored food, condition of protoplasmic proteins, and presence of inhibitory compounds.

14. Viability is the ability of seeds to germinate. The seeds of different species of plants retain their viability for differing periods. Cool, dry storage conditions are more favorable for the retention of viability than warm, moist conditions. The loss of seed viability appears to involve chiefly coagulation of protoplasmic proteins and failure of cell duplication.

15. Seed and fruit dispersal are accomplished by various mechanisms and modes of behavior. Wind, water, animals, and man are the most important agents of seed dispersal.

16. Seeds and fruits furnish man with foods, drugs, oils, and many other economically valuable products.

SUGGESTED READINGS FOR INTERESTED STUDENTS

1. Barton, Lela V., *Bibliography of Seeds*. Columbia Univ. Press, New York, 1967.

2. Barton, Lela V., *Seed Preservation and Longevity*. Interscience Publishers, Inc., New York, 1961.

3. Crocker, William, and Lela V. Barton, *Physiology of Seeds*. Chronica Botanica Co., Waltham, Mass., 1957.

4. Koller, Dov, "Germination." *Scientific American,* Vol. 200, No. 4, pp. 75–84, April 1959.

5. Mayer, A. M., and A. Poljakoff-Mayber. *The Germination of Seeds.* The Macmillan Co., New York, 1963.

6. Porsild, A. E., C. R. Harrington, and G. A. Mulligan. "*Lupinus arcticus* Wats. grown from seeds of Pleistocene age." *Science,* 158 (3797), pp. 113–114, 1967.

7. *Seeds.* The Yearbook of Agriculture, U.S. Government Printing Office, Washington, D.C., 1961.

TOPICS AND QUESTIONS FOR STUDY

1. Describe the structure of a typical embryo and list the functions of its parts.

2. What is endosperm? What is its function?

3. What are the functions of seed coats? What are some of the visible structures or marks of seed coats?

4. What is a micropyle? What is its significance in seed germination?

5. Distinguish between epicotyl and hypocotyl. What do these words mean?

6. List the major structural differences among corn, castor bean, and garden bean seeds.

7. Distinguish between monocotyledons and dicotyledons and name some plants that belong to each group.

8. Describe the principal physiological processes that occur during the germination of seeds.

9. What are the advantages of the early emergence of the hypocotyl during germination?

10. Name and describe briefly the principal external factors that are necessary for the germination of most kinds of seeds.

11. To what extent do seeds depend upon soil nutrients for their germination? Suggest an experiment that would give the answer to this question.

12. Is light necessary for seed germination? For postgermination growth? Explain.

13. Define dormancy, and state when it may be advantageous in some species of plants.

14. Name the major causes of dormancy.

15. Distinguish between dormancy and quiescence. What environmental factors are responsible for quiescence?

16. What factors in nature are responsible for ending the dormancy of seeds?

17. What artificial treatments may be used to shorten or "break" the dormancy of seeds?

18. What is meant by seed viability? What environmental factors favor a prolonged period of viability? What factors tend to decrease the viable period?

19. State two reasons why large masses of seeds, stored in poorly ventilated bins, may lose their ability to sprout.

20. Name the principal structural devices and modes of behavior that promote seed and fruit dispersal. Name the environmental condition or factor in each case that facilitates dispersal.

21. Name some seeds whose cotyledons furnish food to man.

22. Name some seeds whose endosperm furnishes food to man.

23. What advantages do seeds have over vegetables and fruits as sources of food for man?

24. Name some economically important products, other than foods, that are derived from seeds.

3

GROSS STRUCTURE AND ACTIVITIES OF FLOWERING PLANTS

In the last chapter we considered the salient features of seed structure, seed germination, and seed dispersal. We learned that a seed contains a small, immature plant, the embryo, that upon germination grows into a young, active plant, a seedling. A seedling, as a result of continued growth and development, ultimately becomes a mature plant. In this chapter, we will consider the generalized structure of a typical flowering plant, and in subsequent chapters, we will study the details of structure and physiology of flowering plant bodies.

The bodies of most flowering plants are composed of three kinds of organs: **roots, stems,** and **leaves** (see Fig. 3–1). Flowers are not properly termed organs, since they are really specialized shoots, that is, short stems bearing structures that are morphologically comparable to leaves; therefore, flowers are really clusters of organs. An organ may be defined as a major, visibly differentiated part of a plant, a part that performs a single main function or a group of closely related functions. Roots, stems, and leaves are termed the vegetative organs of a seed plant's

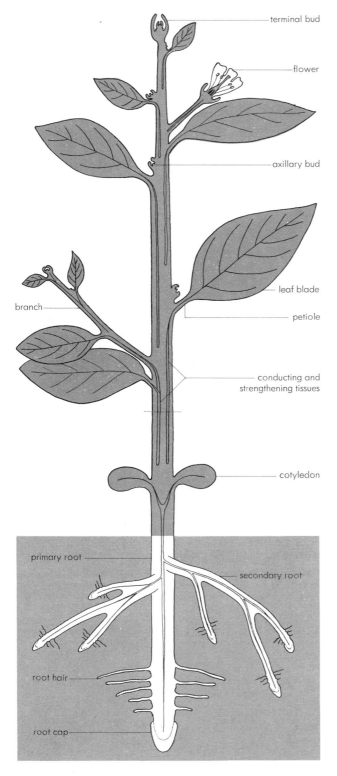

terminal bud

flower

axillary bud

branch

leaf blade

petiole

conducting and
strengthening tissues

cotyledon

primary root

secondary root

root hair

root cap

body because their functions center upon the intake of raw materials, the manufacture of food, and the utilization of food for growth and development. The vegetative organs have no direct role in the fundamental process of reproduction through the formation of seeds, although they may bring about the production of new plants by the growth and development of runners, underground stems, and root "suckers." Such asexual multiplication of plants is termed vegetative reproduction. The reproductive parts of a flower are concerned with the formation of seeds, usually a sexual process. As was stated in the preceding chapter, ovaries of flowers produce structures called fruits within which the seeds are formed.

An intimate relationship exists between the vegetative and reproductive activities of plants. Every plant in its life span, which extends from its inception as a fertilized egg within an immature seed (ovule) to its death, passes through a series of physiological stages. Vegetative activities—the absorption of raw materials, the synthesis of food, and the utilization of foods as sources of energy and building materials for growth—predominate during the greater portion of the life cycle in most plants. After these vegetative activities have proceeded for some time, flowers are formed and seeds are produced. One of the requisites for the development of flowers is a suitable food reserve, which is built up by vegetative processes. When reproductive functions begin, they are often accompanied by a decrease in vegetative activity. This decrease, in part, is a result of the movement of food reserves from vegetative organs into developing fruits and seeds.

The life spans of plants vary from one to many years. **Annual** plants complete their life cycles in a single growing season, **biennial** plants require two growing seasons, and **perennial** plants may live for many years. In annual plants (for exam-

FIG. 3–1. Diagram of the body of a typical flowering plant, showing the major parts.

ple, sweet peas, marigolds), flowers may be produced after relatively little vegetative growth since all food other than that necessary to maintain proper growth and function of the vegetative organs is available for production of flowers and fruits. In biennial plants (for example, beets and carrots), a large food reserve is built up and stored in the roots during the first growing season; then, during the second season, the food available from the first and second years' growth is utilized in flower and fruit production, following which the plant dies. In perennial species (for example, roses, privet, apple trees), a period of one or several years immediately following the sprouting of the seed is exclusively vegetative. When a food reserve has been built up, reproduction may occur. Thereafter during each year of its life the perennial plant carries on both vegetative and reproductive activities, ordinarily forming seeds during each year of its existence.

Roots of most plants are nongreen in color, and they usually grow beneath the surface of the soil. The principal functions of roots are: (1) absorption of water and nutrients from the soil, (2) anchorage of the plant body in the soil, (3) conduction of materials upward into the stem and downward from the stem and leaves, and (4) storage of food, which in plants such as carrots and beets may be accumulated in large quantities. Other, more specialized functions of roots will be considered in a later chapter.

Stems are usually branched axes derived from the meristem originating in the epicotyl; while different from roots in structure, they are continuous with the root system. Their structure varies greatly with different species of plants. The primary functions of stems are: (1) conduction of materials upward, downward, and transversely, (2) production and support of leaves and flowers, and (3) storage of food. The stems of many plants contain chlorophyll and are able to synthesize food. Other, more highly specialized functions of stems will be described later.

Leaves are outgrowths of stems. In their most common form, they are broad, flat, and thin; less frequently they are fleshy, needlelike, or scalelike. The chief function of leaves is the manufacture of food by the process of **photosynthesis**, though specialized types of leaves in some plants perform other functions as well.

The bodies of seed plants, as described in the preceding chapter, are anchored in the soil or other material in which their roots grow. The immobility of plants places certain restrictions upon their activities and markedly influences their entire development and character, and to some degree, their distribution upon the earth's surface. The limitations imposed on plants by immobility significantly influence the operation of their physiological processes; plants can absorb water and various nutrients only from those portions of the soil penetrated by their roots. Diminution or exhaustion of the essential materials within the range of the plant's root systems results in the development of physiological abnormalities that may lead to death.

SUMMARY

1. The bodies of flowering plants consist of:
   a. vegetative organs: roots, stems, and leaves
   b. reproductive structures: flowers
2. Vegetative organs are concerned primarily with the absorption of raw materials, the synthesis and utilization of foods, and growth. Flowers produce seeds.
3. Reproduction of new plants is sometimes brought about by growth from vegetative organs; in this case, it is called "vegetative reproduction."
4. Vegetative processes result in the accumulation of food stores that are necessary for the production of flowers, fruits, and seeds.
5. Annual plants complete their life span in a single year or less.

Biennial plants require two years (or two growing seasons) to complete their lives. Annuals and biennials ordinarily flower and produce seeds only once. Perennial plants live for several to many years, producing flowers and seeds a number of times, commonly once a year.

6. The principal functions of roots are:
    a. anchorage
    b. absorption of water and mineral salts from the soil
    c. conduction of substances
    d. food storage
7. The principal functions of stems are:
    a. conduction of substances
    b. production and support of leaves and flowers
    c. food storage
8. The principal function of leaves is food synthesis.
9. The fixed position of plants restricts their acquisition of nutrients.

TOPICS AND QUESTIONS FOR STUDY

1. What are the vegetative organs of seed plants? What are vegetative processes?
2. What is vegetative reproduction? Name some familiar plants that are propagated by vegetative means and state how each is propagated.
3. Distinguish among annual, biennial, and perennial plants, and name specific plants as examples of each.
4. Describe the functions of roots, stems, and leaves.
5. What is the function of flowers? What is the relationship between flowers and fruits?
6. What problems must higher plants solve as a result of their fixed position in the soil? How do these problems differ from those that animals face?

4

THE MICROSCOPIC STRUCTURE OF PLANTS: CELLS AND TISSUES

THE CELLULAR ORGANIZATION OF PLANTS

When one examines with the aid of a microscope a thin slice of tissue cut from a plant, he observes that the section is composed of very small units or **cells** (Fig. 4-1), each of which consists of a **cell wall** surrounding a tiny droplet of living substance, the **protoplasm.** Microscopic study of all species of plants reveals the same fundamental architectural plan—namely, cells as the basic units of structure. All growth and reproduction of plants is the result of formation and maturation of new cells from preexisting cells.

Even a cursory microscopic examination of plant sections shows that not all cells are alike, but that there is considerable variation in size and form among them. These size and structural differences reflect the different functions that various cells perform. Newly formed cells develop into mature cells through the complex process termed **differentiation** or **maturation.** In this process cells assume specific structural characteristics that are correlated with particular func-

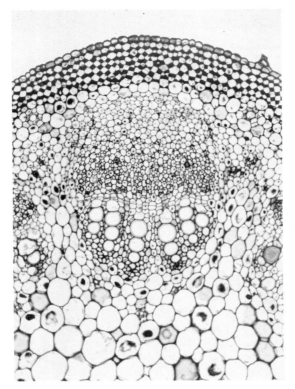

FIG. 4-1. A segment of sunflower (*Helianthus*) stem as seen in transverse section.

tions. They usually retain these structures and functions throughout the life of the organs they belong to. The processes taking place in cell differentiation involve specialization of cells; some cells become food synthesizers; others function in the transport of materials; still others serve for support, food storage, absorption, and other functions.

When botanists and zoologists first became aware that the bodies of plants and animals were composed of cells, they thought the individual cells were of prime importance. They believed that the activities of the whole plant or animal might be considered as a summation of the activities of the individual, constituent cells. This idea was embodied in a concept known as the **cell theory.** Subsequently, another interpretation, known as the **organismal theory,** replaced in part the ideas of the cell theory. According to the organismal theory, the entire organism—and not the individual cells—is the entity of prime importance. The organismal theory emphasizes a biological concept that has developed partly as a result of physiological research upon correlation or coordination of the various tissues and organs of living beings, and upon the mutual interaction between different tissues and organs. In other words, these investigations have shown that the mere summation of the activities of individual cells does not sufficiently explain the behavior of organisms, but that there is a coordination among cells that results in the function of the entire organism as a unit.

The bodies of seed plants are **multicellular** in nature. Moreover, there is a considerable degree of differentiation in structure and function among their many cells. Among certain of the less specialized plant groups there are plants that consist of only a single cell (for example, some algae and fungi). Such organisms are called **unicellular.** Frequently, unicellular organisms remain grouped together in aggregations termed **colonies.** In most colonies, there is little or no specialization among the cells, and the individual members of the colony can continue their life processes if they become separated from the other cells of the colony. In a few types of colonies, the constituent cells are differentiated into two types, vegetative and reproductive cells, and each is necessary to the survival of the other.

THE SIZES OF CELLS

Cells are minute objects, most of them invisible to the naked eye and some of them so small that even under the highest magnifying power of the light microscope they appear merely as tiny spheres or rods. The smallest cells are those of bacteria, some of which are only 0.0002 millimeter, about 1/125,000 inch, in length. The longest plant cells may be several inches in length as, for example, the fiber cells of certain members of the nettle family, some of which may reach a length of 200 millimeters—about 8 inches. Such sizes, however, are extremes among plant cells. The great majority fall within the 0.1 to 0.01 millimeter range. Between 4 and 40 such cells would just span the period at the end of this sentence. A cube one inch on a side could contain more than 15 million spherical cells 0.1 millimeter in diameter, or nearly 15 billion cells 0.01 millimeter in diameter.

THE STRUCTURE OF CELLS

Plant cells are extremely varied not only in size but also with respect to their form, their functions, and the structures they contain. If we examine a living plant cell with the microscope we find structures that can be classified into three groups:

1. the **cell wall,** which encloses the living substance
2. the **protoplast,** or living component of a single cell
3. the **ergastic substances,** nonprotoplasmic products of protoplasmic activity.

Cell Wall   The cell wall is a comparatively strong and semirigid structure arranged in the form of a box or having a more or less spherical, ovoid, cylindrical, much elongated, or occasionally very irregular form. The organization of structural elements in cell walls makes them extremely strong, but in spite of their great strength, plant cell walls possess a considerable degree of resilience, which enables them to be somewhat stretched, compressed, or twisted without being fractured. It is because cell walls are so pliable and at the same time so strong that stems, leaf stalks, and other plant parts may be bent and buffeted by winds and yet return undamaged to their original form and position. In plants, the walls of the cells play a major role in providing support for the plant body.

Plant cell walls have a layered structure and are generally considered to be nonliving (Fig. 4–2). The formation of new walls begins with the deposition of a **cell plate** between daughter nuclei

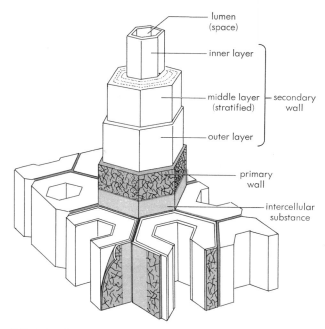

FIG. 4–2.   Diagram illustrating the multilayered structure of the walls of fiber cells. (Adapted from Wardrop & Bland. 1959. The process of lignification in woody plants. Proc. 4th Int'l Cong. of Biochem. Vol. 2, Symp. 2 (*Biochemistry of Wood*), pp. 92–116. Kratzl, K. and G. Billek (Eds.) Pergamon Press, London)

in a dividing cell (see Fig. 6–4). The cell plate appears to consist of pectic substances and forms a filmlike partition across the dividing cell. In this manner the protoplast of the mother cell (the cell that is in the process of division) is subdivided into two daughter protoplasts, each of which participates in the formation of a **middle lamella** by the addition of more pectic substances to the cell plate. The middle lamella consists largely of calcium and magnesium pectates and functions as an intercellular cementing substance that binds together the completed walls of adjacent cells. Pectic compounds are also incorporated into the walls of many cells as incrustations and as deposits between component wall layers. The fruits of many plants contain pectic substances in considerable concentration. Commercial pectin, used

	inch (in)	centimeter (cm)	millimeter (mm)	micron (μ)	angstrom (Å)
inch	1	2.54	25.4	25,400	254,000,000
centimeter	0.393	1	10	10^4	10^8
millimeter	0.0393	10^{-1}	1	10^3	10^7
micron	0.0000393	10^{-4}	10^{-3}	1	10^4
angstrom	0.00000000393	10^{-8}	10^{-7}	10^{-4}	1

Table 4–1. Conversion table for inch and metric units.

in the manufacture of jellies and jams, is usually obtained from apples and citrus fruits.

As each daughter cell grows, other materials are deposited by its protoplast in successive layers upon the middle lamella. The layer that is added directly to the middle lamella is called the **primary wall** and consists chiefly of cellulose, hemicelluloses, and pectic materials. This layer is very elastic and pliable and is capable of growth, extension, and changes in thickness. The primary wall is formed while the cell is still growing and, like the middle lamella, is usually quite thin. Under an ordinary light microscope the middle lamella and the primary walls of two adjacent cells commonly appear as a single layer, the so-called **compound middle lamella.** Many plant cells produce only primary walls. In many other plant cells, however, a **secondary wall** is deposited by the protoplast upon the primary walls. Secondary walls are formed largely after the cell has attained its final size. Cellulose is the chief constituent of secondary walls; non-cellulosic materials are commonly present, although pectic compounds are usually absent. The secondary wall is frequently formed in three or more layers and is considerably less pliable and less elastic than the primary wall.

The physical properties of cell walls are attributable largely to cellulose, which is one of their major constituents and which forms their structural framework. Some of the factors that determine the resilience and toughness of cell walls are the great length of cellulose molecules

FIG. 4-3. Electronmicrograph showing microfibrils. Replica of primary wall including pit membrane area. *Eucalyptus deglupta.* Magnification: 24,750 ×. (Courtesy of Dr. Wilfred A. Coté, Jr., State University College of Forestry at Syracuse University.)

(some estimates suggest 50,000 Angstrom units, that is, about 0.005 millimeter or 1/5000 inch; see Table 4-1); the aggregation of these molecules into partially crystalline, submicroscopic strands called **microfibrils** (Fig. 4-3); the orientation of

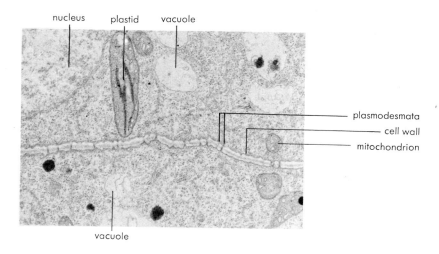

nucleus   plastid   vacuole

plasmodesmata
cell wall
mitochondrion

vacuole

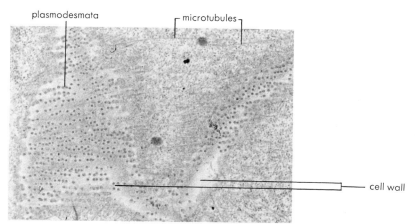

plasmodesmata   microtubules

cell wall

FIG. 4-4. An electron micrograph showing plasmodesmata in the apical cell wall of the moss *Polytrichium,* in transection (above) and face view (below). (Courtesy of Dr. Judith R. Graffius.)

microfibrils in the various wall layers; and wall thickness. Cellulose will not dissolve in water, but it absorbs water in large quantities. As a result, most of the cell walls of living plants are in a highly hydrated or saturated condition. Special properties are often imparted by depositions of noncellulosic substances in the walls of certain cells. For example, the **suberin** found in cork cell walls and the **cutin** in cell walls of the epidermis are related lipids (fatty compounds) with certain waxlike properties that make these walls considerably less permeable to water. **Lignin,** an abundant constituent in the middle lamellae and walls of wood cells, imparts increased strength and hardness.

The thickness of cell walls varies greatly. In many cells, such as the green cells of leaves and the storage cells of roots, the walls remain very thin, rarely more than a few thousandths of a millimeter in thickness. In other cells, such as the outer cells of date seeds and the stone cells of peach fruits, the walls become enormously thickened, so that at maturity the lumen or cavity within each cell is nearly filled with wall material.

The walls of cells throughout the plant body typically have numerous thin areas termed **pits** distributed over their surfaces. Pits result from the failure of secondary wall material to be deposited (Fig. 4-3). They are frequently numerous and

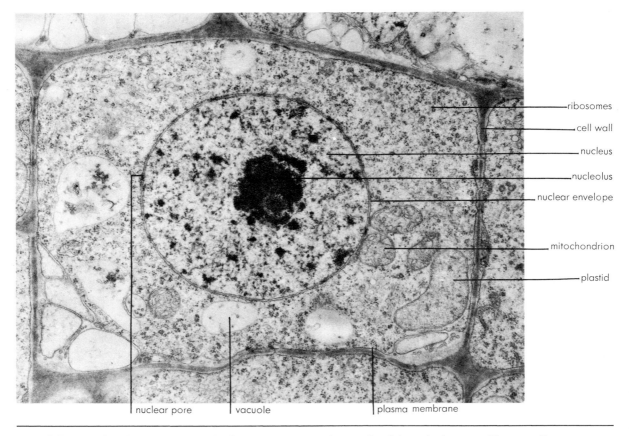

ribosomes
cell wall
nucleus
nucleolus
nuclear envelope
mitochondrion
plastid
nuclear pore   vacuole   plasma membrane

FIG. 4–5. An electron micrograph of a meristematic androgonial cell from the liverwort *Blasia pusilla.*

may be regularly arranged or scattered through-out the wall. At each area of contact between adjacent cells, the pits of the two walls are usually aligned opposite each other to form **pit pairs.** Pits are believed to facilitate the passage of water and dissolved materials from cell to cell.

Canals that are submicroscopic and contain minute strands of cytoplasm extend through ad-jacent cell walls. These delicate, cytoplasmic strands, called **plasmodesmata,** connect adjacent living protoplasts (Fig. 4–4). They are usually present in large numbers within cell walls, and they may be especially abundant in the pits. One study suggests that certain tissues of onion may contain as many as 20,000 plasmodesmata per cell.

Plasmodesmata are presumed to play an impor-tant role in the passage of materials between cells, even including small cytoplasmic organelles (ri-bosomes) and certain of the smaller plant viruses.

Significant changes in the spatial relationships among cells may occur during that phase of tissue growth that is characterized by the cells' increase in volume. To accommodate the stresses of cell enlargement, adjacent cell walls commonly un-dergo slight separation along the middle lamella. Such separations are very evident in corner re-gions where three cells meet. The resulting **inter-cellular space** commonly appears triangular or square when seen in transverse section (Figure 4–1). The system of intercellular spaces may be very extensive and may account for a relatively large proportion of a plant's volume.

Protoplast   Protoplast is a term denoting all the living parts of a cell as they are organized into a single unit. Protoplasm, a general term coined more than a century ago, is the name given to all the living substance that makes up the protoplast. When the term was introduced rather gross examinations showed protoplasm to be viscous, ranging from wateriness to the consistency of semisolid gelatin. It was found also to be elastic, somewhat mucilaginous, and usually transparent and colorless. Although the light microscope showed protoplasm to be of heterogeneous

composition, it was not until studies could be made with the electron microscope that we learned how complex and extensively structured the substance really is (Fig. 4–5). Thus, our concept of protoplasm has changed as we have obtained new knowledge of the structure and function of both the formerly unknown, "invisible" components, and the larger, more conspicuous parts of the protoplast.

NUCLEUS.   Perhaps the most conspicuous of the living protoplasmic components is the **nucleus,** which, in the nondividing condition, appears as a rather large, spherical, ovoid, or elongated structure. The number of nuclei per cell

FIG. 4–6.   Freeze-fracture preparation of the nuclear membrane surface, with pores. (Courtesy of Dr. D. Branton, University of California, Berkeley.)

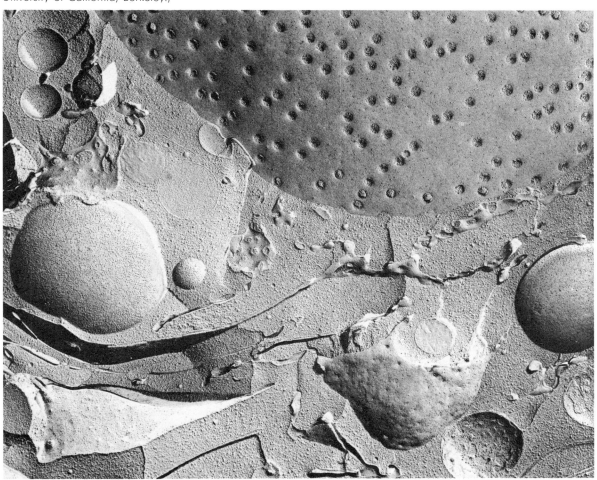

varies according to the organism and the type of tissue; most frequently, each cell contains a single nucleus. The living nucleus is typically colorless, transparent, and generally more viscous than other parts of the protoplast. It may move about within the protoplast and change its shape as it does so. If the cell is treated with suitable fixatives and dyes, it becomes apparent that the nucleus, like the whole protoplast, is not structurally uniform but is made up of several distinct parts.

A very thin **nuclear envelope** delimits the nuclear contents from other portions of the protoplasm. Pictures made with the electron microscope show the nuclear envelope to be a double membrane that is perforated by circular pores approximately 500 A in diameter (Fig. 4–6). It is composed of proteins and lipids and has been shown to be continuous with the cytoplasmic system of membranes. The nuclear envelope is thought to exercise control over the passage of materials into and out of the nucleus. Within the nucleus is the protein-rich **nuclear ground substance** and the **chromatin.** Chromatin, as it appears in stained preparations, has a finely granular texture and is organized into a diffuse, irregular network. It consists chiefly of **deoxyribonucleic acid** (DNA), the material that bears the genetic information of each cell. In addition, chromatin contains relatively small amounts of proteins and another nucleic acid, **ribonucleic acid** (RNA). During nuclear duplication, the chromatin becomes organized into **chromosomes.** Also present within the nucleus are small, spherical **nucleoli.** These structures are produced in association with specific chromosomes, each nucleus commonly having one nucleolus per haploid set of chromosomes. Typically, nucleoli are rich in RNA and proteins but are devoid of DNA; moreover, they lack membranes and usually disappear during nuclear duplication. Electron micrographs show that the nucleolus contains large numbers of nearly spherical particles, each approximately 250 A in diameter. Chemical analyses indicate that most, if not all, the nucleolar RNA is associated with these particles. Considerable uncertainty remains regarding the functions of the nucleolus; however, available evidence suggests that this organelle is primarily involved in nucleic acid metabolism and protein synthesis. There is no doubt, however, that the organized nucleus functions as a primary directive center of the major physiological activities of the cell. Cells from which the nuclei have been removed soon exhibit abnormalities that eventually result in the death of the cells. Among the chief activities controlled by the nucleus is the transmission of hereditary characteristics from one cell generation to the next.

CYTOPLASM   The protoplasmic substance in which the nucleus and other protoplasmic bodies are embedded is called **cytoplasm.** In very young cells, the nucleus and cytoplasm together occupy nearly all the volume of the cell. As plant cells become older and grow markedly in size, the cytoplasm fails to increase proportionately and forms a thin layer lining the wall. In the central region of the cell, inside the cytoplasmic layer, a cavity, or **vacuole,** filled with **cell sap** develops. This watery solution contains various kinds of substances such as sugars and salts, and often pigments, tannins, and organic acids. The vacuole functions as a repository of various nonprotoplasmic materials. It also plays an important part in the maintenance of cell turgidity, as will be described in Chapter 5.

An inner surface film, the **tonoplast** or **vacuolar membrane,** separates the cytoplasm from the vacuole. The **ectoplast** or **plasma membrane** is the surface film that delimits cytoplasm at the outside, that is, next to the wall. Both of these membranes are of cytoplasmic origin, and both are exceedingly important in cellular physiology in that they control in large degree the passage of materials into and out of the living protoplasm. In contrast to the perforate double membrane of the nuclear envelope, the ectoplast and the tonoplast are imperforate single membranes. Typically 75 to 100 A in thickness, membranes have three constituent layers: a central lamella of lipid material sandwiched between two layers of protein. Studies of cell ultrastructure have shown that this trilaminar composition is characteristic of nearly all cell membranes; as a result, biologists commonly refer to them as "unit membranes."

Electron microscopic examination of plant cells also reveals the presence in the cytoplasm of an extensive, interconnected system of membranous tubules, vesicles, and large, flattened sacs, or **cisternae.** This system, the **endoplasmic reticulum,** is continuous with the nuclear envelope; moreover, it occasionally touches the plasma membrane. This system of membranes provides large surface areas over which chemical reactions occur; it may also facilitate both transport and storage of materials throughout the cytoplasm.

In all living plant cells there are large numbers of minute particles called **ribosomes** suspended freely in the cytoplasm and frequently distributed over the outer surfaces of the endoplasmic reticulum. These nearly spherical structures, each approximately 250 A in diameter, consist of about 60 percent RNA and 40 percent protein. Some experimental evidence indicates that ribosomes are formed in the nucleolar region under DNA control and then migrate to the cytoplasm, possibly through the pores in the nuclear envelope. It appears that they are unable to reproduce themselves. Ribosomes function as the major sites for the synthesis of proteins. Individually or in clusters **(polysomes),** ribosomes mediate at their surfaces the assembly of specific sequences of amino acids, the building blocks of which proteins are composed. A detailed account of this process will be found in Chapter 16.

Another kind of cytoplasmic organelle found in all living cells of the plant is the **mitochondrion.** Mitochondria have variable morphology but are commonly rodlike, measuring about half a micron in width and several microns in length. They are dispersed in the cytoplasmic ground substance and may be preferentially distributed in particular regions within the cell. Each of these rodlike organelles, which consist primarily of proteins

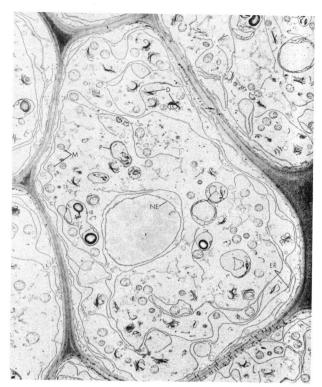

FIG. 4-7. Maize root tip cortical cell showing membranes of dictyosomes (D), endoplasmic reticulum (ER), mitochondria (M), nuclear envelope (NE), and plastids (P). (Courtesy of Dr. H. Mollenhauer, Kettering Res. Lab., Yellow Springs, O.)

and lipids, is limited externally by a double membrane, the inner layer of which is infolded to form numerous fingerlike projections or flattened shelflike extensions called **cristae** (Fig. 4-5). Mitochondria play a vital role in cellular physiology, for they are the sites of respiratory activity. Briefly, the process of respiration releases energy through oxidative chemical reactions within the mitochondria. This energy is immediately transferred to particular molecules, which, in their high energy state, move to other parts of the cell. Then, in a precisely regulated manner, the energy is released wherever it is needed to support the metabolic reactions of the cell.

Living plant cells characteristically contain cytoplasmic organelles called **dictyosomes,** which frequently appear as flat or curved stacks of about six membranous cisternae and associated vesicles (Fig. 4–7). In face view, dictyosomes are approximately circular in outline with margins that resemble an irregular, open meshwork. In transverse section, the cisternae that constitute a stack are seen to lie quite close to each other. The margins of individual cisternae often appear locally inflated, and evidence indicates that the aforementioned vesicles originate by pinching off the margins. While our knowledge of dictyosome function is still incomplete, it is known that these organelles are able to accumulate certain materials from the cytoplasmic ground substance and store them in vesicles that can then be moved elsewhere in the cell, or out of the cell altogether. This mode of action has been recognized in association with wall formation and with both secretory and excretory functions of certain cells.

Another cytoplasmic organelle found in plant cells, the **sphaerosome,** is among those that are least understood. These structures are small, spherical bodies just visible under the light microscope and are often present in considerable numbers. Frequently misidentified as oil droplets or reserve fat bodies, sphaerosomes are limited by single membranes and have rather uniform diameters of about one micron. In contrast, reserve oil droplets in the cytoplasm lack limiting membranes, they coalesce easily, and they are quite variable in diameter. Moreover, there are significant chemical differences between these two structures. Some investigators have suggested that sphaerosomes originate as small vesicles pinched off from the endoplasmic reticulum and that they play an important part in fat synthesis and storage. Others discount this interpretation and suggest quite different roles. Conclusive statements regarding the structure and function of sphaerosomes (and many other organelles) necessarily await further research.

The most conspicuous cytoplasmic organelles found in mature plant cells are the **plastids** (Fig. 4–5). Although they occur in a great variety of shapes, in higher plants plastids are most frequently ovoid or spherical. These organelles are typically larger than mitochondria and much less abundant, ranging from one to several dozen per cell. Plastids may be classified as **chromoplasts** or **leucoplasts,** according to pigmentation. Chromoplasts contain pigment and, therefore, are colored; leucoplasts lack pigment and are colorless. One type of chromoplast, the **chloroplast,** contains the photosynthetic pigments chlorophyll *a* and chlorophyll *b*, which impart the green color to many plant cells. The carotinoid pigments, carotene and xanthophyll, respectively deep and pale yellow, are also present in chloroplasts, but their color is masked by that of the more abundant chlorophylls. The structure and function of chloroplasts as related to photosynthesis will be discussed in Chapter 14. Nonchlorophyllous chromoplasts contain carotenoid pigments, which impart yellow, orange, or red coloration to some flower petals, fruits, and other plant parts. The exact physiological significance of these plastids is not known; however, bright coloration often plays a part in pollination and fruit dispersal. The colorless leucoplasts commonly are identified according to the function they perform; thus, those that synthesize and store starch are called **amyloplasts,** and those that form lipid materials are designated **elaioplasts.** Leucoplasts occur most commonly in storage cells that receive little or no light as, for example, those in roots and underground stems.

It is interesting that, under certain conditions, plastids of one type are transformed into other types. In tomatoes, for example, leucoplasts are present in the tiny, undeveloped fruits. As the fruits enlarge, the leucoplasts slowly develop into chloroplasts, and, in the last phases of ripening, the chloroplasts are changed into chromoplasts, which are responsible for the color of the fully ripened fruits.

The last type of cytoplasmic organelle to be mentioned here is the **microtubule** (Fig. 4–8). These proteinaceous structures are only about 240 A in outside diameter, but they are comparatively long, some individual microtubules having been

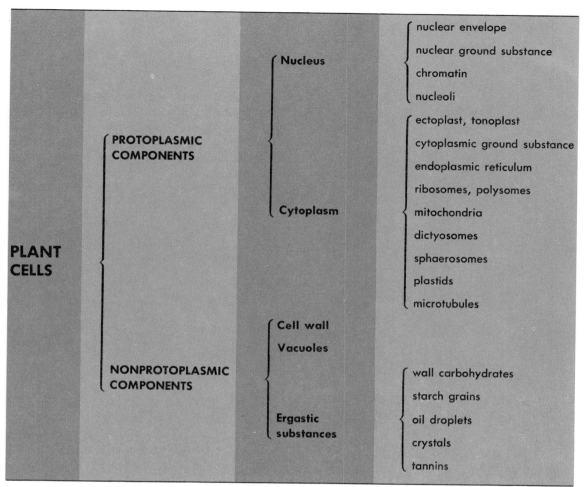

			nuclear envelope
		Nucleus	nuclear ground substance
			chromatin
			nucleoli
	PROTOPLASMIC COMPONENTS		ectoplast, tonoplast
			cytoplasmic ground substance
			endoplasmic reticulum
			ribosomes, polysomes
		Cytoplasm	mitochondria
PLANT CELLS			dictyosomes
			sphaerosomes
			plastids
			microtubules
		Cell wall	
		Vacuoles	
	NONPROTOPLASMIC COMPONENTS		wall carbohydrates
			starch grains
		Ergastic substances	oil droplets
			crystals
			tannins

TABLE 4–2. A classification of cell parts.

traced for several microns. As a class of organelles, microtubules exhibit little structural variation, yet they seem to be involved in several functional roles. They constitute the filamentous strands of the spindle apparatus that forms during nuclear duplication, where they play some part in the movement of sister chromosomes (see Chapter 6). They are found in fixed array inside flagella—whiplike structures that serve to propel certain swimming plant cells. Other microtubules have been shown to impart a static structural support, and to maintain certain asymmetries in cell shape. Further, it appears that microtubules may contribute to cytoplasmic streaming (possibly through an undulatory movement) and that they may be involved in some manner with synthesis of cellulosic microfibrils.

Ergastic Substances   Ergastic substances are nonprotoplasmic components of the cell that have been produced by protoplasmic activity. Some of these products of metabolism play critically important roles in plant structure and function. For example, the form and support of a plant

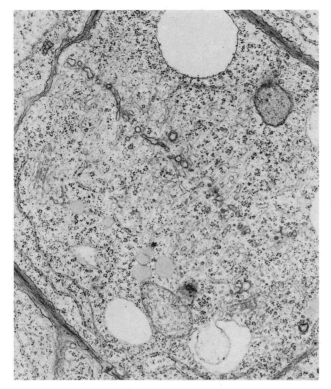

FIG. 4–8. Microtubules associated with a developing cell plate in a primary leaf of a bean seedling, *Phaseolus vulgaris*. Magnification: 45,000 ×. (Courtesy of B. A. Palevitz, U. of Wisconsin.)

are largely attributable to the walls of its constituent cells. The various wall compounds, including cellulose, hemicellulose, lignin, and pectic materials, are all ergastic substances. Starch, which is found within the protoplast, is one of the commonest reserve foods and is thus an ergastic substance of major physiological importance. Other similar substances are certain reserve fats and proteins. Some ergastic substances that naturally occur in the vacuoles and elsewhere include tannins and numerous dissolved salts and sugars. Still others, which are less well understood, include various crystals, resins, gums, and other excretory or secretory products of protoplasmic activity.

Relationships among the cell components described above are summarized in Table 4–2.

TISSUES

As has been emphasized, the cells of plants show great variations in size and structure, differences that reflect their diverse functions in the life of a plant. A group of cells performing essentially the same function or functions and commonly of similar structure is called a tissue. An organ, such as a leaf or root, is composed of tissues. Usually in an organ the various tissues perform interrelated functions. Tissues are classified on different bases: on their origin, their structure, or their physiology. A useful classification, based on morphological and physiological features, is the following:

1. meristematic tissue (growth tissue)
2. permanent tissue (mature tissue)
   A. simple permanent tissue (consisting chiefly of one kind of cell)
      a. epidermis
      b. parenchyma
      c. collenchyma
      d. sclerenchyma
      e. cork
   B. complex permanent tissue (consisting of several kinds of cells)
      a. xylem
      b. phloem

Meristematic Tissue   Meristematic tissue serves chiefly in the production of new cells and is characterized by persistent immaturity. Small masses of meristematic tissue are located near the tips of roots (Fig. 7–6) and in the buds of shoots (Fig. 10–1). Because of the terminal positions occupied by these juvenile tissues, they are called **apical meristems.** The activities of the apical meristems are largely responsible for the increase in length of roots and shoots. Meristematic tissue also occurs as strips or cylindrical sheets of cells located between wood and bark, the **vascular cambium** (Fig. 10–11), and in the outer bark, the **phellogen** or cork cambium (Fig. 4–11). Both of these meristems extend along much of the length of roots and shoots in woody plants, and they are thus classified as **lateral meristems.** The vascular cambium produces complex tissues that conduct water and food; cork cambium, as its name implies, is responsible for the formation of layers of cork (or phellem) cells, which afford protection against excessive water loss and injury. Apical meristem cells are typically small, thin walled, and roughly cubical in form; cambial cells, on the other hand, are often considerably elongated and sometimes have moderately thick walls. Meristematic tissues generally are compact and lack intercellular spaces.

Epidermal Tissue   The epidermis generally may be regarded as the outer layer of cells produced by the apical meristems of roots and shoots. Most commonly this surface layer is only one cell thick (Figs. 4–1, 13–7). It extends over virtually all the plant body and may persist for the life of the plant, as is usually the case in short-lived, non-woody species, or it may soon be replaced by a layer of corky tissue, as happens in trees and shrubs. The epidermis of the aerial parts of plants functions chiefly in conserving the moisture supply of the inner tissues and in offering a certain amount of protection against mechanical damage to internal tissues and against invasion by parasites. The outer walls of these cells, which sometimes are rather thick, are covered by a **cuticle,** a thin layer of waxlike cutin secreted by the protoplasts of epidermal cells. Except for the specialized **guard cells,** which control the openings of epidermal pores, or **stomata,** the epidermal cells lack intercellular spaces and generally are colorless; in some plants, however, red, blue, or purple pigment may be present in the vacuoles of epidermal cells and may give the leaves in which they occur a like color, as in purple-leaved cabbage. In addition to its protective function, the epidermis of roots provides for the absorption of water and nutrients from the soil.

Parenchyma Tissue   Parenchyma tissue is one of the most common and one of the most abundant plant tissues; it occurs in all organs of higher plants. Parenchyma cells usually have long-lived protoplasts, large vacuoles, and relatively thin walls. Depending upon their location and function in the plant, parenchyma cells exhibit a wide variety of shapes. Frequently they are roughly spherical in form, as, for example, in the central portions of certain plant stems; they also occur in elongated, cylindrical, and lobed forms. Parenchyma cells often constitute homogeneous masses of considerable volume, with many intercellular spaces; they also are found intermingled with other types of cells, as in tissues that conduct food and water. The parenchyma tissue of roots and much of that in stems is usually colorless and functions chiefly in the storage of food and water. In leaves and in some portions of stems, the parenchyma cells contain chloroplasts and function chiefly in food synthesis.

Collenchyma Tissue   Collenchyma is found almost exclusively in stems and leaves, where it functions primarily in support. The constituent cells of this tissue are elongated and characteristically have unevenly thickened primary walls that are rich in pectic substances. Collenchyma cells typically occupy a peripheral position in an organ (Fig. 4–1), and they may be aggregated into long strands or into cylindrical layers a few cells in thickness. This tissue of living cells is strong and resilient, and it provides considerable support to relatively young, growing plant parts.

Sclerenchyma Tissue   Sclerenchyma cells, like those of collenchyma, function primarily in support; they differ from collenchyma cells in having thick secondary walls that are usually lignified. Moreover, the protoplasts of sclerenchyma cells may or may not be alive at the tissue's functional maturity. Sclerenchyma cells occur in a wide variety of intergrading shapes and have been conveniently classified into two major groups:

FIG. 4-9. Isolated fiber (left) and vessel member (right) from the secondary wood of beech (*Fagus grandifolia*).

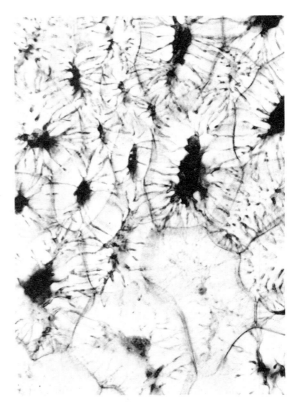

FIG. 4-10. A sectional view of the sclereids comprising the stone of a peach (*Prunus persica*). Notice the numerous pits which traverse the thick secondary walls.

fibers and **sclereids.** Fibers (Fig. 4-9) are much elongated, narrow cells that have tapering ends and possess both great strength and elasticity. Fibers may be aggregated into long strands or layers, or they may be distributed singly or in small clusters in certain parts of the plant. They frequently are intermixed with other cell types to form complex tissues such as those that conduct water and food. The long strands of fibers produced by some plants have sufficient tensile strength to be important in the manufacture of rope, twine, and textiles. Probably the greatest variation in cellular architecture among vascular plant cells is exhibited by sclereids (Fig. 4-10). Some sclereids are nearly spherical, some rodlike or long and filamentous, and others intricately branched and contorted into bizarre shapes. They form the greater portion of seed coats and nut shells and the gritty masses in the pulp of pears. Sclereids also occur in the roots, stems, and leaves of many other plants, where they are presumed to provide strength and support.

Cork Tissue   Cork or phellem is a major protective tissue that usually replaces the epidermis in roots and stems of plants that grow for more than a single season. Cork cells are derived from a lateral meristem, the **phellogen** or **cork cambium,** and are commonly tabular in shape (Fig. 4-11). Collectively they form a compact tissue devoid of intercellular spaces. The cells comprising cork tissue are dead at their functional maturity and may be filled with air or with materials such as tannins or resins. The relative impermeability of cork cells to water is in large measure imparted by the suberin that impregnates their walls. Cork cells, together with old, dead food-conducting tissue, comprise the rough outer bark of woody stems and roots. Cork also serves as an outer protective layer in some fruits, in bud scales, and in certain other plant parts. The prin-

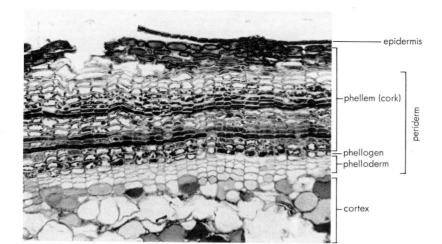

epidermis

phellem (cork)

periderm

phellogen
phelloderm

cortex

FIG. 4-11. Photomicrograph of periderm in the stem of *Erodium macradenum.*

cipal function of cork tissue is reduction of water evaporation from underlying tissues. Cork may also protect inner tissues from extremes of temperature, mechanical injury, and fire. Commercial cork is obtained from the thick, outer bark of the cork oak tree, *Quercus suber,* a species of oak native to the Mediterranean area.

Xylem Tissue   Xylem has two principal functions: conduction and support. It conducts water and various nutrients in solution upward from the roots where they entered the plant, through the stems, and into leaves, flowers, and fruits. This conduction is carried on by **tracheids** and **vessels.** Tracheids are elongated, tapering cells, whose protoplasts die when the cells reach maturity. The walls of tracheids may be thickened by spirals or rings of lignified cellulose, or they may possess pits that facilitate the passage of water and dissolved materials between tracheids. In addition to their function of conduction, tracheids contribute substantially to the strength and support of organs in which they occur. Vessels are not single cells, but longitudinal series of cells called **vessel members.** These elongated, approximately cylindrical vessel members (Fig. 4-9) have common end walls that have been wholly or partly dissolved away, and they are arranged to

form relatively long tubes. The openings in the end walls of vessel members are termed **perforations** and the end walls themselves, **perforation plates.** The presence of these perforations is the major characteristic that distinguishes vessel members from tracheids, which are imperforate. Vessel members have pits in their lateral walls and frequently contain various types of thickenings similar to those of tracheids (Fig. 4-1). Like tracheids, vessel members lack protoplasts at maturity and function both in conduction and support. Other types of cells in xylem tissue are ray parenchyma cells, which conduct substances radially in stems and roots and which sometimes store food; strengthening xylem fibers; and xylem parenchyma, which stores foods.

Phloem Tissue   Phloem, like xylem, is chiefly a conducting and supporting tissue. It conducts food materials from their principal sites of synthesis in leaves to other locations, such as roots and developing fruits, for storage or utilization. The characteristic conducting components of phloem are either **sieve tubes** or **sieve cells.** Somewhat like xylem vessels, sieve tubes are not single cells but longitudinal series of cells called **sieve tube members** (Fig. 4-12). These elongated cells bear on their common end walls one or more

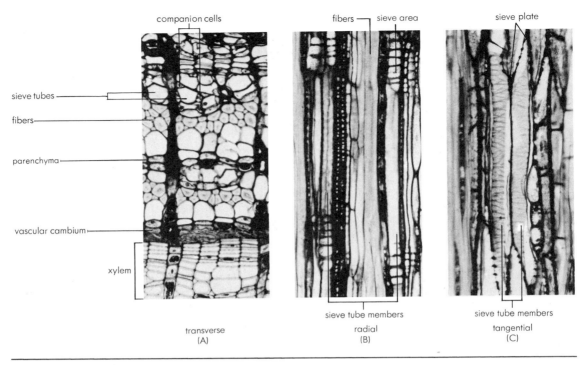

sieve tubes

fibers

parenchyma

vascular cambium

xylem

sieve tube members

sieve tube members

transverse
(A)

radial
(B)

tangential
(C)

FIG. 4-12.   Photomicrographs showing secondary phloem cells of linden (*Tilia*) in three planes of section.

sievelike clusters of pores through which the cytoplasm and vacuolar sap of adjacent cells are continuous. Larger and functionally more complex than plasmodesmata, these minute perforations are called **sieve pores.** The clusters of sieve pores are termed **sieve areas,** and the end walls on which they occur, **sieve plates.** The walls of sieve tube members are rich in cellulose and pectic material, and usually are unlignified. Internally, the functionally mature sieve tube member has a peripheral layer of cytoplasm and a central, vacuolar region from around which the tonoplast has been lost. Each mature cell is characterized further by its lack of a nucleus. Closely associated with sieve tube members are smaller **companion cells.** Usually one or more of these elongated cells lies adjacent to each sieve tube member and is linked with it by plasmodesmatal connections. Companion cells, in contrast to sieve tube members, retain their nuclei, and it has been suggested that these nucleate cells may influence or control the physiological activities of sieve tube members. Sieve cells differ from sieve tube members chiefly in having less specialized sieve areas that are distributed more generally over the walls, and in having tapering or pointed ends that overlap with other, similar cells. Like the more specialized sieve tube members, sieve cells are enucleate at maturity. The conducting cells of phloem tissue typically are accompanied by phloem parenchyma, which serves chiefly in food storage. There also may be present ray parenchyma cells, which function in both food storage and in lateral food conduction, and phloem fibers, which, in plants that do not become woody through prolonged growth, may contribute most of the strength and mechanical support of the stem.

Once permanent tissues are formed, they ordinarily do not undergo pronounced changes in structure or function. Some mature, living tissues, however, retain the capacity for further growth and development. For example, under certain conditions parenchyma cells can revert to a meristematic condition and produce new cells that may differentiate into tissues other than parenchyma. This potentiality for renewed growth has been demonstrated at various levels of structural (and physiological) organization. The practice of plant propagation by means of cuttings, in which new plants or plant parts grow from the cut surface of a mature leafstalk, stem, or other part, illustrates at the level of the *organ* the so-called **dedifferentiation** of mature cells to a meristematic state and the development of new tissues from the meristematic activity that ensues. Botanists also have demonstrated the plant's capacity for dedifferentiation and growth at the *tissue* level by placing small masses of living pith parenchyma cells in flasks containing suitable culture medium. In time, roots and shoots grew from these once mature, "transplanted" cells. The same potentialities for growth have more recently

been demonstrated for isolated *single cells* that, through careful culture techniques, were induced to give rise to complete plants. These successful experiments in the growth of cells and tissues confirm the concept of **cellular totipotentiality**, the inherent capacity of a living cell to express all the characteristics of the whole plant.

A study of the structure of these various tissues strikingly illustrates the close correlation between form and function. Cells that furnish strength and support are thick walled, elongated, tough, and flexible. Conducting cells have in their walls pits or perforations, or both, to facilitate the transport of materials from cell to cell. Protective cells are waterproof so that they reduce or eliminate evaporation of moisture from the underlying tissues. Because of the intimate relationship between form and function, the study of morphology alone, without consideration of physiological activities, is as meaningless as the study of functional processes without reference to the structure of the cells and tissues that perform them.

SUMMARY

1. The bodies of plants are composed of cells.

2. The cell theory regards a plant or animal as an aggregation of cells. The organismal theory regards the whole organism as a unit that is subdivided into functional units, the cells.

3. Some primitive plants consist of single, free cells. Other unicellular plants remain grouped together in colonies in which there is little or no division of labor among the cells. A plant that consists of many interdependent cells is called multicellular. Multicellular plants often have various cell and tissue types in which there is structural and functional differentiation.

4. All growth and reproduction of living organisms result from the formation of new cells from preexisting cells.

5. Cells differ greatly in their structure and functions; these differences develop as a result of processes of differentiation or maturation.

6. The lengths or diameters of most plant cells range from 0.01 to 0.1 mm. (1/2500 to 1/250 of an inch); some cells may greatly exceed these dimensions.

7. A living plant cell typically consists of a small mass of protoplasm, some nonliving inclusions, and an outer, nonliving wall.

8. Cell walls are tough and strong, yet somewhat flexible, and give strength and support to plant bodies.

9. Plant cell walls are rich in carbohydrates and usually have a layered structure. The first-formed layer, or primary wall, is produced while the cell is still enlarging. Primary walls of adjacent cells are held together by the middle lamella, a layer of intercellular cementing substance. In many cells, a laminated secondary wall is deposited against the primary wall.

10. Long cellulose molecules aggregated into crystalline microfibrils form the structural framework of cell walls. Materials such as lignin, suberin, and cutin may impregnate the cellulose framework and impart special characteristics.

11. Both pits (local recesses in the wall) and plasmodesmata (fine cytoplasmic strands passing through cell walls) facilitate passage of substances between adjacent cells.

12. Protoplast is a term denoting all the living parts of a cell as they are organized into a single unit. Protoplasm is a general term given to all the living substance that makes up the protoplast. The structurally complex protoplast contains various organelles, some of which may be seen only with an electron microscope.

13. The nucleus is a conspicuous protoplasmic body that serves as a directive center of most cellular activities. It is separated from the rest of the protoplasm by a perforated nuclear envelope consisting of two closely spaced membranes. Nuclear contents include the DNA-containing chromatin, one or more RNA-rich nucleoli, and nuclear ground substance. Chromatin bears the genetic information of the cell and becomes organized into chromosomes during nuclear duplication.

14. Cytoplasm is the protoplasmic material outside the nucleus. It contains a number of structures, among which are:

a. cytoplasmic membranes, including ectoplast, or plasma membrane; tonoplast, or vacuolar membrane; and the endoplasmic reticulum, a complex system of double membranes that is continuous with the nuclear envelope

b. ribosomes: numerous, minute particles consisting of RNA and protein and serving as the sites of protein synthesis

c. mitochondria: small, often rodlike bodies that function as the centers of respiratory activity, by which energy is released for vital cell functions

d. dictyosomes: organelles that resemble small stacks of membranous, flattened vesicles or cisternae and are thought to play a role in the accumulation and transport of certain materials within the cell

e. sphaerosomes: spherical, membrane-limited bodies that are just visible through the light microscope and that possibly function in the synthesis and storage of fats

f. plastids: commonly spherical or ovoid organelles that may be pigmented (chromoplasts) or colorless (leucoplasts). Chromoplasts that contain green chlorophyll pigments and synthesize food are called chloroplasts. Other chromoplasts may be yellow, orange, or red, and serve generally in the coloration of various plant parts. Amyloplasts and elaioplasts are types of colorless plastids that serve in starch and oil storage, respectively.

15. Ergastic materials are nonliving products of protoplasmic activity and include a wide variety of substances such as cell wall carbohydrates, starch, tannins, crystals, and the cell sap contained in vacuoles.

16. A tissue is a group of cells performing essentially the same function or functions and commonly of similar structure.

17. Meristematic tissues serve chiefly in the production of new cells and may be apical or lateral in position within the plant.

18. Apical meristems are responsible for the increase in length of root and shoot and for the production of leaves. Lateral meristems include vascular cambium and cork cambium, which produce conducting and protective tissues, respectively.

19. Permanent tissues are the differentiated and matured products of meristematic activity. Included among the permanent tissues are epidermis and cork (protection), parenchyma (synthesis, storage), collenchyma and sclerenchyma (support), phloem and xylem (conduction).

20. Living plant cells, even when mature and isolated from other cells, have an inherent capacity to express all the characteristics of the whole plant from which they came. This capacity is termed cellular totipotentiality.

21. Cell structure and cell functions are intimately related; cell structure usually reflects the functions the cells perform.

SUGGESTED READINGS FOR INTERESTED STUDENTS

1. Cutter, Elizabeth G., *Plant Anatomy: Experiment and Interpretation,* Part I, Cells and Tissues. Addison-Wesley, Reading, Mass., 1969.

2. Esau, Katherine, *Plant Anatomy,* 2d ed. Wiley, New York, 1965.

3. Frey-Wyssling, A., and K. Mühlethaler, *Ultrastructural Plant Cytology.* American Elsevier, New York, 1965.

4. Jensen, W. A., *The Plant Cell.* Wadsworth, Belmont, Calif., 1964.

5. Jensen, W. A., and R. B. Park, *Cell Ultrastructure.* Wadsworth, Belmont, Calif., 1967.

6. O'Brien, T. P., and Margaret E. McCully, *Plant Structure and Development.* Macmillan, Toronto, Ont., 1969.

7. Steward, F. C., "The control of growth in plant cells." *Scientific American,* Vol. 209, No. 4, pp. 104–113, October 1963.

8. Voeller, B. R., "The plant cell: Aspects of its form and function." *The Cell,* J. Brachet and A. E. Mirsky, Eds., Vol. IV, Chapter 4. Academic Press, New York, 1964.

TOPICS AND QUESTIONS FOR STUDY

1. What is the basic structural (and functional) unit of a living plant?
2. Define cell differentiation.
3. Distinguish between the cell theory and the organismal theory. Are these theories completely contradictory?
4. Distinguish among unicellular, colonial, and multicellular organisms. What different kinds of problems of existence must be solved by these types of organisms?
5. Are all plant cells microscopic? Explain.
6. Describe the structure and function of the middle lamella. Distinguish between middle lamella and compound middle lamella.
7. Describe the physical properties of plant cell walls.
8. Describe briefly the structure and chemical nature of plant cell walls. How are plant cell walls important in human life?
9. Distinguish between primary and secondary walls in as many ways as you can.
10. Do you think the so-called texture or orientation of microfibrils would influence the physical characteristics of plant cell walls? How?
11. What are the functions of plant cell walls?
12. Describe the structure of pits and comment upon their significance in the life of a plant.
13. What are plasmodesmata? What is their importance?
14. Define these terms: protoplast, protoplasm, cytoplasm, and nucleus. Describe their relationships to each other.
15. Describe the structure and biological importance of nuclei.
16. Name and describe the cytoplasmic membranes.
17. What are ribosomes? Polysomes? Where in the cell are these structures found?
18. Describe the structure of mitochondria. Describe in general terms their function in a living cell.
19. Describe one or two functions attributed to dictyosomes.
20. Distinguish between sphaerosomes and oil droplets.
21. Name and describe the kinds of plastids found in plant cells. State their known or supposed functions.
22. What are chlorophyll, xanthophyll, and carotene? Distinguish among them.
23. What are ergastic substances? Give examples.
24. Characterize meristematic tissue as completely as you can.
25. Name and describe the principal types of permanent plant tissues and state their functions.
26. Distinguish between differentiation and dedifferentiation.
27. What is cellular totipotentiality? What is its significance in terms of plant survival?

5

PHYSIOLOGICAL ACTIVITIES OF PLANT CELLS

CHEMICAL NATURE OF PROTOPLASM

A notable fact concerning the chemical constitution of living protoplasm is the impossibility of classifying the individual materials that compose it as living or nonliving. Every single chemical substance in protoplasm, when it is isolated from all the others, is nonliving. Only when certain of these, chiefly the proteins, nucleic acids, and certain fatty materials, are present together in the proper organization does the living condition exist.

The most careful analyses of protoplasm have never presented a completely accurate account of all the kinds of chemical substances present in it, or of the exact proportions in which they occur. In addition, constant chemical change is an integral aspect of the organization and nature of protoplasm, but it cannot be maintained during ordinary chemical analyses. Such analyses can, however, indicate the kinds of chemical elements present in protoplasm and the relative amounts in which they occur, and they may also provide information concerning the nature and amounts of the more stable chemical compounds present. Only a few techniques have been successfully used to assay certain compounds in living cells or cell parts. The ability of some substances to absorb radiant energy, such as ultraviolet light, may permit their identification within the living cell. Some substances take up certain stains, termed vital stains, and may thus be identified and located. And some substances take up radioactive chemicals, which can sometimes be supplied to living cells or organisms in forms that permit their utilization in place of similar, nonradioactive materials, and these can later be located with suitable detectors. Separation techniques for the removal of living organelles, such as nuclei, mitochondria, ribosomes and plastids, greatly facilitate their chemical and physiological characterization. A great deal of valuable information has been obtained from such studies of living systems, but much more remains to be learned.

Certain chemical elements are present in all living protoplasm of both plants and animals. Most abundant of these are oxygen, carbon, hydrogen, and nitrogen—in descending order of abundance. These four elements ordinarily constitute 95 to 98 percent of active protoplasm. Other chemical elements probably always present (in green plants at least) in smaller quantities are: sulfur, zinc, boron, manganese, phosphorus, calcium, magnesium, potassium, iron, molybdenum, copper, and chlorine. All of these elements are physiologically significant and perform specific functions. Frequently, chemical analyses of plant tissues reveal other elements, such as nickel, gold, tin, and mercury. These elements apparently are not required in the normal metabolism of most plants, and they may in fact be toxic if accumulated in sufficient quantity. Their presence in protoplasm often reflects the fact that they were present in the soil in which the plants grew, and the plants were unable to prevent their absorption. In fact, plants are used to help locate deposits of valuable minerals, such as uranium and selenium. One method involves the use of indicator plants; that is, location and chemical analysis

of plants known to tolerate accumulation of abnormally large quantities of certain minerals. Another technique involves chemical analysis of many or all of the species growing in a test area.

For the most part, chemicals do not occur in elemental form in protoplasm, but are combined with others to form chemical compounds. Chemical compounds are substances consisting of two or more elements held together, or bonded, by attractive forces. Water is a relatively simple compound; its chemical formula, H_2O, indicates that each molecule consists of two atoms of hydrogen (H) bonded to one atom of oxygen (O). Water is the most abundant chemical compound in active protoplasm, varying in amount from 70 to 97 percent by weight, although in dormant structures, such as seeds, the water content may be as low as 4 or 5 percent. Water is very important for the life processes of plant cells. It serves as the solvent for many substances that occur in protoplasm, vacuoles, and cell walls. It is the principal carrier substance for both soluble materials and insoluble particles that are transported from place to place within a cell or within a plant body. Water participates in a number of vital reactions, becoming part of more complex compounds or providing hydrogen and oxygen atoms for their formation. Water also serves a number of mechanical roles; it is involved in support of nonwoody tissues, in enlargement of protoplast and cell wall, and so on.

Many of the compounds important in the life processes of protoplasm are exceedingly complex, often with thousands of constituent atoms. The majority of these substances are synthesized by the plants themselves from simple compounds absorbed from the soil and atmosphere, and all contain large proportions of carbon atoms. Complex, carbon-containing compounds are found only in living cells or cell products, and the chemistry of terrestrial life is based principally upon the chemical and physical properties of carbon atoms. Because such compounds are so closely related to the organic beings that produce and utilize them, both plant and animal, they are

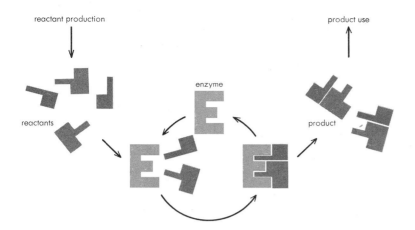

FIG. 5-1. Diagrammatic representations of enzyme-reactant interaction in the formation of a chemical product.

called *organic* compounds. Common kinds of organic compounds found in plants include foods (carbohydrates, lipids, and proteins), structural materials of cell walls, membranes, microtubules, and so on, regulatory chemicals, pigments, genetic material, many ergastic substances, etc.

The most abundant organic compounds of protoplasm are the **proteins.** Proteins are very large molecules (macromolecules) formed by chemical union of simpler substances called **amino acids.** Large numbers of amino acids are linked to one another in precise sequence and spatial arrangement to form the completed protein. Although there are only about twenty common kinds of amino acids, they can be combined in many sequences, ratios, and spatial patterns to form thousands of kinds of protein molecules. The proteins of active protoplasm are very delicate structures that can be altered or irreparably damaged by adverse factors, such as exposure to extremes of alkalinity or acidity or to certain other chemical substances, heat, and radiation. The altered protein molecule is unable to function normally in cell metabolism, and extensive alteration results in death of the cell or organism.

Common among the proteins in living cells are those called **enzymes.** An enzyme molecule may consist of the protein molecule alone, or it may be formed by the union of a protein with a nonproteinaceous substance, the so-called coenzyme,

such as a vitamin or a metal. The enzymes of a cell function as **catalysts,** speeding reactions that would normally occur much more slowly. As catalysts, enzymes are involved in reactions that lead to certain chemical products, but are not changed or altered in any way by the reaction; thus the enzyme emerges from the process ready to participate immediately in subsequent similar reactions (Fig. 5-1). The exact mechanism of enzymatic catalysis is still unknown, but it is presumed to be dependent upon the spatial and electrical properties of both the enzyme and the substances involved in the reactions. Because an enzyme molecule can participate time after time in a particular kind of reaction, only a relatively small number of a given type need be present. Another characteristic of most enzymes is their high specificity; that is, they can only catalyze a particular kind of reaction, or a small number of similar kinds of reactions. Therefore, a great many different kinds of enzymes may be active simultaneously in a single cell. The kinds and amounts of enzymes present in a cell determine, in large part, the things it is capable of doing, and the nature of the cell itself. Much of the study of life processes of organisms involves study of the production, structure, occurrence, and function of enzymes active in those processes.

Many other kinds of chemical compounds are present in living cells, in addition to water, amino acids, proteins, and enzymes. Common among these are sugars, starch, lipids, organic acids, mineral salts, nucleic acids, pigments, and numerous others. Many of these substances, however, are not truly vital constituents of living protoplasm. Some are waste products of physiological processes; others are simple precursors that the protoplasm builds into more complex substances; still others, such as sugars, are foods used as sources of energy.

PHYSICAL NATURE OF PROTOPLASM

The protoplasm of the cell differs in consistency from the watery vacuole, and is usually relatively viscous or gelatinous. It can be characterized as a **colloidal** system, consisting of solid and liquid particles in water. In a typical colloidal system of this kind, the particles may be single, large molecules (such as the macromolecular proteins or enzymes), or aggregates of molecules (such as clustered molecules of lipids, fats, and certain organic acids). A particle is considered to be colloidal when its diameter is 0.001 to 0.1 micron. The presence of colloidal particles may be inferred from the turbidity they give protoplasm, or from the reflection of light rays from their surfaces. Colloidal particles may remain suspended indefinitely in the medium in which they are present, or if the colloid is unstable, they may precipitate in response to slight changes in the chemical or physical nature of the medium. Colloidal systems may be liquid, as in the protein-in-water colloidal system of egg white, or they may be semisolid, as in gelatin desserts. A liquid colloidal state is termed a **sol,** a semisolid one a **gel.** Protoplasm is for the most part a sol, though under certain conditions it loses its liquid quality and becomes a gel. Changes in the colloidal state of protoplasm, which are often reversible, are induced in part by changes in external factors, such as temperature, and by certain types of light rays, and in part by internal changes such as acidity. Sometimes the gelation of a colloidal sol is not reversible, as for example, when egg white

is coagulated by boiling water. Coagulation is an irreversible colloidal gelation that results in the death of protoplasm. In addition to their occurrence in protoplasm, colloidal systems are also found among the solid, structural elements of the cell wall.

The colloidal particles are principally proteinaceous, and the physiological activities of living protoplasm are in large degree dependent upon its colloidal organization. The individual particles of the colloid are not necessarily identical; in fact, the ability of the protoplast to carry on simultaneously a variety of chemical and physical reactions is largely attributable to the heterogeneity of its colloid particles. The colloidal systems of protoplasm and cell walls are often capable of absorbing large quantities of water, and of holding the water tenaciously against drying forces, just as gelatin dessert remains moist even after several days' exposure to dry air.

In addition to its function as the suspension medium for colloidal particles, water serves as the solvent for many substances in true solution in protoplasm. Substances in solution in the aqueous portion of protoplasm are of such a nature that their molecules can freely dissociate and move independently among the water molecules (dissolve). Some molecules, particularly those of substances called electrolytes, break up when in solution to form electrically charged portions called **ions.** Ions may bear positive charges (cations) or negative charges (anions). Many of the elements listed earlier, including sulfur, manganese, potassium, calcium, phosphorus, and so on, are taken into the plant from the soil solution in ionic form. Other substances in solution, such as sugar, some pigments, etc., do not ionize to any great extent. Molecules or ions in true solution are very small, much less than 0.001 micron in diameter; they cannot settle out of solution, and tend to remain dispersed indefinitely. They are too small to reflect or otherwise influence the path of light rays, and true solutions appear clear and without turbidity. Chemicals in solution are ordinarily found in protoplasm, cell walls, and vacuoles, and are often important primary reactants in the chemical processes necessary for life.

In addition to the solution and colloidal systems described above, protoplasm also contains the organelles and ergastic substances described in Chapter 4. Thus, the cytoplasm may be visualized as a complex meshwork of membranes, colloidal particles, and certain organelles, with solutions, other organelles and various nonliving particles filling the spaces between. Within the complicated arrangement of components, thousands of reactions, interactions, and reorganizations are constantly in progress, providing the whole with the dynamic characteristics of life. Of the many physiological activities that go on in plant cells, only two groups of processes will be described in this chapter: the absorption of solutes and the absorption of water. An understanding of these activities is essential to an understanding of the functions and growth of roots, which will be described in the following chapters. Detailed accounts of other important physiological processes, such as photosynthesis, digestion, and respiration, will be deferred until subsequent chapters.

THE ABSORPTION OF WATER BY CELLS

In the performance of their physiological activities, plant cells are continually taking in certain materials and allowing others to pass out. The ability of their cells to act in this manner is prerequisite to all other processes of plants. Of the substances that enter plant cells, water is fundamentally important. Thus, knowledge of how living cells absorb water is necessary to an understanding of the basic processes of plants.

The absorption of water by living plant cells is not thoroughly understood, but it appears to involve at least two processes: **imbibition** and **osmosis.** Both of these are purely physical processes; that is, they occur in nonliving systems as well as in living cells.

When a cell is in contact with water, the cell wall and the protoplasm absorb water by imbibi-

tion, which may be defined as the soaking up of a liquid by solid substances, especially substances in colloidal condition. The process occurs in substances that are porous or have a large amount of surface, and it is caused by the attraction of water molecules to the surface. Imbibition is the phenomenon observed when a dry piece of wood or a piece of gelatin soaks up water. Both of these substances are solids having a large amount of submicroscopic pores that water may enter. Since they are so porous, the amount of solid surfaces in contact with water in the pores is enormous and the water is strongly attracted and bound to the surface. Cellulose, pectic substances, protoplasmic proteins, and other organic compounds in plant cells have great powers of imbibition. Both cell walls and living protoplasm absorb water by imbibition and increase in size as they do so. This may be readily observed in the swelling of dry seeds placed in water. If imbibing materials are confined, they exert considerable pressure as they absorb the liquid and swell. If a glass jar with a tight-fitting lid is partly filled with dry seeds, if the lid is punctured with two or three small holes that admit water, and if the jar is then inverted in a pan of water so that the seeds may imbibe the water, the seeds will burst the jar within 24 hours as a result of the **imbibitional pressure** they exert. The bursting of the seed coats of germinating seeds is the result of imbibitional pressure together with the force produced by the cells of the embryo as they enlarge. The engineers of ancient Egypt, in building the pyramids, split rock masses by hammering thoroughly dried wooden wedges into cracks in the rock and pouring water over the wedges; the wooden wedges slowly imbibed water, swelling as they did so, and exerted sufficient pressure to fracture the rocks.

Osmosis   The phenomenon of imbibition is sufficient to explain the uptake of water by cell walls, and to some extent by protoplasm, but in living protoplasm, additional forces are involved in the process of water absorption. One of these

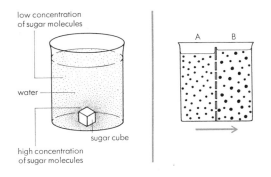

low concentration
of sugar molecules

water

sugar cube

high concentration
of sugar molecules

A   B

FIG. 5-2. (Left). Illustration of diffusion of a solid in a liquid. FIG. 5-3. (Right). Diagrammatic representation of osmosis. The container is divided into two compartments, A and B, by a differentially permeable membrane (color). The membrane permits passage of water molecules (small dots), but prohibits passage of sugar molecules (large dots). Water molecules diffuse in both directions across the membrane, but diffusion is greatest from the region of higher concentration (A), to that of a lower concentration (B). As indicated by the arrow, the *net* movement of water is from A to B, and is increasing the volume of the sugar solution.

is the physical phenomenon of osmosis, which is basically a process of **diffusion.** At normal temperatures the molecules of all substances are in motion. In a liquid, the molecules tumble over each other to produce a gradual mixing. If the space available to a group of like molecules is enlarged, the molecules tend to move into it until they are evenly distributed through both the original and the newly available space. Because a given number of molecules is more concentrated in a small space than in a larger space, the effect of diffusion is often described as the movement of molecules from a place of greater concentration to places of lower concentration. When a lump of sugar is dropped into a beaker of water, the sugar slowly dissolves and there is a net movement of its molecules from the surface of the lump (region of greater concentration) to more remote parts of the water in the beaker (regions

of lesser concentration of sugar), as shown in Fig. 5-2. After a time, the lump of sugar disappears and the sugar particles, having overcome the resistance of the solvent by means of their motion, become equally distributed throughout the surrounding liquid. When the molecules of a substance have become equally distributed through the available space, the system is said to be in equilibrium. Although individual molecules continue to move within the space, their *concentration* throughout that space remains constant.

The ability of molecules or ions to diffuse is dependent upon their capacity for movement; at room temperature this capacity is determined by their **free energy.** This energy is proportional to the concentration of the diffusing particles. The greater the concentration, the more rapidly they tend to move into unoccupied space. Thus, in the sugar experiment just described, the free energy of the sugar molecules is initially greatest near the dissolving lump, since the concentration of sugar molecules is greatest in that space; the free energy is least in the more remote portions of the container, since the concentration of sugar molecules is lower at greater distances from the lump. Both the direction of movement and the speed of movement are influenced by the free energy levels of molecules in different portions of the system. Net change ceases when the free energy levels are the same (i.e., in equilibrium) throughout the system, that is, when the concentration is uniform throughout the system. Another significant feature of diffusion is that a diffusing molecule moves practically independently of other molecules in the available space. If both sugar and salt are added to a beaker of water, the molecules of each of these substances diffuse until they are equally distributed in the liquid. The rate and direction of diffusion of the molecules of one substance in a mixture of molecules of other substances are ordinarily determined by the concentration of each substance considered by itself.

It will be apparent that in the sugar example above, diffusion was not limited to this substance,

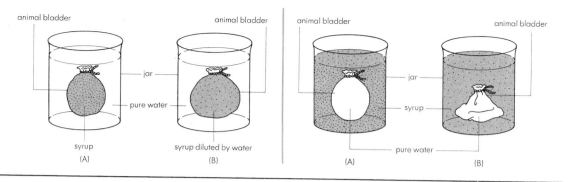

FIG. 5–4. (Left). Osmosis experiment with animal bladder filled with syrup. (A) At beginning of the experiment. (B) After several hours. FIG. 5–5. (Right) Osmosis experiment with animal bladder filled with water and immersed in syrup. (A) At beginning of the experiment. (B) After several hours.

but also involved the diffusion of water. As the sugar molecules diffused among the molecules of water, the water molecules diffused among the molecules of sugar, and the net changes in the concentrations of both substances tended to mix them evenly and to bring the free energy levels into equilibrium.

Osmosis in living systems usually involves the diffusion of water molecules through **differentially permeable membranes.** A differentially permeable membrane is one that allows the passage of certain molecules, but prohibits or restricts the passage of others. A pig bladder is a membrane of this type; it permits, for example, the passage of water but prevents the movement through it of sugar dissolved in water. One of the most noteworthy attributes of living cells is the large number of membranes found in each. In addition to the plasma and vacuolar membranes bounding the cytoplasm, the endoplasmic reticulum is a system of membranes, the cytoplasmic organelles are delimited by membranes, and many of the organelles themselves contain complex, interior membrane systems. As pointed out in Chapter 4, the typical membrane is believed to consist of three layers: two surface layers of protein molecules separated by a lipid layer. These membrane systems provide extensive surface areas upon which reactions occur, and substances that enter and leave cells and organelles must pass through

membranes. The cytoplasmic membranes are of the differentially permeable type. They allow water and certain nutrient particles to pass through readily, but restrict or prevent the movement through them of certain sugars, pigments, and other materials, especially those of organic nature. The state of membrane permeability varies with age, health, vigor, and chemical constitution of the protoplasm, and with various factors in the external environment. The fluctuating permeability of the membranes of living protoplasm is evidence of the sensitivity of living matter, and of its powers of adjustment to rapidly changing internal and external conditions. In nonliving membranes there are no such frequent and continuous alterations of permeability. The effects of a change in the permeability of cell membranes upon protoplasmic contents may be demonstrated by placing a sliced red beet in cold water. The membranes of the beet cells are impermeable to the red pigment and thus prevent its diffusion into the water. The water remains colorless, except for traces of the pigment freed by the cutting of certain cells by the knife. If, however, the beet slices in the water are heated to the death point of protoplasm, the high temperature kills the protoplasm and alters the state of the membranes, which become permeable to most of the red pigment, allowing it to diffuse out of the cells and thus to color the water red.

We may define osmosis as the diffusion of water molecules through a differentially permeable membrane, from a place in which their free energy is greater to a place in which their free energy is lesser. Ordinarily, the place of lesser free energy is one in which the water molecules have been diluted by the addition of solute molecules to which the membrane is impermeable (Fig. 5–3), although factors other than concentration may also influence the free energy level of the water. The phenomenon of osmosis may be demonstrated by the experiments pictured in Figs. 5–4 and 5–5. If a thoroughly cleaned animal bladder or a length of semipermeable dialysis tubing is filled with a highly concentrated sugar solution, such as syrup, if its apertures are tightly bound to prevent leakage, and if it is then immersed in a vessel of water, osmosis into the bladder or the tubing occurs. The volume of liquid inside increases, and the container becomes distended by the pressure of the accumulating liquid; this pressure may become sufficiently great to burst the container. In this experiment, the bladder membrane or dialysis tubing is impermeable to sugar molecules, which remain within it, but is permeable to water. Because of the presence of sugar molecules, the liquid within the container has a lower concentration of water molecules and less free energy than the liquid (pure water) outside. The net movement of water molecules is from the region of high concentration of water (outside the container) toward the region of lower water concentration inside. If conditions of the experiment are reversed by filling the bladder or tubing with water and submerging it in syrup, the net diffusion of water molecules is from the inside to the surrounding syrup, and the container shrinks as a result of loss of the enclosed water; in this experiment, water molecules behave exactly as they did in the first experiment—their net movement is from the region of high water concentration (in the second experiment, inside the container) toward the region of lower water concentration (outside the container). There is an analogy between a plant cell and the simple

physical experiment described above. In a plant cell, the plasma and vacuolar membranes, with the thin layer of cytoplasm between them, behave as a differentially permeable membrane, comparable to the bladder or dialysis tubing. The cell sap is a droplet of water with various materials, especially sugars and salts, dissolved in it. The cell sap is comparable to the sugar solution inside the bladder, for the cell membranes are impermeable to many of the materials dissolved in the cell sap, just as the bladder is impermeable to sugar. Such a cell is in contact with other cells or, if it is an epidermal cell of a root, it is in contact with the water and dissolved materials (**soil solution**) in the soil. The soil solution normally contains a much smaller concentration of dissolved materials than does the cell sap; or, stated conversely, the soil solution contains proportionately more water than does cell sap. The equalization tendency of diffusion prevails, and there is a net movement of water from the place of its greater concentration (or greater free energy)—namely, the soil—into the cell, which is the place of lesser water concentration (or lower free energy). Thus, the soil solution is roughly comparable with the pure water in the dish surrounding the bladder or tubing in our simple physical experiment. In similar manner, water inside a plant may move from a cell with a relatively high concentration of water (low concentration of solutes) into a cell with a lower concentration of water (higher concentration of solutes). The net movement of water from cell to cell or from the soil solution into root cells continues as long as there is a difference in the relative concentrations (or free energy levels) of water between cells or between the soil solution and the root cells. The rate at which water moves into a cell depends chiefly on the difference between its concentrations inside and outside the cell; the greater the difference, the more rapid the movement. The term **osmotic potential** is frequently used to indicate the relative free energy of water in the cell as it is affected by the amount of dissolved materials. When solute concentrations in cells are high, the water concentration is low, and therefore its relative free energy is low. In this situation the cell would be said to have a low osmotic potential. On the other hand, cell sap having few solutes would have a high water concentration, high free energy, and high osmotic potential. It should be obvious that water has a much greater tendency to enter a cell with a low osmotic potential than one with a high osmotic potential, other things being equal. In practice, osmotic potential is given a negative sign and is read much as one reads a thermometer when the temperature is below zero. Pure water has an osmotic potential of zero; as solutes are added to it, the concentration of water drops, its free energy therefore drops, and the osmotic potential of the solution becomes negative. Osmotic potentials are often expressed in negative atmospheres, so that a cell might have an osmotic potential of −10 atmospheres, for example.

It should be emphasized that the comparison between the bladder experiment and the situation in a plant cell is a crude one. The same fundamental principle of diffusion is operative in both cases, but the bladder membrane is a non-living membrane with unchanging properties, whereas the membranes of a living cell are continually undergoing changes in permeability. The concentration of materials in the cell sap varies from one moment to the next, and similarly, the concentration of soil solution or of adjacent cells continually fluctuates. Thus, in the absorption of water by living cells, although the basic physical forces of diffusion are at work, their actual operation is conditioned by the living protoplasm.

TURGOR

Plant cells, except when wilting occurs, contain water in such quantity that the protoplasm is forced outward against the cell walls by the pressure of the water in the cell sap. The extent to which the protoplast can be expanded is, of course, limited by the surrounding wall of cellulose, which can be stretched only slightly by

internal pressure. The pressure exerted by the cell contents against the cell wall is called **turgor pressure.** It is produced by the tendency of water to enter the cell, which is, in turn, a product of the osmotic potential of the cell contents. The osmotic potential determines the theoretical maximum pressure that can be developed in the cell sap solution, which is separated from pure water by a membrane that is permeable only to water. However, the turgor pressure of a cell is always less than this maximum; that is, the cell is never in an environment of *pure* water. The osmotic potential of the cell sap of some species of plants may be lower than −100 atmospheres (1 atmosphere is approximately 15 pounds of pressure per square inch). These low potentials may be found in certain desert plants or in some plants growing in saline soil. In most species of plants, however, the osmotic potential of the cell sap is rarely lower than −25 atmospheres.

A cell whose protoplasm exhibits turgor pressure is said to be turgid or to possess turgidity. Turgidity is responsible for the crisp, rigid condition of lettuce leaves or of celery that is immersed in water. When such vegetables wilt, the protoplasts in their cells lose so much of their water that they no longer exert an outward pressure against the cells walls and the tissues become limp; that is, they lose their turgidity. Turgidity is important in plants in that it aids in the maintenance of form and provides in young cells the pressure that makes growth in size possible. All plant tissues that are well supplied with water and that do not lose water more rapidly than they absorb it are normally turgid.

PLASMOLYSIS

In accordance with the laws of diffusion, there is a net movement of water out of a plant cell when the relative concentration of water outside the cell becomes less than that inside the cell sap. This is a common phenomenon in the transfer of water from one cell to another. In plant tissues, normally, when water moves from cell to cell,

FIG. 5–6. Plasmolysis. (A). Normal, turgid cell. (B). Plasmolyzed cell.

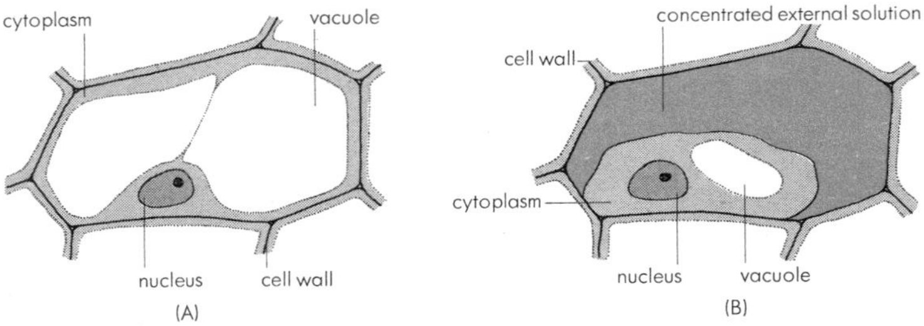

the cell that is losing water is in most cases simultaneously receiving water from some other cell, or from the soil. As a result of this give and take, the water supply of a cell is replenished on one side as it is decreased on another side and the cell retains its turgidity. If, however, water passes out of a cell toward a region of lesser water concentration, and this outwardly moving water is not replenished, the inevitable result is a loss of volume of the protoplast and its consequent shrinkage (Fig. 5–6). The shrinkage of protoplasm away from the cell wall, due to reduced internal pressure as a result of excessive water loss, is termed **plasmolysis.** Plasmolysis may be demonstrated by placing a strip of carrot root or potato tuber in a concentrated salt solution. The relative concentration of water, volume for volume, is less in the concentrated salt solution than it is in the cell sap. Because there is greater free energy of water within the cells, there is a net movement of water from the cell of the potato or carrot into the salt solution. This causes a loss of turgidity, and the plasmolyzed tissues become very limp. Plasmolysis, if it continues too long, causes the death of the plasmolyzed cells. If after a short time, however, the plasmolyzed tissues are transferred from the salt solution to pure water, the direction of net water movement is reversed, for there is now relatively more water outside the cells than there is inside. Water thus passes inward, the protoplasm increases in volume as the turgor pressure of the cell sap increases, and the tissue regains its turgidity.

The principle of plasmolysis is employed in a number of practical ways. In the making of fruit jellies, usually more sugar is added to the juice than the amount needed to achieve the desired degree of sweetness. This raises the solute content of the jelly (decreases the relative proportion of water) to such an extent that decay and fermentation bacteria and the reproductive cells of molds falling into the jelly are quickly plasmolyzed; the water in them diffuses outward toward the region of lesser water concentration, namely into the jelly. Thus, the jelly will not spoil even when exposed to the open air. Through the addition of quantities of salt to meat and fish the same objective is fulfilled. The organisms of decay that come into contact with the salted foods are plasmolyzed and killed, and thus the meat or fish does not spoil. Another application of the plasmolysis principle is found in the spreading of salt on clay tennis courts or in the cracks of brick walks to kill undesired plants. The seedlings of these plants, when they come into contact with the salt, are plasmolyzed and killed. Pasture weeds, such as the obnoxious Canada thistle, that are difficult to uproot, may be destroyed by placing a small quantity of salt about their roots. Plants killed in this manner wilt and turn brown as they die. Because of the wilting and browning of plasmolyzed plants, farmers and gardeners frequently term their manner of death "burning." Residues of insecticidal and fungicidal sprays sometimes cause "burning" of leaves.

If, in the application of fertilizers to soils, excessive amounts are added, the concentration of water in the soil solution may become less than that in the cell sap of plants growing in the soil. As a result, the cells of the plants are plasmolyzed

FIG. 5–7. Effects of plasmolysis on cuttings of *Coleus.* Left: Cutting in water. Right: Cutting after 1 hour in 15% salt solution.

and the plants wilt and die unless the excessive salts are washed away by rain. Directions given for the spreading of fertilizers should be followed carefully if this disastrous effect of plasmolysis is to be avoided.

THE ABSORPTION OF SOLUTES

The absorption of dissolved particles by root cells from the soil solution, as well as by one cell from an adjacent cell, is a complex phenomenon, not all the forces of which are known. Only two of the several processes known to be involved in the absorption of solutes will be discussed here. One of these, simple diffusion, is described as a *passive* process since it requires no energy expenditure by the cell; the other, **active transport,** is an *active* process utilizing energy liberated by metabolism.

Diffusion and Passive Transport   In simple diffusion, molecules of dissolved materials follow the basic law of diffusion; that is, they move from regions in which their concentration is high to regions in which their concentration is lower. The continuation of such movement depends upon the maintenance of a concentration difference of the particles of the diffusing substance; movement by simple diffusion continues only so long as the particles are present in greater concentration in one region than in another. This type of movement occurs in plant cells. In such absorption, solute molecules move into a cell (for example, a surface cell of the root) when their concentration is greater outside the cell than it is inside. As they enter a cell, these molecules usually undergo transformation into other chemical compounds or they move on to other cells; thus, they do not often accumulate to a high concentration within a cell. Such movement, depending only on diffusion, is called **passive transport.**

Active Transport   In this process, ions formed by the dissociation of molecules (for example, NH_4^+ ions and NO_3^- ions formed by the dissociation of ammonium nitrate, or NH_4NO_3 molecules), enter a cell in violation of the basic law of diffusion; that is, they move into a cell even though their concentration may be higher in that cell than in the soil or in adjoining cells. Such movement is in a direction opposite to that which would be maintained in the case of simple diffusion. The result of active transport is that the concentration of some ions becomes many times greater in plant cells than outside the cells. It appears that this process accounts for a much greater part of solute absorption than does simple diffusion. The process is thus an exceedingly important one. This absorption of solute particles against a concentration gradient requires the expenditure of energy by living protoplasm and is directly related to the energy-releasing process of respiration. Experimental evidence indicates that oxygen supply and presence of respirable foods, such as sugars, are closely connected with ion accumulation, and oxygen and foods are essential to respiration. When the oxygen supply is reduced, when food supplies are scanty, or when chemicals that inhibit respiration are added to plant tissues, ion accumulation diminishes or ceases. Relatively little is known about the actual mechanism of active transport. A current theory suggests the existence of a "carrier" that facilitates transport across the membrane. According to this explanation, the ion at the outer membrane surface enters into a temporary chemical union with the carrier; then, after passing through the membrane, the ion and the carrier dissociate. There is considerable controversy regarding the nature of the carrier, and a variety of compounds, including the protoplasm itself, have been suggested.

The molecules of the important mineral salts of the soil, for example, magnesium sulfate, potassium nitrate, and calcium phosphate, dissociate freely in the soil solution. Ordinarily such substances must be dissolved in soil water before they enter a cell, but investigations have indicated that root cells occasionally may absorb molecules and ions directly from soil particles, that is, without dissolution of these particles in soil water.

SUMMARY

1. Protoplasm is a complex system of chemical substances and organized structures.

2. The most abundant chemical elements in living protoplasm are carbon, hydrogen, oxygen, and nitrogen, which constitute between 95 and 98 percent of protoplasm. The remaining 2 to 5 percent is made up principally of small amounts of sulfur, calcium, phosphorus, potassium, iron, magnesium, manganese, zinc, boron, copper, molybdenum, and chlorine.

3. The most abundant compounds of protoplasm are water and proteins; less abundant are sugars, fats, pigments, and others.

4. Water is important as a solvent and as a participant in numerous vital reactions. It also serves mechanical functions in cell enlargement and support.

5. The complex compounds important in life processes contain carbon atoms and are termed "organic compounds."

6. The most abundant organic compounds of protoplasm are the macromolecular proteins. Proteins are constructed of simpler compounds called amino acids. Although there are only about 20 common amino acids, they can be combined to form thousands of kinds of proteins.

7. The majority of proteins appear to function in plant cells as enzymes. Enzymes are highly specific catalysts that promote necessary

reactions within protoplasm; a given enzyme molecule can participate repeatedly in the reaction it catalyzes.

8. Protoplasm is a colloidal system of water and colloidal particles, the most abundant of which are the proteins. In consistency it may vary from a more liquid sol to a more solid gel.

9. In addition to colloidal particles, protoplasm contains many materials found in solution. Molecules of electrolytes break up in solution to form electrically charged fragments called ions.

10. Water enters plant cells principally by means of the special diffusion process called osmosis. Osmosis is the diffusion of water through a differentially permeable membrane from a region of higher water concentration to a region of lesser concentration. Normal osmosis takes place because the watery portions of the cell contain numerous dissolved substances that cannot pass through the differentially permeable membranes and cytoplasm that bound them.

11. If the concentration of osmotically active solutes outside the cell becomes greater than that within, water diffuses out of the cell, turgor decreases, and the protoplast shrinks. Shrinking of the protoplast beyond the minimum volume of the cell cavity is termed plasmolysis; continued or extreme plasmolysis may so upset the normal metabolic processes of the cell as to cause its death.

12. Water and solutes are transported into and within the plant by passive and active transport mechanisms.

13. Passive transport is accomplished by means of intrinsic physical properties of matter. It involves (1) simple diffusion, the net movement of molecules of a substance from a place of their greater concentration and free energy to places of lesser concentration and free energy, and (2) imbibition, the absorption of water by colloids.

14. Active transport is the accumulation of material against a diffusion or free energy gradient; it requires expenditure of energy by the cell. The mechanism of active transport is unknown, but it is believed to involve carrier substances that enter into temporary chemical union with the materials being transported.

15. As the volume of a cell increases through osmotic water uptake, the protoplast swells and presses against the cell wall. The pressure exerted by the cell contents against the cell wall is called turgor pressure. Turgor is important for cell enlargement and support.

SUGGESTED READINGS FOR INTERESTED STUDENTS

1. Bonner, J., and A. W. Galston, *Principles of Plant Physiology.* W. H. Freeman & Co., San Francisco, 1952.

2. Kozlowski, T. T., *Water Metabolism in Plants.* Harper and Row, New York, 1964.

3. Meyer, B. S., D. B. Anderson, and R. H. Böhning. *Introduction to Plant Physiology.* D. Van Nostrand Co., New York, 1960.

4. Ray, P. M., *The Living Plant*. Holt, Rinehart and Winston, New York, 1965.

TOPICS AND QUESTIONS FOR STUDY

1. List 10 elemental chemicals found in protoplasm, including the three most abundant.

2. Can one adequately characterize the nature of protoplasm by listing its chemical constituents? Explain.

3. Does the presence of a particular element in protoplasm signify that that element has a physiological function? Explain.

4. What is "plant prospecting"?

5. Discuss three important functions of water in cell life.

6. What are proteins? What are the relationships between proteins, amino acids, enzymes, and coenzymes?

7. What is catalysis? Discuss the catalytic role of enzymes, including statements concerning specificity for and reparticipation in reactions.

8. What is a colloid? What is a solution? What are the differences in size, reflectivity, and imbibitional properties of colloid and solution particles?

9. Contrast the sol and gel conditions of colloids. Which of these more adequately applies to fried egg white? Would you expect to find a colloidal condition comparable to that of fried egg white in a normal cell? Explain.

10. Distinguish between active and passive transport, and discuss the mechanisms of these two processes.

11. What is imbibition? Imbibition pressure? Describe an experiment to demonstrate imbibition pressure.

12. What is diffusion? Does stirring your coffee promote or substitute for diffusion of the sugar throughout it?

13. Define osmosis. Describe an experiment to illustrate osmosis.

14. What is the role of osmosis in the development of turgor pressure?

15. Of what significance is turgor pressure for cell growth? For support?

16. Is plasmolysis an osmotic process? Distinguish between osmosis and plasmolysis.

17. How might you burn your lawn with a too generous application of fertilizer?

6

CELL DUPLICATION AND THE HEREDITARY MATERIAL

One of the most fundamental and significant of all biological processes is reproduction of living cells. The capacity for cellular duplication, a characteristic of all living things, has its fundamental importance in the fact that organisms not only can but must duplicate cells in order to survive; organisms that lose or lack this ability eventually die from the cumulative effects of aging. Further, cell duplication enables living organisms to effect recovery from different kinds of injuries. A special biological significance lies in the extremely high degree of fidelity that characterizes the self-copying mechanism, for in terms of the heritable genetic information that resides in the nucleus, the two daughter cells resulting from a duplication are alike. Moreover, the genetic similarity between parent and daughter cells may be perpetuated through countless cell generations. Commensurate with the basic importance of cell duplication has been the continuing effort of many biologists and biochemists to understand and explain its complexities. While the progress

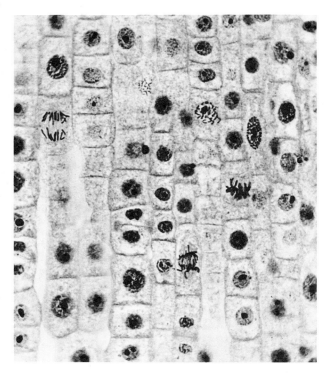

FIG. 6-1. Photomicrograph of meristematic tissue near the tip of a growing root, showing various stages in nuclear and cell duplication. (Courtesy of Triarch Botanical Products, Ripon, Wis.)

of recent years has dispelled many earlier mysteries, our understanding of cell duplication is by no means complete.

THE FORMATION OF NEW CELLS

Cell duplication, commonly termed cell division, consists of two major steps: the duplication (or division) of the parent cell nucleus to produce two nuclei, and the partitioning (or division) of the cytoplasm with the concomitant formation of the cell plate. The process of nuclear division is called **mitosis,** that of cytoplasmic division, **cytokinesis.** In the cells of some plants, several divisions of the nucleus occur without the formation of new walls; this results in cells with more than one nucleus, a condition found chiefly in some lower plants. In higher plants, however, each cell usually has only one nucleus because nuclear duplication is typically followed by cytokinesis and wall formation.

Mitosis   The net result of mitosis is the production of two daughter nuclei that are qualitatively and quantitatively identical; each daughter nucleus possesses the same hereditary materials and potentialities as the parent nucleus before its division. Such an exact distribution is achieved by the duplication and subsequent separation of the hereditary material in the nucleus. Duplication involves principally the molecular replication of deoxyribonucleic acid (DNA), the chief constituent of chromatin. This synthesis of hereditary material occurs in the so-called **interphase nucleus,** that is, the nucleus as it exists between successive duplications. The nuclear structure described in Chapter 4 is that of an interphase nucleus. The chromatin network, which is revealed when an interphase nucleus is treated with a suitable stain, is composed of a group of elongated, slender, twisted chromosomes. During interphase, the individual chromosomes are in their thinnest and most extended condition and are extremely difficult to demonstrate. The numbers of chromosomes per nucleus vary in different species of plants. In flowering plants, the numbers range from 4 to about 200; most species have fewer than 100. The chromosomes usually occur in pairs in most cells of flowering plants (except in some reproductive cells to be described later) and thus their numbers are usually even, for example, 20 in corn, 14 in red clover, 28 in durum wheat. The members of a chromosome pair are called **homologous chromosomes.** Structural and size differences among the various chromosome pairs in a plant are often readily visible under a microscope (see Fig. 6–3). The individuals of any given plant species are generally considered to have the same number of chromosomes in all their nonreproductive, or somatic (body), cells. Nevertheless, variations in chromosome number do occur infrequently in the somatic cells. For example, some

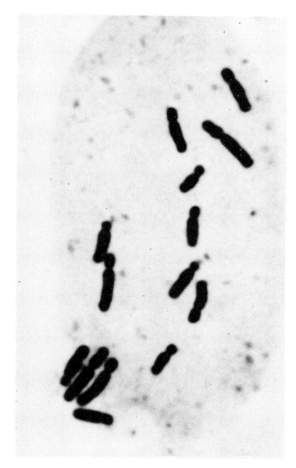

FIG. 6-2. Metaphase chromosomes in a squashed whole cell from the root tip of *Phlox pilosa*. Note the structural differences among the chromosomes. (Courtesy Dr. D. M. Smith, U. of California, Santa Barbara.)

"phases," which gradually merge into each other. A description of the events that take place during the various phases of mitosis follows.

PROPHASE   In this first phase of mitosis, the chromosomes undergo a marked shortening and thickening, developing into rod-shaped structures that are distinctly visible as separate entities and may be only $\frac{1}{20}$ the length of the interphase chromosomes. With these processes of shortening and thickening, the netlike structure in the interphase nucleus disappears. Under the light microscope, each chromosome appears to consist of two longitudinally arranged threads, called **chromatids,** which are often coiled around each other. As mitosis proceeds, the longitudinal separation between chromatids becomes more pronounced. A structure called the **spindle** begins to develop, arising at opposite ends **(poles)** of the nucleus; from the poles, clusters of fiberlike structures (microtubles at the electron microscope level) begin to grow inward toward the nucleus. The nuclear membrane then disappears and some microtubules of the spindle extend through the nucleus from one pole of the spindle to the other. Prior to, or simultaneous with, the beginning of spindle development, the nucleolus typically disappears. The process of spindle formation is incompletely understood. The spindle apparatus is known to contain proteins, fatty substances, and ribonucleic acid (RNA); in plant cells it appears to develop largely from nuclear material and to a much lesser extent from cytoplasm.

METAPHASE   In this phase of mitosis, the chromosomes, now with pronounced longitudinal separations, become arranged in the central, wide portion (equator) of the spindle midway between the poles. The constricted region **(centromere)** of each chromosome appears attached to the poles of the spindle apparatus by strands of microtubules, the so-called chromosomal fibers. These fibrous connections are established in such a way that *sister chromatids are never attached to the same pole;* instead, sister chromatids are always

cells in young roots of various plant species have been shown to contain twice the expected number of chromosomes. This condition is believed to result when cytokinesis fails to occur after mitosis.

For the sake of convenience, biologists usually divide the process of mitosis into a number of phases (see Fig. 6-2), each of which bears a technical name. Actually mitosis is a continuous process with no distinctly marked stages. These "phases" are thus comparable to the moon's

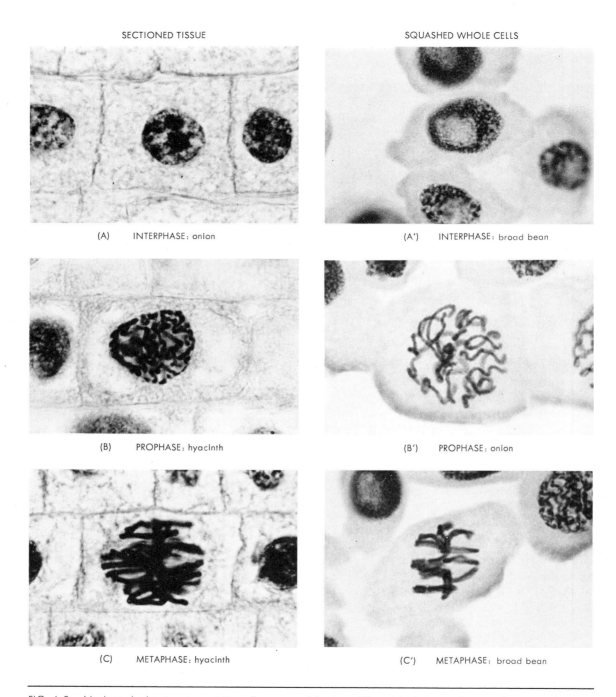

SECTIONED TISSUE   SQUASHED WHOLE CELLS

(A)   INTERPHASE: onion   (A')   INTERPHASE: broad bean

(B)   PROPHASE: hyacinth   (B')   PROPHASE: onion

(C)   METAPHASE: hyacinth   (C')   METAPHASE: broad bean

FIG. 6–3. Nuclear duplication in root tip cells prepared by two different techniques. See text for an explanation of the principal mitotic events.

(D) EARLY ANAPHASE: onion

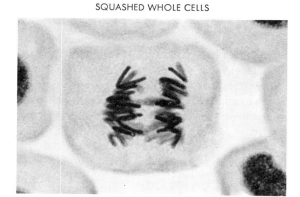

(D') EARLY ANAPHASE: onion

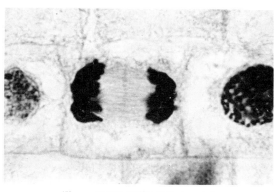

(E) EARLY TELOPHASE: hyacinth

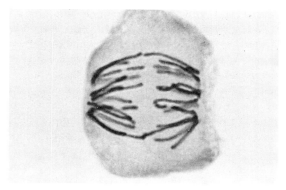

(E') LATE ANAPHASE: broad bean

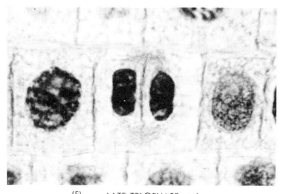

(F) LATE TELOPHASE: onion

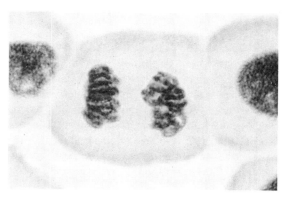

(F') LATE TELOPHASE: onion

linked to opposite poles of the mitotic apparatus. Usually by the end of metaphase, sister chromatids are united only at the centromere. The position of the centromere on a chromosome divides the chromosome transversely into two portions (arms) of equal or unequal length. In metaphase, it is the centromeres that are aligned in the equatorial plane; the chromosome arms may extend in almost any direction.

ANAPHASE   This stage begins with the simultaneous, longitudinal splitting of the centromeres, following which the sister chromatids (now daughter chromosomes) begin to separate. One new chromosome of each pair moves toward one pole of the spindle, and the other chromosome of the same pair migrates toward the opposite pole. Moreover, the spindle itself elongates; that is, there is a further separation of its poles. Little is known about the mechanism of these movements. At the termination of anaphase, two groups of chromosomes are present, one group at each pole of the spindle. The number of chromosomes present in *each* of these groups is the same as the number present in the prophase of mitosis, since each of the prophase chromosomes splits longitudinally by separation of its chromatids and since each of the two chromatids of a prophase chromosome becomes a fully developed chromosome after separation of the chromatids in anaphase.

TELOPHASE   In this phase the two groups of daughter chromosomes are at the spindle poles. The nuclear membranes and nucleoli become reconstituted, and the chromosomes become transformed into the long, slender threads characteristic of the interphase nucleus. Thus, in telophase, two daughter nuclei are formed, one at each end of the spindle. Telophase concludes the process of mitosis.

Cytokinesis   As the reorganization of interphase nuclei proceeds in telophase, the spindle begins to disappear near the nuclei and widens greatly at the equator until it extends almost completely across the cytoplasm. Electron microscopic studies have shown that as the spindle of the plant cell widens, certain organelles migrate to the equatorial plane. These organelles include portions of the endoplasmic reticulum and small, nearly spherical bodies that are thought to play a role in subsequent wall formation. Minute droplets of what may be pectic substances are also deposited in the equatorial plane. In an imperfectly understood manner, this material is then organized into a thin, continuous **cell plate** that extends across the cell, separating the cytoplasm into two portions, each with its new nucleus (Fig. 6–4). The cell plate becomes the middle lamella or intercellular layer upon which the primary walls are subsequently deposited by adjacent daughter protoplasts. The formation of the cell plate marks the end of cytokinesis; wall formation may continue throughout cell enlargement and differentiation.

Some recent research on meristematic tissues has revealed a cytological feature that has some relationship to the orientation of the plane of cell division and thereby may bear a relationship to cell plate formation. Electron microscope studies of dividing cells have revealed the presence of a **preprophase band** of microtubules that encircles the cell in the peripheral cytoplasm. The band is loosely organized and short lived, disappearing just before nuclear prophase begins. Of particular interest is the fact that the band lies in the equatorial plane where, after nuclear duplication, the future cell plate will contact the parent cell wall.

Rate of Mitosis   The time required for the completion of mitosis and cytokinesis varies in different cells and in different species of plants. Its speed is also influenced by varying environmental conditions. At temperatures of 70° F to 80° F, the processes of mitosis and cytokinesis are usually completed within 60 to 90 minutes. Thus it is apparent that the complex processes of chromosome condensation, spindle formation, chromosome splitting, etc., occur rather rapidly.

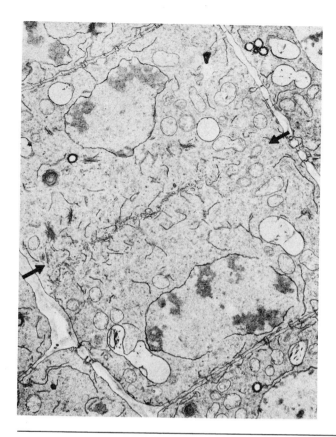

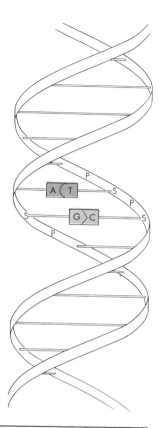

FIG. 6–4. (left). Electron micrograph showing developing cell plate (between arrows) in maize rootcap. (Courtesy of Dr. Hilton H. Mollenhauer, Kettering Res. Labs, Yellow Springs, O.) FIG. 6–5. (right). Diagram representing a portion of the DNA double helix. The "backbone" of each strand is formed from phosphate (P) and sugar (S) groups. The cross bars represent complementary base pairs (A-T, T-A, G-C, C-G), two of which are shown at center.

THE HEREDITARY MATERIAL

The complex nuclear behavior that we call mitosis is a precisely regulated sequence of events that accomplishes equal distribution of the hereditary units, or **genes,** from a parent nucleus to the daughter nuclei developed from it. Evidence indicates that mitosis cannot begin until certain preparative chemical events have occurred, including synthesis of the hereditary material, DNA. To understand how DNA can be replicated with neither change nor loss of hereditary information, and to understand the nature of the information itself, we must consider the chemical composition and physical structure of the DNA molecule.

The modern conception of DNA structure is embodied in the well-known Watson and Crick model advanced in the early 1950s. Using data and techniques from many sources, these men constructed a three-dimensional wire model of a short segment of DNA that agreed with the essential experimental observations. They visualized the molecule as two parallel chains of subunits **(nucleotides)** coiled to form a long helix or, more properly, a right-handed double helix

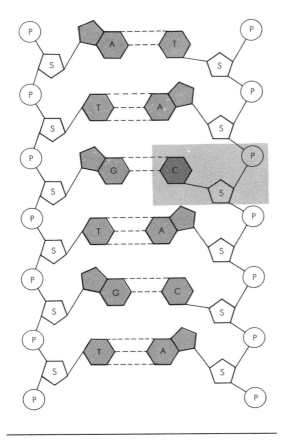

FIG. 6-6. A diagrammatic representation of a short segment of DNA, showing two vertical nucleotide chains linked by hydrogen bonds (dotted lines). The box delimits a single nucleotide.

(Fig. 6-5). The two chains can be compared to a ladder, where each nucleotide represents part of a rung and an upright (Fig. 6-6). Each nucleotide consists of a phosphate group—the 5-carbon sugar, **deoxyribose**—and one of four different nitrogenous bases—**adenine, guanine, cytosine,** and **thymine.** Adenine (A) and guanine (G) belong to a class of compounds called purines, while cytosine (C), and thymine (T) are pyrimidines (Fig. 6-7). The two chains of nucleotides are apposed so that the phosphate-sugar "backbones" (the uprights of the ladder) are on the outside and the bases are directed toward the middle, forming the rungs. Each rung consists of a pair of bases, one a purine and the other a pyrimidine. The purine-pyrimidine bases can pair in only four ways: A-T, T-A, G-C, and C-G. Although the sugar-phosphate backbones are strongly held together, the pairs of bases are only weakly linked—C and its complement G with three hydrogen bonds, A and T with only two.

Molecules of DNA are extremely long—evidence indicates that molecular weights may exceed 100,000,000—and contain great quantities of encoded information. (The nature of the DNA code is described in Chapter 19.) Although there are only four base-pair combinations, the pairs may be arranged sequentially along the length of the molecule in an enormous number of different ways. It is this specific linear arrangement of bases that contains the hereditary information.

FIG. 6-7. Structural representations of the four nitrogenous bases in DNA.

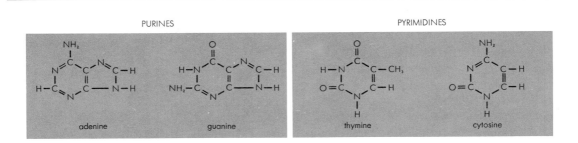

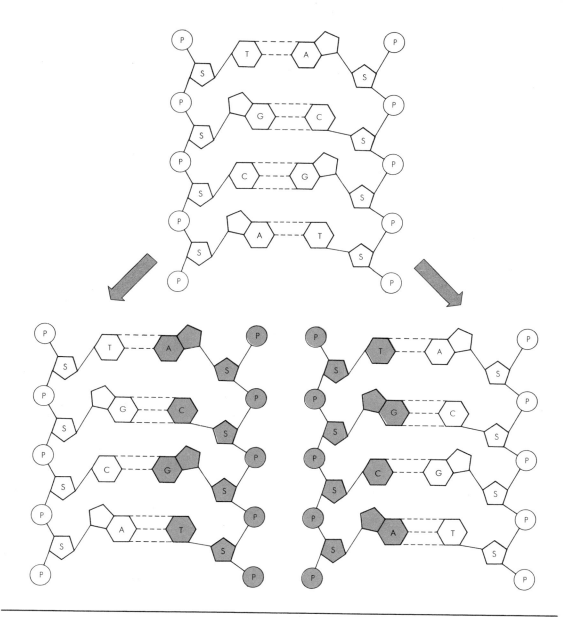

FIG. 6-8. A diagrammatic representation of DNA replication. The two complementary strands of the segment shown at top unwind, and serve as templates to direct the synthesis of new complementary strands (in color).

In addition to information storage, the double helix configuration of DNA allows exact replication of the molecule. Evidence indicates that replication involves the unwinding of the two strands of nucleotides, each strand serving as a template and directing the synthesis of its new complementary strand (Fig. 6-8). Since a particular purine pairs only with a particular pyrimidine, the new strands are exact copies of the ones that formerly occupied the same positions.

SUMMARY

1. Cellular reproduction is necessary for the survival of virtually all living organisms.

2. The duplication (or division) of cells consists of two major steps: mitosis, the duplication of the nucleus; and cytokinesis, the division of the cytoplasm.

3. Interphase, the interval between successive mitoses, is characterized by synthetic chemical activities, including the replication of chromosomal DNA and the production of proteins.

4. Prophase, the first mitotic phase, is marked by shortening and thickening of chromosomes, disappearance of nucleoli, formation of the spindle, and loss of the nuclear envelope.

5. Metaphase is characterized by the migration and orientation of chromosome pairs to the cell's equatorial region, midway between the spindle poles. The centromeres are aligned on the equatorial plane, while the chromosomal arms extend in various directions.

6. Anaphase begins with the splitting of the centromeres, which completes the longitudinal separation of sister chromatids. The members of each homologous chromosome pair then move to opposite poles of the spindle.

7. Telophase concludes mitosis with reconstitution of the nuclear envelope and nucleoli and the progressive attenuation of the chromosomes.

8. The significance of mitosis lies in the qualitative and quantitative equality of the daughter nuclei; each has the same hereditary constitution as the parent nucleus that underwent duplication.

9. Cytokinesis occurs through the deposition and coalescence of pectin-rich vescicular material in the equatorial plane to form the cell plate. This process is accompanied by reconstitution of plasma membranes on both sides of the cell plate.

10. The hereditary information of the cell is contained in the structure of the DNA molecules in the chromosomes.

11. A molecule of DNA consists of two strands of nucleotides forming a double helix. Each nucleotide consists of a phosphate group, a 5-carbon sugar, and one of four nitrogenous bases: adenine, thymine, cytosine, or guanine. The first and second bases (adenine and thymine) and the third and fourth bases (cytosine and guanine) can pair only with each other. The information carried by DNA resides in coded form in the sequence of base pairs along the length of the molecule.

12. The double helix structure of DNA permits exact replication of the molecule by allowing each nucleotide strand to function as a template along which complementary bases are assembled in precise order.

SUGGESTED READINGS FOR INTERESTED STUDENTS

1. Beadle, George, and Muriel Beadle, *The Language of Life.* Doubleday, Garden City, N. Y., 1966.

2. Flagg, Raymond O., and W. R. West, "Plant mitosis and cytokinesis." *Carolina Tips,* Vol. 32, No. 6. Carolina Biological Supply Co., Burlington, N. C., 1969.

3. Haynes, Robert H., and P. C. Hanawalt, *The Molecular Basis of Life.* W. H. Freeman, San Francisco, 1968.

4. King, Robert C., *A Dictionary of Genetics.* Oxford University Press, New York, 1968.

5. Mazia, Daniel, "Mitosis and the physiology of cell division." *The Cell,* J. Brachet and A. E. Mirsky, Eds., Vol. III. Academic Press, New York, 1961.

6. Watson, James D., *The Double Helix.* Signet Books, New American Library, New York, 1968.

7. Wilson, G. B., *Cell Division and the Mitotic Cycle.* Reinhold Publishing Co., New York, 1966.

TOPICS AND QUESTIONS FOR STUDY

1. What is is the significance for species of the high degree of fidelity of chromosome replication?

2. Why do the chromosomes of higher plants usually occur in even numbers?

3. Distinguish between mitosis and cell division.

4. What important synthetic event occurs during interphase?

5. Describe, in the order of their occurrence, the principal events in the process of mitosis.

6. Describe the behavior of the spindle during the various mitotic phases.

7. What is a homologous chromosome?

8. What is a chromatid?

9. What special significance has the sequence of base pairs in a DNA molecule?

10. Describe the major steps in replication of a DNA molecule.

7

ROOTS AND THE RELATION OF ROOTS TO SOILS

It is through their roots that higher plants are in contact with soils, the source of most of their essential mineral nutrients. The major functions of roots include the absorption of water and solutes (consisting principally of nutrient ions) from soils, the firm anchorage of the plant body in the soil, the conduction of substances upward into stems and their conduction downward from stems, and, frequently, the storage of foods and other substances.

THE ORIGIN AND STRUCTURE OF ROOTS

Root Systems   The root system of a flowering plant begins its development in the embryo of a seed. After the seed has absorbed water and its physiological processes have been reactivated, the radicle or embryonic root grows out of the seed to produce the **primary root** of the new plant. The primary root begins to produce branches **(secondary roots)** before it is many days old; these branches in turn give rise to branches of their

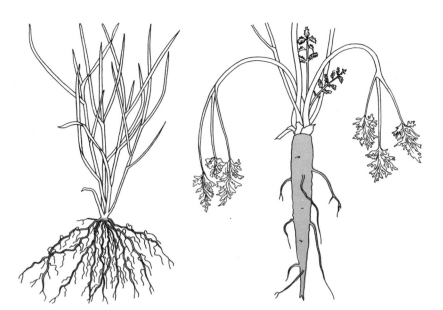

FIG. 7–1. Root systems. (*Left*). Fibrous root system of a grass. (*Right*). Taproot system of a carrot.

FIG. 7–2. Taproot of hickory tree, partly exposed by soil erosion. (Courtesy of Missouri Botanical Garden.)

own. Usually the primary root grows straight downward, whereas the secondary roots and their branches grow out at first in somewhat horizontal positions and may later turn diagonally downward near their tips. Sometimes roots are produced on stems or on various types of leaves; roots of this type, which arise from some structure other than the primary root or one of its branches, are termed **adventitious** roots (see Fig. 7–4). Examples of adventitious roots are the aerial roots of poison ivy, which attach the stems of this vine to a solid support; the roots that grow from bulbs and other kinds of underground stems; and the roots that develop from stem cuttings of roses, geraniums, and many other plants. The vegetative propagation of plants from stem cuttings or from leaves is possible because of the ability of these parts of the plant body to form adventitious roots. The prop roots of corn, which arise from the stem joints at or above the surface of the soil and grow downward into the soil, sometimes form the principal portion of the root system of this plant.

The entire mass of subterranean roots produced by a plant is called its **root system.** The degree of branching, the depth of penetration into the soil, the extent of horizontal spreading of

FIG. 7-3. Undersurface of a mat of blue-grass sod, showing fibrous roots and slender creeping stems (rhizomes). Sods are very effective soil binders. (Photo courtesy of R.B. Musgrave.)

branches, and other features of root systems vary in different species of plants. Botanists distinguish between two common types of root systems: **diffuse (fibrous) root systems** and **taproot systems** (Fig. 7-1, 7-2, 7-3).

Diffuse root systems are composed of numerous, rather slender roots, the main ones being nearly equal in size. Diffuse root systems are often entirely adventitious in mature plants, as in grasses, in which the primary root fails to continue its growth and is replaced by a number of adventitious roots. In other plants with diffuse root systems, the primary root may develop a number of secondary roots that grow more rapidly than it does and ultimately constitute the main part of the root system. Roots of this type are, of course, not adventitious, since they arise as branches of the primary roots. Diffuse roots often remain slender, as in corn and other grasses, in which case they are termed **fibrous roots** (Fig. 7-3). In such plants as the sweet potato and dahlia, the larger diffuse roots become enlarged with stored food; such roots are called **fleshy diffuse roots.** In many trees the diffuse roots become woody after years of growth.

A taproot system is one in which the primary root grows most rapidly and remains the largest root throughout the functional life of the root system. Root systems of this kind are found in carrots, dandelions, and radishes. Taproots may be slender, fleshy, or woody.

The form of root systems and the depth of their penetration into the soil vary with different species and with different soil factors. Each species of plant has, as a rule, a certain characteristic form of root system and often an optimal depth of growth. But both of these features, and especially the latter, are susceptible to the formative effects of the soil. In many types of plants, particularly herbs, the depth of the mature roots is often greater than the height of the stem above ground. In wheat plants, for example, the stem usually reaches a maximum height of 3 to 4 feet, whereas the roots have been found to penetrate 9 feet or more into the soil. Other plants with deep root systems are alfalfa, the roots of which have been

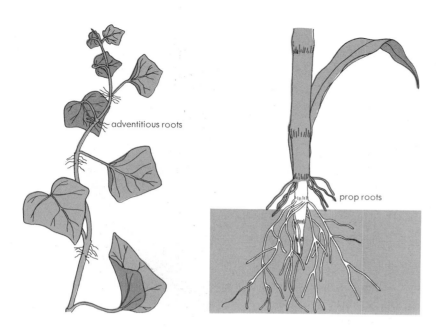

adventitious roots

prop roots

FIG. 7–4. Adventitious roots. Left: English ivy. Right: Prop roots of corn.

reported to reach depths of 12 feet, sugar beets, with roots frequently more than 4 feet long, and bur oak trees, with roots known to penetrate 15 feet into the soil. Many other species of plant, such as corn, bluegrass, and some other members of the grass family, have roots that are confined to the upper layers of the soil, chiefly to those parts within 10 or 20 inches of the surface. Plants with shallow root systems commonly grow in regions of scanty rainfall where only the few upper inches of soil are moistened. Plants with deep root systems, on the other hand, can reach sources of water located deeper in the soil, water that is not ordinarily available to shallower root systems. In some plants there are both abundant roots in the surface layers of soil and roots that penetrate deeply into the lower layers. Plants of this type, of course, have a great advantage over species that have more restricted root systems. Because they are not seen, and because of the difficulty in removing entire root systems from the soil for study, root systems have received little attention. A research publication on the root system of a rye plant presents some astounding figures: the total number of roots is 13,815,762; the combined length of the roots is 387 miles; the total surface area of the roots 2554 square feet. It should be obvious that this is a significant factor in absorption of materials from the soil.

Root Anatomy and Growth   An examination of their external structure shows that roots are typically cylindrical. The tip of a root is usually bare of outgrowths for a length of one to several millimeters; above this bare tip, there is a region in which many of the epidermal cells produce delicate, slender projections called **root hairs** (Fig. 7–6). Functional root hairs are commonly limited to a region a fraction of an inch long above the root tip. They vary in length from sizes imperceptible to the naked eye to more than half an inch. Their special significance lies in the facts that they increase the absorbing surface and anchor the growing tip of the root. The tip of a root is sometimes slightly enlarged. This swelling is the **rootcap,** a thimblelike cap of parenchymatous cells that extends back over the meristematic tissue situated just behind the tip. Rootcaps are present in roots of most plants, but usually are too small to be visible to the naked eye. The

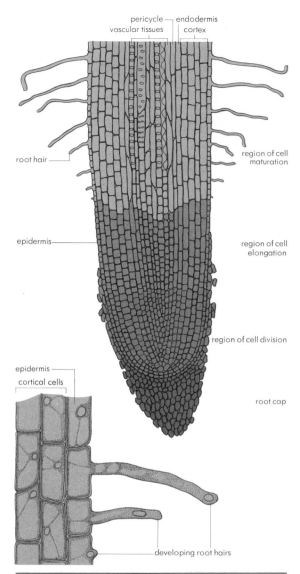

FIG. 7–5 (above). Adventitious roots of screwpine (*Pandanus*). (Photo courtesy of Missouri Botanical Garden.)

FIG. 7–6 (below.) Terminal portion of young root showing terminal rootcap and root hairs, some of which are attached to soil particles.

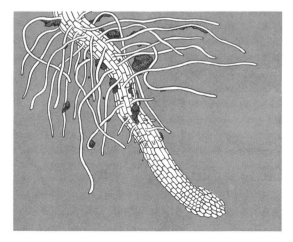

FIG. 7–7. (above). Longitudinal section of a young root of barley. (below). Longitudinal section of root epidermal cells showing stages in root hair development.

rootcap acts as a buffer that protects the delicate meristematic cells located above and partly within it against mechanical injury from contact with rock particles and other hard objects in soils. The crushed rootcap cells also lubricate the paths of rootlets through the soil.

If a longitudinally cut, thin section of the terminal portion of a young root (Figs. 7–7, 7–8) is examined microscopically, four cell regions of rather different aspect are apparent. At the very tip of the root is the protective rootcap, which covers the **meristematic region.** The outer portion of the rootcap is rather rough and uneven because the surface cells are worn away by contact with rock particles as the root tip pushes its way through the soil. The meristematic region just behind the rootcap produces new cells more or less continuously, some of which are added to the inner portion of the rootcap. Thus, the rootcap is built up by new cells on its inner surface as the older cells of the outer surface are worn away. The cells of the meristematic region are small, thin walled, and usually more or less cubical in form. They contain very dense protoplasm, in which the vacuoles are small and usually inconspicuous. When this region of the root is examined with the microscope, numerous cells with their nuclei in various stages of mitosis can be seen. This meristematic region, or growing point, is the cell-forming region, which contributes largely to the growth of the root in length. Above the meristematic region is the **cell-elongation (cell-enlargement) region.** Here the cells newly formed as a result of mitosis and cell division in the meristematic region undergo rapid enlargement, chiefly in the longitudinal direction, and the volume of each cell increases. The protoplasm increases in volume at a slower rate than the cell cavity. The small vacuoles of the meristematic cells combine and enlarge to form usually a single large, central vacuole in each cell of the elongation region. The large vacuole fills the major portion of the cell cavity, with the protoplasm occupying a peripheral position outside the vacuole and against the cell wall. The meristematic and elongation regions together are seldom more than a few millimeters in length. Above these

FIG. 7–8. Photomicrograph of a median section through the root tip of dayflower (*Commelina*). (Courtesy of Dr. James Seago, SUNY, Oswego.)

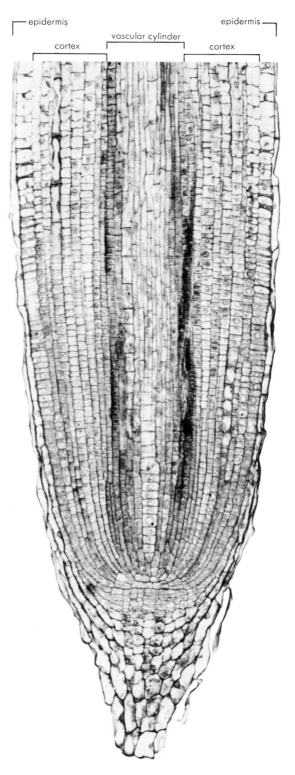

epidermis

cortex   vascular cylinder   cortex   epidermis

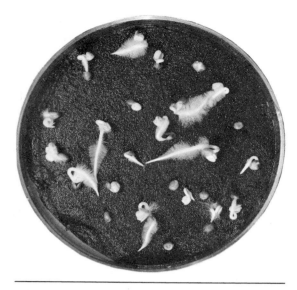

FIG. 7–9.   Germinating radish seeds, and seedlings, 48 hours old. The delicate outgrowths are root hairs.

regions is the **region of maturation** or **differentiation.** Here the growing cells of the elongation region are undergoing division of labor and an accompanying differentiation of structure. Some of them are transformed into parenchyma cells, some into xylem cells, others into phloem cells, and so on. All portions of the root above the maturation zone may be termed the **matured region,** for all these portions are composed of the matured, differentiated tissues of the root system.

Root hairs are produced in the younger part of the maturation region. These structures should not be confused with branch roots, which often appear to be almost as small as hairs. A branch root is a many-celled structure with a rootcap, meristematic region, xylem, phloem, etc., whereas a root hair is an extended portion of a single cell. A root hair begins as a small outgrowth of an epidermal cell near the lower limits of the maturation zone (Fig. 7–7). The rate of growth of root hairs is usually fairly rapid and their life spans are rather short, usually not more than a few days or, rarely, a few weeks. Root hairs grow in great profusion (Fig. 7–9); in some species of plants more than 200 root hairs grow from each square millimeter of root surface in the root hair zone. As the tip grows downward into the soil, the production of new root hairs continues just above the region of elongation of the root, the youngest root hairs developing always at about the same distance above the root tip. The oldest root hairs at the upper end of the root hair zone tend to die at about the same rate that new root hairs are produced at the lower end of the zone; thus the total length of the root covered with root hairs may remain fairly constant.

Root hairs are thin walled and delicate. They will wither and die after a few minutes' exposure to dry air, and their extreme fragility enables them to be easily torn from the roots of a plant being moved to another location. The loss of great numbers of root hairs drastically reduces the water-absorbing surface of the roots. Most water loss from the plant occurs through the leaf surface, and the common horticultural practice of "cutting back" a fairly large portion of the foliage after transplanting compensates for the reduced absorbing surface in the roots. Root hairs are present in most higher types of plants, with the exception of certain aquatic species.

Examination of a transverse or cross section (Fig. 7–10) of a root in the maturation region shows several highly differentiated tissues. The surface layer of cells, the **epidermis,** produces the root hairs and thus is an absorptive tissue, as well as a tissue that furnishes some protection to the underlying cells. The **cortex,** beneath the epidermis, is composed of parenchyma cells that are rather large, thin walled, and roughly spherical or cylindrical in form. Numerous intercellular spaces occur in the cortex; these are important as avenues for the diffusion of water and gases among the cortical cells. The cortex stores much of the reserve food that accumulates in the roots, and it also transports the water and salts absorbed by the root hairs to the conducting cells in the center of the root. Water moves inward from the root hair cells to the outermost cells of the cortex, and from one cortical cell to another toward the conducting tissues as a result of dif-

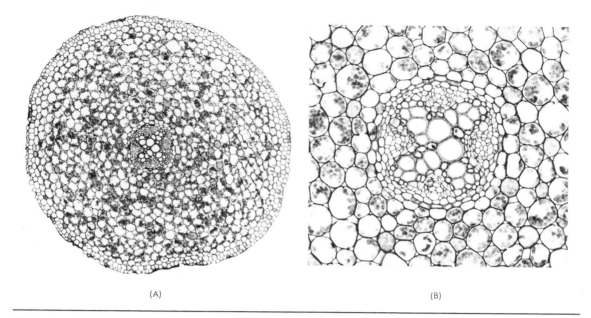

(A)

(B)

FIG. 7-10. Photomicrographs of the dicotyledonous buttercup (*Ranunculus*) root in transverse section showing (A) a low magnification view of the whole organ, and (B) a higher magnification view of the vascular cylinder. Compare with FIG. 7-13.

ferences in the osmotic and diffusion potentials among these cells and of water loss from the aerial parts of the plant. The inward movement of nutrient ions is also attributable in part to differences in the concentrations of those ions in the root hairs and cortical cells, and in part to ion accumulation phenomena.

The innermost layer of cortical cells comprises the **endodermis**. A distinguishing feature of an endodermal cell is the presence, on the radial and transverse walls, of a continuous zone or band (Casparian strip) within which the wall material is impregnated with suberin. The function of the endodermis is not known with certainty but it is believed that the fatty material deposited in these bands blocks the passage of water through the walls. Consequently, all water and solutes moving from cortex to xylem must pass through the living protoplasts of the endodermal cells, where some selectivity or other control may occur. In later stages of development, the radial, transverse, and inner tangential walls commonly

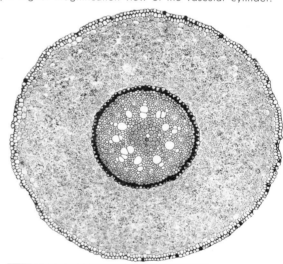

FIG. 7-11. Photomicrograph of a cross section of a monocotyledonous root (*Smilax*), showing an epidermis on the surface, a well-developed cortex, an endodermis, with dark, thickened walls, 10 groups of large-celled xylem, and alternating with them the smaller groups of small phloem cells. The cells surrounding the xylem and phloem tissues are parenchyma cells. (Courtesy of Triarch Botanical Products, Ripon, Wis.)

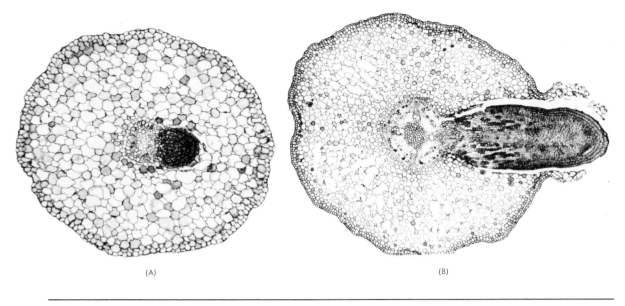

FIG. 7–12. Transverse sections of willow (*Salix*) roots showing (A) earlier and (B) later stages of branch root origin and development.

become thickened and lignified. Occasional thin-walled cells may be found in the older endodermis. These thin-walled cells are believed to facilitate the passage of water and other materials.

Enclosed by the endodermis is the **vascular cylinder,** the principal conducting and strengthening portion of the root. The outermost tissue of the vascular cylinder is the **pericycle,** a layer of small parenchyma cells capable of producing new cells that grow outward to form branch roots. The origin of branch roots is thus internal with respect to cortex and epidermis (Fig. 7–12). All root branches push outward through cortex and epidermis tissues before they reach the soil. Branch roots are similar in structure, growth, and function to the older roots from which they arise.

The xylem and phloem tissues lie beneath the pericycle. As seen in cross section the xylem is usually arranged in the form of a star or in the form of separated groups of cells situated radially, like the spokes of a wheel. The tracheary or conducting cells of the xylem of flowering plants are thick-walled tracheids and vessel members that are joined in longitudinal files to form vessels. The tracheary cells are also responsible for much of the strength of the root. Xylem tissue conducts water and nutrient ions upward into the stem and at certain times may also transport foods previously stored in root tissues. Located between adjacent points of the xylem star or situated in shorter bands alternating with the radially arranged xylem groups are small clusters of phloem cells. These clusters are usually smaller than the xylem masses, and the cells comprising them are typically smaller and thinner walled than those of the xylem. The phloem consists chiefly of sieve tube members, and their associated companion cells. The sieve tubes carry down into the root foods that have been manufactured in the leaves and transported downward through the phloem tissue of the stem. The alternate arrangement of xylem and phloem tissues in young roots is an advantageous one, for such arrangement makes possible ready access of these tissues to the root cortex, through which water and minerals move into the vascular cylinder and in which water and food are commonly stored. In most vascular plants the xylem "star" constitutes the fluted central core. In a smaller number of species, however, the center of the vascular cylinder consists of pith parenchyma.

The tissues thus far described in roots are **primary tissues.** They develop from the meristematic region at the tip of the young root, and their production results in an increase in length of the organ. The roots of most trees, shrubs, and other types of perennial plants have **secondary tissues** in addition to primary tissues. Secondary tissues are those produced by a **cambium;** they are formed radially in stems and roots, as contrasted with primary tissues, which are most often formed in a longitudinal direction. Secondary tissues are therefore involved chiefly in the increase in diameter of roots and stems. In perennial roots of many plants a growth layer termed the **cork cambium** develops in the pericycle tissue. The cells produced by the cork cambium toward the outer surface of the root comprise a layer of **cork.** Young cork cells become suberized and usually die soon thereafter, forming a waterproof, resistant layer. The epidermis, cortex, and endodermis disintegrate as the cork develops, and their protective functions are assumed by the new tissue. The older roots of perennials are thus frequently covered with a corky layer much like that of the outer bark of the stem. In many plants (for example, in some annuals), roots never become thickened beyond the extent of their primary tissues, but in perennials, roots usually grow considerably in diameter as a result of the formation of secondary vascular tissues (Fig. 7–13). These tissues are produced by the growth activity of the vascular cambium that originates from procambial cells lying *between* the xylem and phloem groups and from some of the pericycle cells. By cell division the cambium layer, which is only one cell thick, forms secondary xylem cells toward the center or axis of the organ, and secondary phloem cells toward the outside. These are

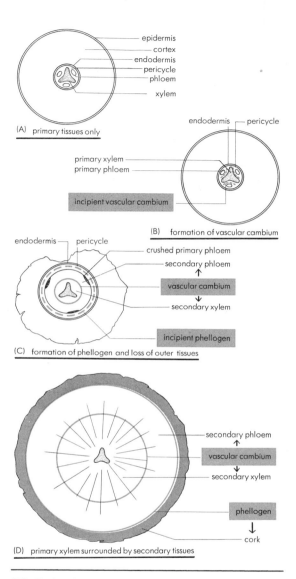

FIG. 7–13. Diagrammatic representation of secondary growth in root of willow (*Salix*).

added to their respective primary tissues, and their continued formation brings about the greater part of the radial growth of the roots of woody plants. The cambium forms xylem cells more rapidly than it does phloem cells, so that ultimately the xylem, or wood, constitutes the greater part of the total volume of such roots.

Older roots with secondary tissues are much like woody stems in structure, with a surface layer of bark, a large woody cylinder beneath the bark, and a cambium layer separating the two.

ECONOMIC SIGNIFICANCE OF ROOTS

The fundamental importance of roots in the scheme of nature and in man's existence needs no further discussion, except to reiterate that the growth of all higher plants would be impossible without roots. It is of interest to mention some specific plants, the roots of which are directly useful to man. Among these are a number of medicinal plants: aconite, asafetida, gentian, goldenseal, licorice, and valerian, all of which are used in pharmaceutical preparations. The principal root crops used as food by man are: beets, carrots, salsify, parsnips, radishes, turnips, rutabagas, sweet potatoes, yams, and cassava (tapioca). Some of these (for example, turnips, beets, carrots) are biennial species; during the first year of their growth, they manufacture abundant food, much of which is stored in the taproot and which is used mainly in the production of flowers and seeds during the second year of their life. Man robs these plants of their food during the first year of their growth by harvesting the root. A beet root is unusual in that it develops several cambium layers that form concentric rings of tissues visible to the naked eye in a beet root cross section. Spices and other aromatic substances are furnished by the roots of several species of plants: angelica, horse-radish, sarsaparilla, turmeric, and sassafras. The roots of madder and alkanna furnish dyes.

SUMMARY 1. The functions of roots are: absorption of water and solutes from soil, anchorage, conduction, and food storage.

2. A root system is the total mass of roots of a plant. Two common types of root systems are taproot and diffuse (fibrous) root systems.

3. A primary root is the root that develops directly from the hypocotyl of an embryo. Secondary roots are branches of primary roots. Adventitious roots arise from some structure other than a primary root or its branches.

4. Root systems differ in their degree of branching, depth of penetration into the soil, lengths, and other features.

5. Roots are typically cylindrical in form.

6. The tip of a root is covered by a protective rootcap.

7. Immediately above the rootcap is the meristematic region (region of cell division) in which new cells are formed. Above this is the region of cell elongation, in which the newly formed cells undergo enlargement, chiefly in length. Above the region of elongation is the region of cell maturation in which the tissues of the root undergo differentiation. Root hairs cover part of the region of maturation.

8. A root hair is a protuberance from a root epidermal cell.

9. Root hairs are very delicate, usually short lived, and easily damaged.

10. In transverse section the maturation region of a young root shows the following regions and tissues, from the outside in:
   a. Epidermis.
   b. Cortex.

c. Endodermis (the innermost layer of the cortex).

d. Vascular cylinder, consisting of pericycle, xylem, phloem, and parenchyma tissue. The primary xylem and phloem tissues are radially arranged.

11. Older roots may develop a cambium tissue from parenchyma cells between the xylem and phloem tissues. The cambium forms secondary xylem and phloem cells and is in large part responsible for the growth of roots in diameter.

12. Both cork cambium and branch roots originate in the pericycle.

13. Roots furnish many economically important products, such as foods for man and other animals, drugs, dyes, and spices.

SUGGESTED READINGS FOR INTERESTED STUDENTS

1. Esau, Katherine, *Plant Anatomy*, 2d ed. Wiley, New York, 1965.
2. Esau, Katherine, *Anatomy of Seed Plants*. Wiley, New York, 1961.

TOPICS AND QUESTIONS FOR STUDY

1. List the functions of roots.
2. What is a primary root? A secondary root? An adventitious root?
3. Distinguish between diffuse and taproot systems.
4. Name six plants that store large amounts of food in their roots.
5. Why is our knowledge concerning the structure and growth of root systems less extensive than our knowledge of structure and growth of stems?
6. Describe the structure, origin, and importance of rootcaps.
7. Describe the structure of a young root as seen in longitudinal section, and describe the functions of the tissues seen in such a section.
8. Describe the growth of roots in length.
9. Describe the structure and origin of root hairs. What is the importance of root hairs?
10. When plants are transplanted, a ball of soil should be kept around the root system. State three reasons for this practice.
11. Describe the arrangement and structure of the tissues seen in a cross section through the maturation region of a young root. State the functions of these tissues.
12. What is cork cambium? Its function?
13. Distinguish between primary and secondary tissues, and name the primary and secondary tissues of roots. Explain how these secondary tissues develop in a root.
14. Describe the importance of roots in human life.

8

THE FUNCTION
OF ROOTS

ROOTS AND SOILS

The roots of most plants live and function in soil. There are many types of soils, each differing in chemical and physical properties, depth, age, and other qualities. Although soils differ widely, those which sustain plant growth share certain characteristics: they are composed of particles of varying kinds and sizes, they possess substances soluble in water, they contain air and moisture, and they are the habitats of soil organisms.

Mineral particles, which form the largest proportions of most soils, vary from microscopic particles of clay to coarse particles of sand and gravel. These particles develop chiefly from the disintegration of rocks by the action of water, wind, and glaciers, freezing and thawing, and from the action of carbonic acid produced from carbon dioxide in the soil. The character of rock particles is important in determining the volume of air space in the soil, the amount of water held by the soil, and the nature of soil solutes. Rock particles are themselves the source of many of the nutrients essential to plant growth, including calcium, iron, phosphorus, magnesium, zinc, and others. Clay particles, which form a kind of structural framework within soil, are especially important. Clay particles hold various nutrient ions on their surfaces—such as calcium, magnesium, and potassium—that are removed by root hairs. Clay particles absorb water readily and swell as they do so, often forcing air out of the soil. Soils with large clay fractions become easily waterlogged and often do not contain an adequate supply of air for roots. As a result, they are unsuitable for the growth of many plants.

Soil air contains oxygen which is essential to root respiration and which is thereby related indirectly to the processes of water and nutrient uptake. Inadequate soil aeration may interfere with root growth, and may cause physiological derangements that lead to stunting and death. Oxygen in soil air is also necessary for the activities of bacteria, fungi, worms, and other soil organisms that decompose dead leaves, bark, wood, animal remains and excreta; through their activities, these organisms contribute to the supply of nutrient solutes required by higher plants. Carbon dioxide is a respiration product of roots, bacteria, fungi, and soil organisms, and is also a component of soil air. Carbon dioxide aids in the absorption of ions from clay particles by roots, but may lead to inhibition of root growth if its concentration becomes excessive. Nitrogen, a normal component of soil air, is converted by certain bacteria in soil and the roots of legumes (such as soybeans, clovers, and alfalfa) into nitrogenous compounds which ultimately increase soil fertility.

Water in soils is derived chiefly from rain and snow. A portion of this water runs off the soil surface into streams and rivers; another portion trickles down through the soil into underground streams and springs; and still another portion remains loosely held within and upon the soil particles and in soil air spaces. When water is abundant in soil, it is easily removed by the plants, and as the water content decreases it gradually becomes more difficult to remove. The water which is available for root absorption and plant growth is principally that amount which lies between the extremes termed **field capacity**

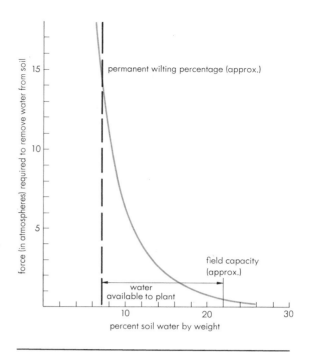

FIG. 8-1. The relationship between amount of soil water and force required to remove it from a representative loam soil. (Adapted from P. J. Kramer, 1949.)

and **permanent wilting percentage.** Field capacity is the amount of water remaining in soil after excess water has drained away. Permanent wilting percentage is that water so tightly adhering to soil particles that roots are unable to remove it. As permanent wilting percentage is approached a plant suffers daily wilt, and at permanent wilting percentage, the plant is unable to recover from wilt during periods of low water requirement (as at night). The amount of water in different soils at field capacity and at permanent wilting percentage varies with the soil type, generally being less in sandy soils with large particle size and more in clay soils with very fine particle size. In a typical loam soil with mixed sand, clay, and organic matter, the amount of water at field capacity is approximately 22 percent of the total weight; and permanent wilting percentage approximately 7.5 percent of the total weight (Fig. 8-1).

Run-off and gravitational water may carry away soil nutrients (a process called **leaching**) and thus may decrease soil fertility; leaching must be compensated for by the addition of fertilizers to soils. There is relatively little movement of capillary moisture from one soil particle to another; thus, as roots absorb water, they dry out the soil particles near them and, unless fresh supplies of water reach the soil, may be unable to absorb moisture.

Soil moisture may be conserved by the use of **mulches** spread over the soil surface; mulches of straw, grass clippings, leaves, manure, and paper are effective in shading the soil, thus lowering its temperature and offering protection against drying winds. Mulches are valuable in other ways: they reduce the growth of weeds, which compete with crop plants for water and nutrients; they protect roots from frost and low temperatures; and some—especially manure and grass clippings—add nutrients to the soils on which they are spread. Glass wool and paper strips have come into recent use as mulches; in Hawaii, paper strips are used as a mulch around pineapple plants, and elsewhere are used to mulch tobacco fields. Straw and paper are valuable mulches for strawberry plants: in addition to the other beneficial qualities of mulches, they prevent contact of the strawberries with the soil, thus diminishing rot damage.

Organic matter consists of decomposing plant remains, such as leaves, stems, roots, and fruits, of dead animal bodies and animal excreta, and of dead micro-organisms. Soils in which plants grow, and on or in which animals live, contain organic matter. Organic matter is not essential as such for plant growth, but is a soil conditioner which modifies soil in ways that improve soil properties and enhance plant growth. It holds large amounts of water that can be absorbed by roots, and it prevents caking and increases porosity and aeration of the soil. Some organic particles hold nutrient ions loosely on their surfaces from which they may be absorbed by roots.

The proteins, fats, cellulose, and other compounds of plant and animal tissues are decomposed by bacteria, fungi, and other soil organisms and are broken down into simpler substances, such as water, ammonia, nitrates, and phosphates. This disintegration of organic matter produces a continuing supply of nutrients that are essential to the fertility of soils and the growth of green plants. The organic content of soils may be increased by the addition of manure, dead leaves, and peat, and by plowing under certain crops, such as alfalfa and cowpeas. Such treatment increases soil nutrients, improves drainage and aeration, loosens the soil and generally renders it more favorable for plant development.

Soil solutes occur in the soil water and on the surfaces of soil particles, and are derived in part from rock disintegration and from decomposing organic matter. These solutes ordinarily occur in low concentrations in soils, although in some areas (as in Utah's Great Salt Desert), the concentration of soil solutes may be so high as to result in plasmolysis of root cells and thus prevent plant growth. Soil solutes include a wide variety of both organic and inorganic compounds—bicarbonates, sulfates, nitrates, and phosphates of calcium, magnesium, potassium, and other elements. Molecules of these inorganic substances undergo dissociation in the soil solution, forming positively-charged ions such as calcium, potassium, iron, and magnesium, and negatively-charged ions such as phosphate, nitrate, and sulfate. Positively-charged ions are usually held on the surfaces of soil colloids, while negatively-charged ions for the most part occur in the soil solution. The nature of soil solutes influences soil acidity or alkalinity, an important factor in influencing plant distribution. Most agricultural crops thrive in neutral or slightly acid soils. Some plants, such as cranberries and rhododendrons, are able to grow only in acid soils, while others, such as cliff ferns and sagebrush, thrive only in alkaline soils. Continued plant growth often causes soils to become more acid. Because of this, limestone and other alkaline chemicals are often added to soils to counteract acidity.

Soil organisms affect the chemical and physical features of soils and thus influence the growth of higher plants. Soil organisms include many types of animals (protozoa, nematodes, earth worms, insects, and others) and many kinds of plants (bacteria, algae, fungi) together with roots and underground stems. Earthworms are especially significant among soil animals in their influences upon soils; they mix and move large quantities of soils, passing them through their bodies, and thereby bring about favorable chemical changes. Charles Darwin found that the earthworms in one acre of soil may pass 15 tons of soil through their bodies in one year. In addition to their chemical effects on soils, earthworms transport soils from deeper layers to the surface; at the same time they form channels that promote drainage and aeration. All soil animals cause movement of soils, thus keeping them open and loose, and all contribute to the organic matter of soils through decay of their dead bodies and feces. Soil algae are green plants that manufacture foods from inorganic sources, thus increasing soil organic matter as they grow, multiply, die, and decompose. Algae are important also in that they serve as food for bacteria, fungi, and animals. Bacteria influence soils in many ways; for example, they attack dead bodies and excreta, converting the complex constitutents into simpler substances that roots of higher plants absorb; their own remains add organic matter to soil; and they transform soil nitrogen into nitrogenous substances which can be utilized by higher plants. This latter function is of extraordinary importance for life as we know it on earth. The amount of protoplasm, including that of plants, animals, and human beings, is absolutely dependent upon nitrogen for formation of all proteins and enzymes, and for many other substances. Under natural circumstances, 95 percent of all such nitrogen is made available by bacteria which live symbiotically in root nodules of legumes and a few other plants; the remaining 5 percent is derived from various other sources. In the United States and many other countries these nitrogen compounds are supplemented by artificially-produced fertilizers, but in some countries there is no significant source other than bacteria.

Mushrooms, molds, and other fungi, like the bacteria, bring about decay of dead bodies and animal wastes and thus increase the soil's supply of essential nutrients. Higher plants also influence the soils in which they grow. If such plants live on the same soil year after year, their fallen leaves and branches, dying older roots, old fruits, and seed coats return to the soil, so that a continuing supply of soil nutrients is ensured. A different situation obtains, however, in soils that are intensively cultivated, for the harvesting of fruits, grains, and other crops results in the net removal of many soil nutrients. If these nutrients are not replaced, the soils become less productive; that is, they lose their fertility. The frequent addition of fertilizers to cultivated soils is essential to replenish the nutrients removed by crops, and it ensures continued productive fertility. Plowing under stubble and other residues compensates in part for nutrients that crops take from the soil.

The absorption of water by roots has marked effects upon soils, for plant growth results in the depletion of soil moisture; thus, if large numbers of plants grow on a given area, they may withdraw so much water that the soil moisture is reduced to a level inadequate to support growth of productive crops. Roots affect soils also in a purely physical manner; lateral root branches growing through the soil tend to keep it open and loose, not only because of the organic matter left by dead roots, but also because of the mechanical effects of roots in penetrating soil lumps and hard soil layers. The roots of many plants, especially grasses, which form dense sods, hold soils in place and thus reduce or prevent soil erosion by water and wind. When sods are plowed up or forests are burned or cut off, their roots are destroyed, their binding effect upon soils is lost, and widespread erosion is the result.

Particularly noteworthy for higher plant nutrition is the presence of the **rhizosphere,** the thin envelope of soil immediately surrounding and

	Principal Cations		Principal Anions	
Macro-nutrients	Potassium	K^+	Nitrate	NO_3^-
	Calcium	Ca^{2+}	Phosphate	$H_2PO_4^-$
	Magnesium	Mg^{2+}	Sulfate	SO_4^{2-}
Micro-nutrients	Iron	Fe^{3+}	Borate	$HB_4O_7^-$
	Manganese	Mn^{2+}	Molybdate	$HMoO_4^-$
	Zinc	Zn^{2+}	Chloride	Cl^-
	Copper	Cu^{2+}		

TABLE 8–1. Principal ionic forms of the 13 essential soil elements required by green plants.

contacting the growing tips of roots. One typically finds a greater concentration of bacteria and fungi in this region. These larger populations are thought to be related to the presence of growth-promoting compounds, such as amino acids, enzymes, and vitamins, that come from the decay of root surface cells, or that are actually exuded by the roots. The increased numbers of these organisms, by their metabolic activities, in turn supply nutrients to the root.

Of widespread occurrence among higher plants is the complex association of roots and fungi termed **mycorrhizae.** This is a symbiotic relationship in which the fungal organism invests or penetrates the outer layer of the root. Metabolic substances provided by the root enhance fungal growth, and the portions of the fungus that extend into the soil bring to the root substances obtained from the soil. There is growing evidence that mycorrhizae are essential for normal growth and development of many vascular plants.

THE MINERAL NUTRITION OF GREEN PLANTS

The Essential Soil Elements   Sixteen elements are known or suspected by plant physiologists to be essential for the normal metabolism of green plants. Three of these (carbon, hydrogen, and oxygen) are obtained chiefly from air and water.

The remaining 13 elements are taken in from solid matter in the soil and include nitrogen, phosphorus, potassium, sulfur, calcium, iron, magnesium, boron, zinc, manganese, copper, molybdenum, and chlorine. These soil elements or soil nutrients are absorbed not in elemental form but as ions that diffuse into root cells or are taken in by active transport as a result of the expenditure of energy by root cells.

The ions originate from the dissociation of various kinds of molecules in soils. Thus, magnesium sulfate molecules ($MgSO_4$) dissociate into magnesium ions (Mg^{2+}) and sulfate ions (SO_4^{2-}) potassium nitrate molecules (KNO_3) dissociate into potassium ions (K^+) and nitrate ions (NO_3^-). When a molecule dissociates, two kinds of ions result: a **cation** bearing one or more positive electric charges, and an **anion** bearing one or more negative electric charges. In the dissociation of potassium nitrate for example, the cation is K^+, the anion is NO_3^-. The essential elements absorbed as ions and their principal ionic forms are shown in Table 8–1. In addition to these, other ions may be absorbed by roots; for example, ammonium (NH_4^+), aluminum (Al^{3+}), carbonate ions (CO_3^{2-} and HCO_3^-), and others. The relative quantities of ions absorbed by plants from the soil vary with differences in the chemical and physical properties of soils and also with different species of plants. Chemical analyses of plant protoplasm

FIG. 8-2. Experiment showing the effect of various nutrients on plant growth. Plants at right rear are receiving more favorable treatment than those in the foreground, as shown by darker color and increased growth. (Courtesy U.S. Department of Agriculture.)

indicate that carbon, hydrogen, and oxygen ordinarily constitute more than 92 percent of living protoplasm. This means that less than 8 percent consists of nitrogen, iron, phosphorus, and others listed in the preceding paragraph. Of the soil nutrients, nitrogen is usually absorbed in larger quantities than all other soil nutrients combined; nitrogen ordinarily makes up about 1 to 2 percent of living protoplasm. Of the other soil nutrients, sulfur, phosphorus, calcium, potassium, and magnesium are required in much smaller quantities than nitrogen. The remaining seven elements (iron, zinc, boron, molybdenum, manganese, copper, and chlorine) are required in such relatively minute quantities that they have become known as the **trace elements,** or **micronutrients.** The contrasting term, **macronutrients,** is applied to the other essential elements.

Determining the Essentiality of Soil Elements
The fundamental researches upon the essential nature of the various soil elements in the nutrition of green plants utilizes an experimental technique known as water culture. In this pro-

cedure, plants are grown not in soil, but in distilled water, in which mineral salts are dissolved. Glazed earthenware jars or hard-glass vessels are used to hold the solution. By omitting various mineral salts and thus various chemical elements, plant physiologists have been able to determine the effects of such omissions upon plant growth; if the omission of a particular element from a water culture results in stunted growth of tops, poorly developed root systems, failure of chlorophyll formation, or some other structural or physiological abnormality, it may be safely assumed that the element is essential for the normal nutrition of the plant (Fig. 8-2). Two important criteria used to determine the absolute requirement for a given element are: 1. Failure of the plant to complete its life cycle when deprived of the element. 2. Recovery and completion of the life cycle when the element is supplied.

When a particular element is present in insufficient quantities in a soil, the soil is said to suffer from a deficiency of that element. Green plants growing in such a soil and exhibiting abnormalities as a result of the deficiency of an essential

FIG. 8–3. (Left). Cucumbers growing hydroponically in sterile desert sand in Puerto Peñasco, Sonora, Mexico. This is part of an experiment in total environment modification using inflated plastic greenhouses (right) that may bring economical fruit and vegetable production to desert regions near the sea. (Courtesy of C. O. Hodge, Environmental Research Lab., Tucson, Arizona.)

element are said to be suffering from a nutrient deficiency. A variation of the water culture technique is that of sand cultures, in which quartz sand or gravel from which all soluble materials have been removed is placed in culture jars along with a suitable aqueous solution of chemicals. Plants in sand cultures stand without external support, whereas plants in water cultures must usually be supported above the jars.

The term **hydroponics** has been applied to growth of plants in water and sand cultures (Fig. 8–3). The solutions used in hydroponic culture must contain all the essential elements for the normal growth and development of green plants and must contain them in the proper proportions and in usable forms. The hydroponic culture of plants has certain advantages, among which are these: 1. The chemical composition of the nutrient solution may be carefully controlled so that the most suitable kinds and concentrations of nutrients may be provided for each crop. 2. There are no soil colloids present to immobilize any of the nutrients through adsorption. 3. Frequent replacement of hydroponic solutions prevents the accumulation of toxic organic decomposition products which may occur in soils. 4. In hydroponic cultures, conditions are relatively unfavor-able for the growth of bacteria, higher fungi, and other organisms that may cause diseases of crop plants. 5. Through pumping devices, the solutions may be circulated and aerated, thus ensuring a regularity of aeration not possible in soils. 6. No tilling is required. 7. There is no weed growth in hydroponic cultures.

Although hydroponic gardening may be satisfactorily and profitably carried on as home gardening or commercial greenhouse projects, this method of crop culture must be regarded as an adjunct to field soil culture, not as a technique that will replace soil culture.

Physiological Functions of Soil Elements   The functions of the various soil elements in plants are not fully known, but the work of plant physiologists has produced rather precise information concerning the importance of some elements. The detailed study of these functions cannot be appropriately included in a course in elementary botany; hence, only a brief list of some of the known or presumed functions of these elements will be included here.

1. *Nitrogen* is a constituent of proteins, and many other organic compounds in plants. Green plants growing in nitrogen-deficient soils most commonly exhibit yellowing, a condition known as chlorosis, in their older leaves, that is, the leaves farthest from the shoot tip.

2. *Sulfur* is a constituent of some proteins and is thus generally distributed throughout the plant. It also occurs in numerous other compounds. When sulfur is deficient in a soil, the plants are frequently yellowish and stunted.

3. *Magnesium* is a constituent of chlorophyll, a pigment necessary for food manufacture. It is also associated with certain regulatory compounds (enzymes). Plants growing in magnesium-deficient soils are a pale, greenish-yellow. In some plants, purplish-red leaves with green veins indicate magnesium deficiency.

4. *Phosphorus* is a constituent of some proteins, of energy-transfer compounds, and of other organic substances and it participates in many physiological activities. Phosphorus deficiency generally retards growth, and in some plants, causes a purplish coloration in leaves and stems.

5. *Calcium* is a constituent of cell walls and of intercellular cementing substance. It is also known to influence cell membrane permeability. Calcium deficiency seriously affects the tissues in the tips of roots and shoots, and results in pronounced growth abnormalities.

6. *Potassium* is apparently not a constituent of the compounds synthesized by green plants, but it does seem to function in a regulatory manner. The principal symptoms of potassium deficiency in many plants include growth retardation, progressive chlorosis that begins along the margins of older leaves and gradually spreads to the younger parts of the shoot, and premature loss of leaves.

7. *Iron* is a constituent of some enzymes and plays a role in respiration and in chlorophyll synthesis (although iron is not a constituent of chlorophyll). Iron deficiency frequently causes chlorosis, especially in the tissue between the veins of young leaves.

8. The functions of *zinc, boron, molybdenum, manganese, copper,* and *chlorine* are inadequately known, but these elements seem to be involved primarily in the regulation of various physiological activities.

In several of the paragraphs above, the locations of the first symptoms of particular deficiency diseases are mentioned. These locations are related to the metabolism of the deficient elements. For example, a plant may utilize calcium so that it cannot be withdrawn from the tissues into which it has been incorporated. The calcium is therefore immobile in the plant, and if calcium becomes deficient during the growing season, the deficiency disease shows up first in the growing points of the plant. Nitrogen can be removed from old plant parts and transported to the meristem. In case of deficiencies, nitrogen is removed from old leaves and brought to the shoot tip. The deficiency disease appears first in older leaves because the mobile nitrogen is withdrawn from the older plant parts in favor of the growing points.

Deficiency diseases may be reduced or eliminated by the addition of suitable mineral nutrients in the form of fertilizers to soils (Fig. 8–4). In some plants, nutrient deficiencies may be corrected by spraying solutions of the appropriate essential nutrients on leaves, a practice commonly referred to as "leaf feeding." An interesting factor in the mineral nutrition of plants is the toxicity of certain essential elements when these are present in soils in excess. For example, magnesium and the micronutrients are essential in minute concentrations, but in larger quantities become poisonous to most green plants. In sufficient quantities nutrient substances may alter the osmotic properties of the soil solution, making it impossible for roots to absorb adequate quantities of water. The enormous amounts of soil nutrients sold each year are used primarily to force greater

FIG. 8-4. Photo showing the effect of fertilizer on plant growth. The central row of corn received little or no fertilizer, and the height of the stalks is about 7 inches, against an average of 40 inches for fertilized stalks. (Courtesy U.S. Dpt. of Agriculture.)

crop yields and, at the same time, to prevent deficiency diseases. In the United States, more than 20,000,000 tons of commercial fertilizers are purchased annually. Most of this total consists of various blends of three macronutrients: nitrogen in organic or inorganic form, phosphorus measured in terms of phosphoric oxide (P_2O_5), and potassium measured in terms of potash (K_2O).

THE ABSORPTION OF MATERIALS BY ROOTS

The absorption of water and solutes by living cells involves a group of complex processes that are still not completely understood. Water absorption results chiefly from imbibition and osmotic action; the uptake of nutrient solutes involves both simple diffusion and active absorption. These processes operate not only in the absorption of water and solutes by root hairs but also in their transfer from the epidermis, across cells of the root cortex, into the vascular cylinder.

In addition to these generalizations, several other conclusions can be drawn from numerous investigations of absorption. Among these are the facts that solutes may be absorbed by roots independently of the direction of movement of water; that the entrance of any particular solute into a root is generally independent of the entrance of other kinds of solutes; and that both water and solutes, as they are absorbed by roots, ultimately move into the xylem cells that carry them upward into stem and leaf cells. Root cells absorb nutrient ions not only from the soil solution, but also directly from the surfaces of soil particles. The cell walls of root hairs, because of their high content of pectic substances, adhere tightly to soil particles. Ionic exchanges occur between the root hairs and the particles they contact so that many of the ions absorbed by root hairs are absorbed from these particles without entering the soil solution.

Very precise experiments have demonstrated that the greater proportion of nutrients are absorbed in the meristematic and elongation regions of the growing root, the rate of nutrient absorption falling rapidly as one approaches the root hair region. A more or less opposite rela-

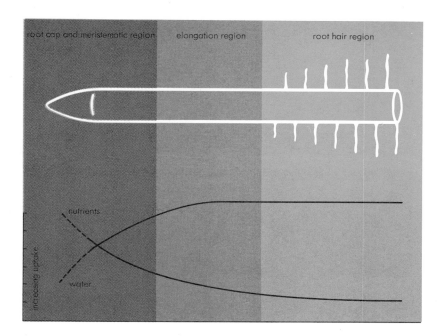

nutrients

water

increasing uptake

FIG. 8–5. Graphic approximation of the relationship between nutrient and water uptake in a root tip.

tionship holds for water intake, the water absorptive ability of the root increasing as one proceeds from the meristematic region into the region of elongation and continuing through the root hair region. This relationship is graphically portrayed in Fig. 8–5.

Botanists have shown that plants take in water by two principal means. Of relative minor importance is **active water absorption** which is accomplished by what is called the root pressure mechanism. Under conditions of abundant soil moisture and very low rate of water loss from the leaves, some plants continue to absorb water until a definite pressure (root pressure) has been developed. Root pressure is related to the ability of living root cells to secrete osmotically active substances into the xylem, thereby raising the osmotic concentration of the xylem liquid. Water then enters the xylem by diffusion, just as it would enter a cell osmotically. The mechanism of secretion requires energy and the phenomenon is in that sense an active one. Root pressure causes the exudation of water in liquid form from the leaves, a process called **guttation** (Fig. 8–6).

It also causes the "bleeding" or exudation of water and solutes from a cut stump following the removal of a shoot from its root. This bleeding may continue for days in certain plants, for example, from the stumps of pruned grape vines.

The second and most important mechanism termed **passive water absorption** occurs when water enters plants by means of physical forces which do not require expenditure of energy. The most important of these is the transpirational pull mechanism. The physical force involved in this mechanism is derived from the tendency of water molecules to cohere. As water evaporates from the surfaces of mesophyll cells in the leaf and diffuses into the surrounding atmosphere, other water molecules move into these cells to replace those lost. These molecules cohere to others in surrounding cells and in the xylem, and this cohesive force extends down through the stem into the living cells of the root. At the surface of the root hair the water molecules cohere to those in the soil solution, so that the loss of water from leaf surfaces results in water intake from the soil solution. The cohesive force that can be devel-

FIG. 8-6. Guttation
in strawberry leaves.

oped in plants as described above has been calculated to be equivalent to as much as the pressure of 70 atmospheres.

The above-mentioned absorptive processes are, of course, affected by numerous external and internal factors. Of these, the rate of water loss from the plant appears to be the most important.

Morphology and Growth of Roots in Relation to Absorption   The rate of absorption of water and solutes from soils by roots is determined not only by such factors as the rate of evaporation of water from leaves, respiration of root cells, osmotic concentration of the soil solution, availability of soil moisture, and osmotic properties of root cells; it is influenced also by the structure and growth of root systems. The form of a root system, the depth of its penetration into the soil, the number of its branches, and the direction of their growth markedly affect the absorption of materials from the soil, since these features determine the amount of root surface and the extent to which roots grow into new soil regions with higher water content. As stated previously, the root systems of many plants are of enormous extent. A single rye plant with its total 387 miles of roots possesses a root surface of over 2500

square feet—about 130 times the surface of the stems and leaves—in contact with the soil; in such a root system, the average daily linear growth of roots is 3.1 miles. A squash plant has been shown to have about 16 miles of roots, with a total surface area of 84,000 square feet. The extent of root growth is vitally important in absorption, since ordinarily there is limited movement of water in soils toward roots; roots obtain additional supplies of water by growing into new regions with greater stores of available water.

Root hairs frequently occur in huge numbers on a single root system; in a rye plant, for example, more than 14,000,000,000 root hairs with a total length of about 6600 feet and a surface of 4321 square feet are present. The enormous number of root hairs, tightly intermingled with and bound to soil particles, anchor the region of maturation and aid forward penetration of the soil by an elongating root tip. This function is important for both germinating seedlings and for development of the extensive root systems of mature plants. As they develop, root hairs penetrate new regions of the soil and help to maintain optimal water absorption, although maximum absorptive capacity is achieved in the region of elongation as shown in Fig. 8–5.

SPECIALIZED ROOTS

Specialized or modified roots perform functions other than the usual root functions of anchorage, absorption, conduction, and food storage. In some plants, roots perform **reproductive** functions. The roots of cherry and apple, for example, produce "suckers" that develop into new plants, and sweet potatoes and dahlias are commonly propagated by means of roots. Some plants, such as corn, screwpine, and banyan trees, produce adventitious prop roots that arise from aerial portions of the stem and grow downward until they reach the soil. The chief function of such roots is to give added support to the stem system. In some plants adventitious roots act as climbing roots, which anchor stems to the walls, fences, cliffs, and trees along which they grow. Roots of this type are found in poison ivy, English ivy, and other species of vines. The spongy **aerial** roots of **epiphytic** orchids (epiphytes are plants that grow nonparasitically upon other plants, wires,

poles, etc.) take water from falling rain and atmospheric humidity, absorb raw materials from the debris that collects about them, and help to anchor the whole plant to the object upon which it grows. Sometimes these aerial roots contain chlorophyll, as in the vanilla plant (which is an orchid), and are thus able to manufacture food. Bald cypress trees in swamps develop peculiar root projections, "cypress knees," that grow upward above the surface of the water or swamp soil in which the trees grow. The function of these "knees" is not understood. Earlier it was believed that they provide aeration for the submerged roots, but more recent evidence tends to discount this idea. Certain parasitic seed plants, such as dodders and mistletoe, absorb their food directly from other plants and do not have contact with the soil during most of their lives. The roots of these plants are modified into **haustoria** that penetrate the tissues of their host plants and absorb food directly from them.

SUMMARY

1.   Soils in which plants grow contain complex particles of different kinds, water, solutes, air, and living organisms.

2.   Mineral particles include clay, sand, and gravel, and furnish many nutrient solutes. Clay particles form the structural framework of soils.

3.   Soil air contains oxygen, essential to root respiration and root growth and functions. Soil air also contains carbon dioxide and nitrogen.

4.   Soil moisture, derived from rain and snow, may run off the surface, trickle downward, or be held by soil particles and in the spaces among soil particles. Roots absorb chiefly the moisture held by soil particles and in soil spaces.

5.   Soil moisture may be conserved by mulches.

6.   Organic matter consists of plant and animal residues and wastes. Organic matter is decomposed by bacteria, fungi, and other soil organisms and is the source of various nutrient solutes. Organic matter promotes water retention and keeps soils loose and open.

7.   Soil solutes arise in part from mineral particles and in part from organic matter, and are absorbed by roots chiefly in ionic form. Some ions are held on soil particles from which roots absorb them; others occur in the soil solution.

8. Soil organisms include bacteria, fungi, algae, worms, insects, rodents, and others. Activities of these organisms improve soil properties in relation to plant functions and plant growth.

9. Roots influence soils in several ways: they absorb materials from soils, they loosen soils, they bind soils against erosive action of wind and water.

10. Crops remove nutrients from soils; adding fertilizers to soils maintains a continuing supply of essential nutrients for plant growth.

11. The rhizosphere is the thin layer of soil surrounding the tips of growing roots and contains higher concentrations of bacteria and fungi than elsewhere in the soil.

12. Mycorrhizae are symbiotic associations of roots and fungi, believed to be mutually beneficial to each organism.

13. There are 16 essential elements for growth of green plants; three of these—carbon, hydrogen, and oxygen—are obtained chiefly from air and water. The remaining 13 elements are obtained from soil and include 6 macronutrients and 7 micronutrients.

14. The soil elements are absorbed in ionic form. Deficiencies in the supply of the essential elements result in deficiency diseases.

15. Plants may be grown in water solutions of essential soil elements. This type of plant culture is called hydroponics.

16. Roots absorb water by imbibition and osmosis, ions by simple diffusion and active transport.

17. Experiments have shown that most water is taken into the growing root in the regions of elongation and root hairs; the same root takes in nutrients in largest amount close to the meristematic region.

18. Active water absorption, a process of minor importance, is accomplished by the root pressure mechanism, an osmotic process associated with the secretion of osmotically active substances into the xylem. This process also requires an energy expenditure.

19. Guttation, or the exudation of droplets of water and solutes from the plant, is caused by root pressure.

20. Most water uptake is accounted for by passive water absorption which requires no energy expenditure by the plant; the evaporative loss of water molecules by transpiration creates a pull on the water column which, in turn, causes water to enter the roots from the soil solution.

21. Specialized roots perform specialized functions other than, or in addition to, the usual functions of roots. Examples of morphologically specialized roots with rather specialized functions are:
    a. prop roots of corn and other plants.
    b. climbing roots of ivies.
    c. spongy, aerial, water-absorbing roots of epiphytes.
    d. haustoria of dodder and mistletoe.

22. Some roots function in vegetative reproduction through their formation of "suckers."

SUGGESTED READINGS FOR INTERESTED STUDENTS

1. Garrett, S. D., *Soil Fungi and Soil Fertility*. The Macmillan Co., New York, 1963.

2. Kramer, Paul J., and Theodore T. Kozlowski, *Physiology of Trees*. McGraw-Hill, New York, 1960.

3. Meyer, B. S., D. B. Anderson, and R. H. Böhning, *Introduction to Plant Physiology*. D. Van Nostrand Co., New York, 1960.

4. *Plant Diseases*. The Yearbook of Agriculture, U. S. Government Printing Office, 1953.

5. *Soil*. The Yearbook of Agriculture, U. S. Government Printing Office, 1957.

TOPICS AND QUESTIONS FOR STUDY

1. Name the principal constituents of soils.

2. In what ways is the clay fraction of soils important in plant growth?

3. Name some of the chemical compounds in the mineral particles of soils.

4. What are the sources of organic matter in soils? What is the importance of organic matter for the growth and functioning of roots?

5. What are mulches? How do they benefit plant growth? Name some common mulches.

6. What is the source of soil water? What type of soil water is most commonly absorbed by roots?

7. Describe the importance of soil air for plant growth.

8. Name some common soil solutes and comment upon their importance for green plants.

9. What are ions? By what processes do roots absorb ions?

10. Name some common soil organisms, and describe their importance for plant growth.

11. Name the soil elements that are essential for the normal development of green plants.

12. In what chemical forms do these elements occur in soils?

13. Name the principal cations and anions absorbed by plant roots.

14. Which soil element is absorbed in greatest quantity by plants?

15. Describe the relative abundance of the various essential elements in plant protoplasm.

16. Describe the experimental demonstration of the essentiality of the various elements.

17. Define the term hydroponic.

18. List the known or supposed physiological functions of the micro-nutrients in plants.

19. What practical applications have resulted from studies by plant physiologists of the mineral nutrition of plants?

20. Why is the burning of dead leaves, straw, and other plant residues biologically wasteful?

21. Describe the processes involved in the absorption of water by roots.

22. What is transpiration? What is its relation to the absorption of water by roots?

23. Name four types of specialized roots and list their functions.

9

THE ORIGIN
AND
GROSS STRUCTURE
OF STEMS

THE ORIGIN AND NATURE OF STEMS

The first stem of a seed plant originates from the
epicotyl portion of the embryo axis in the seed.
The epicotyl is continuous with the hypocotyl—
the portion of the embryo axis located below the
cotyledonary node that gives rise at its tip to the
radicle (embryonic root). The epicotyl is a short,
cylindrical structure bearing a small mass of
meristematic tissue and frequently a pair or more
of tiny leaves at its tip. As was pointed out in
Chapter 2, the epicotyl is interpreted morphologi-

cally as an immature shoot, or leaf-bearing stem.
With resumption of growth following seed germination, the radicle soon penetrates the soil and
continues its development as the first root of the
seedling. Shortly after, the epicotyl emerges from
the seed coat and continues its development as
the first shoot. The entire aerial stem may develop
from the epicotyl as, for example, in garden pea.
In other plants, the garden bean for example, the
upper portion of the hypocotyl rises above the
surface of the soil for several inches, so that the
basal portion of the aerial axis develops from the

FIG. 9–1. False dragon's head (*Physostegia virginiana*), with herbaceous stems.

hypocotyl and the remainder from the epicotyl.

There are two chief functions of stems in flowering plants: the conduction of materials and the production and support of leaves and flowers. Other functions of the stems of certain plants are food storage, food manufacture, and reproduction; these will be described in greater detail later.

As has been mentioned previously, a stem with its leaves is called a shoot; an entire stem with all its branches and leaves is called a **shoot system.** Stems that grow above the soil are termed aerial stems to distinguish them from underground, or subterranean, stems. In flowering plants, stems are chiefly aerial, and in most species they are erect, as in elm trees, petunias, and corn. However, in some species, such as morning glories and grapes, the stems have a climbing habit of growth. In still other species, such as watermelon and cucumbers, the aerial stems are prostrate or creeping, that is, they are not strong enough to maintain an erect position but grow horizontally over the surface of the soil.

THE EXTERNAL STRUCTURE OF STEMS

Stem Types   Stems vary a great deal in different species of plants in their external form, size, internal structure, longevity, and other aspects. From the standpoint of their external structure and their growth habit, aerial stems may be divided into two types: **herbaceous** and **woody.** Herbaceous stems are rather soft and green, with relatively little development of tough, woody tissue, and with relatively little growth in diameter (Fig. 9–1). The tissues of herbaceous stems are largely, sometimes entirely, primary tissues. Herbaceous stems are covered with an epidermis, and as a rule are annual; that is, their life span is only one growing season. Some plants may have annual stems but perennial roots, in which case the stems are usually herbaceous, the roots often woody. This situation obtains in certain types of hibiscus, columbines, and peonies, and the plants live for many years, the perennial roots sending up new shoots each growing season. By contrast, in such plants as peas and squash, both roots and stems are annual and the plants thus live only one season. Some annual stems, such as those of sunflowers, develop moderate amounts of wood, but annual stems are most often distinctly herbaceous. Most woody stems are perennial, remaining alive and active for more than two years. Stems of this type are composed chiefly of secondary tissues, largely xylem or wood. Woody stems become thicker, harder, and tougher than herbaceous stems, and since their surfaces are covered with cork cells, which soon replace the epidermis of very young twigs, they are usually rough in surface texture and lack the green color of herbaceous stems. Also, since they continue growth for a number of years, woody stems are usually much taller and thicker than herbaceous stems. A **tree** is a woody–stemmed plant that possesses a main stem, or **trunk,** which extends some distance above the ground before it branches (Fig. 9–2). A **shrub** is a woody plant in which usually several stems of approximately equal size appear above the soil line (Fig. 9–3).

Buds   An examination of the surface of a stem in active, growing condition shows a variety of structures, most common of which are **buds** and **leaves.** Leaves are usually broad and flattened appendages of stems. The point on a stem

FIG. 9-2. American elm tree (*Ulmus americana*).

FIG. 9-3. Mock orange (*Philadelphus*), a shrub.

FIG. 9-4. Sprouts from adventitious buds on *Catalpa*.

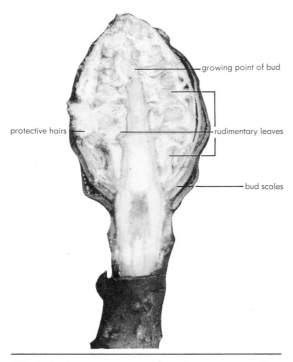

growing point of bud

rudimentary leaves

protective hairs

bud scales

FIG. 9–5. Longitudinal section of horse chestnut (Aesculus) bud.

from which a leaf develops is called a **node,** the segment of stem between two successive nodes, an **internode.** Internodes are sometimes very short, as on spur twigs of an apple tree; in other species such as willows and sunflowers, they may be several inches long. As a rule, buds are located in the upper angle between the point of juncture of a leaf stalk (petiole) with the stem. This angle between the leaf stalk and the stem is termed the **leaf axil,** and the buds found in leaf axils are called **axillary buds,** or since they occur along the sides of a stem, **lateral buds.** At the tip of each stem or twig is usually located a **terminal** bud. Terminal buds and axillary buds are quite similar in structure and in function, the distinction between them being chiefly one of position in most species of plants. Buds occasionally arise at places other than in the axils of leaves or at the stem tip. Buds of this type are called **adventitious.** They sometimes develop as a result of

injury; for example, they frequently are found producing young shoots on tree stumps (Fig. 9–4). Structurally, they are like axillary buds.

A bud (Fig. 9–5) is essentially a convex or cone-shaped mass of meristematic tissue that produces small lateral projections, the **primordia** of leaves; these primordia develop into the mature leaves of the plant as the bud grows. Since a bud contains the primordia of leaves, and, therefore, possesses nodes and very short internodes, it can be regarded as a very short, compact, immature tip of a shoot. In most herbaceous plants and in certain woody species, particularly those of moist tropical regions, the meristematic tissue of the bud is covered and protected only by rudimentary leaves (Fig. 9–6). Buds of this type are called **naked buds.** In woody stems of the drier portions of the tropics and generally in the temperate zones, buds are usually covered with overlapping scales, known as **bud scales.** These scales are modified leaves that grow out from the base of a bud and form a protective cloak over the meristematic tissue. Such scales are often thick and tough, and frequently, as in cottonwoods, are covered with a gummy secretion, or, as in some hickories, with dense growths of hairs. The bud scales protect the meristematic tissue from desiccation and to a certain extent from mechanical injury and from various kinds of parasites.

Buds may also be classified on the basis of their activity, their arrangement on the stem, and the kinds of structures they produce. Those buds that grow are called **active** buds to distinguish them from the occasional buds that remain inactive; the latter are called **dormant** buds and are usually axillary in position and situated some distance below the terminal bud of the twig upon which they occur. Dormant buds of woody stems sometimes develop many years after they are formed; they remain embedded in the bark as the stem grows in diameter and only under an appropriate stimulus grow into branches. More frequently, dormant buds remain undeveloped during the entire life of the plant.

Buds, like leaves, also differ in their arrange-

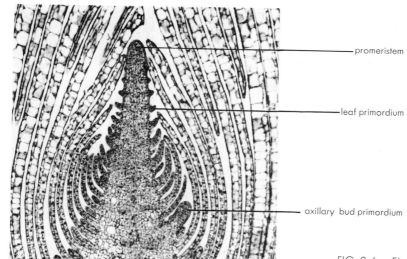

promeristem

leaf primordium

axillary bud primordium

FIG. 9-6. *Elodea* shoot tip in longitudinal section, showing leaf and branch primordia and young leaves.

ment. In most plants, as in elms and apples, they are arranged in **alternate** or **spiral** fashion, that is, one bud occurs at each node and the successive buds from the base toward the apex of a stem may be connected by a continuous spiral line. In a lesser, though still large number of species, including maples, dogwood, ash, and buckeye, the buds have an **opposite** arrangement (Fig. 9-9); that is, there are two buds at a node on opposite sides of the stem. The **whorled** arrangement, in which there are three or more buds more or less equally spaced about the stem at a node, is uncommon, occurring in relatively few plants. An example of a tree with whorled buds is catalpa.

Buds also differ in the structures they produce. Thus, there are **flower buds,** which develop into individual flowers, as in roses and morning glories; **leaf buds,** sometimes also called **branch buds,** which contain only leaf and stem primordia; and **mixed buds** which contain both leaf and flower primordia arranged on the rudimen-

FIG. 9-7. Growing point of young oat stem, enveloped by three young leaves. (Courtesy of Dr. O. T. Bonnet.)

FIG. 9–8. Stages in the opening of the terminal mixed bud of a horse chestnut (*Aesculus*) twig. See p. 109 also.

tary stem. Some of the buds on buckeye and apple trees are the mixed type.

Bud Growth A longitudinal section of a leaf bud usually shows the convex meristematic region with the rudimentary leaves appearing in succession below the meristematic tip (growing point) of the bud. The largest and oldest leaf primordia are at the base of the bud, with progressively smaller leaf rudiments toward the growing point. These leaf primordia are arranged in spiral, opposite, or whorled manner, just as the leaves are in mature twigs, each with a tiny bud rudiment in its axil. A bud is therefore an immature shoot possessing a stem, minute leaves, and axillary bud primordia. In some species, however, the axillary bud primordia are not apparent before the opening of the bud in which they are borne. Increase in length of a stem is brought about largely by elongation of the tiny internodes of the terminal bud as the bud develops. In most annual plants and in many woody plants of the tropics, normal elongation of successive internodes produced in the bud continues through most of the growing season, but in woody plants of cooler regions, elongation of successive

FIG. 9–9. Opposite buds of *Euonymus alatus*.

FIG. 9–8. Continued from p. 108

internodes occurs chiefly during a few weeks of springtime growth, immediately following the opening of the bud scales. The end of the growing season and accompanying onset of adverse environmental conditions bring death to annual plants, and the activity of their buds ends. In woody plants, the end of the growing season finds the buds dormant, usually covered, and physiologically able to survive a period of winter or summer drought.

When a bud of a woody plant opens, the bud scales begin to grow more rapidly on their inner surfaces than on their outer, and, as a result, bend away from the center of the bud. Along with the opening of the scales, bud growth is resumed, including the formation, enlargement, and differentiation of new cells and tissues. The bud scales usually fall away a short time after they have opened. During the growth season the bud primordia in the leaf axils of the new section of twig undergo progressive development, so that at the end of this season enlarged axillary buds are found in all the leaf axils. The terminal bud, similar in structure to that from which the new section of twig grew, is then covered by new bud scales. These buds remain dormant during the remainder of the summer and throughout the following winter, and with the coming of the next spring the active buds begin to grow in the fash-

ion described above. The dormant buds of woody plants are often called **winter buds,** since they live through the winter. The growth of a terminal bud results in elongation of a shoot; growth of an axillary bud produces a branch shoot. When an axillary bud forms a branch shoot, this twig develops its own terminal and axillary buds in the same manner as the main stem of which it is a branch. The axillary buds of this branch may grow subsequently and form a further order of branches of the branch twig. Thus, terminal buds produce growth in length of a twig, axillary buds produce branches of that twig. The origin of stem branches may be described as exogenous since the axillary buds that produce these branches are located on the surface of the stem. This is in contrast to roots in which branch primordia are initiated endogenously as described in the preceding chapter. In many plants, the branches formed by the growth of certain buds are **flowers,** which are highly specialized shoots. Growth of this specialized reproductive branch is different from that of a vegetative branch in that the internodes do not elongate and floral organs are produced instead of leaves. No buds are formed as a rule in the axils of the floral organs and thus no further growth of such a shoot is possible. After fulfilling reproductive functions, certain floral parts commonly wither and fall.

FIG. 9–10.   Effect of disbudding of chrysanthemums. Both stems in the photograph were taken from the same variety of chrysanthemum. No flower buds were removed from the stem at the left. All flower buds except one were removed from the stem at the right.

The form of a whole shoot system is determined in a large degree by the positions, arrangements, and relative activities of the various types of buds. If the axillary buds are opposite, the branches produced by them are opposite; if they are alternate, the branches into which they grow are alternate. If there is a dominant terminal bud and a relatively large number of dormant axillary buds, the branch on which these buds occur will be much elongated with relatively few side branches. If, on the contrary, the terminal bud is slow-growing and the axillary buds are active, the stem grows slowly in length and will possess many, relatively fast-growing branches. By applying his knowledge of bud behavior, a horticulturist can control the shape of plants that he is growing. In a plant with an active terminal bud and with slow-growing or dormant axillary buds, removal of the terminal bud usually stimulates the axillary buds to greater activity, in many cases overcoming their dormancy; thus a bushier

growth of a plant may be induced by pruning away certain of the terminal buds. In peonies all buds on a stem except the terminal one may be removed, a process called **disbudding,** with the result that the single shoot becomes very tall and erect and the flower that develops from the single bud is much larger than it would be were other flower buds allowed to develop. The reduction of competition among many buds for the food manufactured by the plant places all the food at the disposal of the few remaining buds and thus permits them to form unusually large flowers. Disbudding is a common horticultural practice in the culture of plants, such as roses, chrysanthemums, carnations, and asters (Fig. 9–10).

Stem Surfaces   An examination of the surface of an herbaceous stem shows relatively few structures other than buds, leaves, and branch shoots of both vegetative and reproduce nature. There may be **hairs,** which are outgrowths of epidermal cells; **stipules,** small projections of leaf tissue at the point of juncture of a leaf stalk with the stem; and occasionally **spines,** which may be modified branches, leaves, hairs, or stipules. In the woody twigs of trees and shrubs, however, other structures in addition to the above-mentioned features are present (Fig. 9–11). These are **lenticels, leaf scars, bundle scars, bud scars,** and **branch scars.** Lenticels are small masses of loosely compacted cells that are often raised slightly above the surface of the bark on stems and, to a lesser extent, on roots of woody plants. As their name implies, these masses are commonly lens-shaped, although they range in outline from circular to elongated and narrow. Unlike the surrounding corky tissue of which they are part, the lenticels characteristically have abundant intercellular spaces and thus serve as regions through which gaseous exchange between internal tissues and the external atmosphere may occur. A leaf scar is a mark that remains on the stem after the separation of a leaf stalk. Such marks are especially conspicuous on woody twigs in autumn and winter, but they may also be apparent in annual plants if some of the leaves fall away. Leaf scars are variable in form in different species; common shapes of leaf scars are narrow crescents, U's, V's and sometimes circles and triangles. In the twigs of the tree of heaven (*Ailanthus*), the leaf scars are roughly triangular in shape, with sides about ½ inch long. In Hercules' club (*Aralia*), the leaf scars are narrow and elongated transversely, frequently attaining a length of more than an inch. Usually, however, leaf scars do not exceed ¼ to ½ inch in length and are most commonly U shaped or V shaped. Bundle scars appear as tiny raised dots on the leaf scars. Bundle scars are the broken ends of **vascular bundles** (conducting strands) that extended from the twig into the leaf stalk. When a leaf falls, these bundles are broken across at the point of separation of the leaf from the stem and thus are visible in cross-sectional view within the leaf scars. The number, size, and arrangement of bundle scars vary in different species of plants. Bud scars are rings of small, narrow scars left by the bud scales which fall away from the base of an opening bud. Individual bud scale scars are usually inconspicuous, but the ring that the several scars form is readily visible. Most of these bud scars are left by terminal buds, and each of them marks the place at which a terminal bud began its development in a spring season. Since a new terminal bud develops each year from the previous terminal bud of the twig and opens in the following spring, the number of these bud scars on a twig indicates the age of the twig. By counting back from the apex of a stem the number of bud scars present, it is possible to determine the age of any section of the twig. Branch scars are usually circular in outline, often slightly concave, and occur immediately above leaf scars. They mark the points of juncture of fallen branches with the main stem. If the branch produces a flower instead of a vegetative twig, the scar left by the fallen fruit (a fruit develops from a flower) is called a **fruit scar.** Such a scar is similar in form and position to the scars left by vegetative twigs. In many species of woody plants, there is a regu-

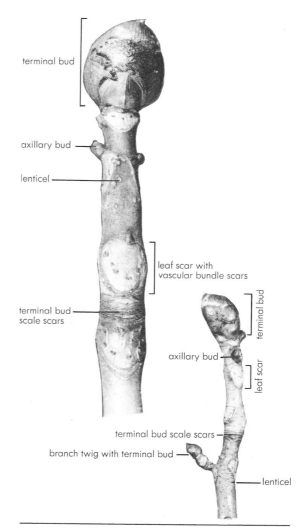

FIG. 9–11. External aspect of horse chestnut (*Aesculus*) twigs. The photograph on the right illustrates the development of a branch from an axillary bud.

larity in the rate at which certain of the twigs and branches fall away from the branches from which they arise. This phenomenon is termed **natural** or **self-pruning** (Fig. 9–12) and is especially noticeable in dense stands of trees where the most heavily shaded twigs and branches fall away while they are still relatively young.

As woody stems grow in diameter, the smooth, young outer bark is split, partly by the formation

FIG. 9-12.   Self-pruning in sycamore (*Platanus*).

Most common of these specialized stems are underground, or subterranean stems, of which there are four principal kinds: **rhizomes, tubers, bulbs,** and **corms.** A rhizome is a horizontal stem that grows at or below the surface of the soil, occasionally with its upper surface exposed to the air. Rhizomes and other types of specialized underground stems sometimes resemble roots superficially; they are, however, true stems, for they have nodes, internodes, buds, and leaves. Leaves and buds occur at the nodes of rhizomes, as do also adventitious roots that grow out usually from the lower surfaces. Rhizomes are sometimes slender, as in quack grass, or much enlarged by abundant stores of food, as in iris. The chief functions of rhizomes are vegetative reproduction and food storage. Most rhizomes are perennial and thus increase in their length year after year, sending up new aerial stems from their nodes. If such rhizomes are separated into pieces, as may happen in hoeing or plowing, each segment is able to develop into a new plant and thus increase greatly the number of plants. Because of this behavior, and also because of the fact that when rhizomatous weeds are pulled up, fragments of

of new tissues of the bark itself, partly by rapid diametric and circumferential growth of the tissues inside the bark. With cracking of the young bark and the growth of new cork layers, the surface of the branch becomes much roughened in most species of trees and the various structures described above are no longer visible. In some species, such as birch and willow, the bark remains rather smooth, even on old parts of the stem, and some of the structures characteristic of the younger twig surfaces, lenticels principally, are still visible on the bark of old branches.

Specialized Stems   Many species of plants have stems that differ markedly in structure and function from the common types of aerial stems described in the preceding section. Such stems are termed specialized or modified stems.

FIG. 9-13.   Longitudinal sections of bulbs, showing roots, a small compact stem and, growing from it, a number of leaves with thickened fleshy bases. In the center of the bulb is a young, growing flower stalk.

Roots

1. Roots grow downward into the soil.

2. Roots do not have nodes and internodes.

3. Root branches arise internally from the pericycle.

4. The growing points of roots are covered by rootcaps.

5. Roots bear absorptive root hairs close to the growing tips.

6. The primary root originates from the hypocotyl of the embryo.

Stems

1. Stems of most plants grow upward above the soil.

2. Stems have well-marked nodes and internodes.

3. Stem branches arise externally, from buds formed on the surface of stems.

4. The growing points of stems are naked or are protected by bud scales.

5. The characteristic appendages of stems are leaves.

6. The main stem (or primary shoot) originates from the epicotyl of the embryo, or in part from the hypocotyl.

TABLE 9–1
External differences between roots and stems.

their rhizomes often remain undetected in the soil, plants with stems of this kind may be very difficult to eradicate. The horticultural propagation of many types of garden plants, such as irises and cannas, is almost entirely by separating large rhizomes into small pieces and planting these.

FIG. 9–14.   Bulbs forming on bulb scales of amaryllis.

In some plants, the growing tips of rhizomes become much enlarged as a result of food storage. Such subterranean stems are called tubers, the best known examples of which are the tubers of Irish potato plants. Starch is the most commonly stored food in tubers, although other carbohydrates, such as **inulin,** are stored in the tubers of certain species. The functions of tubers are food storage and reproduction. Under natural conditions, the rhizomes connecting the tubers with the main stem of the potato plant die in the autumn or winter and the tubers, thus isolated in the soil, are able to produce shoots from their buds the following spring. Shoots develop from buds located at the nodes or "eyes" of the specialized stem, each eye consisting of a cluster of buds in the axial of a subtending, scalelike leaf. Potatoes are also artificially propagated by tuber segments, called "seed pieces." A tuber is cut into pieces, each with one or more "eyes." These segments are planted and each produces a new plant from one of its "eyes."

A bulb (Fig. 9–13) is a single, large, globose bud, with a small stem at its basal end; numerous fleshy, scalelike leaves grow from the upper surface of the small stem, and from the bottom, adventitious roots emerge. Thus, the greater portion of a bulb consists of storage leaves growing from a small, basally situated stem. Bulbs serve primarily for food storage and also for reproduction. Buds frequently develop in the axils of the scale leaves (Fig. 9–14). These buds resemble the parent bulb, from which they may be separated and used

FIG. 9-15. (*left*) A strawberry plant with runners and new plants developed from the runners. FIG. 9-16. (*above*) A cactus garden in California.

for propagation. Familiar plants with bulbs are onion, narcissus, lily, and hyacinth.

Corms resemble bulbs superficially in size and form, but their internal structure differs from that of bulbs. Most of a bulb is composed of modified leaves, but the greater portion of a corm is stem tissue. The leaves are usually thinner and much smaller than those of bulbs. As in bulbs, buds occur in the axils of the thin scale leaves, and adventitious roots grow from the lower surface of the stem. Corms function as do bulbs for food storage and reproduction. Well-known plants with corms are gladiolus and crocus.

Aerial stems, or portions of them, frequently perform unusual functions. In various climbing plants, such as grape and Boston ivy, some of the twigs are modified into climbing organs called **tendrils.** In some plants, the aerial stem grows in spiral fashion about a suitable solid support; such stems, termed **twiners,** are found in the morning glory and sweet potato. Creeping stems that grow horizontally above the surface of the soil and that often develop new plants at their nodes if these touch the soil, are called **runners,** or **stolons.** These occur in strawberry plants (Fig. 9-15) and are used as the common method of propagating this species. The thorns of some plants, such as hawthorn, honey locust, and Osage orange, are modified twigs; these occur in the axils of leaves and may branch, as in honey locusts. These thorns are doubtless of considerable importance in discouraging the visits of herbivorous animals. In most species of cactus (Fig. 9-16), the leaves are reduced in size, or are transitory, withering away a few days after they are formed. In such plants the stems are green and have assumed the chief function of the missing leaves—namely, food manufacture. Cactus stems also store considerable quantities of water. In some plants, such as onion and tiger lily, **aerial** **bulbs** are formed from buds on the aerial portion of the stem. These are similar to subterranean bulbs, and when planted in the soil grow into new plants. In those onions that produce aerial bulbs, the bulbs form in the **inflorescence** (flower cluster) in place of flowers.

EXTERNAL DIFFERENCES BETWEEN ROOTS AND STEMS

Table 9-1 presents in summarized form the principal differences between most roots and stems with reference to their external structure and growth habits.

SUMMARY

1. Aerial stems arise chiefly from the epicotyls (sometimes in part from the hypocotyls) of embryos.
2. The chief functions of stems of flowering plants are:
   a. Conduction of materials from roots to leaves and from leaves to roots and buds.
   b. The production and support of leaves and flowers.
   c. Food storage.
3. A stem with its leaves is called a shoot; an entire stem with all its leaves and branches is called a shoot system.
4. Most stems are aerial; some are subterranean.
5. Herbaceous stems are usually green, with little tough, woody tissue, and usually not much growth in diameter; they are chiefly annual. Woody stems are tough, with well-developed fibers and other types of strengthening cells, are not green, usually show considerable growth in diameter, and are mostly perennial.
6. Stems bear leaves, and in the axils of leaves, buds. The point on a stem from which a leaf or bud arises is called a node. The length of stem between two successive nodes is an internode.
7. Buds that occur at the tips of stems are terminal, those in leaf axils are axillary. Adventitious buds arise in places other than the axils of leaves or the tips of stems.
8. A bud is an undeveloped shoot. A naked bud is covered only by young leaves. A covered bud is protected by overlapping, protective bud scales that are modified leaves.
9. When one bud occurs at a node, bud arrangement is called alternate or spiral. When two buds occur at a node, the arrangement is said to be opposite. When more than two buds occur at a node, the arrangement is called whorled.

10. Leaf buds produce stems and leaves. Flower buds produce flowers. Mixed buds produce stems that bear both leaves and flowers.

11. The opening of a bud results chiefly from the elongation of its internodes and the growth of its leaves. The tip of a shoot is the growing point, the scene of most active growth in a bud.

12. The form of a shoot system is determined largely by the positions and growth activities of its buds.

13. The following structures may be found chiefly on young woody twigs, in addition to buds.

    a. Lenticels—small, porous regions in bark.

    b. Leaf scars—left by the falling away of leaves.

    c. Bundle scars—broken ends of vascular bundles in leaf scars.

    d. Bud scars—rings of scars left by the falling away of bud scales.

    e. Branch and fruit scars.

14. Examples of specialized stems are: rhizomes, tubers, corms, tendrils, runners (stolons), and thorns.

SUGGESTED READINGS FOR INTERESTED STUDENTS

1. Esau, Katherine. *Plant Anatomy*, 2d ed. Wiley, New York, 1965.

2. Trelease, William. *Winter Botany.* 3rd ed. (1931) Reprinted by Dover Publications, New York, 1967.

TOPICS AND QUESTIONS FOR STUDY

1. From what part of an embryo does the stem of a seedling originate?

2. Does the hypocotyl ever form a part of a stem? Cite a specific plant as an example and describe how its stem develops.

3. List the functions of stems.

4. What is meant by the term "shoot"? By "shoot system"?

5. Name some plants with aerial stems. With subterranean stems.

6. List as many differences as you can between herbaceous and woody stems.

7. Are annual stems always herbaceous? Explain.

8. What is the major difference between shrubs and trees?

9. Define: node, internode, leaf axil, terminal bud, axillary bud, adventitious bud.

10. Describe the structure of a bud. What is the most important part of a bud from the standpoint of stem growth?

11. What are the functions of bud scales?

12. Distinguish among active, dormant, leaf, flower, and mixed buds.

13. Describe the common types of bud arrangement. How are these correlated with leaf arrangement?

14. Describe briefly the growth of a leaf bud, and name the structures that it produces. What happens to bud scales when a bud begins to grow?

15. When a bud grows, does all its meristematic tissue become differentiated into mature, permanent tissues? Do all buds behave similarly in this respect?

16. What is meant by "terminal bud dominance"? How is a knowledge of this phenomenon important to horticulturists?

17. What is disbudding? What is its effect?

18. Define and describe: lenticels, leaf scars, bundle scars, bud scars, twig scars, fruit scars.

19. What is the function of lenticels? Why are lenticels usually not visible on tree trunks? Name a species of tree in which lenticels are visible on old trunks.

20. Name four types of subterranean stems, and describe their functions and structure.

21. Describe the structure of a potato "eye."

22. The Irish potato is a tuber, but sweet potatoes are roots. What are the differences between them?

23. List the principal structural differences between roots and stems.

10

THE
INTERNAL STRUCTURE
OF STEMS

The shoot apex within a terminal bud consists of thin-walled cells, many of which divide to produce new cells. These meristematic cells, like those of a root tip, are small, more or less isodiametric, and possess conspicuous nuclei and dense cytoplasm with small vacuoles. Cells formed by divisions in the apex soon undergo enlargement and, as their enlargement approaches its maximum, become differentiated into mature tissues, such as xylem and phloem. Thus, roots and stems share certain similarities in the fundamental pattern of growth and in the arrangement of their apical tissues; in both roots and stems, a zone of meristematic cells is located at or near the tip of the organ, followed by a zone of enlarging cells which in turn is followed by a group of cells undergoing maturation or differentiation. In both stem tips and root tips, then, we may distinguish a region of cell division, a region of cell elongation, and a region of cell maturation. In a root, the meristematic region (region of cell division) is covered by a protective root cap; in a stem, the meristematic region of the tip is naked, but may be partially or wholly covered by bud scales

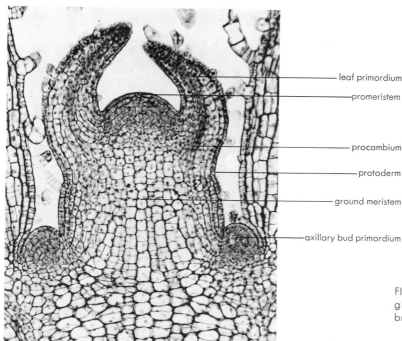

leaf primordium
promeristem

procambium

protoderm

ground meristem

axillary bud primordium

FIG. 10–1. *Coleus* shoot tip in longitudinal section, showing leaf and branch primordia.

or immature leaves, as noted in the last chapter. In the axils of these young leaves, small outgrowths of tissue develop; these typically become axillary buds.

Differentiation begins very early in stem ontogeny, slight structural changes appearing even in the meristematic tissue that underlies the dome-shaped mass of cells at the extreme tip of the stem **(promeristem).** Examination of a longitudinal section of a shoot tip (Fig. 10–1) shows the three meristematic tissues that differentiate from the promeristem:

1. **Protoderm,** the superficial meristem that gives rise to the epidermis.

2. **Procambium,** the provascular meristem, consisting of strands of narrow, slightly elongated cells that develop into primary phloem and xylem.

3. **Ground meristem,** the meristem that produces pith and cortex.

With the development of these meristematic tissues, most of the procambium differentiates into primary phloem and xylem. In many species, however, a single layer of procambial cells may persist, retaining its meristematic condition. This layer of cells, called the **vascular cambium,** functions in stems as it does in roots—namely, in the production of secondary phloem and secondary xylem.

A study of the anatomical features of plant stems furnishes convincing evidence of the inseparability of function and structure in living cells, and of the intricacies involved in the integration of physiological activities with the development of the complex tissue systems of stems. In stems we see the strengthening tissues are composed of elongated cells with thick, tough, yet elastic walls; the conducting tissues with thinner walls in which are present numerous **perforations** and thin areas called **pits** that facilitate the transfer of materials from cell to cell;

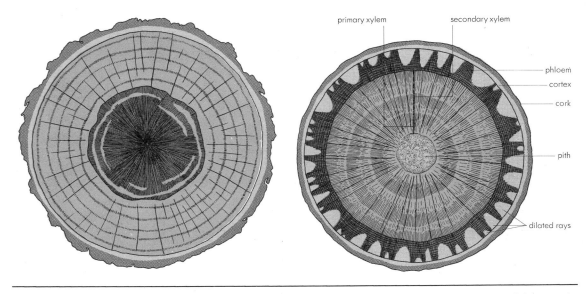

FIG. 10–2. *Left:* Transection of an old tree branch showing dark, inner heartwood, rough bark toward the outside, and the lighter sapwood lying between heartwood and bark. *Right:* Transection of a 3-year old woody stem.

and thin-walled cells within which water, foods, and other materials may be stored. Most of the movement of materials through stems is vertical. Likewise, most of the stresses and strains to which stems are subject are exerted in the longitudinal direction. The architecture of stems seems admirably designed to meet these demands. The conducting cells are elongated parallel to the longitudinal axes of stems, and their pits and wall perforations are located in such manner as to make the upward and downward conduction of materials most effective. Further, strengthening cells are greatly elongated, with tapering ends that fit snugly against the tapering ends of other strengthening cells, and in this arrangement they provide maximum resistance to longitudinal stresses.

It was stated in Chapter 9 that stems could be classified into two rather distinct types—woody and herbaceous. Many anatomical variations are found within these two main types of stems. It is inappropriate to consider in a book of this type the intricacies of structure of the many varieties of plant stems; therefore, we will discuss the

internal structure and development of only the commonest types of stems of seed plants.

Botanists generally believe that among the seed plants woody stems are primitive and herbaceous stems are specialized. Students sometimes have difficulty in remembering this point because old woody stems are structurally more complex than herbaceous stems, and it is an axiom that evolution proceeds from the simpler to the more complex. However, it must be remembered that in many instances simplification is a form of specialization (as with the human coat of fur or appendix), and that, further, many aspects of woody stem complexity are secondary, involving the fact that they continue to grow for many seasons. There is convincing fossil evidence that the first kinds of true seed plants on the earth were perennial, woody-stemmed plants and that the annual, herbaceous type of stem is a relatively recent development from the older, woody type. In accordance with this widely accepted modern interpretation, this chapter will describe first the anatomy of woody stems and later the structure of herbaceous stems.

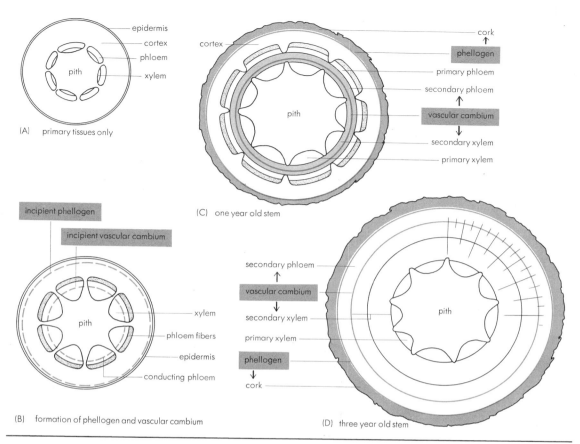

(A) primary tissues only

(C) one year old stem

(B) formation of phellogen and vascular cambium

(D) three year old stem

FIG. 10-3. Diagrammatic representation of secondary growth in a woody dicotyledonous stem.

THE INTERNAL STRUCTURE OF WOODY STEMS

Gross Internal Structure An examination with the naked eye of a **transverse** (cross) section of a mature woody stem more than one or two years old (Fig. 10-2) shows two major groups of tissues: the **bark,** which forms the outer layer of the stem and the wood, or **xylem,** which lies inside the bark. In the center of the stem, surrounded by the wood there is discernible in some species a small core of **pith.** Invisible to the naked eye but exceedingly important in the life of the stem is the **vascular cambium,** a single layer of meristematic cells in the form of a continuous circle between the wood and the bark (Fig. 10-3). The

cambium layer forms new cells radially, and thus causes stems to grow in diameter. The bark is very thin and smooth in young stems, but becomes thicker and usually roughened as stems grow older. This roughening results from splitting or fissuring of the outer bark as it is stretched by the increasing diameter and circumference of the inner bark and xylem. The pattern of fissuring is determined in large part by the nature and growth activity of the **phellogen** (cork cambium), a meristematic tissue in the outer parts of the bark. Although bark becomes thicker with age, its rate of increase is quite slow compared with that of wood, and increase in diameter of woody stems results chiefly from increase in the number of wood cells. As stems grow older, the proportion

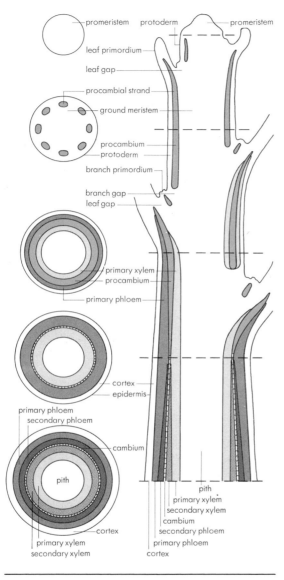

promeristem   protoderm   promeristem
leaf primordium
leaf gap
procambial strand
ground meristem
procambium
protoderm
branch primordium
branch gap
leaf gap
primary xylem
procambium
primary phloem
cortex
epidermis
primary phloem
secondary phloem
cambium
pith
cortex
primary xylem
secondary xylem

pith
primary xylem
secondary xylem
cambium
secondary phloem
primary phloem
cortex

FIG. 10–4. Diagrams depicting longitudinal (*right*) and transverse (*left*) sections of a dicotyledonous shoot.

of wood to bark increases enormously, so that the major part of the volume of the larger limbs and trunks of trees is xylem. This increase of xylem over bark is in part a result of the fact that all the

secondary xylem formed by the cambium is retained within the body of the stem, whereas the outer portion of the bark is slowly and continuously sloughed off.

The Primary Tissues of Woody Stems   In most woody stems of two years old or older, the tissues present are chiefly of **secondary** origin; that is, tissues produced radially in the stem by the activity of cambium and cork cambium. Secondary stem tissues are thus found from the latter part of the first season's growth of the twig through succeeding years. If one examines a cross section of a twig cut in the young part of the maturation region during the early part of the season's growth of that twig, one finds only **primary** tissues present; that is, tissues formed by growth of the meristematic cells of the shoot tip and later differentiated into various mature tissues (Figs. 10–3, 10–4). These primary permanent structures are: 1. **epidermis**; 2. **cortex**; 3. **phloem**; 4. **xylem**; 5. **pith.**

The epidermis is a single surface layer of cells, the outer walls of which are usually cutinized and thus are nearly waterproof. The epidermis is, in part, a protective tissue that serves to prevent excessive evaporation of water from the underlying tissues. The cortex varies in thickness in stems of different species and is composed usually of collenchymatous strengthening cells, just under the epidermis, and parenchyma cells, which function principally in the storage of food and other materials. The **central cylinder** is composed of several tissues or groups of tissues: phloem, cambium, xylem, and pith. Pericycle, the tissue between the phloem and the cortex in roots, is typically absent from the stems of higher plants.

The phloem lies inside the cortex and consists of sieve tubes and their adjoining companion cells, phloem fibers, and parenchyma cells. Sieve tubes are not individual cells, but are rows of elongated, thin-walled living cells (sieve tube members) arranged end to end. Although sieve tube members are living, they typically contain no nuclei at maturity. The end walls (and often side walls) of sieve tube members contain pores through which cytoplasm passes from one cell to another. The wall pores also provide for the passage of foods from one sieve tube member to another. Companion cells are living cells that border upon sieve tube members and in some way participate in the conduction of foods in the sieve tubes. Some of this food is stored in phloem parenchyma. Phloem fibers are thick-walled strengthening cells that are of considerable economic importance; for instance, linen and hemp fibers, obtained from the stems of flax and hemp plants, are phloem fibers. Linen fibers are used in the weaving of fine textiles and in the manufacture of strong threads and cords. Hemp fibers are used chiefly in binder twine, rope, carpets, mats, burlap bags, and upholstery.

Inside the phloem is the vascular cambium, a single layer of meristematic cells that are thin walled, elongated, commonly rectangular, and arranged in a circle, as seen in cross section (Fig. 10-11). The cambium is a meristematic tissue, which, by repeated cell divisions, forms secondary phloem tissue on its outer surface and secondary xylem cells on its inner surface. It is chiefly through this production of secondary tissues by the cambium that stems grow in diameter.

Inside the cambium is the xylem, or wood, which is composed of vessels, tracheids, xylem fibers, xylem parenchyma cells, and vascular rays. These cell types and cell groups were described in Chapter 4. All these types of cells are found in the wood of most flowering plants. In pines and nearly all other gymnosperms, however, vessels and wood fibers are not present, the wood being composed almost entirely of tracheids and ray cells. There are occasionally other types of structures present in the xylem of some species of woody plants—for example, the resin ducts of pines and other gymnosperms. Vessels and tracheids conduct water and dissolved substances and furnish support to the stem; wood fibers function principally as strengthening and supporting cells, and wood parenchyma cells store food. Pith, a tissue located in the center of the stem, is composed of thin-walled parenchyma cells which store food. In some species of woody plants, the pith is alive only when the twig is young. In others it is still alive in older branches of considerable size. Pith rays are broad, radially elongated bands of parenchyma cells between the vascular bundles, that extend from the pith outward to the cortex. In a transverse section of a young twig, rays resemble the radiating spokes of a wheel. The first rays that form in a twig are a result of the growth of the terminal meristem in the bud and are thus primary in origin. Their functions include storage and, presumably, lateral conduction. As the cambium grows and forms secondary tissues, it produces new rays of secondary origin that are called vascular rays. These are thought to be similar in function to pith rays.

The epidermis and cortex are continuous, concentric layers of cells in young stems (Fig. 10-3). However, the xylem and phloem tissues in the young, apical regions of such stems are often not arranged as continuous layers, but may occur as separate strands of cells developed from the apical meristem. Each of these strands is termed a **vascular bundle,** and consists of xylem cells in its inner portion, phloem cells in its outer part. Depending on the species, each bundle may also have a layer of cambial cells lying between the xylem and phloem. This arrangement of the primary xylem and phloem into separate vascular bundles is characteristic of the very young stems of many woody plants but is quite unlike the arrangement in young roots, in which discrete strands of primary phloem and xylem are arranged on alternate radii. In the stems of some woody species the primary phloem and xylem occur as continuous layers with no marked separation into bundles (that is, as concentric cylinders of tissue). Vascular bundles are arranged usually in a single circle, with the cambium present in the bundles and in older stems extending across the pith rays in a continuous layer connecting adjacent bundles.

Most of the above-mentioned tissues of a woody twig in the early part of its first season's

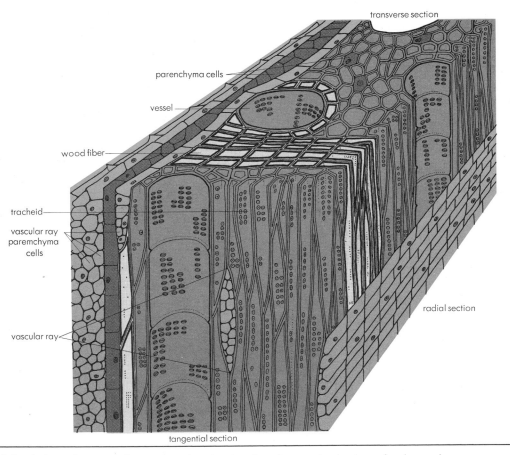

parenchyma cells

vessel

wood fiber

tracheid

vascular ray
paremchyma
cells

vascular ray

radial section

tangential section

FIG. 10–5.   A three-dimensional representation showing the microscopic structure of oak wood.

growth are primary tissues; that is, they have been produced as a result of the division of cells in the shoot tip and of the subsequent enlargement and differentiation of these newly formed cells. The fact that the vascular cambium remains a meristematic tissue and possesses the same ability to produce new cells as the meristematic tissue of the bud is especially noteworthy in these processes of differentiation.

The Secondary Tissues of Woody Stems   After the primary tissues are formed in a young twig, little or no further lengthwise growth of this differentiated portion of the stem is possible. The terminal bud that produced these primary tissues

continues its growth through the growing seasons of successive years in woody stems (or is replaced by axillary buds that function in the same fashion), each year forming a new stem segment with its primary tissues as described above.

The primary tissues of a young twig are completed in the first few weeks of the first year's existence of that twig. Also early in the first year of its life, the twig begins to grow in diameter as a result of **secondary** growth that usually continues through a number of growing seasons, often for hundreds or even thousands of years. With each season's secondary growth, the twig or large branch or main trunk increases further in diameter (Fig. 10–3D).

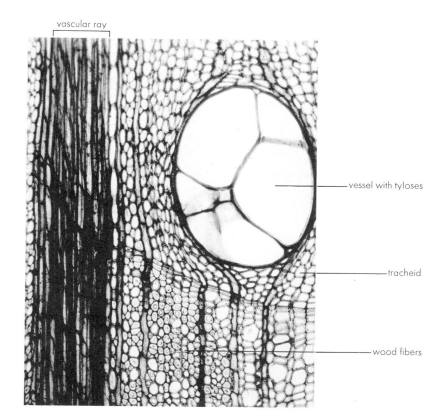

vascular ray

vessel with tyloses

tracheid

wood fibers

FIG. 10-6. Photomicrograph of oak (*Quercus*) wood in transection.

This secondary growth occurs as a result of the continuing division of cambial cells that produce, radially, secondary xylem and secondary phloem cells and, tangentially, additional cambial initials. As the secondary phloem develops, it presses outward, crushing much of the primary phloem. In most species of woody plants, when the cambium produces new xylem and new phloem it does so along its entire circumference; that is, secondary tissues are produced by the portions of cambium in the vascular bundles **(fascicular cambium)** as well as by the portions lying between adjacent vascular bundles **(interfascicular cambium).** Thus, these secondary tissues are formed in continuous layers, as contrasted with the separate bundles in which the primary tissues are commonly formed. The continuous nature of the secondary tissues is usually more noticeable in xylem than in phloem. In the

stems of some woody plants, secondary xylem and phloem are merely added to the primary tissues in the vascular bundles, which thus remain separate and distinct throughout the life of the stem. In these, obviously, the secondary vascular tissues are not formed in continuous layers.

The kinds of cells formed by the vascular cambium are generally the same as those formed by the meristematic tissue of the bud—namely, vessel members, tracheids, wood fibers, and wood parenchyma in the xylem (Figs. 10-5, 10-6), and sieve tube members, companion cells, fibers, and parenchyma in the phloem tissue (Figs. 10-7, and 10-12). The cambium also produces vascular rays. These parenchymatous structures extend from the phloem inward through the xylem for various distances, the earliest formed (oldest) almost reaching the pith. As woody stems grow in diameter, the number of vascular rays formed by the

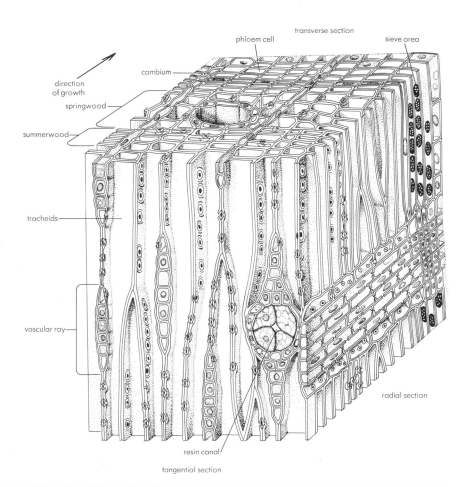

direction
of growth

transverse section

phloem cell

sieve area

cambium

springwood

summerwood

tracheids

vascular ray

resin canal

tangential section

radial section

FIG. 10-7. A three-dimensional representation showing microscopic features of xylem, vascular cambium, and phloem of pine (*Pinus*).

cambium increases, so that the areas of xylem between such rays remain fairly constant. If new rays were not formed, the distance between the younger regions of adjacent, growing rays would constantly increase as the circumference of the stem increased. The continual formation of new rays by the cambium ensures an adequate supply of rays with reference to the increasing circumference of the xylem and phloem. Although the derivatives of cambium cells are formed chiefly in the radial direction, producing secondary tissue on the inner and outer cambial surfaces, there is also a certain amount of cambial growth in a tangential direction, as a result of which the

actual circumference of the cambium increases. The production of new cambial cells in a tangential direction, then, enables the cambium ring to expand in circumference as it is pushed outward by the xylem with each growing season.

Another group of secondary tissues is produced by the **phellogen** (Fig. 10–14), a meristematic tissue that often has, like the vascular cambium, the form of a continuous ring in the stem, as seen in transverse section. In some species of woody plants, several layers of phellogen develop; in such stems, the phellogen layers are not continuous around the stem but occur as short tangential bands of growing tissue. The roughness of the

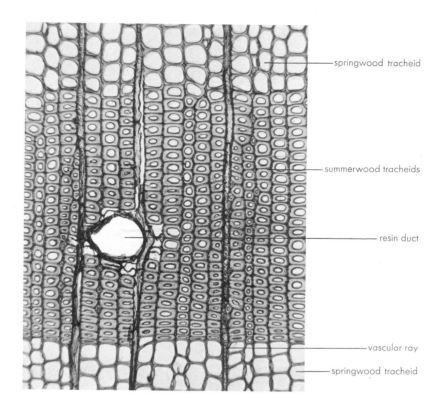

springwood tracheid

summerwood tracheids

resin duct

vascular ray

springwood tracheid

FIG. 10–8. Photomicrograph of pine wood in transection, showing portions of two growth rings.

outer bark of trees is attributable in part to irregular and unequal rates of growth in the numerous patches of cork cambium. The cork cambium usually develops from certain of the parenchyma cells in the outer portion of the cortex. As these cells become meristematic, they produce radially new cells both on the outer and inner faces of the cork cambium. Those cells formed on the outer surface of the meristem become transformed into **cork** or **phellem** cells, which soon become suberized and die. These cork cells prevent the passage of water because of the fatty suberin in their walls, and, as a result, the cells of the cortex and epidermis outside the outer boundary of the cork soon die because they are unable to obtain water. These dead cortical and epidermal cells flake away gradually, partly as a result of rain and wind action and partly because they are split by the outward pressure of the ex-

panding tissues inside them. The cells formed on the inner surface of the cork cambium are called **cork parenchyma** or **phelloderm** cells and are rather like the primary cells of the cortex. Phelloderm cells typically are formed in smaller numbers than the cork cells outside the cork cambium. The phellogen, phellem, and phelloderm cells are collectively called the **periderm.** Thus, as a woody twig grows, the epidermis and outer portion of the cortex (both primary tissues) are sloughed off, and the protection of the internal tissues of the stem against injury and excessive evaporation is assumed by the layers of cork cells. This replacement of stem epidermis and cortex occurs in some species of woody plants during the first year's growth of a twig, in other species, not until several years have elapsed.

The term bark is used for the aggregation of all

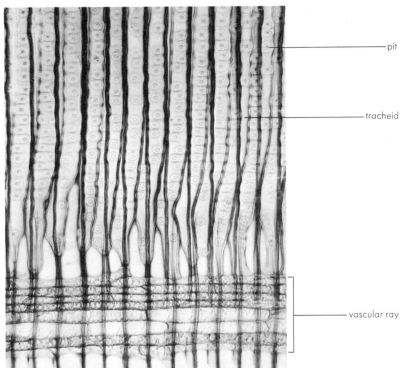

pit

tracheid

vascular ray

FIG. 10-9. Photomicrograph of pine wood in radial section, showing side view of a ray.

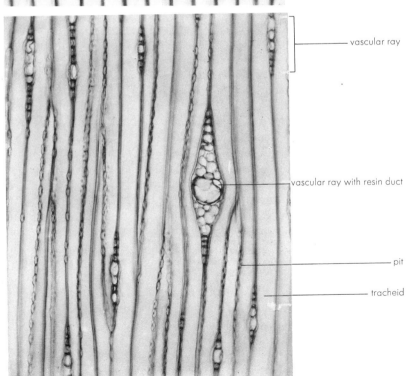

vascular ray

vascular ray with resin duct

pit

tracheid

FIG. 10-10. Photomicrograph of pine wood in tangential section, showing rays in end view.

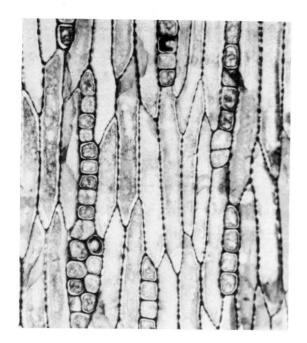

tissues outside the vascular cambium. Accordingly, the young bark of a tree consists of secondary and primary phloem, remnants of the inner portion of the cortex, phelloderm, cork cambium, and cork and epidermal remnants, named in the order of location from the vascular cambium outward. The term outer bark is applied to all those tissues outside the conducting phloem, that is, the periderm and all the tissues isolated by it. Inner bark is the term applied to the actively conducting phloem. Since the phloem of a woody stem is a constituent of bark, another function of bark is the conduction of substances, chiefly foods, to other portions of the stem and into the

FIG. 10–11 (*left*). Walnut (*Juglans*) cambium in tangential section, showing elongated fusiform initials and smaller ray initials. Beaded appearance of walls is caused by the presence of thin areas. FIG. 10–12 (*below*). A three-dimensional representation showing microscopic features of xylem, vascular cambium, and phloem of linden (*Tilia*).

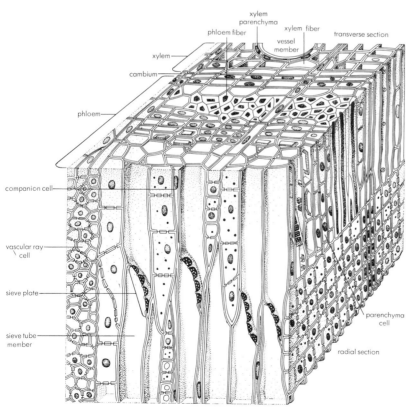

xylem parenchyma

phloem fiber

xylem fiber

vessel member

transverse section

xylem

cambium

phloem

companion cell

vascular ray cell

sieve plate

sieve tube member

parenchyma cell

radial section

tangential section

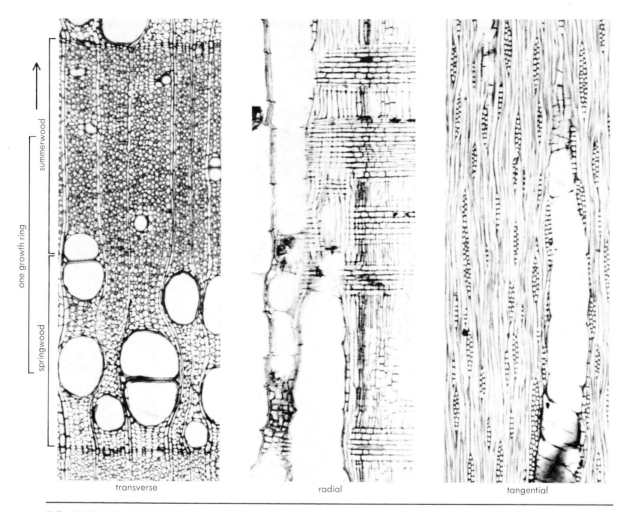

transverse   radial   tangential

FIG. 10–13. Ring porous secondary wood of ash (*Fraxinus americana*) in three planes of section. The transection shows one growth ring and portions of two adjacent rings. The arrow indicates direction of growth.

roots. In the outer bark of some species of trees, as in the cork oak, the periderm is composed of very distinct layers of cork cells. These are usually annual layers; that is, each layer of cork cells is the amount of cork formed by the cork cambium in one season's growth. The periderm of the cork oak tree is the source of commercial cork.

In the young bark of woody stems, lenticels (Fig. 10–14) are present as tiny raised aggregations of loosely compacted cells. As stated in the preceding chapter, lenticels are porous regions through which gaseous exchange between the internal tissues of a stem and the external atmosphere may occur. As a rule, carbon dioxide and other gases formed as physiological byproducts diffuse outward through these lenticels, and oxygen moves inward from the external air to the stem tissues. The brownish spongy streaks that traverse bottle corks are the lenticels of the bark of the cork oak. Lenticels usually develop at the places where the stomatal pores are located in the stem epidermis. A large number of the len-

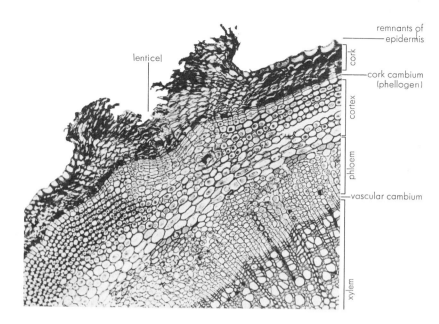

FIG. 10-14. A segment of young woody stem in transection showing the relationship between lenticel and periderm which consists largely of cork.

ticels of twigs occurs at or near the outer ends of vascular rays. As stems grow older and the young bark is furrowed by the growth of the internal tissues, lenticels are no longer apparent on the surfaces of the bark.

In the temperate zones and also in those tropical regions in which marked wet and dry seasons occur, climatic and other conditions are not suitable for the continued growth of the cambium throughout the year. As a result the cambium experiences alternating periods of activity and of dormancy, or relative inactivity. During each of the active seasons, of which there is usually one per year, the vascular cambium forms a new layer of xylem and a new layer of phloem. Since the amount of secondary phloem tissue formed in one growing season is relatively small, it is difficult, often impossible, to distinguish such seasonal layers in the phloem. In xylem, however, which increases much more rapidly than the phloem, the yearly amounts are visible to the naked eye in transverse stem sections as distinct concentric rings, called **growth rings** or **growth layers** (Fig. 10-15). A careful examination of each growth ring, as it appears in most woody species, shows

it to be made up of two fairly distinct bands of xylem cells (Fig. 10-13): an *inner* portion called the **springwood,** in which the vessels and tracheids are relatively large, and an *outer* portion,

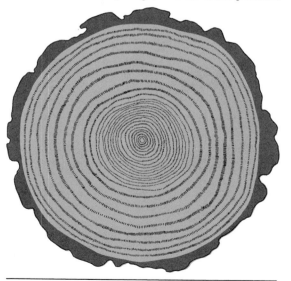

FIG. 10-15. Growth rings of loblolly pine stem. The narrower, inner rings were formed when the young tree was shaded by its neighbors.

the **summerwood,** in which these cells are much smaller in diameter and thicker-walled than those of the springwood. It is the alternating bands of springwood and summerwood in the growth layers of a woody stem that make the growth rings so distinct (Fig. 10–15). As these names imply, the springwood is the portion of each growth layer formed in the spring of the growing season, and the summerwood is that formed during the summer of the same growing period. Springwood appears less dense than summerwood because of its larger cells. The growth ring formed during the first season of a twig's secondary growth is the innermost one, the younger rings being formed in yearly succession, with the youngest ring immediately inside the cambium.

Since ordinarily one ring of xylem is formed each year, the number of such rings in a tree trunk and in a branch indicates the approximate age, respectively, of the whole tree and of the branch. In young twigs in which the first-formed bark has not yet been split, there are thus two methods of determining the age of any portion of the twig—by counting back the number of terminal bud scars from the terminal bud, and by counting the number of growth rings as seen in a transverse section of the twig. The development of a xylem layer begins as the leaf buds form leaves and continues during most of the period that the leaves are present during the growing season. Thus, there is a correlation between a growth layer and a single crop of leaves. Rarely, as a result of the complete destruction of all the leaves of a tree by insect attack or drought, a second crop of leaves may be formed in one growing season. In such event, a second ring of xylem is formed by the cambium as the new crop of leaves develops, and thus *two* xylem rings are formed in one season. For this reason, the number of xylem rings is not always an exact index of the age of a tree. Since the formation of two rings in one season is quite rare, however, the number of rings in most trunks can be regarded as accurately indicating the age of a tree.

The widths of the growth rings in a tree trunk or branches are not uniform. Some rings are very wide, others very narrow. Differences in ring width in the same stem are attributable to the varying climatic conditions that prevailed when the various rings were formed. Probably most influential of the environmental factors affecting ring width is moisture, although light, temperature, and soil aeration are also important. Growth layers formed in seasons of abundant rainfall are usually wider than those produced in years of drought. The growth rings of small trees shaded by large trees are usually narrow; when the large trees are cut and sunlight is able to reach the leaves of the smaller trees, thereby increasing the rate of food manufacture and growth, the new rings become wider. Trees growing in swamps often have narrow rings; if the swamps are drained, thus increasing the oxygen content of the soil, the rings produced in years following the drainage frequently become wider. Especially striking in the relation of growth ring width to these factors is the fact that all individuals of a given species of tree growing under similar environmental conditions produce similar rings in the same season. Thus, a ring formed in a certain season possesses individuality among other growth rings in the tree, and this individuality of ring structure extends to simultaneously formed rings in other trees of the same species that have grown under similar conditions. As a result, the same succession of wide and narrow growth rings may be traced in trees of the same species in the same locality. Not only is the total width of a growth layer influenced by the amount of precipitation, but the relative proportions of springwood and summerwood are affected by the distribution of rainfall through the growing season. Experiments of the U. S. Forest Products Laboratory have shown that the summerwood in certain pines may be considerably increased by providing abundant water in the summer by irrigation.

The widths of growth rings, then, reflect the environmental conditions that prevailed when the rings were formed, and it is thus possible by studying the structure of these rings to read something of climatic conditions of past years. Astronomers have found that there is a remarkable coincidence between sunspot cycles and climatic cycles, as evidenced by growth rings. The late Professor A. E. Douglass, an astronomer at the University of Arizona, and other investigators, have made extensive studies of this type. In his work, Professor Douglass became interested in some of the old Indian pueblos of the Southwestern United States, the ages of which formed for many years a subject of dispute among archaeologists. Douglass made thin sections of wood beams found in the roofs of some of these dwellings and compared them with sections of timbers of known age. By matching the individualistic growth rings in the sections of known and unknown age, he was able to determine the dates in which the roof wood had been cut. Dendrochronologists—specialists who make studies such as the one described above—have reported a bristlecone pine (*Pinus aristata*) that is over 4600 years old, making it the oldest known living individual organism, and one which can extend our year-by-year knowledge of climate as interpreted through growth ring study to nearly 5000 years ago.

As woody stems grow older, physical and chemical changes occur in the oldest growth layers (those nearest the center of the stem) and gradually proceed outward as growth in diameter of the xylem continues in successive years. In many species the protoplasts of the parenchyma cells that surround the vessels and tracheids grow through the pits in the walls of these conducting cells. These balloonlike growths **(tyloses)** (Fig. 10-6) continue to enlarge until they fill considerable portions of the cavities of the vessels and tracheids, forming plugs that prevent further conduction of water and dissolved substances by the cells. In some trees, tyloses may develop in very young growth layers. The older, nonconducting growth rings contain no living cells, are usually darker in color, and are known collec-

FIG. 10-16. Bracket fungus (*Polyporus*) growing on the sapwood of a dead log.

tively as **heartwood;** the younger, actively conducting rings situated outside the heartwood contain many living cells, are usually lighter, and constitute the **sapwood** (Fig. 10-3). Various chemical agents usually not present in sapwood, or present in sapwood in small quantities, become abundant in heartwood: **pigments,** which cause the color of heartwood to darken, **resins,** and **tannins,** bitter substances that discourage the visits of certain wood-rotting organisms. As new growth layers are formed on the surface of the woody cylinder of a tree, the older (innermost) rings of the sapwood are converted into heartwood, usually at about the same rate as the new rings are formed. Thus, the heartwood increases in diameter with the yearly secondary growth of the xylem, whereas the width of the sapwood remains fairly constant in most species. The only benefit that heartwood gives to a woody stem is strength and support. Often the heartwood of a tree is burned out or rotted away and yet the tree continues to live; so long as the sapwood is intact, conduction of materials continues. Trees that have lost their heartwood are structurally weakened, however, and may be blown over.

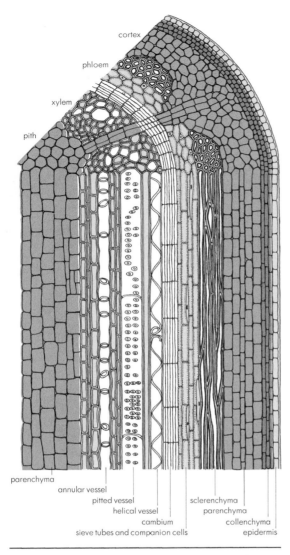

cortex

phloem

xylem

pith

parenchyma
annular vessel
pitted vessel
helical vessel
cambium
sieve tubes and companion cells
sclerenchyma
parenchyma
collenchyma
epidermis

FIG. 10–17. A three-dimensional representation showing microscopic features of a segment of herbaceous dicotyledonous stem.

In the wood of some species of trees—spruce and sycamore, for example—the wood is fairly uniform and there is no structural differentiation of wood into heartwood and sapwood, although only the younger growth rings function actively in conduction. Tyloses are absent from the wood of some tree species; they are rare or absent from the wood of pin oak, for example.

These various chemical and physical changes that result in the transformation of sapwood into heartwood increase the weight and, usually, the hardness and resistance to decay of the wood. The tannins and resins (sometimes called natural preservatives) often repel insects, fungi, and other wood-destroying organisms, the plugged vessels make it more difficult for such organisms to penetrate into the wood, and the absence of living cells reduces the amounts of stored food that might be used by these organisms in heartwood. Thus, heartwood lumber is more durable than sapwood and is more valuable for construction purposes, particularly for timbers, poles, and boards that are exposed to the elements (Fig. 10–16).

THE INTERNAL STRUCTURE OF HERBACEOUS STEMS

The flowering plants are classified in two major groups: *monocotyledons* and *dicotyledons*. Monocotyledons, which include corn, wheat, blue-

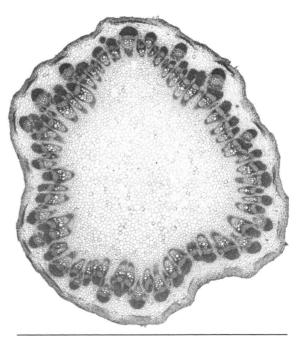

FIG. 10–18. Photomicrograph of a herbaceous dicotyledonous stem in transection, showing extensive pith in center, ring of vascular bundles, a narrow cortex outside the vascular bundles, and the epidermis on the surface of the stem.

grass, and other grasses, lilies, tulips, irises, and orchids, have one cotyledon in their embryos, flower parts usually in threes, and typically long, narrow leaves with parallel main veins. Dicotyledons, which include oaks, maples, castor beans, potatoes, beans, roses, and sunflowers, have two cotyledons in their embryos, flower parts most often in fours or fives, and leaves principally with networks of main veins. Dicotyledons include most woody stemmed flowering plants and, in addition, many thousands of species with herbaceous stems. Monocotyledons are chiefly herbaceous-stemmed plants, although some monocotyledons are trees (for example, palms) or vines (for example, greenbriar). These two major groups of flowering plants have fundamental differences in stem structure which will be described in the following sections.

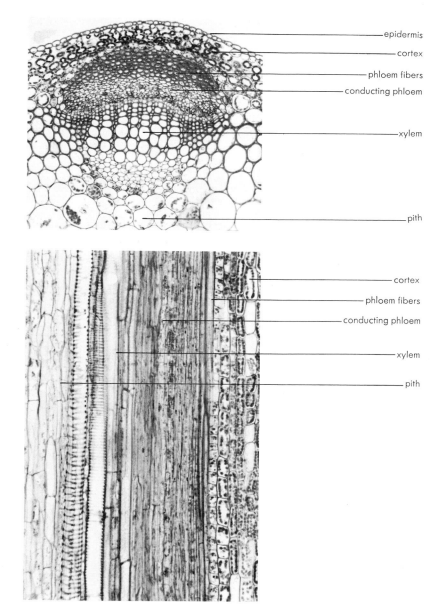

epidermis

cortex

phloem fibers

conducting phloem

xylem

pith

cortex

phloem fibers

conducting phloem

xylem

pith

FIG. 10-19. Photomicrographs showing transverse (*above*) and radial (*below*) sections of a vascular bundle in the stem of clover (*Trifolium*).

135

Herbaceous Stems of Dicotyledons   It has been stated previously that the growth of herbaceous stems is chiefly primary and that ordinarily little or no secondary growth occurs. This is true both of herbaceous dicotyledonous and of monocotyledonous stems.

The herbaceous stems of dicots (Fig. 10–17) are strikingly similar to the young stems of many woody plants before the beginning of the plants' woody secondary growth. In herbaceous dicot stems, as in young woody twigs in the primary state, the terminal bud in its growth forms the following primary tissues: epidermis, cortex, phloem, xylem, and pith (Fig. 10–18). The epidermis in herbaceous dicot stems is a single layer of protective cells, similar to the epidermal cells of a young woody stem; the cortex of a herbaceous dicot is much like that of a woody twig, but is usually thinner. The central cylinder is composed of primary phloem, cambium, primary xylem, and pith, as in a young woody twig. These tissues in a herbaceous dicot stem are arranged either in continuous layers, as in foxglove, or in separate vascular bundles, as in clover and sunflower stems. In some plants, as sunflowers, these central cylinder tissues are in the form of distinct bundles in the young portions of the stem system (Fig. 10–19), and in continuous layers in older parts. In some herbaceous dicots, the vascular cambium is a continuous layer that extends as a complete cylinder both through and between the vascular bundles, while in other species, cambium cells are found only within the vascular bundles, and do not occur between them.

Thus, in general, the anatomy of herbaceous dicot stems is roughly comparable with that of a young woody twig in its first year. The most conspicuous difference between the two is in the relative activity of the cambium: in herbaceous dicot stems it usually produces little secondary tissue, hence relatively little growth in diameter, whereas in woody stems it is very active, producing large numbers of secondary phloem and secondary xylem cells that bring about a marked yearly increase in the diameter of the stem. Her-

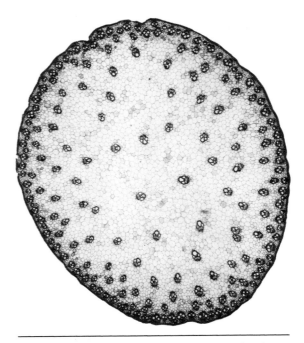

FIG. 10–20.   Transection through an internode of corn (*Zea*) stem.

baceous stems ordinarily live but a single year, as contrasted with perennial woody stems, and hence are smaller and much softer than woody stems. The pith tissue of herbaceous dicot stems ordinarily occupies a much larger proportion of stem volume than it does in woody stems.

Herbaceous Stems of Monocotyledons   Most monocot species (with the exception of certain palms and some members of the lily family) have no cambia in their stems and thus have no secondary growth, their tissues being entirely primary in origin; that is, they all develop from the cells produced by a terminal bud. The xylem and phloem of monocot stems are never arranged in continuous layers, but are in individual vascular bundles that are usually scattered through the stem rather than arranged in a definite circle as in those dicots with their vascular tissues in separate bundles (Figs. 10–20 and 10–21). The vascular bundles are usually surrounded by strengthening

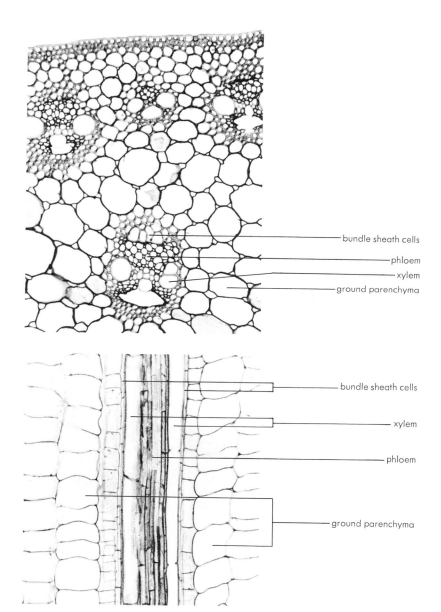

bundle sheath cells

phloem

xylem

ground parenchyma

bundle sheath cells

xylem

phloem

ground parenchyma

FIG. 10-21. Photomicrograph showing transverse (*above*) and tangential (*below*) sections of vascular bundles in corn stem.

cells, which, together with sclerenchyma fibers lying between the outermost vascular bundles and the epidermis, constitute the major strengthening tissues of monocot stems. In the vascular bundles of monocots, as in those of dicots, the phloem is usually in the outer portion of each bundle, with the xylem forming the inner part of each bundle (Fig. 10-21). The surfaces of monocot stems are covered by a protective epidermis, as are the stems of herbaceous dicots. Inside the epidermis and among the scattered vascular bundles is an extensive parenchymatous tissue, usually called ground or fundamental tissue which functions primarily in storage and support.

Because of the absence of cambium in most monocots there is relatively little growth in diameter of monocot stems. The small amount of radial growth that does occur is caused by the increase in size of primary cells, rather than by the formation of new cells. Obviously such growth is limited by the capacities of these primary cells to expand, and is never great.

LEAF TRACES AND LEAF GAPS

At each node of a stem, strands of xylem and phloem diverge from the vascular cylinder, pass out through the cortex, and enter the petiole, or stalk of a leaf. These strands that branch from the vascular system of the stem and enter the petiole are called **leaf traces.** Wherever a leaf trace diverges from the vascular cylinder, a small break occurs in the latter. Such an interruption in a portion of stem vascular tissues is called a **leaf gap** (see Fig. 26-1). The number of leaf traces that enter a leaf varies in different species of plants; in some species there is only one trace per leaf, in others three, five, or even more. These traces continue out through the petioles and as a result of their branching, form the vein system of the leaf. Thus there is a continuation of the vascular tissues of plants from roots through stems into the leaves and likewise into the buds and flowers of stems.

SUMMARY

1. A stem grows in length as a result of formation and enlargement of cells produced by meristematic cells at the stem tip.

2. A growing stem tip, like a growing root tip, exhibits a region of cell division, a region of cell enlargement, and a region of cell maturation.

3. As a stem tip grows, it forms three tissue layers: protoderm, which forms the epidermis of the stem; procambium, which develops into primary xylem and phloem; and ground meristem, which forms pith and cortex.

4. Woody stems are generally regarded as more primitive, though structurally more complex, than herbaceous stems.

5. A transverse section of a woody stem shows the following regions: a) bark, on the outside; b) cambium, just inside the bark; c) xylem (wood), inside the cambium; d) pith, in the center of the stem.

6. In young internodes of woody stems in their first season of life, the tissues present are largely primary, that is, formed by growth and differentiation of cells from the bud. These primary structures, in the order of their arrangement from outside in, are: epidermis, cortex, phloem, cambium, xylem, and pith.

7. Primary xylem and phloem are arranged in vascular bundles, or in a continuous layer, with phloem cells almost always outside the xylem cells, cambium between the xylem and phloem.

8. Secondary xylem and phloem are formed by the cambium, xylem cells being formed on the inside of the cambium, phloem on the outside.

9. Growth in diameter of woody stems is brought about by the production of secondary tissues by the vascular cambium. After the early part of their first season of life, woody stems consist chiefly of secondary

tissues. Secondary xylem is produced more rapidly than secondary phloem by the cambium.

10. Phloem tissue consists of sieve tubes, companion cells, parenchyma, and phloem fibers. Xylem consists of wood fibers, tracheids, vessels, parenchyma, and vascular ray cells. In some plants, one or more of these kinds of cells may be absent from the xylem or phloem.

11. Vascular rays are bands of cells extending radially from the xylem outward into the phloem. They originate in the cambium and conduct substances laterally.

12. A meristematic tissue (one or more groups) called the cork cambium develops from parenchyma cells in the cortex and forms cork cells on the surface of woody stems. Large masses of cork cells constitute most of the rough, outer bark of woody plants. The inner bark consists of actively conducting phloem. Phellogen (cork cambium), phellem (cork), and phelloderm (cork parenchyma) constitute the periderm.

13. The outer bark is primarily a group of protective tissues, the inner bark a group of food-storing and food-conducting tissues.

14. In the temperate zones and in those parts of the tropics with marked wet and dry seasons, the xylem is formed by cambium in definite rings, usually at the rate of one per year. These growth rings near the base of a trunk indicate the age of a tree.

15. Each growth ring in most temperate zone woody plants consists of a layer of rather large cells (springwood) and a layer of smaller cells (summerwood).

16. The thickness of growth rings is usually a reflection of climatic conditions (especially rainfall) that obtained when the rings were formed.

17. As woody stems grow older, the innermost (oldest) growth rings die completely, become plugged up, and undergo chemical alterations. These growth layers are known collectively as heartwood. The outermost (youngest) growth rings, which contain some living cells and which remain open and able to conduct materials, constitute the sapwood.

18. Herbaceous stems grow relatively little in diameter and consist chiefly of primary tissues. The xylem and phloem of herbaceous stems are arranged in distinct vascular bundles, or in a continuous layer.

19. Herbaceous dicot stems usually possess cambium, and have vascular bundles arranged in a single circle or square, as seen in cross section. Monocot stems, which are mostly herbaceous, usually have no cambium and have scattered vascular bundles.

SUGGESTED READINGS FOR INTERESTED STUDENTS

1. Brown, H. P., A. J. Panshin, and C. C. Forsaith, *Textbook of Wood Technology*, Vol. 1. McGraw-Hill, New York, 1949.

2. Esau, Katherine, *Plant Anatomy*, 2d ed. Wiley, New York, 1965.

3. Schulman, Edmund, "Bristlecone pine, oldest known living thing." *National Geographic Magazine,* Vol. CXIII, No. 3, pp. 354–372, March 1958.

TOPICS AND QUESTIONS FOR STUDY

1. Describe briefly how a stem grows in length.

2. Name and describe the tissues formed by the apical meristem of stems.

3. Describe the interrelations between stem structure and stem functions.

4. Describe the gross structure of a mature woody stem as seen in cross section.

5. Distinguish between vascular cambium and cork cambium, from the standpoint of their location and functions.

6. Distinguish between primary and secondary tissues.

7. Name the primary tissues of a woody stem, describe their location, origin, and structure, and state their functions.

8. Describe the location, structure, and function of vascular rays. Distinguish between pith rays and vascular rays.

9. Name the secondary tissues of a woody stem, describe their location, origin, and structure, and state their functions.

10. Explain how stems grow in diameter.

11. In the life of a woody stem, does the cambium produce more xylem cells or more phloem cells? What is the evidence for your answer?

12. Where is the primary xylem in a stem located with reference to the secondary xylem? Which is older?

13. Where is the primary phloem in a stem located with reference to the secondary phloem?

14. What is the physiological importance of the continuing formation of new secondary vascular rays in the outer part of the xylem?

15. Describe the directions in which cambial growth occurs. Does the circumference of the vascular cambium remain constant throughout the life of a woody stem? Explain.

16. Describe the structure of bark, naming the tissues that compose it, and describing their origin and the types of cells of which they are composed.

17. Name three functions of bark.

18. Explain the factors responsible for the rough, furrowed structure of the bark of many woody stems.

19. Why does bark of trees not become as thick as their xylem?

20. What happens to the stem epidermis during cork formation?

21. Define growth ring, and describe the major structural features of growth rings.

22. What environmental factors are responsible for the formation of distinct growth rings? Do all species of woody, perennial plants have growth rings? Explain.

23. What are tyloses?

24. Is the number of growth rings in a tree trunk always an exact indicator of the age of that tree? Explain.

25. Describe two ways of determining the age of a twig.

26. Distinguish between heartwood and sapwood, and describe the structural and physiological changes that occur during the transformation of sapwood into heartwood.

27. How do you explain that, despite the rotting away of their heartwood, many old trees are able to live for long periods?

28. Account for the fact that lumber cut from heartwood is usually more resistant to decay than lumber cut from sapwood.

29. Explain this apparent contradiction: heartwood lumber is more resistant to decay than sapwood lumber, yet, in a living tree, the heartwood may rot away, while the sapwood remains living and functioning.

30. Distinguish between monocotyledons and dicotyledons.

31. Name the primary tissues of a dicotyledonous herbaceous stem and describe their origin and structure.

32. Describe the structure of a typical vascular bundle of a herbaceous stem.

33. Describe the formation and extent of development of secondary tissues in herbaceous stems.

34. Contrast the structure and growth of herbaceous dicotyledonous and monocotyledonous stems.

35. Describe leaf traces and leaf gaps.

11

WOOD AND THE ECONOMIC USES OF STEMS

The stem product of greatest usefulness to man is wood. The uses to which wood is put are determined largely by its chemical, physical, and anatomical properties. In addition to these fundamental qualities, there are many other factors, chiefly of economic, political, and geographic nature, that determine how, when, and where specific kinds of woods are used. A brief discussion of the chemical and physical properties of wood is useful for gaining a better understanding of its economic uses.

CHEMICAL PROPERTIES OF WOOD

Water constitutes from 20 to 50 percent of the weight of live wood. Immediately after cutting, wood begins to lose moisture and may continue to do so until its moisture content becomes as low as 3 or 4 percent. **Cellulose** is the chief dry constituent of wood, occurring in proportions of 60 to 75 percent in various species. Cellulose is the major *structural* component of the plant cell wall, and may be the most abundant organic

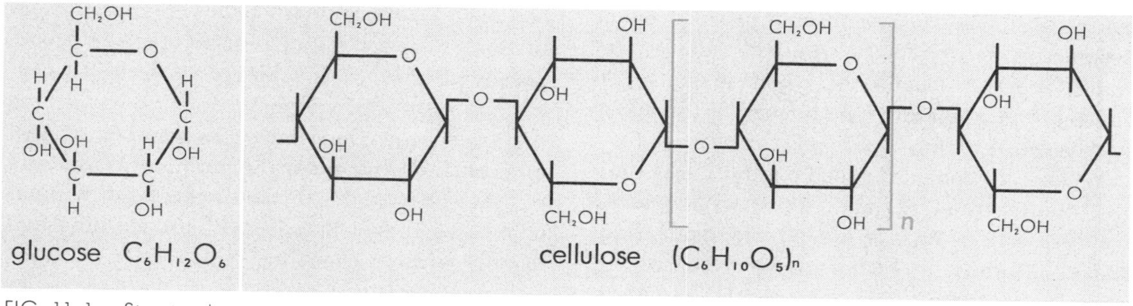

FIG. 11-1. Structural representations of glucose and cellulose. Glucose is a 6-unit sugar. Cellulose is a long chain polymer of glucose units, four of which are shown in simplified form.

compound formed in nature. Chemically, cellulose is a carbohydrate having the empirical formula $(C_6H_{10}O_5)n$. Structurally, the cellulose molecule is composed of numerous glucose sugar units (each with the empirical formula $C_6H_{12}O_6$) joined to form a chain (Fig. 11-1). Aggregations of cellulose molecules make up partially crystalline **microfibrils** that form the structural framework of the cell wall. **Lignin,** another important structural component of many cell walls, is deposited in the microcapillary spaces separating the cellulose microfibrils. Lignin is second to cellulose in quantity, ranging from approximately 15 to 30 percent of the total weight of dry wood. Thus, cellulose and lignin together make up 75 percent or more of all solid materials of wood. Other structural wall components are **hemicelluloses** (noncellulosic carbohydrates of various kinds), certain pectic substances, and minerals. Most woods also contain *nonstructural* materials

or **extractives,** substances that may be removed with various solvents without altering the structural properties. Examples of these extractives are resins, gums, oils, dyes, and tannins.

THE PHYSICAL PROPERTIES OF WOOD

Most important among the physical properties of wood is weight, which is expressed usually in terms of **specific gravity** (weight of 1 cubic centimeter of a substance compared with the weight of an equal volume of water, which is 1 gram). In general, the hardness and strength of wood are proportional to the weight of wood, heavier woods being harder and stronger than lighter woods. The specific gravity of *wood substance* is greater than that of *wood,* for wood is wood substance *plus* a considerable amount of air that is held in its cell cavities. The specific gravities of most woods are less than 1.0; that is, they are

Hardwoods	S.G.
Ash, white	.55
Beech	.56
Hickory	.67
Hard maple	.55
Soft maple	.44
White oak	.61
Black walnut	.52

Softwoods	S.G.
Incense cedar	.33
Bald cypress	.38
Douglas fir	.40
White pine	.36
Western yellow pine	.35
Redwood	.33
White spruce	.32

TABLE 11-1. Specific gravity of woods.

lighter than water. As soon as a piece of wood becomes waterlogged (has its air replaced by water) it sinks because its wood substance is heavier than water and it no longer has the buoyancy given it by air.

In general, woods of specific gravity less than 0.40 are regarded as light; those with specific gravities of 0.40 to 0.59 are termed moderately heavy; and those of 0.60 or above are described as very heavy. Most kinds of wood have specific gravities that range from 0.32 to 0.65. South American balsa wood, the lightest commercially important wood, with a specific gravity of about 0.19, is lighter than cork (specific gravity 0.24) and has been widely used in the construction of airplane models, life preservers, and Hollywood movie sets. At the other extreme are lignum vitae from Santo Domingo and tropical ironwood (*Condalia*) with specific gravities of 1.39 and 1.42 respectively. They are among the heaviest woods known. In the list below the specific gravities of a number of important American woods are given (in dry, or "seasoned" condition).

All the softwoods on this list have specific gravities of less than 0.41, whereas the hardwoods vary from 0.44 to 0.67 in specific gravity. The term **softwood,** as used here and as interpreted by lumbermen, refers to gymnosperm woods such as pine, spruce, fir, cedar, and redwood, while the **hardwoods** are those of angiosperm trees, such as oaks, maples, beech, ash, and others listed in Table 11-1.

Another physical property of woods that is important in determining their treatment and ultimate use is their moisture content. The water content of freshly cut woods varies a great deal in different species. Before woods can be utilized for construction work, for furniture manufacture, and for other finished wood products, their moisture content must be reduced to 10 percent or less. If this process, known as **seasoning,** is not carefully executed, boards and timbers may **warp** and **check.** Warping is an undesired bending or twisting of a piece of wood; checking is the formation of splits along the vascular rays. Both are

obviously undesirable since they result in the loss of shape or cracking of objects made of wood. Seasoning of wood is achieved either by air drying boards in well-ventilated stacks or by drying them in special ovens known as **kilns.** As a result of gradual drying under the mechanical pressure of other boards, the stacked boards dry without change of shape—that is, without warping and usually without checking.

The strength and hardness of wood are determined by a number of factors, chief among which are specific gravity (weight), relative amounts of springwood and summerwood, presence or absence of tyloses, presence or absence of knots, checks, and decay areas, the degree of seasoning, and the relative numbers, lengths, and arrangement of wood fibers. Heavy woods, with large numbers of long, tightly packed wood fibers, with well-developed summerwood in the growth rings, and with numerous tyloses in the conducting cells are generally stronger and harder than woods of lower specific gravity, fewer fiber cells, etc. The principal reason why gymnosperm woods are softer and weaker than most angiosperm woods is that they lack large numbers of thick-walled, heavily lignified fiber cells.

THE DURABILITY OF WOODS

The durability of wood, or the degree to which wood can withstand the forces of decay, has already been referred to in the section on heartwood and sapwood in the preceding chapter. It was stated there that timber and boards made of heartwood are normally more resistant to decay than those made of sapwood. This is so because of the presence of tannins, resins, and other "natural preservatives" in heartwood, the lesser porosity of heartwood, and the smaller quantities of readily available foods in heartwood. Woods vary naturally in their durability. Among very durable woods are red cedar, cypress, black locust, redwood, black walnut, and hickory. Moderately durable are Douglas fir, honey locust, oaks, birch, hard maple, and various

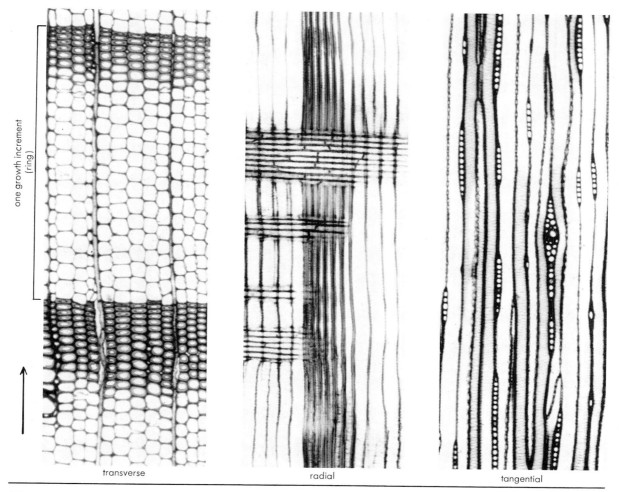

one growth increment (ring)

transverse radial tangential

FIG. 11-2. Nonporous secondary wood of Douglas fir (*Pseudotsuga taxifolia*) in three planes of section. The arrow indicates direction of growth. Helical wall thickenings on the tracheids appear as fine lines in the tangential view.

pines, while cottonwood, basswood, firs, and willows are exceedingly susceptible to decomposition.

Various methods are employed to artificially increase the durability of wood. These methods are of two types: those in which a protective surface layer is applied to wood to retard the entry of moisture and of organisms; and those in which the wood is impregnated with chemicals that are poisonous or distasteful to organisms and discourage their growth.

WOOD SURFACES

The appearance of wood surfaces, as seen with the naked eye, varies with the wood of different species. Each kind of wood has its own characteristic surface markings, by means of which each may be recognized.

Among the prominent features of such markings are the presence or absence of vessels (commonly referred to as "pores") and the arrangement of these vessels in woods. Woods of pine,

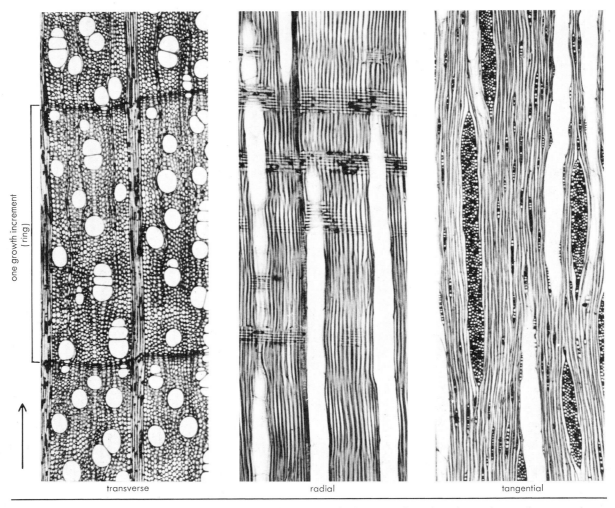

one growth increment (ring)

transverse   radial   tangential

FIG. 11–3. Diffuse porous secondary wood of sugar maple (*Acer saccharum*) in three planes of section. Arrow indicates direction of growth.

firs, spruce, and other gymnosperms are termed **nonporous** because they lack vessels (Fig. 11–2), in contrast to the **porous** woods of angiosperms in which vessels are usually the largest and most conspicuous xylem elements. In some porous wood and are not so variable in size as in ring-differ markedly in size in the springwood and summerwood. Woods in which the vessels are larger and more numerous in the springwood are called **ring porous** (Fig. 10–13). In beech, maple,

birch, and other **diffuse-porous** woods (Fig. 11–3), the vessels are more or less equally distributed throughout both spring- and summerwood and are not so variable in size as in ring-porous woods. The presence or absence of pores, and the distribution of the pores are important characters used to identify various kinds of wood.

The term **wood figure** refers to the surface appearance of wood. The nature of the wood figure is determined by the arrangement and relative numbers and shapes of the constituent cells, and the figure, as it is seen on boards or timbers, on table tops, wall panels, etc., varies within the same species according to the manner in which the boards are cut from the tree (Fig. 11-4). In a **transverse** section, as described in Chapter 10, the growth rings appear as concentric circles and the vascular rays appear to radiate from the center toward the circumference of the wood like the spokes of a wheel. Transverse wood surfaces are seen on cut stumps and on the ends of logs, beams, boards, and railroad ties, never as the large surfaces of boards or beams. Wood is not cut transversely into boards because the size of such boards would be limited by the diameter of the tree; furthermore, sections cut transversely, unless they are several inches or more thick, tend to split along the rays and frequently along the growth rings, so that often the latter begin to separate.

The wood surfaces most commonly visible on the larger expanses of boards, panels, beams, etc., are the surfaces exposed when the board is cut longitudinally from the wood of a tree. Such longitudinal sections may be cut in two ways (Fig. 11-5): along a radius of the log, or the boards may be cut one after another lengthwise through the tree, tangential to a radius of the log. A board cut on the radius, that is, parallel to the rays and across the growth rings, is called a **quarter-sawed** board; one cut at right angles to the rays and tangential to the rings is called a **plain-sawed** or **flat-sawed** board. In radial section the growth rings are seen in *side* view and appear as narrow, longitudinal streaks, groups of wider streaks (springwood) alternating with groups of narrower streaks (summerwood); in such a section the vascular rays are seen in *side* view, as horizontal bands, often wavy and irregular in form, running across the growth layers. In quarter-sawed, or radial, sections, the vascular rays constitute the most conspicuous feature of the figure and many woods are quarter-sawed to produce boards with the characteristic ray figure. Because only a small number of perfect quarter-sawed boards can be

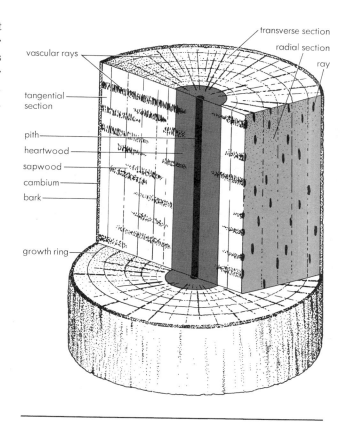

FIG. 11-4.   The three-dimensional appearance of a log illustrating features seen in the three planes of section.

obtained from a log, these boards are rather expensive as compared with plain-sawed boards.

In plain-sawed or flat-sawed boards, the most conspicuous feature is the relatively wide, irregular, alternating light- and dark-colored bands that are portions of growth rings. In plain-sawed wood the springwood and summerwood do not appear in a pattern of concentric rings as in transverse cuts, but in a pattern of parabolas or conic sections (see Fig. 11-5). In most boards, the springwood portions of the growth layers appear dark because their cells are larger and reflect less light than do the smaller cells of the summerwood portions, which appear lighter. In tangential sections, the cut ends of vascular rays are visible

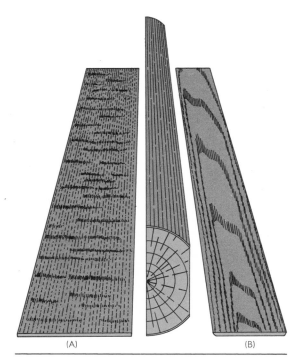

FIG. 11–5. Quarter-sawed (A) and plain-sawed (B) boards from a log. Quarter-sawed boards are obtained by cutting along a radius; plain-sawed by cutting the log tangentially.

as narrow vertical streaks at frequent intervals in the wavy, growth ring bands. Of these three types of wood surfaces, tangential sections are seen most commonly because a plain-sawed log yields the greatest number of board feet, and is the most economical method of sawing.

Knots, which frequently appear in boards, are the basal portions of branches which, during the years, became embedded in the wood of the main trunk by the formation of new growth rings over the branch base. The presence of knots usually weakens the boards or beams in which they occur and thus is not a desirable feature in boards, except those used as ornamental paneling.

THE USES OF WOOD

The uses of wood are so numerous that, within the scope of this book, it is possible only to mention the more important ones. The chief uses may be arranged in three categories: lumber, pulpwood, and fuel. Lumber includes structural timbers (rafters, joists, mine timbers, pilings, etc.), planing mill products (sashes, doors, wall panels, flooring, etc.), boxes and crates, furniture, veneers, railroad ties, cooperage (barrels and casks), and many others. Pulpwood provides wood cellulose which finds widespread use in the manufacture of paper, rayon, cellophane, photographic film, synthetic lacquers, and plastics. Cordwood and charcoal are the principal forms in which wood is used as fuel. Wood is also the source of various non-woody materials of great industrial value; the process of wood distillation results in the formation of wood alcohol, acetone, wood tar, wood gas, oils, and turpentine.

OTHER ECONOMIC USES OF STEMS AND STEM PRODUCTS

The stems of plants furnish many materials, other than woods, that are important in our present civilization. Among these are fibers (flax, jute, ramie, Indian hemp, and others), tannins, dyes, perfumes (sandalwood), medicinal substances (quinine, cascara, slippery elm, ephedrine), cork, rubber, chicle (for chewing gum), gums, lacquer, turpentine, balsams, spices (cinnamon, sassafras), and foods. Among the important plants that produce food for man in their stems are sugar cane, corn (corn syrup), sugar maple, sorghum, Irish potato, asparagus, and kohl-rabi.

SUMMARY 1. Wood is the most useful to man of all stem products.
2. The most abundant structural constituent of dry wood is cellulose.

Second in abundance is lignin. Some nonstructural materials found in wood are resins, gums, oils, starch, dyes, and tannins.

3. Woods vary in their specific gravities from 0.2 to 1.45. Most softwoods (gymnosperm woods) have specific gravities from 0.30 to 0.40; most hardwoods (angiosperm woods) have specific gravities from 0.40 to 0.70. The heaviest commercial wood is tropical ironwood (specific gravity = 1.42), the lightest is balsa (specific gravity = 0.19).

4. Heavy woods are usually hard, light woods soft.

5. Hardwood refers to the wood of angiospermous trees; it is generally porous and contains numerous fibers. Softwood refers to the wood of gymnospermous trees; it is nonporous and lacks fibers.

6. Seasoning is the drying of wood in such a way that it does not warp or check.

7. Factors that determine the hardness of wood are weight, numbers and arrangement of wood fibers, presence of knots, decay areas, etc., and relative amounts of springwood and summerwood.

8. Tyloses are parts of parenchyma cells that grow into the cavities of vessels and tracheids and plug them.

9. The durability of wood is determined in part by the quantities of resins, tannins, and other natural preservatives present.

10. Transverse sections of most woody stems show concentric growth rings, with radially extending vascular rays.

11. Quarter-sawed boards are cut from logs longitudinally along a radius and show the growth rings as vertical, alternating, regular bands of spring- and summerwood, with vascular rays extending horizontally across them as flat, ribbonlike structures.

12. Plain-sawed boards are cut lengthwise tangentially to a radius and show irregular, alternating bands of summer- and springwood, with the ends of vascular rays appearing as streaks in them.

13. Plain-sawed boards are seen most commonly in construction work, because this method of sawing is most economical.

14. Wood is used directly for the manufacture of many industrial products, and is also subjected to wood distillation or chemical treatment to produce many derivative products.

15. In addition to wood, stems furnish fibers, drugs, cork, rubber, gums, resins, spices, foods, and other products.

SUGGESTED READINGS

1. Brown, H. P., A. J. Panshin, and C. C. Forsaith, *Textbook of Wood Technology,* Vol. I. McGraw-Hill, New York, 1949, Vol. II, 1952.

2. Carpenter, C. H., et al. *Papermaking Fibers.* Technical Publication No. 74. State Univ. College of Forestry, Syracuse, N.Y., 1963.

3. Côté, Jr., W. A., Ed., *Cellular Ultrastructure of Woody Plants.* Syracuse University Press, Syracuse, N.Y., 1965.

4. Esau, Katherine, *Plant Anatomy,* 2d ed. Wiley, New York, 1965.

5. Foulger, A. N. *Classroom Demonstrations of Wood Properties,* Forest Products Laboratory, U.S. Dept. of Agriculture, 1969.

6. Hill, Albert F., *Economic Botany.* McGraw-Hill, New York, 1952.

7. Jane, F. W., *The Structure of Wood.* Adam and Charles Black, London, 1956.

8. Schery, Robert W., *Plants for Man.* Prentice-Hall, Englewood Cliffs, N.J., 1952.

9. *Wood Handbook,* Agriculture Handbook No. 72, U.S. Government Printing Office, 1955.

TOPICS AND QUESTIONS FOR STUDY

1. Name the principal chemical compounds that compose wood, and describe their relative abundance in wood.

2. Describe the relation of the chemical nature of wood to the uses made of wood.

3. Describe briefly the specific gravity characteristics of wood.

4. Distinguish between softwoods and hardwoods, and name several specific woods as examples of each.

5. Describe the processes of wood seasoning, and state the reason for seasoning woods.

6. What is meant by the durability of wood?

7. What are the major factors responsible for the strength and hardness of woods?

8. Describe several methods used to increase the durability of woods.

9. What are the major structural differences between gymnosperm and angiosperm woods?

10. Distinguish between ring-porous and diffuse-porous woods.

11. Describe the relation of wood anatomy to the physical properties and economic uses of woods.

12. Why is it easier to split wood lengthwise than crosswise?

13. Describe the gross appearance of the transverse, radial, and tangential surfaces of a block of wood.

14. Why is commercial lumber never produced by the transverse sawing of wood?

15. Which type of sawing, quarter sawing or plain sawing, yields the greater number of usable boards from a tree? Explain.

16. Why are quarter-sawed boards commonly more expensive than plain-sawed boards?

17. Are there any quarter-sawed boards produced by the plain sawing of a tree trunk? Explain.

18. Describe the origin and structure of knots in wood.

19. What is wood distillation? Name its principal products and look up their commercial uses.

20. Name some of the important commercial products derived from wood cellulose.

21. Name the economically important products, other than wood, that originate from plant stems.

12

STEM PHYSIOLOGY AND ITS PRACTICAL IMPLICATIONS

THE FUNCTIONS OF STEMS

In previous chapters, we have described several of the functions of stems, including production of leaf and flower buds, food storage, and strengthening functions. The present chapter will deal principally with the conduction of water and dissolved minerals, the translocation of foods, and some practical applications of knowledge of stem function.

CONDUCTION OF MATERIALS BY STEMS

The processes of movement of liquids and dissolved substances through stems and the paths these substances follow are complex. Although botanists have been able to demonstrate rather conclusively that the upward movement of water and dissolved substances is largely through the xylem, they have not been so successful in explaining the cause of this ascent. Large quantities of water pass out into the air by evaporation from the aerial parts of plants. This evaporated water, plus the water used for food synthesis and growth, rises through the xylem continuously.

Ascent of Sap   The general term sap has been employed both in popular and botanical usage to refer to the water and dissolved materials that move upward, downward, and transversely in stems. Actually, the term is a rather ambiguous one and is used in a variety of ways. Among botanists, the word is applied most commonly to the water and dissolved materials that move upward in the younger growth rings (sapwood) of woody plants. Although sap may contain many substances, they are always greatly diluted by the large amount of water present. The dissolved materials that are carried along are primarily mineral nutrients absorbed from the soil.

During the growing season when plants are in leaf the rate of sap ascent is especially rapid, and even during periods of dormancy there may be a very slow ascent of materials through woody stems. Many external factors of the environment, such as air temperature, humidity, and light intensity, are known to influence the rate of sap rise, but the internal factors influencing this movement are only partly known. It has been shown that the rate of sap ascent is influenced in part by the nature of the woody tissues of the stems. In conifers the rate of sap movement under favorable conditions varies from 0.02 to 0.3 meters per hour; hardwood trees with diffuse-porous wood can conduct water at a rate of one to six meters per hour, while the speed of sap ascent in trees with ring-porous wood may be from 20 to 40 meters per hour. Extremely high rates—in excess of 100 meters per hour—have been measured in vines.

Various types of experimentation support the fact that xylem tissue is the chief avenue of upward movement of water and dissolved substances. The phloem and other tissues external to the cambium may be completely cut away without appreciable diminution in the upward movement of water and solutes. By careful manipulation of a narrow-bladed scalpel, the xylem of a stem can be completely severed with only a slight injury to the phloem. In this case, wilting of the leaves is apparent in a short time. In another experiment the severed lower end of a stem is placed in a solution of some water-soluble dye, with the remainder of the stem above the liquid. Examination of transverse sections of upper portions of the stem soon thereafter reveals the presence of the dye primarily in the tracheary elements and occasionally in the parenchyma cells adjoining them.

It is believed that most inorganic materials (nutrients absorbed from the soil) are carried upward in the xylem, since the removal of the phloem and other tissues outside the cambium does not in most cases interfere with the normal supply of these materials to the leaves. There are some plants in which at least some of these inorganic substances move upward in phloem. It has been demonstrated, for example, that in some trees the removal of the phloem interferes with the movement of nitrogen into the leaves. In addition to mineral nutrients, organic materials such as sugars are frequently dissolved in the water that rises through the xylem. Such materials are especially abundant in the sap in the spring when foods stored in the roots and lower parts of the stem during the preceding growth season move upward, providing the developing buds with substances necessary for proper growth. After the buds have opened and leaves have reached their mature size, relatively little sugar is found in the ascending solution.

An interesting example of ascending sap in early spring is found in the sugar maple. Sap flow from sugar maples results from **stem pressure,** pressure which builds up as the result of high osmotic concentrations which develop in the sap during the spring. With the onset of warm weather, starch previously stored in the root and stem parenchyma is converted into sugar and moved up through the xylem, so that during this period maple sap contains from 2 to 3 percent sucrose. Because of this relatively high sugar content in the xylem, water is rapidly absorbed from the soil. It is the accumulation of this water in the stem that is thought to create stem pressure. Toward the end of the winter season when above-freezing daytime temperatures alternate with near-freezing or lower nighttime temperatures, the trees are tapped by drilling a hole into the sapwood. The positive pressure that forms in the stem under such conditions forces the sap out through the hole. An average tree will yield from 10 to 20 gallons of sap per season and may be tapped for many years without apparent injury. There is still considerable speculation concerning the actual mechanism that causes sap to flow in sugar maples. One interpretation suggests that changes in osmotic concentration induced by ice formation, particularly in the outer layers of sapwood, cause some water to move up the trunk; then, after higher daytime temperatures have warmed the surface tissues and increased the internal pressure, the sap flows out through the opening. In some plants, when fruits are enlarging, sugars in higher concentrations are again present in the ascending sap.

Mechanism of Water Flow to Leaves   One of the earlier attempted explanations of water rise is based upon the phenomenon of **root pressure.** When the rate of water loss from the shoot is low and soil moisture is abundant, sap will frequently exude from the stump following removal of the aerial shoot. Such "bleeding" results from rapid water absorption by the root. It is due to a passive entry of water by osmosis because of relatively high solute concentration in the root sap. These high concentrations appear as a result of active transport of solutes into the root, and represent the accumulation of solutes from the soil solution against a concentration gradient. The magnitude of root pressure, which varies considerably in different species of plants and in the same plant with varying internal and external conditions, is usually not much greater than atmospheric pressure, and only rarely exceeds 2

or 3 atmospheres. There are several objections to the explanation of water rise on the basis of root pressure: 1. Root pressure alone is insufficient to account for the ascent of water because its maximum value under normal conditions (about 3 atmospheres) would only be adequate to push water into the leaves of herbaceous plants and small trees. 2. Root pressures of more than 12 atmospheres would be required to cause water to rise in very tall trees, and forces of this magnitude have not been found under normal conditions. 3. The severed shoots of plants placed with their cut ends in water are usually able to absorb sufficient quantities of water to permit continued growth and food synthesis in the leaves for long periods of time; there is obviously no root pressure in such stems, since there are no roots present, and yet water rise continues. 4. There is usually very little correlation between the magnitude of root pressure and the rate and volume of water movement; root pressure may be high in a plant, and yet the water may simultaneously rise very slowly. 5. Root pressure is not demonstrable in all species of plants. 6. In temperate regions at least, root pressures are usually negligible during the summer when the rate of water rise is most rapid.

Another factor formerly considered to be of importance in contributing to water ascent in stems is **capillarity.** When very fine open glass tubes or tubes of certain other materials, are placed in a vertical position with their lower ends standing in water, ink, or similar liquids, the liquid rises in them to a level *above* the liquid level in the container in which the tubes are standing. The smaller the diameters of the tubes, the higher the level to which the liquids will rise. This phenomenon is caused by the capillary or surface attraction between the molecules of the liquid and those of the tube substance. It has been suggested that this force of capillarity is involved in the ascent of sap, for xylem tracheids and vessels are hollow structures, roughly similar to the glass tubes in the experiment described above, and their walls are able to absorb and hold water by imbibition. Doubtless, a part of the rise of sap in these conducting elements of xylem is attributable to capillary forces, but the diameters of these tubes and the known forces of capillarity are such that their force could cause a sap rise of only a few inches, or at most a few feet. Thus, capillarity may be regarded as relatively unimportant as a possible cause of sap rise.

Another explanation of sap rise, largely discounted at present, is based upon the action of living parenchyma cells adjoining the conducting elements of the xylem. Several plant physiologists have maintained that a pumping action, caused by rhythmic expansions and contractions of these living cells, is detectable in stems and that their pumping force drives the sap upward. This idea, never widely accepted by botanists, received a mortal blow when it was demonstrated that dead stretches of stems, killed by live steam or by poisons such as picric acid, are still able to conduct sap upward in nearly normal fashion. It is extremely doubtful that such pumping action in living cells actually occurs, but it is certain, of course, that water and solutes pass by diffusion from living cell to living cell. It appears, however, that the presence of living cells in a stem is essential to the continuance of normal sap rise, for stems with dead portions, although they may conduct sap for a time in apparently normal fashion, cannot do so indefinitely. The exact nature of the relationship between living cells and the maintenance of normal sap rise is not known.

The explanation generally considered at present to account most satisfactorily for the ascent of sap is based upon the idea that sap is *pulled* up through vessels and tracheids by forces operative in leaves, not *pushed* up from below. Large quantities of water evaporate from the aerial portions of plants, especially from leaves. When the leaf cells nearest the external atmosphere lose water by evaporation, the colloidal materials of their protoplasm are partially dried, and an increase of osmotic concentration in these cells occurs. Since the colloidal materials in protoplasm possess powerful attraction for water, the partly dried protoplasm of these cells absorbs water, chiefly by colloidal imbibition, partly by the osmotic forces of the leaf cells from adjacent cells with higher water content. These cells in turn, as they undergo partial drying, remove water from cells with higher water content adjacent to them, and thus these imbibitional and osmotic forces, initiated by the evaporation of water from leaf cells, are transmitted from leaf cell to leaf cell. This water deficit in the leaf cells creates a pull on the water in the vessels and tracheids in the leaf veins, a pull that is transmitted downward through the xylem cells of the leafstalk and through the xylem-conducting structures of stem and roots. This pull is transmitted through the water column of a plant because of the tremendous cohesive power of water molecules, which remain together with such great mutual attraction that tremendous power is required to separate them. The cohesive force of water in man-made columns similar in size to those in xylem vessels has been found to be almost 300 atmospheres, roughly 10 times the pull required to lift sap to the heights of the tallest known trees. The osmotic pressures of the cells of most leaves vary between 20 and 30 atmospheres, more than enough to furnish this pull as water evaporates from them. One investigator has demonstrated convincingly the pulling effect of evaporation from leaves by removing a terminal portion several feet long from a woody vine and supporting it with its lower end in mercury. When the evaporation of water in the leaves occurred, tensions were exerted on the water columns in the vessels, and these tensions were sufficiently great to cause the mercury to be pulled up into the vessels (because of the adhesive forces between mercury and water molecules) of the stem to a height twice that to which mercury is forced upward by atmospheric pressure.

This explanation known as the **cohesion-tension theory,** is thus based upon several forces and factors all of which have been shown to exist in the shoots of plants: the evaporation of water from leaves; a water deficit created in leaf cells

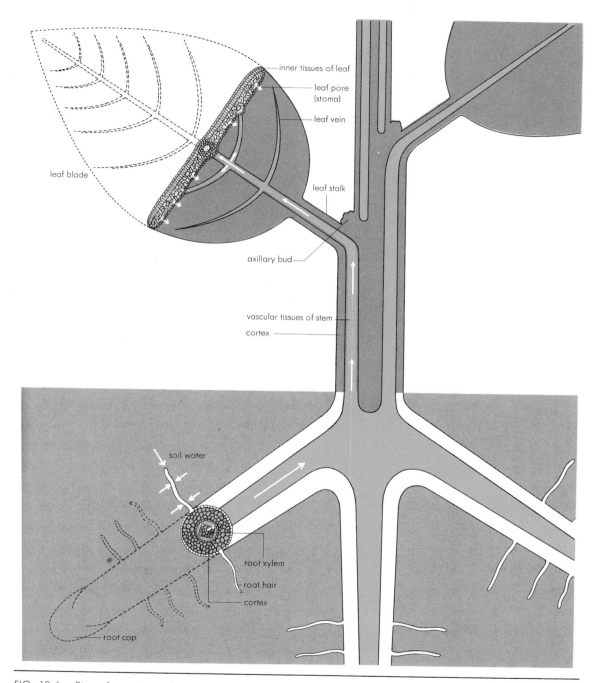

FIG. 12-1. Rise of sap in a plant. The arrows in the soil, root, stem, leaf stalk, and leaf veins indicate liquid water and solutes. The arrows at the leaf pores represent water vapor.

by this evaporation; the passage of water from the xylem cells of the veins into the partly dried leaf cells as a result of colloidal imbibition and osmotic forces; and the transmission downward into the roots of a pull caused by this water deficit, a pull dependent upon the cohesive power of water molecules (Fig. 12–1). There is much indirect evidence in support of this theory. It has been shown that negative pressures of as much as 18 to 20 atmospheres exist in the water columns of stems; that is, these water columns are under tremendous tension from above, which tends to attenuate them or draw them out, as a rubber band is stretched when one end is made fast and the other end is pulled with considerable force. These tensions exist in the vessels because, under conditions of rapid evaporation from leaves, roots cannot supply water to the xylem elements as rapidly as the water evaporates from the leaves. In plants with rather transparent stems—for example, pumpkin and balsam—the diametric shrinkage of the xylem vessels in the stem under conditions of water tension can actually be observed under a microscope.

It is also demonstrable that on hot, bright days when evaporation of water from leaves is rapid, the stems of many plants, both woody and herbaceous, actually shrink in diameter, as a piece of rubber tubing will shrink in thickness if one end is closed and suction is applied at the other. The tremendous pull engendered by water evaporation from the leaves creates "negative pressures" or tensions in the water columns, tensions that result in these slight, though definite decreases in stem diameters. Because of these negative pressures air will rush into the conducting cells in which these tensions exist, if incisions are made into a stem. If air bubbles enter a vessel, the upward rise of water in that vessel is greatly retarded, and may cease. If the tension in a vessel is lowered, the air bubble may be dissolved and the vessel then resumes its upward conduction of water. When cut flowers are brought into a house, an inch or more of the lower ends of their stalks should be cut off under the surface of the

water in the flower bowl or vase. This treatment removes the portions of the stalks into which air bubbles entered when the flowers were cut. With the removal of these air bubbles, the upward movement of water is quickly resumed and the flowers will not wilt as quickly as they would if some of the vessels in their stalks were plugged by air.

It should be emphasized that the cross walls that occur at intervals in vessels and the end walls of tracheids do not hinder appreciably the rise of sap, for these walls are saturated with water and thus masses of water molecules are continuous from cell to cell through these saturated walls. At night, when evaporation from leaves decreases, the negative pressures in stems fall, and a slight expansion in stem diameters is noticeable as the tension in the water columns is relaxed. Further evidence in support of the cohesion-tension theory is found in the structure of xylem vessels, the walls of which are usually thickened, often with rings or spirals; these thickenings are such that they would seem to prevent not the rupture of the vessels by possible upward pressures from below, but rather the collapse of the vessels as a result of the negative pressures in them—in much the same manner as a metal coil in the wall of a vacuum cleaner tube prevents the collapse of the tube when a "negative pressure" is present inside the tube.

Thus the cohesion theory, which is generally accepted by botanists at present, involves chiefly physical forces in its attempt to explain the rise of sap. It should be remembered, however, that the absorption and movement of water and solutes from the soil into the lower ends of the xylem tissues of roots are brought about by the living cells of root epidermis and cortex, and that living cells in leaves are involved in the evaporation of water and the transmission of the imbibitional forces occasioned by the partial drying of these cells. Thus, the presence of living cells seems to be necessary for normal sap rise. Although the forces involved in the upward movement of sap are primarily physical forces, they are, however, subject within limits to physiological control.

It is likely that the evaporation-cohesion force is not the only force operative in the ascent of sap. Root pressure may aid in forcing sap upward for some distance in early spring before buds have opened. Capillary forces in the walls of vessels and tracheids, as mentioned above, doubtless play at least a small role in the upward movement of water. Thus, a variety of physical forces are probably at work in achieving the upward transportation of sap, of which the force produced by evaporation and water cohesion is doubtless the principal one.

Food Translocation   The translocation of foods, which are manufactured chiefly in leaves, is principally through the living sieve elements of the phloem. The movement of foods in the phloem is chiefly downward except during early spring, and also during the events leading to flower and fruit formation when a considerable translocation of food upward into developing buds and flowers occurs. Sugars and various types of proteins are the foods most frequently found in phloem cells. Several types of experimentation have supplied evidence for the belief that the phloem is the principal food-conducting system of stems. Chemical analyses of xylem and phloem tissues demonstrate that both a greater abundance and a greater variety of foods are found in phloem cells than in xylem cells. Girdling experiments (see p. 162), in which a ring of outer tissues including phloem completely encircling a stem is removed inward to the xylem, show that conspicuous swellings develop within a few weeks or months immediately above the girdle. These swellings are caused by the accumulation of downward-moving foods that are halted by the interruption of the phloem and that accumulate just above the cut, thus providing nourishment for the rapid growth of stem cells at this point. A complete girdle on the main trunk of a tree usually results in the death of the tree, for the roots, which are unable to manufacture food,

depend for their nourishment upon food from the leaves and die of starvation when completely severed phloem halts the downward movement of food. Further, it has been observed that certain aphids and other insects that commonly feed on sap from stems and leaves insert their stylets into sieve tubes more frequently than into tracheary cells. This behavior is an additional indication that more food is found in phloem-conducting cells than in xylem.

Investigations of translocation indicate that there may be a considerable amount of upward movement of organic materials through the phloem, particularly in the spring. During the summer or fall some of the foods moving downward through the phloem are transmitted through the vascular rays to the xylem and stored in the parenchyma and ray cells of the latter tissue. During the early spring some of these foods move upward, in part through the xylem, in part upward through the phloem tissue into which they are carried from the xylem through the vascular rays. In some plants, such as mock orange and sumac, the major part of the upward movement of sugars occurs in the phloem, whereas in other species, such as the sugar maple, the greater quantity of the upward-moving sugars rises through the xylem tissue.

The rate at which foods move through the phloem is far too rapid to be explained by simple diffusion. Of the various theories that have been proposed to account for this relatively fast movement, the **mass flow theory** (or pressure flow theory) is perhaps the most widely accepted by plant physiologists. According to this theory, the sugar produced by photosynthesis in leaf mesophyll cells is moved in a special chemical form across cell membranes by active transport to the parenchyma cells lying adjacent to sieve elements. At or shortly before the time of entry into the sieve tubes, the sugar compound is enzymatically converted to another form (sucrose). This sucrose raises the osmotic concentration within the sieve tubes, thus causing water to move in by osmosis, which, in turn, causes an increase in turgor pressure. It is the osmotically-induced turgor pressure that causes a mass flow of both solute (sucrose) and solvent (water). The flow will continue as long as a turgor pressure gradient exists.

A notable feature of the conducting systems of stems is the fact that sieve elements and tracheary elements are remarkably adapted for the translocation of materials vertically (that is, in the direction of the longitudinal axis of stems) but are almost completely unable to carry materials laterally (transversely) in stems. Water, foods, mineral nutrients, and other soluble materials move transversely in stems chiefly through the vascular rays. These vascular rays make intimate contacts with the sieve elements, vessels, and other cells of longitudinal transport. At such points of contact, pits in the walls of the ray cells and those of the sieve elements, vessels, etc., facilitate the interchange of water and solutes among these cells. This transverse conduction by vascular rays is exceedingly important, for it makes possible the movement of foods from the sieve tubes into the dividing cells of the cambium and the enlarging xylem cells of the current growth ring, and also enables foods to pass into the various storage cells of the xylem and phloem. There is also movement of gases (dissolved in

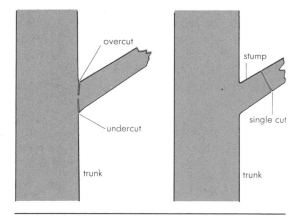

FIG. 12-2. Pruning cuts. *Left*: Branch properly pruned, with undercut made first, followed by overcut; both cuts are parallel to and near the trunk. *Right*: Branch improperly pruned; only one cut has been made, and is in such a position as to leave a branch stump.

water) through the rays; carbon dioxide moves outward toward the lenticels, and oxygen from the external atmosphere moves inward by diffusion and aids in respiratory processes in cambium and living cells of xylem and phloem.

PRACTICAL APPLICATIONS OF A KNOWLEDGE OF STEM STRUCTURE AND PHYSIOLOGY

Floriculturists, orchardists, and others engaged in the practical culture of plants find a knowledge of the basic principles of stem structure and physiology indispensable. Although many men engaged in these vocations do not have a theoretical botanical background, they inevitably learn from practical experience the conspicuous features of stem structure and function.

Pruning   The pruning of shrubs and trees involves a knowledge of conduction in stems and of the location and activity of the cambium and cork cambium. The chief purpose of pruning is to remove broken or diseased branches and thus to prevent the entry and spread of parasites into the main branches or trunks of trees and shrubs. Pruning is also used to give desired shape to ornamental plants, to control or induce flowering, as in grapevines, and to increase the number of branches on a stem by removing the terminal bud. In many plants the terminal bud inhibits the growth of axillary buds of the stem at whose apex it is situated. The fundamental guiding principle in proper pruning is to cut away the branch to be removed as close as possible to the main branch or trunk of which it is an outgrowth, and parallel to the longitudinal axis of the main branch or trunk (Fig. 12-2). In order that the growth tissues of a stem may heal a wound, such as one resulting from pruning, phloem cells must be present in such a position that they can conduct food to the healing tissues surrounding the wound. Since the food that moves downward through the phloem cells comes from leaves above, it is essential that there be leaves above the wound in order that food may reach the cambium and cork cambium at the margins of the wound. When a wound is close to a main branch and parallel to it, food moving downward from leaves borne above the wound reaches the cambium and cork cambium around the wound; the growth of protective tissues then begins from the margin of the wound and proceeds inward, until the wound is eventually completely healed by a layer of bark. Frequently, pruning jobs are performed carelessly or ignorantly, and an undesired branch is cut away at some distance from the main branch, as a result of which a stub of several inches is left protruding from the main branch. A wound at the end of a stub is so situated that healing is usually impossible and the beginning of decay is inevitable. In such a case, the healing of a wound at the end of a stub cannot be promoted by foods passing down the phloem of the main branch, for the movement of foods through this phloem is chiefly downward, and the wound is too far from the main branch phloem to receive food for nourishment of the cambium and cork cambium in the stub. As a result of the failure of a wound at the end of such a stub to heal, fungi and insects may enter the exposed sapwood and phloem of the stub and slowly move downward through the wood of the stub into the wood of the main branch or trunk. It is then necessary to cut away the diseased tissue and to pack the cavity with concrete, if the tree is to be saved (Fig. 12–3). Thus, a knowledge of the path of food transport and of the situation of the meristematic tissue in stems is a prerequisite to proper pruning technique. After a pruning job is correctly executed, the surface of the wound should be painted immediately. This treatment protects the wound against the entry of parasites while healing is in progress.

An additional precaution must be taken in pruning away large branches of a tree. The first sawing cut should be made *upward* from the underside of the branch, after which a sawing cut may be made downward from the upper side of the branch until it meets the undercut. When both cuts meet, the branch falls away cleanly from the main branch or trunk from which it is being removed. If the sawing is done only from the upper side of the branch, the weight of the branch may cause the branch to be torn away from the trunk as the cut deepens; this may strip off a large mass of bark from the main trunk as the pruned branch falls, thus damaging the trunk.

Grafting   Another practical application of a knowledge of stem structure and physiology is found in grafting, an ancient and valuable horticultural practice in which two freshly cut stem surfaces are bound so that their cells grow together and thus form an organic union between the two stem pieces. The usual types of grafting involve the union of a basal, rooted stem, the **stock,** and a distal cutting, or **scion** (Fig. 12–4).

Certain precautions are essential in the making of a successful stem graft. The stock and scion must be placed together in such a manner that their cambium layers are in contact, for the success of the graft depends in large degree upon a union of the cambial layers of the stock and scion. Successful grafts have been made in monocots, which lack cambium, but usually cambial tissue is essential to stem grafts. The cambium layers do not grow together directly, but are united by the development and growth of a new, connecting cambium in the **callus,** a tissue consisting of large, thin-walled cells that are differentiated from certain living cells of the xylem and inner bark, principally from ray cells. The new cambium cells that develop from callus cells connect the cambium of the stock and of the scion, and new phloem and xylem cells, also differentiated from the callus, connect the xylem and phloem of the stock with those of the scion. From the outer part of the callus new cork cells are formed that merge with those of the stock and scion, covering over the wound with a new layer of water-conserving cells. In a graft, stock and scion must be firmly bound together with twine or tape to prevent movement that would interfere with the process of tissue union (Fig. 12–5). The grafted region should be covered with a thick

FIG. 12–3.   Treatment of tree trunk cavities (in linden tree). *Left:* Cavity filled with cement and at an early stage of marginal healing. *Right:* The same, two years later.

FIG. 12-4.   Three common methods of grafting.

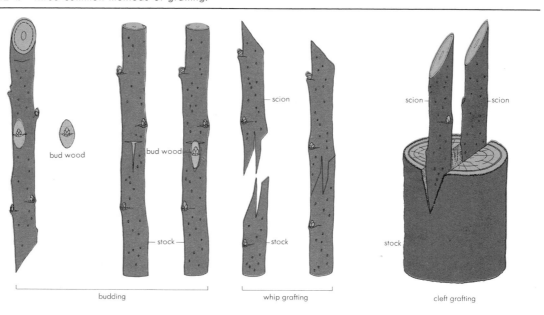

layer of grafting wax to prevent the drying out of the tissues and the entry of fungi. Successful grafts can usually be attained only when stock and scion are members of closely related species or varieties, for only in closely related kinds of plants are anatomical features and growth habits similar enough to ensure tissue union at the joined surfaces. Thus, apples can be grafted on apples, plums on peaches, tomatoes on potatoes; but apple scions could not be grafted on oranges, nor plums on walnuts, for the plants in these cases do not have enough structural and behavioral features in common to produce effective union of their stocks and scions.

There are several methods of grafting, most common of which is known as **cleft grafting** (Fig. 12-4). In this, a notch is made in a stock, and into the notch is placed the tapering end of a scion, cut to fit the notch. Another common method of grafting, termed **budding,** employs a scion composed usually of a single bud with a small amount of adjacent stem tissue. Budding is often employed when the amount of scion material available is small; a single twig may yield a dozen or more buds, each of which serves as the scion in a separate graft. Budding is used widely in the propagation of various fruit and ornamental trees and shrubs. In some plants, a bud will produce a twig that bears flowers or fruits different in some respect from the others on the same plant; an alteration of this kind in a twig is known as **bud sport,** or **bud mutation.** Several important cultivated varieties of plants have arisen as bud sports; for example, the navel orange originated as a bud sport in Brazil in about 1870, and all navel orange trees now cultivated are descendants of the ancestral mutation. Since the navel orange is seedless, it is propagated exclusively by grafting, which perpetuates the characteristics of the variety without change. In budding, a T-shaped slit is made in the bark of the stock, which must be young and slender, and a single bud is inserted in the slit in such a way that the flaps of the T close over its margins. The bud is then bound in place and grafting wax

FIG. 12-5.　A type of grafting known as inarching; either plant could serve as the stock.

applied. Another method of grafting, **bridge grafting,** is used to save trees that have been girdled by the gnawing of porcupines, rabbits, and other animals, or by insects and fungous diseases. The ends of small branches, which are used as scions, are inserted under the bark at the upper and lower borders of the girdle (Fig. 12-6). If such a graft is successful, the phloem of the several branches assumes the translocation functions of the destroyed tree bark, and the tree survives.

Grafting is employed for several purposes, among which the following are common:

1. To propagate seedless varieties of plants, such as navel oranges.

2. To propagate without change hybrid plants, the seeds of which do not all grow into plants like the parents (do not "breed true").

3. To propagate plants, the seeds of which give low percentages of germination.

4. To increase the speed of propagation and induce more rapid fruiting. Many kinds of fruit trees bear fruit within a much shorter time if they are propagated by grafts instead of by seeds.

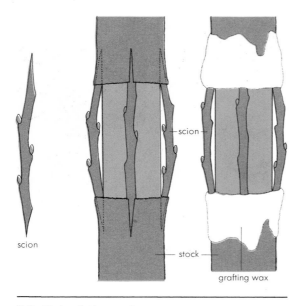

FIG. 12-6.   Bridge grafting.

5. To acclimate species of plants to new environments. For example, cultivated apple varieties are frequently grafted on the stocks of Siberian crab apples, the roots of which are less susceptible to the rigors of harsh winters than are the roots of the cultivated varieties. The roots of plum trees do not grow well in sandy soils, but plums can be successfully grown in such soils by grafting them onto the stocks of peach trees, the roots of which flourish in such soils.

6. To change or control the shape of a plant, as in the umbrella catalpa, Camperdown elm, and others. The maximum stem circumference attained by almond trees is about 5 feet. If almond scions are grafted onto peach stocks, the trunks grow to circumferences of almost 10 feet.

7. To check or eliminate parasites. In France and other parts of Europe, European types of grapes are seriously injured by a kind of root louse that does not attack the roots of American grapes. If scions of European grapes are grafted onto American grape stocks, the European grapes can be grown without damage by root lice.

A common misconception concerning grafting is that it is a method of producing new types of plants. This error has arisen probably because of Burbank's work both with the creation of new varieties of plants and with propagation of plants by means of grafting. Grafting never results in the creation of new kinds of plants. It is exclusively a process of **vegetative** reproduction employed to propagate valuable types of plants *without change.* New varieties arise naturally by **mutation** (a process of sudden unpredictable change) or they are isolated from other varieties by artificial selection or are developed by cross breeding **(hybridizing).** After new varieties have developed, they are frequently propagated by grafting. Since many such varieties are hybrids, their seeds do not "breed true"; that is, all of them do not grow up into plants like their hybrid parents. In order to maintain and propagate such hybrid varieties, grafting, or some other vegetative method of propagation is employed.

That grafting maintains the separate individualities of stock and scion has been shown by every successful graft. Many closely related varieties of scions may be grafted onto one stock, with the result that separate branches of the grafted plant bear different types of fruits or flowers. There are several well-known apple trees in this country, for example, which have as many as 115 apple varieties grafted to them. Each scion continues to produce apples of its variety, with no mixture of the characteristics of the different varieties. Another interesting type of graft can be made between scions of tomato and stocks of potato (Fig. 12-7); the stock continues to produce subterranean tubers, the scion to form typical tomato fruits.

Girdling   Girdling, or "ringing," is another horticultural practice, the success of which depends upon some knowledge of stem structure and functions. As stated earlier, girdling is the removal of a complete ring of bark including phloem down to the cambium or to the wood from a branch or trunk of a woody plant. Girdling interrupts the downward passage of food through the phloem and, as a result, causes food to ac-

FIG. 12-7. Graft of a tomato scion onto a potato stock. A. *Left:* Young scion grafted onto potato stock. *Right:* A three-week-old graft. B. A somewhat older stage. C. Several months later; the scion bears tomato fruits and the stock is producing potato tubers.

cumulate above the girdle. If a girdle is made on a small branch, just below a flower or flower cluster, the fruits produced by the flowers will be unusually large because large amounts of downward-moving food that collect above the girdle pass into the developing fruits. This girdling of small branches is frequently employed in this country to produce extra large grapes or other fruits, chiefly for exhibition purposes. In Europe, girdling is practiced much more extensively than in this country for the production of oversize fruits that command high prices in European hotels and cafés. If, in the girdling of young branches, the cambium is not injured, the girdle is usually healed over by subsequent growth. If a complete girdle is cut through the bark and cambium of a tree trunk, the tree usually dies as a result of root starvation. Girdling of this type was frequently used to kill large numbers of trees preparatory to clearing forest areas for agricultural purposes. Girdling is sometimes employed to force into flowering branches of young trees

that are slow in beginning to flower. Removal of a ring of phloem maintains a high concentration of carbohydrates in branches, a condition related to the beginning of flowering in some species of plants, and may also stimulate the development or accumulation of a flower-inducing hormone in girdled branches.

Stem Cuttings   The vegetative propagation of plants by means of stem cuttings is a horticultural practice that is intimately related to the anatomy and physiology of stems. When stem segments of many species of plants are placed with their lower ends in a suitably moist substance, such as wet sand or soil or, in some species, in water, they develop adventitious roots at these lower ends. Each cutting, upon forming new roots, begins to absorb water and minerals rapidly and becomes established as an independent plant. Many important horticultural species are propagated largely or exclusively by cuttings; among these are carnations, geraniums, coleus, chrysan-

FIG. 12–8. Cutting of yew (*Taxus*). Both sets of cuttings were made and placed in a rooting bench at the same time, but those on the right were treated with a dilute solution of indolebutyric acid to hasten root formation. (Courtesy of P. W. Zimmerman, Boyce Thompson Institute, Yonkers, N.Y.)

not treated   treated

themums, roses, grapes, and English ivy. Stem cuttings of these plants, together with many others, form roots easily and rapidly. In other species, however, the development of roots proceeds so slowly and unevenly that propagation by means of cuttings is rather unsatisfactory. Treatment of the lower ends of cuttings of many of these plants with plant hormones and related substances in water solutions or in lanolin paste stimulates remarkably the formation of adventitious roots, and thus makes possible the large-scale rooting of cuttings of these species (Fig. 12–8). The concentrations of these growth-promoting substances required to accelerate or initiate root formation are remarkably low. For example, a concentration of 1 part of indoleacetic acid in 2000 parts of lanolin is effective in stimulating root production on the cuttings of many species of plants.

In the propagation of plants from stem cuttings, one must take care to reduce evaporation of moisture from the cuttings, for young cuttings, lacking roots, are able to absorb only small quantities of water and would soon wither and die if a compensatory decrease in water loss from aerial parts of the cutting were not made. This reduction in evaporation may be accomplished by removing some of the leaves from cuttings,

by keeping the cuttings in a very humid greenhouse, or by placing over the cuttings waterproof containers, such as glass jars, which retain beneath them a very humid atmosphere thereby reducing the rate of transpiration.

Stem Injection   The injection of chemicals into stems is another interesting application of a knowledge of stem structure and functions. In many types of soils, iron is not present in forms that can be readily utilized by green plants. The leaves of such plants growing in these soils fail to develop normal green color (**chlorosis**) because iron is required for the manufacture of chlorophyll. It has been found that the deposition or injection of water-soluble iron salts into the sapwood of trees promotes the formation of normal quantities of chlorophyll. Poisons such as arsenic compounds and copper sulfate have been injected into sapwood to kill quickly trees on lands to be cleared for agricultural use and also to thin out dense forests. Several investigators have experimented upon the injection into trees of chemicals poisonous to parasites in the hope of controlling the attacks of such organisms on trees. Lithium salts have been injected into chestnut trees in an effort to check the chestnut blight disease and enable the trees to form protective tissues to surround diseased portions of their stems. The injection of zinc chloride, copper sulfate, and other chemicals into the sapwood of trees has been reported to be moderately effective in reducing the depredations of certain kinds of bark beetles. Research on the use of such chemicals to kill or control fungi and insects in woody plants is not very far advanced and at this time the results of such **chemotherapy** must be considered as inconclusive.

SUMMARY

1. Important functions of stems include conduction of water and dissolved minerals, and translocation of foods.

2. The liquid consisting of water and dissolved substances that moves upward in the xylem of stems and other organs is termed sap.

3. The rise of sap in stems proceeds at its greatest rate during periods of rapid growth and vegetative activity, and even during periods of dormancy there is a slow ascent of sap in woody plants.

4. Under certain conditions, the osmotic potential of the sap may be very high, as in the sap of sugar maples in the spring, and osmotic accumulation of water from the soil may actually create stem pressure which forces sap up the xylem, but under normal conditions the osmotic potential of sap approaches zero.

5. A number of factors are believed to contribute to sap movement under usual conditions; among these are:

    a. root pressure, the accumulation of soil solutes in the root xylem by active transport in concentrations high enough to cause water to move into the root xylem more rapidly than it is being lost from the aerial portions of the plant, creating pressure similar to stem pressure;

    b. capillarity, the tendency for water to rise in small tubes because of the attraction between water molecules and the tube walls;

    c. cohesion-tension, a pull exerted along water columns in xylem cell systems extending from the leaf to the root that is dependent upon the cohesive forces which tend to hold water molecules together—as water is lost from the leaves by evaporation from cell surfaces, the cohesive forces between these and other water molecules create tension which pulls water through the plant.

6. Of the above factors, the last-named is believed to be most important, and is termed the cohesion-tension theory. The cohesion-tension theory is supported by demonstration of tension in the water columns of xylem cells during periods of rapid water loss.

7. Living cells appear to be necessary for normal sap movement through plants, although the forces involved are primarily physical ones.

8. Translocation of foods in plants occurs chiefly through the phloem.

9. Food translocation includes movement of foods from the root and stem parenchyma upward to growing tips in the spring, similar movement in the opposite direction during periods of rapid food synthesis and storage, movement of foods from leaves to the non-photosynthetic tissues of flowers and fruits, and so on.

10. Food translocation through phloem is explained principally by the mass flow theory. This theory suggests that sugar accumulated in the phloem by active transport near the sites of photosynthesis raises its osmotic potential and creates a positive pressure by osmotic movement of water into the phloem in such regions; concurrently, removal of sugar from the phloem at sites of sugar use or storage reduces its osmotic potential in these regions, causing a loss of water to surrounding cells. The difference in pressure between areas of sugar input and sugar extraction causes the phloem solution to flow in the direction of sites of sugar utilization.

11. Materials move laterally in stems chiefly through the vascular rays, the parenchyma cells of which are in contact both with xylem and phloem elements and have the capability of passing materials directly to and from these elements and among one another.

12. Our knowledge of the structure and physiology of stems is helpful in many ways, among which are included the important practices of:

a. pruning to remove diseased limbs, to limit leaf production capacity, and to reduce water loss;

b. grafting of desirable scions onto suitable stocks to propagate seedless varieties of plants or varieties which do not breed true, to increase the speed of reproduction of desirable plant shoots, to acclimate plants to otherwise unfavorable environments, to check certain disease organisms and parasites, and so on;

c. girdling of trees or branches by removal of a ring of bark and phloem in order to accumulate food above the girdle, or to kill the plant by starving its root system;

d. propagation of horticultural species by stem cuttings.

SUGGESTED READINGS FOR INTERESTED STUDENTS

1. Crafts, A. S. *Translocation in Plants.* Holt, Rinehart and Winston, New York, 1961.

2. Galston, A. W. *The Life of the Green Plant,* 2d ed. Prentice-Hall, Englewood Cliffs, N.J., 1964.

3. Kramer, P. J., and T. T. Kozlowski, *Physiology of Trees,* McGraw-Hill, New York, 1960.

4. Mahlstede, J. P., and E. S. Haber, *Plant Propagation.* Wiley, New York, 1957.

5. Salisbury, F. B., and R. V. Parke. *Vascular Plants: Form and Function.* Wadsworth, Belmont, Cal., 1964.

6. Steward, F. C., *About Plants; Topics in Plant Biology.* Addison-Wesley, Reading, Mass. 1966.

7. Zimmerman, M. H., "How sap moves in trees." *Scientific American,* Vol. 208, No. 3, pp. 132–142, 1963.

TOPICS AND QUESTIONS FOR STUDY

1. Review the major functions of stems.

2. What is sap? Is there a difference between stem "sap" and cell "sap"? Explain.

3. In what portion of the xylem of woody plants does most sap rise occur? In tapping a sugar maple tree, how far into the trunk does the tapper bore? Explain.

4. What is stem pressure? How is stem pressure associated with production of maple syrup?

5. What is root pressure? How does root pressure develop? What reasons can you give that suggest root pressure is of relatively little importance in sap ascent?

6. What is capillarity? Does capillarity appear to be an important factor in ascent of sap? Explain.

7. Does the removal of a complete ring of bark from a stem interfere with the ascent of sap? Explain.

8. Summarize the presently accepted theory that attempts to explain the ascent of sap, and describe the experimental evidence supporting this theory.

9. If you are careless with your lawn mower and damage the bark around the base of a tree, why may the tree die?

10. Why is it a good idea to immerse the stems of freshly cut flowers and cut off the lower portions underwater?

11. Through what tissues would you expect:
    a. water to move from the soil region to the leaves?
    b. food to move from the roots to the developing leaves in spring?
    c. food to move from the leaves to the roots in summer?
    d. food to move from the leaves to the maturing fruits in fall?
    e. food to move from the bark to the pith of the stem?

12. Define mass flow in the phloem, and explain the physical factors which influence mass flow.

13. Why do horticulturists frequently prune a proportion of the foliage of stems from cuttings which they are attempting to root?

14. Describe the proper way to prune a large branch from a tree.

15. What is girdling? Describe two ways in which girdling could be useful.

16. If a branch is girdled immediately below a flower, that flower may produce an unusually large fruit, but if the girdle is made immediately above a flower, the flower may wilt and fall, without producing a fruit. Explain.

17. What is grafting? Describe three types of grafts and list one way in which each would be useful.

18. Why is it that some species of plants (for example, some varieties of fruit trees, carnations, and chrysanthemums) are propagated only by grafting, cuttings, or some other vegetative method? Explain.

13

THE ORIGIN AND STRUCTURE OF LEAVES

Leaves are the food-making organs of higher plants, and thus are vitally important to the plants themselves and to animals which eat them. All foods used by living organisms (except for a few species of bacteria) are products of leaves or other green parts of plants. Herbivorous (plant-eating) animals, such as cattle, sheep, and horses, obtain their food directly from leaves or other plant parts; carnivorous (flesh-eating) animals, such as lions, tigers, and wolves, derive their food from the tissues of other living animals which eat other herbivorous or carnivorous animals. Non-green

plants, such as fungi, also are dependent for their nutrition upon foods synthesized by green plants.

THE NATURE, ORIGIN, AND ARRANGEMENT OF LEAVES

Leaves are the most characteristic appendages of aerial stems. They are usually expanded and flattened in form, although they may vary greatly in shape, size, and internal structure, and may even vary from one part of a plant to another. Leaves are joined to stems at nodes and usually

FIG. 13-1.   Leaf arrangement. A. Alternate arrangement of redbud (*Cercis*). B. Alternate arrangement of Japanese quince (*Chaenomeles*) showing large stipules. C. Whorled leaves similar to catalpa. D. Opposite leaves of maple (*Acer*).

have buds in their axils. As stated in Chapter 9, leaves originate as lateral protuberances of the apical meristems of buds. With the opening of a bud, these leaf primordia begin to grow rapidly as a result of cell division, cell enlargement, and cell differentiation until they become mature leaves.

Because of the occurrence of a bud in the axil of each leaf, leaves are arranged on stems in the same manner as buds (Fig. 13-1). Only one leaf commonly occurs at a node, and buds are therefore **alternate** or **spiral** in their arrangement as in elms, lindens, and apples. The **opposite** arrangement, in which two leaves are produced at

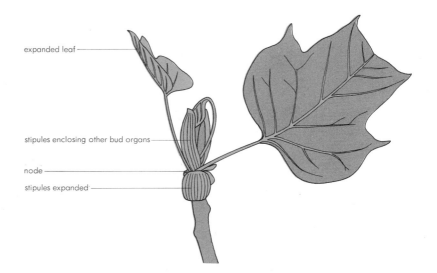

expanded leaf

stipules enclosing other bud organs

node

stipules expanded

FIG. 13-2. Twig of tulip tree (*Liriodendron*).

a node, usually on opposite sides of the stem, as in maples, carnations, and buckeye, is less common. In the **whorled** arrangement, three or more leaves are produced at a node, usually more or less equally spaced around the stem; this arrangement occurs in catalpa, in some species of lilies, and in a number of other woody and herbaceous plants, but it is the least common type. It is apparent that the arrangement of leaves is such that their weight is more or less equally distributed on all sides of the stem and that there is a minimum degree of mutual shading.

EXTERNAL STRUCTURE OF LEAVES

The most common type of leaf consists of a leaf stalk, or **petiole;** a usually flattened, expanded portion at the end of the petiole, the blade, or **lamina;** and in many species of plants, small green appendages called **stipules** at the juncture of petiole with stem. Stipules are absent from the leaves of many plants, and in others fall off shortly after the buds open and the leaves begin to expand. Stipules are seemingly not of fundamental importance in the physiology of most plants, but in some woody species, such as the tulip tree, beech, and linden, they furnish protec-

tion for developing buds in leaf axils (Fig. 13-2). In Japanese quince (Fig. 13-1) and in garden pea, the large, green stipules persist for the life of the leaf, and add considerably to the plant's total photosynthetic surface. Some leaves lack petioles, their laminae growing directly from the stem. Petioles are usually slender and cylindrical in form, but in some plants, they are flattened; in certain species of *Acacia* the petioles are broad, flat, and green, and replace the leaf blades as the principal photosynthetic surface. Vascular tissue in petioles conducts water and solutes from stems into leaf blades, and transports foods manufactured in the blades to the stem. Many petioles retain the ability of differential growth for a long period, and are thus able to move the blades they support into positions of favorable light concentration. The toughness and flexibility of petioles permits movement of leaves in wind without damage.

Leaf laminae are usually flat, thin, and broad, with a conspicuous system of **veins** forming the structural framework of the blades. These veins branch at the juncture of petiole and lamina, and are composed principally of strands of xylem and phloem which are continuous with the conducting tissues of the petiole and stem. Thus, in addi-

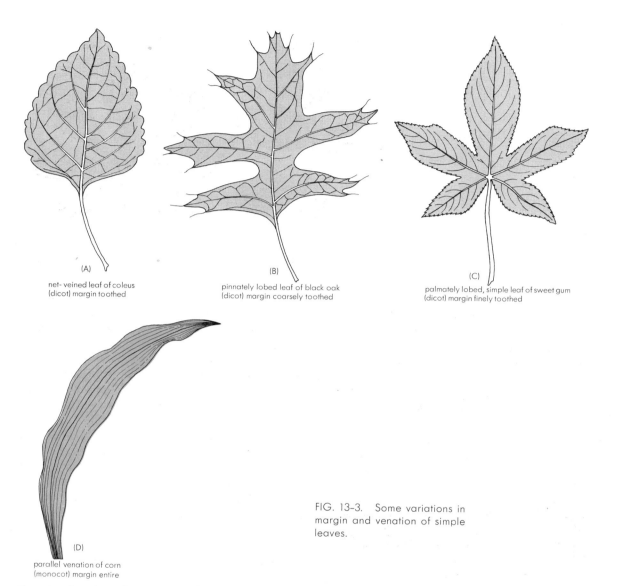

(A)
net-veined leaf of coleus
(dicot) margin toothed

(B)
pinnately lobed leaf of black oak
(dicot) margin coarsely toothed

(C)
palmately lobed, simple leaf of sweet gum
(dicot) margin finely toothed

(D)
parallel venation of corn
(monocot) margin entire

FIG. 13–3. Some variations in margin and venation of simple leaves.

tion to forming the structural framework of blades, veins are the ultimate branches of the conducting tissues that pass into leaves from the vascular tissues of stems. The arrangement of veins **(venation)** varies in leaves of different species of plants, but usually conforms to one of two major types: **parallel venation** and **net venation.** In leaves with parallel venation, such as those of iris, lilies, and corn, the main veins are parallel with each other and are arranged lengthwise (Fig. 13–3). In leaves with net venation, such as those of maple, lettuce, geranium, and bean, the main veins branch from the tip of the petiole in such manner that they are not parallel to each other but form a network (Fig. 13–5). In most net-veined leaves, such as those of elms and oaks, there is one central vein, the midrib, to which the principal lateral veins are attached in the same fash-

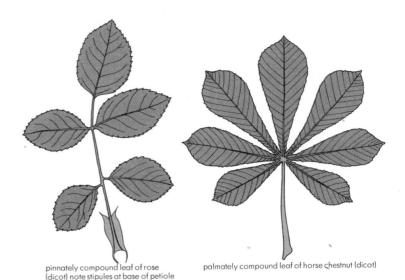

FIG. 13–4. Compound leaves of rose (*Rosa*) and horse chestnut (*Aesculus*).

pinnately compound leaf of rose (dicot) note stipules at base of petiole

palmately compound leaf of horse chestnut (dicot)

ion as the barbs of a feather extend outward from the central rib. In a net system of this type the venation is termed **pinnate.** In leaves with **palmate** venation, such as those of sycamore, cucumber, and maple, there are several main veins that branch into the leaf blade from the tip of the petiole. Generally, parallel-veined leaves occur in monocotyledons, and net-veined leaves in dicotyledons, although both groups of flowering plants contain numerous exceptions.

Leaf laminae vary greatly in shape, size, the nature of their margins, and in amount of lobing

FIG. 13–5. Pinnately compound leaves of honey locust (*Gleditsia*).

or blade division (Fig. 13–3). In some plants, for example clovers, roses, and locusts, the leaf blade is not a single structure but is divided into a number of separate segments. A leaf of this type is termed **compound** and the individual blade segments are called **leaflets** (Figs. 13–4, 13–5). More common than compound leaves are **simple** leaves, in which the blade is a single structure, as in peach, elm, and oak. Each compound leaf, like each simple leaf, typically is associated with a single axillary bud; in contrast, buds are not found in association with individual leaflets.

The leaves of iris, corn, dogwood, and nasturtium have **entire margins,** that is, smooth margins that lack indentations. Many leaves, however, have **toothed margins;** the teeth vary greatly in size and shape among various plants, but usually have some definite orientation with respect to the marginal vein endings of the blades. **Lobed** leaves such as in maple, sweet gum, and red oak, are those in which the marginal indentations are deep, often extending inward almost to the main veins.

The forms of leaf blades vary from **linear,** as in blue-grass and wheat, to **circular,** as in nasturtium, with many intergrading forms, such as **lanceolate** (willows), **heart-shaped** (redbud), **ovate**

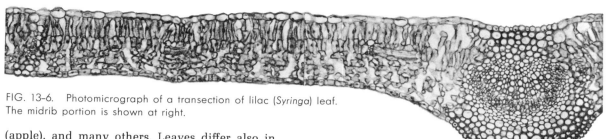

FIG. 13–6. Photomicrograph of a transection of lilac (*Syringa*) leaf. The midrib portion is shown at right.

(apple), and many others. Leaves differ also in size, from a fraction of an inch in length and width, as in tamarisk, to 12 to 50 or more feet long and 1 to 2 feet or more wide, as in certain palms and in banana plants. These various features of leaves—size, division of the blade, nature of the margins, blade form, and venation—are characters by which botanists may quickly recognize or identify many species of plants.

Of the many variations in leaf form, venation, margins, and shapes, there is apparently no single pattern that renders any one kind of leaf more successful or more efficient than other kinds of leaves. The fact that there exists such diversity in the external structure of leaves attests an apparent lack of significance in such diversity; all leaves are relatively efficient food-making organs, so long as they are provided with chlorophyll.

THE INTERNAL STRUCTURE OF LEAVES

Microscopic examination of a transverse section of a leaf shows three groups of tissues: **epidermis, mesophyll,** and **conducting** (Fig. 13–6). The epidermis is a single layer of cells forming the surface skin of the leaf. Its chief functions are the protection of the inner tissues from excessive moisture loss and the admission of carbon dioxide and oxygen to these internal tissues. In some leaves the epidermis may furnish some protection against the entry of parasites. The outer walls of epidermal cells are frequently thickened and are usually covered with a layer of waxy cutin that is secreted on the outer surface of the cell

Plant	Upper Surface		Lower Surface	
	/ sq. mm.	/ sq. in.	/ sq. mm.	/ sq. in.
Waterweed (*Elodea canadensis*)	0	0	0	0
Coleus (*Coleus blumei*)	0	0	141	90,970
Lilac (*Syringa vulgaris*)	0	0	330	212,900
Oat (*Avena sativa*)	25	16,130	23	14,840
Corn (*Zea mays*)	94	60,650	158	101,940
Sunflower (*Helianthus annuus*)	175	112,900	325	209,680
Bean (*Paseolus vulgaris*)	40	25,810	281	181,290
Water Lily (*Nymphaea alba*)	460	296,770	0	0

TABLE 13–1 Average numbers of stomata on the upper and lower leaf surfaces of some familiar plants.

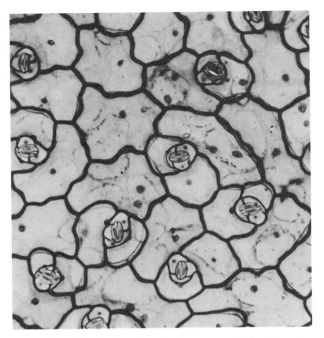

FIG. 13-7. Leaf epidermis of stonecrop (*Sedum*), showing guard cell pairs and other epidermal cells.

walls by the protoplasts of epidermal cells and that is in large part responsible for the effectiveness of the epidermis in conserving moisture. Ordinary epidermal cells usually lack chloroplasts and are colorless, but in some plants, such as purple cabbage, anthocyanin pigments are present in the cell sap of leaf epidermal cells. Certain specialized cells of the epidermis, the **guard cells,** do, however, contain chloroplasts. The guard cells are somewhat bean shaped, as seen in surface view, and occur in pairs, distributed among the more numerous, ordinary epidermal cells, chiefly on the lower surfaces of leaves (Fig. 13-7). Each pair of guard cells encloses a small pore, or **stoma** (*pl.* stomata) (Fig. 13-8), through which gaseous exchange between the inner tissues of a leaf and the external atmosphere occurs. These paired guard cells expand and contract with changes in their water content, and, as they do so, the size of the stoma that they enclose changes. When the guard cells are ex-

panded, the stomata are open; when the water content of guard cells decreases and they contract, the stomata are nearly or completely closed. Stomata in most leaves are partially or completely open all day or during the greater part of the day and are closed or nearly closed during all or most of the night. Stomatal numbers per unit of leaf area vary greatly in different species; also, the numbers of stomata on upper and lower surfaces of the same leaf show considerable differences. Examples of these differences are shown in Table 13-1.

This table gives the average number of stomata per unit area of leaf surface and also indicates the variation in their distribution. In some species (coleus, lilac) stomata occur on the lower leaf surface only; in other species they occur on both upper and lower surfaces, in nearly equal numbers (oat) or, more commonly, with a greater number on the lower epidermis (corn, sunflower, bean). The stomata of water lily are restricted to the upper sides of the leaves which characteristically float on the surface of the water. The absence of stomata exemplified by the leaves of *Elodea*, is correlated with the habitat of this and numerous other submerged aquatic plants. The average areas of most stomata when fully opened are between 0.000092 and 0.0001 square milli-

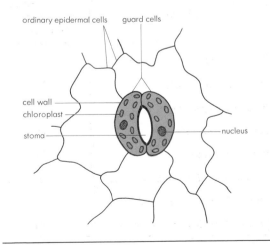

FIG. 13-8. Portion of leaf epidermis.

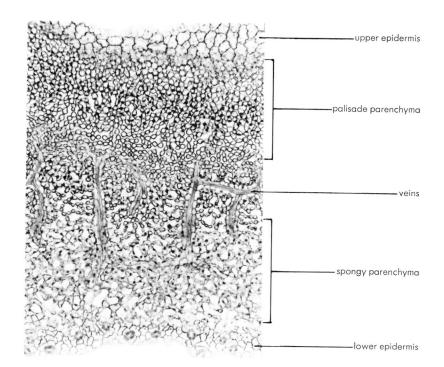

upper epidermis

palisade parenchyma

veins

spongy parenchyma

FIG. 13-9. Paradermal section of lilac (*Syringa*) leaf.

lower epidermis

meters (remember that a millimeter is $\frac{1}{25}$ inch); clearly, stomatal areas are exceedingly small.

In many plants **hairs** occur as outgrowths of leaf epidermal cells, as in tomato and tobacco. In some plants, petunia, for example, the terminal cells of these hairs are glandular and secrete sticky materials that give the leaves a clammy texture. In other species, epidermal hairs soon die and become dry and grayish or white, as in mullein. Hairs appear to serve a variety of functions. They reduce air movement at the surface of the leaf and, thus, slow the rate of water loss; they may be spiny, as in many of the thistles, and inhibit grazing animals from eating plants thus covered, and the secretions of glandular hairs may repel animals and reduce evaporative water loss.

The upper and lower epidermal layers of leaves are usually much alike in their detailed structure, except that in most flowering plants, stomata are more numerous on the lower surface, as shown above, and that the cutin layer **(cuticle)** is com- monly thicker on the upper epidermis than on the lower. The thicker cuticle and smaller number (or absence) of stomata on the upper surface of a leaf are doubtless an advantageous arrange- ment, for the upper surfaces of leaves are more directly exposed to the drying action of the sun's rays than are the lower epidermal cells.

The **mesophyll** consists of thin-walled paren- chyma cells (sometimes called chlorenchyma) that characteristically contain numerous chloroplasts and is the food-making tissue of leaves. The meso- phyll cells nearest the upper epidermis are cy- lindrical, loosely packed, and arranged at right angles to the leaf surface. These constitute the **palisade** layer of the mesophyll. In the leaves of most plants, there are one or two palisade layers just beneath the upper epidermis. Beneath the palisade cells is a second group of parenchyma cells of different form; these cells are typically quite variable in shape and are very loosely ar- ranged so that there are numerous air spaces among them. These cells constitute the **spongy**

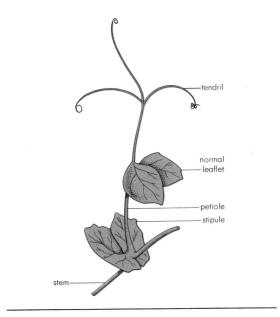

FIG. 13-10. Compound leaf of pea (*Pisum*).

FIG. 13-11. Development of plantlets in leaf notches of air plant (*Bryophyllum*).

layer of the mesophyll. Like palisade cells, spongy cells contain numerous chloroplasts and function in food synthesis. The numerous air spaces of the mesophyll facilitate gas diffusion through the internal tissues of leaves, for they connect with the spaces underlying the stomata. The type of mesophyll differentiation just described is characteristic of most leaves that grow in a horizontal or oblique position. In some grasses, irises, and other species in which the leaves stand in a more or less vertical position, there are palisade layers under both epidermal layers with spongy tissues between them.

Veins are vascular bundles that branch out from the vascular bundles of the petiole. The main veins frequently appear in relief on the lower surfaces of leaves and often as shallow depressions in their upper surfaces. Each vein consists of both xylem (vessels and tracheids) and phloem (sieve tubes, chiefly), which conduct, respectively, water and minerals upward into leaf blades and foods manufactured in mesophyll downward into the petiole for transfer to the stem and roots. In leaves of most plants, the xylem cells form the upper portion of the veins, that is, the portion closest to the upper epidermis, whereas the phloem cells are situated in the lower portions. Each vein is surrounded by a group of cells, known as a **bundle sheath,** which gives support and strength to the vein; these cells are sometimes thick-walled. Some experimental evidence suggests that bundle sheaths may also participate in conduction. The degree of branching of leaf veins is such that no mesophyll cell is far removed from a veinlet. It has been estimated that there may be as many as 25,000 veinlet endings within 1 square inch of leaf surface (Fig. 13-9).

SPECIALIZED LEAVES

There are several kinds of leaves that perform functions other than food synthesis or in addition to food synthesis and that possess corresponding structural features reflecting these specialized

FIG. 13–12. A tropical pitcher plant (*Nepenthes dominii*).

functions. Of most common occurrence among the various kinds of specialized leaves are the protective **bud scales** of many woody plants, and the various floral organs, including sepals, petals, stamens, and carpels. In barberry and certain species of cacti, **spines** are morphologically specialized leaves, for they bear buds in their axils; these spines discourage grazing animals. In black locust the spines occur in pairs at the nodes, and are modified stipules. In onion and lily bulbs, the **bulb scales** are leaves specialized for the storage of food. The leaves of *Portulaca* ("moss rose"), of *Sedum* and other members of the live-for-ever family, and of century plants, are very thick and succulent because of the large quantities of water they store. The leaves of some plants function wholly, or in part, as **tendrils** (Fig. 13–10), structures that twine about solid objects and thus aid in supporting their weak stems. In peas, some of the leaflets of the compound leaves are slender tendrils. Among the leaves of seed plants there are some that provide for **vegetative reproduction,** as well as for food manufacture (Fig. 13–11). Plantlets formed from meristematic tissue at the

leaf notches of *Bryophyllum* become detached from the leaf, fall to the soil, and, if their roots reach moisture, grow into new plants.

Doubtless, the most highly specialized and most amazing of all kinds of leaves are the insectivorous or carnivorous leaves of approximately 200 species of angiosperms. These plants grow principally in bogs, the soil of which is either deficient in certain essential elements such as nitrogen or contains these elements in forms not readily available to most green plants. Insectivorous plants secure certain of these elements by trapping and digesting insects and other small animals. Insectivorous plants are chlorophyllous and make their own food; their use of animal tissues as a source of nutrients is merely supplementary, and they are able to develop in apparently normal fashion, without digesting insects, if their roots receive the required mineral nutrients. In some species of these plants, the leaves apparently secrete enzymes that digest the soft parts of insect bodies; in other species, bacteria inhabiting the insectivorous leaves produce these digestive enzymes.

FIG. 13-13. A pitcher plant (*Sarracenia*) in flower. Note the pitcher-shaped leaves; from Northeastern United States.

The pitcher plants have leaves that are tubular or pitcher shaped and that hold a liquid containing digestive enzymes. Insects are attracted to the pitchers by their colors or odors, and crawl into them, passing over a number of stiff, downward-pointing hairs inside the pitcher. When they attempt to crawl out, they are frequently unable to climb upward over the bristly hairs and eventually fall into the liquid and drown. The soft portions of their bodies are then digested and absorbed by leaf cells. Some of the Malayan species (Fig. 13-12) have leaf pitchers that are 18 inches long and may hold a quart of liquid. There

are pitcher plants in the United States, of which the Sarracenias (Fig. 13-13) occur in bogs in many of the midwestern and eastern states. The leaves of one species may be a yard in length.

The sundews are another interesting group of insectivorous plants. In these, the leaf blades possess many glandular hairs that grow upward from their upper surfaces. These tentacles secrete sticky substances containing digestive enzymes. When an insect alights on one of these leaves, it is smeared by the mucilaginous secretions of

FIG. 13-14. *Drosera filiformis,* a species of insectivorous sundew.

the glands at the tentacle tips. Simultaneously, some of the tentacles, which are sensitive to contacts of as little as 0.000822 milligram (0.0000000287 ounce), bend inward and surround the body of the insect. The movement of these tentacles is quite rapid, in some cases requiring only 3 or 4 minutes for completion. The fluid with which the body of the insect becomes covered contains digestive agents that convert the nitrogenous substance of the insect into forms that the plant can utilize (Figs. 13–14, 13–15).

FIG. 13–16. Plants of Venus'-flytrap (*Dionaea*).

FIG. 13–15. Leaves of the insectivorous sundew, *Drosera rotundifolia,* enlarged.

The Venus' flytrap has specialized leaf blades each of which is supplied with 12 to 20 marginal, bristly teeth about ½ inch long. On the inner (upper) surface of the blade there are several slender hairs that are sensitive to touch. If an insect, alighting on the leaf, contacts the sensitive hairs, a stimulation is initiated that causes the two halves of the leaf to suddenly move together in the same manner as a book is closed. The marginal bristles interlock and the insect is securely held within the trap. Glands on the inner surface of the leaf then digest the entrapped body. After digestion is completed, the leaf opens again, ready for another victim. The time required for the closing of the leaf halves is very brief, frequently as short as 1 second (Figs. 13–16, 13–17).

In many other species of insectivorous plants, there are no highly specialized leaves of the types

FIG. 13–17. Various stages in the capture of a fly by a leaf of Venus'-flytrap.

described above. In such species, the surfaces of the leaves are covered with sticky, glandular hairs, upon which insects become glued. Some of these glands secrete juices that partially digest the bodies of captured insects. One of the species of this type is used in rural districts of Portugal as a substitute for fly paper. The plants are hung in doorways and, by means of their sticky leaf secretions, firmly hold insects that alight upon them.

There are many superstitions about insectivorous plants, chief of which is that there exist plants able to entrap the bodies of large mammals, including man. Occasionally stories of this nature find their way into the columns of tabloids, but they have never been authenticated by reputable scientists. The known carnivorous plants trap only small insects, occasional crus-

taceans, and, infrequently, very small amphibians.

ECONOMIC IMPORTANCE OF LEAVES

The fundamental importance of leaves to man lies in their ability to make foods that he and other animals can utilize. Of the many kinds of plants that furnish food for cattle, sheep, and horses, most valuable are the grasses, which form dense mats of leafy vegetation over vast stretches of the prairies and plains of the world. The leaves of some plants are used directly by man as a source of food: these are artichoke, cabbage, collards, Brussels sprouts, celery, Chinese cabbage, endive, lettuce, rhubarb, spinach, and water cress. Economically important products other than foods are derived from the leaves of many other species. Among such materials are various dyes (indigo and henna), aromatic oils for perfumes, soaps, spices, and flavoring extracts (geranium, citronella, bay, marjoram, peppermint, sage, spearmint, thyme, parsley, wintergreen, and tansy), drugs (belladonna, cocaine, digitalis, eucalyptus, witch hazel, and senna), tobacco, tea, chlorophyll (used as a dye in foods, soaps, candles, and beverages), and waxes used in polishes for furniture, shoes, and automobiles.

SUMMARY

1. The chief function of leaves is food synthesis.

2. Leaves are usually flattened, expanded structures, although in some plants they are needle- or scalelike.

3. Leaves develop as lateral protuberances of the apical meristem in buds.

4. Leaves are arranged in the same manner as buds: spiral (alternate), opposite, and whorled. Buds are formed in the axils of leaves.

5. A typical leaf consists of a petiole (stalk), blade, and, in some species, a pair of stipules at the base of the petiole.

6. Leaves vary greatly in their sizes, forms, margins, venation, and degree of division of their blades.

7. Leaves with parallel main veins are characteristic of most monocotyledons, those with net main veins are typical of most dicotyledons.

8. The epidermis consists of a continuous outer layer of cells that extends over the entire leaf.

9. Between upper and lower epidermises of leaves are the mesophyll tissues. These consist typically of vertically oriented cylindrical palisade cells, situated usually in one or two layers beneath the upper epidermis, and a spongy layer, located below the palisade cells. The spongy tissue consists of loosely packed, rather irregular cells. Extensive intercellular spaces occur throughout the palisade and spongy tissues. Running through the mesophyll are veins that branch out from the apex of the petiole or its continuation in the blade, the midrib.

10. Epidermal cells usually have cutinized outer walls and serve primarily in protecting the mesophyll against excessive drying. Occurring in pairs in the epidermis are green guard cells, each pair enclosing a pore, or stoma, through which gas exchange occurs.

11. Palisade and spongy mesophyll cells are rich in chlorophyll and are the chief food-making cells of a leaf.

12. The xylem cells of veins conduct water and minerals into leaves, and the phloem cells of veins conduct foods downward into stems.

13. Examples of structurally and functionally specialized leaves are: bud scales, floral organs, certain types of spines and tendrils, bulb scales, storage leaves, and insectivorous leaves.

SUGGESTED READINGS FOR INTERESTED STUDENTS

1. Darwin, Charles, *Insectivorous Plants*. Murray, New York, 1884.
2. Esau, Katherine, *Plant Anatomy*, 2d ed. Wiley, New York, 1965.

3. Hill, A. F., *Economic Botany,* 2d ed. McGraw-Hill, New York, 1952.
4. Lloyd, F. E., *Carnivorous Plants.* Ronald Press, New York, 1942.

TOPICS AND QUESTIONS FOR STUDY

1. Describe the origin and development of leaves, and state their major functions.

2. Name and describe some common types of leaf arrangement.

3. Why is the fact that all leaves do not grow from one side of a stem important?

4. Describe the external structure of a typical angiosperm leaf.

5. What are the functions of stipules?

6. Distinguish between parallel venation and net venation. Are venation differences of any importance in plant classification and identification? Explain.

7. Distinguish between pinnate and palmate venation.

8. What is the physiological importance of leaf veins?

9. Distinguish between simple and compound leaves. Do you think that either of these types of leaves is better or more efficient than the other? Explain.

10. How do you most frequently identify different species of flowering plants, by their leaves or their flowers? Explain.

11. Describe the structure of the epidermis of a typical leaf. What is the significance of the cuticle?

12. Describe the structure of guard cells, and state their relation to stomata and stomatal function.

13. If one coats the upper surface of a detached leaf of rubber plant with Vaseline and places it on a laboratory shelf, the leaf wilts and dries out completely in two or three days. If one coats the lower surface of a detached rubber plant leaf, then places it on the shelf, it remains moist and turgid for a week or more. Explain.

14. Describe variations in the distribution of stomata on leaf surfaces, and comment upon the significance of this distribution.

15. What is the meaning of "mesophyll"? Describe the structure of mesophyll of a typical angiosperm leaf.

16. What is the major function of mesophyll tissues?

17. Name five kinds of specialized leaves and list their functions.

18. Describe the structure of leaf veins.

19. Some types of specialized leaves are similar structurally and physiologically to certain types of specialized stems. State how you would determine whether such structures are leaves or stems.

20. List some of the economically important uses of leaves and leaf products.

14

PHOTOSYNTHESIS AND THE PHYSIOLOGY OF LEAVES

PHOTOSYNTHESIS

Photosynthesis is the fundamental process of food synthesis in green plants, and it occurs primarily in the leaves. Sugar, one of the products of photosynthesis, is the basic food substance which supports plant and animal life. Oxygen, which is required by virtually all living organisms, is liberated during photosynthesis, and all the oxygen of the atmosphere has been accumulated in this way. With the exception of a few species of bacteria, photosynthesis makes possible the existence of all living things. Thus, if any one physiological process of plants can be designated as "most important," photosynthesis is that process.

The development of our understanding of the photosynthetic process is one of the most exciting chapters of the history of plant physiology. For many centuries, scholars believed that green plants derived all their nourishment from the organic materials of the soil. This interpretation of plant nutrition, called the humus theory, was challenged and disproved by the Belgian physician, Jean van Helmont. Around 1630 he began a most revealing experiment. He placed exactly 200 pounds of completely dried soil into a vessel and planted in the soil a willow shoot weighing 5 pounds. For five years van Helmont added rain water to the soil at regular intervals; he added no fertilizer, nor did he remove any soil during this period. At the end of the five years, he removed the willow tree, now grown large, scraped all the soil from its roots, returned this soil to the vessel, removed all water from the willow tree by drying it, and carefully weighed the willow tree. He then dried the soil thoroughly and weighed it. He found that the willow tree weighed 169 pounds and 3 ounces, a gain of approximately 164 pounds during the five-year interval, and that the soil weighed 199 pounds and 14 ounces, indicating a loss of only 2 ounces during the same period. Van Helmont concluded that the willow tree built its substance from water alone. Although his critical experiment demonstrated the falsity of the humus theory, his explanation of the results was only partially correct since he did not understand the roles of light and atmospheric carbon dioxide. Within the next thirty years, the experiments of Ingenhousz, Senebier, and de Saussure showed that sunlight was necessary, that only green plant parts were capable of liberating oxygen, and that carbon dioxide was taken from the atmosphere. These works thus provided the rough outline of photosynthesis. Since that time numerous observations and experiments have been added to this foundation. Among the important discoveries were identification of the green pigment chlorophyll and demonstration of its necessity, identification of sugar glucose as the principal food product, and demonstration of the effects of various environmental factors on photosynthesis. In recent years, particularly since World War II, work with isotopes and other techniques have greatly added to our understanding of the essential biochemical and biophysical processes of photosynthesis.

The overall process of photosynthesis may be summarized as follows:

1. Photosynthesis is an energy-requiring process; it uses light as the source of energy and therefore can occur only when light shines on the plant.

2. Photosynthesis transforms light energy into chemical energy.

3. The raw materials, or reacting substances, in photosynthesis are carbon dioxide (Fig. 14–1), absorbed from the air, and water (Fig. 14–1), absorbed chiefly from the soil.

4. The green pigment chlorophyll a (Fig. 14–1) is the principal light-absorbing material of most plants.

5. The principal food product of photosynthesis in higher plants is the carbohydrate glucose (Fig. 14–1).

6. Oxygen in molecular form (O_2) is released from green plant tissues in the process.

7. Photosynthesis is not a single, simple chemical reaction, but is a series of many complex chemical reactions, some of which are only partially known.

8. Photosynthesis is important in the entire world of living organisms in two fundamental ways: (a) it is the only major process of food manufacture in the world; (b) it is the only major source of oxygen in the earth's atmosphere at the present time.

The Course of the Process   Photosynthesis may be represented by this simplified chemical equation:

$$6CO_2 + 6H_2O \xrightarrow{\text{CHLOROPHYLL}} + 673\text{kcal}$$

(carbon dioxide)   (water)   (light energy)

$$\longrightarrow C_6H_{12}O_6 + 6O_2\uparrow$$

(glucose)   (oxygen)

This equation indicates the raw materials and products in the proportions in which they occur. It shows that for a net input of 6 molecules of carbon dioxide and 6 molecules of water, there is a net output of 1 molecule of sugar and 6 molecules of oxygen. It further shows that 673 kilocalories (kcal) of energy are utilized in the

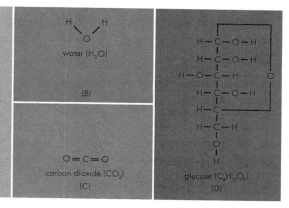

FIG. 14-1. Structural formulas for chlorophyll a, water, carbon dioxide, and glucose.

Of the 12 water molecules in this equation, only 6 actually become a part of the glucose sugar. The other 6 are chemically transformed and then reformed at a later point in the process.

The carbon dioxide used in photosynthesis in higher plants enters leaves by diffusion through the stomata of the leaf epidermis (Fig. 14-2). Carbon dioxide dissolves easily in water and thus

chlorophyll a ($C_{55}H_{72}O_5N_4Mg$)

(A)

process. (A kilocalorie is the quantity of energy required to raise the temperature of 1000 grams of water 1°C.)

Actually, water is both broken down and reformed in the process of photosynthesis (Fig. 14-5). Consequently, the photosynthesis equation is better restated:

$$6CO_2 + 12H_2O + 673\text{kcal}$$

(carbon dioxide)   (water)   (light energy)

CHLOROPHYLL

$$\rightarrow C_6H_{12}O_6 + 6O_2\uparrow + 6H_2O$$

(glucose)   (oxygen)   (water)

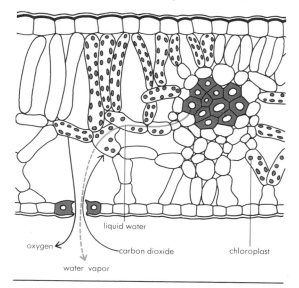

FIG. 14-2. Cross section of a common type of leaf, showing movement of water and gases during photosynthesis. Water vapor and oxygen leave the leaf through the stomata, while carbon dioxide enters.

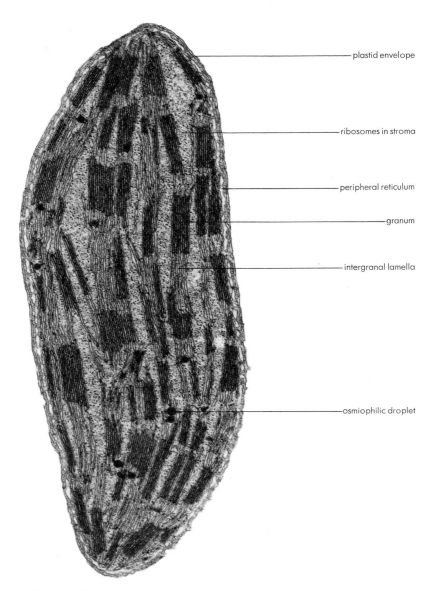

plastid envelope

ribosomes in stroma

peripheral reticulum

granum

intergranal lamella

osmiophilic droplet

FIG. 14–3. Electron micrograph showing a sectional view of a chloroplast from the mesophyll of a 15-day old leaf of corn (Zea). (Courtesy of Raymond Chollet, U. of Illinois, Urbana.)

readily enters the green mesophyll cells of leaves through their moist cell walls. As photosynthesis proceeds, the absorption of carbon dioxide molecules by mesophyll cells results in a lowered concentration of carbon dioxide molecules in the air of the intercellular spaces of the mesophyll. The concentration of carbon dioxide molecules, then, is higher in the air surrounding the leaf, and carbon dioxide molecules, according to the laws of diffusion, continue to diffuse into the leaf through the stomata.

The energy that is essential to photosynthesis is absorbed by chlorophyll in chloroplasts and is normally supplied by sunlight. The chloroplasts are membrane-limited and contain small, chlorophyll-bearing structures **(grana)** embedded in a

FIG. 14-4. Electron micrograph of chloroplast grana. (Courtesy of Dr. L.K. Shumway, Washington State University, Pullman.)

colorless matrix, or **stroma.** Electronmicrographs show the grana to consist of flattened membranous vesicles or sacs **(lamellae)** aligned in such a way that they bear a superficial resemblance to a small stack of coins (Fig. 14-3, 14-4). The membranes that comprise the grana vesicles are believed to be composite structures, each consisting of two films of protein between which are a layer of chlorophyll and a layer of fatty material. Some lamellae extend through two or possibly more grana.

Of the light that strikes a leaf, a portion is reflected from leaf surfaces, a portion passes through the leaf without being absorbed, and a portion is absorbed by green cells of the leaf. Experiments have indicated that only 5 to 8 percent of the total light energy which strikes the leaf is converted into the chemical energy of foods in photosynthesis.

If sunlight passes through a glass prism (or at certain angles through droplets of moisture, as in a rainbow), it is separated into its component types of visible light as a continuous colored light band called a **spectrum;** a sunlight spectrum shows red, orange, yellow, green, blue, and violet light, in that sequence. If sunlight passes through a chlorophyll solution and then through a prism, the resulting spectrum shows chiefly green, yellow, and some orange color, indicating that the chlorophyll has absorbed most of the red and blue-violet light rays. The rays that are most completely absorbed by chlorophyll are the ones that are most effective in photosynthesis. Leaves are green principally because green light is both reflected and transmitted by chlorophyll. Only a relatively small amount of green light is absorbed.

As stated earlier, photosynthesis is not a single chemical reaction but a complex series of reactions not all of which are understood. A diagrammatic summary of its principal steps is presented in Fig. 14-5. The process is subdivided into **dark** and **light reactions.** A dark reaction may be described as purely *chemical* in that the reaction rate is doubled with each 10°C increase in temperature, whether in darkness or light. This characteristic applies to photosynthesis when light, carbon dioxide, and other factors are adequate, that is, not *limiting* the process by their shortage. On the other hand, the light reactions are *photochemical* because they require only light energy in order to proceed and are unaffected by changes in temperature (within limits). When the intensity of light is low enough to be a limiting factor, the rate of photosynthesis is not influenced by changes in temperature.

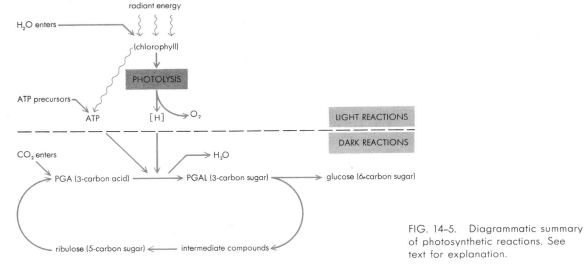

FIG. 14–5. Diagrammatic summary of photosynthetic reactions. See text for explanation.

LIGHT REACTIONS

Chlorophyll has been shown to participate in at least two major photochemical processes in which light contributes energy to chlorophyll molecules and this energy is transferred to energy-carrying compounds (Fig. 14–5). One of these processes yields a compound that provides readily available energy for use in further photosynthetic reactions. This compound, **adenosine triphosphate,** or **ATP,** has been called the energy currency for living cells because it is the chemical carrier of energy for most metabolic reactions which require energy. ATP has three phosphate portions linked in series; the energy content of ATP—high because of the special characteristics of the chemical bonds between the two terminal phosphates—may be transferred to other metabolic processes by transferring the high-energy terminal phosphate to other molecules.

The second photochemical process in photosynthesis results in the cleavage of water molecules in a process termed **photolysis.** When light strikes a chlorophyll molecule it is temporarily raised to a higher energy level. The energy of chlorophyll in this excited state is that which is used to remove hydrogen from water. The water molecule is believed to be split into two parts, one of hydrogen, and one containing oxygen and

hydrogen. The hydrogen enters into a temporary chemical union with molecules of a carrier compound, this complex being represented as [H]. The oxygen-hydrogen fragments are combined in a series of intermediate reactions to form molecular oxygen (O_2), given off at the time of photolysis, and water, reconstituted during the dark reactions. The photochemical processes allow photosynthesis to perform a dual function: (1) by conversion of light energy to a chemical form (ATP), it supplies some of the energy required by the cell for subsequent photosynthetic steps and for other processes; and (2) photolysis uses light energy to produce hydrogen needed in subsequent dark reactions.

DARK REACTIONS

The dark reactions (Fig. 14–5) are carried out in the stroma of the chloroplast. Here carbon dioxide, a 1-carbon compound, is combined with another compound containing the 5-carbon sugar, ribulose. This reaction is believed to produce an unstable 6-carbon substance that quickly decomposes to form 2 molecules of phosphoglyceric acid (PGA), each molecule of which contains 3 carbon atoms. The hydrogen removed from water in the light reactions is transferred to PGA to produce a 3-carbon sugar compound, phosphoglyceraldehyde (PGAL). The energy of some of the ATP produced during the light reaction phase is used to promote these reactions. Several of the 3-carbon PGAL molecules then undergo a complex series of reactions which ultimately produce two substances: (1) the 6-carbon sugar, glucose (Fig. 14–1), and (2) the 5-carbon ribulose needed to repeat the cycle. With the production of glucose, photosynthesis is complete.

The speed at which sugar is manufactured in photosynthesis varies in different species of plants and with changing environmental conditions. In bright light and warm temperature, leaves of most plants manufacture sugars at the rate of 0.5 to 1.8 grams per hour per square meter of leaf surface. These values represent averages and may fluctuate from hour to hour during the day. The sugar manufactured in photosynthesis may be utilized in a variety of ways. Some of it is oxidized (respired) to provide energy for living cells; some is converted into starch, the most common storage carbohydrate food in plants; and some of it is used in the formation of cellulose, proteins, fats, and other compounds necessary for growth and for the formation of new protoplasm.

In most species of plants, as sugar molecules are formed in photosynthesis, they are enzymatically converted almost immediately into starch which accumulates as small grains in leaf cells during the daylight hours. This behavior is advantageous because starch is insoluble in water and does not affect the osmotic properties of cells. Furthermore, the conversion of sugar into starch results in a decrease in volume; that is, starch does not occupy as much space as sugar. During the night, much of the starch stored in the mesophyll cells during the day is enzymatically transformed back into sugars, a portion of which is translocated through the veins and petioles to the stems and other portions of plant bodies to be utilized in various processes that will be described in the next chapter.

Factors Influencing Photosynthesis Photosynthesis, as a complex of chemical and physical reactions involving phenomena both inside and outside a plant, is affected by a variety of factors. Among those factors that exert direct influences on photosynthesis and that have been extensively studied are the chlorophyll content of leaves, the intensity of the light shining on leaves, the availability of moisture, and the carbon dioxide content of the air.

The synthesis of chlorophyll depends on a number of factors: the availability in suitable form of the chemical elements that constitute the chlorophyll molecule; the presence of light; the activity of certain chemical regulators; and hereditary factors. The carbon, hydrogen, and oxygen of chlorophyll molecules are derived from sugars. The first chlorophyll synthesized in a seedling is formed at the expense of foods and minerals stored within the seed. As the seedling grows and begins to carry on photosynthesis, its subsequently formed chlorophyll is built up from sugars manufactured as a result of the seedling's photosynthetic activity, and from nitrogen and magnesium derived from nitrate and magnesium ions absorbed by roots from the soil. Iron also is essential to chlorophyll formation, although it is not a part of the chlorophyll molecule. When plants become yellowish as a result of deficiency of magnesium or iron or nitrogen in the soil, they are termed **chlorotic.** If plants do not receive light most of them fail to form chlorophyll. They are thus white or pale yellowish, and they show certain structural peculiarities, such as weak succulent stems and undeveloped leaves. This condition is known as **etiolation.**

Light intensity influences the rate of photosynthesis. For every plant there is a range of light intensities within which photosynthesis can proceed. Within this range an increase or decrease in light intensity results in a corresponding increase or decrease in photosynthetic rate. Furthermore, different levels of photosynthetic activity may occur in different leaves on the same plant, a condition that is at least in part related to light intensity differences; leaves at stem tips ordinarily receive more light than leaves borne lower on a branch in positions shaded by other branches and leaves.

Most chloroplasts cannot use all the light energy available from full sunlight. For instance, the photosynthetic process in many common crops—including cotton, tobacco, and soy beans—is saturated with light at approximately 30 to 50 percent of full sunlight. However, there are exceptions to this generalization: experiments indicate that, among the important crops, corn and sugarcane would be able to utilize even more light than is available from full sunlight. This partly explains their high productivity.

Water is not ordinarily a limiting factor for photosynthesis unless plants are in a period of extreme drought. So long as their tissues are turgid and water is being absorbed by roots and translocated into leaves, plants do not suffer variations in their photosynthesis as a result of minor fluctuations of water in their mesophyll cells.

Carbon dioxide makes up approximately 0.03 to 0.04 percent, or 3 to 4 parts per 10,000 parts, of air. Carbon dioxide is added to the air as a result of plant and animal respiration, of the combustion of fuels, of volcanic activity, and of rock weathering. Green plants ordinarily have abundant light, chlorophyll, and water for photosynthesis, but the supplies of CO_2 available to them are limited by the small concentration of this gas in the atmosphere. Because the speed of the photosynthetic process under conditions of abundant light and moisture is usually limited by the low concentrations of carbon dioxide available, carbon dioxide is often termed the "limiting factor" in photosynthesis. It has been shown experimentally that an increase of as much as twenty times in the normal atmospheric concentration of carbon dioxide induces a corresponding increase in the rate of photosynthesis in some plants. Several greenhouses in this country are equipped with devices to increase the carbon dioxide content of their air, for a more

rapid rate of photosynthesis results in more rapid growth and frequently in greater yields of flowers, fruits, vegetables, and other crops. Experiments have also shown that the yield of certain field crops is increased if the air around them is enriched by the addition of carbon dioxide from pipes laid in or on the ground. It should be emphasized that, although carbon dioxide is commonly the limiting factor in photosynthesis in plants growing in full sunlight and with readily available moisture, other factors may become limiting agents of this process. Thus, on the poorly illuminated floor of a forest, light, rather than CO_2, may limit the rate of photosynthesis.

Leaves as Photosynthetic Machines   The leaves of most plants are well constructed for photosynthesis. They are usually broad and thin, and light readily penetrates all cells of the mesophyll. Their epidermal layers contain numerous stomata, through which carbon dioxide diffuses into the intercellular spaces of the mesophyll. These spaces afford ready paths of diffusion of carbon dioxide to all green cells of leaves. The cuticles of leaves aid in the conservation of water, which is a raw material of photosynthesis, and in the maintenance of turgidity, which is a necessary condition for rapid and continuing photosynthesis. Furthermore, the numerous ramifications of the vein systems carry water to all cells of leaves. Finally, the numerous chloroplasts of the mesophyll cells constitute the machinery in which the manufacture of sugar occurs.

Each stoma is enclosed by a pair of guard cells (Fig. 13–11), in which turgor changes produce expansion or contraction of the cells and thus open or close the stoma. Guard cells characteristically contain chloroplasts. The inner walls of the guard cells—that is, the walls bordering on the stoma—are frequently much thicker than the outer walls—that is, those that touch on other epidermal cells. When the turgor pressure within the guard cells increases, the outer thinner walls expand more rapidly than the thick inner walls and pull the inner walls away from each other, thus opening the stoma. With a decrease in the turgor pressure, the thick inner walls straighten and move toward each other, closing the stoma. The factors responsible for turgor changes in guard cells are not fully known. An explanation of stomatal opening favored by many physiologists suggests a sequence of events beginning with illumination of the plant. The light induces photosynthesis in guard cells and, as a result, CO_2 concentrations inside the leaf drop. By an unknown mechanism, the reduced CO_2 level brings about an increase in turgor and, ultimately, stomatal opening. The stomata of most plants are usually open to the greatest extent during the day; during this time, photosynthesis proceeds actively. At night, the turgor within guard cells decreases as CO_2 levels rise, and the guard cells straighten and close the stomata. In some leaves (for example, those of potato), stomata may be open for part of the night.

THE COLORS OF LEAVES

The predominating green color of leaves is caused by the presence of the pigment chlorophyll, which is essential in food synthesis. All higher plants and some of the algae contain chlorophyll that consists of two closely related pigments, chlorophyll a ($C_{55}H_{72}O_5N_4Mg$) and chlorophyll b ($C_{55}H_{70}O_6N_4Mg$). For the sake of convenience, these two pigments are commonly referred to by the single name chlorophyll. Chlorophyll a constitutes about three fourths of the total chlorophyll of leaves and is bluish green in color. Chlorophyll b is a yellowish green. Light is a necessary factor in chlorophyll synthesis in most plants, and when seedlings of these plants are grown in darkness, they do not become green. Moreover, when healthy green plants are placed in the dark, they lose their green color and become yellowish, or etiolated. Chloroplasts contain, in addition to chlorophyll, pigments belonging to a class of compounds called the carotenoids. These pigments are generally found in the grana along with the chlorophylls. The carotenoids include a rela-

tively large group of yellowish pigments, the xanthophylls, and a much smaller group of yellowish orange ones, the carotenes. Carotenoids are usually present in relatively small quantities as compared with chlorophyll; hence, their colors are usually masked. When larger amounts of xanthophyll and carotene pigments are present, the leaves may appear yellowish green.

Chlorophyll and carotenoid pigments are insoluble in water and occur chiefly in plastids. Infrequently they may be found dispersed in the cytoplasm, but never in the cell sap. The physiological role of carotenoids in plants is poorly understood. Experiments have shown that in certain groups of plants, the carotenoid pigments in chloroplasts absorb light energy that is then contributed to the photosynthetic process. The carotenoids in chromoplasts impart bright coloration to many flowers, fruits, and seeds. Thus, they probably aid in attracting insects, birds, and other animals that are agents of pollination and seed dispersal.

The red, blue, lavender, and purple colors of various plant parts are attributable principally to water-soluble pigments known as anthocyanins. These pigments belong to a group of organic compounds called glycosides, which, upon partial decomposition, yield sugar (usually glucose) in addition to a nonsugar component. Anthocyanins are found dissolved in cell sap and are never present in plastids. These pigments occur commonly in the petals of flowers and are also frequently present in leaves (purple cabbage), roots (garden beet), fruits (grapes), and occasionally in stems. Little is known about the direct significance of these pigments in the physiology of plants. The widespread occurrence of such colored compounds in flowers indicates that they are probably important in attracting insects that are necessary for pollination.

TRANSPIRATION

Transpiration is the evaporation of water from the aerial parts of plants, especially the leaves.

This process goes on at all times, except possibly when the air is saturated with moisture during or immediately following rains. The quantities of water lost by transpiration are often very great. It has been determined that a single sunflower plant during a growing season of approximately 140 days loses about 145 pounds of water by evaporation from its aerial portions, an average daily loss of more than 1 pint of water. A single corn plant has been found to lose by transpiration over 50 gallons of water (more than 400 pounds) during its life span of 100 days. An acre of corn plants, transpiring in this same degree, evaporates into the air over 300,000 gallons (about 1200 tons!) of water in a 100-day growing season. Calculations of the quantities of water transpired by large apple trees indicate that a single, full-grown apple tree loses by evaporation as much as 1800 gallons of water in a growing season of about six months. The tremendous amounts of water vapor transpired by such extensive masses of vegetation affect air temperatures, increase the moisture content of the air, and thus influence the frequency and quantity of rainfall.

Ordinarily about 90 percent or more of the water that evaporates from leaves passes out into the air through the stomata; the remainder of the water vapor lost diffuses outward through the lenticels and the cuticle. These three types of transpiration are termed **stomatal, lenticular,** and **cuticular transpiration,** respectively. The relative amounts of water vapor lost by these methods show that stomatal transpiration is by far the most abundant and hence the most important.

The actual conversion of liquid water into water vapor does not occur at or through the stomata, for the latter are merely openings in the epidermal layer. Liquid water passes into vapor from the wet walls of the mesophyll cells at the places where such walls are exposed to the intercellular spaces. As water vapor collects in these spaces, it moves outward through the stomata into the external air, in accordance with the laws of diffusion.

Transpiration proceeds more rapidly during the day than at night. This is chiefly because the stomata of most plants are open widest during the day and also because the environmental factors that prevail during the day favor rapid evaporation of water. At night, when stomata are partially or wholly closed and when temperatures are lower than during the day, the rate of transpiration is considerably less. The nocturnal rate of evaporation from leaves is frequently from 3 to 20 percent of the daytime rate.

The principal external factors that influence the rate of transpiration in plants are light, temperature, humidity, wind velocity, and soil factors.

Transpiration is more rapid in bright light than in diffuse light or in darkness, partly because certain light rays raise the temperature of leaf cells and thus increase the rate at which liquid water is transformed into vapor, partly because bright light causes opening of stomata.

High temperatures favor more rapid transpiration not only because evaporation and diffusion occur faster in warm air but also because warm air is capable of holding more water vapor than is cold air. At moderate or low temperatures, the rate of transpiration is markedly less than it is when the temperature of the surrounding air is high.

When the external atmosphere is very humid, the evaporation of water from leaves is reduced, for the difference in water vapor concentration in the inner spaces of leaves and in the outside air is so slight that the net outward diffusion of water molecules from leaves is very slow. The rate of transpiration is roughly proportional to atmospheric humidity; thus, the drier the air, the more rapid is the rate of evaporation from leaves. It is known that plant organs, particularly leaves, become larger when they grow in humid atmosphere than in dry air. The greater the atmospheric humidity, the lower the transpiration and the greater is the amount of water retained within the plant.

Where there are no breezes, the motionless air near transpiring leaves becomes very humid and, as a result, the rate of water evaporation decreases. Moving air currents continually bring fresh, drier masses of air in contact with leaf surfaces and thus maintain a high rate of transpiration. However, the rate of transpiration is not directly proportional to wind velocity, for closure of the stomata frequently begins when the wind velocity exceeds 25 or 30 miles per hour, and thus the transpiration rate may be lowered at high velocities.

Soil temperature, the solute concentration of the soil solution, the water content of the soil, and other soil factors influence the rate of transpiration indirectly in that they affect the rate at which roots absorb water. If plants cannot absorb water readily, the rate of their transpiration is correspondingly low. If water is more easily absorbed, the transpiration rate is higher.

Other factors of importance in controlling transpiration are those inherent in the physiological and structural organization of plants. Among these internal factors regulating transpiration is stomatal behavior. Under natural conditions, even small changes in stomatal opening will change transpiration rates, and the stomata are very sensitive to changes in turgor; when turgor drops, the guard cells straighten to reduce the stomatal aperture. During periods of severe wilt stomata may be closed throughout the day as a result of low leaf turgor, even though the leaves are in bright sunlight. Under these circumstances, water loss is strongly curtailed, and the probability of survival of the tissue until water is more plentiful is enhanced.

The colloidal materials in protoplasm hold water very tenaciously, and when transpiration has proceeded for some time at a rapid rate, the water-retaining power of these colloids frequently causes a marked decrease in transpiration rate. Many desert plants, such as various species of cacti and acacias, have colloidal mucilaginous materials in large quantities in their tissues.

Structural modifications in many species of plants growing in desert soils of low water content frequently conserve water. Plants that grow in such regions and that possess structural features that reduce transpiration are termed **xerophytes** to distinguish them from **hydrophytes** (plants growing in water) and **mesophytes** (land plants growing in soils with moderate amounts of available moisture). Among the characteristic structural features that conserve water in xerophytes are: heavy layers of cutin on leaves and stems, reduced numbers of stomata, stomata sunken in cavities below the surfaces of leaves or surrounded by hairs, abundance of water-storage tissues, and reduction in size of or absence of leaves. Some xerophytes produce leaves during the rainy season and lose them as soon as dry weather begins.

The importance of transpiration to plants is a much debated question. It has been suggested that transpiration lowers the internal temperatures of leaves on hot days, since evaporation of liquids is known to exert a cooling effect. The large quantity of heat dissipated by transpiration results in considerably cooler leaf temperatures than would otherwise be the case. On bright days transpiration may lower the leaf temperature as much as 20 degrees. Even with transpirational cooling, however, a leaf in bright light usually remains several degrees above air temperature. Conversely, leaves may actually become somewhat cooler than the nighttime air, bringing about condensation of water vapor from the air and the formation of dew on their surfaces.

It has been argued by some plant physiologists that transpiration may be regarded as having a beneficial effect in plants in that it furnishes the pull in leaves that is principally responsible for the rise of sap. It should be noted, however, that if there were not such tremendous water loss from leaves, plants would not need to lift such large quantities of water into their leaves. It appears that in most plants less than 10 percent of the total water absorbed by the roots and passed through stems is actually used in photosynthesis and in the maintenance of turgor. In many tropical plants, which grow in almost constantly saturated air, transpiration is slight and sap rise is slow; yet sufficient water ascends to the leaves to maintain photosynthesis and growth.

It is sometimes stated that rapid transpiration favors a correspondingly rapid absorption of nutrient ions from soil. There is little experimental evidence in favor of such a supposition, although it is true that rapid transpiration promotes the upward movement of ions in the xylem *after* they have entered roots.

The chief disadvantage to plants of transpiration lies in the fact that it frequently causes excessive loss of water, resulting in wilting and often death. If the rate of water absorption by roots equals or exceeds that of transpiration, no wilting occurs, but if transpiration overbalances water absorption, wilting is inevitable.

Transpiration is sometimes called "unavoidable," a statement that is doubtless true, for plants have no way of preventing the escape of water vapor from the leaves when their stomata are open. It should be emphasized here that a primary role of stomata is their admission to mesophyll cells of the carbon dioxide necessary for photosynthesis. Stomata are open and admit carbon dioxide during the light hours of the day. In the intake of carbon dioxide, plants must expose wet cell walls to the air; carbon dioxide molecules become dissolved in the water of the cell walls and diffuse into the enclosed protoplasm. Simultaneous with the intake of carbon dioxide is the unavoidable escape of water molecules from the leaf cell walls and their diffusion from intercellular spaces of leaves through stomata into the outside air.

Stomata are also important for conserving water during drought. Rapid water loss under these conditions can result in death of leaf tissue if the stomata remain open. However, as water becomes unavailable to the plant, the stomata close and protect the leaf tissue against extreme desiccation.

Transpiration and Plant Cultivation Farmers, horticulturists, and others engaged in large-scale plant culture employ certain practices that control water balance. One of the commonest of these is the removal of weeds from the vicinity of cultivated plants. Weeds, like other plants, transpire and thus deplete water supplies of the soil. When weeds are removed, the water in the soil that they would have used is reserved for the use of the desired plants. Weeds are removed for other reasons as well: they shade cultivated plants and thus interfere with their photosynthetic activities; they use soil nutrients that are thus lost to crop plants; and they crowd and frequently stunt root growth of cultivated plants.

Horticulturists whitewash their greenhouses during the summer to reduce the intensity of sunlight and to lower the greenhouse temperature. They usually water the walks, floors, and walls of the greenhouses several times during hot summer days to maintain a high degree of humidity in the air. These practices result in a decrease in the rate of transpiration of plants growing in these houses.

When horticulturists propagate plants from cuttings, they remove some of the leaves before planting the cuttings or they cover them with glass jars. The reduction of leaf surface in the first case diminishes water loss from the cuttings and thus prevents wilting. The glass jars exclude air currents and maintain humid air around the cuttings, thus decreasing transpiration and at the same time allowing light to reach the leaves.

One of the major reasons for windbreaks of trees planted about fields and gardens, particularly in regions where there are dry summers and frequent winds, is to break the force of the hot winds and thus to prevent excessive transpiration from the leaves of cultivated plants growing behind the windbreaks. In addition, windbreaks offer protection against the mechanical force of strong winds.

LEAF FALL

Many plants are subjected to annual periods of drought or high water stress. In temperate zones

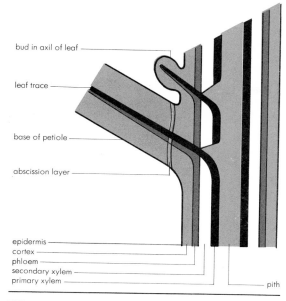

bud in axil of leaf ⎯

leaf trace ⎯

base of petiole ⎯

abscission layer ⎯

epidermis ⎯
cortex ⎯
phloem ⎯
secondary xylem ⎯
primary xylem ⎯

⎯ pith

FIG. 14-6. Portion of twig and petiole, showing position of abscission layer.

this period is during the winter when air humidity is low and much of the water is frozen and unavailable for plant use. Woody plants often survive such drought periods by losing their leaves, thus greatly reducing their transpirational surfaces. Such plants are termed **deciduous.** The leaves of deciduous plants fall off the branches at the end of their growing season, as contrasted with those of **evergreens,** in which the leaves persist for several seasons, often for two years or longer. Evergreens do not retain the same leaves always, but shed them gradually. They do not annually lose their leaves because they are specially modified for water retention. Leaf fall, technically termed **leaf abscission,** involves more than the physical separation of a leaf from a branch; it includes complex structural and physiological changes that, in effect, prepare the plant in advance for this event. Prior to actual leaf drop, a **separation,** or **abscission, layer** is formed across the base of the petiole in a region called the **abscission zone** (Fig. 14-6). This layer is only a few cells thick and is characterized by structural

weakness attributable, in part, to chemical alteration of cell walls and intercellular material. A somewhat thicker **protective layer** is formed by deposition of suberin and other substances in intercellular spaces and walls of cells situated beneath the separation layer. The factors responsible for these changes are not completely understood. Evidence indicates that the **photoperiod,** or relative duration of night and day, to which plants are exposed is a major factor in the initiation of abscission. A decrease in production of auxins (a kind of growth-regulating substance) in leaves is also believed to promote abscission. The existence of a special abscission hormone has recently been proposed; since then, two investigators have succeeded in isolating from cotton burs a hormone (**dormin,** or **abscisin**) that has accelerated abscission in experimental plants. A decrease in available soil moisture is another factor involved in leaf abscission in some species, as, for example, in many tropical regions where there is marked alternation between wet and dry seasons and in temperate zones in periods of serious drought.

The separation layer begins to disintegrate shortly after its formation, as a result of the separation or the dissolution of its cells, or both. Disintegration continues until the leaf is held to the stem merely by the vascular bundles of the petiole. With the repeated swaying caused by winds and also as a result of frost action, the vascular bundles break and the leaf falls. In woody plants, the protective layer is later replaced by periderm that forms beneath it. It should be emphasized that frost is not a factor that initiates the formation of a separation layer; the differentiation of this layer commonly precedes the first frosts of autumn and occurs in tropical regions where there is no frost.

When abscission and protective layers form, tyloses may grow in the vascular bundles and impede the conduction of materials into and away from leaf blades. Through such interference with the translocation of nitrogen, magnesium, iron, and other substances into leaves, chlorophyll synthesis is retarded. It is believed by some plant physiologists that bright light causes the decomposition of chlorophyll in leaves and that the decrease in movement of the above-mentioned elements into leaves prevents the synthesis of new chlorophyll in place of that destroyed by light. This explanation is scarcely tenable, however, since there is no clear evidence that light destroys chlorophyll in living leaf cells. At present, all that we can justifiably say is that in late summer and autumn, certain factors, not thoroughly understood, cause leaf chlorophyll to decompose more rapidly than carotene and xanthophyll; the latter pigments, persisting longer than chlorophyll, and freed from the masking effect of the more abundant chlorophyll, become apparent, causing leaves to exhibit yellowish and golden colors.

The flaming red and purple colors characteristic of the autumn leaves of sumacs, hard maples, sweet gums, and numerous other species of plants are attributable to the formation of anthocyanins not previously present in the leaves, probably as a result of the accumulation of certain waste products. The details of the development of these pigments are not known, but their appearance is correlated with the presence of considerable quantities of sugars in leaves. Light seems to promote the formation of these red pigments, as do also very sudden drops in temperature. If the main vein of a leaf is severed in early autumn, the portion of the blade beyond the cut becomes a deeper red than other portions of the leaf, for the disjunction of the vein prevents or retards sugars from leaving this part of the leaf and thus promotes anthocyanin formation. The sudden decrease in temperature usually accompanying frost inhibits the removal of sugars and often deepens the colors of the anthocyanins in leaves, but the frequent appearance of yellow, orange, and red colors *before* the first frost indicates that frost is not essential to the development of these hues.

With the death of all the cells of leaves, these pigments decompose and leaves become brown.

SUMMARY

1. Photosynthesis is the fundamental process of food manufacture by green plants. Without photosynthesis, life as we know it would not be possible.

2. Photosynthesis involves trapping of light energy and incorporation of a portion of this energy into food substances manufactured from simple chemicals available to the plant.

3. The fundamental food product of photosynthesis is glucose ($C_6H_{12}O_6$), made from carbon dioxide (CO_2) and water (H_2O).

4. An important second product given off as a "waste" material from the photosynthesis process is oxygen (O_2). All the oxygen in the earth's atmosphere has been accumulated in this way.

5. Photosynthesis takes place principally in the chloroplasts of the leaf mesophyll cells. It is made possible by the energy trapping abilities of the green pigment chlorophyll found on the grana lamellae of the chloroplasts.

6. The process of photosynthesis can be divided into two phases:
   a. The light reactions, so-called because the reactions involved are light dependent and uninfluenced by temperature under normal conditions. During the light phase, water is split by photolysis to provide the high-energy [H] particles used to reduce carbon

dioxide during glucose production, oxygen gas is evolved as a by-product, and the energy substance, ATP, is formed.

b.   The dark reactions, so-called because they do not require continued input of light energy. During the dark reactions glucose is formed in a complex cycle of reactions, and water is given off as a by-product.

7.   Factors which influence photosynthesis include the chlorophyll content of leaves, the intensity of light striking the leaves, and the availability of water and carbon dioxide.

8.   Chlorophyll is normally not synthesized without light. Plants grown in the dark are typically yellow or whitish (chlorotic), spindly, and succulent (etiolated).

9.   Light intensity requirements vary from plant to plant. For most species the photosynthetic process becomes light saturated at approximately one half full sunlight.

10.   Carbon dioxide is the common limiting factor under normal, favorable conditions for photosynthesis. This substance comprises only approximately 0.03 to 0.04 percent of air, and if additional amounts are supplied, the photosynthetic abilities of most plants are enhanced.

11.   The design and cellular organization of leaves is well suited to the process of photosynthesis. This statement applies to leaf shape, venation, mesophyll structure, and guard cell operation.

12.   Transpiration is the evaporation of water from the aerial parts of plants; it occurs principally through stomata but also involves water loss from lenticels and from the cuticle.

13.   Transpiration is normally increased by bright light, high temperatures, low relative humidity, increased wind velocity, and plentiful supplies of available water in the soil.

14.   Plants which live in arid habitats, xerophytes, often show several modifications for water retention (reduction of transpirational water loss). These include reduction in size or absence of leaves, thick cuticles, reduced numbers of stomata, sunken stomata, an abundance of surface hairs, and an abundance of water-storage tissues.

15.   It appears probable that the large amounts of water lost from most plants by means of transpiration is largely unavoidable; the necessity for openings into leaves to facilitate carbon dioxide exchange for photosynthesis also permits diffusion of water vapor from the intercellular spaces of the mesophyll into the surrounding atmosphere.

16.   Many plants lose their leaves during annual periods of intense water stress or drought; in temperate regions this period is during the winter. Such plants are termed deciduous.

17.   Leaves are lost in the process of leaf fall, or leaf abscission.

18.   The abscission zone at the base of the petiole includes a structurally weakened separation layer through which actual physical separation of the leaf occurs; this layer is underlain (on the stem side) by a protective layer of scar tissue or periderm that seals the portion of stem exposed after abscission.

19. Activation of the abscission zone is accomplished by growth-regulating substances and is controlled in temperate regions by changes in length of the photoperiod.

20. With the approach of abscission in the autumn, the amount of leaf chlorophyll diminishes, allowing the red and gold pigments present in the blade to be seen.

SUGGESTED READINGS FOR INTERESTED STUDENTS

1. Arnon, D. I., "The role of light in photosynthesis." *Scientific American,* Vol. 203, No. 5, pp. 104–118, Nov. 1960.

2. Bassham, J. A., "The path of carbon in photosynthesis." *Scientific American,* Vol. 206, No. 6, pp. 88–100, June 1962.

3. Galston, A. W., *The Life of the Green Plant,* 2d ed. Prentice-Hall, Englewoods Cliffs, N.J., 1961.

4. Leopold, A. C., *Plant Growth and Development.* McGraw-Hill, New York, 1964.

5. Rabinowitch, E. I., and Govindjee. "The role of chlorophyll in photosynthesis." *Scientific American,* Vol. 213, No. 1, pp. 74–83, July 1965.

6. Ray, P. M., *The Living Plant,* 2d ed. Holt, Rinehart and Winston, New York, 1972.

7. Rosenberg, J. L., *Photosynthesis.* Holt, Rinehart and Winston, New York, 1965.

TOPICS AND QUESTIONS FOR STUDY

1. What is the dual function performed by photosynthesis?

2. What is the humus theory? What is its present status?

3. What conditions must be present in a plant and in its environment in order for photosynthesis to occur?

4. What are the raw materials of photosynthesis? What are its products?

5. State a simple, balanced chemical equation that indicates the raw materials and products of photosynthesis.

6. Distinguish between a light and a dark reaction.

7. Why is chlorophyll green?

8. What light rays are most effectively absorbed by chlorophyll?

9. Describe two ways in which photosynthesis is essential to the animal kingdom.

10. List several ways in which the carbohydrates formed in photosynthesis are utilized by plants.

11. What is a "limiting factor" in any physiological process? What is usually the limiting factor in photosynthesis? How would you demonstrate this experimentally?

12. Do other factors ever become limiting factors in photosynthesis? Name some of these potentially limiting factors, and describe the conditions under which they may become limiting.

13. What is the usual concentration of carbon dioxide in the atmosphere?

14. Would you expect the carbon dioxide concentration of the soil air to be greater or lower than that of the air above the soil? Explain.

15. What process accounts for the movement of carbon dioxide into leaves? Explain.

16. Describe briefly the structure and operation of guard cells.

17. What is the source of the water used in photosynthesis? How does it reach leaves?

18. Perennial weeds, such as dandelions, may be killed by repeatedly cutting off their leaves before the leaves enlarge. Explain.

19. Distinguish between chlorosis and etiolation.

20. Explain this statement: "Most of our machines and engines are powered by photosynthesis." Can you think of any machines that are not powered by photosynthesis? Explain.

21. Define transpiration.

22. Where in a leaf does water evaporation occur?

23. List the principal environmental conditions that influence transpiration, and describe how they affect this process.

24. What is the relation of stomata to transpiration? Is the major function of stomata and guard cells to control transpiration? Explain.

25. Distinguish among hydrophytes, mesophytes, and xerophytes.

26. Describe some of the precautions that are taken to reduce transpiration in the cultivation of plants.

27. If you were to plant a rootless cutting in soil, would it be better to cover the cutting with a glass jar or a tin can? Explain.

28. Distinguish between transpiration and guttation.

29. Distinguish between deciduous and evergreen plants.

30. Describe briefly the causes of leaf fall. To what extent does frost influence leaf fall? Explain.

31. Name the principal leaf pigments and describe their colors. Which of these pigments occur in flowers or other plant parts?

32. Explain briefly the causes of the familiar autumnal coloration of leaves. To what extent does frost influence this coloration?

15

METABOLIC ACTIVITIES OF CELLS

Protoplasm is a mixture of hundreds or thousands of chemical substances interacting in highly intricate and coordinated ways. Some of the chemical reactions of living protoplasm are relatively simple and can easily be duplicated in the laboratory whereas others are exceedingly complex and organized in long series of interdependent, enzyme-mediated events which can only be duplicated outside the cell with great difficulty. An example of such a series is the process of photosynthesis discussed in the preceding chapter.

The total of all the chemical reactions involved in the physiological activities of living organisms is termed **metabolism.** By means of certain metabolic processes organisms accumulate organic substances from which they obtain energy, or materials to produce, maintain, and repair cells; these organic substances are called **foods.** The basic food, glucose, is synthesized during photosynthesis. Glucose can be used to synthesize other foods and nonfood molecules needed for structural purposes and can also be broken down in the process of **respiration** to yield energy. Photosynthesis and respiration are complementary metabolic processes; the former transforms radiant energy to chemical energy and stores it in the structure of certain molecules; the latter releases this energy to drive reactions needed to sustain life. Some metabolic activities result in the synthesis and elaboration of additional or more complex substances. Other metabolic activities result in degradation of complex substances to simpler forms which may be required for other processes or which may be waste products. Photosynthesis and respiration are, respectively, special synthetic and degradative activities which, because of their importance, are usually considered separately from other metabolic processes. In this chapter we shall deal principally with respiration and food utilization.

RESPIRATION

Respiration is probably the most fundamental life process. It is analogous to combustion of fuel in an automobile engine in which fuel is explosively combined with oxygen to release energy—combustion transforms the energy stored in fuel to energy that drives the engine and results in motion. Like fuel combustion, respiration is essentially a process of oxidation, but it differs in being relatively slow and occurring at a much lower temperature.

Respiration by plants and animals that live in air usually involves removal of oxygen from air, and the combination of this oxygen with the carbon, hydrogen, and oxygen of the food molecules being respired produces carbon dioxide and water. The more easily measured aspects of this process are consumption of oxygen and release of carbon dioxide. Because these processes are ordinarily associated in animals and man with inhalation and exhalation, respiration is frequently used synonomously with "breathing" (for instance, as in "artificial respiration"). However, respiration is a process which goes on within *all* living, functioning cells. The central characteristic of respiration is oxidative chemical reactions, not the associated exchange of oxygen and carbon dioxide between the cell and the atmosphere.

Respiratory processes vary somewhat in different kinds of plants, but all types of respiration have certain common attributes: the chemical breakdown of foods and certain other substances involved in respiration, the incorporation of some of the energy released during respiration into the energy-rich substance **adenosine triphosphate, ATP,** and, usually, the production of carbon dioxide. ATP is made by combination of phosphate and the precursor substance adenosine diphosphate, ADP. The energy of ATP is a property of the bonds binding the phosphate portions to the molecule. Transfer of phosphates from ATP to other substances in the process of *phosphorylation* transfers these energy characteristics to those substances. Phosphorylation permits the receiver molecules to readily undergo reactions or transformations which would otherwise have been improbable or slow. In giving up its terminal phosphate group in phosphorylation of another molecule, ATP is converted to ADP, which may serve again as one of the precursors in ATP formation.

Respiration that involves utilization of atmospheric oxygen is termed **aerobic respiration.** However, some cells carry on a type of respiration that involves only the removal of hydrogen from foods. This hydrogen is subsequently attached to some substance other than oxygen for removal from the cell; such nonoxygen-requiring respiration is termed **anaerobic respiration** or **fermentation.** The processes of anaerobic and aerobic respiration are summarized in Fig. 15–1 and 15–2.

Both aerobic and anaerobic respiration involve the breakdown of the simple sugar glucose ($C_6H_{12}O_6$), or some glucose product, into smaller molecules containing fewer carbon atoms. In aerobic respiration the carbon atoms are ultimately released singly in carbon dioxide (CO_2), whereas in anaerobic respiration some of the carbon atoms of glucose are released in larger molecules, typically ethyl alcohol (C_2H_5OH), or sometimes other substances such as lactic acid. In both aerobic and anaerobic respiration, however, the initial chemical changes are the same. By means of these reactions, glucose is split into

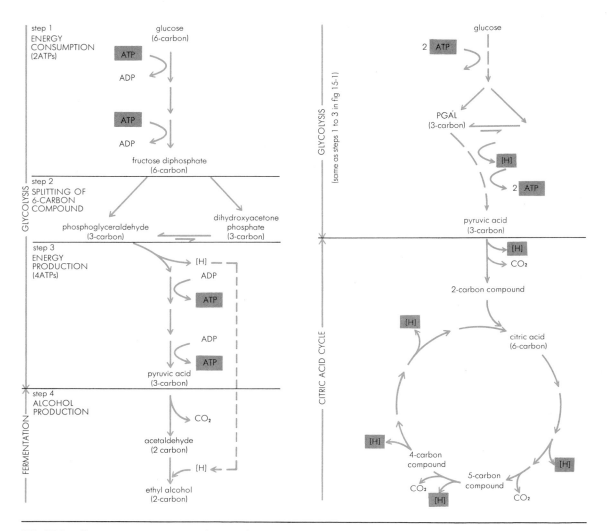

FIG. 15–1. Diagrammatic summary of anaerobic respiration. Note that glycolysis has a *net* yield of 2 ATPs because step 3 occurs twice for each 6-carbon sugar metabolized. Since no oxygen is available for the reaction, [H] is used in alcohol production. FIG. 15–2. Diagrammatic summary of aerobic respiration. The citric acid cycle occurs twice for each 6-carbon sugar compound metabolized. Since oxygen is available, [H] may be taken to represent energy made available as ATP during oxidative phosphorylation of the [H] to produce ATP and H_2O.

two 3-carbon molecules of pyruvic acid. This phase of respiration is termed **glycolysis,** from the Greek meaning "to split sugar." During initial phases of glycolysis, two ATP molecules are used to phosphorylate glucose (Fig. 15–1). Later in glycolysis two ATP molecules are produced for *each*

of the 3-carbon derivatives. Thus, during glycolysis, 2 ATPs are utilized and 4 ATPs are produced, giving a net yield of 2 ATP molecules for each glucose molecule which enters the process. Also during the later stages, hydrogen atoms are removed (shown as [H] in Fig. 15–1). If respiration is completed without available oxygen to form ethyl alcohol, the hydrogen is attached to an intermediate compound (acetaldehyde), after which this material is expelled from the cell, and anaerobic respiration is complete.

If oxygen is available, the pyruvic acid is completely oxidized to carbon dioxide and water (Fig. 15–2). In this series of oxygen-requiring reactions, 1 molecule of carbon dioxide is removed from the pyruvic acid, and the 2-carbon residue is combined with a 4-carbon acid present in the cell to form the 6-carbon citric acid. The net result of the subsequent reaction is that the carbon, hydrogen, and oxygen of this 2-carbon material are gradually removed, and the 4-carbon acid needed to repeat the cycle is reconstituted. Because citric acid is the first substance formed in this postglycolysis phase of aerobic respiration, the cyclic series of reactions is often termed the **citric-acid cycle.**

The hydrogen atoms removed from pyruvic acid in the citric-acid cycle are transferred to a series of pigments called **cytochromes** and are passed from pigment to pigment. At three steps in this series, energy is released to phosphorylate ADP to form ATP in the process of **oxidative phosphorylation** (Fig. 15–3). The hydrogen is eventually combined with oxygen from the atmosphere to form water. Since 6 [H] are produced from both 3-carbon compounds derived from glucose, oxidative phosphorylation results in the production of 36 ATPs; this is in addition to the 2 molecules of ATP formed during glycolysis. Thus, nineteen

times as much ATP energy is made available to the cell by means of aerobic respiration as by anaerobic respiration. The energy for these reactions is contained in [H]. Sunlight provides energy to split [H] from water and incorporate it into glucose; respiration releases the [H] and its energy and results in incorporation of the energy into ATP.

The sites of cellular respiration are the mitochondria that are found suspended in the protoplasm. It is believed that glycolysis occurs outside the mitochondrion and that the series of reactions in the citric-acid cycle takes place within. Oxidative phosphorylation to produce ATP is thought to take place on the surface of the cristae, the interior projections of the mitochondrial membrane system (Fig. 4–2). To complete the process it is necessary for some of the materials to move into and out of the mitochondria.

In aerobic respiration, the summary equation for the chemical changes that occur may be written:

$$C_6H_{12}O_6 + 6O_2 \rightarrow 6CO_2 + 6H_2O + \text{energy}$$

(glucose)   (oxygen)   (carbon dioxide)   (water)

Thus, aerobic respiration is essentially the reverse of the process of photosynthesis, although the chemical pathways involved are quite different. The two processes are compared on p. 204.

The gaseous exchange between green plants and the external atmosphere during the day is different from such exchange at night. During the day, both photosynthesis and respiration occur in leaves. Photosynthesis uses carbon dioxide and releases oxygen whereas respiration uses oxygen and releases carbon dioxide. Photosynthesis proceeds more rapidly, however, than respiration, so that the carbon dioxide produced in respiration is immediately used in green tissues in photosynthesis. The oxygen released in photosynthesis is in excess of that used by respiration, so a part of this oxygen escapes into the outer air. Thus, during the day, green plants give off oxygen

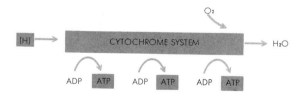

FIG. 15–3.   The general scheme of oxidative phosphorylation by which three ATPs are formed from each [H] in aerobic respiration. All of the [H] produced in Fig. 15–2 passes through this set of reactions.

PHOTOSYNTHESIS	RESPIRATION
1. Absorbs water and carbon dioxide	1. Releases water and carbon dioxide
2. Liberates oxygen	2. Absorbs oxygen
3. Makes sugar (and other compounds)	3. Breaks down sugar (and other compounds)
4. Increases dry weight of tissues	4. Decreases dry weight of tissues
5. Stores energy in foods	5. Releases energy from foods
6. Proceeds in green cells only	6. Proceeds in all living cells
7. Proceeds only in light	7. Proceeds in light or darkness

and take in carbon dioxide. This makes it appear as though only photosynthesis were going on, for the gaseous exchange during the day is the characteristic gaseous exchange of photosynthesis. At night, photosynthesis ceases and respiration continues. Thus, at night, green plants give off carbon dioxide and take in oxygen, a condition which seems to be exactly the reverse of that during the day.

Some of the glucose produced during the day is stored in various forms within the plants, or it is used to manufacture wall material and other substances which are not immediately respired to maintain the life of the cell at night. Some of these stored foods can be utilized by nonphotosynthetic organisms, such as man, and the oxygen in the atmosphere originally released during photosynthesis can be used to oxidize them. In a manner of speaking, the respiration which makes life possible for man and other nonphotosynthetic organisms is simply delayed respiration of photosynthetic products synthesized by plants.

Some of the energy of respiration is released in the form of heat energy, even by plants, and this heat is often measurable. In the growth of flower clusters of certain tropical plants called aroids and in masses of sprouting seeds, temperatures are occasionally as much as 80°F higher than those of the outside air. Respiration proceeding rapidly in a poorly ventilated space may generate sufficient heat to cause fire. For exam-

ple, if moist hay is stored in a tightly walled barn loft, the respiration of living hay cells and of the bacteria and molds that grow on the hay may develop enough heat to cause the hay to burst into flame. Frequently the burning of barns is attributable to this "spontaneous combustion."

Relation of Aerobic to Anaerobic Respiration Anaerobic respiration releases less energy from the same quantity of sugar than does aerobic respiration because one of its products is incompletely oxidized. In sufficiently high concentrations, the organic substances resulting from anaerobic respiration are often toxic to the organisms that produced them. Yeast plants may produce alcohol to a concentration of 12 to 16 percent before their growth is inhibited. One of the factors that restricts the growth and reproduction of many bacteria is accumulation of the toxic products of their anaerobic respiration.

The most familiar example of anaerobic respiration is **alcoholic fermentation** of sugars by yeasts, which are minute one-celled fungi. Yeasts derive their energy from the anaerobic respiration of sugars, releasing carbon dioxide and ethyl alcohol in the process. Even in the presence of free oxygen, yeasts continue to produce alcohol; that is, they are unable to complete a process of aerobic respiration because they lack certain enzymes essential to aerobic respiration. In the presence of free oxygen and the alcohol produced by yeasts, certain bacteria will utilize the ethyl alcohol as an energy-yielding food, oxidizing the alcohol to acetic acid. These bacteria, often present on the skins of grapes and other fruits, convert wines (fermented fruit juices) to vinegar.

Anaerobic respiration is apparently of general occurrence in living cells. In many lower organisms, such as yeasts and some bacteria, anaerobic respiration is the only type of respiration normally carried on, and these organisms, called **anaerobes,** commonly live only in the absence of free oxygen. Most higher plants, if deprived of oxygen, will respire anaerobically for a time. When higher plants are deprived of oxygen for a few hours, their tissues develop small amounts of some of the intermediate products (for example, acetaldehyde) of anaerobic respiration. Also, when seedlings in air are given fermented sugar solutions, their respiration rate increases, indicating that they can respire products of alcoholic fermentation. However, although higher plants may respire anaerobically, they can live normally only in the presence of oxygen. If such plants are kept in oxygen-free atmosphere for more than two or three days, they begin to show growth abnormalities as a result of the accumulation of toxic products of their anaerobic respiration. Corn seedlings, for example, under anaerobic conditions for so short a time as 48 hours, suffer severe injury. One effect of the waterlogging of soil is the accumulation in and around roots of toxic products of anaerobic respiration. Some investigators have reported traces of alcohol in soil water around plant roots under anaerobic conditions.

Anaerobic respiration is important to man in many ways. The manufacture of industrial alcohols, alcoholic beverages and vinegar, the spoilage of many types of foods, the manufacture of cheese and other dairy products and of sauerkraut, and the preparation of ensilage (fermented green plant material, such as chopped cornstalks and leaves) in silos are the results of processes of anaerobic respiration by microorganisms. Much of the decomposition of dead plant and animal bodies in soil and water and of their waste products is attributable to the anaerobic respiration of these materials by certain anaerobic bacteria and fungi. These anaerobic organisms produce certain organic compounds as their respiratory products and, in so doing, obtain energy necessary for their life processes. Aerobic soil organisms may then respire the organic products of anaerobic organisms, thereby obtaining energy in the process and forming water and carbon dioxide as their respiratory products. The processes of decomposition result in the ultimate restoration to the soil and air of the simple substances that constitute the organic compounds of plant and animal bodies and are thus important in maintaining soil fertility.

THE USE OF RADIOACTIVE ELEMENTS AND HEAVY ISOTOPES IN THE STUDY OF METABOLISM

In addition to its common form, a chemical element may occur in forms having similar chemical properties but different atomic weights. For example, the common form of oxygen has an atomic weight of 16 and accounts for about 99.7 percent of oxygen atoms. In addition to O^{16}, there are two naturally occurring heavier forms (O^{17} and O^{18}) and three artificially synthesized forms (O^{14}, O^{15}, and O^{19}). These heavier and lighter forms are called **isotopes.** Artificial isotopes tend to be highly unstable; in their spontaneous transformation to more stable forms, they emit radiant energy and are spoken of as **radioactive.** Most of the naturally occurring isotopes are either stable or only slightly radioactive.

A widely used technique of studying plant nutrition and other phases of metabolism is the use of radioactive isotopes of certain chemical elements. In some suitable form these are placed in the medium in which roots grow or are otherwise introduced into plant bodies. The subsequent movement and physiological behavior of radioactive compounds in plant tissues may be studied by photographic methods or by the use of a Geiger-Muller counter or some similar device

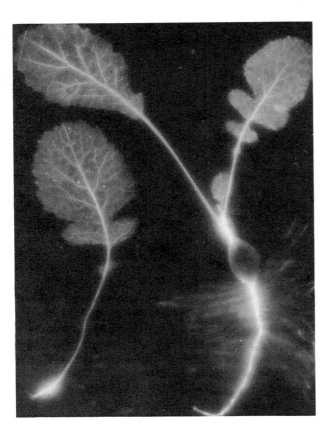

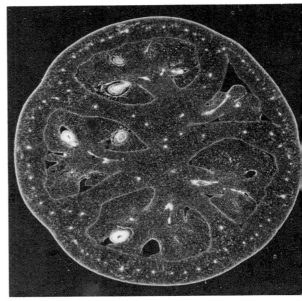

FIG. 15–4. Autoradiographs showing accumulation of radioactive material in radish plant (*left*) and tomato fruit (*right*). (Courtesy American Smelting and Refining Co.)

for measuring radioactivity. Radioactive isotopes of carbon, hydrogen, phosphorus, sulfur, and other elements have been used in investigations of absorption, translocation, photosynthesis, and other activities and have produced much information about these phenomena. The use of radioactive elements has demonstrated the rapid exchange of potassium and phosphorus by living cells during absorption, a phenomenon that was unknown before the use of these "tracer" elements (Fig. 15–4).

Nonradioactive isotopes also are used in the attack on physiological problems. For example, a study of photosynthesis involving the use of water containing the heavy oxygen isotope, O^{18}, showed that all the oxygen liberated in this process comes from water and that the oxygen that enters into carbohydrates is derived from CO_2.

FOODS AND FOOD SYNTHESES

The word "food" is frequently used to designate all types of substances that enter the bodies of living organisms and that are used by them. In this sense, "food" is commonly used by florists, horticulturists, and farmers to refer to the inorganic materials absorbed by plants from soil. Most botanists prefer a more restricted use of the word food—to refer, namely, to those organic compounds synthesized by living plants and used to supply energy and to construct and repair living tissues. In terms of this more limited definition, nutrient ions, water, and carbon dioxide absorbed from the soil and air by plants are not foods but are the raw materials from which green plants synthesize three kinds of foods: **carbohydrates, fats,** and **proteins.**

Carbohydrates   Carbohydrates are always composed of carbon, hydrogen, and oxygen, with the hydrogen and oxygen in the same proportion (2 to 1) as they are in water. Most carbohydrates in plants contain in their molecules 6 carbon atoms or some multiple of 6: common carbohydrates in plants are glucose, or grape sugar ($C_6H_{12}O_6$); fructose, or fruit sugar ($C_6H_{12}O_6$); sucrose, or cane sugar ($C_{12}H_{22}O_{11}$): maltose, or malt sugar ($C_{12}H_{22}O_{11}$); and starch and cellulose, both with the basic formula ($C_6H_{10}O_5)_n$. The fact that different carbohydrates (for example, glucose and fructose) may have the same chemical formula means that the differences between them are attributable to differences in the *arrangement* of their constituent atoms, *not* to differences in the kinds or number of their atoms. Many carbohydrates, such as sugars, are soluble in water, can be moved readily from one part of a plant to another, and influence the osmotic properties of the cell fluids in which they are dissolved. Starch, however, is insoluble in water, cannot be translocated in plants unless first converted into sugars, and has no influence on osmotic potentials. Starch is the commonest reserve carbohydrate in plants and is found stored as small, colorless starch grains in large amounts in the cells of fruits such as bananas, in the cells of seeds such as corn and wheat, and in the cells of various types of roots (carrots) and stems (potato tubers) (Fig. 15–5). Sugars are also stored in considerable quantities in the tissues of certain plants, as in sugar cane, sugar beet, and sugar maple. The chief uses of carbohydrates in plants are: to supply energy, to furnish materials from which other organic substances, especially fats and proteins, are made, and to build the structural framework of plants (cellulose).

Fats Fats and oils are similar to carbohydrates in that they are composed of the same chemical elements: carbon, hydrogen, and oxygen. The arrangement of the atoms of these substances in fat molecules differs markedly from that in carbohydrate molecules, and the proportion of hydrogen to oxygen in fats is much higher than the 2-to-1 ratio of carbohydrates. The

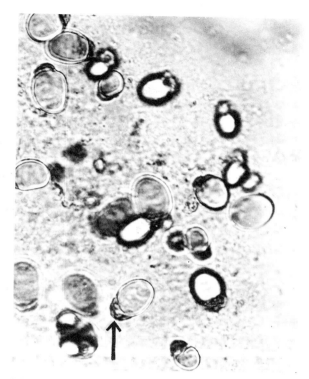

FIG. 15–5. Starch grains forming in chloroplasts of the stem of *Pellionia*. The arrow indicates a chloroplast.

chemical formulas of two plant fats, stearin and palmitin, are respectively $C_3H_5(CO_2C_{17}H_{35})_3$ and $C_3H_5(CO_2C_{15}H_{31})_3$. From these formulas can be seen the relatively small proportion of oxygen in these substances. It is largely because of this low percentage of oxygen that fats are able to provide about twice as much energy as sugars, weight for weight; that is, fats can be oxidized to a greater extent. In plants, fatty substances occur most frequently as oils; that is, they are liquid at ordinary temperatures. All fats and oils are insoluble in water. Fats are chiefly reserve foods that are stored in various plant structures, especially seeds (peanut, coconut, and castor bean) and fruits (banana, avocado, and paw-paw). When these reserve foods are about to be utilized, they may be converted into sugars. Certain complex fatty compounds are constituents of living protoplasm,

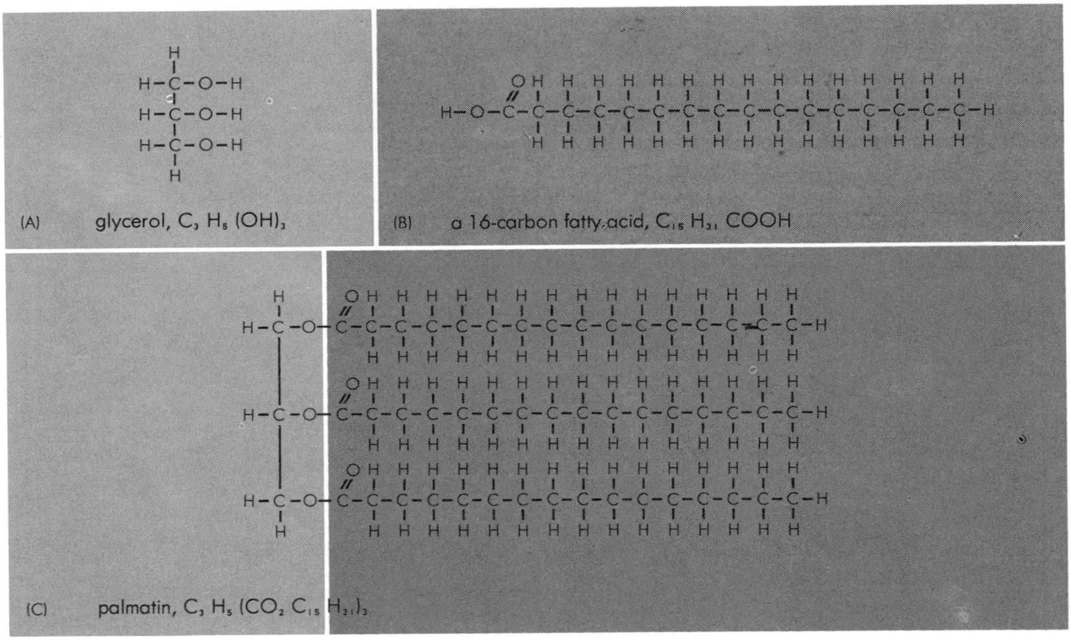

FIG. 15-6. Structural formulae of A, glycerol; B, a fatty acid; and C, the plant fat palmatin.

particularly of cytoplasmic membranes, and are thus important in membrane permeability and absorption phenomena.

Fats are produced by uniting glycerol (glycerine) and fatty acids (Fig. 15–6), both of which are substances derived from sugar precursors. When they are to be utilized in living cells, their molecules are broken down into the constituent fatty acids and glycerols prior to entry into the respiration processes. Carbohydrates and fats can be interconverted, and the fat and carbohydrate contents of plant tissues are often inversely related. Thus, in the maturation of many kinds of seeds, the carbohydrates decrease in quantity as the fats simultaneously increase. Conversely, in the germination of many seeds, the fatty foods decrease in quantity as the carbohydrates increase.

Proteins   Proteins are the most complex organic substances in living organisms. Their molecules are exceedingly large, as is shown by two plant proteins, **zein** from corn and **gliadin** from wheat, the formulas of which are respectively $C_{736}H_{1161}N_{184}O_{208}S_3$ and $C_{685}H_{1068}N_{196}O_{211}S_5$. The molecular weights of some proteins approximate 500,000 as compared, for example, with 342 for sucrose and 180 for glucose. Proteins, like fats, are made from carbohydrates and thus always contain carbon, hydrogen, and oxygen, as do carbohydrates. In addition to these chemical elements, proteins always contain nitrogen and frequently also contain sulfur or phosphorus or both. The nitrogen, phosphorus, and sulfur in proteins are derived chiefly from nitrate, phosphate, and sulfate ions absorbed from the soil.

In the synthesis of proteins, the carbon, hydrogen, and oxygen derived from carbohydrates are combined in complex chemical reactions with nitrogen to form **amino acids,** which may be regarded as the building blocks from which protein molecules are constructed. As shown in Fig.

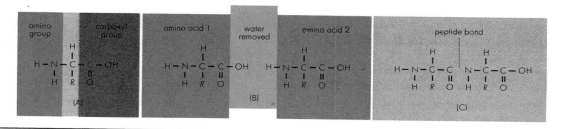

FIG. 15-7. A. A diagrammatic representation of an amino acid. B. and C. Union of two amino acids through formation of a peptide bond with concomitant loss of a molecule of water.

15-7A, an amino acid has two chemically reactive **functional groups:** a carboxyl, or acid, group (COOH), and an amino, or basic, group (NH$_2$). It has, in addition, a characteristic side group (R) that is different in each of the twenty-odd amino acids isolated from plant tissues. For example, in the simplest amino acid (glycine), R represents a single hydrogen atom; in another (alanine), it represents CH$_3$. Plants are able to synthesize all the amino acids required in their metabolism. From these compounds, the hundreds of proteins occurring in the plant are synthesized as a result of the chemical linkage of amino acid molecules with other amino acid molecules. The union of two amino acids, a process involving the removal of a molecule of water and the formation of what is termed a peptide bond, is schematically outlined in Figs. 15-7B and 15-17C. Proteins consist of many amino acids joined to form chains and are characterized in large part by the kind, number, sequence, and spatial relationships of these amino acid components.

Proteins form the fundamental structure of protoplasm and thus are found in all living cells. Many proteins are stored as reserve foods in plant cells, usually in the form of distinct bodies called **aleurone grains.** Aleurone grains are especially abundant in certain cells of grains, such as corn and wheat. Reserve proteins occur in large concentrations in many other types of seeds, such as beans, peas, and soybeans. The proteins stored in seeds are used chiefly in the formation of protoplasm in new cells when seeds germinate. The chief function of proteins is the construction

and repair of protoplasm. Proteins may also be used as sources of energy, but such utilization ordinarily occurs only after available carbohydrate and fat reserves have been exhausted.

As discussed in an earlier chapter, many of the proteins of protoplasm function as enzymes. Enzymes are organic catalysts which influence the rates at which certain chemical reactions occur; as such they mediate many cellular activities and many metabolic processes. Often the products of a reaction catalyzed by one enzyme become the reactants for reactions mediated by other enzymes. Usually the various steps in processes discussed in this and other chapters—such as photosynthesis, respiration, and ATP formation—are promoted by enzymes. Because of the many hundreds of such reactions and the specificities of particular enzymes for particular reactions, many hundreds or thousands of enzymes may be functioning simultaneously in an active cell. Some enzymes can function appropriately only when they are associated with a nonproteinaceous **coenzyme.** Inorganic materials such as copper and iron, and organic compounds such as vitamins are known to function as coenzymes. Another characteristic of enzymes is their sensitivity to heat. Many of them are weakened or inactivated at temperatures of 70°C (158°F), and most of them are quickly destroyed by temperatures near the boiling point of water 100°C.

Enzymes, chiefly those from plants, are important in many industrial processes; in some of these living tissues are employed, in others the enzymes are extracted from the living cells and are then allowed to act on certain substances of economic significance. The following partial list of uses made of enzymes attests to their great economic value: the preparation of sizing for textiles and paper; the removal (retting) of fibers from the stems of flax, hemp, and other plants; the degumming of silk; the preparation of skins for tanning; the brewing and clarification of beer; the clarification of syrups and pectin solutions; the making of bread; cheese manufacture; the production of syrup from sweet potatoes and corn; the manufacture of soy sauce; the fermentation of pulp to remove it from cocoa seeds; the preparation of medicinal diastase and pepsin for human digestive disturbances; and the manufacture of infant foods. In the brewing of beer, barley grains (or other types of cereal grains) are most commonly used as a source of carbohydrates. The grains are soaked in warm water and germinated. During this sprouting, the amylase in the grains becomes active and converts the stored starch into maltose, a sugar that is readily acted upon by yeasts and converted into alcohol. Sprouted barley is known in the brewing industry as malt. A protease enzyme, papain, from leaves and fruits of the tropical papaya is used to tenderize meats because the enzyme digests some of the meat proteins. Papain is sometimes used medicinally for patients whose own proteases show diminished activity.

ORGANIC COMPOUNDS OTHER THAN FOODS

Plants produce, in addition to carbohydrates, fats, and proteins, a great variety of other organic substances. Some of these (chlorophyll, xanthophyll, carotene, anthocyanins, suberin, and others) have already been discussed. Only a few other groups of organic substances remain to be considered in this introductory text.

Vitamins   These are complex organic compounds, most of which are synthesized only by plants. Although the chemical structure of some vitamins is known and the laboratory synthesis of certain vitamins has been accomplished, information concerning their specific functions in plants is rather meager. It is probable that most vitamins contribute to the formation of enzymes or function as coenzymes (see above). Some are believed to function in growth regulation, while other vitamins or vitamin derivatives serve as hydrogen carriers in respiration.

Hormones   These are organic compounds synthesized by living protoplasm and involved principally in the regulation of certain processes of growth and development. A fuller account of these hormones and of their behavior follows in the chapter on growth (Chapter 16).

Essential Oils   These are organic compounds that occur widely in plant tissues and that are generally regarded as waste products of plant metabolism. Although they are called "oils," they are chemically different from true oils and fats; most of them are members of a group of organic compounds called **terpenes,** which are made up of carbon and hydrogen only, with no oxygen. The essential oils are aromatic substances that are responsible for the characteristic odors and flavors of many plant parts, such as fragrant flowers, mint leaves, cinnamon bark, clove buds, sandalwood, nutmeg seeds, and pine needles. The essential oils are economically important in perfumes and cosmetics, food flavoring, varnishes, medicines, and many other products. Essential oils in some plants become partially or wholly oxidized into substances called resins, of which turpentine, balsams, and copals are examples.

Organic Acids   All living plant cells contain organic acids of various types. Among the common organic acids of plants are citric, malic, oxalic, pyruvic, succinic, tannic, and tartaric acids. These are variously important in plant metabolism. Some organic acids are obviously waste products of certain metabolic activities of plants and often accumulate in sufficient concentrations in plant tissues to give them a sharp, sour taste (for example, oxalic acid in rhubarb and sourdock leaves). Also, the sour or tart taste of many fruits is the result of relatively high organic acid content (for example, malic acid in apples and citric acid in lemons and grapefruit). Tannic acid is probably a metabolic waste product that accumulates in certain plant tissues and becomes transformed into tannins. Tannins occur in many types of wood (chestnut and oak), in bark (hemlock and oaks), in leaves (tea and sumac), and in seeds and unripe fruits (acorns, persimmons, plums, and bananas). Tannins are important economically in the tanning of animal hides and in the manufacture of tannin inks. Some organic acids are intermediate products in respiration and may be oxidized with the release of energy.

DIGESTION

Digestion is the process whereby foods that are insoluble in water or are very complex chemically are converted into foods that dissolve readily in water or that are simpler chemically. Digestion of insoluble storage products is prerequisite to translocation because only water-soluble foods can be moved from one part of a plant to other parts. It is also important as a preliminary to other processes, such as respiration, that ordinarily occur only when the foods involved in them are dissolved in water.

Digestion proceeds in virtually all living cells but is especially active in cells that store considerable quantities of foods. Thus, it is a conspicuous feature in most seeds, tubers, rhizomes, and other storage structures, particularly when they are beginning or resuming growth after a dormant period. The principal kind of digestion that occurs in green plants is **intracellular;** that is, it proceeds within the protoplasm of cells. In some plants, such as many fungi and insectivores, digestive enzymes diffuse out of the cells that produce them and act on foods outside cells in which they developed. This type of digestion, which also occurs in cotyledons, is termed **extracellular.**

Digestion involves the uptake of water during the conversion of complex foods into simpler foods, as is shown by the equation representing the transformation of malt sugar to grape sugar:

$$\underset{\text{(malt sugar)}}{C_{12}H_{22}O_{11}} + \underset{\text{(water)}}{H_2O} \longrightarrow \underset{\text{(grape sugar)}}{2C_6H_{12}O_6}$$

Thus, from the chemical standpoint, digestive processes are processes of **hydrolysis.** The mere physical addition of water to complex foods in the cell is not sufficient to cause their transformation into simpler foods, for these complex substances are so stable that they require the action of enzymes to bring about their alteration.

The action of some hydrolytic enzymes is reversible; that is, they not only convert complex foods into simpler ones, but they may also build up the corresponding complex foods from the simpler types. The enzyme **maltase,** for example, digests maltose (malt sugar) into glucose (grape sugar) and is also able to synthesize maltose from glucose molecules. The reversible action of some enzymes is very important in translocation and food storage. An insoluble food in one part of a plant may be digested by a particular enzyme into soluble food, which may then be moved to some other portion of the plant and converted back into insoluble form by the same enzyme.

HETEROTROPHIC NUTRITION

Plants that manufacture their own foods from simpler substances are called **autotrophic;** those that depend on ready-made, externally supplied foods are **heterotrophic.** Most important and most common of autotrophic plants are those that manufacture their basic foods by photosynthesis—in other words, all green plants. There are several species of photosynthetic bacteria that, although they lack chlorophyll, contain purple or green pigments and are able to synthesize their own food from carbon dioxide and hydrogen sulfide (H_2S). Some other species of bacteria are able to manufacture their own food by **chemo-**

synthesis, a process in which energy for food synthesis is obtained by various oxidation or reduction reactions that the organisms carry out. For example, certain bacteria oxidize free sulfur to sulfate, whereas others reduce sulfate to sulfide. Still others use iron and nitrogen compounds as substrates for oxidation or reduction reactions. However, the number of species of chemosynthetic bacteria is small as compared with that of more advanced photosynthetic plants.

There are two main types of heterotrophic plants: **parasites** and **saprophytes.** Parasites are organisms that obtain their food directly from the living bodies of other organisms. Beechdrops, dodders, and various fungi that cause animal and plant diseases are examples of parasites. Some species of plants are partial or semiparasites. Mistletoe, for example, contains chlorophyll and can therefore manufacture food; however, it obtains water and mineral nutrients from the trees on which it grows. Saprophytes are organisms such as breadmold, most kinds of mushrooms, and puffballs, which obtain their food from the dead bodies or waste products of living organisms or from other nonliving organic materials. Many species of very adaptable organisms can live either parasitically or saprophytically. Certain fungi behave as parasites when they attack the living tissues of their **host** (the organism that they parasitize) but later live saprophytically on the dead tissue of the host.

The curious and unusual methods of obtaining supplementary food employed by insectivorous plants deserve mention again in connection with the other methods by means of which plants make or acquire foods.

SUMMARY

1.   Metabolism is the total of all the chemical reactions involved in the physiological activities of living organisms. It includes manufacture and transformations of foods and the utilization of foods as energy sources during respiration.

2.   Respiration is the complementary process of photosynthesis and usually involves:
    a.   The chemical breakdown of foods to release energy.
    b.   The incorporation of some of this energy into the energy-rich substance adenosine triphosphate (ATP).
    c.   The production of carbon dioxide.

3.   Respiration that involves utilization of atmospheric oxygen is termed aerobic respiration; respiration that occurs without utilization of atmospheric oxygen is termed anaerobic respiration.

4.   In both aerobic and anaerobic respiration, the first phase consists of a series of reactions in which glucose is broken down into two 3-carbon molecules (pyruvic acid); this phase is known as glycolysis.

5.   During glycolysis, there is a net production of two molecules of ATP for each molecule of glucose which enters the process.

6.   In anaerobic respiration, hydrogen atoms removed during glycolysis are attached to intermediate derivatives of glucose; this material (ethyl alcohol, lactic acid, and so forth) is expelled from the cell, and respiration is complete.

7.   In aerobic respiration, pyruvic acid produced by glycolysis is fed into a cyclic series of reactions called the citric-acid cycle.

8. Hydrogen atoms removed from pyruvic acid in the citric-acid cycle are transferred to a series of pigments called cytochromes. As the hydrogen is passed from pigment to pigment, energy is released that is used to form ATP.

9. Through the operation of the citric-acid cycle and the cytochrome system, 36 molecules of ATP are produced for each molecule of glucose respired, in addition to the 2 molecules of ATP produced during glycolysis.

10. In aerobic respiration, the hydrogen removed is eventually combined with oxygen from the atmosphere to form water, while the carbon and other atoms which were in the original glucose molecule are combined with additional oxygen to produce water and carbon dioxide.

11. Aerobic respiration is essentially the reverse of the process of photosynthesis. The empirical formula for aerobic respiration may be written: $C_6H_{12}O_6 + 6O_2 \rightarrow 6CO_2 + 6H_2O +$ energy (as ATP).

12. During the day, green plants produce more glucose and oxygen by means of photosynthesis than is simultaneously respired, and there is a net production and liberation of O_2. During the night, only respiration occurs, and there is net utilization of atmospheric O_2 and production of CO_2.

13. Under favorable conditions, the net production of glucose and oxygen over an average period of 24 hours is more than is utilized by the plant for its life processes. This residuum of food and oxygen is available for use by animals and other nonphotosynthetic organisms.

14. Some of the energy of glucose is not recovered as chemical energy during aerobic respiration but is released as heat.

15. The most familiar example of anaerobic respiration is alcoholic fermentation of sugars by yeasts to produce ethyl alcohol and carbon dioxide. The brewing and baking industries, respectively, make use of these products.

16. If oxygen is not available, the cells of most plants and animals can respire anaerobically for at least a short time, but the cells of most aerobic organisms are damaged if deprived of oxygen for long periods.

17. A food is an organic substance that furnishes energy or is used in building protoplasm. Three classes of foods are carbohydrates, fats, and proteins.

18. Carbohydrates supply energy, build cell walls, and are the sources from which fats, proteins, and other organic compounds of plants are constructed. Carbohydrates consist of carbon, hydrogen, and oxygen, with twice as many hydrogen atoms as oxygen atoms in each molecule. Carbohydrates include sugars, starches, and cellulose.

19. Fats are chiefly storage foods and constituents of protoplasm. Fats contain carbon, hydrogen, and oxygen, with a lower proportion of oxygen to hydrogen than in carbohydrates. Fats result from the reactions of glycerol with fatty acids.

20. Proteins are the chief solid constituents of living protoplasm and contain carbon, hydrogen, oxygen, and nitrogen, and often phosphorus or sulfur or both. Proteins result from the linkage of amino acid molecules.

21. Autotrophic plants manufacture their own food by photosynthesis or chemosynthesis. Heterotrophic plants are unable to make their own food; they are parasites (which obtain foods from tissues of other living organisms) or saprophytes (which obtain foods from dead or nonliving organic matter).

22. Organic compounds other than foods produced by plants include chlorophyll, carotenoids, enzymes, hormones, vitamins, organic acids, and essential oils. Some of these perform vital functions, others are metabolic wastes.

23. Enzymes are highly specific, proteinaceous catalysts that promote a great variety of reactions.

24. Organic acids may be metabolic waste products or intermediate compounds in food syntheses and respiration.

25. Digestion is the conversion of complex or water-insoluble foods into simpler or water-soluble foods. Digestive processes are processes of hydrolysis.

26. Plants which manufacture their own foods are termed autotrophic; those which depend on external sources of food are termed heterotrophic.

27. The most important and abundant autotrophic plants are those which manufacture food by means of photosynthesis, that is, green plants; a few bacteria are chemosynthetic, using energy released from chemical reactions to manufacture food.

28. The two main types of heterotrophic plants are saprophytes, plants which take food from the nonliving substrates on or within which they grow, and parasites, plants which take food from living hosts.

SUGGESTED READINGS FOR INTERESTED STUDENTS

1. Galston, A. W., *The Life of the Green Plant,* 2d ed. Prentice-Hall, Englewood Cliffs, N.J., 1964.

2. Goldsby, R. A. *Cells and Energy.* The Macmillan Co., New York, 1967.

3. Kennedy, D., Ed., *The Living Cell.* W. H. Freeman, San Francisco, 1965.

4. McElroy, W. D., *Cell Physiology and Biochemistry,* 2d ed. Prentice-Hall, Englewood Cliffs, N.J., 1964.

5. Ray, P. M. *The Living Plant.* Holt, Rinehart and Winston, New York, 1965.

6. Salisbury, F. B., and R. V. Parke, *Vascular Plants: Form and Function.* Wadsworth, Belmont, Cal., 1964.

7. Steward, F. C. *About Plants: Topics in Plant Biology.* Addison-Wesley, Reading, Mass., 1966.

TOPICS AND QUESTIONS FOR STUDY

1. Define metabolism, food, and respiration.
2. Contrast and compare photosynthesis and respiration.
3. What is ATP? Why is it important for metabolic processes?
4. How much ATP is produced by anaerobic organisms? How much by aerobic ones?
5. What is glycolysis?
6. Explain the action of the citric acid cycle. What relationship has this to the cytochrome system?
7. Where in cells does respiration occur?
8. From where do the food and oxygen necessary to sustain human life come? Can you suggest reasons why these substances were not utilized first by the organisms which produced them?
9. Compare anaerobic and aerobic respiration.
10. What is an isotope? Of what importance are isotopes in the study of metabolism?
11. Compare the three major classes of foods with respect to their
    a. Molecular structure.
    b. Synthesis by plants.
    c. Utilization by plants.
12. What is the relationship between proteins and enzymes? What is the function of enzymes? What are coenzymes?
13. List three kinds of substances other than foods that are produced by plants, and discuss their importance in human life.
14. Define digestion.
15. Define heterotrophism and autotrophism.
16. Contrast parasites and saprophytes.

16

PLANT GROWTH

Growth is a fundamental process in living organisms and generally represents synthesis of new living material as a result of the energy-yielding reactions of metabolism. These reactions can be traced ultimately to the energy of sunlight that is incorporated into cellular substances. Such substances cannot be produced without large amounts of photosynthetic tissue which, in order to function, requires water and minerals from the soil and gases from the atmosphere. Thus, leaves, stems, and roots must be built as the machinery which makes it possible for a plant to produce and store food in large quantities. The building of this cellular machinery is a fundamental attribute of growth.

THE NATURE OF PLANT GROWTH

The word "growth" usually signifies to the layman increase in size. To biologists, however, growth is a complex phenomenon with many more implications than mere enlargement. The biological interpretation of growth includes both quantitative and qualitative concepts. Quantitatively, growth is an irreversible increase in size of a cell, tissue, organ, or organism and is usually accompanied by an increase in the amount of protoplasm and in dry weight. The qualitative aspect of growth, sometimes called development, includes all the structural changes that occur as growth proceeds. Three fairly distinct growth phases are recognized: first, the formation of new cells by the processes of mitosis and cell division; second, the enlargement of the newly formed cells; and third, the differentiation or maturation of these enlarging cells into the mature tissues of a growing organ. There are no sharp lines of demarcation among these stages of growth; each phase merges gradually into the next. The terms "cell division," "cell enlargement," and "cell differentiation" refer to these characteristic stages in a continuous process. Extremely important in the growth of living organisms are the coordination of physiological activities and the subordination of these activities to the growth plan of each species, whereby differentiation and the orderly development of tissues and organs occur. Growth without coordination results in **hypertrophy,** the formation of abnormal growths such as tumors. Various internal maladjustments and external conditions, such as insect or fungus attacks, may interrupt normal growth processes and thus cause hypertrophies.

Growth occurs ordinarily only when foodmaking activities of plants exceed food-consuming processes, for the formation of new cell walls and protoplasm requires food both for construction and for energy. Thus, photosynthesis is prerequisite to growth. If respiration exceeds photosynthesis through a period of days or weeks, food utilization exceeds food manufacture, and growth conspicuously declines. Under such conditions, there may occur a considerable decrease in volume of plant organs and in weight of protoplasm. Thus, growth is closely related to plant nutrition and can occur only when sufficient quantities of cellulose for wall building, sugars for energy, and amino acids and proteins for the construction of protoplasm are present in living tissues.

Growth Rates and Measurement   The rate at which growth occurs varies in different species and in different organs, if growth is measured in terms of increase in size, as is frequently done. In some plants, such as desert junipers and cacti, the rate of growth is exceedingly slow, so slow, in fact, that measurement of growth is almost impossible except over a period of many months or years. In other plants, the growth rate may be phenomenally rapid; for example, the young leaf sheath of banana grows for a time at the rate of almost 3 inches per hour; wheat stamens for a brief time grow at the rate of 1.8 millimeters (about $\frac{1}{14}$ inch) per minute, and bamboo stems have been observed to grow as much as 2 feet per day. In most species of plants the rate of growth lies between these extremes. The rate of growth depends on a complex of factors: the hereditary nature of the plant, temperature, nutrition, water supply, and many others to be discussed later. Most commonly, growth begins slowly, then enters on a period of rapid enlargement, following which it gradually decreases until no further enlargement occurs.

Distribution of Growth   Growth does not occur simultaneously in all parts of plant bodies but, as indicated in earlier chapters, proceeds chiefly in certain tissues, known as meristematic tissues. These are normally the growing points of the tips of roots and the buds of stems, the cambium, cork cambium, and root pericycle. The growth of roots and stems is **indeterminate,** which means that the meristematic tissues of the buds and root tips do not become completely transformed into mature, differentiated tissues but retain their meristematic character, continuing to cause growth of the stems and roots for as long as those organs live. These small masses of meristematic tissues in buds and root tips are called terminal meristems; they do not themselves increase in volume but form new tissues that are left behind; as they carry on this growth activity the growing points are carried upward (in buds) or downward (in roots) by the tissues they have produced. A striking example of indeterminate growth is furnished by palm trees. In a palm, such as the coconut tree, the terminal bud, which continues its growth for the entire life of the tree (a period of many years), is a direct continuation of the meristematic tissue of the epicotyl of the embryo. The growth of cambium in woody stems may be regarded also as indeterminate in nature. Some plant organs, after reaching their mature sizes, cease their growth and enlarge no more, all their meristematic cells having been transformed into differentiated, mature tissue. Such growth, called **determinate,** is characteristic of leaves, flowers, and fruits.

In many plants, certain differentiated cells, particularly parenchymatous cells, occasionally undergo a process of **dedifferentiation;** that is, they are transformed from matured cells into meristematic cells and are capable of further growth that may result in the production of adventitious roots, buds, and the like. In all these growing parts of plants, the same sequence and pattern of growth phases occur—cell formation, cell enlargement, and cell differentiation.

INTERNAL FACTORS AND PHENOMENA ASSOCIATED WITH PLANT GROWTH

Growth is a resultant of numerous physiological processes, including the absorption of water and of soil nutrients, the manufacture of food, the digestion, translocation, and assimilation of food, the release of energy by the process of respiration, the construction of cell walls from pectic substances and cellulose, mitosis, and regulating influences of plant hormones. Growth is, therefore, affected by the diverse internal and external factors that influence these metabolic activities. These factors will be considered briefly in this and the next section of this chapter.

The internal factors that affect growth are chiefly those inherent in the protoplasm of a species (hereditary factors) or that have been previously induced in the protoplasm by external factors. It is not always easy to distinguish be-

tween internal and external factors in their effects on growth; for example, the amount of food stored in the roots of a perennial plant is an important internal factor in determining in large part the features of the next season's growth. The food thus stored, however, depends on the amounts of water, light, carbon dioxide, and so forth available at the time when it was synthesized in the preceding growing season.

HEREDITARY NATURE OF PLANTS

The hereditary potentialities of individual species of plants are important internal factors that regulate growth. Some species of trees, such as poplars and willows, grow very rapidly in the presence of favorable external conditions; pines, white oaks, and sweet gums exposed to similarly advantageous conditions grow much more slowly. Morning-glories are by nature twining vines with weak stems, and although their rate of growth may be markedly influenced by variations in their external environment, they always remain weak-stemmed twiners. The buds of black-locust trees produce leaves that are pinnately compound; the rate of growth of such leaves is subject to environmental variations, but the compound nature of the leaves cannot be changed by alterations in moisture, temperature, and so forth. The time of flowering of cocklebur plants may be shifted by changes in the daily duration of light to which they are exposed, but the plants always remain recognizably cocklebur plants, with the traits and potentialities of the cocklebur species. Thus, variations in environmental factors can induce certain changes in gross structure, anatomical features, reproductive phases, and so forth, but the degree and quality of these changes are limited in the final analysis by that most important internal controller—the hereditary nature of the species. Such a constitution is always liable to amendment but rarely to fundamental change.

Hereditary control of the processes and products of growth can be traced ultimately to the

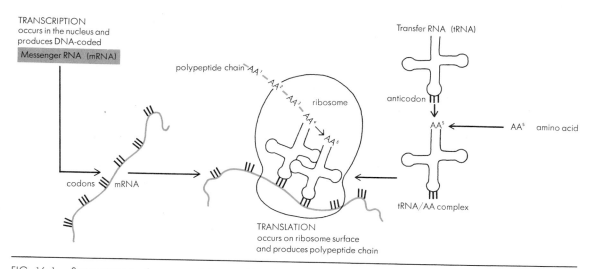

TRANSCRIPTION
occurs in the nucleus and
produces DNA-coded
Messenger RNA (mRNA)

polypeptide chain

ribosome

codons   mRNA

TRANSLATION
occurs on ribosome surface
and produces polypeptide chain

Transfer RNA (tRNA)

anticodon

AA⁵ ← AA⁵ amino acid

tRNA/AA complex

FIG. 16-1. Some steps in the sequential assembly of amino acids to form a polypeptide chain.

genes of the chromosomes in the nuclei of an organism's cells. As pointed out in an earlier chapter, the chemical substance which contains genetic information in the chromosome is deoxyribose nucleic acid or DNA. Information is stored in DNA in sequences of nitrogenous bases which are precisely paired to complementary bases in the double-stranded DNA molecules. Within the nucleus, this coded information in DNA is transferred to other molecules called **ribose nucleic acids,** or **RNA,** a process termed **transcription.** Like DNA, RNA molecules have incorporated into their structure precise sequences of nitrogenous bases; unlike DNA, RNA is largely a single-stranded molecule, and the nitrogenous base **uracil** is substituted for thymine. Because of the template-product relationship the synthesis of RNA is under the control of DNA, and specific kinds and amounts of information in DNA are incorporated into RNA at the time of transcription. Three forms of RNA are synthesized in the nucleus: **messenger RNA (mRNA),** which is of relatively high molecular weight and which migrates to the surfaces of the ribosomes in the cytoplasm; **transfer RNA** or **tRNA** (sometimes called soluble RNA) of smaller molecular weight; and **ribosomal RNA (rRNA)** a structural constit-

uent amounting to approximately 60 to 70 percent of the ribosomal substance. With the help of certain enzymes, tRNA molecules in the cytoplasm become linked with the particular amino acids for which they are coded. These amino acid-tRNA units migrate to the ribosomes where they are precisely aligned according to the structure (that is, the base sequence) of the mRNA molecules on the ribosome surfaces. The amino acids are then enzymatically joined one by one in a series of reactions to form protein molecules. The assembly of amino acids into protein molecules is termed **translation** since DNA information is thus "translated" into nonnucleic acid substances. This sequence of events is summarized diagramatically in Fig. 16-1.

In the series of reactions described above, DNA molecules inherited by cells from their precursor cells are responsible for production of RNA molecules, and these in turn are responsible for assembly of protein molecules. Information borne in a cell's DNA is transcribed to the structure of its mRNA, and this is translated into specific proteins through mRNA and tRNA activity at the surface of ribosomes. The proteins, in their roles as enzymes, regulate metabolic processes (including manufacture of new DNA and RNA), and, thereby, the activities, structure, and growth of the cells and of the organisms the cells comprise. The intracellular environment, affected in varying degrees and ways by factors of the external environment, controls what RNA messages are sent to the ribosomes from the nuclear DNA and thus what kinds of proteins, cells, and tissues will be produced. The regulation of this internal cellular environment is still not fully understood, but it is known that substances manufactured within the cells, or which enter the cells from the external environment or from sources in other cells and tissues, may affect the RNA message by activating or deactivating certain DNA elements. Such substances are termed **inducers** and **repressors,** respectively. Possible roles of the growth regulating substances known as plant hormones are as inducers and repressors.

GROWTH REGULATORS

Plant **hormones** constitute another of the important internal mechanisms that regulate plant growth. Characteristically, a hormone is synthesized in one region of the plant and is translocated to another region where, in extremely minute amounts, it exerts a physiological effect. Although the existence of a growth-regulating substance had been postulated as early as 1881 by Charles Darwin, it was not until 1926 that such a substance was isolated from plant material. About ten more years elapsed before investigators were able to determine its chemical identity: **indoleacetic acid,** an organic compound of the formula $C_{10}H_9O_2N$. Unfortunately, the minute amounts of indoleacetic acid (IAA) in a plant could not be accurately determined with usual chemical techniques. Investigators finally devised a suitable test for hormone activity by measuring the response of *living tissue* to hormone, a technique known as **bioassay.** A widely used bioassay for IAA and related growth substances is the **Avena test,** so named because seedlings of oat (*Avena sativa*) are employed in its use. The hormone to be tested is collected in a small agar block that is then placed on one side of the tip of a decapitated oat coleoptile. The growth substance moves down into the tissues immediately beneath the agar block and stimulates the cells of that region to elongate. This, in turn, produces a curvature in the coleoptile. The degree of curvature is a measurement of hormone activity, since the response of living coleoptile tissue is almost directly proportional to the amount of hormone present. The development of this now standardized test has greatly facilitated research efforts.

In recent years a number of growth influencing substances have been extracted from plants. Some of these behave like indoleacetic acid—that is, they cause curvature of oat coleoptiles—and, together with IAA, are called **auxins.** Another group of substances promotes tissue enlargement but lacks the marked ability to induce coleoptile curvature, and is called **gibberellins.** A third group of compounds influences tissue differentiation and cell division (cytokinesis), and is termed **cytokinins.** In addition to these classes of compounds, two other substances, **dormin** and **ethylene,** are naturally produced compounds which influence growth and development. Dormin promotes dormancy and is known to be of importance for stimulating leaf abscission; ethylene also promotes leaf abscission and stimulates fruit ripening. A number of these chemical growth regulators plus synthetic compounds not normally found in plant tissues but which have hormonelike activity are discussed below.

Auxins   Auxins are synthesized chiefly in young, physiologically active parts of plants, such as root and shoot apices. In these regions, an amino acid (tryptophan) is enzymatically converted into indoleacetic acid, which is then translocated to other parts of the plant. Experiments have shown that auxin transport is polarized; that is, it moves away from root and shoot apices but cannot move toward them. The specific effects of auxins on the metabolic activities of plant cells are not well understood, but some of them are known at least in part. One of the cellular phe-

not treated   treated

FIG. 16–2. Effect of a growth-promoting substance, indolebutyric acid, on the rooting of cuttings of American holly (*Ilex*). *Left:* Cuttings placed in rooting bench without treatment. *Right:* Cuttings treated with indolebutyric acid, then placed in rooting bench for same length of time as plants at left. (Photo by P.W. Zimmerman, Boyce Thompson Institute.)

nomena influenced by auxins is structural alteration of the wall to enable a cell to take up more water and increase its size.

Auxins regulate many growth and developmental processes of plants. Some of the more fundamental of these processes include the following.

1. Tissue and organ growth generally seems to be regulated by auxins. The growth of buds, the enlargement of leaf primordia, the growth of flower buds into mature flowers, cambial growth, and the growth of roots are some of the processes under auxin control. Researches on the effects of auxins on these growth phenomena have led to rather important commercial applications. For example, the treatment of stem cuttings, particularly the more basal parts, with solutions, pastes, or powders containing small concentrations of plant auxins, or chemically related substances, promotes rapid and extensive rooting of cuttings (Figs. 16–2 and 16–3). This method is now used on an extensive commercial scale to hasten the formation of roots on stem cuttings of hard-to-root cultivated plants.

2. Cell division in some tissues seems to be affected by auxins. Cell division of the cambium,

before treatment

control   treated

FIG. 16–3. Tubers of Jerusalem artichoke (*Helianthus tuberosus*) showing acceleration of development following treatment with a growth substance. *Upper row:* Tubers before treatment and planting. *Bottom row:* Tubers after a period of growth; the four at left were soaked in water for 24 hours before planting, while the four at right were soaked in a dilute solution of naphthaleneacetic acid for 24 hours before planting. (Photo by P.W. Zimmerman, Boyce Thompson Institute.)

FIG. 16–4. Spraying tomato flowers with growth substances to produce seedless fruits.

FIG. 16–5. Cross sections of squash and tomato fruits. Fruits at the left were developed by normally pollinated flowers and contain seeds. Fruits at right were developed without seeds as the result of treatment of the flowers with beta-naphthoxyacetic acid, a growth substance. (Photo by P.W. Zimmerman, Boyce Thompson Institute.)

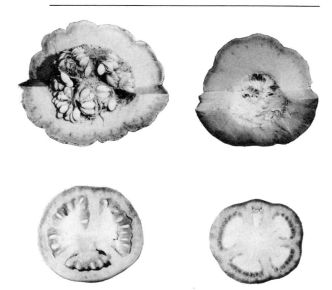

for example, is stimulated by auxins diffusing downward in stems from apically situated buds and young leaves. The beginning of division of cambial cells in woody stems usually coincides with the beginning of bud growth; at this time, auxin production by the developing buds increases rapidly. The application of hormones to the tips of decapitated stems accelerates the division of cambial cells located in more basal portions of the stems.

3. Abscission of leaves, flowers, and fruits is in part controlled by auxins. The abscission of leaves, for example, is the result in part of a decrease in supplies of hormones moving from leaf blades downward through leaf petioles. If a leaf blade is removed from a petiole and an auxin preparation is applied to the cut end of the petiole, abscission of the petiole is delayed, often for a long period of time. Abscission of fruits is apparently also related to diminishing auxin supply; if young fruits are sprayed with solutions of growth substances, their fall is often retarded. This fact has been applied commercially to delay premature fruit drop in apple trees; spraying of young apple fruits with auxins prevents premature fruit drop, a major source of fruit loss. When high concentrations of such sprays are used on fruits, abscission of some immature fruits may be promoted, resulting in a thinning out of fruits. This effect is sometimes valuable in preventing overproduction, which may weaken a plant or cause it to bear a negligible crop in the year following a heavy crop production.

4. The development of fruits from the ovaries of flowers and the ripening of ovules into mature seeds after fertilization are controlled in part by auxins. The first evidence that chemical regulators play a role in fruit development was secured in 1910 by a plant physiologist who discovered that, if a water extract of orchid pollen grains (in lieu of the pollen grains themselves) was placed on orchid ovaries, the ovaries enlarged just as though they had been pollinated. These ovaries, of course, contained no seeds, since no fertilization of ovules had occurred. More recent

studies have shown that auxins and related growth substances, when applied to ovaries of flowers in liquid sprays (Fig. 16–4) or in a lanolin paste or injected into the ovaries, cause the development of ovaries into seedless fruits (Fig. 16–5). This phenomenon has been demonstrated in a number of species of plants. Watermelons, tomatoes, and squashes are particularly sensitive to this treatment and develop parthenocarpic fruits readily when subjected to it. There is a close relation between the fertilization of ovules and the growth of the ovary into a ripened fruit, a relation that is doubtless hormonal. In most species of flowering plants, ovaries do not develop into fruits unless the ovules are fertilized and mature into seeds; the sizes of the fruits are usually related to the numbers of seeds that develop within them. These phenomena may be interpreted on the basis of movement of auxins from developing seeds into ovary tissues.

5. Various **correlation** phenomena are the result of auxin-induced effects. Correlation may be defined as the mutual interaction of plant parts. For example, in many kinds of stems, the terminal bud is the dominant bud—that is, it grows more rapidly and is physiologically more active than the lateral buds; the dominance of the terminal bud prevents or retards the development of lateral buds. This correlation phenomenon, called bud inhibition, may be demonstrated strikingly in a potato tuber. If a whole potato is planted, only the terminal cluster of buds develops into sprouts, the lateral buds remaining inactive; if the tuber is cut into several pieces, all or most of the lateral buds, removed from the inhibitory effects of the terminal bud cluster, sprout. Similarly, in aerial stems, the development of branches is related to this **apical dominance.** So long as the terminal bud is present, the lateral buds usually develop slowly or remain dormant; the removal of the terminal bud commonly results in growth of the lateral buds. Auxin interactions between terminal and lateral buds are responsible for this bud correlation.

6. Many of the growth movements termed **tro-**

FIG. 16–6.   Successive stages in the positive phototropic bending of a radish seedling. Exposures were made on the same plate at intervals of 40 minutes.

FIG. 16–7.   Leaf mosaic of rhododendron. The arrangement of each leaf for maximum light reception is the result of phototropic bending of the petioles.

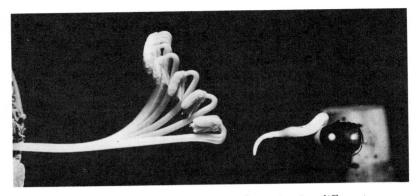

FIG. 16–8 (*left*). Negative geotropism in a bean seedling. Composite photo with successive exposures made every 40 minutes. FIG. 16–9 (*right*). Positive geotropism in a primary root of bean.

pisms are brought about by auxins. Tropisms are growth responses to unidirectional stimuli, that is, stimuli that affect one portion of a plant more strongly than another. Tropisms are common throughout the plant kingdom; they occur in many fungi, in mosses and ferns, and in all seed plants. Since tropisms result from differences in growth rates in different parts of organs, they are usually rather slow, requiring from one hour to several days or longer for their completion. Tropisms are named on the basis of the stimuli that initiate them. Thus, **phototropism** is the growth reaction of plant organs to light, **geotropism** is the growth reaction to gravity, **chemotropism** to chemical agents, and so forth. In phototropism, stems and leaves usually bend toward light; roots may bend away from light. In geotropism, stems usually bend upward away from the earth's gravitational force, and roots usually bend downward. A reaction toward the source of a stimulus is a **positive reaction;** one away from the stimulus is a **negative reaction.** Thus, the bending of a stem and leaves toward light is positive phototropism, and bending of roots away from light is negative phototropism. Tropisms constitute the chief means of advantageous adjustment of most plants to environmental factors. It is obviously advantageous in the life of a plant, for example, that stems and leaves usually grow upward and toward light and that roots grow downward into the soil as a consequence of geotropism.

Growth responses of plant cells and organs are at least partially related to accumulation of different amounts of auxin in different areas, thereby stimulating different growth rates. The various stimuli may affect the rate of manufacture of auxin in different portions of the tissues responsible for their production and thus, indirectly, the amounts accumulated in nearby reaction sites, or they may affect translocation phenomena and thereby modify accumulation rates in reaction sites. The presence of relatively large amounts on one side of a stem usually causes more rapid elongation of this side and results in bending of the stem toward the side with lesser concentration. However, the higher concentrations may actually be inhibitory for some tissues, as in roots, and result in more rapid elongation of the tissues on the side with lower concentrations. The interplay of stimuli on auxin synthesis and accumulation, and inhibition or stimulation of growth rates, results in growth toward, away from, or at right angles to the stimulus.

Phototropism is a growth movement made in response to illumination and is best demonstrated by the growth of stems toward unidirectional light sources (Fig. 16–6) and the adjustments made by leaves resulting in optimal light exposure for the blades (Fig. 16–7). Auxin produced in the stem tips or leaf primordia migrates to the elongating internodes and petioles, where it promotes cell elongation. If the axis is receiving light from one side, the accumulation of auxin is greatest on the unlighted side. The tissues there elongate more rapidly, and the result is curvature which bends the stem or petiole toward the source of illumination. The mechanisms which control differential accumulation of auxins in response to light and other stimuli are not fully understood, but there is evidence that auxin may migrate to the areas of lesser illumination. The turning of stems and leaves toward a light source are examples of positive phototropism. In some organs, however, the higher concentrations of auxins on the darkened sides may actually inhibit cell elongation in those areas and result in curvature away from the direction of illumination. Such negative phototropism is illustrated by roots and by the stems of many climbing vines, the latter thereby being continually induced to grow toward their supports.

Geotropism is auxin-induced growth movement in response to gravity. The effect of gravity is to increase auxin concentrations on the underside of the axis. In aerial stems, the underside is thus stimulated to develop more rapidly, bringing about an upward curvature (Fig. 16–8) and growth of the stem away from the direction of gravitational pull (negative geotropism), but in roots (Fig. 16–9) the higher concentrations are inhibitory to elongation and the underside grows more slowly, resulting in bending of the root downward (positive geotropism). A number of perennial plants produce rhizomes which exhibit lateral geotropism, that is, growing at right angles to the direction of gravitational pull. Thus, in a plant such as iris, geotropism simultaneously plays roles in the upward growth of leaves and flower stems, the lateral growth of rhizomes, and the downward growth of roots.

In studying tropisms, students should take care that they do not attribute foresight or purposeful reaction to plants. One should not say that plants bend toward the light *in order* to secure light, which they need, or that roots grow downward *in order* to reach the soil. More nearly correct interpretations of these growth reactions are that stems grow toward light because light is a stimulus that affects their growth in such a way as to cause them to bend toward it and that roots grow downward because gravitational force in-

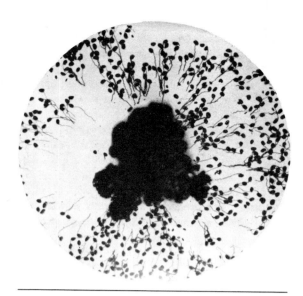

FIG. 16–10.   Chemotropism in pollen tubes, which are shown growing toward a crushed stigma.

fluences their growth in such a manner that they bend downward.

Gibberellins   Japanese rice farmers have long been familiar with the "foolish seedling" disease in which the shoot of a rice plant becomes extremely elongated. The cause of this disease, infection by the sac fungus *Gibberella fujikuroi,* was discovered in 1926 and about 10 years later, the growth-promoting substance was isolated and named **gibberellin.** It was not until after World War II that American investigators began intensive studies of this hormone and its effects on plant growth and development. To date about 20 different gibberellins have been isolated, some from the fungus only, some from seeds of certain green plants, and one from both of these sources.

As was previously shown, plants treated with auxins exhibit a variety of responses. This is also true for plants treated with gibberellin. The commonest effect is extreme elongation of the stem. On an experimental basis, gibberellin has also been used to increase cambial activity, to inhibit the development of floral and vegetative buds, and to shorten the period of dormancy of seeds of some species. One of the most surprising responses to gibberellin treatment is the induction of flowering in long-day plants that are on a short-day photoperiod. Photoperiodism is discussed later in this chapter and in Chapter 17. Gibberellin appears to act as an inducer of protein synthesis during seed germination. The enzyme α-amylase is necessary for breakdown of starch during germination of cereal grains. The embryo triggers α-amylase production by releasing gibberellin to specialized cells which manufacture it. The breakdown products which form as a result of α-amylase action on starch provide food for the developing embryo.

Cytokinins, the third class of plant hormones, act in a number of ways to influence growth and development, but their most striking effects are induction of cell division and promotion of tissue differentiation. Although they may also act to promote cell elongation, their action is usually weak, and under many circumstances cytokinins actually inhibit elongation. Cytokinins can induce development of roots and shoots from parenchyma masses grown in sterile cultures but inhibit the formation of roots on cuttings. They often have all-or-nothing effects on differentiation, so that no response may occur at a given concentration whereas at a slightly different concentration they may promote large changes. Cytokinins exert a controlling influence on the translocation of nutrients in intact plants and tissues, can delay the normal processes of deterioration in leaves, may increase the tolerance of plants to adverse temperature conditions, and promote synthesis and utilization of RNA and proteins. Thus, like auxins and gibberellins, the cytokinins exhibit multiple effects. In addition, specific activities of cytokinins may be promoted or blocked by the activities of other hormones, and they may, in turn, promote or block the activities of other growth substances. The study of such antagonistic (opposed) or synergistic (enhancing) effects of growth substances under various conditions is only now being explored.

Dormin, or abscissic acid $(C_{15}H_{20}O_4)$, is a growth substance presently under intensive investigation. As the name implies, this substance is strongly associated with dormancy phenomena and acts to induce leaf senescence and formation of bud scales and induces leaf drop and dormancy of seeds and apical meristems. In ways that are not fully understood, dormin appears to inhibit growth and suppress the action of auxins, gibberellins, and cytokinins as growth promoters.

Ethylene is a simple organic compound with the formula C_2H_4. It appears to be produced normally during cell metabolism and has a number of growth effects. It stimulates respiration and fruit ripening and has been used commercially to promote rapid ripening of green fruits during or after shipment. Ethylene represses bud development and enhances leaf abscission. There is evidence that at least part of the auxin-controlled suppression of lateral buds in the apical dominance phenomenon is due to the ability of auxin to promote ethylene formation. The action of ethylene can be blocked by application of cytokinins.

Flowering of plants appears to be related to hormone activity. Information concerning the hormonal initiation of flowering is still meager, since it has not been possible to isolate chemically a flower-inducing hormone or to demonstrate conclusively that the known auxins are related to flower production.

The practical applications of research on growth regulators illustrate an important feature of scientific work, namely, that many of the economically valuable procedures in agriculture and industry are the results of the labors of scientists who explore the secrets of nature to satisfy their intellectual curiosity, without compulsion to seek practical benefits. The plant physiologists who made the fundamental discoveries concerning plant hormones were motivated simply by their consuming desire to learn more of plant growth, not by a wish to make cuttings root more rapidly or to cause apples to cling longer to the branches. We now know many of the physiological func-

FIG. 16–11. Asparagus plot, showing clear area at right in which a chemical weed killer related to indoleacetic acid has destroyed all weeds; area at left has not been treated. (Photo by Michigan State University.)

tions and operations of auxins and many of the intricacies of plant growth. New practical applications of this knowledge are still being developed and will probably continue to expand in the future with further basic research on growth regulators. Consider one of the practical benefits of such research—the use of 2,4-D (2,4-dichlorophenoxyacetic acid) and related compounds as selective weed killers. Some of these substances are toxic to broad-leafed plants and have little or no effect on most monocotyledons, such as cereal crops and lawn grasses. Thus, they may be sprayed or dusted on lawns and fields of asparagus (Fig. 16–11), wheat, corn, rice, oats, and other cereals, with killing effects on dandelions, plantains, bindweeds, milkweeds, poison ivy, and other noxious weeds, without damaging the valuable monocotyledons. These growth substances have an exaggerated hormonelike effect on susceptible plants; they stimulate respiration and accelerate the depletion of stored carbohydrates, until the plants die of physiological exhaustion.

It should be emphasized that plant hormones do not bring about their effects in a simple, direct manner but that their functions are related to, and dependent on, other physiological processes. Thus, auxin activity is related to respiratory processes that release from foods the energy required

for growth. Also, the growth of cells requires such substances as cellulose, sugars, and proteins that are used in the synthesis of cell walls and protoplasm. In the absence of these structural materials, hormone-controlled processes cannot be carried on.

THE EXTERNAL FACTORS THAT INFLUENCE GROWTH

The principal external factors that affect growth and configuration of plants are **light and other types of radiations, temperature, moisture, soil nutrients, foods, oxygen, carbon dioxide and other gases, poisons, gravity,** and **the attacks of parasites.** A noteworthy feature of this list is the fact that most of these environmental conditions that influence plant growth likewise exert profound effects on the development of animals. The susceptibility of all living organisms to the same features of their environments is another indication of the fundamental unity of all living protoplasm.

These factors of the external environment affect plants in various ways: they influence the rate of growth of their tissues; they affect food manufacture, digestion, respiration and other physiological activities; they exert influences on the form and structure of certain organs (limited, of course, by the internal organization of each species); they affect reproduction; and, if they act in different intensity from different directions, they frequently induce movements of various plant organs.

Light and Other Radiations   The sole source of energy for green plants is the radiant energy from the sun. The visible portion of this radiation, called **light,** is the most important type of radiation in plant life. Light affects the germination of certain kinds of seeds, photosynthesis, the rate of growth of various organs, the synthesis and distribution of auxins, the initiation of reproduction, transpiration, the sizes of various plant organs, the activity of enzymes, the synthesis of chlorophyll, and the physicochemical condition of certain protoplasmic proteins. Many species of plants are very exacting in their light requirements. Grasses, sunflowers, goldenrods, tomatoes, and milkweeds usually thrive under bright, direct sunlight and grow poorly in diffuse, dim light. Most ferns and mosses and many woodland wildflowers grow best in low light intensities and are retarded in their growth or killed by the intensity of full sunlight. Still other plants—such as columbines, phlox, periwinkles, and roses—are tolerant of wide ranges of light intensity and grow well both in bright and diffuse light.

Light has pronounced morphological effects on the leaves and stems of plants. Plants that grow in darkness are characterized by long, succulent, weak stems, undeveloped leaves, and pale, yellowish, chlorophyll-less tissues; this condition is called **etiolation.** Excessive intensities of light frequently cause a stunting of stems and of leaves. Plants grown in moderate light intensities usually have longer internodes, with larger, more succulent, less tough leaves than those growing in intense sunlight. Most of us have observed that leaves growing in shade, such as tree leaves growing on inner, shaded branches, are appreciably larger and more tender than those growing in full sunlight. Several species of crop plants, such as tobacco and lettuce, are frequently cul-

tivated under cheesecloth screens to reduce the intensity of light reaching them, and thus to produce larger, more succulent leaves.

The duration of daily exposure to light profoundly affects various developmental processes in plants. The most striking effects of daily **photoperiods** become evident when plants begin to flower (discussed in Chapter 17). Daily photoperiod duration also affects certain purely vegetative activities. For example, many potato varieties form few tubers in long days but undergo rapid tuberization in short photoperiods (temperature is also involved in tuber formation in potatoes); soybeans undergo tuberization when the photoperiod is shortened below the optimum for stem growth or flowering; yams experience extensive tuberization under short days but show little tuberization under long photoperiods. Research on the photoperiodic responses of plants has led to important applications in practical plant growing. For example, by controlling photoperiods through the use of shading or of supplemental illumination at night, commercial growers can accelerate or delay the flowering of greenhouse crops. Complete shading of most chrysanthemum and poinsettia plants during a portion of the long days of summer accelerates flowering, while supplemental illumination of these species by electric lights at night prolongs vegetative growth and causes later flowering. The flowering of snapdragons, stocks, and other plants which require long days may be hastened during the short days of autumn, winter, and early spring by illumination at night.

Temperature   Growing plants are constantly influenced by variations in the temperature of the soil in which they grow and of the surrounding air. Most species of plants in active condition develop best in temperatures between 20°C and 32°C and cease growth when air and soil temperatures approach freezing or rise much above 38°C(100°F). Dormant (relatively inactive or resting) structures with low water content, such as seeds or spores, are much more resistant to extremes of temperature than are actively growing organs. The maximum, minimum, and optimum (best) temperatures for seed germination and plant growth vary, of course, with different species of plants, with age, with other environmental conditions simultaneously operative, and so forth. In general, plants of tropical and subtropical origin have higher temperature requirements than do those of higher latitudes. Thus, rubber, quinine, and orange trees require higher temperatures for their best growth than do apple, pine, and birch trees, which are natives of the north temperate zone.

Plants that are able to survive exposure to subfreezing temperatures are termed **hardy.** Elms, apple trees, maples, irises, pines, and strawberries, for example, are hardy in the Middle West. Hardiness is fundamentally an inherent characteristic of different species, although it is subject to considerable modification by varying environmental conditions. Winter hardiness depends upon several physiological factors—increased soluble carbohydrate content of tissues, great stability of protoplasmic proteins, reduced water content of tissues, and a high proportion of colloidally bound water, which is incapable of freezing. The hardiness of many kinds of plants such as cabbage, tomatoes, and alfalfa may be increased by suitable manipulation; thus, cabbage plants moved from a warm greenhouse directly to outdoor temperatures slightly below freezing suffer pronounced cold injury; if cabbage plants are first moved from a warm greenhouse to a cool greenhouse or a cold frame with a temperature of about 2° to 4°C, and are kept at the cool temperature for 5 to 6 days, they are then able to withstand outdoor temperatures slightly below freezing for several days without injury. Many other species of plants may be subjected to this **hardening** treatment with a similar beneficial result, namely, increased ability to withstand low temperatures. Plants may also be hardened by severe pruning, which deprives them of actively growing parts that are especially susceptible to cold injury, and by manipulation of photoperiods

to reduce vegetative growth and to cause storage of soluble carbohydrates.

Temperature has many other effects upon plant growth that are too numerous and too complex for discussion in an elementary textbook. In some species, for example, susceptibility to disease varies with different temperatures. Another striking temperature effect is found in the differentiation of flower buds; certain plants, such as varieties of winter wheat, beets, cabbage, and celery, do not flower if they are grown continuously at temperatures of 20°C or above; brief low temperature exposures **(vernalization)** are needed for formation of flower primordia in these plants. Temperature is also an important factor in ending the dormancy of their flower buds; grown in subtropical climates in the absence of low winter temperatures, apple and peach trees normally do not flower. Other species of plants flower only at higher temperatures; rice and cotton usually do not flower unless they are exposed to temperatures above 27°C.

Water   The importance of water in the life of plants has been considered in earlier chapters. The relation of plants to water is complex and involves problems of osmosis, water transport, transpiration in relation to water absorption by roots and to wilting, atmospheric conditions, and so forth. The amounts of water available to plants influence markedly their growth and form. Since water is one of the raw materials of photosynthesis, its availability is related to the quantities of food manufactured in plants. The growth of cell walls and the formation of new protoplasm depend directly on the amount of food formed in photosynthesis. Chiefly through its effects on these processes and on the turgor of cells, the water supply of plants influences growth rate and the ultimate size attained by various tissues and organs.

Most species of plants possess minimum, maximum, and optimum soil moisture concentrations that influence their growth. Plants may be stunted in their development by too much water as well as by too little. In mesophytes, a scarcity of water results in stunted growth because of reduced food synthesis and assimilation. An excess of water in the soil may likewise stunt growth through the exclusion of oxygen necessary for root development. Growth is best promoted by moderate supplies of water that are sufficient for rapid food manufacture and assimilation and yet do not exclude oxygen from the soil. In addition to its effect on the rate of growth, water supply frequently exerts a direct influence on specific morphological features of plants. For example, the roots of corn plants grown in water cultures do not produce root hairs; in damp soil or in saturated air, root hairs develop in great abundance. In several species of water plants, leaves borne above the surface of the water are morphologically very different from those produced below the water surface. This structural difference is apparently related to dissimilar conditions of the aerial and submerged habitats.

Gases   Oxygen is required for normal root growth and for respiration, and its absence is soon indicated by abnormalities in growth. Carbon dioxide is a raw material of photosynthesis and hence its presence is necessary for the manufacture of carbohydrates. A moderate increase in the carbon dioxide content of air usually accelerates photosynthetic activity. If the percentage of atmospheric or soil carbon dioxide becomes excessive, plants may be injured as a result. Some other gases influencing plant growth are sulfur dioxide, ethylene, and carbon monoxide, which escape into the air from smelters and factories, usually as products of the combustion of coal and of other fuels involved in industrial activities. These gases frequently cause serious injury to plant tissues and often kill plants, particularly evergreens, which are more susceptible than most other plants to such injury because they retain their leaves during the winter, when the smoke and gas content of the air near congested industrial centers is highest. Plants are exceedingly susceptible to small traces of illuminating gas.

One of the reasons for the poor growth of many kinds of plants in houses is the presence in the air of minute amounts of illuminating gas escaping from stoves and other appliances. These traces of gas are so small that they are harmless to human beings, but they stunt the growth of plants and cause premature fall of leaves, retardation of growth, and often death. Extremely low concentrations of ethylene gas hasten the ripening of fruits and are used commercially to speed the ripening of citrus fruits, bananas, and other kinds of fruits.

Chemical Agents in Soils   The quantities and kinds of nutrient elements available to plants exert tremendous influences on growth. Failure of plants to obtain the elements necessary for food syntheses, chlorophyll formation, the construction of protoplasm, and other metabolic activities results in pronounced physiological aberrations. The effects of deficiencies and excesses of these essential nutrients on plant growth have been briefly described in the preceding chapter and will not receive further attention here.

In addition to these essential nutrients, soils often contain substances that are toxic to plants and that may cause their injury or death. Some of these toxic compounds are inorganic substances of mineral derivation; compounds of selenium, copper, and other elements occur in some soils in sufficient concentrations to injure plants. Some toxic inorganic compounds accumulate in soils as a result of certain agricultural and industrial practices; for example, arsenic residues from insecticidal sprays sometimes reach sufficient concentrations to cause injury to plants. Some toxic substances in soils are organic compounds produced by the decomposition of dead plants and their parts, and animal bodies; these substances often stunt the growth of plants or otherwise adversely affect them. An interesting feature of the toxicity of such organic compounds is the fact that the poisonous compounds produced by the decomposition of dead leaves, roots, fruits, and other parts of one species are usually more

FIG. 16–12. A sensitive plant, *Mimosa pudica*, showing rapid turgor movements. *Left:* Plant in unstimulated condition. *Right:* Plant after being struck with a pencil.

toxic to other plants of the same species than they are to plants of other species. Thus, the growth of successive crops of oats on the same soil results in a progressive deterioration of later oat crops, despite the periodic addition of fertilizer; if, after a crop of oats is harvested, clover, corn, or some other crop is grown in the same soil, no harmful effects of the decomposition products of oats on the second crop are apparent. The formation of toxic organic decomposition products in soils is an important factor in crop rotation and may likewise play an important ecological role in cyclic fluctuations of plant populations in nature.

Other Living Organisms   Higher plants are frequently attacked by parasitic fungi, worms, insects, and other living organisms. Such attacks exert profound effects on the growth and structure of the attacked plants. The harmful effects

of parasites are the results of several physiological disturbances: the theft of food from the tissues of parasitized plants, destruction of leaves and the consequent reduction of the food-making ability of the host plants, stoppage of vascular tissues and interference with sap rise and food translocation, injury to roots and thus abnormalities in absorption, and so forth. The attacks of parasites often result in accelerated local growth of host tissues, with the formation of galls and tumors.

The growth of plants is affected also by higher animals. The trampling of hoofs of cattle, sheep, and other domesticated animals injures the shoots of grasses, churns up and destroys their roots, and often causes their death. Also, the browsing of animals exerts marked effects on plants. Domesticated herbivorous animals eat the leaves of plants and thus reduce their photosynthetic activity. Rabbits, porcupines, and other wild ani-

FIG. 16–13. Sleep movements of *Oxalis stricta*. *Left:* Day position of leaflets. *Right:* Night position of leaflets.

mals eat bark and frequently girdle the trunks of young trees, causing their death.

RAPID MOVEMENTS OF PLANTS

Plant reactions or movements are usually too slow to be observed by the human eye but that they actually occur can be demonstrated by time-lapse motion picture photography or, more simply, by observing reacting plants at intervals of several hours and noting changes in position of the various organs. All kinds of plants exhibit reactions to environmental stimuli. The reactions of plants differ in their speed, direction of movement, the nature of the mechanisms that bring them about, and in other respects. Despite the many variations among the diverse kinds of plant movements, there are certain features common to most kinds of reactions, chief among which are reception of stimuli, the transmission of growth hormones, and changes in certain cells or tissues that actually bring about a reaction or movement. However, **turgor reactions,** in which the reaction results from changes of turgor pressure of certain tissues of plant organs, are of a different nature. These changes of turgor pressure are usually rapid, so that turgor movements may be completed within a fraction of a second or, at most, within a few seconds. In contrast with most growth movements, turgor movements in many species of plants seem to have little advantageous significance for the plants in which they occur. Unlike most tropisms, turgor movements are reversible; that is, when the stimulus has disappeared, the plant organ returns shortly to the position it held before stimulation.

Sleep movements occur chiefly in leaves of various plants, such as clovers, beans, locusts, wood sorrel, and peas and result from turgor changes induced by alterations of light intensity, usually in specialized tissues at the bases of leaflets and leaves. In white clover, for example, leaflets assume a horizontal position in bright light and move upward into a nearly vertical

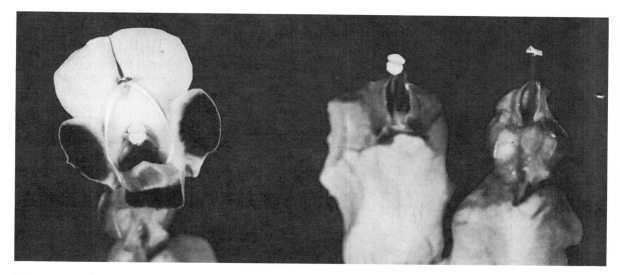

FIG. 16–14. *Left:* Flower of *Torenia*, showing 2-lobed stigma in center of corolla tube. *Right:* Unstimulated and stimulated stigmas of *Torenia* (corollas removed).

position as light disappears. Wood sorrel leaflets occupy a horizontal position during the day, assume a vertical hanging position at night, and return to the horizontal position at sunrise (Fig. 16–13). The benefits of sleep movements in plants are unknown.

Contact movements are turgor movements, chiefly of leaves and flower parts, that result from contact stimuli. The closing movements of the leaf halves of the Venus'-flytrap are contact turgor movements. This reaction is one of obvious advantage to this species, since it increases the effectiveness of insect trapping. The rapid movement of certain flower parts, such as the stigmas (the tips of the pistils, the innermost floral parts) of *Torenia* flowers, are turgor movements that are beneficial in promoting insect pollination. In the flowers of *Torenia*, catalpa, and trumpet creeper, the two-lobed stigmas are sensitive to contact and fold together quickly when they are touched (Fig. 16–14). If the stigmas are not covered with pollen during their stimulation, they open after a several minutes' closure. If, however, as normally occurs, the stigma lobes are covered with pollen, they remain closed, securing the pollen grains firmly between them.

Doubtless the most spectacular of all turgor movements is the rapid infolding of the leaflets and the sudden drooping of the whole leaves of the sensitive plant. *Mimosa pudica* (Fig. 16–12). This leaf reaction, which is initiated by various stimuli, such as sudden contact and rapid temperature change, is completed within a few seconds. After one leaf drops and folds its leaflets, other leaves above and below the stimulated leaf react successively in similar fashion. After a period of some minutes, the leaves return to their original positions. It appears that these spectacular reactions of *Mimosa* leaves possess little if any biological significance. Experiments carried out on *Mimosa* plants indicate that stimulation of a leaf releases or activates a chemical agent that moves rapidly to other leaflets of the plants, inducing them to respond in the same manner.

SUMMARY

1. The fundamental aspect of growth is the production of tissues and organs that function to maintain life processes.

2. The growth process has both qualitative and quantitative aspects. The qualitative aspects include all the structural changes that accompany growth—formation, enlargement, and differentiation of new cells into the permanent tissues of the plant. Quantitatively, growth is an irreversible increase in size of a cell, tissue, organ, or organism and is usually accompanied by an increase in dry weight.

3. Growth can continue over an extended period of time only when photosynthesis exceeds respiration.

4. The rate of growth varies in different species of plants and in different organs of the same plant.

5. Growth in plants occurs principally in root tips, buds, cambium, cork cambium, and root pericycle. The more or less continuous growth of root tips, buds, and cambium is called indeterminate growth. The growth of leaves, flowers, and fruits, which ceases after maturity, is called determinate growth.

6. Growth is influenced by a number of internal conditions, such as the hereditary nature of the plant, supply of growth hormones, reserve foods, and vitamins.

7. The hereditary nature of a plant is determined by its genetic constitution.

8. Genetic information contained in DNA is made effective through the action of derivative messenger and transfer RNA molecules, which, with the ribosomes, translate the DNA code into assembled protein molecules.

9. Enzymes mediate metabolic activities, including the production and action of the growth-regulating substances called plant hormones.

10. Hormones are naturally occurring growth-regulating substances. Characteristically, they are synthesized in one part of a plant and translocated to other parts where very small amounts of the regulators produce physiological effects.

11. Plant hormones include several kinds of compounds: auxins, gibberellins, cytokinins, dormin, and ethylene. Several plant hormonelike substances have also been synthesized artificially by man.

12. Auxins influence many growth processes, including cell division, root formation, abscission, fruit development, and phenomena involving correlation of growth activities, such as apical dominance and growth movements or tropisms.

13. Tropisms are regulated by accumulation of growth promoting or growth inhibiting concentrations of auxin on different sides of the growing organs in response to various stimuli; this results in growth of the organ toward, away from, or at right angles to the stimulus.

14. Readily observed tropisms are phototropism, the usual growth of stems and leaves toward and roots away from light, and geotropism,

the usual growth of shoots upward and roots downward in response to gravity.

15. Gibberellins also influence many growth processes, including stem elongation, cambial activity, bud development, and flowering.

16. Cytokinins influence cell division (cytokinesis) and tissue differentiation; at least a portion of the action of cytokinins appears to be linked to their roles as inducers of protein synthesis.

17. Dormin affects dormancy phenomena, including leaf senescence and leaf drop, formation of bud scales, and dormancy of seeds and apical meristems.

18. Ethylene is a normal by-product of cell metabolism, and influences respiration, fruit ripening, bud development, leaf abscission, and apical dominance.

19. The action of any one hormone may be influenced by others, and they may act together (synergistically) to promote growth phenomena or in opposition to one another (antagonistically).

20. Several practical applications have been made of growth regulators: in the rooting of cuttings, the production of seedless fruits, the prevention of premature fruit drop, and weed killing.

21. Growth of plants is also influenced by many external factors, among which are light, temperature, water, gases, chemical agents, and other living organisms.

22. Turgor movements of plants are brought about by changes in turgor pressure of certain tissues and include the sleep movements of the leaves of many plants, plus the rapid contact movements of some floral organs and of the leaves of the sensitive plant and Venus'-flytrap.

SUGGESTED READINGS FOR INTERESTED STUDENTS

1. Allard, H. A. "Length of day in relation to the natural and artificial distribution of plants." *Ecology*, Vol. 13, pp. 221–234, 1932.

2. Galston, A. W. *The Life of the Green Plant*, 2d ed. Prentice-Hall, Englewood Cliffs, N.J., 1964.

3. Leopold, A. C. *Plant Growth and Development*. McGraw-Hill, New York, 1964.

4. Letham, D. S. "Cytokinins and their relation to other phytochromes," *Bioscience,* Vol. 19, pp. 309–316, 1969.

5. Ray, Peter M. *The Living Plant,* Holt, Rinehart and Winston, New York, 1965.

6. Salisbury, F. B., and R. V. Parke. *Vascular Plants: Form and Function,* Wadsworth, Belmont, Cal., 1964.

7. Sinnott, E. W. *Plant Morphogenesis*. McGraw-Hill, New York, 1960.

8. Steward, F. C. *Growth and Organization in Plants*. Addison-Wesley, Reading, Mass., 1968.

9. Torrey, J. G. *Development in Flowering Plants*. The Macmillan Co., New York, 1967.

1. Discuss the relationship between sunlight and plant growth.

2. What are the quantitative and qualitative concepts associated with a biological interpretation of growth?

3. Describe briefly the methods of measuring the growth of various plant organs.

4. In what sense is the measurement of dry weight increase a better criterion of growth than increase in fresh weight, increase in length, or increase in some other dimension?

5. May growth occur in plants without increase in size? Explain.

6. Where in plants is growth most pronounced?

7. Distinguish between indeterminate and determinate growth.

8. List the principal internal factors that influence plant growth.

9. What is the relationship between heredity and growth phenomena in species?

10. What substance is responsible for the hereditary nature of plants? Where in the cell is nearly all of this substance located?

11. Describe the manner in which the information of DNA is translated into enzyme regulators of metabolism.

12. What are inducers and repressors? What substances act as inducers and repressors in plants?

13. Define the term "plant hormone."

14. List the major groups of plant hormones, and describe their actions.

15. Distinguish between growth and tropism; between phototropism and geotropism; between positive geotropism and negative geotropism.

16. What plant hormones are principally active in regulating phototropism and geotropism? Describe this action for geotropism.

17. What is "foolish seedling" disease of rice? What organism causes it?

18. What is 2,4-D? How does it act, and how is it used commercially?

19. List several economic applications of our knowledge of plant hormone activity, including the hormone type used in each instance.

20. What is photoperiodism?

21. Comment briefly on the ecological aspects of photoperiodism.

22. What practical applications have been made of photoperiodic studies? Explain how the study of photoperiodism may be important in the selection of crops for cultivation in different parts of the world.

23. Describe briefly the relation of temperature to flowering.

24. What is the effect of reduced transpiration on plant growth?

25. What are the effects of industrial gases on plant growth?

26. Name some of the organisms that parasitize flowering plants. In what ways do these parasites harm the plants upon which they grow?

27. What effects do grazing animals exert on plants?

28. How would you account for the fact that grazing animals eagerly eat some species of plants but avoid others?

29. List and describe briefly the chief differences between turgor movements and growth movements.

17

THE STRUCTURE
AND FUNCTIONS
OF FLOWERS

THE DEVELOPMENT AND
STRUCTURE OF FLOWERS

The activities thus far considered in flowering plants are termed **vegetative activities.** They involve the absorption of raw materials from the atmosphere and the soil, the synthesis of foods and other complex organic substances from these raw materials, the translocation of foods and water, the release and utilization of the potential energy of foods, and the processes involved in growth, differentiation, and reaction. Vegetative

processes serve primarily in maintaining the life of the individual. Ordinarily, vegetative activities begin in sprouting seeds and continue for a varying period of time before reproduction commences.

The **reproductive activities** of flowering plants center on the propagation of the species through the formation of offspring. The reproductive processes of flowering plants may be divided into two categories: **asexual,** or **vegetative reproduction,** and **sexual reproduction,** which is typically associated with seed formation. Vegetative re-

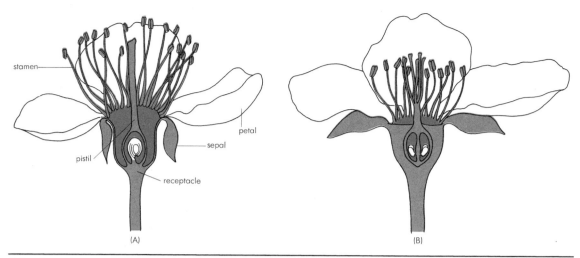

FIG. 17-1. Longitudinal sections of complete flowers. A. With superior ovary (plum). B. With interior ovary (apple).

production includes the formation of new plants by runners, rhizomes, tubers, bulbs, and corms, the development of new individual plants as root suckers, and various human-controlled processes such as grafting, layering, and the rooting of cuttings of stems and leaves. Sexual reproduction involves, in part, the fusion of a male gamete, or **sperm,** with a female gamete, or **egg,** in the ovule of a flower. This fusion process, called **fertilization,** results in the formation of a fertilized egg, or **zygote,** that develops into the embryo of a seed.

In the angiosperms, the characteristic reproductive structures are **flowers.** A flower is regarded by botanists as a specialized shoot, some parts of which are directly involved in reproduction, others of which are only indirectly concerned with reproductive activity. Some of these floral organs are leaflike in development and structure, whereas others have the developmental and anatomical characteristics of stems.

Flowers develop from buds, as do vegetative shoots. Some buds produce only flowers (lilac, tulip, morning-glory, and poplar); others produce both flowers and leaves (buckeye and apple), and bring about increase in the lengths of stems in addition. Flowers differ from vegetative shoots in that there is virtually no elongation of their internodes, as a result of which floral organs are bunched together and are not distributed at obvious intervals along the floral axis. Moreover, growth of the flower is determinate; that is, no further apical growth occurs after the floral parts have been formed, whereas apical growth of the vegetative shoot is indeterminate. Flowers also differ from vegetative shoots in that buds normally do not develop in the axils of floral organs as they do in the axils of green leaves of vegetative twigs. The parts of a flower develop as lateral protuberances of a bud's terminal portion in much the same way as do foliage leaves. The lowermost floral organs usually develop first, followed in order by the more apically situated parts, those nearest the tip of the bud enlarging last. The tip of a floral stalk, from which floral organs grow, is called the **receptacle.**

The most familiar types of flowers, such as those of snapdragons, morning-glories, roses, irises, and petunias, are **complete** flowers; that is, they bear on their receptacles four kinds of floral parts: **(1)** sepals, **(2)** petals, **(3)** stamens, and **(4)** pistils (Fig. 17–1). Botanists commonly regard these structures as highly modified leaves. The outermost (lowermost) of these are the sepals, which in most kinds of flowers are small, green, leaflike structures. The sepals enclose and protect the other floral parts in the bud before they are fully developed. The sepals collectively are called the **calyx.** Above (inside) the sepals are the usually showy, often brightly colored **petals,** known collectively as the **corolla.** The number of petals in a flower is usually the same as that of the sepals or sometimes a multiple of the sepal number. Iris flowers have three sepals and three petals, and magnolia flowers have three sepals and six petals. Petals serve primarily to attract insects, the visits of which are important in the reproductive functions of flowers. Petals secure the attention of insects in several ways. The bright colors of many flowers are attractive to insects. Some petals have glands **(nectaries)** that secrete nectar, a sweet liquid which provides food for bees and other kinds of flower-visiting insects. The odors of the essential oils and other substances produced by the petals of many species of plants constitute another means of luring insects to flowers. In many species, floral fragrances are very plesant to the human sense of smell as well. The characteristic odors of jasmine, rose, lavender, sweet pea, carnation, and other flowers arise from substances secreted by petals, and many of these substances are of importance in perfume manufacture. In a few species, such as skunk cabbage and Dutchman's pipe (*Aristolochia*), the floral odors are strong and exceedingly unpleasant. These offensive odors attract chiefly flies and other kinds of insects that commonly visit decaying animal flesh and other rotting, ill-smelling organic matter. Many flowers of this type are reddish brown in color. The insects that visit pleasantly scented flowers are not attracted to them.

Inside (above) the petals are the **stamens,** which produce **pollen grains.** A stamen usually consists of a slender stalk, or **filament,** that bears at its apex a single, enlarged, often more or less cylindrical or ovoid, **anther.** Within the anthers develop the pollen grains which later lead to the formation of male reproductive cells, or **sperms.**

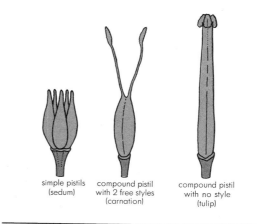

simple pistils
(sedum)

compound pistil
with 2 free styles
(carnation)

compound pistil
with no style
(tulip)

Fig. 17-2. Types of pistils.

In the center of a complete flower is a **pistil** (or pistils), which consists usually of three fairly distinct portions: an enlarged basal **ovary,** within which the seeds are formed; an elongated, slender **style,** which rises from the top of the ovary; and at the top of the style, a slightly enlarged **stigma,** where pollen gains fall or are brought previous to the fertilization of the immature seeds, or **ovules.** Stigmas are frequently very rough or bristly, and sometimes they are covered with a sticky fluid, by means of which pollen grains are more securely held on the stigmatic surfaces. A pistil is composed of one or several **carpels,** or ovule-bearing organs. A pistil made up of one carpel—as in the flowers of peas, beans, and buttercups—is called a **simple pistil.** In the flowers of tulips, snapdragons, lilies, and many other species, two or more carpels are fused together into a single **compound pistil** (Fig. 17-2).

Inside the ovary of a pistil are structures called **placentae,** to which the ovules are attached, each by a short stalk or **funiculus.** The placentae usually are of the same number as the carpels in the pistil. The arrangement of placentae in an ovary varies in different species of plants; some of the common types of placentation are illustrated in Fig. 17-3. The number of ovules in an ovary varies from one, as in corn, to many hun-

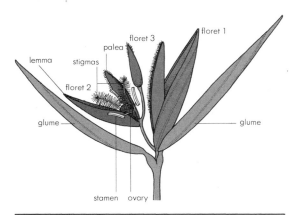

FIG. 17-3. Three types of placentation, as labeled. The two drawings at left show free central placentation as seen with longitudinal (*upper*) and transverse (*lower*) sections of the ovary.

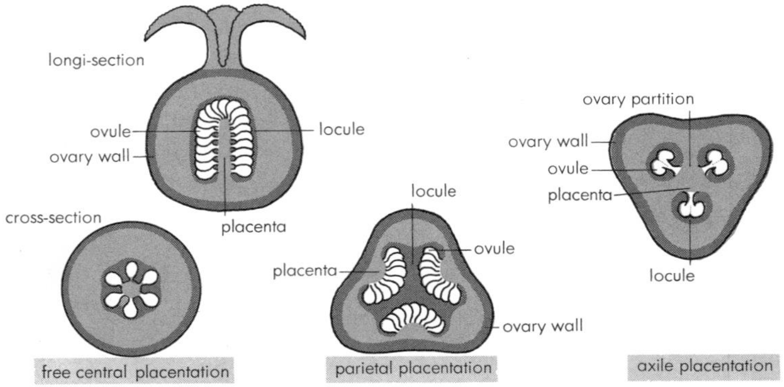

longi-section
ovule
ovary wall
cross-section
locule
placenta
free central placentation

locule
placenta
ovule
ovary wall
parietal placentation

ovary partition
ovary wall
ovule
placenta
locule
axile placentation

dreds, as in foxgloves, or more than a million, as in some orchids. An ovary cavity, within which ovules develop, is called a **locule.**

Sepals and petals are termed the **accessory parts** of flowers because they are not directly concerned with reproductive processes. Stamens and pistils are the **essential parts** of flowers for they are involved directly in the production of seeds. The accessory parts are frequently of indirect importance in reproduction in that they attract insects necessary for the pollination of many types of flowers.

The four kinds of floral parts described above —sepals, petals, stamens, and pistil(s)—are present in all complete flowers. Not all flowers are complete, however; in some plants, such as anem-

one and clematis, there are sepals, stamens, and pistils present but no petals. In oat flowers, stamens and pistils are present, but sepals and petals are lacking (Fig. 17–4). In corn and willows, there are two kinds of flowers, some that bear stamens, others that bear pistils; in both types, neither sepals nor petals are present. All flowers, such as those of willow, corn, clematis, and anemone, that lack one or more of the four kinds of floral parts, are called **incomplete.** Species, such as willow, corn, walnut, and cottonwood (Fig. 17–5), in which the stamens and pistils are produced in separate flowers, are said to have **imperfect flowers.** Imperfect flowers that bear stamens are termed **staminate;** those that contain pistils are called **pistillate flowers.** In willows, cottonwoods, hemp, and many other species, staminate flowers and pistillate flowers are borne on separate plants, a condition described as **dioecious.** The staminate and pistillate flowers of other species, such as walnut, oaks, and corn, are produced by the same plant; such plants are **monoecious.** Tulips, lilies, roses, sweet peas, and orchids have flowers in which both stamens and pistils are present; such flowers are termed **perfect flowers.** A flower may be perfect but incomplete; for example, oat flowers are perfect because they bear both stamens and pistils, and they are incomplete because they lack sepals and petals. Obviously all imperfect flowers are incomplete.

floret 3
floret 1
palea
lemma
stigmas
floret 2
glume
glume
stamen
ovary

Fig. 17-4. Oat spikelet and details of single flower.

FIG. 17-5. *Above:* Staminate flowers of cottonwood. *Below:* Pistillate flowers of cottonwood. These flowers are imperfect.

There are many other kinds of variations in the structure of flowers of different species of angiosperms. The number of parts, the size and color of petals, the relative position of the various floral parts, and the degree of fusion among parts are chief among the varying characteristics of the flowers of different species of plants.

The flowers of monocotyledons (about 50,000 species) generally have their flower parts in threes or multiples of three (Fig. 17-6). In tulip flowers, for example, there are three sepals, three petals, six stamens, and a pistil of three fused carpels. In iris flowers, the same numbers of parts are found, except that there are only three stamens. The same basic numbers of parts are found in most other monocot families—rushes, amaryllises, bananas, pineapples, palms, and orchids. In dicotyledons (about 200,000 species) flower parts are chiefly in fours or fives (Fig. 17-1), less frequently in twos, and in only a few families in threes. In the flowers of *Sedum* and certain other members of the live-forever family, there are five sepals, five petals, ten stamens, and five separate, simple pistils. The flowers of evening primroses have four sepals, four petals, eight stamens, and a compound ovary of four fused carpels. In members of the bleeding-heart family, the flowers have usually two sepals, four petals, six stamens, and a compound pistil of two fused carpels. Magnolias and pawpaws are among the relatively few dicotyledons in which the sepals and petals are in multiples of three.

Floral parts vary greatly in their size, color, and arrangement. In buttercups, petunias, and roses, the petals and other floral parts are equal in size and are equally spaced in position, so that the flowers are built on a circular plan, as viewed from above. This type of symmetry is termed **radial symmetry** (Fig. 17-1). In other flowering plants, such as sweet peas, snapdragons, orchids,

FIG. 17-6. *Lilium canadense,* a monocotyledon. (Photo by the Carolina Biological Supply Company.)

Fig. 17-7. The bilaterally symmetrical flowers of the dove orchid, a monocotyledon. The head of the "dove" is the column, which is a structure composed of a pistil, bearing a functional stamen near its apex.

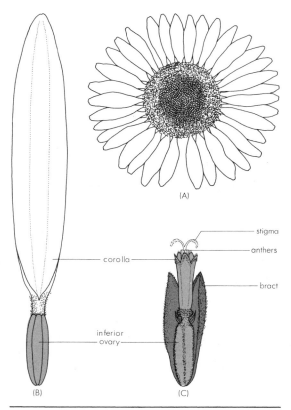

FIG. 17-8. Inflorescence of a composite (sunflower). A. Head. B. Ray flower. C. Disc flower.

and mints, the floral parts vary in size and are unequally spaced, so that flowers of this type are constructed on a right-and-left plan rather than a circular plan. This right-and-left plan of construction is called **bilateral symmetry** (Fig. 17-7).

In many flowers, such as roses and magnolias, the floral parts are all separate and distinct from each other. The flowers of petunias, phlox, and sunflowers, on the contrary, show a considerable degree of fusion among their floral parts. In petunia and phlox flowers, the petals are fused into trumpet-shaped corollas. In sunflowers the petals are fused, and the stamens are likewise fused by their anthers into a tube around the style. The degree of fusion of various flower parts thus differs widely among different species of flowering plants.

In some kinds of flowers, such as magnolias and water lilies, the floral parts are arranged in **spiral** fashion on the receptacle; that is, all the floral parts from lowermost to uppermost can be connected by a continuous, spiral line or several spiral lines. In lilies, phlox, and many other species, the flower parts are arranged in distinct circles or cycles on the receptacle and cannot be connected by a spiral line. This **cyclic** arrangement of parts is more common than the spiral arrangement among flowering plants.

Flowers vary also in the positions of their ovaries with respect to the places of attachment of sepals and petals on their receptacles. In snapdragons and morning-glories, the sepals and petals are attached to the receptacle just *beneath* the point of attachment of the ovary to the recep-

FIG. 17-9. Composite head of goatsbeard, in which all flowers are ray flowers. (Copyright, General Biological Supply House, Chicago.)

tacle. In evening primroses and honeysuckles, in contrast, the sepals, petals, and stamens grow out from the *top* of the ovary, which is sunken in the receptacle. Ovaries situated above the points of origin of sepals and petals are termed **superior ovaries.** Ovaries of the second type, with sepals and petals arising at their crests, are called **inferior ovaries** (Fig. 17-1).

Flowers vary also in their relative positions on the plants that produce them. In magnolias, most roses, and tulip trees, each flower is solitary, borne on a single stalk at some distance from other flowers. In snapdragons, lilacs, and asters, several or many flowers are borne in a cluster. These flower clusters, or **inflorescences,** differ markedly in the number of flowers they bear, the number and arrangement of their branches, and in other respects.

A type of inflorescence called a **head** is characteristic of members of the daisy, or composite family (Figs. 17-8 and 17-9). In a head, the flowers are small and are tightly crowded on a flattened or convex, disc-shaped compound receptacle. The corollas of the marginal flowers on these discs are much enlarged and brightly colored in most composites. These **rays** are commonly and erroneously called petals. Each of these so-called petals of a sunflower head, for example, is really the corolla of a ray flower. The flowers that occupy the central part of a sunflower head have much smaller, less conspicuous corollas than do the ray flowers; furthermore, these **disc** flowers are radially symmetrical whereas ray flowers are bilaterally symmetrical. In sunflowers, as in many other composites, the disc flowers produce seeds, while the ray flowers

FIG. 17–10.   Inflorescences of dogwood (*Cornus florida*). Each inflorescence consists of several very small flowers subtended by four large, white bracts.

These bracts are sometimes small, as in snapdragons, or they may be large and brightly colored, as in poinsettias and bougainvillea. There is commonly a gradual transition from typical foliage leaves to bracts. One may find a graded series of such structures in snapdragons and foxgloves, and in poinsettias in which there are leaves intermediate between the green leaves and the bright red bracts. Bracts sometimes attract insects or offer protection to flowers, but commonly they seem devoid of function.

The flowers of grasses merit brief description because of the abundance of grasses in the earth's vegetation and of their great economic importance. A grass inflorescence bears flowers in separate, small clusters called **spikelets** (Fig. 17–4). At the base of a typical spikelet is a pair of chaffy bracts called **sterile glumes.** A slender, short stalk projects above the glumes, and at its joints other pairs of bracts are borne. The larger bract of each of these pairs is the **lemma,** the smaller the **palea.** Within each such pair is borne a single flower. In most grasses a flower consists of a single pistil with two feathery, long styles and three stamens with long, slender filaments. In a few species, the flowers are imperfect, as in corn, in which the pistillate flowers are borne on the ears and the staminate in the tassels. A spikelet may bear only one flower, as in barley, or several flowers, as in oats. Pollination of grass flowers is by wind, the long, feathery styles capturing wind-borne pollen (Fig. 17–22, A) shed by the long, dangling stamens which protrude beyond the enveloping bracts. The "chaff" of many grains consists of lemmas and paleas that adhere to the grains. Threshing removes the chaff, freeing the grains.

The many diverse features of flower structure furnish the chief criteria used to distinguish among various species of flowering plants and to classify such plants into related groups. On the basis of their study of plant fossils, of the anatomy of flowers of living plants, of the developmental histories of flower parts, and of other features of floral structure, botanists have demonstrated that evolution has occurred among the

are sterile. A whole sunflower is thus not a single flower but an inflorescence bearing many dozens of tiny flowers. In some composites, for example, dandelion and goatsbeard, the inflorescence is made up entirely of ray-type flowers (Fig. 17–9); in other composites, for example, ageratum and blazing star, the head is composed entirely of disc flowers.

In many kinds of inflorescences, special, leaf-like structures called **bracts** grow out from the main stalk **(peduncle)** of the inflorescence (Fig. 17–10). A bract may grow from the base of the peduncle, or from the juncture of each individual flower stalk **(pedicel),** with the peduncle, in such fashion that the flower is in the axil of its bract, just as a vegetative twig is in the axil of a leaf.

anther

stigma

filament

FIG. 17–11. A. An oat spikelet, showing two flowers ready for pollination. B. An enlarged view of a single flower. (Courtesy of Dr. O. T. Bonnet, U. of Illinois, Urbana.)

angiosperms and that certain types of floral structure are to be regarded as primitive while others are more advanced. Table 17–1 lists some primitive and advanced characters of flowers.

Among plants that are considered to have primitive or intermediate types of flowers are magnolias, buttercups, barberries, tulip trees, and roses. Species that have more advanced types of flowers are mints, petunias, snapdragons, morning-glories, potatoes, and sunflowers.

THE POLLINATION OF FLOWERS

Pollination is one of a series of processes that result in the formation of seeds and thus is ex-

ceedingly important in the lives of angiosperms. Pollination in angiosperms is the transfer of pollen grains from an anther to a stigma. The transfer of pollen from the anther of one flower to the stigma of a flower of another plant is termed **cross-pollination.** In **self-pollination,** pollen is carried from an anther to the stigma of the same flower or to another flower of the same plant. In some species (for example, orchids), only cross-pollination occurs; in others (for example, peas), self-pollination is the rule.

Flowers that produce seeds following self-pollination are termed **self-fertile,** and those that form seeds only as a result of cross-pollination are **self-sterile.** Flowers of pears, grapes, and

Primitive Characters	Advanced Characters
1. Large, variable numbers of parts	1. Smaller, constant numbers of parts
2. Spiral arrangement of parts	2. Cyclic arrangement of parts
3. Solitary flowers	3. Flowers in inflorescences
4. Parts separate	4. Parts partly or wholly fused
5. Superior ovaries	5. Inferior ovaries
6. Radial symmetry	6. Bilateral symmetry

TABLE 17–1 Characteristics of flowers

FIG. 17–12. Portion of staminate inflorescence of corn, showing dangling stamens. (Copyright, General Biological Supply House, Chicago)

apples are chiefly cross-pollinated. If cross-pollination fails, self-pollination of these flowers often occurs, with the result that some fruits and seeds are formed. These are usually fewer and sometimes smaller than fruits and seeds resulting from cross-pollination. Horticulturists advise the establishment of beehives in or near orchards in order to ensure cross-pollination of flowers so

FIG. 17–13. Bees entering snapdragon flowers. (Photo by C. F. Hottes.)

FIG. 17–14. Tip of mature style ("silk") of corn, showing pollen grains. (Courtesy of Dr. O. T. Bonnet, U. of Illinois.)

FIG. 17–15. Flowers of *Clerodendron*. *Left:* The stamens are mature, the style is immature and is still curled downward. *Right:* Stamens have shed their pollen and have begun to dry up, and the style is now erect and capable of receiving pollen.

that the resulting fruit crop may be large and of superior quality.

The natural agents of pollination are most commonly **wind** and **insects,** less frequently **birds** and **water,** rarely bats, snails, and other animals. Bees, butterflies, and moths are the most common insect visitors of flowers (Fig. 17–13). Various kinds of birds, particularly hummingbirds in search of nectar, are important in pollinating flowers of some species. In most flowering plants, insects are the most common agents of pollination. Insect-pollinated and wind-pollinated flowers have certain fundamental structural and behavioral differences that reflect their different modes of pollination. Wind-pollinated flowers, such as those of cottonwoods, oaks, corn, wheat, and cattails, are usually borne in rather dense clusters, produce copious pollen, and have stigmas that are greatly enlarged or that are equipped with long hairs that catch and hold pollen grains as they are blown through the air (Fig. 17–14). Flowers of roses, orchids and apples, which are pollinated by insects, generally possess rather large and showy petals, produce nectar or aromatic substances or both, form smaller quantities of pollen than do wind-pollinated flowers, and usually have stigmas that lack bristles and hairs and that are smaller than those of wind-pollinated flowers (Fig. 17–1). Many insect-pollinated flowers lack showy corollas but have brightly colored sepals (four-o'clock), showy stamens (willow, eucalyptus), or large bracts (dogwood, poinsettia). In many cases, the individual flowers of an inflorescence are relatively small and inconspicuous, but the inflorescence itself is showy, as in lilacs, phlox, milkweeds, and forget-me-nots. In composites, the flowers are tiny, but the heads in which they occur are usually conspicuous, chiefly because of the large corollas of the ray flowers.

A cross section of an anther shows usually four pollen sacs, within which the pollen grains are produced. When an anther reaches maturity, the pollen sacs open, usually by longitudinal slits, and the pollen grains are thus exposed and are ready for transfer to a stigma.

In many species of plants, it seems that greater vigor is shown by the offspring of cross-pollinated

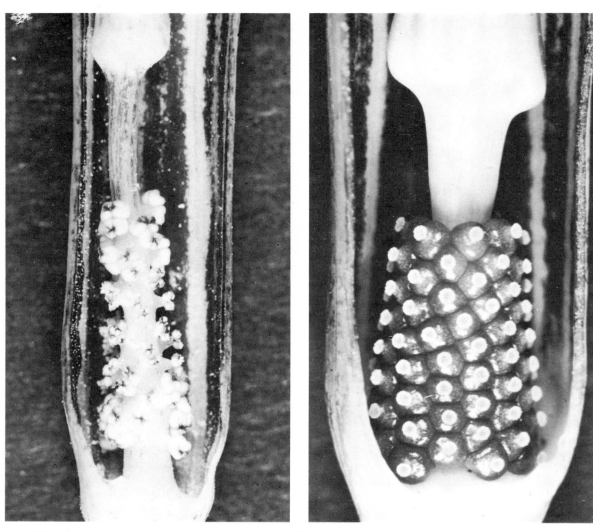

FIG. 17-16. Inflorescence bases of jack-in-the-pulpit (*Arisaema*). *Left:* Staminate flowers from inflorescence of male plant. *Right:* Pistillate flowers from inflorescence of female plant. The enveloping sheaths are bracts. (Copyright, General Biological Supply House, Chicago.)

flowers than by those of self-pollinated flowers. This fact, together with the facts that the flowers of most species of angiosperms are cross-pollinated and that there exist in these flowers many modes of behavior and highly specialized devices to ensure cross-pollination, indicates that this type of pollination is highly advantageous. Among the ingenious methods that ensure cross-

pollination or make it more effective are the following: imperfect flowers (Figs. 17-5 and 17-16), chemical incompatability between pollen and stigma of flowers on the same plant, differences in time of maturation of stigmas and stamens (Fig. 17-15), and a specialized floral structure that keeps the stamens out of proximity to the stigma in the same flower.

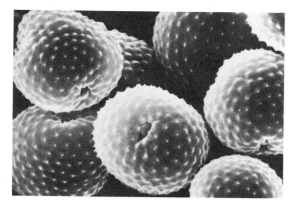

FIG. 17–17. Electron micrograph of pollen grains of the cocklebur (*Xanthium*) showing germinal pores. (Courtesy of Jean Schoknecht and A. J. Hicks, U. of Illinois, Urbana.)

FERTILIZATION IN FLOWERS

After pollen grains (Fig. 17–17) are deposited on a stigma, swellings appear in the thin places in their walls. The pollen grains absorb water, sugars, and other materials from the stigma and use these substances, together with the foods stored within them, in the production of **pollen tubes** (Figs. 17–18 and 17–19). Each pollen grain normally produces a single tube, which grows downward through the style. The lengths attained by pollen tubes vary in different species of plants, depending on the lengths of the styles through which they must grow. In some flowers, such as those of willow and beet, the styles are only about $\frac{1}{10}$ inch long, and the pollen tubes are accordingly short. In some lilies, the styles are 5 inches long, and in the pistillate flowers of corn the styles (silks) are frequently 16 to 20 inches long, with pollen tubes necessarily somewhat longer. In many short-styled flowers only a few hours are required for the complete growth of pollen tubes whereas in many long-styled species, several weeks may be required for the full growth of pollen tubes. The length of the style is not always a controlling factor in determining the time required for a pollen tube to complete its journey

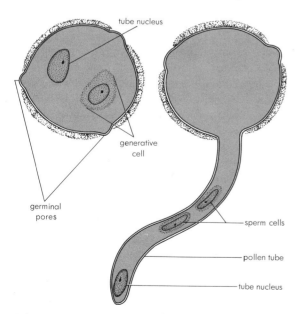

FIG. 17–18. Diagram of pollen grain (*left*) and germinating pollen grain with pollen tube (*right*).

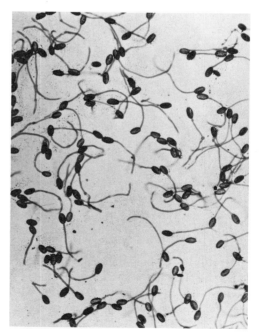

FIG. 17–19. Germinating pollen grains, with their pollen tubes.

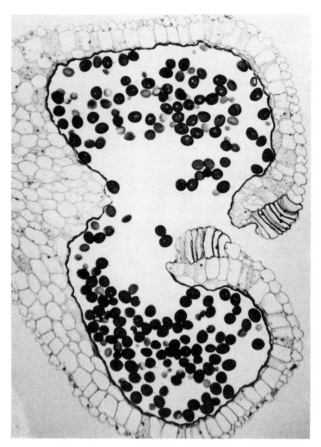

FIG. 17-20. Portion of *Lilium* (lily) anther in transverse section, showing numerous pollen grains.

pollen grain is usually a two-celled structure, consisting of a tube cell and a generative cell. In the growing pollen tube, the tube cell nucleus usually precedes the generative cell and controls the growth of the pollen tube. At some time during the development of the tube the generative cell nucleus undergoes a single mitotic division, following which two sperm cells are formed. Each of these is directly involved in the complex fertilization process that occurs in the ovule. In some pollen grains, the sperms are formed prior to the development of the pollen tube.

A pistil is composed of one or more carpels. A carpel is interpreted by many botanists as a much modified leaf which is folded along its midrib and fused at its margins to produce an elongate hollow structure. Ovules are produced from the surface within the chamber, usually near the margins. If the simple pistil (a single carpel) of a pea is opened along the line of marginal fusion and is spread out flat, it bears a striking resemblance to a foliage leaf, from which it differs in that it has ovules attached to its edges.

In compound pistils, two or more carpels are fused together into one pistil. In some species, such as lilies, there are as many cavities in the ovary of the compound pistil as there are carpels; in a lily ovary, there are three fused carpels, each fundamentally like the one-carpellate pistil of pea but combined into a compound pistil with three separate cavities, within which the ovules are borne. In other species, carpel fusion is such that there are no walls between the locules; the ovary of such a pistil, although it is composed of two or more carpels, has but a single cavity. In most flowering plants the number of styles, or of style or stigma branches, coincides with the number of carpels in their pistils. In lilies, for example, there are three stigma branches and three carpels in a pistil, in cherry flowers one style and one carpel, in morning-glories two style branches and two carpels. There are some exceptions to this correspondence; in a tomato flower, for example, there is a two-carpellate pistil with but a single, unbranched style.

through the style. In oak flowers, for example, pollen tubes require several months to grow through the styles, which are about $\frac{1}{8}$ inch long whereas in corn the pollen tubes often complete their growth through more than a foot of style within 36 hours.

Pollen tubes continue their downward growth through the style until they reach the ovary cavity, within which the ovules are contained. The pollen tubes grow along the inside of the ovary wall until they reach the ovules, which they enter. Although many pollen tubes reach an ovary, only one pollen tube usually enters each ovule. A

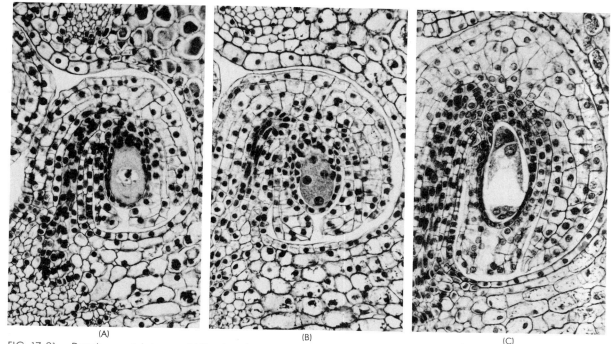

FIG. 17–21.   Developmental stages of *Lilium* female gametophyte. A. Ovule showing large diploid megaspore mother cell. B. Ovule showing four haploid megaspore nuclei. C. Ovule showing 8-nucleate stage, 4 triploid nuclei above, and 4 smaller, haploid nuclei below.

An ovule, or undeveloped seed, is attached to the inside of the ovary in which it is borne by a short stalk (Fig. 17–3). The outer cells of an ovule form one or two fairly distinct layers termed **integuments,** which, after fertilization, become differentiated as the seed coats. At one end of the ovule there is a tiny pore in the integuments, the **micropyle.** Inside the integuments and other outer cells of an ovule is a somewhat ovoid **embryo sac** (Fig. 17–21), which usually occupies the greater part of the volume of an ovule. A typical embryo sac at the time when it is ready for fertilization contains the following structures: an **egg cell** (female gamete) and two **synergid cells** at the micropylar end of the embryo sac, two **polar nuclei** in the central region, and three **antipodal cells** opposite the micropylar end (Fig. 30–5).

When a pollen tube after its growth down a style reaches an ovule, it penetrates the micropyle and enters the embryo sac, into which it dis-

charges a portion of its contents, most important of which are the two sperms. One of the sperms fuses with the egg. The other fuses with the two polar nuclei to form the **endosperm nucleus.** The remaining five cells of the embryo sac (three antipodals and two synergids) usually disintegrate after fertilization is completed. The term **double fertilization** is applied to the two fusion processes in which the sperms engage.

After fertilization, the ovary usually begins to enlarge into the **fruit,** and as it does so the ovules also develop. As stated in Chapter 16, pollination and fertilization are stimuli that initiate the enlargement of the ovary. The zygote by numerous cell divisions and differentiation processes becomes the embryo within the seed. The nutritive **endosperm tissue** is formed by mitotic divisions of the endosperm nucleus and subsequent cell formation.

In summary, the complex series of events involved in pollination and fertilization in flowers is as follows:

1. Pollination is accomplished by transfer of pollen grains from a stamen to a stigma by wind, insects, or some other agency.

2. Pollen grains absorb water from the stigma and produce pollen tubes, which grow down through the style into the ovary.

3. Each pollen tube has a tube nucleus, which controls the growth of the tube, and a generative cell, which divides into two sperm cells.

4. A pollen tube enters an ovule through the micropyle, a pore in the integuments of the ovule.

5. In an ovule there is an embryo sac, which at the time of fertilization contains an egg cell and two synergid cells at the micropylar end, three antipodal cells at the opposite end, and two polar nuclei in the central part of the sac.

6. A pollen tube penetrates the embryo sac where it discharges its two sperms.

7. One sperm fertilizes the egg, forming a zygote, which by subsequent growth develops into the embryo of the seed.

8. The other sperm fuses with the polar nuclei, forming the endosperm nucleus, which after numerous mitotic divisions gives rise to the endosperm or food storage tissue of the seed.

9. The developing seed enlarges as a result of growth of the endosperm and of the embryo and the movement of food into it, the integuments harden into the seed coat, and the fruit undergoes enlargement.

10. When the fruit reaches maturity, it splits open, or, if there is no definite splitting, its walls disintegrate, and the mature seeds are freed.

The enlargement of ovaries into fruits and of ovules into seeds requires much food. Soluble foods, such as sugars, amino acids, and simple proteins, move rapidly through vascular tissues that connect flower parts with stems into the cells of the ovules and of the ovary walls. When these foods reach their destination, they may be converted into insoluble storage foods, such as starches, complex proteins, and fats. In this process, the water content of maturing ovules, and often of fruits, decreases markedly, so that mature seeds contain a low percentage of moisture, usually not more than 10 percent.

The maturation of fruits and seeds often has an inhibitory effect on the growth of vegetative organs, especially of annual and biennial plants, usually leading to their death—in annuals at the end of one season of growth, in biennials during the second season of their lives. In some perennials, such as century plants (*Agave*) there is a vegetative period from 5 to 60 years or more, following which the plants flower once and die. If the maturation of seeds and fruits in such plants is prevented by removal of the flowers as they appear, there is usually no inhibition of vegetative growth, which may continue for many weeks or months. Many of us have practiced the gardener's advice "to keep picking the sweet pea flowers if you want the plants to keep flowering." This valuable admonition applies not only to sweet peas but to pansies, stocks, larkspurs, and many other garden annuals as well. It has long been thought by plant physiologists and horticulturists that this inhibition of vegetative growth and the frequent death of plants following seed and ovary maturation result from exhaustion by the rapidly growing seeds and fruits of food reserves stored in vegetative organs. However, there is evidence to indicate that this inhibition must be at least in part attributable to some physiological cause other than exhaustion of food reserves. It has been suggested that young, developing fruits produce a hormone that in some manner retards vegetative growth. There is insufficient information as yet concerning the nature of this supposed hormone or the manner of its action.

Usually the development of ovules into seeds and the growth of an ovary into a fruit follow only after pollination and fertilization have occurred. In most species of flowering plants, failure of pollination results in failure of fruit and seed production. This frequently occurs if pollinating insects are not active or if destruction of pollen occurs. In many kinds of fruit trees, if heavy rains fall during the time when pollen grains are maturing, they are washed out of the flowers, pollination does not occur, and, as a result, few or no flowers "set fruits." The action of pollen on ovaries is at least twofold: the pollen grains produce the sperm cells that fertilize the eggs within the ovules and thus lead to the development of embryos within the seeds, and they stimulate a hormonal reaction that controls the enlargement of ovaries into fruits. If an extract of pollen grains is prepared and is placed on the stigmas of flowers ovary enlargement commonly occurs. The same result, as described in the last chapter, may be obtained by spraying growth-promoting substances on, or injecting them into, ovaries of many species of plants. This type of fruit development is called **artificial parthenocarpy.** This treatment leads to the production of seedless fruits that are often more succulent and more desirable than normal, seed-containing fruits. Some kinds of plants produce seedless fruits naturally, that is, without treatment of their pistils with growth-promoting substances. In navel oranges, bananas, and pineapples, for example, ovaries normally develop into seedless fruits, a type of fruit development called **natural parthenocarpy.**

Now that our study of the biology of flowering plants has brought us back to the subject of seeds, students should review seed structure and germination.

THE INITIATION OF FLOWERING

One of the major unsolved problems in the study of plant physiology is that of the factors responsible for the initiation of flowering. For a long time, plant physiologists regarded flowering as the result of accumulation of food reserves within the vegetative organs of plants. According to this interpretation, the production of flowers requires large quantities of food and is able to begin only when a sufficient amount of food has been synthesized and stored. This explanation of the cause of flowering is acceptable so far as it goes, for flower formation does require the

mobilization of foods in flower buds, but it is inadequate because it does not explain many of the phenomena associated with flowering.

Our knowledge of the reproductive process was greatly advanced in 1920 when it was discovered that the length of the day and night plays an important role in floral initiation and that the dark period of each 24-hour day is the principal factor in control of flowering. This response of plants to the duration of alternating periods of light and dark is known as **photoperiodism.** Certain species of plants (for example, poinsettias, most chrysanthemums, certain soybean varieties, cosmos, asters, dahlias, and violets) produce flowers only when the daily photoperiod is shorter than a critical length, usually about 14 hours; these plants are called **short-day plants** (Fig. 17–22). Other species (for example, lettuce, beets, spinach, wheat, clovers, delphiniums, gladiolas, and coreopsis) flower only when the daily photoperiod is longer than a critical length; these plants are termed **long-day plants** (Fig. 17–23). If short-day plants are exposed to long photoperiods, they do not produce flowers or their flowering is much delayed. Similarly, if long-day plants are exposed to short photoperiods, they fail to flower or their flowering is delayed. Some species, termed **indeterminate** species, flower irrespective of the photoperiods to which they are exposed; examples of such plants are buckwheat, tomatoes, carnations, cotton, and dandelions. During the past 50 years, the efforts of many investigators have yielded considerable data on the physiological and morphological changes associated with flower initiation, including hormone activity, and, more recently, the first substantial clues regarding the timing mechanism inherent in photoperiodism.

The mechanism by which plants respond to photoperiod duration is still not fully understood, but there is increasing evidence that flowering may be linked, at least in part, to the activities of the pigment complex known as the phytochrome system. The light-sensitive pigment **phytochrome** is present in leaves and exists in

FIG. 17–22. Milmi (*Amaranthus edulis*), a food plant of the Andes mountains, is a short-day species. The plant at left was grown on 8-hour daily photoperiods. The central plant was grown in 14-hour daily photoperiods. The plant at right was grown on 24-hour photoperiods. Only the plant grown with short photoperiods has flowers.

two forms: one which absorbs red light and is designated P_R, and another which absorbs far red light and is designated P_{FR}. The two forms are interconvertible; exposure of P_R to red light converts it to P_{FR}, and exposure of P_{FR} to far red light converts it to P_R. Under conditions of natural daylight, conversion of P_R to P_{FR} occurs to such an extent that a P_{FR} level is attained which effectively influences the metabolism of the plant. It has been suggested that during the night P_{FR} spontaneously converts to P_R and that the level of P_R thus increases with lenghtening night periods. In short-day plants, experiments have shown that it is P_R which promotes flowering, while P_{FR} inhibits flowering. In order to flower, short-day plants must experience a daily, uninterrupted dark period of sufficient length to allow conversion of a quantity of inhibitory P_{FR} to the noninhibitory P_R; with this system in operation, the plant is able to "measure" night length (or its converse, day length). The dark period must be continuous, for if it is interrupted by even a brief flash of light, no flowers are produced. Investigation of this phenomenon by researchers in the U.S. Department of Agriculture showed that exposure of a short-day plant to a flash of red light was more effective in the prevention of flowering than exposure to other colors. They also learned that brief exposure to far red light, when applied immediately after a flash of red light, would reverse the inhibitory effect. Long-day plants exhibit responses to P_R and P_{FR} levels which appear to be essentially the opposite of short-day plants; they, thus, require a relatively short dark period.

Although phytochrome has been isolated and chemically characterized as a protein, the exact mode of its action is still unknown. Also, it appears that other substances which are dependent on the phytochrome system are also involved in

Fig. 17-23. Photoperiodism in the China Aster, a long-day plant. The plant at left received normal short winter days, plus 9 hours each night of electric illumination of 10 foot-candles intensity. The central plant received a similar treatment, but the intensity of the night illumination was only 0.1 foot-candle. The plant at right received normal short winter days without supplementary night illumination.

flower initiation. Notable among these is the flowering hormone, **florigen.** Although the chemical nature of florigen is unknown, its presence has been demonstrated by experimentation. For example, the cocklebur, a short-day plant, will not flower when grown under a regime of long days and short nights; conversely, cocklebur plants grown with short days and long nights are induced to flower. When two plants growing under these different conditions are grafted together, a flowering stimulus, which must be the chemical substance florigen, is transmitted from the induced to the noninduced plant, causing the latter to flower. Further experimental evidence indicates that florigen is synthesized in leaves. Although the relationship between phytochrome and florigen action is unclear, it seems probable that phytochrome acts as a timer, while florigen transmits the timer signal to meristems which subsequently differentiate to produce inflorescence and flower primordia. A balance between the carbohydrate and nitrogenous constituents of the tissues of some plants seems also to be related to the initiation of flowering. A high carbohydrate content in relation to nitrogen content seems to favor early flowering in some species; in others, a shift in the carbohydrate-nitrogen ratio appears to occur after flower production has begun.

Other factors of the external environment also exert some effect on flower production. Plants growing in fertile soils, and thereby supplied with all essential nutrients, are more likely to undergo normal flowering than plants growing in poor, exhausted soils. Also, temperature is an important external factor in the flowering of many species. For example, cotton plants require fairly high minimum temperatures before they flower whereas other species may flower at much lower temperatures. Many spring-flowering plants of temperate regions require an exposure to low temperatures during the preceding winter to initiate flowering. Many species of plants come into flower quickly when some environmental condition, or combination of conditions, assumes an unfavorable aspect; sudden drops in temperature, drought, and crowding by other plants are some of the factors which often act as stimuli to flowering.

SUMMARY

1. Leaves, stems and roots function primarily in maintaining the life of the individual plant, although some of them carry out vegetative reproduction (rhizomes, runners, and tubers).

2. Seed formation involves a sexual process and is the function of flowers.

3. Flowers develop from buds, the floral parts arising as lateral protuberances of the growing points of buds.

4. A flower cluster is an inflorescence.

5. A flower is interpreted as a reproductive shoot bearing parts, some of which are similar to leaves in their origin and structure.

6. A complete flower consists of a receptacle, to which are attached four kinds of floral parts: sepals (calyx collectively), petals (corolla collectively), stamens, and pistil(s). A pistil consists of one or more carpels. The enlarged base of a pistil is the ovary; this contains ovules that develop into seeds after fertilization.

7. Sepals protect the inner parts of young flowers, petals attract insects, stamens produce pollen grains, and carpels produce ovules.

8. There are many variations in the structural and physiological features of flowers: numbers of parts, size and form of parts, color, kinds of parts present, and so forth.

9. Pollination is the transfer of pollen grains from a stamen to a stigma. Self-pollination is the transfer of pollen from a stamen to the stigma of the same flower or another flower on the same plant. Cross-pollination is the transfer of pollen from a stamen to the stigma of a flower on another plant. Cross-pollination is the more common.

10. Pollination is brought about mainly by insects and wind, to a lesser extent by water, birds, and other agents.

11. Many kinds of flowers have specialized mechanisms or modes of behavior that attract insects or increase the effectiveness of insect pollination.

12. Structural differences often distinguish wind-pollinated and insect-pollinated flowers.

13. The events that occur from pollination through fertilization and seed development are summarized on pages 251 and 252.

14. A seed is a matured ovule. A fruit is a matured ovary.

15. Pollen affects ovaries in two ways: it provides the sperms that bring about fertilization in the ovules, and it stimulates the formation or activity of auxins that induce the enlargement of ovaries into fruits.

16. The maturation of fruits and seeds often inhibits the growth of vegetative organs and sometimes leads to the death of plants, especially annuals and biennials. The cause is probably twofold: depletion of food reserves and activation of hormones with an inhibitory effect.

17. The enlargement of a fruit without fertilization is called parthenocarpy. Parthenocarpy occurs naturally in some fruits; in others it can be induced by the application of auxins to the pistil.

18. The causes of flowering are not fully known, but both external and internal factors are involved. Probably the most important cause is the duration of the alternating periods of dark and light, with the length of the dark period being the principal controlling factor.

19. Based on their flowering response to the duration of light and dark periods, plants fall into three categories: short-day plants (those requiring short days and long nights); long-day plants (those requiring long days and short nights) and indeterminate plants (those which will flower under any regime of light and dark periods). These flowering responses are known as photoperiodism.

20. The photoperiodic response is due to the presence of a light-sensitive pigment, phytochrome, and also to floral hormones, one of which has been termed florigen. Other factors associated with the initiation of flowering are the accumulation of foods, suitable temperatures, and nutrient supplies of the soil.

SUGGESTED READINGS FOR INTERESTED STUDENTS

1. Bonner, Bruce, "Phytochrome and the red, far-red system." *Plant Biology Today—Advances and Challenges,* 2d ed. William A. Jensen and Leroy Kavaljian, Eds. Wadsworth, Belmont, Cal., 1966.

2. Eames, A. J., *Morphology of the Angiosperms.* McGraw Hill, New York, 1961.

3. Echlin, Patrick. "Pollen." *Scientific American,* vol. 218, No. 4, pp. 80–90. April 1968.

4. Hillman, William S., *The Physiology of Flowering.* Holt, Rinehart and Winston, New York, 1962.

5. Leopold, A. Carl, *Plant Growth and Development.* McGraw-Hill, New York, 1964.

6. Salisbury, Frank B., "The flowering process." *Scientific American,* Vol. 198, No. 4, pp. 108–117, April 1958.

7. Scagel, R. F., et al., *An Evolutionary Survey of the Plant Kingdom.* Wadsworth, Belmont, Cal., 1965.

8. Torrey, John G., *Development in Flowering Plants,* Current Concepts in Biology Series. The Macmillan Co., New York, 1967.

TOPICS AND QUESTIONS FOR STUDY

1. Contrast the vegetative with the reproductive activities of flowering plants.

2. Indicate the order in which these activities occur in the life of a flowering plant.

3. Describe several methods of vegetative reproduction. How does such reproduction differ from reproduction by seeds?

4. Summarize our knowledge concerning the physiological causes of flowering. Cite specific experiments as evidence.

5. Describe briefly the development of flowers.

6. Distinguish between complete and incomplete flowers.

7. Name and describe the parts of a complete flower, and state their functions.

8. How do flowers attract insects?

9. Distinguish among carpel, pistil, simple pistil, and compound pistil.

10. Define placentation.

11. What are ovules? Describe the structure of an ovule.

12. What is the major difference between flowers of monocotyledons and those of dicotyledons?

13. Distinguish between radial and bilateral symmetry. Name several specific plants to illustrate each type of floral symmetry.

14. Distinguish between spiral and cyclic arrangement of flower parts.

15. Distinguish between superior and inferior ovaries.

16. Describe in detail the structure of a composite inflorescence (head).

17. Describe the structure of a grass spikelet and of a grass flower.

18. List and describe briefly the structural differences between primitive and advanced types of flowers.

19. Define pollination, and list the principal agents of pollination.

20. Distinguish between self-pollination and cross-pollination.

21. Nursery catalogs frequently advise that a person desiring to have a fruit tree in his garden should buy two fruit trees and plant them near one another. Explain.

22. Horticulturists advise keeping beehives in or near orchards. Explain.

23. List the principal differences between wind-pollinated and insect-pollinated flowers.

24. List and describe briefly some of the features of flowers that promote cross-pollination.

25. List and describe (in the order of their occurrence) all the events that take place in the reproductive processes of flowers, from the time of pollination through the formation of mature seeds.

26. What is double fertilization?

27. It is often stated that the embryo sac has more effect on the endosperm of a seed than the pollen grain. Explain.

28. Fruit trees may flower profusely but form few fruits. Describe the conditions that might be responsible for this.

29. Fruit trees may produce very light crops following a season of heavy yield. Explain.

30. When DDT is extensively used outdoors as an insecticide, fruit production in nearby orchards may be reduced, even though DDT may not reach the trees. Explain.

31. Name and describe two effects of pollen on pistils.

32. Name some plants that produce naturally parthenocarpic fruits.

18

FRUIT DEVELOPMENT AND STRUCTURE

FRUIT DEVELOPMENT

As described in the preceding chapter, a fruit is a matured **ovary** and a seed is a matured **ovule,** which is produced inside a fruit. The term "fruit" in its technical botanical sense is thus any kind of ripened ovary within which seeds are formed and includes such diverse structures as bean and pea pods, squashes, grapes, peaches, corn grains, tomatoes, dandelion "seeds," cucumbers, and watermelons. The popular usage of "fruit" differs somewhat from the botanical usage, in that it refers only to matured ovaries that are sweet and more or less pulpy. According to this popular definition, only grapes, peaches, and watermelons of the above list are fruits; bean and pea pods, corn, squashes, tomatoes, and cucumbers are popularly termed "vegetables," although botanically they are ripened ovaries or fruits.

The development of an ovary into a fruit is a complex phenomenon that involves many physiological activites. As described in the chapter on growth, hormones play an important role in fruit development. Pollen grains contain

FIG. 18-1. Berries. Tomato (above) with thin exocarp, and orange (below) with thicker, leathery exocarp. (Copyright, General Biological Supply House, Chicago.)

auxins that directly stimulate the growth of ovaries or initiate a chain of reactions that cause an increase in the auxin concentration of ovary tissue and thus stimulate ovary growth. The development of ovaries into fruits involves many other physiological changes. Foods of various types are translocated into ovary tissues, some of them accumulating in the ovary tissues, others moving into the growing ovules. Sugars, amino acids, soluble proteins, and other foods commonly

increase in ovary tissues during ripening. The increase of sugar supplies in maturing fruits is responsible for the sweetness of many fruits, such as grapes, peaches, and bananas. The sugar content increases in the early development of corn and wheat grains (one-seeded fruits), then decreases with maturity as the sugars are converted into starch. In avocados and olives, fats and oils accumulate in large quantities in the growing tissues. The accumulation of water is often very great in fleshy fruits, such as tomatoes and watermelons: in others, such as string beans and walnuts, the water content of the fruit decreases sharply as maturity is reached. Coincident with these changes in food and water content there is often a change in the pigmentation. In tomatoes, for example, chlorophyll disappears and is replaced by carotenoid pigments as the fruits approach maturity. In Concord grapes, Jonathan apples, and many types of plums, anthocyanin pigments accumulate as ripening progresses and give the fruits their characteristic colors.

The physiological processes involved in the late stages of fruit ripening are even less understood than those occurring in the early stages of fruit development. It was discovered some years ago that ethylene, a gas, hastened the ripening of citrus and other types of fruits, a discovery that was soon applied in a practical manner to the accelerated commercial ripening of green fruits by brief storage of such fruits in chambers containing a very low concentration of ethylene. More recently it has been demonstrated that normally ripening fruits, as well as flower parts, leaves, and other plant organs, produce ethylene in minute quantities. Thus, the so-called "artificial ripening" of fruits by ethylene treatment is seemingly only an acceleration of a normal physiological ripening process. The way in which ethylene brings about fruit ripening is not known.

FRUIT STRUCTURE

As an ovary ripens into a fruit, its wall **(pericarp)** often becomes differentiated into three rather

FIG. 18-2. Drupe of peach. *Left:* Section of fruit showing intact pit (endocarp) and fleshy mesocarp. *Right:* Section of fruit with endocarp opened to show seed.

distinct layers of tissues: the **exocarp, mesocarp,** and **endocarp.** The exocarp is the outermost layer and consists usually of a single layer of epidermal cells, although in some species it may consist of several cell layers. The mesocarp is the middle layer of tissue and varies in thickness from a single layer of cells to a mass of tissues several inches thick. The endocarp, or innermost layer of the pericarp, likewise varies greatly in struc-

ture, texture, and thickness in the fruits of different species (Fig. 18-2).

There are many different kinds of fruits, which are classified principally on the basis of their structure and of the number of ovaries comprising them. A classification of some common types of fruits and brief descriptions of them are given in Table 18-1.

It is obvious from studying the classification

FIG. 18-3. Capsules of *Yucca.* (Copyright, General Biological Supply House, Chicago.)

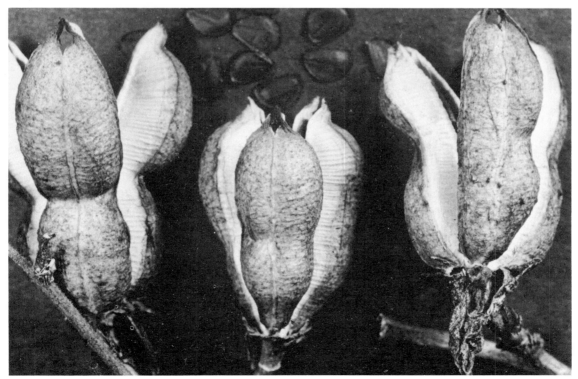

I. Simple Fruits. A simple fruit consists of single ripened ovary. The fruits of most angiosperms are simple fruits. The major types of simple fruits are:

A. Fleshy fruits, in which all or most of the pericarp is soft and fleshy at maturity. Seeds escape from fleshy fruits as a result of the decomposition of the fleshy tissues.

    1. **Berry,** in which the pericarp is fleshy throughout or nearly so. Examples: grape, banana, tomato, watermelon, orange, cucumber, and currant (Fig. 18–1).

    2. **Drupe,** in which the exocarp is a thin skin, the mesocarp is thick and fleshy, and the endocarp hard and stony. The endocarp ("stone" or "pit") encloses one, rarely two or three seeds. Examples: peach, plum, olive, cherry, apricot and coconut (Fig. 18–2).

B. Dry fruits, in which the entire pericarp becomes dry and often brittle or hard at maturity.

    1. **Dehiscent fruits,** which split open along definite seams or at definite points at maturity. Contain several to many seeds.

        a. **Legume,** consisting of one carpel, which usually splits open along two seams. Examples: pea, bean, and locust (Fig. 18–4).

        b. **Follicle,** consisting of one carpel, which splits open along one seam. Examples: larkspur, columbine, peony, and milkweed.

        c. **Capsule,** consisting of two or more fused carpels and splitting open in various ways. Examples: lily, snapdragon, tulip, and violet (Figs. 18–3 and 18–7).

        d. **Silique,** consisting of two fused carpels that separate at maturity, leaving a persistent partition between. Examples: mustard, shepherd's-purse, and cabbage (Fig. 18–8).

    2. **Indehiscent fruits,** which do not split open along definite seams or at definite points at maturity. Usually contain only one or two seeds.

        a. **Achene,** bearing only one seed which is separable from ovary wall, except at point of attachment of seed to inside of pericarp. Examples: sunflower, buttercup, dandelion, and smartweed. (Fig. 18–7).

Table 18–1

and descriptions of Table 18-1 that the common names of many kinds of fruits do not indicate their correct botanical nature. Thus, blackberries and raspberries are not berries but are aggregates of tiny drupes; the mulberry is not a berry but a multiple fruit composed of tiny nutlets that are surrounded by fleshy sepals; the strawberry is not a berry; neither is it, in the strict botanical sense, a fruit but a much enlarged receptacle, bearing on its convex surface a number of dry fruits, the achenes. An apple is not merely a fruit but is a true fruit (the core, plus a thin layer of fleshy tissues immediately surrounding it) embedded in an extensive mass of edible fleshy, succulent tissue, which is the product of the fused bases of the other floral organs. The popular term "nut" is, in most cases, not properly descriptive of the botanical nature of the fruits to which it is applied. Thus, a peanut is not a nut, but is a legume fruit. A walnut is not a nut, but a drupe, the fleshy husk of the walnut being the outer part of the pericarp, and the walnut "shell" the inner part of the pericarp; the "meat" of a walnut is the seed, with two large, much-convoluted co-

b. **Caryopsis**, or **grain**, bearing only one seed, the coat of which is completely fused to the inner surface of the pericarp. Examples: corn, wheat, and oats.

c. **Samara**, a one- or two-seeded, achenelike fruit, the pericarp of which bears a flattened, winglike outgrowth. Examples: elm, maple, ash, and wafer ash (Fig. 18–5).

d. **Nut**, a one-seeded fruit, much like an achene, but usually larger and with a thickened, very hard pericarp. Examples: acorn (oak), hazelnut, and chestnut (Fig. 18–6).

II. **Aggregate Fruits.** An aggregate fruit is a cluster of several to many ripened ovaries produced by a single flower and borne on the same receptacle. The individual, ripened ovaries may be drupes (as in raspberries and blackberries, Fig. 18–9), achenes (as in buttercups, Fig. 18–7), and so forth.

III. **Multiple (Compound) Fruits** (Fig. 18–10). A multiple fruit is a cluster of several to many ripened ovaries produced by several flowers crowded on the same inflorescence. As in aggregate fruits, the fruitlets of a compound fruit may be drupes, berries, or nutlets. Examples: mulberry, Osage orange, and pineapple.

IV. **Accessory Fruits.** Accessory fruits are structures that consist of one or more ripened ovaries together with tissues of some other floral part, such as calyx or receptacle. In an accessory fruit, these additional tissues are often extensively developed to the point of constituting the major part of the structure popularly called the "fruit." Among familiar accessory fruits are strawberries (Fig. 18–12), in which the individual fruits are achenes, borne upon an extensively developed, sweet, red, succulent receptacle. Another common type of accessory fruit is a **pome** (Fig. 18–11), exemplified by apples and pears, in which the matured ovaries (sections of the core) are surrounded by enlarged receptacle and calyx tissues in which large amounts of food and water are stored. Thus, in strawberries, apples, and pears, edible portions are not true fruits; that is, they are not the matured ovaries, but they are stem and calyx tissues in which or on which the matured ovaries, or true fruits, are embedded.

tyledons, a tiny epicotyl and hypocotyl, and a thin, papery seed coat. A Brazil nut is a seed, borne along with several other seeds in a large, thick-walled capsule; a coconut is a drupe; and an almond shell is the "stone" (hardened endocarp) of a drupe, with a single seed, rarely more.

FRUIT AND SEED DISPERSAL

The majority of higher plants have evolved definable mechanisms to facilitate dispersal of their seeds. Although there are numerous special mechanisms and many modifications of the common ones which make it impossible to present a complete discussion here, the more usual ones and a few of special interest can be mentioned briefly.

The majority of fleshy fruits are sweet and pleasantly flavored and are eaten by animals. Two common adaptations are encountered with such fruits:

1. The seeds are small and are eaten with the fruit pulp, passing unharmed through the animals'

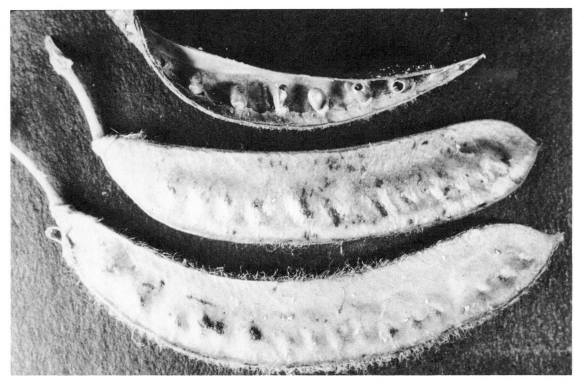

FIG. 18–4.   Legume fruits of broom (*Cytisus*). (Copyright, General Biological Supply House, Chicago.)

FIG. 18–5.   Samaras of maple (*Acer*). (Copyright, General Biological Supply House, Chicago.)

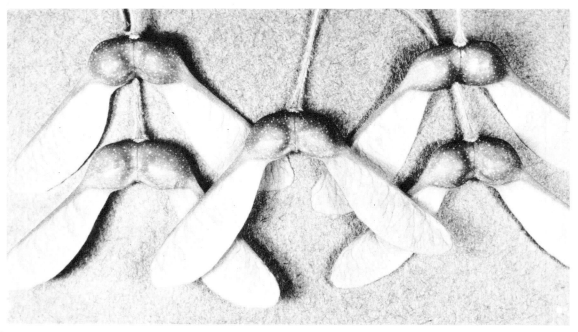

FIG. 18-6. Nuts of hazel (*Corylus*). (Copyright, General Biological Supply House, Chicago.)

digestive tracts and voided in the feces at some distance from the place of ingestion. This mechanism has the added advantage of providing the seedling with a ready supply of fertilizer. Dispersal via this mechanism is characteristic for strawberries, figs, raspberries, mulberries, and so forth.

2. The seeds are large and tend to be rejected by the animal when it eats the fruit. Because the site at which the pulp of the fruit is eaten may be some distance from the parent plant, the seeds are effectively dispersed. Fruits having large seeds not usually ingested include those of pawpaw, persimmon, banana, and the drupaceous fruits of peach, cherry, and olive.

The seeds of dry fruits are disseminated in many ways. Often, dry fruits are one-seeded

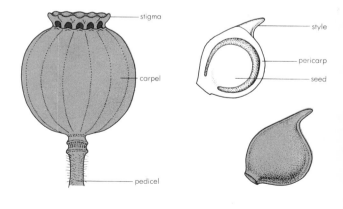

FIG. 18-7. *Left:* Capsule of poppy. *Right:* Achenes of buttercup.

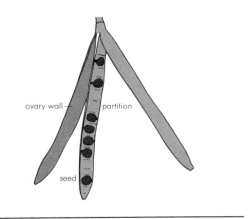

FIG. 18-8. Silique.

(achenes, nuts), thus, dispersal of individual fruits also accomplishes dispersal of individual seeds.

Among the common dispersal agencies are:

1. *Gravity*—Dry fruits, or seeds liberated from fruits, simply fall to the ground to await favorable growing conditions in subsequent seasons. Examples include the fruits and seeds of many weeds, such as pigweed, goosefoot, ragweed, most members of the mustard family (Fig. 18-8), most grasses, and the unspecialized seeds of many capsular fruits, such as those of violet, purslane, and poppy (Fig. 18-7). Seeds of such plants often accumulate in great quantities in soil.

2. *Water*—Many dry fruits and seeds are buoyant and may be carried short or long distances by streams, run-off rivulets, wave action, and the like. Often this mechanism reinforces others. The large fruits and seeds of coconuts can survive prolonged immersion in salt water and may be carried great distances by ocean currents.

3. *Wind*—Many seeds and small fruits are provided with wings or plumes which slow their rates of descent through air and permit them to be carried by air currents. Winged fruits are exemplified by the samaras of maples (Fig. 18-5) and elms, and by the bract-winged fruits of linden; winged seeds include those of catalpa and pine. Plumed fruits are exemplified by those of dandelion and clematis, and plumed seeds by those of milkweed, willow, and cottonwood. The seeds of orchids are so tiny that, although they are not provided with wings or plumes, they are carried in air as dust.

FIG. 18-9. Aggregate fruits of raspberry (*Rubus*). Note the styles extending from the small drupes. (Copyright, General Biological Supply House, Chicago.)

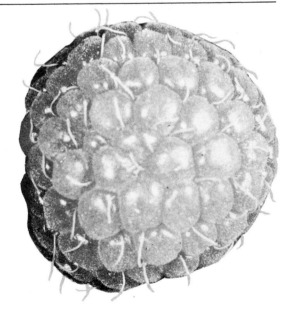

4. *Animals*—Many dry fruits possess straight or hooked spines or spiny hairs by means of which they can cling to the fur or skin of animals. Spiny fruits include those of cocklebur, beggar's ticks, burdock, buffalo bur, and unicorn plant (Fig. 33-1). Some fruits are commonly gathered and buried by squirrels and other rodents to serve as future stores of food. Many such cached fruits are abandoned or forgotten, having thus been "planted" by the animals. This device is effective in dispersing many nuts, achenes, and grains.

5. *Man*—Certainly the most effective seed dispersal agent ever to have appeared on earth is man. He intentionally transports seeds of many crop and ornamental plants to all areas of the earth where they can be grown, and he inadvertently carries seeds on his vehicles, in soil, and as contaminants, in other seed materials.

Among the many special dispersal mechanisms which have been evolved, the following are sufficiently well known, or unusual, to be mentioned here:

1. Some plants fling their seeds considerable distances by spring mechanisms or explosive pressures. Examples of the former, in which seeds are thrown through the air as tensions developed during fruit maturation are suddenly released, are jewel weeds, geraniums, and witch hazel. An example of the latter is the squirting cucumber, the fruits of which suddenly rupture at one end, expelling the watery contents and seeds for several feet.

2. The well-known tumbleweed of arid regions of the western United States have a special abscission region at the base of the stem. At maturity the more or less globular shoot system of the entire plant breaks away from the root and blows about the countryside, scattering seeds along the way. The inflorescences of some grasses are similar in their action.

3. One of the most unusual devices for seed implantation is that of the peanut. This leguminous plant produces flowers resembling those of the pea, but after pollination the flower stalk

young shoot

single fruit element

stem

FIG. 18–10.   Multiple (compound) fruit of pineapple.

FIG. 18–11.   The apple is a pome (accessory) fruit.

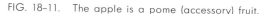

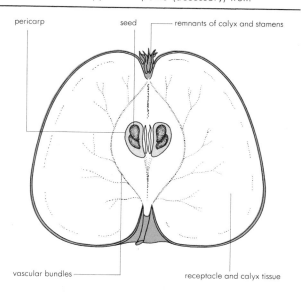

pericarp

seed

remnants of calyx and stamens

vascular bundles

receptacle and calyx tissue

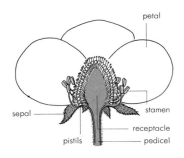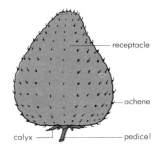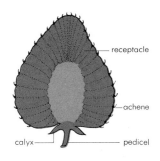

FIG. 18–12. *Left:* Longitudinal section of strawberry flower. *Right:* Accessory fruit of strawberry: whole fruit and section.

elongates greatly, carrying the developing legume to the soil and forcing it beneath the surface. There the seeds grow to maturity, and if not dug by animals, are effectively "planted" (Fig. 18–13).

ECONOMIC IMPORTANCE OF FRUITS

The importance of fruits as sources of food for man is so obvious that it needs little comment. Many fruits consist largely of water, with very small quantities of sugars, other foods, minerals, vitamins, and other organic compounds in their tissues. Such fruits are important in the human diet chiefly for their flavor and for the vitamins they contain. Apples, pears, cherries, oranges, watermelons, and many other fruits of this type have little food value in terms of calorie content. Avocados, bananas, cereal grains, and plantains, on the other hand, contain high concentrations of starches and fats and thus possess high food value, as well as the accessory dietary advantages derived from vitamins and minerals.

Many products other than foods are supplied to man by fruits. Dyes (Persian berries and sap green), oils (castor oil and palm oils), waxes (bay-berry and myrtle waxes), vegetable ivory (from the hard fruits of several palm species), drugs (morphine from the opium poppy and cubebs from a climbing Asiatic pepper), and spices (allspice, capsicums or red peppers, black pepper, vanilla, anise, caraway, and dill) are among the economically important products of fruits.

FIG. 18–13. Peanut plant, showing the fruits (legumes) that develop underground after the flowers, which are borne and pollinated above the soil, bend downward, burying the young fruits. (Photo by Missouri Botanical Garden.)

SUMMARY

1. A fruit is a matured ovary.

2. The maturing of an ovary into a fruit involves a series of complex physiological activities, including the acceleration of tissue growth under the influence of auxins, the translocation of foods and often water into fruits, and changes in pigmentation.

3. In some little-known manner, ethylene appears to be involved in fruit ripening.

4. A fruit wall is called a pericarp. A pericarp may consist of three tissue layers: exocarp (outer layer), mesocarp (central layer), and endocarp (inner layer). The relative development, texture, and other features of these layers vary in the fruits of different species.

5. A classification of fruits is presented in this chapter.

6. The common names of fruits frequently do not indicate their botanical nature.

7. Many mechanisms are effective for disperal of fruits and seeds. Common mechanisms involve modifications to facilitate having the seeds carried by animals, man, wind, water, and gravity to sites distant from the parent plants.

8. Fruits are important to man in many ways. They provide food, drugs, dyes, waxes, spices, and other products.

SUGGESTED READINGS FOR INTERESTED STUDENTS

1. Esau, Katherine, *Plant Anatomy*, 2d ed. Wiley, New York, 1965.

2. Leopold, A. Carl, *Plant Growth and Development*. McGraw-Hill, New York, 1964.

3. Porter, C. L., *Taxonomy of Flowering Plants*, 2d ed. Freeman, San Francisco, 1965.

TOPICS AND QUESTIONS FOR STUDY

1. List the common dispersal mechanisms for fleshy and dry fruits.

2. Postulate the dispersal mechanisms for the seeds of ten species not mentioned in the text.

3. Of what benefit to plants are mechanisms for seed dispersal?

4. Discuss an example which is known to you of inadvertent seed dispersal by man.

5. Contrast the popular and scientific meanings of "fruits."

6. Describe the physiological processes involved in the growth of an ovary into a fruit.

7. Explain the fact that some fruits become sweeter as they ripen (for example, bananas) whereas others (for example, corn grains) become less sweet as they mature.

8. Describe the effects of fruit growth on the vegetative organs of some plants, and explain the physiological causes of these effects.

9. Comment on the relation of ethylene to fruit ripening.

10. Define pericarp, and describe the structure of a typical pericarp.

11. Distinguish among simple, aggregate, and compound fruits, and name specific plants to illustrate each type.

12. Describe the structure of each of the following types of fruits: berry, drupe, legume, follicle, capsule, achene, caryopsis, samara, and nut. Name specific plants to illustrate these fruit types.

13. What are accessory fruits?

14. Describe the structure of a pome, and name some pome fruits.

15. Describe the structure of a strawberry "fruit."

16. List the economically important products derived from fruits.

19

GENETICS AND PLANT BREEDING

One of the most striking qualities of living protoplasm is its ability to beget protoplasm of the same kind. When a plant or animal reproduces, its offspring are always like their parents in their fundamental character. Robins produce more robins; snapdragons produce seeds that grow into snapdragon plants. The tendency of progeny to resemble their parents in all fundamental features of structure and behavior is called **heredity.** All organisms inherit the characteristic attributes of their species from their parents. Not only are they recognizably members of the same species as their

parents, but they often inherit certain peculiarities and thus resemble their parents more than they do other individuals of the same species. Despite the fact that all organisms are fundamentally like their parents, they usually differ from them in certain minor respects. No child is ever a perfect duplicate of his mother or father. He is a member of the human species, as are his parents, and he may show a marked resemblance to one or both of them but he is at the same time an individual who is different, if only so slightly, from them. White elms are all white elms, yet each tree is an individual living organism that differs in some quality or degree from other white elms. This tendency of organisms to differ from their parents is called **variation.**

Variation   Variations within a certain plant or animal species are of three common types: variations induced by **environmental conditions,** variations resulting from **hybridization** (breeding together of organisms differing from each other in one or more features), and variations resulting from **mutations.** Plants of the same species often vary from each other as a result of being subjected to different environmental conditions. Plants grown in poor soils do not grow as large or produce as much food as plants of the same species that grow in fertile soils. Plants exposed to bright sunlight manufacture more food than those growing in dim light. These variations caused by differences in moisture, light, soil nutrients, and other environmental factors are not inherited; that is, they are not transmitted to the offspring of the plants subjected to the varying environmental conditions. The seeds of Bonny Best tomatoes, whether they are from tall plants grown in fertile soil or stunted plants in poor soil, usually produce plants of the same quality if they are planted and allowed to grow under similar environmental conditions. The variations induced by environmental factors are thus not a part of the inheritance of the species and are limited in their extent and quality by the hereditary characteristics of the species.

The type of variation which results from hybridization, is the product of the breeding of closely related, although somewhat different, types of organisms. This "crossing" of two different varieties or types of parents typically produces offspring exhibiting a combination of characteristics of both parents. The offspring resulting from a cross between two individuals differing in at least one characteristic is called a **hybrid.** Variations resulting from hybridization differ from those induced by environmental influences in that variation seen in hybrids are determined by factors carried in the sex cells of the parents to succeeding generations, whereas environmentally induced variations are the result of the response of body cells to the environment.

Defined broadly, mutations are changes in the genetic material that can be detected and that are not attributable to ordinary gene recombination. These changes are frequently difficult to recognize, but in some instances they are so marked that the offspring that arise by mutation are notably different from their parents.

GENETICS

The scientific study of heredity and variation is called **genetics.** It is one of the recent fields, since there was little exact knowledge of the principles of inheritance prior to 1900.

THE STUDIES OF MENDEL

The foundation of modern genetics was laid by an Austrian monk, Gregor Mendel, who in 1866 published the results of his far-reaching experiments on inheritance in garden peas. The value of Mendel's experiments was not recognized until 1900, some years after his death, when several biologists realized the significance of the experiments described in his brief publication. Mendel's work differed from that of his predecessors in that he studied the inheritance of single characteristics one at time, instead of attempting to trace the inheritance of a number of traits simultaneously, a task of great complexity. Mendel proceeded differently in another respect, in that he kept very accurate records of the pedigrees of every plant with which he worked. He thus knew the parents, grandparents, great grandparents, and the more remote ancestors of every individual plant involved in his experiments. Mendel established another precedent in genetics: he studied not only the *kinds* of variations that developed from his cross-breeding experiments but also the *numbers* of the types of offspring produced. Thus, his study was both *qualitative* and

FIG. 19–1.   Gregor Mendel (1822–1884). (Courtesy of the Hunt Botanical Library Collection, Carnegie-Mellon University, Pittsburgh, Pa.)

quantitative, a fundamental feature of the scientific method of investigation.

Mendel chose peas for his study because they grow quickly from seed to maturity, because the hybrid offspring are fertile, and because their flowers are normally self-pollinated. This latter feature was an important one in his choice, for foreign pollen from unknown sources usually does not reach the stigmas of pea flowers and thus cannot introduce unknown factors into breeding experiments. Finally, he investigated only characteristics that were constant and clearly recognizable.

The methods used by Mendel in performing his crosses are the same methods employed today. In order to prevent self-pollination, he removed the immature stamens from a pea flower that was to serve as the female parent. Next he placed on the stigma pollen from the plant being used as the male parent. He then covered the hand-pollinated flowers to prevent foreign pollen from reaching the stigma and fertilizing the eggs in the ovules. In such experiments, it is important to know whether a particular characteristic can be transmitted by both egg and sperm. Mendel determined this in each case by making a **reciprocal cross** in which the parents were reversed. For example, when the experimental cross consisted of applying pollen from a dwarf plant to the stigma of a tall plant, the reciprocal cross was made with pollen from the tall plant and the stigma of the dwarf variety.

Following such cross-pollination, the ovaries produce seeds. These seeds, when planted, grow into the first generation of offspring from the cross, called the **first filial generation,** or F_1 generation. The F_1 individuals are allowed to self-pollinate and produce offspring that constitute the **F_2** or **second filial generation;** the offspring of the F_2 are known as the F_3 generation, and so on.

Monohybrid (Single-Character) Crosses.   In one of his experiments, Mendel crossed a race of garden peas that were tall (6 to 7 feet in height) with a race of peas that were dwarf ($\frac{3}{4}$ to $1\frac{1}{2}$ feet in height). The seeds from this cross grew into an F_1 generation, all plants of which were tall. This was surprising, for Mendel expected that the plants in this first filial generation would be intermediate in height between the parents of the cross. Mendel then permitted these tall F_1 plants to be *self-pollinated,* and, in the resulting F_2 generation, he found that 75 percent of the plants were tall and 25 percent were dwarf (Fig. 19–2). The actual count was 787 tall and 277 dwarf plants; that is, the F_2 ratio of tall to dwarf plants was 3:1. Mendel allowed these dwarf individuals to carry on *self-pollination,* and he found that in the F_3 generation all the progeny of the F_2 dwarf individuals were dwarf. However, when the tall individuals of the F_2 were permitted to carry on self-pollination, one third always produced tall pea plants in the F_3, while two thirds produced tall and dwarf plants in the F_3 in a 3:1 ratio as had the plants of the F_1 generation.

Units of Heredity On the basis of this and similar experiments, Mendel concluded that there must be determiners in a plant that control the inheritance of characters such as height. These determiners he called factors. He concluded that these factors must occur in *pairs* because from the F_1 he recovered both tall and dwarf individuals in the F_2, and, therefore, the F_1 individuals must have had a tall factor and a dwarf factor. In modern genetic parlance these hereditary units that govern the expression of all characteristics of an individual are termed **genes.**

Dominance Mendel concluded further, on the basis of the cross just described and of similar crosses, that one gene in a pair may mask the expression of the other. When he crossed a tall pea plant with a dwarf, all the F_1 plants were tall, but both tall and dwarf types appeared in the F_2. Thus, the F_1 plants must have carried a gene for dwarfness, which was obscured by the one for tallness in the F_1 plants. This condition, wherein one gene of a pair may mask or inhibit the expression of the other, is called **dominance.** In the cross described above, the factor for tallness is the **dominant** gene; the dwarf factor that is suppressed is the **recessive** gene.

Figure 19-3 is a diagram representing Mendel's cross between tall and dwarf pea plants. Capital letter T is the symbol that represents the gene controlling tallness; lower case t represents the gene controlling dwarfness. The tall parent is shown as TT because these hereditary factors occur in pairs; similarly, the dwarf parent is shown as tt. Each of these parents produces gametes that contain only *one* factor of each pair—a result of the process of meiosis, to be explained later in this chapter.

The tall parent produces only gametes with one T, or one factor for tallness; the dwarf parent produces gametes with t, or one factor for dwarfness. The gametes unite in pairs at fertilization and produce zygotes, which have both factors and which develop into new individuals, those of the F_1 generation. The plants of the F_1 generation are shown as Tt; that is, each F_1 plant bears in its cells one gene for tallness and one for dwarfness, derived from the tall and dwarf parents, respectively. At maturity, the F_1 plants produce male and female gametes. Half the male gametes have T, the gene for tallness, half have t, the gene for dwarfness. Similarly, half the female gametes have T, half have t. Thus, the F_1 hybrid parent produces eggs and sperms, each with a single set of chromosomes and having gametic ratios of 1:1 for tallness and dwarfness. Following self-pollination, the gametes unite at random and produce zygotes that grow into the plants of the F_2 generation. In this random combination, a male gamete with T may unite with a female gamete with T, thus producing an F_2 individual with TT; or, a male gamete with T may unite with a female gamete with t, producing an F_2 plant with Tt. Also, a male gamete with t may unite with a female gamete bearing a T gene, forming a plant with Tt, and a male gamete with t may fertilize a female gamete with t, producing an offspring with tt. These are the only four possible combinations resulting from the union of these gametes. The plant with TT is tall because it has only genes for tallness. The two plants with Tt are also tall, since the T gene dominates the recessive t gene. The plants with tt are dwarf because they possess only genes for dwarfness. Thus, there are three tall plants and one dwarf pea plant in the F_2 generation or a ratio of 3 to 1 (Figs. 19-3 and 19-4). In his experiments, Mendel permitted these F_2 plants to carry on self-pollination, and the individuals with TT always produced tall individuals. Similarly, the plants with tt always produced dwarfs. The individuals with Tt behaved as the F_1 plants, producing tall and dwarf plants in a ratio of 3:1.

This experiment shows that individuals similar in external appearance, or **phenotype,** may actually differ in their genetic constitution, or **genotype.** It is frequently necessary in breeding exper-

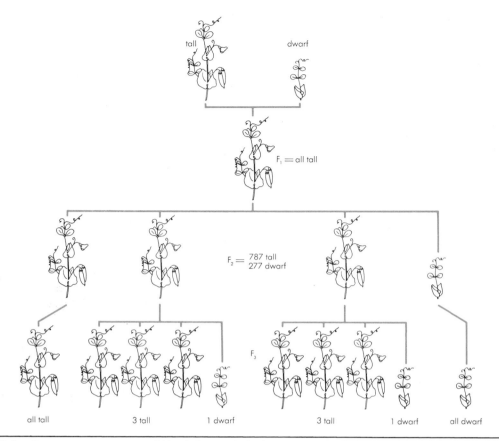

FIG. 19-2. Diagrammatic summary of Mendel's monohybrid crosses illustrating dominance of tallness over dwarfness in garden pea. See FIG. 19-3 for the genotypic interpretation of the above experiment.

iments to know which of the phenotypically similar offspring are **homozygous,** that is, contain identical genes, and which are **heterozygous,** or contain a dominant and a recessive gene. This may be determined by backcrossing the unknown hybrid with a homozygous recessive, a procedure known as a **test cross.** If homozygous dominant *TT* is crossed with homozygous recessive *tt,* all the offspring will be tall; if the heterozygous *Tt* is crossed with *tt,* half the resulting offspring will be tall and half will be dwarf.

Law of Segregation   Mendel's work led also to the establishment of the **law of segregation,** which states that the genes making up pairs are separated from each other prior to the formation

of gametes. In other words, only one gene of each pair goes into a given sperm or egg (Fig. 19-3). This means that the two genetic kinds of gametes will be formed in equal numbers.

Dihybrid (Two-Character) Cross   A dihybrid cross is one between two individuals differing in two distinct characters. For example, one of Mendel's experiments involved a cross between two varieties of peas differing in color and and shape of their seeds; one had seeds that were yellow and round, the other, seeds that were green and wrinkled. Mendel found that yellowness and roundness were dominant, greenness and wrinkledness recessive. As Fig. 19-5 illustrates, the genes of one parent may be represented

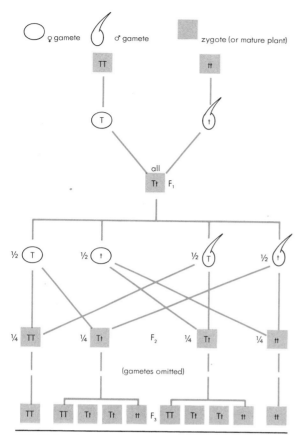

FIG. 19-3. A genotypic interpretation of Mendel's monohybrid crosses illustrating dominance of tallness over dwarfness in garden peas as summarized in FIG. 19-2. T represents the gene for tallness, t the gene for dwarfness. Note that the F_2 progeny appear in the ratio of 3 tall to 1 dwarf.

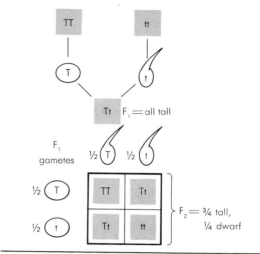

FIG. 19-4. A more conventional summary of the genotypic analysis presented in FIG. 19-3.

gametes combine at fertilization to produce zygotes. The results of chance combinations of the various types of gametes are shown in Fig. 19-5.

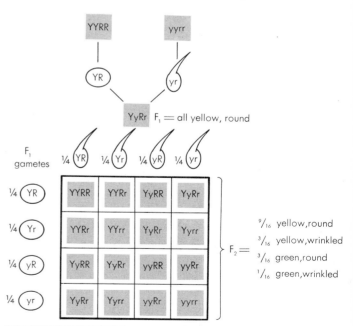

FIG. 19-5. Diagram representing a dihybrid cross between two varieties of peas that differ in two characters.

by $YY\ RR$, those of the other parent by $yy\ rr$. The parent with the dominant traits produces gametes with YR, the other produces gametes with yr. When these gametes unite, the zygotes bear the genes $Yy\ Rr$; phenotypically, the plants produced by these zygotes all have yellow, round seeds because of the dominance of yellowness and roundness; these F_1 plants may be described as heterozygous yellow and heterozygous round. Both the male and the female gametes produced by heterozygous F_1 plants are of four types: YR, Yr, yR, and yr. Following self-pollination, the

Nine of the F_2 plants have yellow, round seeds, three have yellow, wrinkled seeds, three have green, round seeds, and one has green, wrinkled seeds. Thus, the phenotypic ratio of the F_2 plants is 9:3:3:1. The actual numbers obtained by Mendel from these crossing experiments were: 315 yellow, round; 101 yellow, wrinkled; 108 green, round; and 32 green, wrinkled.

Law of Independent Assortment   On the basis of this dihybrid cross, Mendel concluded that the entrance of the yellow factor and round factor together into a cross does not mean that they remain together when the gametes are formed by the F_1 plants. This conclusion is called the **law of independent assortment,** which, in modern form, states that the genes representing two or more contrasting characteristics are segregated to the gametes independently of each other and that these gametes then combine with each other at random at the time of fertilization.

THE CYTOLOGICAL BASIS OF INHERITANCE

Every organism that develops as a result of sexual reproduction begins its existence as a single cell termed a zygote, which is the product of the fusion of gametes. All the traits that parents transmit to their offspring are carried in these gametes; therefore, the gametes constitute the sole hereditary link between parents and offspring. The basic characteristics of an organism are thus mapped out for its entire life at the time when the zygote is formed. As stated earlier in the chapter, the fundamental nature of the hereditary characteristics is normally not affected by external factors but the expression of these characteristics is frequently modified by environmental conditions. We may say, then, that an organism inherits from its parents certain structural and functional potentialities; the development of these potentialities is conditioned largely by the environment of the individual.

There is no doubt that most hereditary determiners are carried by the chromosomes in cells. Convincing evidence in support of this statement comes, in part, from close parallels in the behavior of genes, as determined by various breeding experiments such as those mentioned earlier, and in the behavior of chromosomes, as determined by observation with the microscope. Studies of the sexual cycle of a plant in relation to its chromosomes show that at fertilization two sets of chromosomes are combined in a single cell (zygote). One set comes from the paternal parent by way of the male gamete, or sperm; the other set is contributed by the maternal parent in the female gamete, or egg. Each of the paternal chromosomes has a matching counterpart in the maternal chromosome complement. The members of such matching pairs are said to be **homologous.** The number of chromosomes in a gamete is called the haploid, or n number, while the number of chromosomes in the fertilized egg, or zygote, is the **diploid,** or $2n$ number. In onions, for example, each gamete contains 8 chromosomes and the diploid zygote contains 16. The multicellular plant body that develops from the zygote is essentially a diploid structure, since all or most of its cells contain two sets of homologous chromosomes—copies of the originals brought together at fertilization. In each mitotic division, the chromosomes are duplicated without undergoing qualitative change. In this way, the morphological identities of chromosomes are preserved, as is the genetic information they carry. Diploid body cells, however, do not function as gametes. In all sexually reproducing organisms, there occurs at some time prior to gamete formation a process called **meiosis,** in which the diploid chromosome number is reduced to the haploid number. In angiosperms this process occurs in the formation of microspores in anthers and in the formation of megaspores in ovules. Meiosis is just as essential to sexual reproduction as is the process of fertilization, for in the absence of either, the sexual cycle cannot be completed. Moreover, meiosis plays a significant role in inheritance by recombining genes in various ways. In contrast with mitosis, in which there is one chromosomal duplication and one nuclear division, meiosis involves one duplication and two divisions. Chromosomal duplication in meiosis is thought to occur most commonly in early prophase of the first meiotic division (prophase I) or in the preceding interphase. Following duplication, each chromosome consists of two chromatids.

Prophase I affords visible evidence of two characteristic meiotic events: **pairing** and **crossing over** (Fig. 19-6). In pairing, homologous chromosomes come together in a zipperlike manner and soon lie parallel to each other along their entire length. Each part of one chromosome is adjacent to the corresponding part of the other member of the homologous pair. The visible evidence of crossing over is an exchange of matching *segments* of two homologous chromatids; that is, two of the four chromatids may break at the same gene locus and rejoin to the broken ends of the homologous chromatids, with the result that a chromatid of one chromosome will then carry a portion of a chromatid from the other chromosome and vice versa. The exact time when crossing over occurs is not known with certainty; however, crossovers are visible under the microscope after the chromatids have become shortened and thickened. At metaphase I, the chromosomes are arranged in the equatorial region of the cell; in anaphase I, the members of a homologous pair of chromosomes migrate to opposite poles, an event known as **disjunction.** Disjunction is the cytological basis for the genetic law of segregation. Anaphase is usually followed by telophase, during which the nuclear membranes are formed. The second meiotic division then follows a brief interphase. This second division bears a superficial resemblance to mitosis, but, of course, the chromatids that separate are not necessarily perfect duplicates, and they are present in the haploid number. Meiosis ends with the completion of telophase II. The single duplication and two divisions of meiosis have produced four nuclei, each with the haploid number of chromosomes. The gametes that are formed subsequently

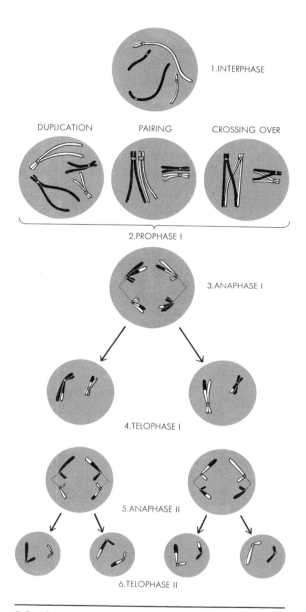

FIG. 19-6. Schematic representation of meiosis. Interphase shows two pairs of homologous chromosomes; that is, $2n = 4$. In telophase I, each cell contains two chromosomes, each consisting of 2 chromatids. The four haploid cells shown at telophase II each have two chromosomes. Metaphase I, prophase II and metaphase II have been omitted.

are derivatives of these haploid meiotic products. Union of gametes at fertilization produces a diploid zygote and initiates the next reproductive cycle. The genetic significance of meiosis lies in the "reshuffling" of genes. This is accomplished in part by the random separation of homologous chromosomes in anaphase I and II and is the cytological basis for the genetic law of independent assortment. When a plant forms gametes, the chromosomes that came from its male parent do not all go to a particular gamete nor do the chromosomes from its female parent. Rather, because of independent assortment, the homologous chromosomes are incorporated into the gametes by chance. Further reassortment of genes is brought about by crossing over, to be discussed in more detail in a later section.

During the fertilization process, the respective haploid chromosome sets come together in the zygote. When a homozygous individual forms gametes, these are all of the same type because the homologous chromosomes that are separated in meiosis are alike; that is, they carry identical genes. In the production of gametes by a heterozygous organism, however, the chromosomes that separate at meiosis do not all bear similar genes, for they have been contributed to the heterozygous individual by different types of parents. Thus, the gametes produced by heterozygous organisms are of different kinds with respect to various genes they carry, rather than of the same kind, as in homozygous organisms. As the result of the chance unions of the different kinds of gametes formed by hybrids, different characters are brought together, and thus different types of offspring are produced.

The control of characters in inheritance is the function of genes, which are located on the chromosomes. In the garden pea, the gene controlling roundness of seeds is located on one chromosome, and the gene controlling wrinkledness is located on the homologous chromosome. On another pair of chromosomes, there are the gene for yellowness and the gene for greenness, on a third pair of chromosomes the gene for tallness and the gene

for dwarfness. There are striking parallels between the genes and the chromosomes. Thus, the genes occur in pairs, just as do the chromosomes. These genes occur in pairs because half of them come from the male parent and half come from the female parent. Likewise, there is a segregation of factors prior to the formation of gametes, and there is a corresponding disjunction of chromosomes during meiosis. Finally, just as there is independent assortment of genes, so there is independent assortment of chromosomes.

The examples given thus far are based on diploid plants in which each body cell contains *pairs* of homologous chromosomes and which bear related, alternative genes or **alleles** (such as T and t) at corresponding loci on the homologous chromosomes. Some other plants, such as the green alga *Chlamydomonas* and the mold *Neurospora,* are naturally haploid organisms; that is, they have only a *single* set of chromosomes in each of their body cells. Union of gametes in these plants produces a diploid zygote which then undergoes meiosis and produces a quartet or **tetrad** of haploid cells. In haploid plants a cross between individuals having A and a alleles will, after meiosis, produce a tetrad consisting of equal numbers of each gene type; therefore, the ratio for A and a is 1:1.

THE CHEMICAL BASIS OF INHERITANCE

As the carriers of hereditary traits, chromosomes have been intensively studied in an effort to determine the chemical basis of inheritance. Analyses have shown the principal constituents of chromosomes to be proteins and two kinds of nucleic acids: deoxyribonucleic acid (DNA) and ribonucleic acid (RNA). The nucleic acids account for approximately 40 percent of the total, of which about 1 percent is RNA. One of the fundamental problems was therefore to determine which of these materials bore the hereditary determiners.

Convincing evidence that DNA carried the genetic information was presented in 1944. This work was based on extensive studies of pneumococci, the bacteria that cause pneumonia. Each of these pathogenic cells has a thick outer capsule of polysaccharide material. The numerous strains of pneumococci are recognized on the basis of certain genetically controlled properties of their capsules. When cultured on agar, the virulent strains produce smooth colonies. Occasionally, there arises a mutant form that lacks a capsule and produces colonies described as rough. In addition, the rough forms are nonvirulent. Rough mutants may occasionally mutate back to the smooth form, producing capsules characteristic of the original strain. For example, cells of smooth strain II may mutate to rough, which may then revert to smooth II. It was found by earlier workers that when a *mixture* of heat-killed smooth III bacteria and living rough bacteria derived from strain II was injected into a mouse, the mouse contracted the disease. Living pneumococci recovered from the animal were found to be virulent *smooth III*. This strain did not arise through mutation, for rough could mutate only to smooth II. However, under the influence of the heat-killed cells, there occurred a heritable **transformation** from one genetically controlled strain to another. Years of research were required in order to learn the identity of the transforming agent, which has been shown to be deoxyribonucleic acid. It is now thought that the DNA carrying the genetic information relating to capsule formation is incorporated into a rough cell. This cell (and its descendants) then synthesizes a capsule according to the new "instructions." Other examples of genetic transformation in bacteria have been described, but, to date, none has been discovered elsewhere in the plant or animal kingdoms.

As described in Chapter 6, molecules of DNA are very large and contain great amounts of coded information. The structure of a DNA molecule is that of two helically coiled strands of nucleotides. Each nucleotide consists of a phosphate group, the 5-carbon sugar, and one of four nitrogenous bases (Fig. 6–1). Nucleotides of the two complementary strands are arranged so that the base adenine is always paired with the complementary base thymine and that the base guanine is always paired with the complementary cytosine. Weak hydrogen bonds hold these base pairs (and, therefore, the two strands of nucleotides) together. The number of ways in which the four different pairs of bases (A-T, T-A, G-C, and C-G) can be arranged along the length of the double helix is enormous, and it is the *sequence* of base pairs that imparts the tremendous capacity for variation among DNA molecules.

The significance of the sequence of bases in DNA and RNA becomes clear when we consider the nature of the genetic information carried in these molecules. Earlier we saw that specific information in DNA is transcribed into messenger RNA which, in turn, directs the step-by-step assembly of amino acids to form polypeptide chains (translation). Such elaborate syntheses obviously require highly specific, accurate directions. It has been shown in recent years that the necessary directions are an extrinsic property of the nucleic acid base sequence as expressed in a triploid code. Briefly stated, such a code consists of three linked nucleotides which, in a specific combination, can select for a particular amino acid. For example, one such base triplet or **codon,** AAA, selects for the amino acid lysine; another, GGG, is specific for glycine. Actually, with four different bases and a triplet code, we have more than enough codons to select for the 20 different amino acids; nevertheless, the triplet code is the simplest system that provides enough codons to do the job. A single base code could select for only four amino acids, and a double base code could select for only 16 (that is, 4^2), but a triplet code produces 64 codons (4^3). With the triplet code some amino acids can be specified by more than one codon; for example, lysine is specified by AAG as well as AAA, and glycine is specified by GGA and GGC as well as GGG. The accomplishment of deciphering this genetic code has been one of the major triumphs of modern biological research.

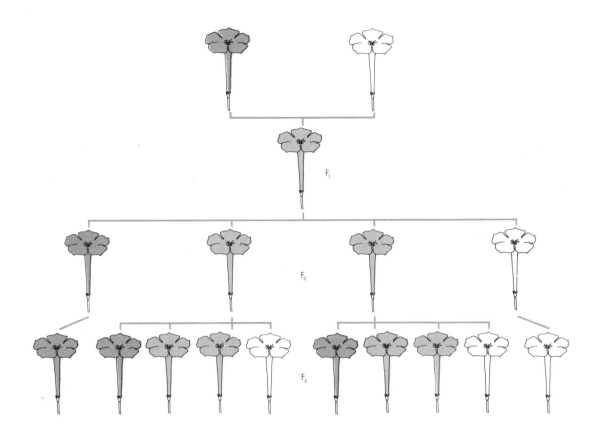

FIG. 19-7. Diagram illustrating incomplete dominance in flower color of four-o'clock plants. The F_1 progeny of a cross between red and white parents are all pink, while F_2 generation plants have the ratio of 1 red: 2 pink: 1 white.

A close relationship between genes and biochemical reactions was confirmed initially through experiments with the mold *Neurospora*. Normal spores of *Neurospora* may be germinated and molds grown on chemically defined, minimal culture medium, that is, a substrate containing only those nutrients essential for the growth of the organism. Mutations were induced in normal spores by x-ray treatment, after which the spores were transferred to an enriched culture medium that contained the nutrients of minimal medium plus other amino acids and vitamins. Following germination and mold growth, a portion of each

mold was subcultured on minimal medium where it was found some were unable to grow. Each mutant form was later shown to require, in addition to the nutrients in minimal medium, one other substance that prior to mutation it was able to synthesize. For example, the mutation of a particular gene prevented the organism from synthesizing the amino acid citrulline; another specific gene mutation prevented the formation of another amino acid, arginine.

The biosynthesis of these compounds is a stepwise process, each step of which is enzymatically regulated. It has been postulated that a given gene directs the synthesis of a particular enzyme which, in turn, catalyzes a specific reaction. This is called the one-gene, one-enzyme hypothesis.

SOME OTHER GENETIC MECHANISMS

Incomplete Dominance   Genetic studies made after Mendel's work have shown that although dominance occurs in many cases, it is rarely if ever absolute. It is now known that dominance may be influenced by a variety of external and internal factors and that the phenotypic expressions of offspring are commonly intermediate between the phenotypes of their parents. This may be illustrated by a cross between red-flowered and white-flowered four-o'clocks. In these plants, red flowers are the expression of a homozygous dominant condition (RR), and white flowers are a homozygous recessive condition (rr). However, all the F_1 offspring (Rr) are pink-flowered (Fig. 19-7). When two of the pink F_1 plants are crossed, the resulting F_2 ratio is 1 red, 2 pink, and 1 white.

Multiple Genes   The blending effect obtained in crossing four-o'clocks resulted from the interaction of only two genes. A far more common cause of blending is the interaction of multiple, incompletely dominant genes. This may be illustrated by a cross between two varieties of wheat, each of which has four genes that influence coloration of the kernels. A plant homozygous for dark red kernels ($R_1R_1R_2R_2$) is crossed with one homozygous for white kernels ($r_1r_1r_2r_2$). All the F_1 offspring produce kernels of a medium red color ($R_1r_1R_2r_2$). However, most of the F_2 progeny have kernels of various shades of red. Analysis of the F_2 reveals a phenotypic ratio of 1 dark red: 4 red: 6 medium red: 4 light red: 1 white. These results reflect the cumulative effect of R genes for redness, as follows:

$$RRRR = \text{dark red}$$
$$RRRr = \text{red}$$
$$RRrr = \text{medium red}$$
$$Rrrr = \text{light red}$$
$$rrrr = \text{white}$$

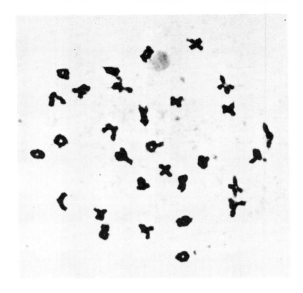

FIG. 19-8.   Meiotic prophase chromosomes of *Pityrogramma triangularis*, the California gold-back fern, showing 30 pairs of chromosomes. (Courtesy of Dr. Dale M. Smith, U. of California, Santa Barbara)

With each additional pair of interacting genes, there is an increase in the number of F_2 phenotypes and, therefore, an increase in variability among the offspring. But in terms of expected numbers of individuals, the proportions of F_2 phenotypes change rapidly with an increase in pairs of interacting genes. For example, when only 2 genes interact, the probability of obtaining an F_2 individual similar to one of the homozygous parents is 1 in 4; with 4 genes, it is 1 in 16; with 6, it is 1 in 64; with 8, it is 1 in 256, and so on. This explains why geneticists, when dealing with large numbers of multiple genes, find it difficult or virtually impossible to recover in the F_2 a single individual similar to one of the parental types. It also explains why earlier workers who knew nothing of this genetic mechanism were unable to account for their experimental results. Continuing research is conducted on multiple gene inheritance because of the importance this genetic mechanism has in plant and animal breeding.

Linkage   An exception to Mendel's law of independent assortment was discovered when it

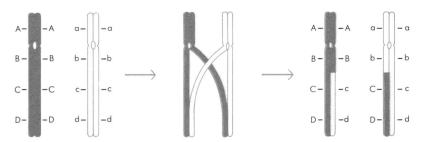

FIG. 19-9. Diagram illustrating crossing over. To the left are two homologous chromosomes, each consisting of two chromatids. The letters, A, B, C, D indicate genes with their homologs a, b, c, d. In the center of the figure, the chromosomes are shown at synapsis (pairing), with one chromatid twisted over a chromatid from the other chromosome. The portion to the right shows the distribution of genes following exchange of segments between the two chromatids.

was shown that certain groups of genes tended to be inherited together. This behavior is attributable to the fact that each gene of a particular group is located on the same chromosome. Since a chromosome moves in meiotic division as a unit, all the genes on that chromosome move together. This phenomenon, in which certain genes (and the characteristics they determine) are inherited in groups, is called **linkage.** The genes that are borne on the same chromosome are said to be linked. It was a remarkable accident that, even though Mendel studied seven pairs of characters in peas, all the genes of these characters were located on different chromosomes and therefore showed no linkage; thus, Mendel found no exceptions to independent assortment.

Crossing Over   Shortly after the discovery of linkage, it was found that the characteristics whose genes are on the same chromosome do not always remain linked. This phenomenon is explained by crossing over. As described earlier, the cytological basis for crossing over lies in the interchange of segments of homologous chromatids. The effect of crossing over on the distribution of genes is diagrammatically illustrated in Fig. 19-9. Crossing over may be regarded as an exception to linkage, which in turn is an exception to independent assortment.

Through careful analysis of crossover data, it has been possible to determine the locations of

specific genes on a chromosome and thus to construct "chromosome maps." The positions of genes may be deduced by determining the percentage of crossing over. If two genes are close together, there is less chance for a crossover between them than if they are more distantly separated. Therefore, if the percentage of crossing over between two particular genes is high, those genes are relatively far apart. On the other hand, if the percentage is low, the two genes are relatively close together.

Sex Inheritance   One might suppose, since genes control the inheritance of various characteristics, that there might be a gene controlling the characteristic of sex; however, such is not the case. In animals and in some plants, there are sex-determining chromosomes. In a human, for example, the diploid number is 46. Two of these chromosomes are **sex chromosomes;** the remaining 22 pairs are called **autosomes.** The two sex chromosomes in the female are similar and are designated X chromosomes. Males have one X chromosome, and a dissimilar Y chromosome. As can be seen in Fig. 19-10, the female (XX) produces only gametes with single X chromosomes, whereas the male (XY) produces gametes of two types, one with a single X chromosome, the other with a Y chromosome. These gametes fuse at random, and, thus, when two gametes with X chromosomes unite, a female results, and when

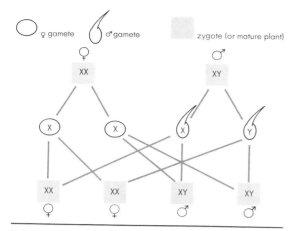

FIG. 19-10. Genetic mechanism of sex inheritance in certain dioecious plants, in man, and in certain other animals. Explanation in text.

a gamete with an X chromosome unites with a gamete with a Y chromosome, a male results. Males and females are thus produced in a ratio of 1:1. A similar mechanism is known to operate in some dioecious plants.

Mutations   As defined earlier, mutations are changes in the genetic material that can be phenotypically detected and that are not attributable to ordinary gene recombination. These changes are frequently difficult to recognize, but in some instances they are so marked that the offspring that arise by mutation little resemble the parents with respect to the characters involved. The characters that develop by mutation are usually passed on by mutating organisms to their offspring; that is, they are heritable and persist from generation to generation as permanently established variations. Mutations occur in plants raised from seeds, or they may develop from individual buds on a stem. These are known, respectively, as **seed mutations** and **bud mutations.** In a mutation that develops in a bud, the twig that grows from the bud differs in some manner from all other twigs of the plant. Many important varieties of cultivated plants have had their origins in mutations. Among these are navel oranges, cer-

tain varieties of Boston ferns, weeping willows, nectarines, many kinds of double-flowered plants, and some sweet pea and chrysanthemum varieties. Bud variations are usually propagated by bud grafting by some other means of asexual propagation.

It is known that many mutations are due to changes in single genes, and it is in this sense that most geneticists use the term mutation. Other mutations are produced by the development of extra sets of chromosomes. Plants with extra sets of chromosomes are known as **polyploids;** those with $3n$ chromosome numbers are called triploids, those with $4n$, tetraploids, and so on. Other mutations are caused by a single extra chromosome produced by imperfect reduction division; still other mutations are produced by the inclusion or omission of fragments of chromosomes or by the inversion of pieces of chromosomes. Mutations occur in nature as well as in the laboratory, although the rate of successful establishment is apparently not very high.

Mutations can be induced experimentally. Some widely used techniques include exposure of the organism to radiations such as ultraviolet, x-rays, and gamma rays, or to chemical mutagenic agents such as acridine orange, colchicine, nitrogen mustard, and nitrous acid. Not all the mechanisms of gene alteration are fully understood; however, the net effect of some of the mutagens is to change the base sequence of the nucleic acid, commonly by addition, substitution, or deletion of nucleotides. Also, some mutagens can alter slightly the structure of a base so that that codon becomes meaningless. Finally, it should be emphasized that individual mutations are random and are not predictable.

PLANT BREEDING

One of the important techniques of plant breeding is **selection,** a very old method of improving the quality of domesticated organisms. It is based on the fact that organisms of the same species or variety vary among themselves and tend to pass

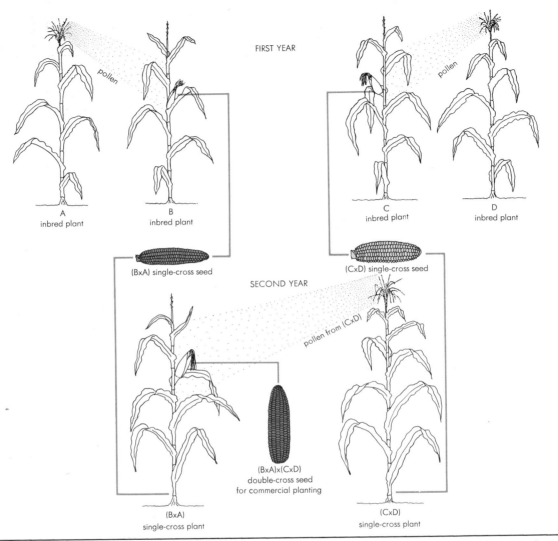

FIRST YEAR

A
inbred plant

B
inbred plant

C
inbred plant

D
inbred plant

pollen

pollen

(BxA) single-cross seed

(CxD) single-cross seed

SECOND YEAR

pollen from (CxD)

(BxA)x(CxD)
double-cross seed
for commercial planting

(BxA)
single-cross plant

(CxD)
single-cross plant

FIG. 19–11.   Crossing to produce hybrid corn. Plants A, B, C, and D are the offspring of four inbred lines. Strain A is crossed with strain B and strain C is crossed with D. The products of these two crosses are then crossed to produce the hybrid corn seed. Wide use is currently made of male-sterile plants (B, C, and B × A in diagram) which do not require detasseling.

on to their offspring many of these variations. It is a matter of common knowledge, for example, that certain families of human beings rank unusually high in intelligence and that the members of successive generations of these families generally possess superior mental ability. In other families, low intelligence prevails and is a common feature of its members though many generations. Some plants are more resistant to diseases than others of the same species, and their offspring sometimes inherit, in part at least, the greater resistance of their parents. Some plants yield better crops than other plants of the same species and often pass this more desirable feature on to

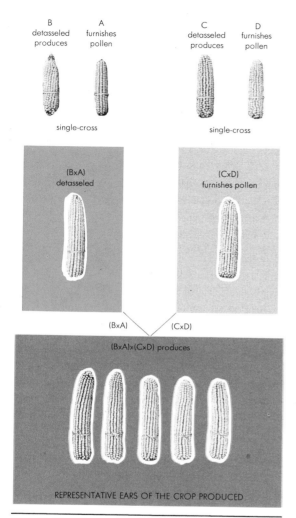

inbred parent strains

| B detasseled produces | A furnishes pollen | | C detasseled produces | D furnishes pollen |

single-cross   single-cross

(BxA) detasseled

(CxD) furnishes pollen

(BxA)   (CxD)

(BxA)x(CxD) produces

REPRESENTATIVE EARS OF THE CROP PRODUCED

FIG. 19-12. Corn ears illustrating the crosses represented in FIG. 19-11.

their progeny. From a large group of plants of the same variety or species, the individuals that possess the desired qualities in greatest degree are selected. Their seeds are planted and selections again made from the plants that these seeds produce. This selection process is often continued through many generations until a superior type of plant, with respect to a single character or group of characters, is isolated. Luther Burbank

(1849–1926) employed this method with conspicuous success in the development of the giant Shasta daisy and the "stoneless" plum. The production of the latter illustrates the method of selection. First, Burbank selected from a large collection of plums one which had a thin "pit" or stone. He permitted this tree to carry on pollination and to set fruit. Then, he chose from this tree a few plums that had the thinnest stones. The seeds from these he planted, and when the resulting trees fruited, he again selected the fruits with the thinnest stones. These were planted and when the resulting trees matured, Burbank again selected the fruit with the thinnest "pits." After several selections of this type, he produced a plum with an extremely thin stone; this was marketed as a "stoneless" plum. In this method, advantage is taken of all the desirable variations and modifications, and the undesirable types are discarded.

In some kinds of plants, the practice of selection entails difficulties. Sometimes selected varieties gradually revert back to less desirable ancestral forms, and thus the process of selection must be carried on constantly to assure a continuance of superior varieties. Further, the rate of progress in selection toward a desired type is often very slow, so that long periods of time are required in some plants to achieve the wanted improvements. In spite of these limitations, selection has developed many valuable types of plants, such as Reid's Yellow Dent corn, Leaming corn, Red Fife wheat, and various oat and tobacco varieties. Of course, an intelligent breeder, while carrying on this work, is alert for the appearance of any desirable mutations or "sports," which he would then select for further work. He would also carry on hybridization to achieve wanted recombinations of characters.

Inbreeding   Another method of plant breeding is illustrated by the work of a breeder who desires to obtain a variety of plant that is both productive and resistant to a destructive disease. He first selects those plants that produce very large yields and then permits them to carry on self-pollination. This procedure of selection followed by self-pollination might be carried on for several generations. This type of breeding in which self-pollination is carried on or in which closely related individuals are crossed is known as **inbreeding.** By this method a **pure line** is established; that is, the plants become more or less homozygous for productivity and hence produce offspring that are also highly productive. There are dangers in inbreeding, for, as a result of this crossing of closely related individuals, undesirable recessive characters may appear. However, if the stock is good and lacks these recessives, the method is successful.

Hybridizing   While this pure line of very productive plants is being developed, the breeder has been carrying on similar procedures with plants selected for desirable resistance until he has obtained a more or less pure line for disease resistance. He then crosses the two lines, thus obtaining offspring with a combination of disease resistance and high productivity. In addition, the offspring resulting from a cross between two such inbred lines often show a marked increase in vigor and productivity, called **hybrid vigor.**

Similar methods are used in the production of hybrid corn, which is the product of crosses between two or more carefully inbred lines. As is well known, hybrid corn may give a yield much greater than that of the parent varieties. Yet, if the seed produced by plants grown from hybid corn grains is planted, the crop is very poor. This illustrates another characteristic of hybids of this type; that is, their seeds are low in productivity, and they do not breed true to the parent type because in the reproductive process assortment of genes occurs and their offspring are of different types. Thus, desirable hybids must be propagated vegetatively by cuttings or grafting, or must be produced repeatedly. Such vegetative propagation is used in reproducing hybrid fruit trees, rosebushes, carnations, and many other types of plants that have been developed as a result of cross-breeding or hybridizing. Corn plants cannot, however, be propagated by such methods. Farmers must purchase fresh hybrid corn seed each year (Figs. 19–11, 19–12).

Mutation   In all these methods, the alert breeder is constantly on the watch for desirable mutations, for these are the only really "new" characters and types that appear. Selection of desirable variations can only be carried so far, and hybridization merely recombines old characters. Mutations are thus the new traits that are the stepping stones for the production of new types of plants; mutations also play a similar role in the production of new species in nature. The Shirley poppy, dwarf sweet peas, numerous double-flowered plants, as well as the red dogwood, have appeared as a result of mutation.

SUMMARY   1. Heredity is the tendency of offspring to resemble their parents; variation is the tendency of organisms to differ from their parents.

2. Variations may result from changes in environmental conditions, from hybridization, and from mutations. Organisms inherit potentialities; the environment affects the development of these inherited potentialities.

3. A genetic hybrid is the offspring resulting from a cross between two parents differing in at least one characteristic.

4. Mendel crossed tall peas with dwarf peas. All the F_1 peas were tall, and when these were permitted to self-pollinate, the F_2 plants were in a ratio of 3 tall to 1 dwarf. When the F_2 peas were self-pollinated,

the dwarf pea plants always produced dwarf pea plants. One third of the tall peas always produced tall peas, the other two thirds produced tall and dwarf plants in a 3:1 ratio, as did the F_1 plants.

5.   Genes are the hereditary units that govern the expression of all characteristics of an individual. They occupy fixed positions on the chromosomes and, in diploid cells, occur in pairs.

6.   Dominance is the condition wherein one gene of a pair may mask or inhibit the expression of the other.

7.   Mendel's law of segregation states that each gene of a pair of genes separates from the other so that, ultimately, only one gene of each pair goes into sperm or egg.

8.   Mendel's law of independent assortment states that the members of different pairs of genes are assorted or distributed independently to the gametes and that the gametes then fuse randomly in fertilization.

9.   A gene that is expressed is called a dominant gene; a gene that is masked is called a recessive gene. The external apparance of an organism is referred to as its phenotype; its genetic constitution is known as its genotype. When the two genes of a pair are similar, they are said to be homozygous (TT or tt); when the two genes of a pair are unlike, they are said to be heterozygous (Tt).

10.   Monohybrid crosses involve two parents differing in one character; a dihybrid cross involves two organisms differing in two characters. In the latter, the F_2 ratio is 9:3:3:1, in the case of two dominants.

11.   Every cell in a flowering plant body is a descendant of the zygote that resulted from the fusion of egg and sperm. Each of these gametes contributes a set of chromosomes, and hence the zygote has two sets of homologous chromosomes; that is, it is $2n$ or diploid, whereas the gametes are n or haploid. The zygote undergoes mitosis, in which the chromosomes are duplicated. In meiosis, the diploid or $2n$ chromosome number is reduced to the n or haploid chromosome number of the gametes.

12.   In meiosis, homologous chromosomes duplicate and then pair. Chromatid segments of homologous chromosomes are interchanged in a process called crossing over. In the first division of meiosis, the homologous chromosomes (each consisting of two chromatids) separate. In the second division, the two chromatids separate and move to different cells. Thus, the four cells produced by these two divisions have the haploid or n chromosome number.

13.   The actual migration of chromosomes to opposite poles at anaphase is termed disjunction and serves as the cytological basis for genetic segregation. The *random* separation of homologous chromosomes at anaphase is the cytological basis for the genetic law of independent assortment.

14.   Genes are located on chromosomes in linear order. The following are some of the similarities that occur between the genes and the visible

chromosomes: both are duplicated, both are in pairs, both are segregated in meiosis, and both undergo independent assortment.

15. Chromosomes consist chiefly of DNA, RNA and proteins; of these, DNA has been shown to carry the heritable genetic information.

16. A molecule of DNA is viewed as two strands of nucleotides forming a double helix. Each nucleotide consists of a phosphate group, a 5-carbon sugar, and one of four nitrogenous bases: adenine, thymine, cytosine, or guanine. The first two of these bases (adenine and thymine) can pair only with each other; the other two (cytosine and guanine) also can pair only with each other. The information carried by DNA resides in coded form in the sequence of base pairs.

17. The genetic code is based on triplets of nucleotides or codons, each of which can specify the assembly of a particular amino acid during enzyme synthesis.

18. The one-gene, one-enzyme hypothesis postulates that the DNA of a given gene directs the synthesis of a specific enzyme that then controls a particular biochemical reaction.

19. In incomplete dominance both genes are expressed phenotypically, neither gene masking the expression of the other.

20. Multiple gene inheritance produces blending among the offspring through the cumulative effect of more than two genes that influence the same trait. This mechanism is far more common than incomplete dominance between two genes and is important in plant and animal breeding.

21. Linkage, or the inheritance of characters in groups, is due to the location of genes for these characters on the same chromosome. Linkage is an exception to independent assortment.

22. Crossing over is an exception to linkage and is the result of exchange of parts between homologous chromosomes. Crossing over results in the separation of some genes that were linked.

23. Sex in some dioecious plants and in animals is determined at the time of fertilization by sex chromosomes. In the usual type of chromosome behavior, the presence of two X chromosomes produces a female, and an X and a Y chromosome result in a male.

24. Defined broadly, mutations are changes in the genetic material that can be detected phenotypically and that are not attributable to ordinary gene recombination. They may result from alterations of genes or from chromosome aberrations such as extra chromosomes or sets of chromosomes. Experimentally they are commonly induced by various radiations and by treatment with various chemicals.

25. Selection is the choosing of desirable individuals generation after generation for breeding purposes. Hybridization results in recombination of characters. Inbreeding is the crossing of closely related organisms, leading the production of a "pure line," that is, a line of organisms that are more or less homozygous for certain desirable traits.

26. Crossing two inbred lines produces offspring with a combination of the characters of the two lines and, in addition, a special vigor known as hybrid vigor.

27. Hybrid corn is the product of crossing two or more carefully inbred lines.

28. Hybrid plants do not breed true if they are propagated by seeds. If they are to be propagated without change, they must be reproduced by cuttings, grafts, or some other asexual method.

SUGGESTED READINGS FOR INTERESTED STUDENTS

1. Briggs, F. N., and P. F. Knowles, *Introduction to Plant Breeding.* Reinhold, New York, 1967.

2. Burns, George W., *An Introduction to Heredity.* The Macmillan Co., New York, 1969.

3. Cook, Stanton A., *Reproduction, Heredity and Sexuality.* Wadsworth, Belmont, Cal., 1964.

4. King, Robert C., *Genetics.* Oxford Univ. Press, New York, 1962.

5. King, Robert C., *A Dictionary of Genetics.* Oxford Univ. Press, New York, 1968.

6. Levine, Robert P., *Genetics,* 2d ed. Holt, Rinehart and Winston, New York, 1968.

7. Rhoades, M. M., "Meiosis." *The Cell,* J. Brachet, and A. E. Mirsky, Eds., Vol. III. Academic Press, New York, 1961.

8. Strickberger, Monroe W., *Genetics.* The Macmillan Co., New York, 1968.

9. Sturtevant, A. H., *A History of Genetics.* Harper & Row, New York, 1965.

TOPICS AND QUESTIONS FOR STUDY

1. Why was Mendel more successful than his predecessors in experiments on inheritance?

2. Define gene, dominance, segregation, and independent assortment.

3. Using genetic symbols, work out a monohybrid cross in which one factor is dominant, such as in a cross between tall and dwarf peas. Assuming that the F_1 and F_2 individuals are self-pollinated, carry your analysis through the F_2 and F_3. What is the F_2 phenotypic ratio? What is the F_2 genotypic ratio?

4. Repeat for a dihybrid cross in which two factors are dominant. What is the F_2 phenotypic ratio? The F_2 genotypic ratio?

5. Repeat for a monohybrid cross in which there is incomplete dominance. What are the F_2 ratios?

6. Explain the terms phenotype, genotype, homozygous, and heterozygous.

7. Compare mitosis and meiosis.

8. Define and give an example of bacterial transformation.

9. What special significance has the sequence of base pairs in a DNA molecule?

10. What is a codon?

11. What is the anticodon of GAC?

12. Why would a doublet code be inadequate for protein synthesis?

13. What is the one-gene, one-enzyme hypothesis?

14. Define and explain linkage and crossing over.

15. Explain the mechanism of sex inheritance. In view of your knowledge of sex determination, comment on the belief that a mother may "will" the sex of her unborn child; that environmental conditions may influence the sex of a child.

16. Discuss mutations with reference to their nature, causes, examples, and horticultural and evolutionary significance.

17. Explain the methods of selection, inbreeding, and cross-breeding.

18. Explain how hybrid corn is produced. Why is it important that hybrid corn seed be secured each season, rather than using the seed from the previous year's crop?

19. Why are hybrid fruit trees propagated by vegetative methods rather than by seeds?

20. Discuss the respective roles of environment and heredity in determining the traits of organisms.

20

THE PRINCIPLES
OF PLANT
CLASSIFICATION

THE CLASSIFICATION AND
NAMING OF PLANTS

The tendency to arrange organisms or objects into some kind of systematic grouping is one of the basic traits of intelligent man. We constantly classify things in accord with certain relationships that we perceive to exist among them. The classification and identification of plants is primarily the responsibility of the branch of botany known as **taxonomy.** There are about 350,000 known kinds of plants, which botanists arrange into groups of varying size and relationship. Botanists and nonbotanists alike classify plants, the former to achieve orderly and significant arrangement and to facilitate retrieval of information about them, the latter chiefly to distinguish among plants that are beautiful, edible, noxious, ugly, weedy, poisonous, and so on.

The aim of a scientific classification of plants is to indicate, wherever possible, the real relationships among the plants being classified. Such a **natural system,** based on evolutionary relationships, is the ultimate goal of taxonomic research.

An **artificial system** of classification is one that is based on convenience rather than on actual relationships. Artificial systems are often employed to classify organisms whose kind and degree of relationship are not known; these are likewise used for convenience and simplicity in grouping organisms for purposes of identification. A common artificial system of plant classification is one that separates all plants into herbs, shrubs, and trees to speed identification. Obviously such an arrangement is not natural, for totally unrelated plants often have similar growth habits and external forms. Apple trees are more closely related to strawberry plants than they are to elm trees; yet, in this artificial system of classification, elms would be grouped with apples, and strawberries would be in a separate, herbaceous group.

Criteria of Classification   The classification of various groups of living organisms may be based on a number of criteria—size, color, manner of obtaining or making food, anatomy, external form, methods of reproduction, and so on. The criteria considered to be most significant for purposes of classification are structural features of vegetative parts, especially with reference to anatomy, the structure of reproductive parts, and the nature of reproductive processes. Reproductive criteria are especially significant as bases of classification because they are least susceptible to the molding effects of fluctuating environmental conditions. The sizes of leaves, lengths of stems, amounts of root growth, colors, and other features vary widely with external factors, but the structure of flowers, fruits, seeds, and other reproductive parts is relatively constant. Often totally unrelated kinds of plants have almost identical vegetative structure. For instance, some members of the cactus, milkweed, and spurge families, growing in arid and semiarid regions, have barrel-shaped stems, thick cutin layers, spines, and other morphological similarities. However, plants of these groups differ widely in the structure of their flowers and fruits. If they were classified according to the form of their vegetative parts, they would be considered as closely related, but differences in their flower structure indicate that their relationships are actually very distant.

Units of Classification   Botanical classification involves the separation of different kinds of plants into groups of varying size and nature. The basic classificational unit in plant (and animal) taxonomy is the **species.** A species may be defined simply as a single *kind* of living organism—for example, silver maple is a species, red clover is a species, the coconut palm is a species. Biologists usually consider a species as the smallest unit in the classification system whose individual members are structurally similar, can readily interbreed without loss of fertility of their progeny, have common ancestors, and maintain their characteristic features *in nature* through innumerable generations.

A group of closely related species is called a **genus** (plural, **genera**). For example, all kinds of roses together constitute the rose genus, *Rosa*. The individual varieties and species of roses differ among themselves in various ways, but they all possess a common quality of "roseness" that stamps them as very closely related kinds of plants. Another example of a genus is the pine genus, *Pinus*, composed of many species of pines —white pines, sugar pines, slash pines, yellow pines, etc.—that vary among themselves but that all possess a fundamental assemblage of characteristics that distinguishes them as pines.

A group of closely related genera is called a **family.** For example, the rose family is composed of many genera, among which are the rose genus, the apple genus, the cherry genus, and the strawberry genus. All these genera have certain basic similarities in their floral structure but differ among themselves in rather well-marked ways. The scientific names of most families end in "aceae"; thus, the technical name of the rose family is **Rosaceae,** of the pine family, **Pinaceae,** and so forth.

A group of related families constitutes an **order,**

the scientific name of which ends in "ales." Thus, the rose order **(Rosales)** is composed of the rose family **(Rosaceae)**, the legume family **(Leguminosae)**, the stonecrop family **(Crassulaceae)**, and others, all of which have certain common, basic features of floral structure that indicate a close relationship among them. Orders are grouped into **classes,** and a group of classes constitutes a **division.** All the plant divisions together comprise the **plant kingdom (Plantae).** Often these major classificational units are split into subgroups; thus, there are subclasses, subdivisions, subfamilies, subspecies, and so on in the taxonomic system.

As illustrations of the mutual relationships of the classification units or **taxa** (singular, **taxon**) just described, the complete taxonomic categories of two common plants, prairie rose and corn, are presented below.

Kingdom—Plantae
  Subkingdom—Embryophyta
    Division—Anthophyta
      Class—Dicotyledonae
        Order—Rosales
          Family—Rosaceae
            Genus—*Rosa*
              Species—*Rosa setigera*

Kingdom—Plantae
  Subkingdom—Embryophyta
    Division—Anthophyta
      Class—Monocotyledonae
        Order—Graminales
          Family—Gramineae
            Genus—*Zea*
              Species—*Zea mays*

Scientific and Common Names By international agreement, every plant's species name consists of two words: the first corresponds to the genus name, the second (or **specific epithet**) indicates the particular kind within that genus. The generic name is a Latin or Latinized noun usually equivalent to a generalized common name, as: *Rosa,* rose; *Pinus,* pine; *Acer,* maple; *Pisum,* pea. The specific epithet is a modifying adjective that

FIG. 20-1.   Carolus Linnaeus, Swedish systematist (1707–1778).

often describes the plant further, as: *rubra,* red; *alba,* white; *albacaulis,* white-stemmed; *saccharum,* sweet. Frequently the generic name or specific epithet will commemorate a renowned scientist, as *Linnaea,* a genus named in honor of Carolus Linnaeus, or *michauxiana,* a specific epithet honoring André Michaux. Often specific epithets will indicate the place of discovery of the species, as in *canandensis, virginiana,* and *mexicana,* or indicate the habitat type in which the plant is usually found, as in *aquaticus.* Because the generic name is a proper noun, it is always capitalized; the adjectival specific epithet is not capitalized. By convention, Latin names, like other foreign words, are italicized.

In using scientific names, biologists do not employ the complete taxonomic pedigree of living organisms outlined above but use simply the species names. The hierarchical system is sufficiently simple that anyone familiar with it knows or can find the appropriate higher categories from the genus alone.

The system of using two words as the scientific name of a species is termed the **binomial system** and is used for both plant and animal names. The binomial system was first used for all organisms by the great Swedish botanist Carolus Linnaeus (1707–1778) Fig. 20–1. Following the scientific name of each species is an initial or abbreviation, which indicates the name of the scientist who first described and named the species. For example, *Zea mays* L. was named by Linnaeus, as were also *Pisum sativum* L. (garden pea) and *Solanum tuberosum* L. (Irish potato). *Rosa virginiana* Mill. was described and named by Philip Miller, *Rosa setigera* Michx. by André Michaux, and *Eriogonum harperi* Goodman by George J. Goodman.

People unfamiliar with the use of scientific names sometimes regard them as an unnecessary evil since common names with which they are more familiar may already be available. Common names are often useless for scientific purposes, however, for several reasons. They are composed of words from the native language of the country in which they are used; thus, in England, Australia, and the United States, common names consist of English words; in Mexico and Peru, they are chiefly of Spanish origin, and, in Japan, they are Japanese words. To an English or American botanist, common names in Japanese and Spanish would be meaningless; similarly, a Greek or German botanist unfamiliar with English would be puzzled by such common English names as snapdragon, milkweed, and bachelor's-buttons. Another disadvantage of common names for scientific purposes is their frequent variability within the borders of a single country or even of one state. Thus, the name lady's-slipper is commonly applied to several dozen species of orchids, as well as to another plant in a family not closely related to the Orchidaceae. The name lily is given such members of the lily family as Easter lily and tiger lily; it is also used in the common names water lily, spider lily, and calla lily, none of which belongs to the lily family. Thus, one common name may be applied to several distinct species of plants, and, also, a single species of plant may be designated by several common names. Obviously, common names are often confusing and lack the standardization and precision required by scientists. The advantage of scientific names over common names is that they are governed by rules established by international congresses of biologists and are thus uniformly regulated and applied. Since they are based on Latin, with which all biologists are presumably somewhat familiar, they are the same in all parts of the world. Although a German botanist might not know the meaning of the English name black walnut, he would immediately recognize the name *Juglans nigra* L.; similarly, an American botanist, ignorant of the Spanish word *cebolla*, would recognize the binomial *Allium cepa* L., the scientific name of onion.

REPRODUCTION IN PLANTS

Since the chief criteria of classification are based on body structure and reproductive processes, an understanding of the basic features of reproduction is prerequisite to a study of plant classification. Reproduction is a process whereby organisms produce offspring and thus maintain their species. Plants reproduce themselves in many ways. These reproductive methods are usually separated into two types: **sexual reproduction** and **asexual reproduction.** Sexual reproduction involves both **meiosis** and **fertilization.** The cell produced by the fusion of two gametes is called a **zygote.** In a few primitive plants, the gametes are alike in size and structure, although they may differ in their physiology. Such gametes are called **isogametes,** and the process of reproduction in which they participate is termed **isogamy.** The more common and more advanced type of sexual reproduction, termed **heterogamy,** involves gametes that are unlike in size and structure as well as in certain physiological characteristics. These **heterogametes** are called **eggs** (female gametes) and **sperms** (male gametes). Eggs are usually larger than sperms and are most frequently nonmotile; sperms are often equipped with whiplike locomotory processes called **cilia** or **flagella** and are in such cases able to swim in a liquid medium. The fusion of an egg and a sperm in the embryo sac of an angiosperm ovule is an example of heterogamous sexual reproduction.

In asexual reproduction, neither meiosis nor fusion of gametes is involved. A portion of a plant body separates from a parent body and grows into a new individual. Among the common types of asexual reproduction in plants are **fission, budding, fragmentation, spore formation,** and **vegetative propagation.** Fission is the method of reproduction in many primitive plants; it is the division of a single-celled organism into two new single-celled organisms. Budding is a method of asexual reproduction in which a small protuberance forms on the surface of a one-celled organism, nuclear division occurs, and one daughter nucleus migrates into the protuberance which continues to grow until it is almost as large as the parent cell; a wall is then formed between the parent cell and the "bud," and the two cells may separate, as in yeasts. Fragmentation is the breaking of a multicellular plant body into segments, each part of which is then able to grow into a complete new plant. Spores are usually one-celled, specialized structures that are produced by various plants. A spore separates from the parent plant and is able by repeated cell divisions to grow into a complete new plant. The structure within which spores are produced is called a **sporangium.** In many water plants, such as aquatic fungi and algae, the spores possess cilia or flagella that move in undulating fashion and propel the spores through the water. Such motile spores are called **zoospores.** Vegetative propagation is reproduction by means of runners, tubers, root sprouts, and so on.

In some plants—certain algae, for example—the zoospores and isogametes are almost indistinguishable in structure, differing only in size. Because of this, many botanists think that sexual reproduction may have originated from asexual reproduction through fusion of zoospores.

ALTERNATION OF GENERATIONS

A conspicuous feature of sexual reproduction in most plants is a phenomenon called **alternation of generations.** This means that the complete *sexual* life history (life cycle) of a plant consists of two phases or generations, one of which (the **sporophyte**) produces spores while the other (the **gametophyte**) produces gametes. Intimately associated with and characteristic of the sexual cycle are two significant processes, meiosis and fertilization, each of which must occur before the cycle can be completed. An understanding of the relationships that exist between the structures and processes mentioned above may be obtained by considering the sequence of major events in a generalized life history, such as that shown diagrammatically in Fig. 20–2. Fertilization, the fusion of a female gamete (egg) with a male gamete (sperm), gives rise to a zygote. Since each gamete nucleus is haploid (or $1 n$), that is, contains a single set of chromosomes characteristic for the species, the zygote contains two sets of homologous chromosomes at fertilization, and is, therefore, diploid (or $2 n$). The diploid zygote grows into a sporophyte that likewise has the diploid chromosome number in all its cells. When the sporophyte is mature, certain of its cells (spore mother cells) undergo meiosis and produce **meiospores.** Meiosis *reduces* the chromosome complement from the diploid to the haploid condition and thereby marks the beginning of the gametophyte generation. The gametophyte into which a spore grows contains the haploid chromosome number in all its cells, including the gametes that it produces. Fertilization then re-establishes the diploid chromosome number in the zygote and marks the beginning of the sporophyte generation.

In all vascular plants, bryophytes, and some lower plants (thallophytes), both gametophytes

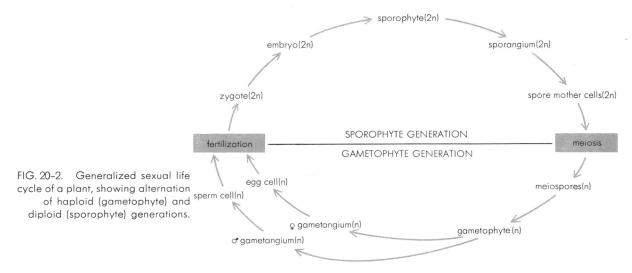

FIG. 20-2. Generalized sexual life cycle of a plant, showing alternation of haploid (gametophyte) and diploid (sporophyte) generations.

and sporophytes are multicellular structures, usually quite unlike in relative size and appearance. In other thallophytes the zygote does not develop by cell divisions into a multicellular plant but instead undergoes meiosis directly; thus the single diploid cell (the zygote) represents the sporophyte "generation." In still other thallophytes the zygote develops into a diploid vegetative phase that ultimately produces gametes by meiosis. In this type a single haploid cell (the gamete) represents the gametophyte "generation." In each of the above cases there is a cytological alternation between the haploid and diploid conditions; however, many botanists believe that alternation of generations in a morphological sense requires the alternation of multicellular haploid and diploid phases.

As you study the various plant groups you will encounter many types of plants with which you are unfamiliar. Moreover, these plants will appear to have many differences in their life histories. Remember that in all plant groups with alternation of generations, the same basic sequence of events occurs: haploid gametes fuse at fertilization to form a diploid zygote that grows into the sporophyte plant; the sporophyte produces diploid spore mother cells that undergo meiosis, giving rise to haploid meiospores; each meiospore

grows into a haploid gametophyte plant that then produces gametes. If you will trace these basic similarities through all the groups having alternation of generations, the differences among them will become simple to comprehend.

ORGANIZATION OF CHAPTERS ON PLANT DIVISIONS

In your study of the various plant divisions listed in the next section of this chapter, you will encounter many new facts about these divisions. To facilitate your study, descriptions of these groups and the plants they encompass will be organized and summarized under the following headings wherever possible.

1. *General characteristics:* major features of external and internal structure of the plants in each division.

2. *Reproductive characteristics:* descriptions of reproductive methods and structures representative of each division.

3. *Habitat and distribution:* an account of the places in which members of the divisions grow— fresh water, salt water, deserts, woodland, and so on—and of their geographical distribution.

4. *Representative members:* description of selected orders, families, or genera of each division.

I.   Subkingdom **THALLOPHYTA**—plants not forming embryos.
   Division 1—**Schizophyta** (bacteria)
   Division 2—**Cyanophyta** (blue-green algae)
   Division 3—**Chlorophyta** (green algae)
   Division 4—**Euglenophyta** (euglenophytes)
   Division 5—**Chrysophyta** (diatoms and others)
   Division 6—**Phaeophyta** (brown algae)
   Division 7—**Rhodophyta** (red algae)
   Division 8—**Myxomycophyta** (slime fungi)
   Division 9—**Eumycophyta** (true fungi)
      Class 1—**Phycomycetes** (water molds and others)
      Class 2—**Ascomycetes** (sac fungi)
      Class 3—**Basidiomycetes** (club fungi)

II. Subkingdom **EMBRYOPHYTA**—plants forming embryos
   Division 10—**Bryophyta** (mosses and relatives; terrestrial
                  plants lacking vascular tissues)
      Class 1—**Musci** (mosses)
      Class 2—**Hepaticae** (liverworts)
      Class 3—**Anthocerotae** (hornworts)
   Division 11—**Psilophyta** (whisk-ferns and their relatives; rootless, terrestrial, vas-
                  cular plants, almost entirely extinct)
   Division 12—**Lycopodophyta** (club mosses and their relatives; with simple con-
                  ducting systems and scalelike leaves)
   Division 13—**Arthrophyta** (horsetails and their relatives; with simple conducting
                  systems, scalelike leaves, and jointed stems)
   Division 14—**Pterophyta** (ferns and their relatives; with complex conducting
                  systems and large, conspicuous leaves)
   Division 15—**Coniferophyta** (pines and their relatives; seed-producing plants with
                  specialized cones and simple leaves)
   Division 16—**Ginkgophyta** (ginkgo and its relatives; with fan-shaped leaves and
                  fleshy seeds)
   Division 17—**Gnetophyta** (gnetophytes; seed-producing plants with broad leaves
                  and conelike reproductive structures)
   Division 18—**Cycadophyta** (the cycads and their relatives; with fernlike leaves and
                  large cones)
   Division 19—**Anthophyta** (the flowering plants)
      Class 1—**Dicotyledonae** (flowering plants producing seeds with two cotyledons)
      Class 2—**Monocotyledonae** (flowering plants producing seeds with one cotyledon)

TABLE 20—1   A system of plant classification.

5. *Relationship to other organisms:* accounts of the known or supposed affinities with other groups of plants, with emphasis on evolutionary relationships.

6. *Importance in nature and in human life:* importance of each group in relation to soil binding, soil fertility, sources of food for animals, and so on, and in providing food, drugs, fibers, and other products useful in human life.

A MODERN SYSTEM OF PLANT CLASSIFICATION

The taxonomic system used in this book is a phylogenetic system based on recent results of botanical research on the structure, reproductive methods, and apparent relationships of living and extinct plants. However, it should not be regarded as the final word in the classification of the major plant groups. There are still gaps in our knowledge of the precise relationships of some of the taxa—for example, the origin of angiosperms—and it is likely that changes will be made in this system as the future brings more information about these groups.

As a prelude to the systematic study of the major groups of the plant kingdom, this system is presented in Table 20–1 to give orientation to students.

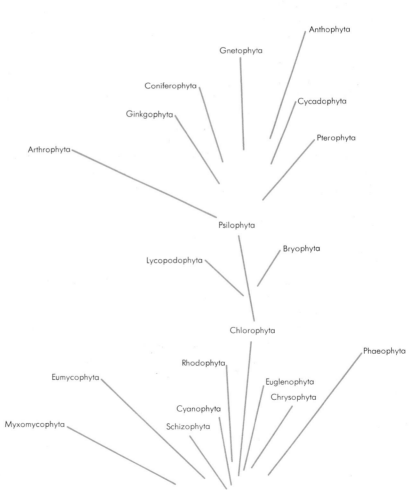

FIG. 20-3. Diagram illustrating possible relationships among the major plant groups.

SUMMARY

1. There are approximately 350,000 known species of plants living on the earth at present. Taxonomy is the branch of botany concerned with the classification, identification, and evolutionary relationships of plants.

2. The principal criteria used in classifying plants are features of their structure and reproduction.

3. The basic unit in the classification of living organisms is the species. A group of closely related species constitutes a genus, a group of closely related genera comprises a family, a collection of related families is an order, orders are grouped into classes, classes constitute divisions, and divisions are grouped into subkingdoms. Any of these categories may be divided into subgroups.

4. Common names of organisms are of little value for scientific purposes because they vary from language to language, they are often used in loose, indefinite ways, and they are frequently variable in meaning.

5. A scientific species name consists of two words, the first the name of the genus, the second the specific epithet. Such a name is called a binomial.

6. Scientific names are made of Latin or Latinized words and are the same in all parts of the world.

7. The two types of reproduction in plants are sexual and asexual. Sexual reproduction involves meiosis and gametic fusion. Asexual reproduction includes all methods that do not involve these two processes.

8. Isogamy is sexual reproduction by means of structurally similar gametes. Heterogamy is sexual reproduction by means of structurally dissimilar gametes.

9. A female gamete is called an egg, a male gamete a sperm.

10. Among common types of asexual reproduction are fission, budding, spore formation, fragmentation, and vegetative reproduction.

11. Alternation of generations is a phenomenon in which the complete, sexual life cycle of a plant consists of two phases or generations: a gametophyte generation that produces gametes, and a sporophyte generation that produces spores. By means of fusion of gametes at fertilization and spore formation at meiosis, each generation in turn gives rise to the other. Alternation of generations occurs in most groups of plants.

12. The gametophyte generation has the haploid chromosome number, the sporophyte generation has the diploid number.

SUGGESTED READINGS FOR INTERESTED STUDENTS

1. Bell, C. R., *Plant Variation and Classification*. Wadsworth, Belmont, Cal., 1967.

2. Cronquist, Arthur, *The Evolution and Classification of Flowering Plants*. Houghton-Mifflin, Boston, Mass. 1968.

3. Heslop-Harrison, J., *New Concepts in Flowering Plant Taxonomy*. Harvard University Press, Cambridge, Mass. 1964.

4. Heywood, V. H., *Plant Taxonomy*. St. Martin's Press, New York, 1967.

5. Lawrence, G. H. M., *Taxonomy of Vascular Plants*. The Macmillan Co., New York, 1951.

6. Porter, C. L., *Taxonomy of Flowering Plants*, 2d ed. W. H. Freeman, San Francisco, 1967.

TOPICS AND QUESTIONS FOR STUDY

1. Define taxonomy.
2. Distinguish between natural and artificial systems of classification.
3. What are the major criteria of classification?
4. Define species, genus, family, order, class, and division.
5. How may one readily recognize the names of families? Of orders?
6. What are the objections to the use of common names of organisms for scientific study?
7. What is the binomial system?
8. What are the advantages of scientific names over common names?
9. Define: sexual reproduction, asexual reproduction, gamete, zygote, isogamy, heterogamy, meiospore, fission, budding, fragmentation, and vegetative propagation.
10. Define and describe briefly alternation of generations.
11. At what points in alternation of generations do chromosome numbers change? Explain.

21

THALLOPHYTA: ALGAE

DIFFERENT GROUPS WITHIN THE THALLOPHYTA

The subkingdom Thallophyta consists of the algae, fungi, and bacteria. Algae in general have chlorophyll and are photosynthetic and autotrophic, whereas all the fungi and the great majority of bacteria lack chlorophyll and are not photosynthetic but are parasitic or saprophytic. The Thallophyta is a large assemblage of very diverse plants which range from microscopic, unicellular forms to large, multicellular plants 200 feet or more in length. Most of the divisions of plants grouped in the subkingdom Tallophyta are not related. Because the majority of them are more similar to one another than they are to the more highly evolved land plants, they have simply been segregated from land plants—that is, the Embryophyta—and put into a separate group, the Thallophyta. The plants comprising the Thallophyta are structurally the least complex of the plant kingdom. Their simple bodies or **thalli** (singular: **thallus**) consist of a single cell or a chain of cells or a mass of cells arranged in various degrees of organization. The vascular, epidermal, and other specialized tissues characteristic of higher plants, as well as the typical organs—roots, stems, and leaves—are absent in the Thallophyta. The gamete-producing structures (gametangia) and spore-producing bodies (sporangia) are essentially unicellular and are rarely enveloped by a jacket of protective cells such as occurs in higher plants. None of the thallophytes form multicellular, embryonic stages within the female gametangia of a parent plant.

Algae are chiefly aquatic plants, many of which live suspended in or floating near the surface of water as **plankton;** others live in the deeper or benthic zones submerged and attached to some object in the water. In some groups of algae such as the reds, browns, blue-greens, and diatoms, the great majority of species are marine. In other groups, such as the greens, golden browns, and euglenoids, most members live in fresh water or in some terrestrial environment. In the latter they may be found on or within moist soil, rock, or tree bark; on or under snow and ice; in hot springs; on or within the bodies of other plants and animals; and in communal association with fungi to form lichens. Algae play a major role in the supply of energy for the biological world. The energy comes almost entirely from photosynthesis which converts the nonusable radiant energy of the sun into usable chemical energy. Algae, by their sheer numbers alone, account for 90 percent of this capture of the sun's energy and its conversion to a storable chemical form. Most of the earth's surface (71 percent) is covered by the seas—140 million square miles. Another 10,000 square miles are covered by lakes and rivers. This is almost three times as vast as the mere 57 million square miles of land; thus, aquatic habitats are huge photoreceptor regions for the absorption of the sun's rays. The algae of these waters account for approximately 3.6 billion tons of carbon fixed into organic compounds annually by photosynthesis. Algae also furnish much of the oxygen necessary to animal life.

In man's search for new sources of food to sustain the ever-expanding human population, he

Algal Division	Auxiliary Pigments
Cyanophyta (blue-green algae)	Phycocyanin predominantly, plus phycoerythrin and carotenoids
Chlorophyta (green algae)	Chlorophyll *b* predominantly, plus carotenoids
Euglenophyta (euglenoids)	Chlorophyll *b* predominantly, plus carotenoids
Chrysophyta (diatoms and others)	Fucoxanthin predominantly, plus chlorophyll *c* and *e*
Phaeophyta (brown algae)	Fucoxanthin predominantly, plus chlorophyll *c* and carotenoids
Rhodophyta (red algae)	Phycoerythrin predominantly, plus phycocyanin, carotenoids and chlorophyll *d*

TABLE 21–1 Auxiliary photosynthetic pigments of the algae

is looking more and more seriously at algae as a relatively unexploited source of food, either from the algae directly or from the myriad of animal life that is supported by the algae.

A great diversity of photosynthetic pigmentation is found among algae in contrast to the higher land plants which are remarkably uniform in the pigments they contain. The different groups of algae have characteristic colors that are the basis of the common names of the divisions—the blue-green algae, the reds, the browns, and the golden browns. These colors are due to the presence of chlorophyll *a* in association with certain auxiliary photosynthetic pigments—namely chlorophylls *b*, *c*, *d*, and *e*—and two major groups of nonchlorophyllous pigments, the carotenoids and phycobilins. Carotenoid pigments include orange-yellow carotenes and yellow or brownish xanthophylls; the phycobilins include red phycoerythrin and blue phycocyanin. Table 21-1 presents a summary list of the auxiliary pigments found in the various algal divisions. These auxiliary pigments are believed to facilitate photosynthesis under the conditions of illumination found at various depths. Sunlight is composed of many wavelengths, certain ranges of which are visible as the colors of the spectrum: violet, blue, green, yellow, orange, and red. When sunlight passes into a body of water such as an ocean or lake, its component wavelengths are selectively filtered out and absorbed at different depths. First to be absorbed at shallower depths are the longer wavelengths of red, orange, and yellow; last to be absorbed at deeper levels are the shorter ones of green, blue, and violet. The pigment involved in conversion of light energy to chemical energy during photosynthesis is chlorophyll *a*, a green pigment that functions principally in absorption of red and blue light from the sunlight spectrum. Chlorophyll *a* tends to predominate in the pigment complements of those plants growing where full sunlight is available for photosynthesis, as on land or in very shallow water, and the plants commonly appear green. At greater depths in water, however, chlorophyll *a* does not efficiently absorb the available wavelengths. Photosynthesis is possible at these depths because of the presence of the auxiliary pigments which absorb the energy of the light waves present and pass it on to chlorophyll *a*. However, these auxiliary photosynthetic pigments cannot substitute for chlorophyll *a* in its catalytic role of converting light energy to chemical energy. Thus, in the seas and in bodies of fresh water we see a vertical distribution of algae which is related to their chromatic adaptation to the wavelengths of light available at different depths of water. Although there are, of course, numerous exceptions, it can be said that, in general, green algae occur in upper or shallow water zones, red algae grow at depths as great as 800 feet in the sunny tropics, and brown algae grow best in water of about 10 to 60 feet in depth and in the intertidal zone where they are particularly abundant.

SIZE INCREASE, GROWTH FORMS, AND REPRODUCTION

Evolution in the plant and animal kingdoms has followed several major trends. One such trend is gradual increase in size and complexity of organisms. Major advantages of increased size for the Thallophyta probably include increased photosynthetic capability and increased reproductive ability. Another possible advantage is reduced susceptability to depredation by animals. A unicellular organism must produce sufficient food to maintain its own life and must also produce all the food necessary for production of reproductive bodies (spores and gametes). Increase in size and photosynthetic capacity of unicellular organisms is ordinarily limited by problems of metabolic control within a single-cell unit. But increase in size can readily be accomplished by cohesion of the derivative cells resulting from cell division to form colonial or multicellular organisms. In such organisms the majority of cells may be involved in food production and other vegetative functions for their own needs and the needs of the entire plant, while, usually, a smaller

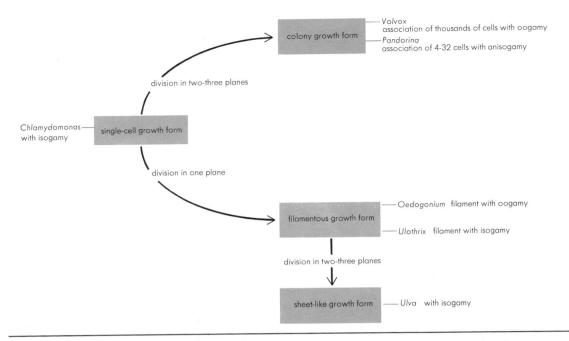

FIG. 21-1.   Some of the different forms of green algae illustrating some of the probable stages of evolution.

number of cells have the special function of reproduction. Each vegetative cell contributes directly or indirectly toward the development of the reproductive cells, and the likelihood of successful reproduction by the individual is thereby increased.

Within the algae the general evolutionary trend of size increase is recognizable in the existing growth forms (body types). These growth forms illustrate some of the stages in evolution. Each form represents a successful way of life that, within certain limits, has survived to the present. Among the algae, the trend of size increase has followed different lines, proceeding from unicellular to colonial to multicellular thalli (Fig. 21-1). The growth of a plant reflects the amount of division of vegetative and reproductive labor among the cells of the organism and the manner in which cell division proceeds. Unicellular organisms are those in which a single cell performs all the necessary functions of the organism and in which cell division is followed by separation of the daughter cells so that each becomes an

independent individual. Colonial organisms usually display little, if any, division of labor or cellular differentiation for vegetative or reproductive activities; each cell of a colonial organism is usually identical to all of the others, each may function at different times for either vegetative or reproductive roles. Colonial organisms in which cell division occurs predominantly in only one plane are filamentous; those in which cell division occurs in two or three planes are, respectively, sheetlike or three dimensional, as, for example, a sphere. Multicellular organisms usually display conspicuous division of labor between vegetative cells and a smaller proportion of reproductive cells. As with colonial organisms, the thalli of multicellular organisms may be filamentous, flattened, or three dimensional. In summary, the algal thallophytes may be unicellular, colonial, or multicellular, and the colonial and multicellular organisms may be filamentous, flattened, or three dimensional in form.

Reproduction of all organisms may be either asexual or sexual. Asexual reproduction is

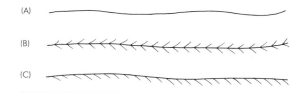

(A)

(B)

(C)

FIG. 21-2. Flagellum types among algae. A. Whip-lash type. B. and C. Tinsel types.

thought to be the least specialized and involves either the simple breaking of the thallus into two or more smaller portions, each of which can grow into a larger thallus comparable to that from which it was derived, or the formation of special cells called spores that can divide and grow to form a thallus like that of the parent. Sexual reproduction involves the exchange and mixing of genetic information from two individuals by fusion of their gamete nuclei. The gametes of higher plants, of most multicellular animals, and of many thallophytes are clearly differentiated into a larger, nonmotile egg and a smaller, motile sperm. This type of reproduction involving such a differentiation of egg and sperm is termed **oogamy.** The simplest sexual process is that in which the fusing sex cells are identical morphologically (though not genetically); this is termed **isogamy.** Another process is that in which one gamete is smaller and the other larger, though both are motile; this is called **anisogamy.** Anisogamy and oogamy are grouped under the term **heterogamy** (sexual reproduction involving unlike gametes). Isogamy is thought to have preceded heterogamy in the evolution of the thallophytes and anisogamy to have preceded oogamy.

The majority of algae are themselves motile or produce motile reproductive cells. In some instances, motile cells move somewhat in the manner of amoebae, and in a few groups the method of movement is unknown, but most motile cells or colonies swim from place to place by the action of minute, threadlike projections called **flagella.** There are two general types of flagella among algae: the whiplash type (Fig. 21-2, A) in which the flagellum is smooth and lacks branches, and

the tinsel type (Figs. 21-2, B and C) in which the flagellum has many fine branches either on one or both sides. Several variations of these basic types exist, and they are of importance in differentiating the algal groups.

DIVISION CYANOPHYTA (BLUE-GREEN ALGAE)

General Characteristics Of all the algae, the Cyanophyta are simplest in organization and reproduction, and their simplicity is usually interpreted as strong evidence that they are the most primitive of the algal groups. The protoplast of a blue-green algal cell has less structural differentiation than the protoplast of any other green plant. Neither chromatin nor chlorophyll-bearing lamellae is delimited by membranes, so the cells have neither organized nuclei nor chloroplasts. True vacuoles are also absent, but small gas vacuoles can occur. Cell duplication in the Cyanophyta differs from that in other algae in that discrete chromosomes are not organized from the chromatin material prior to the time of cell division, a type of cell replication termed **amitotic.** The cells themselves are usually invested by pectic, mucilaginous sheaths which are secreted through the cell walls.

The blue-green algae are so named because of the predominance of the blue pigment phycocyanin, which, in combination with chlorophyll and other pigments, gives many members a blue-green color. Color alone, however, may not be sufficient to distinguish the blue-green algae from members of other divisions because relatively large amounts of other pigments, notably phycoerythrin, may make certain Cyanophyta appear red, brown, black, or purple. For example, the Red Sea got its name from the periodic abundance of a blue-green alga which is red due to large quantities of phycoerythrin. The majority of Cyanophyta are photosynthetic and autotrophic, but a few species are parasitic or saprophytic. Some autotrophic species become heterotrophic if sufficient organic nutrients are available in their environment. Some species are able to incorporate atmospheric nitrogen into organic compounds (nitrogen fixation), a process better known in certain bacteria. The principal reserve foods of blue-green algae are a carbohydrate called cyanophycean starch and a proteinaceous material (cyanophycin) which occurs in the form of minute granules dispersed in the cytoplasm.

There are unicellular, colonial, and filamentous genera of blue-green algae, and the plants are characteristically surrounded by a gelatinous or mucilaginous sheath. Typically, large numbers of individuals grow clustered together, and their dense growth, along with their combined mucilaginous sheathes, produces stringy or bulbous masses of slimy material.

Reproductive Characteristics   Reproduction is largely, if not wholly, asexual. Some observations suggest that an exchange of genetic material may occur between some plants, but this is not accomplished by the formation and fusion of gametes, and the process may resemble gene exchange mechanisms known for bacteria. Unicellular genera reproduce by cell division, each daughter cell constituting a new, independent organism. In filamentous algae, new individuals commonly are produced by the fragmentation of the filament into shorter pieces which are motile and capable of forming new filaments. These fragments, called **hormogonia** (Fig. 21–3) arise when weak points are created in the parent filament by the death of certain cells. Other fragments are formed when certain modified cells called **heterocysts** (Fig. 21–3) cause a section of the parent filament to become pinched off.

Some filamentous algae reproduce by means of spores. Spores are single cells with little or no water content and highly thickened walls. They are formed by the modification of certain cells of the filament; they break away from the chain and are dispersed. When provided with suitable conditions for gowth, their walls split open, the protoplasts absorb water, divide, and grow into new filaments. Commonly, spore formation occurs when adverse environmental conditions

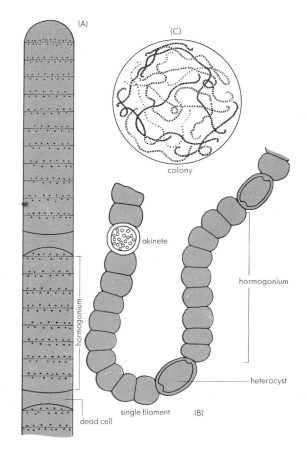

FIG. 21–3.   Filamentous blue-green algae. A. *Oscillatoria* with a hormogonium formed between two dead cells. B. *Nostoc* showing two types of reproductive bodies: the unicellular akinete and the multicellular hormogonium, formed between two heterocysts. C. Colony of *Nostoc* filaments in typical mucilaginous mass (drawn here highly reduced).

arise or when certain physiological changes occur in the cells of the filament. The most common spore type formed is the **akinete** (Fig. 21–3), which is a vegetative cell transformed by a thickening of its wall.

The dissemination of blue-green algae is mainly passive, the plants being borne about by water or air currents, although some filamentous forms are capable of limited motion through oscillatory or rotating movements. Unlike most other algal groups, the Cyanophyta do not produce any flagellated vegetative or reproductive cells.

Habitat and Distribution   Over three fourths of the blue-green algae are marine or live in brackish waters. In tidal marshes and mud flats they are the dominant algal type present. Many fresh-water species can be found in lakes, ponds, rivers, springs, or open tanks of water. Along with the diatoms, the blue-green algae are the most numerous algae found growing on soil surfaces or wet rock or on the outside of flower pots. They show a high degree of adaptation whereby they can adjust to various light intensities. Some species are found growing in caves having low light levels whereas others can live in bright sunlight. Tolerance to temperature extremes is typical of the group. About 150 genera thrive in hot springs and geyser basins where the temperatures may range between 75° C and 82° C. In such places the algae typically precipitate calcium and magnesium salts out of the hot waters and deposit them as colored **travertine** rock (Fig. 21–4). Depositions of rock as thick as 5 centimeters a year can be laid down by these algae. At the other extreme, there are blue-green algae thriving in the ice of the Arctic. Some fresh-water species cause the precipitation of carbonates from the water to form small limy stones—oolites. On the other hand, many marine species live in and on limestone rock, and by their borings into such rock they can cause significant degrees of erosion. Symbiosis is common within the group: some species live within the tissues of flowering plants; some live in the intestines of animals, including man; and others live in association with fungi to form lichens.

Representative Members   *Gloeocapsa* (Fig. 21–5) is a genus of very simple plants, the species usually being considered unicellular. Each cell is surrounded by a relatively thick, mucilaginous capsule and when the cell divides, both daughter

FIG. 21–4.   Travertine terraces and thermal springs in Yellowstone National Park. (National Park photo.)

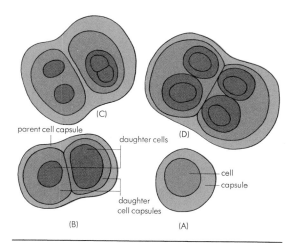

FIG. 21–5.   *Gloeocapsa.* Cells embedded in mucilagenous capsules. A. Single cell. B. Two cells of unequal size, each embedded in its own capsule as well as that of the parent cell. C. and D. Older colonies with cells and capsules embedded in parent cell capsules.

cells may remain enclosed by the parent cell's capsule for some time. Each daughter cell also secretes a new capsule of its own, and when these cells divide, they, too, may be retained within the original capsule. In this manner colonies of four, eight, or more cells are frequently developed (Figs. 21–5, C and D). *Gloeocapsa* commonly occurs on moist rock, soil surfaces, and dripping cliffs, where it often forms extensive, dark-colored slimy masses.

Oscillatoria (Fig. 21–3) is a very common blue-green alga in which the species are filamentous. Filaments grow in length by the division of their component cells and increase in numbers by the formation of hormogonia. As they float in the water, they commonly exhibit an oscillating or rotating movement—hence the name *Oscillatoria*. Extensive growths of *Oscillatoria* are common on wet rock, soil surfaces, and flower pots.

Nostoc (Fig. 21–3) is another genus of filamentous plants occurring in fresh water and moist terrestrial habitats with hundreds of filaments embedded in large globose or filmy masses of mucilage whose dimensions may reach several centimeters. Fragmentation in *Nostoc* occurs by the formation of heterocysts.

Relationship to Other Organisms   The relationships of the Cyanophyta with other organisms are obscure, but most workers agree that their lack of specialization denotes a primitive level of evolution. Fossils as old as 1.7 billion years found in southern Ontario consist of several forms identified as blue-green algae. Blue-green algae are considered by some authorities as possibly related to bacteria because they share several characteristics. These include lack of organized nuclei and plastids, lack of sexual reproduction involving gametes, amitotic cell division, ability to fix nitrogen, tendency to flourish in water with high quantites of organic matter, and, in some species, the ability to form endospores. (See Chapter 22 on bacteria). On the other hand, blue-green algae also share certain characteristics with red algae; these include lack of flagellated cells and the presence of phycocyanin and phycoerythrin. Thus there might be some relationship to the red algae.

Importance in Nature and in Human Life   Blue-green algae may serve as sources of food for fish and other aquatic animals, some of which provide food for man. The dead thalli of soil-living Cyanophyta add organic matter to the soil, increasing its fertility and promoting the growth of bacteria and other organisms whose activities also increase the soil fertility. Many soil species of blue-green algae can capture atmospheric nitrogen and, as valuable soil conditioners, they sometimes play a role equal in prominence to the nitrogen-fixing bacteria. Probably of more far-reaching importance to man are the undesirable effects of blue-green algae. Many species contain or exude foul-smelling products which in some cases are quite toxic. These toxins, as well as the abundant growth of the organisms themselves, commonly ruin water supplies and recreational areas. Farm animals and birds have been killed or made seriously ill after drinking water containing these toxins. The preferential growth of many species in polluted waters, coupled with the undesirable substances they release, greatly increases the pollution level. Their profuse growth also clogs screens and sand filters in water systems and their subsequent decay depletes the oxygen content of water, causing suffocation of fish and other animals.

DIVISION CHLOROPHYTA (GREEN ALGAE)

General Characteristics   The Chlorophyta, with approximately 400 genera and 7000 species, is second only to the diatoms in numbers of species. They display more diversity of size, form, and complexity than any other algal group, but in their general structure and reproductive characteristics they show less evolutionary advance than the red and brown algae. The organization

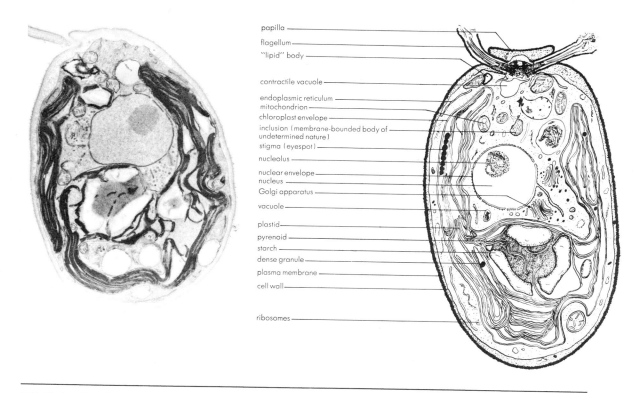

papilla
flagellum
"lipid" body

contractile vacuole
endoplasmic reticulum
mitochondrion
chloroplast envelope
inclusion (membrane-bounded body of undetermined nature)
stigma (eyespot)
nucleolus
nuclear envelope
nucleus
Golgi apparatus
vacuole
plastid
pyrenoid
starch
dense granule
plasma membrane
cell wall

ribosomes

FIG. 21-6.   The ultrastructure of the green alga *Chlamydomonas eugametos*. *Left:* Electron micrograph (approximately × 25,000). *Right:* Line drawing of same (Photo and drawing courtesy of Dr. Patricia L. Walne.)

of the protoplast is quite like that of higher plants; it has the typical inclusions or organelles we have studied earlier, including nuclei and chloroplasts (Fig. 21-6). Cell division is typically mitotic.

Green algae have a pigment complement identical to that of higher plants. Here again, however, color alone is inadequate to distinguish the members of this division because many genera in other divisions are also green. The food reserve is true starch, which is synthesized and stored in the chloroplasts, sometimes in association with small bodies called **pyrenoids**. The cell wall is cellulosic, and the electron microscope has revealed that in many genera the wall is identical to that of higher plants (Fig. 21-6). Growth forms of the thallus include unicellular, colonial, and

multicellular types. In spite of the general lack of tissue differentiation found in thallophytes, some green algae approach the structural complexity of simple land plants. The motile cells of green algae are flagellated, but some genera produce amoeboid gametes.

Reproductive Characteristics   Green algae reproduce both sexually and asexually, and many species have an alternation of haploid and diploid generations. In marine species the generations may be relatively massive and multicellular, but all fresh-water species are small plants and are unicellular, filamentous, or colonial.

Asexual reproduction of unicellular Chlorophyta is by cell division or spore formation; fila-

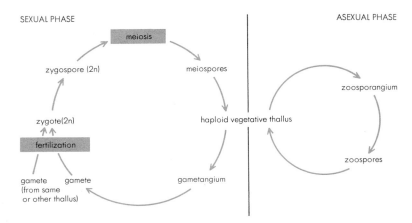

SEXUAL PHASE

meiosis

zygospore (2n)

meiospores

zygote(2n)

haploid vegetative thallus

fertilization

gamete   gamete
(from same
or other thallus)

gametangium

ASEXUAL PHASE

zoosporangium

zoospores

FIG. 21–7. Generalized life cycle of fresh water green alga.

mentous forms can be readily fragmented by water movement or other mechanical agitation to produce pieces that can grow to typical length by cell division. Green algae do not form hormogonial fragments as do filamentous bluegreens. Spore formation is another important method of asexual reproduction among the colonial and multicellular greens, with usually a small number of zoospores being formed within a parent cell, which is thus transformed into a zoosporangium. After release from the zoosporangium, a zoospore may swim to a favorable site, attach itself to the substrate, lose its flagella, and by cell division grow into a new individual similar to the parent plant.

Sexual reproduction among the greens may be isogamous, anisogamous, or oogamous, and fertilization may involve those gametes produced by a single plant **(homothallism)** or may be restricted to gametes produced by different thalli **(heterothallism).** Many marine species undergo regular alternation of generations—the haploid plant producing gametes, the diploid plant that grows from the zygote giving rise to haploid spores by means of meiosis. Most fresh-water green algae do not display such an alternation of generations. In this group the haploid thallus produces gametes that fuse to form a zygote, and the zygote secretes a resistant outer wall to become a diploid **zygospore.** This cell is able to survive prolonged periods of adverse physical or physiological con-

ditions. When conditions again become suitable, the zygote undergoes meiosis and germinates. Meiotic division of the zygote produces four haploid, motile **meiospores,** each of which grows into a new haploid plant. Figure 21–7 shows a generalized life-cycle diagram for fresh-water green algae.

Habitat and Distribution   The Chlorophyta are among the most conspicuous algae of fresh water and terrestrial areas, but in the sea they are far less prevalent. Only 13 percent of green algae are marine. A large variety of species live in lakes, rivers, reservoirs, creeks, and in soil and snow, on moist tree bark, rock, and flowerpots. The "moss" seen growing on the north side of trees is commonly a green alga. Many Chlorophyta have spores which become airborne, and open water bottles in the laboratory or open tanks outdoors may develop lush growths of green algae as a result of the germination of these spores.

Representative Members   *Chlamydomonas* (Fig. 21–8) is a unicellular, fresh-water genus of motile organisms, each cell bearing two anterior flagella. The thallus is typically sperical or ovoid, and a posterior, cup-shaped chloroplast fills most of the cell. A red or orange, light-sensitive pigmented body, the **eyespot,** is located on the chloroplast near the anterior end of the cell, and one to several pyrenoids occur within the

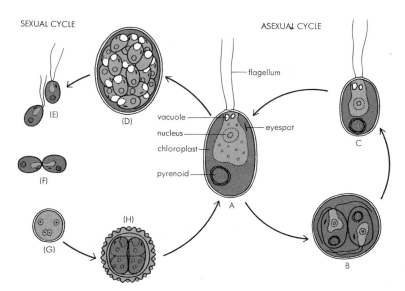

SEXUAL CYCLE

ASEXUAL CYCLE

flagellum

vacuole

nucleus

chloroplast

pyrenoid

eyespot

(E)

(D)

(F)

(G)

(H)

A

B

C

FIG. 21–8. *Chlamydomonas* life cycle. A. Mature vegetative cell. Asexual reproduction at the right. B. Two daughter cells formed by bipartition of parent cell. C. Zoospore. Sexual cycle at left. Numerous daughter cells D. formed by the parent cell become isogametes E. which fuse F. forming a zygote G. which develops into a heavy-walled zygospore H. that undergoes meiosis, forming cells which later become vegetation cells A.

chloroplast. Two contractile vacuoles are located near the bases of the flagella. The *Chlamydomonas* life cycle shown in Fig. 21–8 follows the typical scheme for fresh-water green algae. In asexual reproduction the protoplast divides to form two, four, or eight zoospores that are liberated from the parent cell. Each zoospore is smaller than the parent cell but similar to it in other respects, and, after liberation, grows to the size of its progenitor. During sexual reproduction the protoplast divides to form eight, sixteen, or thirty-two daughter cells that resemble the vegetative cells and zoospores but are still smaller. These cells function as isogametes, and after their release into the water they fuse in pairs to form zygotes. Each zygote develops a thick, resistant wall to become a zygospore. If favorable conditions prevail, a zygospore will undergo reduction division to produce four motile meiospores, each of which, after its release, grows into a mature *Chlamydomonas* plant.

Pandorina (Fig. 21–9) is a simple colony of chlamydomonas-like cells that illustrates a level or phase in a probable line of evolution within the Chlorophyta. Here the increase in size of the thallus is achieved by cohesion of a number of unicellular plants. The various species of *Pan-*

dorina illustrate colonies ranging from four to thirty-two cells, surrounded by a gelatinous envelope. Each colony swims about by means of coordinated movements of its flagella.

Volvox (Fig. 21–10) is another colonial plant form, similar to *Pandorina* in being composed of chlamydomonaslike cells, but is the most specialized of this group. In *Volvox* the plant body is

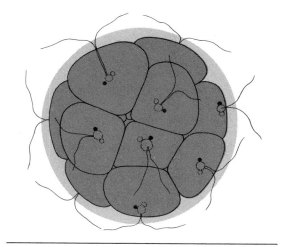

FIG. 21–9. *Pandorina*. Mature colony made up of chlamydomonas-like cells surrounded by gelatinous envelope.

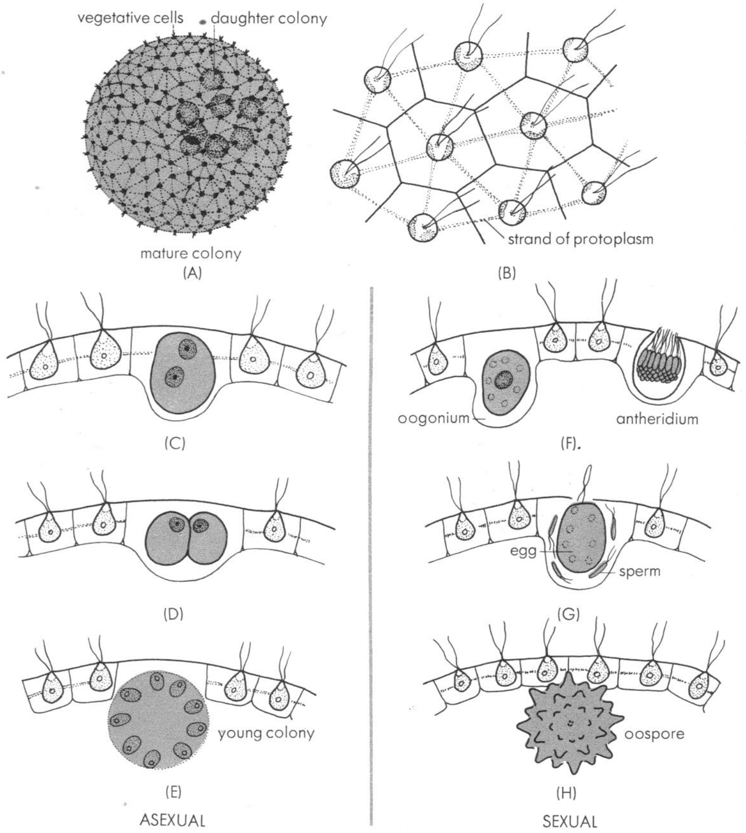

vegetative cells · daughter colony

mature colony
(A)

strand of protoplasm
(B)

(C)

oogonium   antheridium
(F)

(D)

egg   sperm
(G)

young colony
(E)

ASEXUAL

oospore
(H)

SEXUAL

FIG. 21-10. *Volvox*. A. Mature colony with daughter colonies within. B. Surface view of cells. C-E. Asexual formation of new colonies. C. Enlarged vegetative cell. D. Enlarged cell now divided. E. Further division to form young colony within parent colony. F-H. Sexual reproduction. F. Oogonium and antheridium. G. Fertilization. H. Diploid, thick-walled oospore resulting from fertilization. Following the death of the parent colony, the oospore undergoes meiosis and then gives rise to a new colony.

composed of a large number of cells, ranging in different species from approximately 500 to 50,000 cells and organized to form a hollow sphere. The flagella project from the surface, and their action enables the colony to move by rolling slowly through the water. Each cell is enveloped by an individual gelatinous sheath which contributes to a colonial matrix, and the cells are connected to their neighbors by delicate protoplasmic strands. There is some differentiation or division of labor among the cells of *Volvox*; only certain cells at the posterior or trailing portion of the colony have reproductive abilities, and those cells at the anterior or forward end have larger eyespots and may have a greater role in the colony's response to light. *Volvox* reproduces asexually (Fig. 21-10) by the development of daughter colo-

nies from cells that divide *in situ* at the periphery of the colony and later migrate to the center of the parental colony. Small daughter colonies of this kind are often seen floating in the center of larger colonies. Sexual reproduction in *Volvox* is of the most advanced, oogamous type (Fig. 21-10).

Ulothrix plants are fresh-water algae whose bodies consist of unbranched, multicellular filaments (Fig. 21-11). The basal cell of the filament is a **holdfast,** which attaches the plant to a solid object in water. Each filament cell has a single nucleus and a collar-shaped chloroplast. Asexual reproduction is by fragmentation or zoospores. The life cycle is shown in Fig. 21-11. In asexual reproduction, certain cells become transformed into zoosporangia, each of which commonly pro-

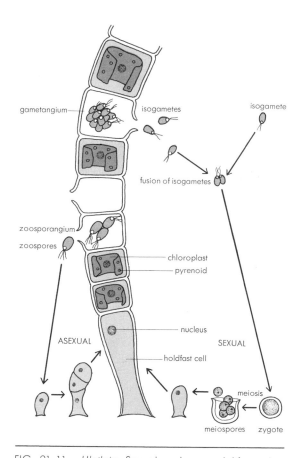

gametangium
isogametes
isogamete

fusion of isogametes

zoosporangium
zoospores

chloroplast
pyrenoid

nucleus

ASEXUAL
SEXUAL

holdfast cell

meiosis

meiospores
zygote

FIG. 21-11. *Ulothrix.* Sexual and asexual life cycles.

duces four or eight quadriflagellate zoospores. After liberation, these swim about, then attach themselves to objects in water and grow into new filaments. Sexual reproduction is isogamous, and both homothallic and heterothallic species occur. These motile sex cells resemble zoospores in structure, except that they bear only two flagella and are smaller. After their release into the water, the gametes fuse in pairs. *Ulothrix* species are said to be homothallic or heterothallic, depending on whether the gametes that fuse are produced by the same or by different parent filaments. After a rest period, the zygote undergoes reduction division and produces four meiospores which, when liberated from the zygospore, swim

about for a time, settle, attach themselves to objects in the water, and grow into new filaments. All cells of *Ulothrix* are haploid, except the zygote, which is diploid.

Oedogonium species are fresh-water algae of common occurrence. The plant body is a multicellular, unbranched filament that is attached by a holdfast cell to some solid object in water (Fig. 21-12). Each vegetative cell has a netlike chloroplast and a single nucleus. Asexual reproduction is by fragmentation or by zoospores which are produced singly in zoosporangia and have a crown of about 120 flagella. After a period of swimming, zoospores become attached to solid objects, form holdfast cells, and grow into new filaments. Sexual reproduction is heterogamous, and both homothallic and heterothallic species occur. The antheridia are short cells that usually produce two sperms each; the sperms resemble zoospores but are much smaller. Oogonia are globose cells, each of which bears a single egg. An oogonium develops a wall pore through which a fertilizing sperm may enter. Fertilization occurs within the oogonium, the zygote becoming thick walled. After liberation and a period of rest, a zygote undergoes meiosis to form four haploid meiospores which develop into new filaments. Some heterothallic species (Fig. 21-13) produce dwarf male filaments that develop from special zoospores that become attached to female filaments. A dwarf male filament produces one or two antheridia from which sperms are liberated; these fertilize the eggs in the oogonia of the larger female filament.

Spirogyra (water silk) (Fig. 21-14) is a genus of unbranched, filamentous green algae that grow commonly in bodies of fresh water. The smooth or slimy feel, characteristic of these plants, is imparted by a slippery sheath that surrounds every filament. Each cell has one or more conspicuous, beautiful, spiral chloroplasts, and a central nucleus. Asexual reproduction is by fragmentation only. In sexual reproduction, the cells of two filaments in contact with each other form tubes that meet and push the filaments slightly

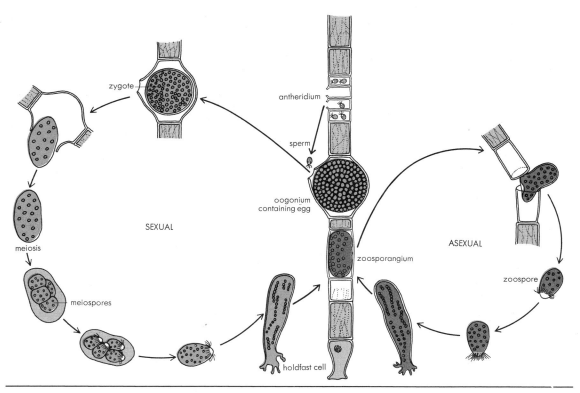

FIG. 21-12. *Oedogonium.* Sexual and asexual life cycles.

FIG. 21-13. *Oedogonium.* Two dwarf male filaments attached below two oogonia. (Courtesy Carolina Biological Supply Co.)

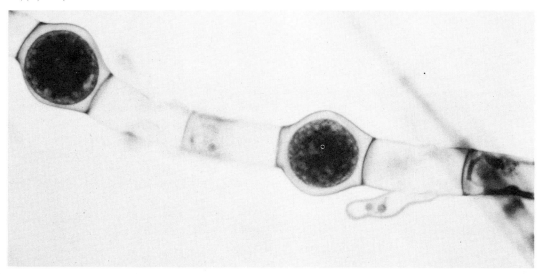

apart. An opening develops at the contact points of two tubes, and the protoplast of one cell, behaving as a gamete, moves through the tube and fuses with the protoplast of the opposite cell in the other filament. This protoplasmic fusion forms a zygote which, after release from the surrounding cell wall and a period of rest, undergoes meiosis. Of the four nuclei formed, three disintegrate, and the cell with the remaining nucleus grows into a new filament. The type of sexual reproduction illustrated by *Spirogyra* is termed **conjugation,** in which one isogamete migrates through the connecting **conjugation tube** and unites with an isogamete of the opposite mating type that has been retained within its parent cell. Thus, in their behavior these morphological isogametes bear some resemblance to heterogametes. In heterothallic species, conjugation occurs between cells of different filament; in homothallic species, it occurs between adjacent cells of the same filament.

Protococcus is one of the most (if not the most) common green alga (Fig. 21–15). The species may be irregularly filamentous when grown in water but are most often encountered as unicellular organisms that form greenish growths on tree bark, damp soil, and rocks. Each cell has a single chloroplast and a nucleus. Reproduction is exclusively asexual by cell division. Often the cells cohere after division, forming colonies of varying size and form.

Ulva or "sea lettuce" is a green alga with a parenchymatous thallus body (Fig. 21–16). The thallus is an expanded sheet two cells in thickness and may be a foot or more in length.

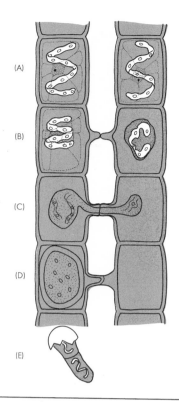

FIG. 21–14. *Spirogyra.* Two filaments showing sexual reproduction. A. Vegetative cell. B. Formation of conjugation tubes. C. Migration of protoplast from one cell to other, with fusion of the nuclei and protoplasts. D. Thick-walled zygote. E. Following meiotic reduction, the haploid germinates to form new filament.

FIG. 21–15. *Protococcus,* a genus of green alga that may be a single cell or may divide to form packets or colonies of two, three, four, or more cells.

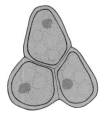
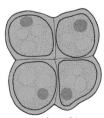

single cell   colony of 2   colony of 3   colony of 3   colony of 4

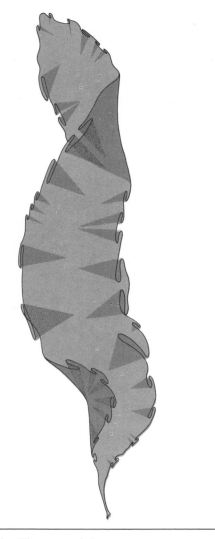

FIG. 21-16. *Ulva* or sea lettuce.

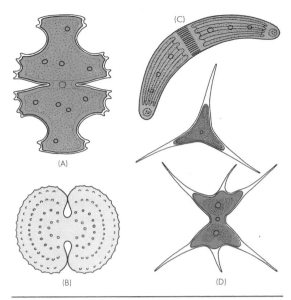

FIG. 21-17. Desmids. A. *Micrasterias*. B. *Cosmarium*. C. *Closterium*. D. *Staurastrum*.

Special Groups of Fresh-Water Green Algae

Of unusual interest for the beauty of their cells and chloroplasts are the unicellular (rarely colonial) Chlorophyta known as the desmids (Fig. 21-17). Most desmids are characterized by a central constriction which defines two opposed halves, and they are often ornamented by spines, blunt projections, and pores. Many of the unicellular forms are capable of a jerky, apparently random movement. Desmids are related to *Spirogyra* because of their mode of reproduction and the absence of flagella.

Chara (Fig. 21-18) is a fresh-water genus, the species of which show a structural organization that superficially resembles the bodies of higher plants. A multicellular stalk is attached to the substratum by a system of branched rhizoids, and the stalk at intervals bears whorls of branches, resembling the "node-internode" organization of advanced land plants (Fig. 21-18, B). Of special interest are the gametangia produced at the nodes. Although they are themselves unicellular as in other Thallophyta, both male and female gametangia are surrounded by jackets of sterile cells. Most botanists agree that *Chara* and its relatives are not related to the land plants of today but that the basic morphology of higher plants quite probably had its origins from ancestral green algae whose morphological complexity was comparable to that seen today in the genus *Chara*.

Relationship to Other Organisms

The Chlorophyta are well represented in the fossil record, their earliest known occurrence being in late Precambrian rocks whose age is estimated to be

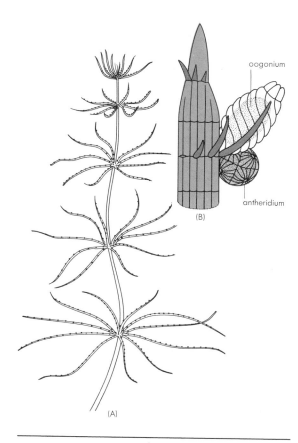

oogonium

antheridium

(B)

(A)

FIG. 21-18 *Chara*. A. Branch of plant. B. Enlarged section of plant with sex organs.

between 700 and 900 million years. Older algal-like fossils have been found, but their specific identity has not been determined. In many structural features and evolutionary tendencies, the green algae parallel other algal divisions. Some authorities believe that all algal groups except the red and the blue-green have evolved from the Chlorophyta; others think that the Chlorophyta are the latest group of algae to have evolved and hence are not ancestral to the other groups. It is quite generally held that the green algae are ancestral to the Embryophyta. Of all the algal divisions, only the greens have certain characteristics in common with the Embryophyta, namely, the presence of both chlorophylls *a* and *b*, storage of true starch reserves within the chloroplasts, and the general occurrence of cellulosic cell walls and flagellated reproductive cells.

Importance in Nature and in Human Life   In fresh water, green algae are an important source of food and oxygen for fish and other animals. Not only is the oxygen produced by algal photosynthesis vital to aquatic animals, but it also promotes the activities of aerobic bacteria that are involved in the decomposition of organic matter in water. Thus, when rivers and lakes become silt-laden (an increasingly common condition today), the amount of sunlight available to the algae is reduced or even cut out completely. When this happens, algal photosynthesis slows or stops, and hence there is no longer an oxygen supply for the animals and aerobic bacteria. These organisms die and are replaced by anaerobic decay bacteria whose activities lead to foul waters not fit for any other life. Soil-living green algae provide food for soil animals and increase the organic matter, and thus the fertility, of soil. Some green algae are eaten by humans, particularly in the Orient, India, and the Polynesian Islands. They are chiefly used in salads or in addition to rice and fish. Some marine green algae secrete calcium salts that develop into oceanic reefs. Green algae are sometimes the cause of clogged filters in water-purifying plants. Their excessive growth can lower the oxygen potential of bodies of water and thus endanger the animal life.

DIVISION EUGLENOPHYTA (EUGLENOIDS)

General Characteristics   All genera of Euglenophyta are unicellular, although a few marine forms and one fresh-water genus produce stalked, branched colonies of independent cells. Of the approximately 400 species, most are green and photosynthetic but a few are colorless. Euglenoids lack cell walls but are supplied with a rigid or flexible layer called the **periplast** at the periphery of the cell. The cells are motile, with flagella attached at the bases of invaginations in the anterior ends. One of the two flagella in *Euglena* is of the whiplash type and is very short, rarely extending beyond the mouth of the anterior invagination; the other is long and branched. Spiral movement of the elongated flagellum draws the cell rapidly through the water. Many euglenoids also have the ability to contract and elongate and can squeeze themselves through narrow openings and along crevices. In chlorophyllous forms the predominant pigments are chlorophyll *a* and *b*, carotene, and xanthophyll, as in the green algae; in addition, these forms possess a pigmented eyespot located near the bases of the flagella. Both green and colorless euglenoids store their reserve food as **paramylum,** a carbohydrate unique to this division.

Reproductive Characteristics   Reproduction of most euglenoids is asexual by longitudinal division of the cell. Sexual reproduction, if any, is apparently rare, and reports of its occurrence are not well documented. During unfavorable periods, some species can transform themselves into thick-walled, nonmotile, dormant cells, and when favorable conditions return, these germinate to produce motile, physiologically active cells.

Habitat and Distribution   The Euglenophyta are fresh-water plants; only 3 percent of the species occur in the sea. The rare colorless euglenoids are heterotrophic and depend on food substances in the surrounding medium for their nutrition. Chlorophyllous euglenoid species manufacture food, but all species that have been studied are unable to grow normally in a medium that is devoid of organic substances. Euglenoids are especially common, therefore, in diluted sewage and other water that is rich in organic materials. It has been demonstrated that under certain experimental conditions some chlorophyllous species can lose their green pigment and grow as heterotrophs, while retaining the ability to revert to the chlorophyllous condition under other circumstances. All colorless species are totally de-

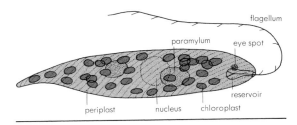

FIG. 21-19.   *Euglena.*

pendent on external food sources, and a few colorless euglenoids live in the intestines of amphibia.

Representative Members   *Euglena* (Figs. 21–19 and 21–20) is a green form that is commonly studied. Its unicellular nature is typical of the group as a whole. Members of this genus consist of elongate, tapering cells containing numerous chloroplasts, paramylum grains, a single eyespot, and a nucleus.

Relationship to Other Organisms   Botanists consider the green euglenoids to be plants because they contain chlorophyll and are photosynthetic. Certain botanists think that the colorless euglenoids are also plants because such forms can be derived experimentally from green forms. Pigmentation similarities suggest possible relationship to the Chlorophyta. Zoologists consider the euglenoids to be a primitive group within the Protozoa, a phylum of single-celled animals. A third, intermediate interpretation of the euglenoids is that the group consists of organisms, some of which show plant characteristics and others of which are animal-like. Under this third interpretation, the organisms are held as not being rigidly classifiable as either plant or animal. Regardless of the interpretation, all Euglenophyta share three features which tie the division together: production of paramylum, longitudinal cell division, and the characteristic organization of the anterior end of the cell.

Importance in Nature and in Human Life   The Euglenophyta are an important source of food

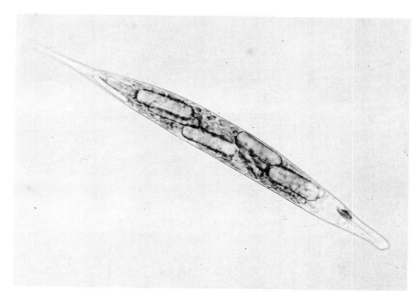

FIG. 21-20. *Euglena acerbissima.*
(Photo by Eric V. Grave, Photo
Researchers, Inc.)

for fish and other aquatic animals. Their unique ability to undergo reversible changes between heterotrophic and autotrophic forms is important in photosynthesis studies. Species of *Euglena* require vitamin B_{12}, which they cannot manufacture, and they have been used as assay agents to analyze substances for vitamin B_{12} content.

DIVISION CHRYSOPHYTA (GOLDEN-BROWN ALGAE)

General Characteristics   The division Chrysophyta contains between ten and eleven thousand species and thus, in numbers of species, surpasses any other group of algae. The plants are chiefly unicellular, but a small percentage of colonial and filamentous forms are included. Special features common to most members of the group are siliceous cell walls composed of two overlapping segments, reserve foods stored as oils, and as **leucosin,** a carbohydrate occurring dissolved or as whitish lumps in the cytoplasm, and accessory photosynthetic pigments which include chlorophylls *c* or *e,* carotene, and xanthophylls. A few species are flagellated or give rise to flagellated spores or gametes, and many genera can produce

silicified, dormant cyst stages. The most abundant and widely distributed members of the Chrysophyta are diatoms, (between six and ten thousand species). They are the only group which will be discussed here.

The diatoms are essentially unicellular although a few are weakly colonial. They occur in two basic forms: the **centric** type, in which the cell has radial symmetry and is circular or triangular in face view (Fig. 21-21); and the **pennate** type, in which the cell has bilateral symmetry and is elongate. Diatom cell walls consist of two overlapping, siliceous halves, called **valves,** that fit together as the two parts of a pillbox (Fig. 21-22). The walls are hard and brittle (silica is the principal ingredient of glass) and are ornamented by pores, grooves, and ridges arranged in intricate and often beautiful patterns that can be used to identify the species. Figure 21-23 shows several cell shapes and some of the variety in cell size and wall patterns among them. The elongate, pennate forms are capable of a smooth, gliding motion which is believed to be associated with the system of pores and median grooves on the two flat faces of the valves. Although the action is not completely understood, it

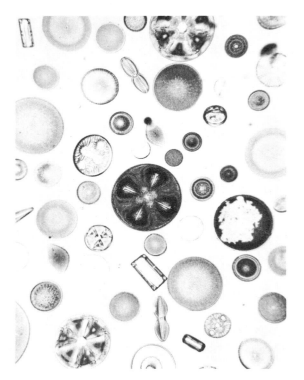

FIG. 21-21. A variety of marine diatoms showing both centric and pennate forms. (Courtesy of Dr. R. L. Smith.)

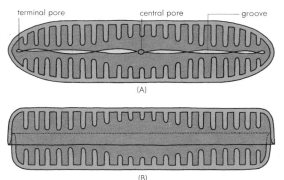

FIG. 21-22. *Pinnularia,* a pennate diatom. A. Top or valve view, showing pores and longitudinal groove. B. Side or girdle view showing overlapping valves.

is thought that exposed protoplasm flows along the grooves from the median or terminal pores, creating friction with the surrounding water or against a substrate. Whatever the mechanism, the pennate diatoms are able to glide forward or backward in the direction of their long axes and turn in other directions. The protoplasts of all diatoms are uninucleate and contain one or more conspicuous chloroplasts that are golden- or greenish-brown.

Reproductive Characteristics Among the diatoms, asexual reproduction is by cell division (Fig. 21-24). The protoplast divides into two, and when these separate, one remains in the outer valve and the other in the inner valve of the parent cell. Each of the daughter protoplasts secretes a new valve that fits inside the old one, so that both of the old valves persist as outer valves of the new cells. As a result, one daughter cell is the same size as the parent cell whereas that

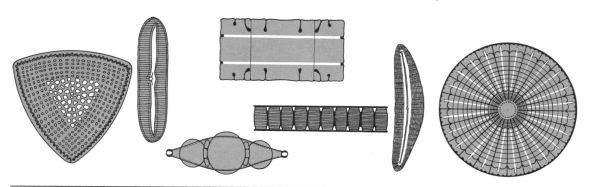

FIG. 21-23. An array of diatoms.

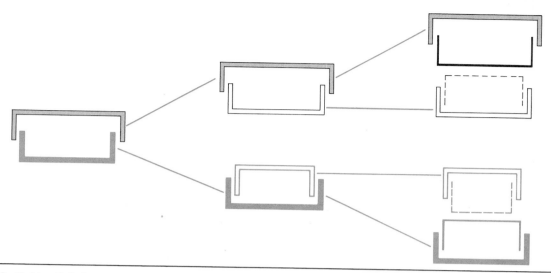

FIG. 21-24. Cell division (asexual reproduction) in diatoms. Note that the new valve forms within the old one, and therefore some of the resultant diatoms are smaller than others.

daughter cell associated with the inner valve of the parent is slightly smaller. With successive divisions there is a constant decrease in size in half of the progeny, and for this reason one may find considerable size variation among the members of a single-species population. Continued decrease in size is halted by a shift to sexual reproduction. In sexual reproduction the protoplast of the cell undergoes meiotic division and forms one or two gametes which cast off the old cell wall. Two gametes from the same or from different parental cells fuse to form a naked zygote (that is, one without cell walls). The zygote enlarges to the maximum size of the species before secreting new outer and inner valves. Vegetative reproduction in some species may proceed for as long as five years before sexual reproduction occurs.

Habitat and Distribution   The majority of diatoms are aquatic and of these 30 to 50 percent are marine. Species of diatoms are the most abundant algae found on the surface of the soil; others can be found on wet rock, in rivers, in lakes, and in hot springs. The pennate forms are found in both fresh water and the sea; the centric species are almost exclusively marine. Diatoms in astronomically large numbers make up a large proportion of the plankton of the seas, and a few also exist as benthic forms. The planktonic forms exhibit a semiannual peak growth, one in the fall and one in the spring.

Representative Members   One of the many genera of fresh-water diatoms of North America, *Pinnularia* is shown in Fig. 21-22.

Relationships to Other Organisms   The affinities of the Chrysophyta are uncertain. Relationships to both the green algae and to the brown algae have been suggested on the basis of certain similarities of pigmentation and food reserves.

Importance in Nature and in Human Life   The diatoms are very abundant plants, so much so that even though they are tiny, microscopic, single-celled plants, it has been estimated that diatom protoplasm exceeds in total mass that of all other plants combined. They are the major, single source of photosynthetically produced food and

FIG. 21–25. Diatomaceous earth quarry near Lompoc, California. (Photo courtesy of the Celite Division, Johns-Manville Corporation.

oxygen in the world. In midocean, the diatoms and dinoflagellates (division Pyrrophyta) are usually the only algae present. Diatoms are the principal primary food producers of the seas; they form the basic link in all the marine food chains. As such, they have appropriately been called the "grass of the sea." Furthermore, they play an extremely important role in that they absorb the nutrients present in the silt-laden river waters discharged along the continental shelves. Such nutrients, if not absorbed by the diatoms, would be carried down to the bottom of the sea and forever lost from the food cycle of life. The diatoms, however, by absorbing and storing these nutrients, serve as a food bank receiving and augmenting nutrients and in turn supplying nu-

trients to marine animals. Diatoms are also abundant in fresh water; it has been estimated, for example, that 1 cubic yard of Illinois river water may contain 35 million diatoms, and in these abundant numbers they are a supply of food for aquatic animals.

The empty siliceous valves of diatoms are essentially glass and are not used as food by fungi or other decomposing organisms. As a result, the gradual rain of empty diatom valves can cover the ocean floors to great depths. In many parts of the world, cubic miles of such deposits occur on land above the surface of the sea as the result of geological processes of uplift. These rocklike deposits (Fig. 21–25), known as diatomaceous earth, are mined and used in the manufacture of metal polishes and as the abrasive ingredient in scouring cleansers. Diatomaceous earth is used in insulation for steam pipes, for refrigeration systems, and for blast furnaces, in filters for clarification of oils, sugar syrup and other liquids, in dynamite as an absorbent for nitroglycerin, in concrete, and in the manufacture of certain kinds of glass. Bricks are often cut from diatomaceous earth for construction purposes because of their light weight; the dome of the church of St. Sophia in Istanbul was constructed of such bricks. Diatom valves are often associated with oil-bearing sands, and some geologists believe that oil-storing diatoms may have aided in the formation of petroleum deposits.

DIVISION PHAEOPHYTA (BROWN ALGAE)

General Characteristics   The Phaeophyta are chiefly marine and include the vegetatively most complex of all the algae. Approximately 225 genera and 1400 species are known, all of which are multicellular. Their pigments include chlorophyll *a* and *c*, carotene, and xanthophylls, of which the distinctive pigment fucoxanthin is the most abundant, exceeding even the amount of chlorophyll and carotene. These pigments give most of the species a rich brown or greenish-brown color, from which the division takes its name. The food reserve is the carbohydrate **laminarin,** a soluble sugar dissolved in the cytoplasm. The cell walls are of cellulose, often reinforced with deposits of stiff, gelatinous material which gives the plants a tough, leathery texture. The motile, reproductive cells are pear shaped and are supplied with two lateral flagella, one whiplash, and one tinsel.

Reproductive Characteristics   All brown algae have a well-developed alternation of generations. Three classes of Phaeophyta are distinguished, each characterized by a particular life-cycle type. In the first class, the life cycle consists of two generations of identical vegetative morphology alternating with each other; one generation consists of a haploid plant that produces gametes,

the other of a diploid plant that produces spores. Because the generations in this first class are so similar in appearance, they are described as isomorphic. In the second class, the life cycle consists of two multicellular generations, but the haploid generation is a microscopic, filamentous plant, whereas the diploid is large and often structurally complex. Alternation of these unlike generations is termed heteromorphism. In the third class of Phaeophyta, only the diploid phase exists as a multicellular organism, the haploid phase being represented only by the gametes. Algae representing these three classes of Phaeophyta are described in the section on representative members.

Habitat and Distribution   All but three species of brown algae are marine plants. They grow mostly in the cooler oceanic waters and are abundant, for example, in the Arctic and Antarctic oceans, on the Atlantic coasts of Europe and New England, and the Pacific coast of the United States. A few species thrive in warmer oceanic waters of tropical regions. Filamentous brown algae grow attached to rocks or stones or as epiphytes attached to other plants. The larger forms often grow attached to rocks or reefs in fairly shallow water, and some species grow in intertidal zones; that is, they are submerged or floating during high tides and exposed to the air at low tide. Such species are mainly those plants known as kelps and rockweeds, and they are the typical "seaweeds" of the ocean coasts. *Nereocystis* (Figs. 21–29 and 21–30) and *Pelagophycus* (Fig. 21–31) are large kelps that live attached to the ocean bottom in water depths of about 15 to 20 meters, and by means of their long stemlike stipes and large air bladders, they are able to float their blades on the surface of the water. A few species are unattached and float at or near the water surface, in some regions forming masses of plants of enormous extent. For example, the Sargasso Sea is a mass of *Sargassum* plants (Fig. 21–35) that occupy an area in the Atlantic Ocean east of the West Indies approximately twice the size

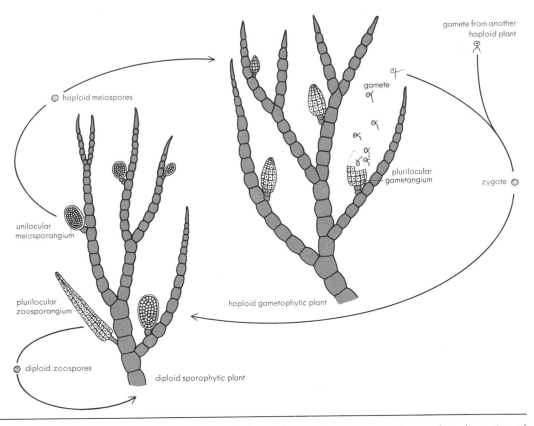

FIG. 21-26. *Ectocarpus* life cycle. Two generations of identical vegetative structure — isomorphic alternation of generations.

of the state of Texas, or about one half million square miles.

Representative Members *Ectocarpus* (Fig. 21-26) is an example of that class of Phaeophyta in which the life cycle consists of two generations of plants of identical vegetative structure alternating with each other—isomorphic alternation. The plant body consists of branching filaments, the entire thallus being only about 2 centimeters in length. The plants grow submerged and attached to other algae or to stones or shells. The haploid gametophyte plant produces multicellular reproductive structures, the plurilocular gametangia, so-called because they are multicellular and each cell becomes one biflagellate gamete.

Two gametes from different haploid plants fuse to form a zygote, which grows into a diploid sporophyte. The sporophyte produces two types of sporangia, plurilocular and unilocular. The plurilocular sporangium is multicellular (as in the case of the plurilocular gametangium), and each of its cells becomes transformed into a diploid zoospore. These give rise to new diploid plants. The production of diploid zoospores provides for rapid increase in the number of plants during favorable growth periods. In a unilocular sporangium of the diploid plant, all the spores lie together in a single cavity, and, because meiosis takes place in this sporangium, the spores formed are haploid cells or meiospores. Meiospores germinate into haploid plants.

Laminaria (Fig. 21–27) is a common "kelp" and, as is typical for all the kelps, has an alternation of dissimilar generations. The haploid plant is microscopic and filamentous and is either male or female. Sperms and eggs fuse to form zygotes that grow into diploid plants. The diploid plant may be very large and is composed of three portions: a holdfast, an elongated stemlike part or stipe, and a flattened, leaflike blade. This plant produces meiospores, each of which grows into a haploid, male or female, filamentous plant. The bodies of kelps (and also of rockweeds) have abundant mucilage either within the thallus or covering it or both. This mucilage protects the plants against desiccation during periods of exposure to the air at low tide. Many species have air bladders; these are gas-filled vesicles which buoy the plant. The kelps have a higher degree of internal differentiation than is found in any other group of algae. In some, for example, there are elongated cells with perforated end walls which apparently conduct food and which strongly resemble the sieve tube members in the phloem of higher plants. Most kelps are perennial; usually the terminal portion of the blade wears away and is replaced each spring by the activities of a meristem located at the base of the blade.

Fucus (Fig. 21–32) is a typical "rockweed," species of which are abundant along the seacoasts where they grow attached to rocks in shallow water. A typical *Fucus* thallus may reach a length of 30 centimeters or more and consists of a holdfast and a branching stipe, the terminal portions of which are flattened, ribbonlike structures bearing air bladders. Sexual reproduction is oogamous. The inflated tips of the branches are termed **receptacles,** and each receptacle is usually covered with small, raised pores that lead into

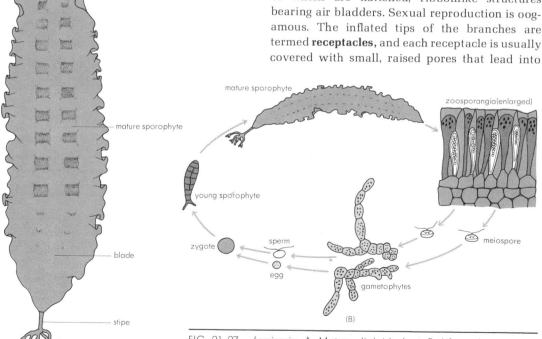

FIG. 21–27. *Laminaria.* A. Mature diploid plant. B. Life cycle.

FIG. 21–28. *Fucus*, a common rockweed of the tidal zone.

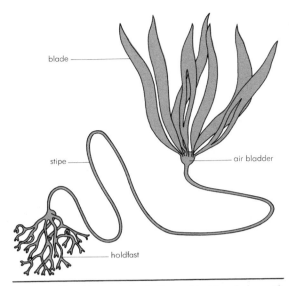

FIG. 21–29. *Nereocystis*, bull or bladder kelp with branched holdfast, long stipe, single bladder and many blades.

cavities called **conceptacles,** in which the gametangia are produced (Figs. 21–33 and 21–34). In some species the sperm-producing antheridia and egg-producing oogonia are formed on separate plants; in others they are borne on the same plant, sometimes within the same conceptacle. Following meiosis, each oogonium produces eight eggs, each antheridium numerous, biflagellate sperms. Eggs and sperms are discharged from the conceptacles into sea water, where fertiliza-

tion occurs. The zygotes grow into new, mature *Fucus* plants. Thus, *Fucus* has no true alternation of diploid and haploid generations since only the sperms and eggs are haploid.

Relationship to Other Organisms   Because of their usually motile reproductive cells, the Phaeophyta are thought to be descendants of

FIG. 21–30.   *Nereocystis* floating on the waters of Puget Sound. (Courtesy of the New York Botanical Garden.)

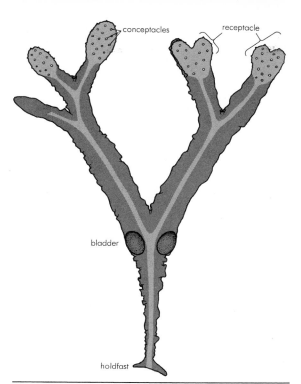

FIG. 21–31. (Above). Kelp on beach. (Courtesy David Donoho, Photo Researchers, Inc.) FIG. 21–32. (Right). *Fucus* with basal disc or holdfast, dichotomus thallus, paired bladders or floats, and inflated tips or receptacles. On the surface of the receptacles are pores opening into the conceptacles.

some early flagellated, unicellular algae. Their relationships to other contemporary algal groups, if any, are not known. Although they have developed highly complex bodies that resemble land plants in some ways and also show some degree of tissue development, particularly in their "phloem," they are not considered ancestral to land plants because their pigmentation and food reserves are quite unlike those of land plants.

Importance in Nature and in Human Life   In many coastal regions farmers have traditionally harvested brown algae as food for cattle, sheep, and chickens. The production of such cattle feed is commercialized in some parts of the world. Since World War I, seaweed meal factories in

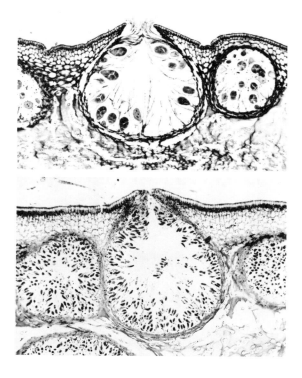

FIG. 21–33. (Above right). Sectional view of *Fucus* receptacle showing female conceptacles containing oogonia. FIG. 21–34. (*Below right*). Sectional view of *Fucus* receptacle showing male conceptacles containing antheridia.

FIG. 21–35. Sargassum gulf weed, with stemlike stipe, leaflike blades and berrylike bladders or floats.

south Pacific and in Japan and China, where they are widely cultivated on bamboo stems pushed into the sand in shallow coastal waters. Brown algae are quite valuable for their mineral contents and particularly because of this they are commonly used as soil fertilizer. They are either spread out on fields and plowed under, or they may be dried and burned and their ash used as fertilizer. Some species have been used as a commercial source of iodine for medicinal use. Certain carbohydrate derivatives of brown algae, known as alginates, have widespread use in industry, for example, in the production of rubber, paints, ice creams, and confections. As a harmful effect, brown algae, along with barnacles and other animals, become attached to ship hulls. The result of such fouling is a substantial reduction in the ship's speed and maneuverability.

DIVISION RHODOPHYTA (RED ALGAE)

General Characteristics   Red algae in numbers of species are the most abundant of all the seaweeds. Of the approximately 4000 species, more than 90 percent are marine. The red pigment phycoerythrin occurs in all members, and many of the species are bright red or pink, but color is not always a reliable diagnostic feature because

California have been processing kelps for the production of supplementary feed for farm animals. A modern kelp-harvesting ship operating off the Pacific coast is shown in Fig. 21–36. Although, in general, brown algae are not used as food for humans because of their leathery texture and indigestible components, there are some species that are eaten by human beings especially in the

FIG. 21–36.   Kelp harvester. (Courtesy of the Kelco Company, San Diego, California.)

A.

B.

C.

in some species the red pigment may be so masked by the abundance of other pigments present that the alga may appear bright green — or brown, as in brown algae. The plants are typically delicate, branched, tufted filaments or of some membraneous or fleshy leaflike form (Fig. 21-37). In general, they are much more delicate and smaller than the green and the brown algae; rarely does any reach a size of 2 or 3 feet in any dimension. None is free floating; all grow attached either to rock or to another alga. The cells have nuclei and plastids, and, in addition to phycoerythrin, they contain phycocyanin, chlorophyll, and carotenoids. The reserve food formed from photosynthesis is a carbohydrate called **floridean starch.**

Reproductive Characteristics   Some of the most complex and uniquely different life histories occurring in nature are to be found within the red algae. Sexual reproduction is heterogamous, and a conspicuous feature of the group is the lack of flagellated reproductive cells. Typically, the female gametangium produces an egg and develops a long slender, hairlike protuberance, the trichogyne. A sperm, carried by the current, adheres to the trichogyne; the sperm nucleus then enters the trichogyne and fuses with that of the egg to form a zygote. Depending on the species, the zygote may or may not directly undergo meiosis, and different species may have one or two intervening spore and filamentous stages before arriving at the egg- and sperm-producing filamentous stage again.

Habitat and Distribution   Red algae are most abundant in temperate and tropical marine waters, where they outnumber the brown and green algae. They grow attached to rocks or other marine plants and are commonly found in the calmer, deeper waters below the tidal zone, although some do live at shallower depths. Because

FIG. 21-37.   Red algae. A. *Centroceras.* B. *Acanthophora.* C. *Halimeda.* (Algae courtesy of Oren F. Lackey, Photo by W. R. Kennedy.)

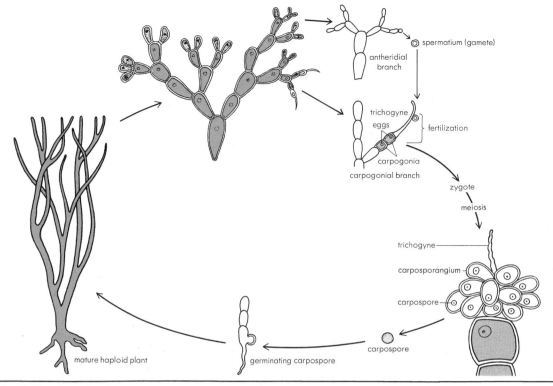

FIG. 21–38. *Nemalion* life cycle.

of their red pigment, they can grow in the deeper and thus less illuminated depths of the sea. In tropical waters red algae have been found growing at depths as great as 800 feet, which are reached only by the blue wavelengths of sunlight.

Representative Members   *Nemalion* is a genus of red algae which are attached to rocks of sea coasts. A *Nemalion* plant has a cylindrical, branching body (Fig. 21–38) with a basal holdfast. Some branches bear short filaments whose tips produce antheridia, each with one nonmotile male gamete called a spermatium. Other branches bear the characteristic female gametangia (carpogonia) of red algae, each with a single egg and a trichogyne. Meiosis occurs immediately after zygote formation, and the resulting haploid nuclei migrate into budlike outgrowths which develop in the carpogonial wall. Short filaments grow from

the cells thus produced, and the terminal cell of each functions as a sporangium (carposporangium) that has a single, nonmotile spore (carpospore). After its release, a carpospore becomes attached to a suitable substrate and grows into a characteristic *Nemalion* plant.

Other red algae have somewhat more complex life cycles, which will not be considered here. In many species a definite alternation of a free-living gametophyte plant with a free-living sporophyte plant occurs.

Relationship to Other Organisms   The origins of the red algae, as well as their relationships to other algae are unknown. In some respects, namely, in their blue and red pigments and in their lack of flagellated cells, they are similar to the blue-green algae. In other ways, certain red algae resemble certain fungi (the rusts) in the

FIG. 21–39. Irish moss (*Chondrus*) (Courtesy Russ Kinne, Photo Researchers; Inc.)

character of their life cycles. Although these similarities exist, there is no evidence that they reflect interrelationships among the plants.

Importance in Nature and in Human Life The red alga *Porphyra* has been eaten by man for thousands of years in China, Japan, Hawaii, Malaysia, and Indonesia. In North America, too, it was used as a food by the Indians of the Pacific shores. In Japan, present-day cultivation and processing of *Porphyra* supports thousands of workers. About one-half million tons of this alga are harvested each year from nets strung between bamboo stems pushed into the ocean bottom in shallow waters. *Chondrus*, or Irish moss (Fig. 21–39), has been used in Europe for the past few centuries as a gelling agent in making puddings and other desserts. The colloid carrageenin extracted from *Chondrus* is extensively used commercially for its gelling properties, and a relatively large industry concerned with collecting and processing the plant has grown up in Maine and the Maritime Provinces of Canada. Carrageenin is used as a stabilizing and thickening compound for ice cream, puddings, candies, syrups, canned milk, chocolate milk, creamed soups, and toothpaste. Several red algae, chiefly species of *Gelidium*, produce a gelatinous material called agar-agar, which has a large and varied number of uses: as the chief ingredient in the preparation of media for the laboratory culture of bacteria and fungi; as a sizing material for textiles; as a solidifying agent in ice cream and dairy products; as an antidrying agent in bakery goods; as an ingredient in the manufacture of a number of products among which are shoe polish, shaving creams, laxatives, cosmetics, and candies. Some red algae, known as the coralline forms, secrete calcium carbonate which encrust the thallus with a coat of lime. In some species,

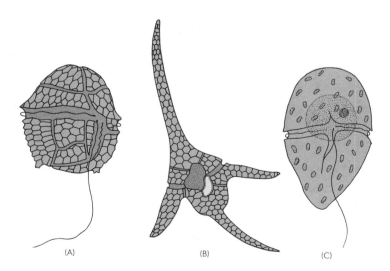

FIG. 21–40. Dinoflagellates. A. *Peridinum*. B. *Ceratum*. C. *Gymnodinium*.

(A)   (B)   (C)

certain regions of the plant remain uncalcified, producing an articulated thallus. In other species, the entire thallus becomes calcified. In tropical seas, coralline algae form limestone reefs and islands that are comparable in size to reefs and islands formed by coral animals.

DIVISION PYRROPHYTA

The majority of Pyrrophyta are microscopic, unicellular, motile plants known as dinoflagellates (Fig. 21–40), and most of them are marine. Their most obvious and identifying characteristic is the presence of two flagella that both lie in grooves on the cell surface: one flagellum encircles the body in a transverse groove and the other runs vertically down one side of the cell in a vertical groove and also extends beyond the cell like a tail. Vibrations of the transverse flagellum and undulations of the vertical flagellum propel the cell in a whirling motion through the water. Some cells are naked, but the majority have cell walls made of small plates of cellulose. Chlorophyll is present, and the auxiliary carotene and xanthophyll pigments color many members golden brown. Many others are luminescent. They occur in astronomically large numbers as photosynthetic plankton, and they, with the diatoms, comprise the basic supply—the initial producers of food—for all the food webs of the sea. Some species secrete toxins that cause the death of fish during periods of abundant growth or bloom of the dinoflagellate. These blooms are popularly known as the Red Tide. Dinoflagellate toxins absorbed by shellfish that are in turn eaten by man may kill that person in a matter of 2 to 24 hours.

SUMMARY

1. The subkingdom Thallophyta contains the structurally simplest and most primitive plants. Their bodies lack true roots, stems, and leaves; they lack vascular tissues (except for some brown algae that have sieve tube cells); they do not form embryos; and their gametangia are usually unicellular. The Thallophyta constitute a somewhat artificial subkingdom.

2. The name algae is applied to those divisions whose members contain chlorophyll and carry on photosynthesis. The fungi and bacteria are divisions that lack chlorophyll and obtain their food chiefly as saprophytes or parasites.

3. Algae are chiefly water plants, a minority of species living on damp soil, tree bark, moist rock, and on other land substrata.

4. The different colors of algae are due to the presence of auxiliary photosynthetic pigments. These pigments absorb the energy from light of wavelengths different from those absorbed by chlorophyll a. This energy is then transferred to chlorophyll a, for use in photosynthesis.

5. Reproduction of algae is by a variety of methods. Asexual reproduction is chiefly by fission, cell division, spores, and fragmentation. In many aquatic algae, swimming zoospores are produced. Both isogamous and heterogamous sexual reproduction occur in algae. Some algae are homothallic, others heterothallic. Male gametangia are called antheridia, female gametangia oogonia (carpogonia in red algae).

6. Many algae have a definite alternation of generations. In alternation of generations the chromosome number is doubled as a result of the union of gametes. The fertilized egg or zygote grows into a mul-

ticellular, diploid, sporophyte plant that later produces haploid spores by a process involving meiosis. These spores then develop into haploid gametophytes that, in turn, produce gametes. In other algae, meiosis occurs when the zygote germinates, in which case the zygote is the only diploid phase of the life cycle.

7. The division Cyanophyta, or blue-green algae, has the following distinguishing characteristics: bodies unicellular or colonial; no organized nuclei; chromatin scattered; no chloroplasts; chlorophyll diffused in cytoplasm; a blue pigment, phycocyanin, and a red pigment, phycoerythrin, present in addition to chlorophyll; reproduction exclusively asexual, chiefly by fission, in a few species by spores; no flagellated reproductive cells; cells often embedded in a slime sheath; reserve food cyanophycean starch; chiefly inhabitants of seas, other species in fresh water.

8. The division Euglenophyta, or euglenoids, has the following distinguishing characteristics: definite nuclei and chloroplasts in cells; grass-green color; reserve foods paramylum and fats; most species naked, unicellular plants with flagella inserted in a gullet; reproduction chiefly by cell division; fresh-water plants.

9. The division Chlorophyta, or green algae, has the following distinguishing characteristics: grass color; definite nuclei and chloroplasts; cellulose cell walls; reserve food chiefly starch; motile cells with flagella of equal length at anterior ends; unicellular, colonial, or multicellular plants, reproduce asexually by cell division, fragmentation, zoospores, or immobile spores; reproduce sexually by isogamy or heterogamy; gametangia always unicellular; chiefly fresh-water plants.

10. The division Chrysophyta—or yellow-green algae, golden-brown algae, and diatoms—has the following distinguishing characteristics: considerable concentrations of yellowish and brownish pigments along with chlorophyll; definite nuclei and plastids; food reserves chiefly oils; cell walls of two overlapping halves, often impregnated with silica; flagella when present of unequal length with minute branches; unicellular, less frequently colonial or multicellular plants; reproduction by cell division, zoospores, immobile spores, and isogamy; widely distributed in fresh and salt water and in soils.

11. The division Phaeophyta, or brown algae, has the following distinguishing characteristics: brownish in color because of masking of chlorophyll by brown pigment, fucoxanthin; definite nuclei and plastids; multicellular, often complex in structure with holdfasts, stipes, and blades; air bladders often present; motile reproductive cells pear shaped and with two lateral unequal flagella; most have alternation of generations; in some species, one generation is limited to only a few cells whereas in others, both generations consist of similar plants of equal size; sieve tube cells and cambiumlike cells occur in some species; reproduction is by fragmentation, zoospores, immobile spores, isogamy, and heterogamy; almost exclusively marine plants.

12. The division Rhodophyta, or red algae, has the following distinguishing characteristics: green color of chlorophyll usually masked by a red pigment, phycoerythrin; reserve food is floridean starch; multicellular plants often ribbonlike or feathery, usually with holdfasts; rarely exceed 3 feet in length; no flagellated reproductive cells; the female gametangium is a carpogonium with a trichogyne; many have alternation of generations; chiefly marine plants.

13. The division Pyrrophyta is made up of unicellular, microscopic plants known as the dinoflagellates. These plants, along with the diatoms, comprise a very large percentage (if not all) of the marine photosynthetic plankton and constitute the basic food supply for all the food webs of the sea.

14. Algae are important in nature and in human life in the following major ways: as sources of food for fish and for other aquatic animals and for soil animals; as sources of oxygen in water; as agents of water pollution; as formers of travertine and coral reefs; as human food; as food for cattle and sheep; as sources of iodine, potash, magnesium, and other substances important in medicine or in soil fertilizers; as causal agents of fouling of ships and clogging of filters in water purification plants; as sources of agar-agar and other gelatinous material for bacteriological media, soups and desserts, shoe polishes, cosmetics, shaving cream, laxatives, and textile sizings. Fossil diatoms are important ingredients in polishes for metals and other materials, in some tooth powders, in insulation of steam pipes, refrigeration systems, and blast furnaces, in dynamite, in filters for clarifying liquids, as construction materials; diatoms of past ages probably contributed to the formation of petroleum.

15. The relationships of the various algal divisions with each other are not known. It is generally thought that they are parallel series that have developed independently of each other, possibly from a common ancestral stock.

16. The Chlorophyta are regarded as the source group from which higher plants probably evolved.

SUGGESTED READINGS FOR INTERESTED STUDENTS

1. Bold, H. C., *Morphology of Plants,* 2d ed. Harper & Row, New York, 1967.

2. Dawson, E. Y., *Marine Botany,* Holt, Rinehart and Winston, New York, 1966.

3. Prescott, G. W., *The Algae: A Review.* Houghton-Mifflin, Boston, Mass., 1968.

4. Scagel, Robert F., et al., *An Evolutionary Survey of the Plant Kingdom.* Wadsworth, Belmont, Cal., 1965.

5. Smith, G. M., *Cryptogamic Botany,* Vol. 1, *Algae and Fungi.* Mc-Graw-Hill, New York, 1938.

6. Smith, G. M., *The Fresh Water Algae of the United States*, 2d ed. McGraw-Hill, New York, 1950.

7. Smith, G. M., Ed., *Manual of Phycology*. Ronald Press, N.Y., 1951.

8. Tiffany, L. H., *Algae, The Grass of Many Waters*. Charles C. Thomas, Springfield, Ill., 1938.

TOPICS AND QUESTIONS FOR STUDY

1. Characterize the Thallophyta as a whole.

2. Distinguish between algae and fungi. Why are the algae considered an artificial group?

3. List the distinguishing characteristics of the following algal divisions: Cyanophyta, Chlorophyta, Euglenophyta, Chrysophyta, Phaeophyta, Rhodophyta, and Pyrrophyta.

4. List and describe all asexual methods of reproduction in the algae.

5. List and describe the methods of sexual reproduction in the algae.

6. What is alternation of generations? State two differences between gametophyte and sporophyte generations.

7. Describe briefly the distribution and habitats of algal divisions.

8. Make a list of ways in which algae influence human life.

9. Differentiate among unicellular, colonial, and multicellular organisms.

10. Describe the structure and reproduction of *Gloeocapsa, Oscillatoria,* and *Nostoc.*

11. Describe the economic importance of the Cyanophyta.

12. Why is *Euglena* classified both as a plant and as an animal?

13. Describe the structure and reproduction of *Euglena.*

14. Contrast the Chlorophyta and the Cyanophyta.

15. Describe the structure and reproduction of *Chlamydomonas, Ulothrix, Oedogonium, Protococcus,* and *Spirogyra.*

16. Compare the reproduction of *Ulothrix* and that of *Oedogonium.*

17. List the ways in which Chlorophyta are important in human life.

18. Characterize the Chrysophyta.

19. Describe the structure and reproduction of diatoms.

20. List the economic uses of diatoms.

21. Describe the structural features of brown algae.

22. Describe the body structure and reproduction of *Ectocarpus* and *Fucus.*

23. Describe alternation of generations in the brown algae.

24. List the ways in which brown algae are important in human life.

25. Describe the habitats and distribution of brown algae.

26. Describe the habitats and distribution of red algae.

27. Describe the structure and reproduction of red algae.

28. Describe the structure and reproduction of *Nemalion.*

29. List the ways in which red algae are important to man.

22

THALLOPHYTA: SCHIZOPHYTA (BACTERIA)

Bacteria constitute a rather well defined but heterogeneous group of organisms which are unique in their extremely small size. They are the smallest of all known living organisms and, superficially at least, are very simple in structure. About 1700 species are known and are placed in the division Schizophyta. The scientific divisional name of the bacteria, Schizophyta, refers to the fission method of reproduction. The prefix *schizo* is derived from a Greek word that means to split or cut; its use in the naming of this group of organisms refers to the characteristic splitting of bacterial cells to form two cells—a process known as binary fission. Thus, Schizophyta means plants that split.

Most are saprophytic or parasitic heterotrophs, but a few are able to synthesize foods from inorganic matter by means of either chemosynthesis or a type of photosynthesis that involves pigments other than the chlorophyll of green plants. Such autotrophic bacterial species constitute a minute segment of the total number of bacteria in the world today. Within the division Schizophyta, ten orders are recognized, and of these, the order

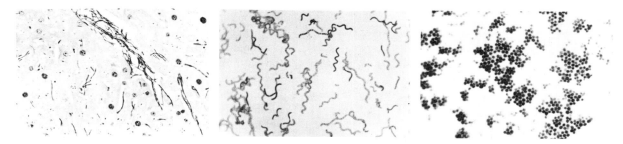

FIG. 22-1. *Left: Bacillus anthrax*, the anthrax bacterium. *Center: Spirillum rubrum*, a bacterium found commonly in water. *Right: Staphylococcus aureus*, cause of boils and skin infections.

Eubacteriales contains those bacteria that are possibly the simplest in overall form and life history. Our discussion of the bacteria will concern mainly the members of the Eubacteriales.

General Characteristics The Eubacteriales are single-celled organisms occurring in two basic forms: spherical, known as the *coccus* type, and oblong or cylindrical, known as the *bacillus* type. The latter is sometimes twisted or curved, in which case it is called the *spirillum*. These cells multiply exclusively by transverse fission and grow either isolated or in colonies (Figs. 22–1 and 22–2). In size they commonly average 2 microns in diameter, with the length of the cylindrical types ranging from 5 to 500 microns. A few species of bacteria are only about 0.15 micron (1/165,000 inch) in diameter! Of these smaller bacteria, 900 placed side by side would just cover the printed period at the end of this sentence. Bacteria are thus visible only under considerable magnification by high-power microscopes (Figs. 22–6, 22–7).

The wall of a bacterial cell is a rigid structure, consisting principally of amino acids, polysaccharides, and some lipids; no cellulose is present. Outside the wall of most, if not all, bacteria is a coat of slimy material which may take the form of a thin layer, a loose film, or a thick and viscous **capsule.** This slime material protects the bacterium against desiccation or other harmful effects of the environment. The protoplast of bacteria appears to be much simpler structurally than that of all other organisms, except the blue-green algae, which show a comparable level of organization. No mitochondria, endoplastic reticulum, or plastids are present, few if any vacuoles exist, and the cytoplasm is comparatively immobile. The nucleus or chromatin body is not enclosed by a nuclear membrane. It consists of DNA that can be extracted from the cell as a single, continuous loop or strand which may be considered a single chromosome. During cell division, no mitotic apparatus is present. The cytoplasm contains abundant ribosomes but few other organ-

FIG. 22-2. Left to right: coccus, bacillus, and spirillum forms of bacteria, illustrating some of the flagellate forms.

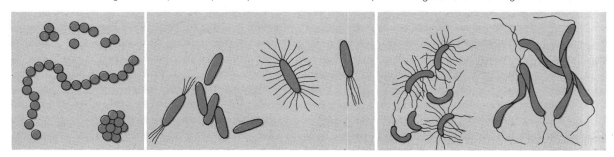

elles. The plasma membrane frequently infolds into the cytoplast, and some of these membranous invaginations are thought to be analogous to the endoplasmic reticulum of cells of other organisms.

Respiratory activities are mediated by enzymes situated in the plasma membrane. Often cytoplasmic granules can be seen. These have been identified as reserve materials the nature of which varies with the organism. Many kinds of bacteria are able to move about in the liquids in which they live. The movements of bacteria are usually the result of the rhythmic, wavelike or screwlike motions of slender flagella. These extremely thin appendages are often several times as long as the cell to which they are attached. The numbers and positions of flagella vary in different species of bacteria; thus, some have only one flagellum (for example, cholera bacterium), others have a tuft of flagella at one end or in some cases a tuft at each end (for example, several species of *Spirillum*), and still others have flagella covering the entire body surface (for example, typhoid bacillus) (Fig. 22–4).

Most bacteria, since they lack chlorophyll, are unable to manufacture foods from inorganic substances and thus live as saprophytes or parasites, utilizing foods manufactured originally by green plants: the growth, physiological activities, and reproduction of bacteria depend on adequate supplies of food and moisture, on a favorable temperature, and on certain other environmental factors.

A minority of bacterial species is autotrophic, that is, capable of synthesizing organic compounds from carbon dioxide and other simple, inorganic substances. Such autotrophic species thus resemble green plants, which are also autotrophic. Autotrophic bacteria may be separated into two groups: (a) chemosynthetic species, which obtain the energy required for synthesis of organic compounds from the oxidation of certain chemicals such as iron compounds and hydrogen sulfide, and (b) photosynthetic species, which utilize light energy in promoting their

food-making processes. The few species of photosynthetic bacteria contain purple and greenish pigments by which they utilize light energy in the synthesis of foods. On the basis of their color, photosynthetic bacteria fall into two groups: green and purple bacteria. The chlorophyll of green bacteria is chemically very similar to that of higher plants, whereas the chlorophyll of purple bacteria is not. The color of purple bacteria is due to the particular combination of other pigments present.

Although these chemosynthetic and photosynthetic bacteria form a distinct minority of all bacterial species, they are widely distributed, and their importance in nature is tremendous. Sulfur bacteria, for example, are responsible for the conversion of hydrogen sulfide, a common product of protein decay, to sulfur and then to sulfuric acid, which undergoes chemical reactions in soils to form sulfates, the principal source of sulfur for green plants. The sulfur bacteria thus play a very important role in nature. Without their activity, most of the sulfur in nature might be locked up in hydrogen sulfide, and the supply of sulfates, necessary for the nutrition of higher plants, might disappear. This important activity of sulfur bacteria proceeds not only on land but likewise in fresh water and salt water, with the result that hydrogen sulfide is constantly being transformed into sulfur compounds that both land and sea plants can utilize. Many biologists believe that the world's iron ore deposits were produced by iron-oxidizing bacteria; thus, iron bacteria of past ages have been important in determining the chemical nature of portions of the earth's crust.

The photosynthetic and chemosynthetic bacteria utilize carbon dioxide as the principal source of carbon required for the synthesis of carbohydrates, fats, proteins, and other organic compounds. Parasitic and saprophytic bacteria are unable to synthesize organic substances from carbon dioxide and live at the expense of organic compounds manufactured by other organisms. Some parasites, called **obligate parasites,** can survive only when they are able to absorb foods from the tissues of a **host,** the organism that they parasitize. **Facultative parasites** usually live on the living tissues of a host but may, under certain circumstances, derive nourishment from nonliving organic matter. Saprophytes utilize organic compounds present in nonliving matter, such as the decomposing bodies of animals, dead leaves, bark, wood, roots, and fruits, unsterilized and unrefrigerated meat, vegetables, pastries and other foodstuffs, and animal feces.

Some bacteria are very specific in the types of organic compounds they utilize, deriving their nourishment from certain specific substances, whereas other species can use a great variety of organic substances. Many bacteria live largely on carbohydrates, whereas others utilize proteins, fats, and amino acids. In general, the common types of saprophytic bacteria that are responsible for processes of decomposition in nature are rather cosmopolitan in their nutritional requirements, obtaining nourishment from a variety of organic substances. Many parasitic, disease-producing bacteria are very specific in their food requirements and can utilize only a few types of organic compounds. Thus, certain parasitic bacteria can live only in blood, different species requiring different types of blood, or in certain specific tissues of host plants or animals.

Like other kinds of plants, bacteria manufacture digestive enzymes by means of which complex or water-insoluble foods are converted into simpler or water-soluble compounds. The enzymes of bacteria include amylase, which converts starch to malt sugar; lipases, which digest fats into fatty acids and glycerol; invertase, which transforms cane sugar into glucose and fructose; maltase, which digests maltose into glucose; and proteases, which digest proteins into amino acids. Some of the enzymes are secreted by the bacteria into the surrounding medium, where they promote digestion; the bacterial cell then absorbs the digested material through its walls.

Like all other living organisms, both plants and animals, bacteria carry on respiration and the oxidation of foods to release energy necessary for growth, reproduction, and other cellular processes. Anaerobic bacteria, which thrive in the absence of free, gaseous oxygen, usually carry on anaerobic respiration or fermentation, in which, under the control of certain respiratory enzymes, foods are broken down, with the formation of carbon dioxide and intermediate organic compounds, such as alcohols and organic acids, and with the release of energy. Most aerobic species of bacteria, which live only in an environment containing free oxygen, complete the process of respiration through the aerobic phases, liberating carbon dioxide, water, and energy. Some facultative anaerobes, under anaerobic conditions, form carbon dioxide and organic compounds; given sufficient free oxygen, however, these organisms may complete the oxidation of these compounds to water and carbon dioxide.

As a result of their metabolic activities, different species of bacteria form different types of products, such as lactic, butyric, and acetic acids; gases (including carbon dioxide, methane, hydrogen sulfide, and others); red, yellow, orange, and blue pigments; and other substances. These products are often important in distinguishing among different species of bacteria.

Reproductive Characteristics   Sexual life cycles comparable to those common in other plants have not been observed in bacteria. However, transfer of genetic material from one bacterium to another is known to occur in numerous species. Of the transfer processes that are known, all, however, have been observed only under the controlled growth conditions of the laboratory; therefore, there is some question as to whether they occur regularly under natural conditions. Three of these observed processes are conjugation, transformation, and transduction.

Conjugation occurs in many different bacteria but is best known in *Eschericia coli.* During conjugation, two bacterial cells pair and one of the cells forms a conjugation tube leading into the other cell. This tube-forming cell, interpreted as the "male" cell, transfers a portion, not all, of its genetic material into the recipient "female" cell. There is no mutual exchange of genetic material between the cells, only a transfer from the donor "male" cell to the recipient "female" cell. Following conjugation, therefore, the recipient cell contains duplicate genes for several characters. Generations of cells arising from this cell often show combinations of characteristics of both the donor and recipient cells.

In the process known as **transformation,** DNA released from cells of one bacterial strain diffuses into the culture medium and directly enters the living cells of another strain. Among the progeny of this second strain will be some individuals that have inherited the properties of the first strain.

In the process of **transduction,** bacterial viruses (bacteriophages) are involved. When a virus infects one strain of bacteria, it may absorb DNA from the cells of that strain and later, when this same virus infects cells of a second strain of bacteria, it transfers this DNA to these cells. Subsequently, some of the progeny of this second strain will exhibit characters of the first.

The practical value of sexual reproduction in bacteria is not easily agreed on. One interpretation is that these transfer processes may function to spread entire groups of adaptive characteristics through populations in new or very different environments. More commonly, a generally high mutation rate ordinarily ensures that a small percentage of the cells in any population will be able to survive and reproduce under new environmental conditions. Consequently, simple binary fission is an adequate means of reproduction for almost all bacteria. In binary fission, one bacterial cell divides and forms two new individuals.

The cell undergoes DNA replication, followed by cytoplasmic division, processes analogous to mitosis and cytokinesis but with no stages resembling the mitotic phases. In bacillus and spirillum forms, the division plane is typically transverse, that is, at right angles to the long axis of the cell (Fig. 22–7). After division, the newly formed cells

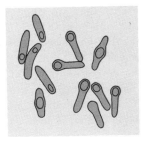

FIG. 22–3. Sketch showing various types of bacterial endospores.

often remain together, forming colonies of varying forms and sizes. Some of these are filamentous, or threadlike, others are cubical, platelike, or of some other shape. The forms of these colonies are relatively constant in some species, and bacterial identification may thus often be aided by observing the structure of colonies (Fig. 22–5). Under favorable conditions of temperature, food, and moisture supply, fission occurs as often as every 20 minutes. A cholera bacterium, reproducing at its most rapid rate, would, in 24 hours, produce *offspring numbering 4,700,000,000,000,- 000,000,000 and weighing about 2000 tons!* This exceedingly rapid reproduction is only theoretically possible, however, for inadequacy of food supply in any one place and the accumulation of toxic waste products of metabolism prevent such unlimited multiplication.

Some species of bacteria can form highly resistant **endospores** (Fig. 22–3), thus enabling the organisms to survive adverse environmental conditions that would kill cells in the vegetative state. Endospore formation is initiated as physical and/or chemical conditions for growth become progressively unfavorable, for example, through desiccation, depletion of the food substrate, and temperature change. An endospore is formed within a vegetative cell by condensing the protoplasm into a spherical or ovoid mass that then develops a relatively thick wall. Accompanying this condensation is a loss of some water so that the resulting spore has a lower moisture content than the vegetative bacterial cell. When the endospore is mature, it is commonly liberated by the rupture or disintegration of the wall of the old vegetative cell. With the return of favorable environmental conditions, the spore germinates and eventually grows into a vegetative cell of the type from which it was formed.

Some bacteria have special means by which they can reproduce asexually. For example, a process called **segmentation** occurs in some species; this involves the production by bacterial cells of tiny bodies called **gonidia,** which, upon encountering a suitable environment, grow into mature bacterial cells. Also, some filamentous bacteria produce small spores called **conidia,** usually in chains at their tips (Fig. 22–10).

Habitat and Distribution   As a result of their heterotrophic mode of life, most bacteria are limited to places where organic substances are readily available. According to their particular complement of enzymes, bacteria live within and on the bodies of other living things, in soils and water, in foodstuffs, in dead bodies, and in sewage and debris of all kinds. Since most bacteria do not carry on photosynthesis, they are independent of light and can live either in light or in darkness; many species, in fact, thrive in darkness and are injured or killed by exposure to sunlight. Bacteria require considerable amounts of moisture for their growth, and thus flourish in damp places, such as the tissues of other organisms, moist soils, manures, and foodstuffs with high water content. The occurrence of aerobic and anaerobic bacteria is conditioned by the presence or absence of free oxygen in the surrounding medium. Bacteria are probably the most widely distributed of all living organisms.

Representative Members   The classification and identification of bacteria involve certain difficulties not found in other groups of plants. These difficulties spring in part from the very small size of bacteria and the consequent difficulty of recognizing clearly their structural characteristics and in part from the relatively restricted range of morphological differences

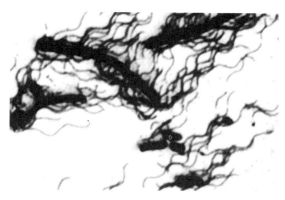

Fig. 22–4. Highly magnified photograph of *Eberthella typhosa*, a rod-shaped bacterium that causes typhoid fever in man. Notice the numerous, long flagella.

among different species. Such morphological differences include number, length, and position of flagella (Fig. 22–4), body form (rods, spheres, or spirals), and size. Another group of bacterial characters includes the shapes, colors, and structures of the colonies they form (Fig. 22–5). These differences are used, of course, in distinguishing among certain groups of bacteria, but they are often inadequate taxonomically since several bacterial species may resemble each other in

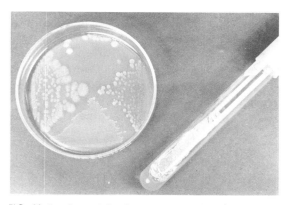

FIG. 22–5. Bacterial colonies growing in culture media in Petri dish (left) and test tube (right). The medium, consisting of agar, a gelatinous material, plus minerals and suitable organic compounds (sugars, blood, proteins, or others) is poured into the dishes and tubes, then sterilized, then inoculated with bacteria. (Photo by W. R. Kennedy.)

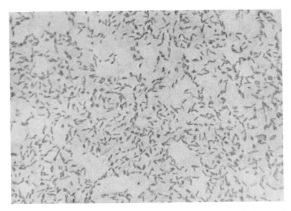

FIG. 22-6. *Pseudomonas aeruginosa,* a rod-shaped bacterium. Magnified ×1700. (Courtesy D. W. McNeill, Nancy Palmer Photo Agency.)

their external morphology and colony appearance. Thus, bacteriologists must often depend on physiological differences to identify and classify bacterial species and must, therefore, investigate the types of organic compounds that bacteria utilize, the kinds of organic acids, gases, pigments, and other compounds produced in their metabolism, their growth in relation to oxygen supply, and their reactions to various biological stains and antibiotics.

Bacteria are presently separated into ten orders, the largest of which, the Eubacteriales, includes most of the typical coccus, bacillus, and spirillum forms. Other orders include the sulfur bacteria, iron bacteria, spirochaetes, and others. The order Actinomycetales is especially known for the production of certain antibiotic drugs by some of its members.

Relationship with Other Organisms Nothing is known of the historical origin of bacteria on the earth's surface, and little is known positively concerning their relationships with other groups of living organisms. There is no doubt that bacteria constitute a group of great antiquity. This fact, together with their structural simplicity and small size, has led many biologists to consider them as possibly the first living organisms. Recent speculations seem to favor the view that the first living things were less complex heterotrophs than the bacteria of today. The morphological and reproductive similarities among bacteria, blue-green algae, and certain true fungi are believed by some biologists to indicate close relationship among these groups. Other biologists regard these groups as having had a more or less parallel development from some unknown common ancestral stock. Still others prefer to regard bacteria as degenerate organisms derived by evolutionary reduction from some more ancient and complex stock, similar perhaps to the blue-green algae.

Importance in Nature and in Human Life

Beneficial or advantageous activities of bacteria The beneficial activities of bacteria far outweigh their damaging effects on mankind. Among the most valuable are the following.

1. The metabolic processes and products of bacteria are important in many industries. The manufacture of vinegar, of butter, of certain kinds of cheese, and of sauerkraut, the tanning of leather, the curing of black tea, coffee, and cocoa beans, the removal of flax fibers from the stems of flax plants, the curing of vanilla pods, and the

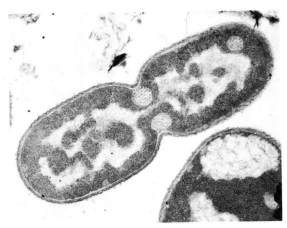

FIG. 22-7. A dividing cell of *Achromobacter* (×26,000). Courtesy W. J. Wiebe and G. B. Chapman, *J. Bacteriol.,* **95**:1874–1886 (1968).

production of ensilage through the fermentation of fodder are examples of industrial and agricultural activities promoted by bacteria. Bacteria utilize in their metabolism various sugars, proteins, and other organic compounds, and in their metabolic activities excrete products, some of which have important commercial uses. Among these products are acetone, an ingredient used in the manufacture of explosives, photographic film, rayon, and other products; butyl alcohol, a commercial solvent especially valuable in the manufacture of synthetic lacquers; lactic acid, of special usefulness in the tanning industry; citric acid, employed as a flavoring in lemon-flavored confections, beverages, and other foodstuffs; and vitamins, useful in medicines and foods.

The manufacture of vinegar is one of the oldest processes in human history that involves bacterial metabolism. Vinegar production begins with the fermentation of apple juices by yeasts, the carbohydrates in the juice being converted to alcohol. In the presence of oxygen, species of the vinegar bacterium, *Acetobacter*, oxidize the alcohol to acetic acid. Other alcoholic substrates used in vinegar making are cider, wine, beer-wort, and the fermented juice of sugar beets.

Ensilage is an important product of bacterial metabolism. Green plant parts, such as chopped corn stems and leaves, are packed into a silo, where they are fermented by bacteria. During this fermentation, organic acids, especially lactic acid, are produced. These acids have a preservative action that prevents the spoiling of the ensilage. Ensilage, or silage as it is sometimes called, is a nutritious food in the diets of cattle and other domesticated animals during those seasons when fresh, green plant tissues are not available for feeding.

2. Bacteria bring about the decomposition of proteins, fats, carbohydrates, and other complex organic compounds in the bodies of plants and animals and in their waste products. Thus, they clear the earth of organic debris and return to the soil and air the simple substances necessary for the maintenance of soil fertility and for the

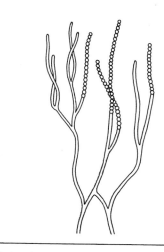

FIG. 22-8. Sketch of filamentous bacterium, *Actinomyces*, showing chains of conidia.

continued food-making activities of green plants.

The bacteria involved in the decomposition of nitrogenous organic compounds are so important in the maintenance of soil fertility that they deserve more detailed description. The groups of bacteria involved in nitrogen transformations in the soil are **ammonifying bacteria, nitrifying bacteria, nitrogen-fixing bacteria,** and **denitrifying bacteria.** Ammonifying bacteria transform various proteinaceous substances into ammonia (NH_3) in the soil, in a process called **ammonification.** The ammonia thus formed usually reacts with other substances in the soil to form ammonium salts, for example, ammonium sulphate. Under certain conditions some plants can obtain nitrogen from the soil in the form of the ammonium ion (NH_4^+), which is taken in through the roots. Green plants obtain most of their nitrogen by the absorption of nitrates into the roots. Certain bacteria in the soil convert ammonia to nitrites ($-NO_2$) whereas other bacteria oxidize the nitrites to nitrates ($-NO_3$); this process is called **nitrification.** Ammonifying and nitrifying bacteria are, therefore, directly concerned in the transformation of protein compounds of nonliving organic matter into nitrates and thus play a major role in the maintenance of soil fertility. Nitro-

FIG. 22-9. Winter pea plants. *Left:* Plants grown from seeds inoculated with proper strain of nodule bacteria. Note the nodules in the upper parts of the roots. *Right:* Plants grown from uninoculated plants. Note size.

gen-fixing bacteria contribute to soil fertility by incorporating atmospheric nitrogen (which green plants cannot utilize) into organic compounds, a process called **nitrogen fixation.** There are two types of nitrogen-fixing bacteria: saprophytic, soil-inhabiting species, and others that live in small swellings or **nodules** (Fig. 22-9) on the roots of various seed plants, chiefly legumes such as alfalfa, clover, and soybeans. The saprophytic bacteria must die and be decomposed before their fixed nitrogen can be converted to nitrates as described above. The relationship between the nodule bacteria (genus *Rhizobium*) and the plants

they infect is one of **mutualism,** a state of more or less mutual benefit. The bacteria obtain food from the tissues of the host plant, and the host plant obtains nitrogen that has been fixed by the bacteria. It is because of this relationship and activity that leguminous plants usually enrich the soil in which they grow. In order to ensure the development of nodule bacteria, pure cultures of various strains of such bacteria are prepared commercially in laboratories and are mixed with the proper types of seeds before planting or are added to the soil in which the seeds are to be sown (Fig. 22-10). Although these symbiotic bacteria are widely distributed in soils, they cannot fix atmospheric nitrogen unless they are associated with a suitable host plant. Inoculation of seeds or soil with the proper strain of bacteria results in a higher percentage of infections than would result from chance contact with naturally occurring soil organisms and has the added advantage of bringing together the seeds and the particular strain of bacteria best suited to the kind of seeds planted. The three processes mentioned above directly or indirectly increase the nitrate content in soil.

A discussion of the beneficial effects of bacteria in relation to soil fertility should also emphasize the work of **sulfur bacteria,** which, as described earlier in this chapter, convert hydrogen sulfide, a product of protein decay, through intermediate compounds into sulfuric acid, which undergoes transformation into sulfates. Still other bacteria are able to oxidize elemental sulfur to sulfates that plants can use. Sulfates are the major source of sulfur, an essential element for the metabolism of green plants. Were it not for the sulfur bacteria, the supply of sulfates in soils would become exhausted, and the growth of green plants might become impossible.

3. Bacteria promote digestive and possibly other physiological processes in the intestinal tracts of animals. The digestion of cellulose by such herbivorous animals as horses and cattle results in part from cellulose-digesting enzymes

FIG. 22-10. Austrian vetch. *Left:* Plants grown from seeds inoculated with proper strain of nitrogen-fixing nodule bacteria. *Right:* Plants from uninoculated seeds.

excreted by bacteria inhabiting the intestines of these animals. Bacteria also dwell in large numbers in the human intestinal tract, particularly in the lower part of the small intestine and in the large intestine. The activity of these bacteria in the human gut and the significance of this activity are not known positively; some physiologists believe that these bacteria carry on certain digestive activities of value to the human body, whereas others believe that lactic acid and other metabolic products of these normally occurring bacteria inhibit the growth of putrefactive and possibly certain pathogenic bacteria. Whatever may be their specific physiological significance, it is certain that the maintenance of a normal bacterial flora in the human intestinal tract is essential to the health of the human organism and that any major disturbance in this intestinal bacterial flora results in derangements of health. It is interesting that from 30 to 40 percent of the dry weight of human feces consists of bodies of microorganisms, chiefly the colon bacterium, *Escherichia coli*. Pathogenic bacteria

sometimes dwell in the human digestive tract and pass out with the feces; bacteria that cause typhoid fever and certain types of dysentery are often spread through feces. For this reason, the use of human feces as a fertilizer for soils, a practice common in many parts of the world, often contaminates carrots, potatoes, lettuce, radishes, and other vegetables and thus spreads typhoid fever and dysentery.

Harmful or disadvantageous activities of bacteria

1. Bacteria cause many serious diseases of man, for example, tuberculosis, meningitis, pneumonia, lockjaw, typhoid fever, cholera, diphtheria, and dysentery.

2. Bacteria cause diseases of domesticated animals, for example, tuberculosis of cattle and hogs, anthrax of sheep, chicken cholera, pneumonia, glanders in horses and sheep, and septicemia in cattle.

3. Bacteria cause many diseases of cultivated plants, for example, fire blight of pears, citrus canker, cotton root rot, potato black leg, celery, cucumber, and eggplant rot, and wilt diseases (caused chiefly by the stoppage of vascular tissues by bacteria) of tomatoes, potatoes, cucumbers, squash, and cantaloupes. These diseases cause large crop losses, the value of which reaches many millions of dollars annually.

4. Bacteria cause the spoilage of large quantities of human foodstuffs: the souring of milk, the rotting of meat, the spoilage of butter, potatoes, vegetables, and fruits, both fresh and canned. In their growth in these foodstuffs, bacteria frequently excrete waste products (**toxins**) that are toxic to human beings and frequently cause severe, even fatal, poisoning in persons who eat such bacteria-contaminated foods.

5. Denitrifying bacteria, which are especially abundant and active under anaerobic conditions in wet soils and soils with high organic matter content, break down nitrates through intermediate compounds to free nitrogen gas, which escapes into the air. Denitrifying bacteria thus

reduce soil fertility by depleting the nitrogen content of soils.

CONTROL OF BACTERIA

An important objective of bacteriology is the control of harmful bacteria wherever they may occur. Some control techniques are designed to kill the bacteria, hence are **bactericidal;** others are **bacteriostatic,** that is, they prevent the growth of bacteria without actually killing them. The methods most commonly used include high and low temperatures, chemical treatment, drying, and irradiation. One principal type of heat treatment used in the preservation of food and in many other processes is **sterilization.** In sterilization, all bacteria (vegetative cells and spores) are killed. Steam under pressure in an autoclave is commonly used to provide a sufficiently high temperature that is then maintained for a time determined by the nature of the material being sterilized. It should be noted that the temperature of boiling water (212°F) is sufficient to kill all vegetative cells but *not* high enough to kill all kinds of bacterial spores. Canned foods are commonly heat treated after they have been sealed in the container. Improper sterilization or sealing may result in contamination of the food, which, if eaten, could cause serious food poisoning. One of the most dangerous types of food poisoning is **botulism.** The causal agent of this disease is a toxin secreted by *Clostridium botulinum,* an anaerobic, spore-forming bacterium that occasionally contaminates food. Another method of heat treatment used in the preservation of food is **pasteurization.** In this process the temperature of the material being treated (milk, for example) is raised for 30 minutes to approximately 145°F, as a result of which certain bacteria are destroyed but not necessarily all species. Most types of pathogenic bacteria, including *Mycobacterium tuberculosis,* are destroyed by this treatment. Another pasteurizing process raises the temperature to about 160°F for 15 seconds. Prolonged heating at high temperatures would adversely alter the properties of the material being treated. Pasteurization is commonly applied to milk, cream, beer, and wines. Many products, such as foods and drugs, are frequently kept refrigerated since low temperatures inhibit bacterial activity. Subfreezing temperatures of freezers and food lockers are very effective in preserving foods.

Chemical agents used as food preservatives act chiefly in two ways.

1. They reduce the amount of available moisture to a level at which bacteria in these foods are inactivated or killed. The effectiveness of salt in preserving meats and fish and of sugar in preserving jellies and jams depends almost entirely on their withdrawal of water from the microorganism.

2. Other chemical agents added to foods have a direct killing effect on bacteria; among such bactericides are benzoic and salicylic acids and their salts, boric acid and borates. Caution must be used in the addition of these preservative substances to foods, since if their concentration becomes too high they may exert harmful physiological effects on human consumers.

Chemicals are widely used against bacteria in medicine, hygiene, public health, and other fields. Those chemicals that kill bacteria are called **germicides** or **disinfectants;** others inhibit or prevent the growth and activities of bacteria and are called **antiseptics.** These terms, although generally useful, require some qualification since a bactericidal compound at a sufficiently low concentration may exhibit bacteriostatic properties instead. Other factors—for example, kind and number of bacteria, temperature, and length of exposure to a particular chemical—also influence the effect of chemical treatment. Among the best-known drugs used to combat bacterial infections are the **sulfonamides** (for example, sulfanilamide and sulfadiazine) and the **antibiotics.** Antibiotics are the products of metabolism of certain fungi and soil bacteria that exert a bacteriostatic effect. Examples of antibiotics are penicillin from the mold *Penicillium;* tyrothricin, bacitracin, and polymyxins from species of *Bacillus.* About fifteen commercially available antibiotics are obtained from species of the branched, filamentous bacterium, *Streptomyces,* including aureomycin, chloromycetin, streptomycin, and terramycin. These antibiotics have been so effective in the treatment of diseases that they are popularly called "wonder drugs."

Drying, especially of foods, makes bacterial growth difficult or impossible, since bacteria require considerable amounts of water for their metabolism. Various techniques are used in drying foods for preservation, and different types of foods are dried to differing moisture contents. Thus, "dried" prunes, raisins, and apricots may contain as much as 25 percent moisture. Despite this considerable moisture content, most bacterial growth is virtually impossible, since the high-sugar content of these fruits serves to withdraw water from the bacterial cells, thereby inhibiting their growth. Other foods are dried completely for preservation purposes; for example, dehydrated vegetables, powdered eggs, powdered milk, and dried meats and fish. Some foods, such as cereals, beans, and nuts, undergo a marked decrease in moisture content as they mature, so that they naturally contain a very low moisture content by the time of harvest or shipment; thus, they are naturally protected against bacterial decomposition. Foods with high water content, such as tomatoes, beef, bananas, and fresh fish, are quickly decomposed by bacteria.

The bactericidal effect of certain kinds of radiant energy has been used with varying degrees of success for some time. Such radiations include ultraviolet rays, x-rays, gamma rays, and powerful electron beams. Ultraviolet rays are widely used for surface sterilization and air purification; moreover, they are relatively safe and inexpensive to produce. The other radiations are used in special applications requiring higher energies and greater penetrance. In recent years, food preservation experiments have involved exposure of wrapped foods to radioactive energy which kills bacterial cells and leaves the packaged food more or less permanently sterile.

VIRUSES

General Characteristics   Viruses are infective agents which are characterized by their submicroscopic size (up to 300 millimicrons) and by their ability to propagate only within living cells. They are particles of matter existing on the threshold between life and nonlife. When they are within the living cell, existing in concert with its enzymes and other factors, viruses exhibit genetic functions and the ability to reproduce, but outside the living cell they are simply molecular complexes whose properties can be described in terms of organic chemistry. Viruses, therefore, cannot live independently but must parasitize the cells of plants, bacteria, and animals. In some instances the parasitism is a mild one causing no injury or definable disease in the host, but in other cases serious metabolic disturbances occur which are often severe enough to kill the host. Insects or other biting animals commonly serve as carriers, transmitting viruses from one organism to another. Also, some viruses can be carried in the air or can be transmitted directly by contact with infected individuals. Common virus diseases of man are poliomyelitis, meningitis, measles, mumps, chicken pox, the common cold, warts, rabies, small-pox, yellow fever, infectious hepatitis, cat-scratch fever, and infectious mononucleosis. Virus diseases in animals include distemper in dogs, hog cholera, foot-and-mouth disease in cattle, fowl plague, and infectious myxomytosis in rabbits. Among plants, viral diseases are legion, and many are of immense economic importance causing millions of dollars in damage in the United States each year. Important crops affected by viral diseases are corn, tomato, tobacco, sugar cane, apple, sugarbeet, wheat, rice, peach, banana, sweet potato, and others.

Composition and Behavior of Viruses   Viruses are made up of a nucleic acid core of genetic material enclosed in and protected by a protein coat. In plant viruses the nucleic acid is RNA;

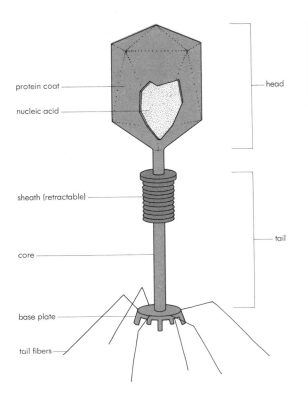

protein coat

nucleic acid

head

sheath (retractable)

core

tail

base plate

tail fibers

FIG. 22-11.   Bacteriophage (bacterial virus). *Left:* Drawing showing major components of a T-series type. *Above:* Electronmicrograph of same (Courtesy of Virus Lab, U. of California.)

FIG. 22-12.   Bacteriophage infecting *Eschericia coli* (×210,000). (Courtesy of Councilman Morgan, M.D.)

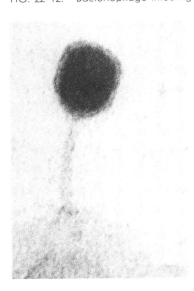
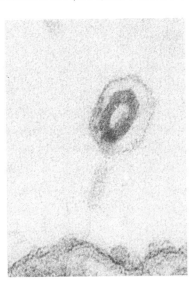
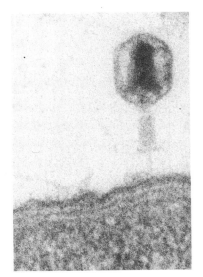

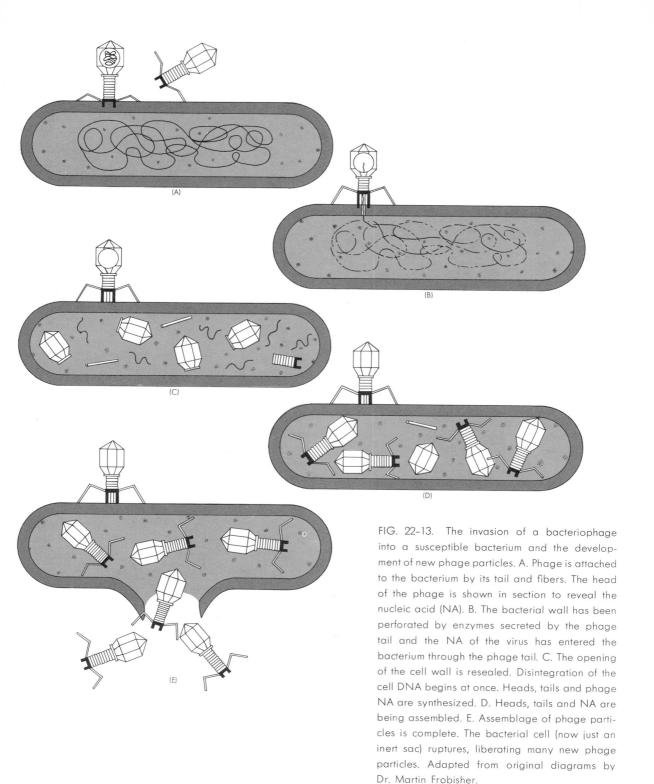

FIG. 22-13. The invasion of a bacteriophage into a susceptible bacterium and the development of new phage particles. A. Phage is attached to the bacterium by its tail and fibers. The head of the phage is shown in section to reveal the nucleic acid (NA). B. The bacterial wall has been perforated by enzymes secreted by the phage tail and the NA of the virus has entered the bacterium through the phage tail. C. The opening of the cell wall is resealed. Disintegration of the cell DNA begins at once. Heads, tails and phage NA are synthesized. D. Heads, tails and NA are being assembled. E. Assemblage of phage particles is complete. The bacterial cell (now just an inert sac) ruptures, liberating many new phage particles. Adapted from original diagrams by Dr. Martin Frobisher.

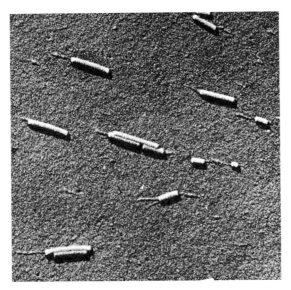
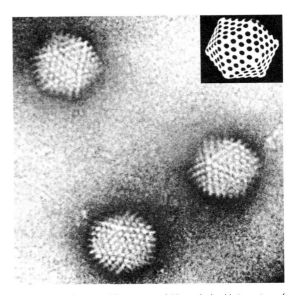

FIG. 22-14. Electronmicrograph of tobacco mosaic virus, a rod-shaped virus. (Courtesy of Virus Lab, University of California.) FIG. 22-15. Electronmicrograph of a polyhedral form of virus, showing a model in the upper right-hand corner. (Courtesy of Dr. Joseph L. Melnick.)

in bacterial viruses (bacteriophages) (Fig. 22–11), with some exceptions, it is DNA; among vertebrate viruses, it is either DNA or RNA, and among insect viruses it is chiefly RNA. Viruses are capable of entering a living cell and harnessing its metabolic pathways so that the cell produces primarily virus constituents instead of cell constituents (Fig. 22–13). Viruses themselves have no metabolism and most lack enzymes. The protein coat of the virus acts as a protective package for the nucleic acid so that it may survive extracellularly, and it also facilitates entry of the viral nucleic acid into the host cell. Upon entry of the cell, the DNA or RNA core is freed of its protein coat and then initiates production of replicas of itself and of its protein coat by the machinery of the host cell. Although viruses can take any of several shapes, every shape is but a variant of two basic morphologies of the protein coat: a rod shape (Fig. 22–14) or polyhedral shape (Fig. 22–15). Viruses are visible only with an electron

microscope, and much of what is known about their structure has been obtained by x-ray diffraction methods.

Relationship of Viruses to Other Organisms Our knowledge of the origin and relationship of viruses is based only on speculation. Several hypotheses have been advanced: one holds that viruses are the degenerate forms of organisms formerly much more complex, and which have become totally adapted to a parasitic life; another view suggests that viruses were once components of normal cells and resemble genes that have gotten out of normal controls; a third theory supposes that they are the modern day descendents of those primitive and earliest evolved self-replicating organic compounds; and still another theory holds that viruses have evolved from pathogenic bacteria through a process of retrogressive evolution.

SUMMARY

1. Bacteria are the smallest of all living organisms, rarely exceeding 5 microns in length.

2. Most species of bacteria are saprophytes or parasites; a few species are capable of carrying on photosynthesis and chemosynthesis.

3. There are three common body forms among the eubacteriales: spheres, rods, and spirals.

4. A few species of bacteria have a filamentous body form.

5. The wall of the bacterial cell is made up chiefly of amino acids and sugars; cellulose is absent. The wall is rigid and maintains the characteristic shape of the cell.

6. The bacterial protoplast typically lacks vacuoles, cytoplasmic movement, mitochondria, and plastids. Its nuclear material apparently is a single chromosome of DNA—the chromatin body which is not enclosed by a nuclear membrane. Ribosomes are abundant.

7. The plasma membrane is the site of several enzyme systems and, with its invaginations into the cytoplasm, is active in respiration and in maintaining the osmotic integrity of the cell.

8. Many bacteria bear flagella, the rhythmic movements of which cause bacteria to move in liquids in which they may occur.

9. There are two types of autotrophic bacteria: chemosynthetic species and photosynthetic species.

10. Chemosynthetic species oxidize various chemicals, obtaining energy from this oxidation. This energy is utilized in food synthesis. They include sulfur bacteria, iron bacteria, and nitrifying bacteria.

11. Photosynthetic species utilize light energy in food syntheses. They include purple and green bacteria.

12. Obligate parasites can live only in parasitic fashion, facultative parasites usually live parasitically but may also live as saprophytes.

13. Heterotrophic bacteria vary greatly in the kinds of organic compounds they utilize. They also vary in the products of their metabolism.

14. Bacteria produce many types of enzymes, the functions of which are similar to those of higher plants. Bacteria carry on various types of respiration.

15. The common method of reproduction in bacteria is fission, or simple cell division. After successive divisions, bacterial cells often cohere to form colonies.

16. Certain forms of sexual reproduction involving the transfer of genetic material from one bacterium to another have been observed in many different bacterial species grown in culture media in laboratories. The three best known transfer mechanisms are conjugation, transformation, and transduction.

17. Some bacteria form resistant endospores enabling them to survive unfavorable environmental conditions that would kill cells in the vegetative state.

18. Some bacteria form reproductive bodies called gonidia and conidia.

19. Bacteria are probably the most widely distributed of all organisms.

20. The principal growth requirements of most bacteria are: favorable temperature, abundant moisture, and a supply of organic matter. Most bacteria are independent of light; many species are injured or killed by light.

21. Aerobic bacteria thrive only in the presence of oxygen, anaerobic bacteria in the absence of oxygen.

22. Bacteria show certain structural and reproductive similarities with blue-green algae and some true fungi. The significance of these similarities is not definitely known.

23. Bacteria exert many beneficial influences on human life. Among these are: the production of industrially important chemicals, the production of foodstuffs such as sauerkraut, cheese, vinegar, and ensilage, the curing of cocoa and other beverages, the production of vitamins, the decomposition of dead bodies of plants and animals and of their wastes, and the maintenance of soil fertility through the activities of ammonifying bacteria, nitrifying bacteria, nitrogen-fixing bacteria, and sulfur bacteria. Some bacteria are beneficial inhabitants of animal digestive tracts.

24. Bacteria exert harmful or disadvantageous effects on human life, among which are these: they cause diseases of man, of his domesticated animals, and of crop plants; they cause food spoilage; they are frequently responsible for food poisoning; and cause a loss of nitrogen from soil.

25. Pathogenic, or disease-producing bacteria, form poisonous substances called toxins, which injure or kill host tissues.

26. Bacteria may be destroyed by exposure to sunlight and other types of radiations and by chemical agents called disinfectants or germicides. Antiseptics inhibit the growth and activity of bacteria but do not necessarily kill them.

27. Pasteurization of foods will kill certain bacteria but not necessarily all species; heat sterilization kills all bacteria (vegetative cells and spores).

28. Foods may be preserved by cold storage, freezing, dehydration, and preservatives such as salt, sugar, benzoic acid, and benzoates.

29. Physiological characteristics are very important in the classification and identification of many types of bacteria.

30. The bacteria are separated into ten orders, of which the Eubacteriales is the largest. The order Actinomycetales contains some bacteria that produce important antibiotic drugs.

31. Viruses are ultramicroscopic infective particles propagating only when within a living cell and so small that they are visible only with an electron microscope.

32. Structurally a virus consists of a core of DNA or RNA—the infective agent—enclosed in a protein coat which serves as a protective package during periods of extracellular existence of the virus.

33. Viruses exhibit genetic functions which commandeer the metabo-

lism of the host cell so that the cell produces viral DNA or RNA and protein instead of normal cell constituents.

34. Outside the living cell, a virus exhibits no metabolism and is a stable molecular complex.

35. Viruses have been variously interpreted as degenerate, highly parasitic forms of formerly more complex organisms, or as "escaped" cell components which resemble genes, or as descendents of the first evolved self-replicating compounds, or as highly reduced forms of pathogenic bacteria.

SUGGESTED READINGS FOR INTERESTED STUDENTS

1. Andrews, Christopher H., *The Natural History of Viruses.* Norton, New York, 1967.

2. Cairns, John, "The bacterial chromosome." *Scientific American,* Vol. 214 No. 1, pp. 36–44, January, 1966.

3. Doyle, William T., *Nonvascular Plants: Form and Function.* Wadsworth, Belmont, Cal., 1965.

4. Fraenkel-Conrat, Heinz, *Design and Function at the Threshold of Life:* The Viruses. Academic Press, New York, 1962.

5. Fraser, Dean, *Viruses and Molecular Biology.* The Macmillan Co.. New York, 1967.

6. Frobisher, Martin, *Fundamentals of Microbiology.* Saunders, Philadelphia, Pa., 1968.

7. Jawetz, Ernest, Joseph L. Melnick, and Edward A. Adelberg, *Review of Medical Microbiology.* Lange Medical Publications, Los Altos, Cal., 1966.

8. Scagel, Robert F., et al., *An Evolutionary Survey of the Plant Kingdom.* Wadsworth, Belmont, Cal., 1965.

9. Sistrom, W. R., *Microbial Life,* Modern Biology Series, Holt, Rinehart and Winston, New York, 1969.

10. Thimann, Kenneth V., *The Life of Bacteria.* The Macmillan Co., New York, 1963.

TOPICS AND QUESTIONS FOR STUDY

1. Describe the size and shapes of the bacteria belonging to the Eubacteriales.

2. What are the chief constituents of the wall of bacterial cells? How does the composition of the wall differ from that of most other plants?

3. Contrast the protoplast of the bacterium with that of most other plants and animals.

4. What nucleic acid is found in most species of bacteria? Describe the chromatin body of the bacterial cell.

5. What factors favor a high level of physiological activity in bacteria?

6. Distinguish between aerobic and anaerobic bacteria. List some of the places in which you would find these types of bacteria growing.

7. Describe briefly how bacterial movement is caused.

8. Name some common types of chemosynthetic bacteria, and briefly describe their activity.

9. What are photosynthetic bacteria? Describe their activity.

10. Describe the methods of reproduction that occur in bacteria.

11. What factors favor rapid reproduction of bacteria? What factors may cause a decrease in the rate of bacterial reproduction?

12. Why are bacteria thought to be related to blue-green algae? Why to true fungi?

13. Why do bacteriologists consider physiological differences in the classification of bacteria? Name some of the physiological activities that bacteriologists use in differentiating among bacteria.

14. List some of the harmful activities of bacteria in human life.

15. State two reasons why the drying of foods, of bedding, of freshly washed clothing is best done in sunlight.

16. Sewage contains large numbers of bacteria, and the water in streams into which sewage is poured is rich in bacteria near the point of entrance of sewage. A few miles downstream, however, the bacterial content of the water may be greatly reduced. Explain.

17. In many parts of the world, where agriculture is very intensive, it is dangerous to eat vegetables that have grown in, or have been in contact with, soils unless the vegetables are cooked or treated with disinfectants. Explain.

18. How do salt and sugar preserve foods?

19. List some of the important chemicals produced by bacteria. What important human foods owe their flavor and other qualities to bacterial action?

20. Describe fully the importance of bacteria in the maintenance of soil fertility. Describe the work of sulfur bacteria and of the various bacteria that bring about nitrogen transformations in the soil.

21. Describe the principal methods used to preserve foods, and explain why each is effective.

22. List all the precautions that are taken in a hospital to destroy or prevent the growth of bacteria; in a food cannery; in a swimming pool; in a well-operated restaurant.

23. What methods of personal hygiene may be used to prevent the spread of bacteria?

24. List the chief characteristics of viruses.

25. Describe the general structure of viruses.

26. Describe the method by which a virus is replicated.

27. Are viruses living organisms?

28. List some of the differences between bacteria and viruses.

29. What major groups of organisms are parasitized by viruses?

30. What is the name given to viruses that attack bacteria?

31. List some viral diseases of man; of animals.

23

THALLOPHYTA: MYXOMYCOPHYTA (SLIME MOLDS) AND EUMYCOPHYTA (TRUE FUNGI)

As an assemblage of intrinsically interesting organisms, the fungi have long held a special fascination for man. As the agents of enormous harm and benefit, they have long commanded his attention. These unusual plants live a heterotrophic existence as saprophytes and parasites because, like most bacteria, they lack chlorophyll. In contrast to bacteria, the fungi are larger and chiefly multicellular, they possess well-defined nuclei and other subcellular organelles, they show re-

markable diversity in the formation and structure of their thalli and spores, and their reproduction usually includes some kind of distinct, sexual process.

DIVISION MYXOMYCOPHYTA

General Characteristics   The Myxomycophyta consist of a small number of organisms whose life cycle includes an animal-like vegetative stage,

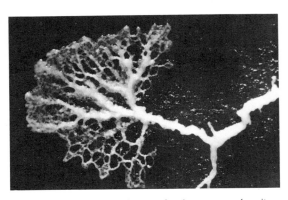

FIG. 23-1. The plasmodium or feeding stage of a slime mold, *Physarum polycephalum,* growing upon agar. (Courtesy of D. A. Eggert, U. of Illinois, Chicago Circle.)

the **plasmodium,** (Fig. 23-1) and a plantlike reproductive stage consisting of one or several sporangia. The plasmodium is a thin mass of viscous, naked, multinucleate protoplasm that may be white, yellow, red, orange, or violet. Depending on its age and growth, it may be microscopic in size, or it may have an area of many square centimeters. As it grows, the mass of protoplasm typically becomes finely branched and netlike in its organization. At the leading edge of the growing plasmodium the protoplasm is separated from the external environment by only a thin membrane. In the older parts of the plasmodium the protoplasmic mass is differentiated into a network of tubules or veins within which the cytoplasm flows in interconnecting streams. This flow of cytoplasm is easily observed under the microscope and can often be seen to proceed in one direction for a minute or two, then stop abruptly and resume its flow in the opposite direction. Commonly the flow may even occur as two currents of cytoplasm moving simultaneously in opposite directions within the same tubule. During the growth of the plasmodium, protoplasm accumulates at the leading edge and is withdrawn from other areas, causing it to creep over the substratum. As it moves, the plasmodium absorbs dissolved food materials and also ingests solid food particles such as bacterial cells, spores, and yeasts. Ingested particles are confined to

vacuoles where they are digested and assimilated into the cytoplasm. The numerous nuclei are diploid, and all undergo synchronous mitosis a number of times during the life of the plasmodium. Although most species of slime molds are saprophytes, a few are parasitic on algae, true fungi, flowering plants, and other hosts. Saprophytic species typically live under dead bark or leaves, in darkness or diffuse light.

Reproductive Characteristics   Following a period of food intake and growth, the plasmodium moves to an exposed site and undergoes a complete structural change: the prostrate plasmodium is transformed into one or more sporangia (Fig. 23-2). Sporangium formation is unusual in slime molds in that the entire multinucleate body is converted into sporangia and spores. The cytoplasm becomes concentrated into one or many small mounds, each of which will become a sporangium. In some species meiosis occurs within the sporangium followed by cytoplasmic cleavage isolating each nucleus in a separate cell which will become a haploid spore. Usually, a complex network of noncellular threads (called the **capillitium** is secreted within the sporangium during spore formation. These capillitial threads support the sporangia and spores, and in many species assist in spore liberation. Often the capillitial threads are intricately toothed, lobed, or convoluted and, together with the shapes and colors of sporangia and spores, provide bases for classifying and identifying the species. The sporangia are usually large enough to be seen with the naked eye and are often considered to be among the most strikingly beautiful objects in the plant kingdom (Fig. 23-3).

After liberation, the spores germinate on dead leaves, fallen logs, soil, or other substrates. Each spore produces one to four naked, uninucleate flagellated **swarm cells** or nonflagellated **myxamoebae** cells. These cells may function immediately as gametes or may divide repeatedly by mitosis, giving rise to cells that later function as gametes. Fusion of a pair of these cells ordinarily

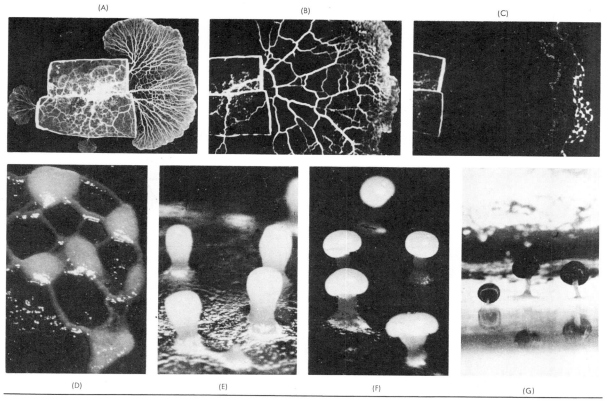

FIG. 23-2. Formation of sporangia by the slime mold *Didymium iridis* (duration approx. 20 hrs.) (A) Plasmodial fans creeping off blocks of agar containing yeast food; (B) First visible evidence of fruit forming, protoplasm collecting into broad band along front; (C) Plasmodium separating into droplets; (D) Higher magnification of stage (C). droplets still connected by veins; (E) Stalks of young sporangia forming from droplets; (F) Sporangia well separated into head and stalk; stalk contracting, protoplasm moving into head; (G) Mature fruit, spore head black. (Courtesy of Dr. A. L. Cohen.)

produces an amoeboid zygote which grows to form the plasmodium. In some other species, the details of structure and reproduction vary somewhat from those just described. The life cycle of *Physarum polycephalum* is shown in Fig. 23-4.

Habitat and Distribution Saprophytic slime molds occur chiefly on dead and rotting logs and leaves, on dung, and in soil. They appear in greatest abundance in temperate zone forests following warm, rainy periods, especially in late spring,

FIG. 23-3. Two examples of sporangial types found among slime molds. *Hemitrichia vesparium* fruiting on rotting wood. *Physarum polycephalum* fruiting on a leaf. Specimens courtesy of Alan Parker. (Photos by W. R. Kennedy.)

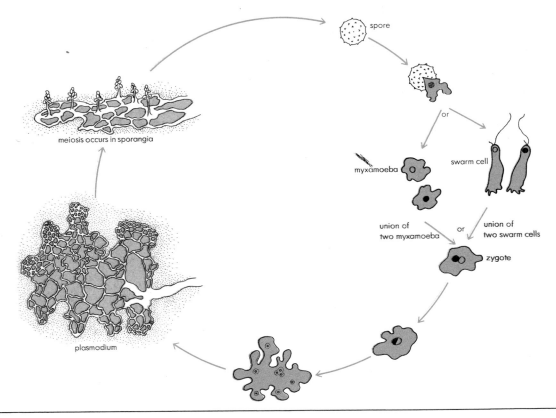

FIG. 23–4.   The life cycle of a slime mold *Physarum polycephalum*.

and they also occur in considerable numbers in humid, tropical forests. During their vegetative or assimilative phase, plasmodia usually inhabit dark or dimly lighted, moist areas, moving into drier, more exposed habitats as reproduction begins. Parasitic species live within or on the bodies of their hosts.

Representative Members   *Physarum polycephalum* (Figs. 23–1, 23–3 and 23–4) is a common slime mold which is easily cultured in the laboratory. Another species is *Hemitrichia vesparium* whose sporangia are shown in Fig. 23–3.

Relationship to Other Organisms   The origin and relationships of the Myxomycophyta are ob-

scure. They possess both plant and animal characteristics and are considered by some authorities to be intermediate between plants and animals. Others view them as animals and place them in the Phylum Protozoa. Those who view them as plants place them in a division by themselves, separate from, but probably most closely related to, the bacteria and true fungi. This point of view is supported by the presence of cellulose walls which enclose the spores. The Myxomycophyta are commonly referred to as the plasmodial slime molds to distinguish them from the more animal-like cellular slime molds.

Importance in Nature and in Human Life   Slime molds like many bacteria and true fungi are involved in processes of decomposition of organic materials that lie on or in the soil. Among the economically important species are *Plasmodiophora brassicae* which attacks the roots of cabbage and other members of the mustard family causing a disease called clubroot, and *Spongospora subterranea* which causes the powdery scab disease of potato tubers.

DIVISION EUMYCOPHYTA (TRUE FUNGI)

General Characteristics The Eumycophyta comprise over 50,000 known species of widely diverse form, size, physiology, and reproductive method. Although a few species are unicellular, most have a vegetative phase consisting of a mass of microscopic, profusely branching filaments called **hyphae.** Hyphae are commonly colorless and collectively have a whitish, cottony appearance, but in some species they are red, orange, yellow, brown, or otherwise pigmented. A mass of hyphae is called a **mycelium.** In some species, the mycelium is composed of tubular hyphae lacking cross walls so that the cytoplasm is continuous throughout the hyphae. Such a nonseptate multinucleate mycelium is termed **coenocytic.** In the majority of species, the mycelium is subdivided by cross walls or septa and is thus multicellular. The constituent cells of such septate hyphae may be uni-, bi-, or multinucleate. In some cases the septa have central pores through which cytoplasm extends between adjacent cells; hence, septate hyphae are to some degree coenocytic like nonseptate hyphae. A mycelium is commonly extensive, permeating the organic substrate from which it takes its foods, or enveloping, covering, or infiltrating the body of an organism on which the fungus is parasitic. In many species the mycelium grows completely hidden within the substrate or host organism. The familiar mushrooms, puffballs, and other similar visible structures of the higher fungi are only the spore-producing, reproductive bodies. In many fungi, the individual fruiting bodies are microscopic or scarcely visible to the naked eye but are typically produced in great numbers and together form masses large enough to be readily seen. The structure and in many cases the color of the fruiting body is distinctive for different species. Thus, the fruiting body is of great importance in the identification of fungal organisms.

Most true fungi are obligate saprophytes but many are facultative parasites and a few are obligate parasites. Although most species are aerobic, a few are facultatively anaerobic. Fungi develop best in the presence of abundant moisture, in temperatures between 20°C and 25°C, and with abundant food supply. Fungi absorb their food in predigested form. The substratum supporting mycelial growth is gradually decomposed by extracellular enzymes secreted by the fungal hyphae, and the dissolved matter is then absorbed. Hyphae remain constant in diameter and grow by increasing their length at the tips or by forming branches. Some types of fungi that parasitize plants develop special absorbing hyphae called **haustoria** which penetrate into the interior of the host's cells. It has been found that different species of fungi exhibit a variety of responses to light. Vegetative growth in some is inhibited by light, in others it may be accelerated, or in still others it may be unaffected. For the vast majority of fungi, we have no information on the influence of light. The formation and growth of sporangia and fruiting bodies is also variously affected by light in different species.

Reproductive Characteristics Reproduction of fungi is most frequently carried out by asexual processes, chief among which is the production of spores. Sexual reproduction occurs in most species only once a year and then usually after the mature mycelium has already produced many new generations asexually. Asexually produced spores are of two types, **conidia** and **sporangiospores.** Conidia are pinched off one at a time from the exposed tips of hyphae and often occur in short chains. Sporangiospores are produced enclosed within saclike structures called sporangia. Conidia are never motile, but sporangiospores may be motile or nonmotile, depending on the

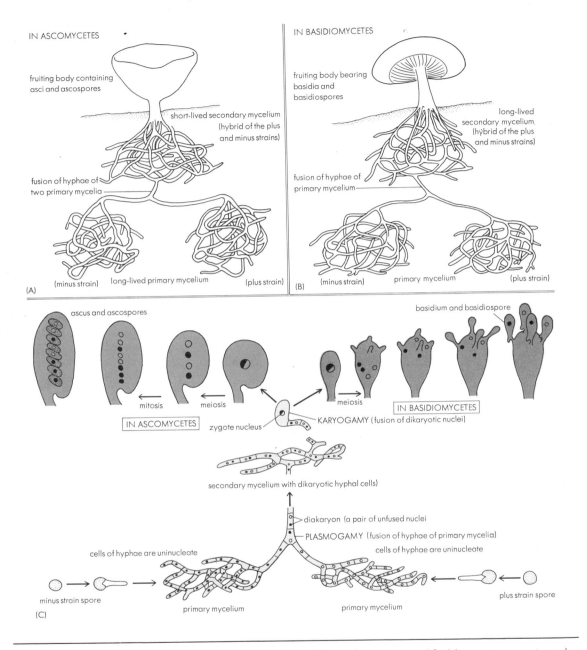

FIG. 23-5. Generalized steps in sexual reproduction of the *Eumycophyta*, as exemplified by an ascomycete and a basidiomycete. A. Outline of sexual reproduction in a cup fungus (ascomycete). B. Outline of sexual reproduction in a mushroom (basidiomycete). C. Composite diagram of the microscopic detail of some of the major events in sexual reproduction in a cup fungus and a mushroom.

species. Unlike asexually formed spores whose genetic make-up is identical to that of the parent mycelium, sexually formed spores bear genetic combinations that are different from those of the parent mycelia. Sexual reproduction in fungi (Fig. 23-5) involves a merging of vegetative hyphae followed by a succession of stages each characterized by a certain nuclear behavior or condition. In the merging of the protoplasts of two hyphae, a process termed **plasmogamy,** compatible nuclei of two strains are brought together within one protoplast. For varying lengths of time, they remain as pairs of closely associated but unfused nuclei. Such a pair is termed a **dikaryon.** The members of a dikaryon then undergo repeated mitotic divisions to produce additional dikaryons. Ultimately, the dikaryotic nuclei fuse to form a zygote nucleus which is diploid; this fusion is termed **karyogamy.** Later, the zygote nucleus undergoes meiosis, and each of the resulting haploid nuclei participate directly (or after mitotic duplications) in the formation of spores. The spores are formed within or on special structures that are distinctive for each fungus division; these structures, in turn, are borne on fruiting bodies. The variety in size, shape, and color of fungal spores is very great and exceeds that of any other plant group. In addition to reproduction by spores, virtually all fungi can and often do reproduce themselves by means of vegetative propagation. This is accomplished usually by fragmentation or, in unicellular species, by budding or cell division.

Representative Classes of Eumycophyta   The true fungi are separated into nine classes of which we will study only five, namely the (1) Oomycetes; (2) Zygomycetes; (3) Ascomycetes; (4) Basidiomycetes; and (5) Deuteromycetes.

CLASS OOMYCETES (THE WATER MOLDS, WHITE RUSTS AND DOWNY MILDEWS)

Both unicellular and filamentous species occur in this class of true fungi. The mycelium of the filamentous species consists of coenocytic hyphae in which septa are formed only at the bases of reproductive organs. The unifying characteristic of the class is the production of biflagellate spores by all members. These spores are produced mitotically in sporangia which are modifications of hyphal tips and which in some cases are deciduous. In unicellular species the entire thallus changes into a sporangium. At the time of sexual reproduction most multicellular species produce morphologically distinct antheridia and oogonia which are formed on special hyphal branches. In unicellular species, the entire thallus is converted into a male or female gametangium. No motile gametes are produced by members of this class, and cellulose appears to be the chief component of their cell walls. Recent investigations of the life cycle of certain Oomycetes have indicated that the class may be unique among the true fungi in having diploid mycelia with the gametes the only haploid cells in the life cycle.

Habitat and Distribution   Some Oomycetes live in water, others in the soil, and others (the most advanced species) as parasites on seed plants. In these habitats the various species may be facultative or obligate parasites or saprophytes.

Representative Members   The Oomycetes that grow in water, the water molds, are widely distributed, and they are commonly described as examples of the class. Of these, *Saprolegnia* (Fig. 23–6) is representative. The mycelium of *Saprolegnia* consists of diaphanous, cottony, coenocytic hyphae which invade and envelop the bodies of dead insects, seeds, or other organic objects in the water. Asexual reproduction begins when an elongate, ovoid sporangium forms at the tip of a vegetative hypha. A sporangium is formed when a multinucleate mass of cytoplasm accumulates at a hypha tip and becomes isolated from the rest of the hypha by a cross wall. Inside the young sporangium, the nuclei, each surrounded by a small quantity of cytoplasm, become isolated from each other by walls to form spores. When

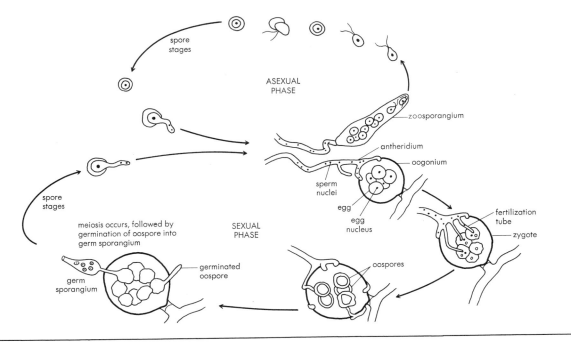

FIG. 23–6.   Life cycle of the water mold, *Saprolegnia*, an oomycete.

the spores have matured, a pore develops at the tip of the sporangium and the pear-shaped, **primary spores** escape. Each has two anterior flagella, one whiplash and one tinsel. These spores swim about and then encyst; later, each produces a kidney-shaped, **secondary spore** with two lateral flagella. These also swim about and then encyst. Finally these encysted spores germinate and produce hyphae, the growth of which initiates new mycelia.

Sexual reproduction occurs when conditions are no longer favorable for asexual reproduction or when other conditions stimulate the organism to undergo sexual reproduction. When this happens, the vegetative hyphae produce antheridia and oogonia, sometimes on the same hypha and sometimes on different hyphae. Antheridia and oogonia develop from vegetative cells whose protoplasm has undergone repeated divisions to form smaller nucleated units which serve as sperm or eggs. Antheridia come into contact with an oo-

gonium, pores are formed in the oogonial wall, and fertilization tubes grow from the antheridia to the eggs. Karyogamy occurs immediately after plasmogamy to produce diploid zygotes. The wall of each zygote thickens, converting it into an **oospore** which enters a period of dormancy. Eventually, the oogonial wall disintegrates, liberating the oospores, each of which develops a hypha that forms a sporangium at its tip. Diploid spores from this sporangium produce new mycelia.

Relationship to Other Organisms   The origins of the Oomycetes are obscure. According to various theories, they could have originated from either algal or protozoan stock. The number and the kinds of flagella they have seems to some authorities to indicate close relationship with either the brown or the chrysophycean algae, both of which also have biflagellated cells exhibiting whiplash and tinsel-type flagella.

Importance in Nature and in Human Life In nature, Oomycetes play an important role as decomposers. All bodies of water, both fresh and marine, invariably are found to contain water molds living on plant and animal debris. Water mold infections of living fish and fish eggs are the cause of heavy losses among fish populations in natural bodies of water and in hatcheries and farm fish ponds. Some species of water molds subsist on the organic wastes of sewage and if, therefore, they are found in a city's water supply, they provide evidence of contamination by sewage. The economy and the history of man have been seriously affected by the activities of certain Oomycetes. Oomycetes cause the downy mildew diseases of grapes, onions, tobacco, lettuce, sugar cane, and other crop plants. Particularly significant is the historical fact that the wine industry of France was almost totally destroyed by the oomycete *Plasmopara viticola.* The disease was brought under control by the timely and inadvertent discovery in Bordeaux in 1882 of a solution of copper sulfate, lime and water (Bordeaux mixture) which inhibited the growth of the fungus. Another oomycete, *Phytophthora infestans,* is the cause of the late blight disease of the white potato. During 1845, 1846, and 1847, because of a series of unusual climatic conditions, the growth of this fungus was so great that it destroyed the potato crops of much of Europe and eastern North America. In Ireland where a large proportion of the people subsisted almost entirely on potatoes, a nationwide famine occurred resulting in the death of 500,000 people and the emigration of another two million to England and the Western Hemisphere, representing a loss of more than a quarter of Ireland's population.

CLASS ZYGOMYCETES (THE BREAD MOLDS AND FLY FUNGI)

General Characteristics The Zygomycetes include the common bread molds and the fly fungi, as well as a host of other forms which live in soil and on manure. Their name is based on the fact they produce resting spores called **zygospores** following plasmogamy and karyogamy. More often, however, most members are recognized by their asexually produced sporangia. The thalli are filamentous and form extensive mycelia, except for the parasitic species in which the thallus consists of large individual cells or clusters of cells. The hyphae are generally coenocytic, but as a mycelium grows older, they become septate and in some species both young and old hyphae may be septate. No flagellated cells are produced. Chitin is the chief component of the wall, although cellulose may also be present. Sexual reproduction is achieved by the fusion of gametangia that are identical in form and often in size. Asexual reproduction is by means of sporangiospores or conidia.

Habitat and Distribution Zygomycetes are predominantly terrestrial organisms. The vast majority are saprophytes living on dung or in soil on the decaying organic matter of plants and animals. Many are predaceous—trapping, killing, and digesting round worms (nematodes) and amoebae. Others are parasites on green plants, or they may live in partnership with green plants as symbionts in their root systems.

Representative Members The best-known representative of the Zygomycetes is the bread mold *Rhizopus stolonifer* (Fig. 23–7). The fungus is **heterothallic;** that is, sexual union will occur only between hyphae from two genetically different mycelia. These different breeding strains of mycelia are commonly designated as "plus" and "minus" strains. Recent studies show clearly that each strain secretes at least three sets of hormones which act as attractants to the opposite strain to induce union through the formation of conjugating sexual hyphae. Sexual reproduction occurs as follows: when different strains of mycelia come into proximity, they mutually evoke formation of sexual hyphae. The tips of these hyphae, called **progametes,** abut, and each soon becomes enlarged and filled with many

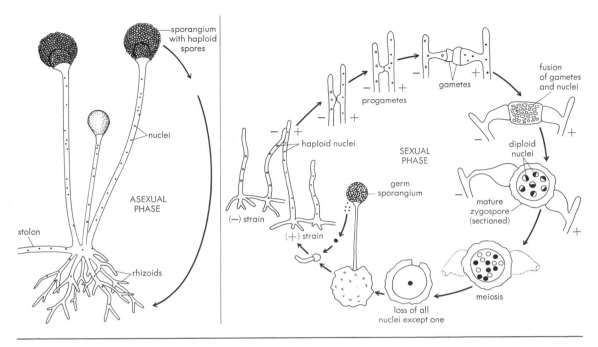

FIG. 23-7. *Rhizopus* life cycle.

nuclei and cytoplasm which move into it from other portions of the hypha. The progametes grow in length and diameter, and the terminal portion of each is cut off from the rest of the hypha by a wall. These terminal portions then behave as gametes: the wall between them disintegrates,

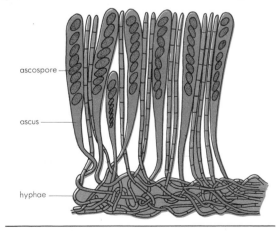

FIG. 23-8. Asci and ascospores of a sac fungus.

plasmogamy occurs and is quickly followed by fusions of nuclei of the two different strains. As a result, many zygote nuclei are formed. The structure containing these nuclei is the zygospore, and it develops a thick, resistant wall. One to three months later, the zygospore germinates; at the same time meiosis takes place, producing many haploid nuclei but of these, all but one abort. This remaining nucleus, either a plus or minus type, then undergoes many mitotic divisions to produce many plus or minus nuclei. A single hypha is produced which develops a sporangium at its tip. Within this sporangium cytoplasmic cleavage occurs around each of the nuclei resulting in formation of numerous plus or minus spores. Germination of these results in the development of plus or minus mycelia.

Relationship to Other Organisms   The origin of the Zygomycetes is unknown. Some think that they arose from the Oomycetes; others suggest they evolved from protozoanlike ancestors.

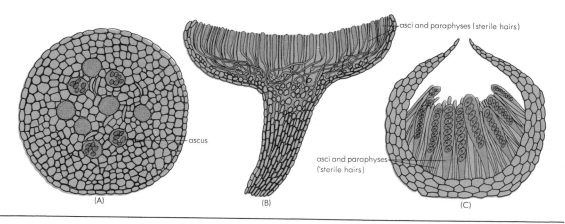

FIG. 23-9. Three common types of sexually produced ascocarps or fruiting bodies found among ascomycetes. A. cleistothecium. B. apothecium. C. perithecium.

CLASS ASCOMYCETES

General Characteristics This largest class of fungi includes at least 30,000 species with great diversity of structure, size, nutrition, and reproduction. Many of them are of great economic importance in industry and agriculture, and several are exceedingly valuable in medicine. The classes Ascomycetes and Basidiomycetes are commonly referred to as the higher fungi because they have evolved greater complexity than the fungi considered so far. Most species are filamentous with profusely branched hyphae, but a few species, such as the yeasts, are unicellular. The unifying characteristic that distinguishes Ascomycetes from all other fungi is the **ascus** (plural, asci), a saclike structure within which meiospores are produced (Fig. 23-8). Commonly, asci are

FIG. 23-10. Microscopic details of the sexual and asexual reproductive cycles of an ascomycete. *Left:* Asexual cycle. *Right:* Sexual cycle showing plasmogamy, karyogamy, and ascospore formation. The fruiting bodies which contain these structures are not shown.

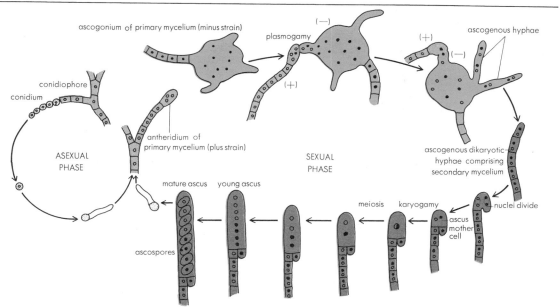

borne on fruiting bodies called **ascocarps** of which there are three basic forms: (1) the apothecium (Fig. 23–9,A) which is cup shaped and in which the asci line the inner surface of the cup; (2) the cleistothecium (Fig. 23–9,B), which is spherical and in whose central cavity a cluster of asci are produced; and (3) the perithecium (Fig. 23–9,C) a more or less flask-shaped structure with an apical opening and a cluster of asci in the basal part. The general pattern of sexual reproduction (Fig. 23–10) found in many Ascomycetes is as follows. The hyphae of a developing ascocarp form male antheridia and female ascogonia. Depending on the species, these antheridia and ascogonia, and the hyphae which produced them, may be of the same strain or of two genetically different strains. Each ascogonium produces a hairlike extension that makes contact with an antheridium. A pore develops at the point of contact and through this the male nuclei of the antheridium migrate, mingling with the female nuclei but not fusing with them. The ascogonium forms fingerlike extensions termed ascogenous hyphae into which the ascogonial and antheridial nuclei migrate. Here the nuclei divide once, following which septa are laid down in the hypha in such a way that each cell contains two nuclei, one from the ascogonium and one from the antheridium. The tip of each ascogenous hypha forms a hook-shaped cell whose two nuclei undergo mitosis. Septa are formed which isolate two nuclei, one male and one female, in a cell called the ascus mother cell. These nuclei fuse, and the resulting zygote nucleus immediately undergoes meiosis to form four haploid nuclei. The ascus mother cell enlarges, and the nuclei may be either directly embodied in four **ascospores** or they may each divide by mitosis producing eight nuclei which are then embodied in eight ascospores. The enlarged ascus mother cell becomes the ascus. In the majority of Ascomycetes the ascogenous hyphae branch a number of times, each branch becoming an ascus, with the result that clusters of asci are formed. These clusters are produced within the ascocarp which is constructed of the interwoven somatic hyphae of the mycelium (Fig. 23–11). Ascospores are released from the ascus simply by its disintegration or, as occurs in a large number of Ascomycetes, they are forcibly ejected. The mechanisms for forcible discharge are influenced and triggered by changes in temperature, light, relative humidity, and air currents.

Asexual reproduction is most commonly achieved by means of conidia (Fig. 23–12) borne on special hyphae that may arise individually on somatic hyphae or may be organized into definite fruiting bodies of various forms. No motile cells are produced by any Ascomycetes, not even by aquatic species.

The mycelium of Ascomycetes is composed of cells which have haploid nuclei. The cells are often uninucleate but multinucleate cells occur in some mycelia. The zygote nucleus constitutes the entire diploid phase of an Ascomycete. A large proportion of the hyphal walls is composed of chitin.

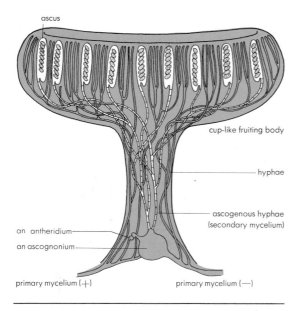

ascus

cup-like fruiting body

hyphae

ascogenous hyphae
(secondary mycelium)

an antheridium

an ascognonium

primary mycelium (+)   primary mycelium (—)

FIG. 23–11. A cut-away view of the internal organization of a cup fungus (ascomycete) showing the growth and formation of ascogenous hyphae and the cup-like fruiting body containing the asci.

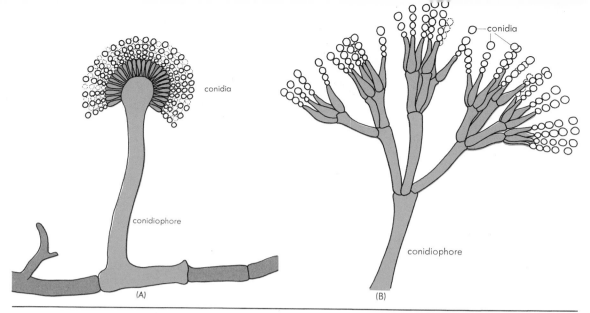

FIG. 23-12.   Two types of conidiophores. A. *Aspergillus*. B. *Penicillium*.

Representative Members and Their Economic Importance   The order Endomycetales includes the **yeasts,** essentially unicellular, spherical or ovoid fungi in which reproduction is chiefly asexual by budding. In budding, a blob of protoplasm squeezes out of a cell through a hole in the wall and forms a naked bud. At the same time, the nucleus of the cell divides, and one daughter nucleus remains in the parent cell while the other passes into the bud. Later, as the bud enlarges, it lays down a cell wall and ultimately is cut off from the parent cell by a constriction that forms between the two. Often a daughter cell will itself produce a bud while it is still attached to the original parent cell, or the original cell will divide again to produce one or more additional buds. *Saccharomyces cerevisiae* (brewer's yeast) is an important species whose life cycle is shown in Fig. 23-13. Generations of ovoid, relatively larger, diploid cells alternate with generations of spherical, relatively smaller, haploid cells. It is the cells of the diploid generation that comprise the yeast cultures used commercially. The populations of cells in such cultures are continually enlarged by budding. If growth conditions for a population become less favorable, the nucleus of a diploid cell may undergo meiosis to form four haploid nuclei around which the cytoplasm cleaves to form four ascospores each with its own cell wall; the wall of the original cell thus forms the ascus. The ascospores are later released from the ascus and increase in number by budding, thereby forming a haploid population of cells. These cells are round and smaller than the ovoid cells of the diploid generation; they are of two different genetic strains or mating types, that is, plus and minus. After a period of vegetative reproduction by budding, cells belonging to different mating types will fuse to form diploid cells which by budding give rise to a diploid population.

If one were to make a list of all the economically valuable products that are obtained from yeasts, it would be extraordinarily long and varied. By far the most important use of yeast is in the manufacture of industrial alcohol which, except for water, is the most widely used raw material in the chemical industry. Yeasts, of

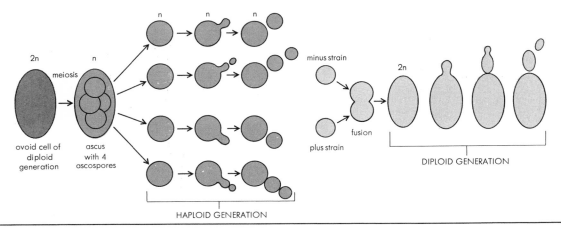

FIG. 23-13. Life cycle of brewer's yeast (*Saccharomyces cereviciae*). Haploid and diploid generations alternate.

course, are responsible, too, for the fermenting processes involved in manufacture of beer, wine, whiskeys, and other liquors. All these alcoholic compounds are a result of the highly controlled use of cultures of yeasts which, in their respiration, convert sugars to alcohol. Yeasts are also important sources for many of the vitamins of the B group and of vitamin D. Yeast contains about 50 percent protein, and when it is dried it is used as a food supplement for man and animals. Another valuable industrial compound obtained from culturing yeast is glycerol, although most of the glycerol of industry is obtained in the process of soap making. Carbon dioxide liberated during yeast respiration is used to leaven dough in the baking of bread. Some yeasts are parasites, and several species of the genus *Torula* are pathogens which cause serious diseases in man.

Another order, the Eurotiales, contains fungi whose bodies consist chiefly of loose masses of hyphae of indefinite extent that grow in and on the substratum. To this order belong the various bluish, greenish, and yellowish molds, chiefly of the genera *Penicillium* and *Aspergillus* which grow on foodstuffs, leather, and other organic materials in damp places. Reproduction of these fungi is most often by conidia. These conidia are variously colored, and the colors of these fungal colonies are due chiefly to their conidial masses (Fig. 23-12). The microscopic conidia are produced in enormous numbers; they are almost always present in air and dust, and when they encounter organic material and moisture, they quickly germinate. Thus, old shoes, wooden objects, books stored in a damp basement, or a stale lemon or orange left in a damp place will show growths of *Aspergillus* or *Penicillium*. Sexual reproduction of most species of *Penicillium* and of *Aspergillus* has not been observed.

Various members of the Eurotiales, notably certain species of *Aspergillus* and *Penicillium,* play extremely important roles in man's economy. These organisms are responsible for the spoilage of tremendous quantities of foods including fruits, vegetables, bread, and other baked goods. They produce discoloration and deterioration of paper, books, lumber, fabrics, leather, and other products. Some members have long been used to render beneficial services to man. *Penicillium roquefortii* and *P. camembertii* impart the characteristic odors and flavors to well-known types of cheese, and the bluish-green splotches in roquefort or blue cheese are masses of fungal conidia. In Japan, *Aspergillus* has been used for centuries in the manufacture of sake, a rice wine. This fungus converts the starch of the rice grains to sugar which is then acted on by yeasts to

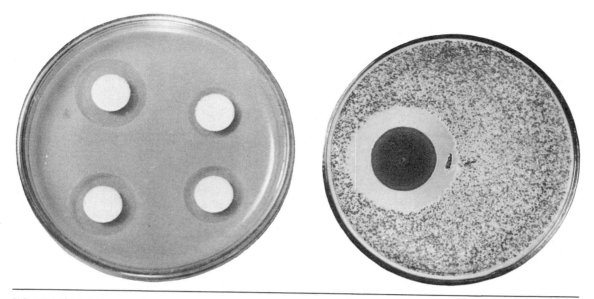

FIG. 23–14.   *Left:* Action of penicillin on bacteria. White filter paper discs containing penicillin solution are placed on agar culture of bacteria; penicillin diffusing from the discs destroys bacteria, leaving clear zones in the agar. The clouded portions of the agar have not been reached by the penicillin and still contain living bacteria. *Right:* Antibiosis between two species of *Penicillium.* The clear area on the agar medium is a zone of mutual antagonism, resulting from the secretion of antibiotic substances by these fungi.

produce alcohol. Another species of *Aspergillus* is used in the manufacture of citric acid which is widely utilized in industry. *Penicillium notatum* and *P. crysogenum* are important organisms from which we obtain penicillin, a "wonder drug" that exerts a strong inhibitory (bacteriostatic) effect on the growth of certain bacteria and, to a lesser extent, acts as a bactericidal agent (Fig. 21–14). Penicillin belongs to a group of organic substances called antibiotics, or substances that are synthesized by one kind of organism and that inhibit or destroy other kinds of organisms. Antibiosis often appears when two species of fungi grow in the same culture dish, where one often inhibits the growth of the other, or both may exert mutual inhibition (Fig. 23–14).

The order Erysiphales of the Ascomycetes includes the **powdery mildews,** which are parasites chiefly on leaves of higher plants, such as clovers, roses, lilacs, apples, dandelions, and grapes. The hyphae on leaf surfaces form asci enclosed by

small, usually dark-colored cleistothecia (Fig. 23–15) that are just large enough to be visible to the naked eye. Usually they are mild parasites causing slight damage to host plants, but a few species sometimes cause severe losses in grapes,

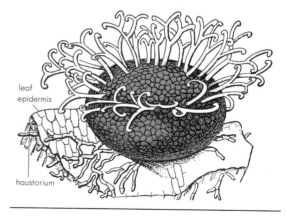

leaf epidermis

haustorium

FIG. 23–15.   Cleistothecium of a powdery mildew on the surface of a host leaf.

FIG. 23-16. Cup fungus (*Peziza*) on rotting wood.

cherries, cucumbers, and other cultivated plants.

The order Pezizales, the **cup fungi** (Fig. 23-16), is composed of saprophytic fungi that have fleshy, apothecial ascocarps. They are found commonly in soils and on dead trunks, branches, and stumps of trees, the decaying tissues of which are penetrated by the mycelia from which the visible reproductive bodies develop. These ascocarps vary in size from barely visible forms of only a few millimeters to large structures of 10 centimeters. In color they may be grayish white, dark brown, black, or brightly colored, especially in shades of red and orange. The ascocarps are cup shaped with the asci lining the inner surface of the cup. Morels (Fig. 23-17) are highly prized edible fungi that have stalked spongelike or saddle-shaped ascocarps.

FIG. 23-17. *Morchella esculenta* (morel) a fleshy, edible sac fungus. (Photo by W. R. Kennedy)

The order Sphaeriales contains the pink bread mold *Neurospora,* a saprophytic filamentous ascomycete widely referred to in biological publications because of the important role it has played in the study of biochemical genetics. It was in research using *Neurospora* that scientists were first able to show how genes control enzymes. The ascus of *Neurospora* is narrow and cylindrical in shape with the spores arranged in a single row. Their order in the row corresponds to the arrangement of the nuclei during the meiotic division of the zygote nucleus. Because of this, they provide an ideal means for elucidating the segregation of genetic characters. The fungus has also proved exceedingly useful in determining certain aspects of the biochemistry of metabolism.

Other orders of Ascomycetes include fungi of great biological or economic interest; among these are the parasites that cause such well-known plant diseases as Dutch elm disease, apple scab, apple canker, chestnut blight, oak wilt, and peach leaf curl. An ascomycetous fungus called ergot (*Claviceps*) causes a serious disease of rye and other cereals. The ergot disease transforms rye grains into enlarged purplish bodies filled with hyphae which contain an alkaloid called ergotoxine. If humans or animals ingest the contaminated grain, they develop ergotism, a disease which is partly characterized by eclampsia, or powerful, spasmotic contractions of smooth muscle, and which may result in agonizing death. Valuable drugs derived from ergot are often used at childbirth as stimulants that induce uterine contractions. Also in the Ascomycetes are the truffles, subterranean edible fungi that are frequently hunted by dogs or hogs trained to locate them by scent. Truffles are popular in Europe.

Relationship to Other Organisms   According to one view, Ascomycetes may be closely related to red algae because of similarities in structure and reproduction. Another interpretation holds that Ascomycetes are probable descendents of certain Zygomycetes. This view is based on similarities between the development of the ascus in

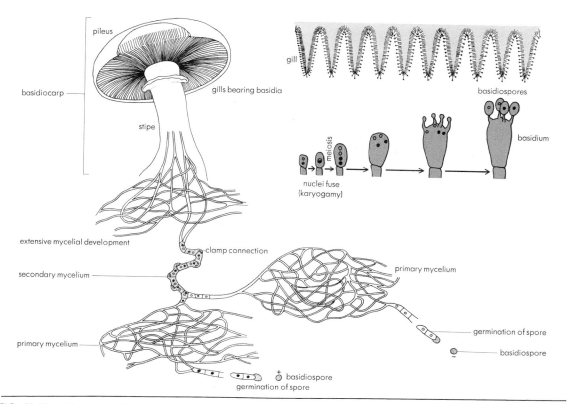

FIG. 23–18.   Life cycle of a mushroom (basidiomycete). Compare with Fig. 25–5, B and C, and Fig. 23–19.

certain primitive Ascomycetes and the development of the sporangium from the zygote in certain Zygomycetes. Whatever their origins may be from lower fungi, there is good evidence that the Ascomycetes are probably rather closely related to the Basidiomycetes. The two groups closely resemble each other in several characteristics; for example, the dikaryon, the formation of hook-shaped cells, and the development of their sexually produced asci and basidia.

CLASS BASIDIOMYCETES

General Characteristics   The Basidiomycetes comprise the second largest group of true fungi (25,000 species) and to it belong the large and conspicuous mushrooms, shelf fungi, puffballs, stinkhorns, and jelly fungi found in fields and woods. The group also contains many microfungi, among which are the economically important smuts and rusts. The unifying character common to all members of this class is the reproductive structure, the **basidium** (Figs. 23–5,C and 23–18). A basidium is usually an enlarged, terminal, club-shaped cell of a hypha. It develops four meiospores (rarely two) called **basidiospores** which at maturity are situated singly at the tips of minute stalks. In a minority of species a basidium is four-celled, each cell producing a single basidiospore. Basidiomycetes reproduce chiefly by basidiospores, but some species, such as the smuts, commonly propagate by conidia. No differentiated gametangia are formed, the sexual function being assumed by vegetative hyphae.

In the Basidiomycetes vegetative growth consists of a relatively short-lived primary mycelium

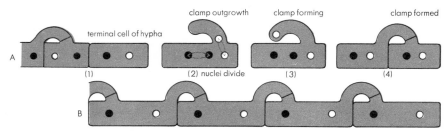

FIG. 23-19. Diagrams of the growth (A) and the appearance (B) of a hypha of the secondary mycelium of a basidiomycete showing the typical clamp connections. (A) Growth of hypha. (1) Terminal cell at right not yet divided, preceding cell at left already divided; (2) nuclei of terminal cell divide and a clamp-like outgrowth forms; (3) nuclear distribution occurs as shown; (4) clamp fuses with cell and walls are laid down, separating nuclei as shown. (B) Section of mature hypha showing clamp connections.

of uninucleate cells followed by a much longer-lived secondary mycelium of binucleate cells. The secondary mycelium of many species is perennial, periodically producing fruiting bodies called **ba-sidiocarps,** which bear basidia (Fig. 23-18). The organized, specialized tissues that comprise the fruiting bodies represent the tertiary mycelium. This is in contrast to the Ascomycetes, in which the uninucleate primary mycelial phase predominates; the binucleate ascogenous hyphae, constituting the secondary mycelial phase, are relatively short-lived. The life cycle of a common basidiomycete is shown in Fig. 23-18. The germination of a basidiospore produces hyphae of haploid uninucleate cells which form the primary mycelium. After a short period of growth, the hyphae of two compatible primary mycelia fuse (plasmogamy), and an extensive secondary mycelium is subsequently produced. The nuclei of the fusing hyphae remain distinct in the resulting cells as dikaryotic pairs, each nucleus of the dikaryon having come from one of the primary hyphae. As the secondary mycelium develops, cell formation is accompanied by simultaneous division of the dikaryotic nuclei, and their separation is such that each daughter cell remains binucleate. This distribution of the daughter nuclei is facilitated by a special outgrowth extending laterally from cell to cell, the clamp connection (Fig. 23-19). Clamp connections are characteristic for the secondary mycelia of the basidiomycetes.

After a period of extensive growth, the secon-dary mycelium forms hyphae in highly organized arrangements which result in the formation of the basidiocarps. These are quite varied in complexity, color, size, and texture according to the particular species and range from microscopic sizes to 3 feet or more in diameter. In texture they may be fleshy, corky, woody, papery, spongy, or gelatinous. A basidium typically develops from a two-nucleate cell at the tip of a hooked hypha in the basidiocarp (Fig. 23-18). As the cell enlarges, haploid nuclei of the dikaryon fuse (karyogamy) to form a single-diploid zygote nucleus that then divides meiotically to produce four haploid nuclei. The growing basidium produces four protuberances, into each of which one nucleus passes; when a nucleus reaches the apex of the protuberance, the tip enlarges and becomes walled off to form an uninucleate basidiospore. At maturity the basidiospores fall or are ejected from their stalks.

Representative Members and Their Economic Importance The order Agaricales includes a large number of saprophytic species whose fruiting bodies are commonly known as **mushrooms** or **toadstools.** They derive their nourishment from decomposing organic matter in soils and from dead leaves, dung, and dead or dying bark and wood. A small number of species are parasitic on seed plants. The vegetative body consists of a loose and perennial growth of hyphae (composing the secondary mycelium) that penetrates the

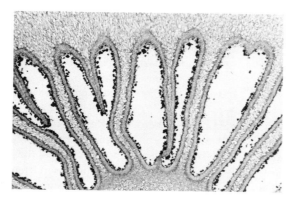

FIG. 23-20. Transverse section of *Coprinus pileus* (inky cap fungus) showing gills. The small black objects are basidiospores.

FIG. 23-21. A mushroom (*Pleurotus*) growing from tree trunk. Notice the gills. (Photo by Thomas W. Martin from Rapho Guillumette.)

soil, bark, or other substratum. When temperature and moisture conditions are favorable and the hyphae have absorbed sufficient food, the fruiting bodies grow upward or outward into the air and produce basidia and basidiospores. Spores are often produced in enormous numbers; a common field mushroom (*Agaricus campestris*) liberates about one million spores per hour for several hours. Basidiocarps of the Agaricales are commonly fleshy and less frequently woody. The largest family of Agaricales is the gill fungus family. In the **gill fungi,** the mature fleshy basidiocarp consists typically of a stalk, **stipe,** surmounted by a broad umbrella-shaped cap, the **pileus** (Fig. 23-18). On the undersurface of the

cap are **gills,** thin, radiating plates which bear basidia and basidiospores on their surfaces (Figs. 23-20 and 23-21). After the basidiospores are shed and if conditions are favorable, they germinate to form primary mycelia which by plasmogamy with other compatible primary mycelia produce secondary mycelia and so on (Fig. 23-18).

Another family of Agaricales is that of the **pore fungi,** whose basidiocarps often resemble those of mushrooms but differ from them in that the underside of the basidiocarp contains hundreds of tiny tubes, which appear as pores on the lower surface of the cap. The cap hyphae surrounding these tubes produce basidia and basidiospores; the latter escape through the pores and are dis-

FIG. 23-22. (a) Shelf-like basidiocarps of a pore fungus (*Fomes*). (b) Portion of basidiocarp of *Fomes* enlarged and sectioned on edge to show the mass of vertically oriented canals whose linings produce basidiospores which are then released through the porous horizontal surface here below the canals. (Photo by W. R. Kennedy.)

persed by wind and insects. Some pore fungi grow in soils, others are parasites or saprophytes on trees and stumps. The hyphae of the tree-inhabiting species secrete enzymes that digest the hard tissues of bark and wood and absorb organic compounds from these tissues. After a period of vegetative activity, these hyphae form basidiocarps that, in many species, grow horizontally as shelves from the surface of the tree trunk or post on which they grow. Such fungi, which are often tough and woody, are called shelf fungi or bracket fungi (Fig. 23–22).

Economic Importance of Agaricales   Many species of Agaricales are edible and are prized for their delicate aromas and flavors. Some edible species are extensively cultivated, especially the common mushroom, *Agaricus campestris*. Several species of mushrooms produce toxic compounds that poison humans or animals that eat them; often this poisoning results only in illness, but it sometimes causes death. Careful study and observation are necessary to distinguish among edible and poisonous species, and only persons who are thoroughly familiar with mushrooms can, with any degree of certainty, know whether wild mushrooms are safe to eat. Pore fungi are common and active agents of wood decomposition, and the parasitic species damage and kill

FIG. 23-23.   Puffballs on rotting wood. Notice the rhizomorphs (compact strands of vegetative hyphae) penetrating the wood.

trees. Among the important wood-rotting pore fungi is *Merulius lacrymans,* which causes a type of wood decomposition known as dry rot; this fungus is a common destructive agent of wood in buildings. Few species of pore fungi are poisonous, but most species are so tough that they cannot be eaten.

The order Lycoperdales includes the puffballs (Fig. 23–23) and related fungi, which are very similar to the Agaricales in many respects; they are chiefly saprophytes, obtaining their food from dead leaves, animal wastes, and decomposing bark and wood; their vegetative hyphae grow extensively through the soil or other substratum; and their fruiting bodies, at least when young, are fleshy. The principal difference between members of the Lycoperdales and those of Agaricales is in the structure of their basidiocarps, which in the lycoperdales are very often globose, pear shaped, or ovoid, with a rindlike surface layer. The basidia and basidiospores develop on hyphae beneath this layer which, at maturity, ruptures or opens by a pore to liberate the spores. The puffballs vary greatly in size, color, form, and texture in different species. In some species they are very small whereas in others they may attain diameters of 4 feet. No poisonous species of puffballs are known, and the young fleshy basidiocarps of many species are edible. As puffballs mature, they become dry and leathery or powdery and are no longer palatable. A sharp blow with a stick on a matured puffball causes a great cloud of spores to burst forth; a single large puffball may produce as many as 7,000,000,000,000 spores, about two thousand times the human population of the world.

Members of the order Ustilaginales are known commonly as smuts because of the sooty color of their spore masses. Smuts are obligate parasites chiefly of grasses, such as corn, oats, wheat, and barley. The bodies of smuts consist of irregular masses of hyphae in host tissues. The hyphae develop smut spores, especially in the ovary tissues of the hosts, so that the growing grains are usually transformed into sooty, ill-smelling

 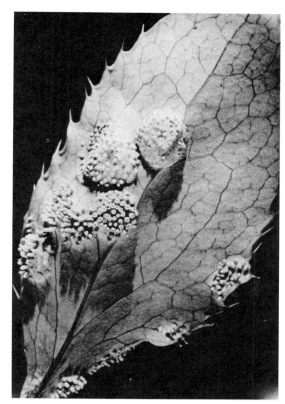

FIG. 23–24. (*Left*). Uredial stage of stem rust (*Puccinia graminis*, var. *tritici*) on wheat. FIG. 23–25. (*Right*.) Aecial stage of stem rust on wheat. Both photos courtesy of the Canada Dept. of Agriculture Research Station, Winnipeg.

masses of spores. The smut spores may infect other plants or may remain dormant until spring when they germinate, forming hyphae that produce basidiospores which then infect host plants. Smut fungi cause large crop losses in grains.

The rust fungi (order Uredinales) are obligate parasites of certain seed plants and ferns. They are called rusts because of the reddish-brown color of some of their spores, which are produced chiefly on the surfaces of host leaves and stems. A remarkable feature of the rusts is the fact that many of them must parasitize two different hosts in order to complete their sexual reproductive cycle, a condition known as **heteroecism.** One of the most destructive and most extensively studied rusts is *Puccinia graminis* var. *tritici,* the wheat

rust fungus. The hyphae of this fungus live in stem and leaf tissues of wheat plants in spring and summer. During the summer, they produce surface pustules called **uredia** (Fig. 23–24), which are many one-celled, reddish-brown spores **(urediospores)** that are carried by wind to other wheat plants where infection occurs. The spread of infection by urediospores is an asexual reproductive process sometimes called the "repeater stage" because new uredia (hence new urediospores and new infections) are produced at approximately two-week intervals through much of the summer. At about the time the wheat grains begin to mature, the uredia begin forming black **teliospores** in addition to urediospores. The proportion of teliospores in new pustules increases

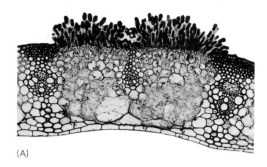

(A)

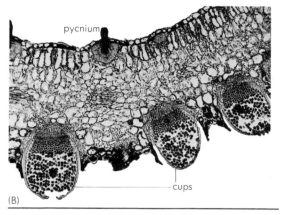

pycnium

cups

(B)

FIG. 23-26. Wheat rust. A. Teliospores breaking through epidermis of wheat leaf. B. Aeciospores forming in cups on barberry leaf. A pycnium protrudes from the upper epidermis. (Photos courtesy of Triarch Botanical Products.)

until they alone are produced. Pustules containing only teliospores are called **telia** (Fig. 23–26). Many of these two-celled, resistant teliospores remain on wheat stubble throughout the winter. Teliospores germinate in the spring and produce basidia and basidiospores. Basidiospores are then carried by wind to the common barberry, which becomes parasitized. The hyphae produced after basidiospore germination consist of uninuclear cells that grow in the internal leaf tissues, forming flask-shaped structures called **pycnia** (Fig. 23–26,B) that open onto the upper leaf surface and from which are produced small **pycniospores** and **receptive hyphae.** The same mycelium produces small masses of cells **(aecial primordia)** close to the lower leaf surface. When a pycnio-

spore of one physiological strain comes in contact with a receptive hypha of the opposite physiological strain, its nucleus migrates through a pore into the hyphal cell, where it divides. The wall separating adjacent hyphal cells has a small central perforation, through which one of the daughter nuclei migrates. Again the nucleus divides, and again one of the daughter nuclei migrates to the next cell. This process **(dikaryotization)** is repeated until virtually all the hyphal cells have become binucleate. Cells of the aecial primordia then begin to divide, forming both binucleate **aeciospores** and an outer, cellular jacket, collectively referred to as an **aecium.** The enlarging aecium ruptures the lower leaf epidermis, the cellular jacket splits open, and the aeciospores are released (Figs. 23–25 and 23–26,B). The sexual cycle is completed when the aeciospores are carried to wheat plants in the spring. The essential cytological details are shown in Fig. 23–27.

Wheat rust is an extremely virulent parasite, frequently causing extensive crop damage. Eradication of the barberry host has long been practiced as a means of control, especially in cooler regions of the temperate zone. The fungus is then unable to complete its sexual life cycle, for the urediospores ("summer spores") cannot survive cold winters, and the teliospores ("winter spores") and basidiospores cannot infect wheat plants. However, urediospores can survive the mild winters of the southern temperate regions and infect wheat plants in the spring. The summer spores are then carried northward by the wind. Most of the new races of rust fungus originate through hybridization, which is prevented by the destruction of barberry. However, the complete elimination of this alternate host would not stabilize the disease, since new races also originate through mutation. A second feasible approach to the problem of control is found in the disease resistance of certain wheat varieties. Extensive breeding programs are maintained to develop additional resistant varieties in an attempt to "keep ahead" of the disease.

Another common rust is cedar-apple rust,

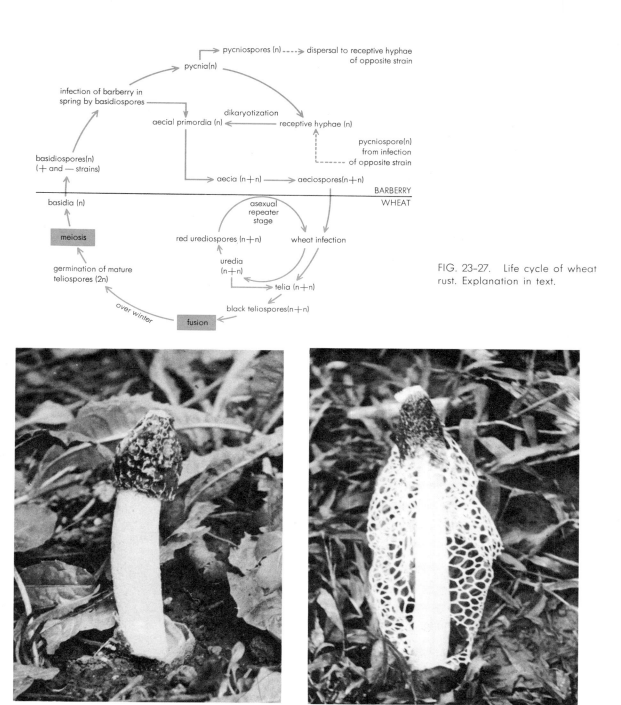

FIG. 23-27. Life cycle of wheat rust. Explanation in text.

FIG. 23-28. *Left:* Basidiocarp of a stinkhorn fungus (*Ithyphallus impudicus*), a member of the order Phallales of the basidiomycetes. *Right:* Basidiocarp of a net fungus (*Dictyophora phalloidea*), of the order Phallales.

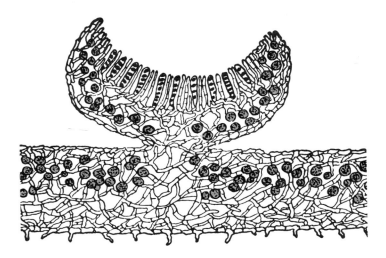

FIG. 23–29. Cross section of a lichen showing the small round algal cells enmeshed in the hypha of the fungus. The cup-shaped reproductive body bears asci with ascospores.

which lives for a part of the year on cedars and another part of the year on apples, hawthorns, and related plants. White pine blister rust alternates between white pine trees and wild gooseberries and currants; it causes serious damage to white pines and may be in part controlled by the eradication of the alternate hosts, the wild gooseberries and currants. Other species of rusts cause diseases of rye, oats, corn, pears, peaches, cherries, plums, firs, hemlocks, figs, coffee, asparagus, carnations, and snapdragons.

Other orders of Basidiomycetes include the bird's-nest fungi, in which the basidiocarps are cup shaped with enclosed ovoid basidia-producing bodies, and the stinkhorns, which have stalked basidiocarps with spongelike structures at the apices of their stalks (Fig. 23–28 shows examples). These spongelike caps bear the basidia and basidiospores and are covered by a slimy material that is greenish or brownish in color and has a vile stench attractive to flies; these crawl over the slimy caps and aid in the dispersal of spores. Closely related to the stinkhorns are the net fungi; in the latter, the basidia and spores are borne on the conspicuous and beautiful net.

Relationship to Other Organisms   Most mycologists regard the Basidiomycetes as a group of

fungi that have evolved from Ascomycetes, since the Basidiomycetes resemble Ascomycetes more closely than any other class of fungi. Their hyphal structure is similar, and the development of asci and of basidia is very similar in the two groups. In both groups of fungi, fusion of protoplasts from two cells occurs, bringing together compatible nuclei which will later fuse to form zygote nuclei. Most mycologists believe that a basidium is an evolutionary development from an ascus. The fact that some Ascomycetes produce asci, which, like the basidia have only four spores, is considered further evidence of relationship between these two classes of fungi.

CLASS DEUTEROMYCETES (IMPERFECT FUNGI)

The Deuteromycetes is a heterogeneous assemblage of many types of fungi which have only been observed to reproduce asexually, usually by conidia. In the absence of sexual stages (also called perfect stages) or marked resemblance to other groups, these species cannot be assigned to the other classes of fungi that have already been described. Mycologists generally believe that most imperfect fungi are Ascomycetes in which sexual reproduction has not been found or in which sexual stages never occur.

Some imperfect fungi are very important in human life. A number of species are parasitic on higher plants, causing serious diseases of apples, cabbage, corn, tomato, tobacco, celery, wheat, oats, citrus fruits, cowpeas, strawberries, flax, lettuce, peaches, garden beans, and many other crop plants. The imperfect fungi also include species that are parasites of man, causing a number of diseases, many of them very serious. The genus *Candida (Monilia)* includes species that cause pulmonary infections, diseases of the nails and of the mucous membranes of the genital organs, various types of skin diseases, sprue, a widespread intestinal disease of the tropics, and thrush, a disease of the throat and mouth. The imperfect fungi also include a group called Trichophytoneae, or ringworm fungi, which parasitize man and other animals, causing diseases of the hair follicles, hair, skin, nails, feathers, and horns. Many of the skin diseases caused by these fungi are known by such popular names as ringworm, barber's itch, and athlete's foot. These diseases are widespread and, although they infrequently become serious, they are irritating.

MYCORRHIZAE

One of the most interesting and important relationships between fungi and vascular plants is that found in mycorrhizae. A mycorrhiza is a compound structure composed of root tissue and fungus mycelium living together in physiological union. There are two general types of mycorrhizae: one in which the fungal hyphae grow intracellularly in the root tissue and one in which the fungal hyphae form a mantle over the root tips and grow between the cells of the outer regions of the root tip. Mycorrhizae are limited to those regions of the root tip that are young and not yet mature enough to have woody tissues present. Mycorrhizae occur in many species of trees, shrubs, and herbs in all parts of the world. There is abundant evidence that they are not an exceptional occurrence but may be the rule.

Fungi of mycorrhizae belong to the various classes of fungi already described. In woody plants the fungus is typically a basidiomycete. Roots of plants with mycorrhizae differ in certain structural features from those of plants without them. They are often short and thick, commonly lack root caps and root hairs, and they sometimes do not branch.

The physiological and biological significance of mycorrhizae is not fully understood. Some botanists regard mycorrhizal fungi as parasites on the roots they inhabit and thus consider mycorrhizae as purely pathological structures. Other botanists believe that the relationship between these fungi and the roots they inhabit is more complex than direct parasitism and that both fungi and roots benefit from their close association. According to this latter view, the fungi receive food from root tissues and in turn facilitate certain physiological activities of roots. Some investigators believe that these fungi may increase water absorption by roots, others that mycorrhizal fungi promote the absorption of certain organic nitrogenous substances from the soil or that they carry on nitrogen fixation in much the same manner as nitrogen-fixing bacteria. Studies of plants growing in the Amazon forests indicate that mycorrhizae may digest dead organic litter and pass minerals and food substances from their hyphae directly to living root cells. This direct cycling of minerals and organic compounds from dead leaf and wood litter back to the living trees and shrubs without dissolution into the soil appears to explain the presence of the lush climax forest growth of this tropical region even though the soils show nutrient deficiencies.

The view that the fungi have beneficial effect on roots is supported by a number of other observations and experiments. In some species of plants, particularly certain species of trees, shrubs, and orchids, the mycorrhizal association is seemingly universal; that is, it occurs in all individuals of the species. The invariability of this occurrence may be interpreted as indicating a condition of mutual benefit. Controlled experiments also have indicated that some species of higher plants derive benefit from the mycorrhizal

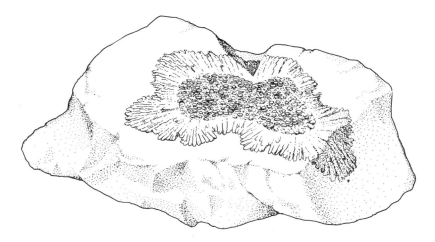

FIG. 23–30. Crustose lichen growing on a rock.

relationship. If seedlings of certain species of pine trees, for example, are grown in sterile soils or in soils that do not contain suitable species of mycorrhizal fungi, the growth of the seedlings is slow and weak; if the soil is inoculated with these fungi and if the fungi then infect the roots, the growth of the seedlings quickly and conspicuously improves.

LICHENS

Lichens, which are estimated to number about 15,000 species, are plants composed of an association of certain algae and fungi that live together in a close structural and physiological combination. Their relationship involves a mutual dependence of one on the other and is termed **symbiosis.** The fungus obtains foods, minerals, and some vitamins from the alga; its hyphae encircle the algal cells and permeate them with haustoria. This parasitism by the fungus is a mild one, the algal materials being extracted so gradually that several new generations of algae are formed before the old, infected ones die. The alga receives from the fungus water, minerals, and protection against high light intensities. Either alga or fungus is capable of living independently, and the association between the two exists only as long as

growth conditions are unfavorable for both. Structure of the lichen is determined by the fungus which is the dominant morphological partner (Fig. 23–29). The fungus is commonly an ascomycete and forms fruiting bodies characteristic of the Ascomycetes. These ascocarps are important features in identifying lichens. Less commonly the fungus is a basidiomycete. Algal components are chiefly members of the Cyanophyta (blue-green algae) and Chlorophyta (green algae). A lichen is a composite plant whose structure is quite different from that of either its algal or fungal component when these are grown separately under experimental conditions. Reproduction is by fragmentation of the lichen body or by **soredia.** Soredia appear as small powdery masses on the surface of the lichen and consist of a mass of hyphae enveloping one or more algal cells. Air currents disperse them to new habitats where they may develop into new plants. Both fungal and algal components can also reproduce independently, the fungus by means of the ascospores formed in the fruiting bodies and the alga by cell divisions.

There are three general types of lichens based on their gross appearance. If the lichen forms a crustlike growth closely appressed to the substratum, it is termed a **crustose** lichen (Fig. 23–30),

FIG. 23–31. Foliose thallus of the lichen *Parmelia caperata.* Numerous cup-like fruiting bodies are present. (Photo by W. R. Kennedy.)

if a leafy growth projecting from the substratum, a **foliose** lichen (Fig. 23–31), and if a branching, bushy growth mostly free from the substratum, a **fruticose** lichen (Fig. 23–32). Colors of lichens vary; some are grayish green, others are white, orange, yellow, yellowish-green, brown, or black. Commonly lichens occur on rocks, tree trunks (Fig. 23–33), certain types of poor soils, shingles, fence posts, and other unpainted weather-exposed objects. Some lichens are able to withstand low temperatures and long periods of drought. Such species are abundant on high mountain elevations, in the arctic tundra, in desert regions, and in many other environments where conditions are too severe for the growth of most other types of plants.

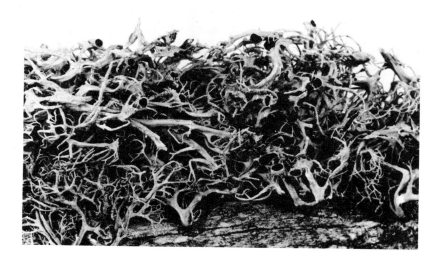

FIG. 23–32. Fruticose thallus of the lichen *Letharia vulpina.* (Photo by W. R. Kennedy.)

FIG. 23–33. Lichen growing on a tree. (Photo by Russ Kinne.)

ECONOMIC IMPORTANCE

Although they do not usually form a conspicuous part of the vegetation, except in such exposed habitats as those mentioned above, lichens play important roles in nature and in human life. Particularly noteworthy is the fact that they initiate soil-forming processes by disintegrating rock surfaces. They mechanically break off little pieces of rock when, during dry spells they lose water and contract, pulling up small bits of rock to which the moist lichen had tightly adhered. They also excrete organic acids that disintegrate the rock surface into small, loose particles. Such rock particles, together with bits of dead lichen, comprise a simple soil which serves as the substratum in which plants other than lichens may take root. Tundra lichens are valuable sources of food for reindeer, caribou, musk ox, and other animals.

In Lapland, Iceland, and other subarctic regions, as well as in India, Japan, and other parts of the Orient, lichens are harvested and dried to be used as human food and sometimes as food for cattle, swine, and horses. It is generally believed that the manna of the Bible was a lichen, *Lecanora esculenta*, which is still eaten by desert tribes of Asia Minor. Fragments of lichens found with foodstuffs in Egyptian tombs indicate that lichens were used as human foodstuffs in ancient Egypt. Assorted medicinal benefits have been ascribed since pre-Christian times to various lichens. They have been used in the treatment of jaundice, diarrhea, fevers, epilepsy, and skin diseases. Most of these supposed medicinal benefits are now known to be without scientific foundation; however, a lichen known as "Iceland moss" produces a mucilaginous substance that has some value as a laxative. It is also an ingredient in salves, puddings, and culture media for bacteria, as well as in sizings for paper. Some lichens produce dyes that have been used for centuries in coloring fabrics and paints. Among these dyes are orchil, a beautiful blue dye, used since pre-Christian times, cudbear, another blue dye, and various brown and yellow dyes. The dye known as litmus, used in chemical work as an indicator of acidity and alkalinity, is obtained from certain lichens. Some lichens contain tannins and are used for tanning animal hides in France and other European countries.

SUMMARY   1.   Members of the Myxomycophyta and Eumycophyta are nonchlorophyllous saprophytic or parasitic plants, most of which reproduce sexually.

2.   The Myxomycophyta, or slime fungi, possess both plantlike and animal-like characteristics. Their life cycle includes an animal-like stage, which has amoeboid movement and the ability to ingest solid food particles, and a plantlike stage with sporangia and spores.

3.   Myxomycophyta are chiefly saprophytes, occasionally parasites. The vegetative body consists of a naked, multinucleate plasmodium which eventually produces spores within sporangia. The spores germinate, producing microscopic myxamoeba and swarm cells that creep for a time, then fuse in pairs to form zygotes. A zygote grows into a new plasmodium. No hyphae are present.

4.   Eumycophyta comprise groups of fungi in which the body consists typically of fungus filaments, or hyphae, and in which no true plasmodia are formed.

5.   Eumycophyta are separated into nine classes, five of which are discussed in this chapter: Oomycetes, Zygomycetes, Ascomycetes, Basidiomycetes, and Deuteromycetes.

6.   Eumycophyta require moisture, favorable temperature and an abundance of organic matter for their growth. Most species are aerobic obligate saprophytes.

7.   Eumycophyta are important in nature and to man in many ways:
    a.   Some species produce enzymes, drugs, alcohols, organic acids, vitamins, and other substances useful in industry, medicine, and research.
    b.   Some species are eaten by man and other animals and have long been used to impart special flavors to cheeses.
    c.   Some species cause serious diseases of man, animals, and plants.
    d.   Some species cause food spoilage.
    e.   Some species cause rotting of wood, wood products, leather, fabrics, and other organic materials.
    f.   Most species cause decay of dead bodies and of animal dung, thus helping to rid the earth of this organic debris and contributing to the maintenance of soil fertility.

8.   Oomycetes, which include the water molds, white rusts, and downy mildews, range from unicellular forms to filamentous ones composed of loosely arranged coenocytic hyphae. The asexually formed spores are typically biflagellate; gametes are nonflagellate. Morphologically distinct gametangia are formed by most species.

9.   Zygomycetes, which include the bread molds and fly fungi, commonly have hyphae that are nonseptate and coenocytic and comprise the vegetative phase of the plant. The hyphae do not form compact bodies of definite shape but extend through or over the substratum in

loose mats of varying extent. Asexual reproduction is achieved by sporangiospores or conidiospores, sexual reproduction by zygospores. Many species are heterothallic.

10. Ascomycetes range from one-celled fungi to those in which the body consists of multicellular, septate hyphae. During their sexual reproduction all species produce small sacs called asci in which are enclosed usually eight ascospores. In many species asci are borne on special fruiting bodies termed ascocarps. which are of definite form for each species.

11. Among the familiar ascomycetes are yeasts, blue and green molds, powdery mildews, cup and sponge fungi, and truffles.

12. Basidiomycetes are many celled fungi, in which the hyphae have cross walls. The distinguishing characteristic of the group is the basidium, a reproductive structure that develops following nuclear fusion and that bears usually four basidiospores externally on stalks. In some species basidia are borne in or on fruiting bodies called basidiocarps. Conidia and related types of spores are produced in some species.

13. Among the familiar basidiomycetes are mushrooms, pore fungi, puffballs, rusts, and smuts.

14. Basidiomycetes are usually considered to have evolved from Ascomycetes.

15. Deuteromycetes, or imperfect fungi, are a miscellaneous group of species in which sexual or perfect stages do not occur or have not been found; most species are believed to be Ascomycetes in which sexual fusion and ascus formation have disappeared.

16. Mycorrhizae are symbiotic associations of certain fungi with roots of higher plants. Most mycorrhizae are believed to be mutually beneficial associations, in which fungi obtain nutrients from the roots and promote the absorption by the root of water or organic nitrogen compounds.

17. Lichens are symbiotic associations of certain algae and fungi. It is thought that the fungus obtains foods, minerals, and some vitamins from the alga, while the alga, in turn, receives water, minerals, and protection against high light intensities.

SUGGESTED READINGS FOR INTERESTED STUDENTS

1. Alexopoulos, Constantine J., *Introductory Mycology,* 2 ed. Wiley, New York, 1962.

2. _____, and Harold C. Bold, *Algae and Fungi.* The Macmillan Co., New York, 1967.

3. Ahmadjian, Vernon, *The Lichen Symbiosis.* Blaisdell, Waltham, Mass., 1967.

4. Ahmadjian, Vernon, "The fungi of lichens." *Scientific American,* Vol. 208, No. 2, pp. 122–132, February 1963.

5. Atkinson, George F., *Mushrooms,* 2 ed. Hafner, New York, 1961.

6. Christensen, Clyde M., *The Molds and Man.* University of Minnesota Press, Minneapolis, Minn., 1951.

7. ———, *Common Fleshy Fungi,* rev. ed. Burgess, Minneapolis, Minn., 1955.

8. Garrett, S. D., *Soil Fungi and Soil Fertility.* The Macmillan Co., New York, 1963.

9. Gray, William D., *The Relation of Fungi to Human Affairs.* Holt, Rinehart and Winston, New York, 1959.

10. Ingold, C. T., *Dispersal in Fungi.* Oxford University Press, New York, 1953.

11. Smith, Alexander H., *The Mushroom Hunter's Fieldguide,* rev. ed. University of Michigan Press, Ann Arbor, Mich., 1963.

TOPICS AND QUESTIONS FOR STUDY

1. List the principal differences between bacteria and true fungi.

2. List the distinguishing characteristics of Myxomycophyta.

3. Why do some biologists regard Myxomycophyta as animals? As plants?

4. Describe the life history of a typical slime fungus.

5. How are slime fungi important in human life?

6. List the differences between Eumycophyta and Myxomycophyta.

7. Comment on the distribution of Eumycophyta in nature. What environmental conditions are essential to their growth?

8. Define the following terms: saprophyte, parasite, autotrophic, heterotrophic, obligate parasite, facultative parasite, hypha, and mycelium.

9. Since the beginning of World War II, U.S. government agencies have conducted extensive investigations on fungous growth in the tropics. How might such fungi affect the operations of a military force?

10. List all the major ways in which fungi influence human life.

11. How are fungi important in nature?

12. Comment on this statement: In one major respect, fungi are more like animals than they are like plants.

13. How does the exchange of gases between fungi and the atmosphere differ from that between green plants and the atmosphere?

14. Describe briefly the structure and reproduction of Oomycetes.

15. List some of the economic importances of the Oomycetes.

16. Describe briefly the structure and reproduction of Zygomycetes.

17. Describe the life cycle of *Rhizopus stolonifera.* Why are the gametes of this fungus not called eggs and sperms?

18. A loaf of bread as it comes from a hot oven is sterile. Within a few hours after cooling, however, bread mold may begin to grow on it. From where does the fungus come?

19. Name some Zygomycetes that are important in human life.

20. State the ideas concerning the evolutionary origin of Zygomycetes.

21. Characterize briefly the Ascomycetes.

22. Describe briefly the development and structure of an ascus.

23. It has been said that many Ascomycetes are losing their ability to reproduce sexually. Explain.

24. List and describe briefly the common asexual reproductive methods of Ascomycetes.

25. Name some of the principal orders of Ascomycetes and distinguish among them.

26. Make a complete list of the ways in which Ascomycetes influence human life.

27. Describe briefly a *Penicillium* fungus, and describe how species of this genus are important to man.

28. State the present ideas concerning the relationships of Ascomycetes.

29. Describe briefly the development and structure of a basidium. How does a basidium differ from an ascus?

30. Name the principal orders of Basidiomycetes, and characterize them briefly.

31. Describe the structure, nutrition, and reproduction of a typical mushroom; of a pore fungus.

32. What is the generally accepted idea concerning the evolutionary origin of Basidiomycetes?

33. Characterize the Deuteromycetes. Why is this class sometimes called the "fungal wastebasket"?

34. How do members of the Deuteromycetes affect human life?

35. Describe the structure of mycorrhizae and summarize the ideas concerning the physiology of mycorrhizae.

36. Contrast symbiosis and antibiosis.

37. Describe the structure and reproduction of lichens. What are the physiological relationships between the algal and fungal components of lichens?

38. Describe briefly the importance of lichens in nature and in human life.

39. List as many similarities as you can between algae and fungi. Name some algal and fungal species (or orders) that strikingly resemble each other.

40. Most of the hyphae of a mushroom are subterranean, but the basidiocarps grow upward into the air before their spores mature. Of what advantage is this behavior?

41. How would you proceed to grow mushrooms commercially?

42. The hyphae of fungi are slender, soft, delicate structures, yet they are able to penetrate with ease such hard materials as wood. Explain.

24

EMBRYOPHYTA: BRYOPHYTA (MOSSES, LIVERWORTS, AND HORNWORTS)

EMBRYOPHYTA AS A WHOLE

The plant divisions that remain to be studied are members of the **Embryophyta,** the second of the two plant subkingdoms. Plants of the Embryophyta have the following characteristics in common.

1. The gametangia of the Embryophyta are always multicellular. Male gametangia are called **antheridia,** as in the thallophytes; female gametangia are termed **archegonia.** Each of these re-

productive structures possesses an outer wall of sterile cells that provides nutrients and protection for the gametes, zygote, or developing embryo within. In contrast, thallophyte gametangia are unicellular or, if multicellular, lack sterile walls. The absence of gametangia in many seed-bearing embryophytes is thought to have resulted from evolutionary reduction of an ancestral stock that had multicellular gametangia.

2. The zygotes in all Embryophyta are retained in the female gametangia, or elsewhere in the

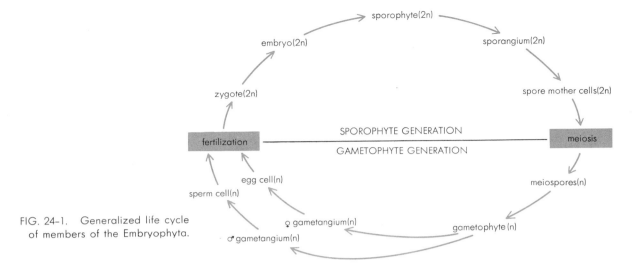

FIG. 24-1. Generalized life cycle of members of the Embryophyta.

female gametophyte if archegonia are lacking, where they develop parasitically into multicellular embryos. Retention of the zygote has several advantages for life on land, chief among which is protection of the embryo from desiccation and mechanical injury. This is in striking contrast to the condition in the green algae which are believed to have given rise to the embryophytes. In green algae, the zygote is released soon after fertilization and survives in the surrounding medium as a single, free cell having a protective wall and a small supply of stored food. It appears that one of the first and very necessary adaptations for survival on land was the establishment of a protective structure, initially the archegonium, for housing the zygote and, subsequently, the embryo.

3. All embryophytes have heterogamous sexual reproduction.

4. All members of the Embryophyta have the potential for regular (usually annual) alternation of generations. In the reproductive cycle, the diploid sporophyte plant produces diploid **spore mother cells.** These undergo meiosis to produce haploid spores (meispores), and the spores produce **gametophyte** plants which form gametangia and gametes. Fusion of gametes produces the diploid zygote which grows into the **sporophyte** plant. The change from diploid to haploid conditions occurs with formation of meiospores, and the change from the haploid to the diploid chromosome number occurs with the fertilization of an egg by a sperm. A diagram of a typical embryophytic life cycle is presented in Fig. 24–1.

5. All members have multicellular sporangia whose walls consist of one or more layers of sterile cells.

In addition to these features found in all members of the Embryophyta, *most* members of this subkingdom have certain other characteristics, among which are the following.

1. They are chiefly land plants, with few species living in water.

2. They possess the vascular tissues xylem and phloem and, because of this, are considered to have true roots, stems, and leaves (the exception being the Bryophyta which lack such elaborate conducting tissues).

3. The sporophytes and often the gametophytes have a cuticle. The cuticle is exceedingly important in land plants, since it conserves moisture and thus retards drying of leaves and other organs exposed to air.

4. They possess chloroplasts whose pigments are the same as those of green algae, and they also produce true starch.

5. The sporophyte is larger and more complex (that is, dominant) than the gametophyte (with the exceptions of the bryophytes).

DIVISION BRYOPHYTA
(MOSSES AND ALLIES)

General Characteristics This division, with approximately 900 genera and 23,600 species, consists of the mosses and their allies, all of which are small plants that rarely exceed 20 centimeters in height or length (Fig. 24–2). In all embryophytes other than the Bryophyta, the sporophyte generation forms the conspicuous and vegetatively dominant plant body; it is the sporophyte that typically has vascular tissue and the relatively large photosynthetic, supportive, and storage organs. In the bryophytes, however, it is the gametophyte generation that forms the more conspicuous and longer-lived plant body performing the functions of photosynthesis, support, and storage. However, the gametophyte generation of the bryophytes (as of most other Embryophyta) lacks xylem and phloem, and this absence of vascular tissues for support and rapid water conduction limits the gametophyte's growth potential. Thus, the typical, vascularized organs of higher plants—root, stem, and leaf—are lacking in bryophytes. Instead, the bryophyte gametophyte has "substitute" parts that superficially resemble these organs (Figs. 24–4 and 24–9). Their function is the same as that of the roots, stems, and leaves of vascular Embryophyta, but their complexity, by comparison, is far less. The majority of species have short, slender, stemlike structures that bear tiny, green, leaflike scales. Hairlike anchoring structures, called rhizoids, attach the plant to its substrate and resemble roots in appearance, but in most bryophytes the rhizoids have little or no absorptive function. Cuticle development in the gametophyte is slight or absent, and the plants are, therefore, subject to dessication during dry

FIG. 24–2. *Polytrichum ohioense*—entire plant with sporophyte growing out of the leafy gametophyte. Inset shows the hairy capsule covering typical of the genus. (Photo by W. R. Kennedy.)

periods, but when moisture again becomes available, this lack of cuticle permits rapid reabsorption of moisture by all surfaces. The sporophyte generation grows parasitically on the gametophyte and consists primarily of a spore-bearing capsule which is usually supported by a stalk that is embedded in the gametophyte plant (Figs. 24–4, 24–12, and 24–16).

Reproductive Characteristics A single gametophyte may produce both archegonia and antheridia (monoecious species), or archegonia and antheridia may be borne on separate female and male gametophytes (dioecious species). An antheridium is typically ovoid or cylindrical and produces numerous sperms (Figs. 24–3,A and 24–11).

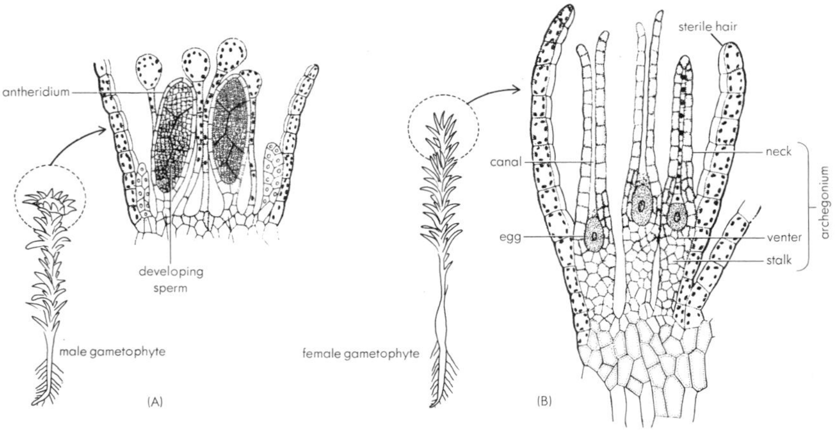

FIG. 24-3. Gametophytes and gametangia of moss (*Polytrichum* sp.). (A) Male gametophyte bearing at its tip antheridia and sterile hairs, shown enlarged. (B) Female gametophyte bearing at its tip archegonia and sterile hairs, shown enlarged.

An archegonium is usually shaped like a bowling pin, with a long slender **neck** and a somewhat enlarged hollow base **(venter),** within which a single egg is produced (Figs. 23–3,B and 24–12). When an archegonium is mature, its neck develops a central canal, which opens at the apex of the neck. Sperms reach the archegonia by swimming through water or by being carried to the archegonia in splashed water; they then swim through the neck canal to the venter, where a single sperm fertilizes the egg. The zygote then undergoes cell division and begins to grow into the embryo sporophyte *within the archegonium.* During its growth, the embryo develops a basal structure called a **foot,** which becomes embedded in the gametophyte tissue and absorbs nutrients and water from it. The upper part of the young embryo ultimately becomes the major part of the sporophyte, which commonly consists of a stalk **(seta)** and at the apex of the stalk a **capsule,** within which spore mother cells are produced, reduction division occurs, and meiospores are formed (Fig. 24–4). In some bryophytes, the sporophyte consists only of a capsule. At maturity, the capsule opens, liberating the spores that, if deposited in a suitable environment, germinate. As a result of growth, the germinated spores form gametophyte plants, which then reproduce in the manner described above, completing the life cycle. In Bryophyta, the sporophyte remains attached to the gametophyte and depends on the gametophyte for its nourishment; the gametophyte is always larger and forms the main photosynthesizing generation of the plant.

Habitat and Distribution   Although a few species of bryophytes are aquatic and some others are adapted to living in dry, sunny, exposed places, the majority occur in moist, shaded habitats. They grow on damp soil and rocks and on the moist bark of trees in diffuse light. Thus, they may be found in greatest abundance in forests and in deep, shaded ravines. They are widely distributed over the earth's surface, from arctic regions through the temperate zones to equatorial forests. In tropical regions, mosses often form dense epiphytic growths on the trunks and branches of trees, on posts, and on the roofs of buildings. Mosses often grow in dense mats, which may attain areas of many square yards or acres, especially on the damp soil of northern forests and in bogs and swamps.

Representative Members   The division Bryophyta consists of three classes: Musci—the mosses, with about 14,500 species; Hepaticae—the liverworts, with about 9000 species; and Anthocerotae—the hornworts, with about 100 species.

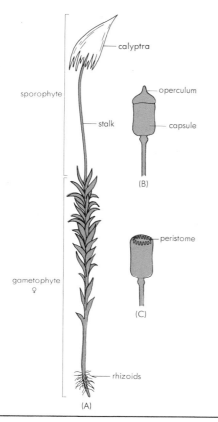

FIG. 24-4. Moss plant (*Polytrichum* sp.). (A) Mature sporophyte on the female gametophyte. The gametophyte is green and leafy with rhizoids. The sporophyte is made up of a slender stalk and a capsule. The capsule is covered by the shaggy calyptra—a remnant of the archegonium. (B) After loss of the calyptra, the capsule is seen to be capped by a lid, the operculum. (C) Loss of the operculum reveals the ring of teeth—the peristome—which controls release of the spores that are within the capsule.

CLASS I—(TRUE MOSSES) *General Characteristics* Mosses are small plants with usually erect stemlike axes bearing small, green, leaflike scales and anchored in the soil at their bases by rhizoids (Figs. 24-2 and 24-4). This "leafy shoot" or "moss plant" is the principal portion of the gametophyte generation of a moss species. The leafy shoot bears antheridia or archegonia, or both, at its apex (Fig. 24-3). In some species of mosses, both antheridia and archegonia are produced on the same gametophytes; in other species they are borne on separate male and female gametophytes. When the gametangia are mature and are covered by a layer of water or are struck by rain, the antheridia discharge their biflagellate sperms, which swim to the archegonia and enter the neck canals, a single sperm reaching and fertilizing an egg. The zygote grows into the sporophyte, which is attached by its foot to the gametophyte from which it absorbs food and water (Fig. 24-4). The sporophytes of mosses usually contain small amounts of chlorophyll, so that they are able to synthesize some food; however, they depend chiefly on the gametophytes to which they are attached for their nourishment and water.

A moss sporophyte (Figs. 24-2 and 24-4) has a slender stalk (seta) that rises from the apex of the gametophyte and bears a spore-producing capsule (the sporangium) at its tip. The capsule is often covered by a caplike structure, the **calyptra,** which is a remnant of the archegonial neck and upper part of the venter and which is carried upward by the growth of the sporophyte. The calyptra usually falls off or disintegrates as the capsule matures, exposing the capsule lid, or **operculum.** Beneath this lid is the **peristome,** a ring of teeth that, depending on the species, may assist in the release of spores from the capsule. These teeth are hygroscopic; that is, they change shape in response to differences in atmospheric moisture. Release and dispersal of spores is most efficient when the air is dry. In dry weather the hygroscopic teeth curve outward, opening the capsule and allowing the release of spores; in wet weather, the teeth curve in, closing the capsule.

An immature capsule contains spore mother cells, each of which undergoes meiosis, forming four haploid meiospores (Fig. 24-5). After germination, a spore produces a branched, prostrate, algalike filament, the **protonema** on which buds develop (Fig. 24-5). Each bud grows into a new erect gametophyte which then produces gametangia and gametes as described earlier. In alternation of generations in mosses, the gametophyte

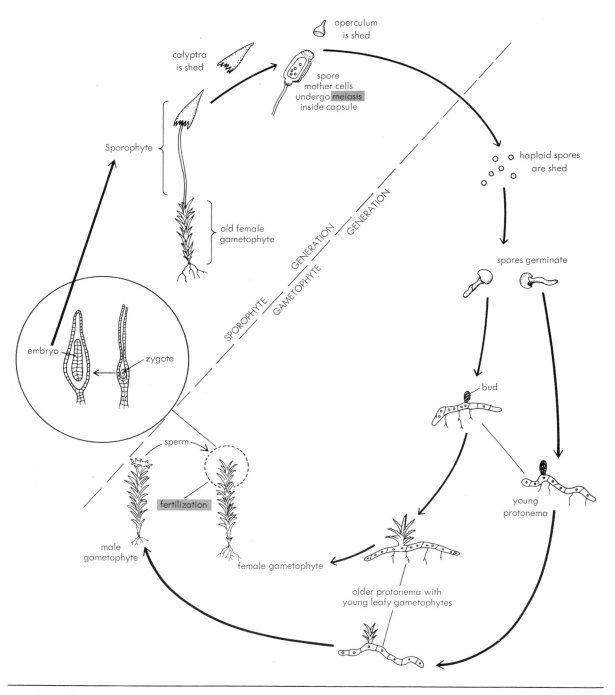

FIG. 24-5. Moss life cycle.

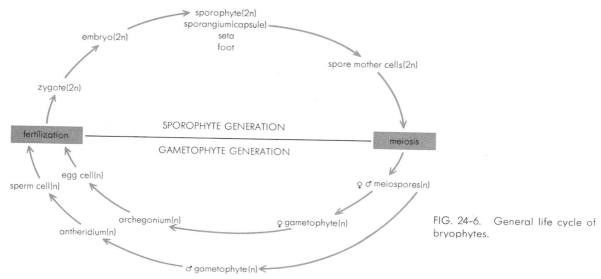

FIG. 24-6. General life cycle of bryophytes.

begins with the haploid spores and includes the protonema, leafy shoot, gametangia, and gametes; the sporophyte begins with the zygote and includes the foot, seta, capsule and its parts, and spore mother cells. All gametophyte structures are haploid, all sporophyte structures diploid. The sexual life cycle of a typical moss is shown in Fig. 24-5 and outlined in Fig. 24-6. Mosses may also reproduce by fragmentation; that is, a portion of a leafy shoot may break away from other portions of the plant, form rhizoids, and become a new individual. In addition, the protonemal stage developed from a single spore may become relatively extensive and produce numerous buds, each of which develops into an independent upright shoot.

Representative Members   Common and well-known genera of mosses are *Polytrichum*, the hairy cap moss (Figs. 24-2 and 24-4), and *Sphagnum* or peat moss (Fig. 24-7). Species of *Polytrichum* are dioecious; that is, they have two kinds of gametophytes, male and female which produce antheridia and archegonia, respectively (Fig. 24-3). In such mosses, two types of spores are formed by the sporophyte, one kind producing male gametophytes, the other female gameto-

phytes. These two kinds of spores are identical in size and structure but different in their genetic constitution. Various features of *Polytrichum* and its life cycle are shown in Figs. 24-2 to 24-5.

In *Sphagnum*, antheridia and archegonia may be borne on separate gametophytes, or they may be borne on the same "leafy" shoot. *Sphagnum* is most interesting and well-known for its great capacity to absorb liquids. The gametophyte plant can hold up to twenty times its own weight in water. Figure 24-8 shows the leaf cells of *Sphagnum* with dead cells modified for water storage and interspersed among them, the living, green, photosynthetic cells.

CLASS II—HEPATICAE (LIVERWORTS)   *General Characteristics*   Numerous characteristics serve to distinguish liverworts from mosses. Some of the more general differences are listed in Table 24-1. The name liverwort was given to the plant centuries ago because of its supposed resemblance to the liver lobes of animals. The term "wort" is an old Anglo-Saxon word for plant; hence these plants were thought of as liver plants.

Leafy liverworts are delicate, horizontal or erect plants, usually with three rows of leaves, two lateral rows of larger leaves and a third

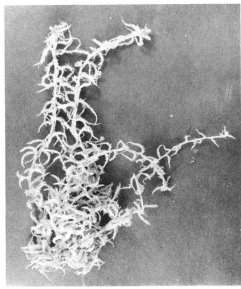

FIG. 24-7. *Sphagnum* or peat moss shown here in its natural bog habitat where it forms a mat supporting the growth of bog-dwelling seed plants such as the shrubs whose leaves and twigs appear on the left and upper right and the pitcher plant at left. Photo at right shows the plant in detail. (Photos by W. R. Kennedy.)

FIG. 24-8. Leaf cells of *Sphagnum*. Above: Surface view of cells. Below: cells seen in cross section.

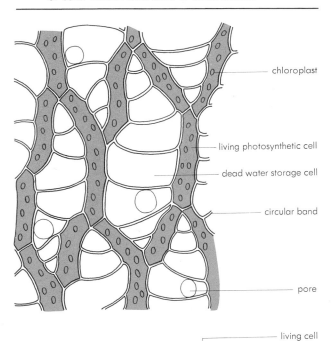

— chloroplast

— living photosynthetic cell

— dead water storage cell

— circular band

— pore

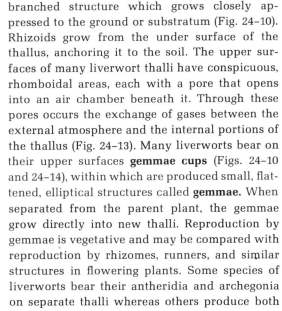

— living cell

— dead cell

ventral row of smaller leaves (Fig. 24–9). The thallose liverwort body is a flat, ribbonlike, fork-branched structure which grows closely appressed to the ground or substratum (Fig. 24–10). Rhizoids grow from the under surface of the thallus, anchoring it to the soil. The upper surfaces of many liverwort thalli have conspicuous, rhomboidal areas, each with a pore that opens into an air chamber beneath it. Through these pores occurs the exchange of gases between the external atmosphere and the internal portions of the thallus (Fig. 24–13). Many liverworts bear on their upper surfaces **gemmae cups** (Figs. 24–10 and 24–14), within which are produced small, flattened, elliptical structures called **gemmae.** When separated from the parent plant, the gemmae grow directly into new thalli. Reproduction by gemmae is vegetative and may be compared with reproduction by rhizomes, runners, and similar structures in flowering plants. Some species of liverworts bear their antheridia and archegonia on separate thalli whereas others produce both antheridia and archegonia on the same thallus. The gametangia, similar in structure to those of mosses, may be embedded in the thallus, opening at maturity onto the upper surface of the thallus, or may be borne on specialized stalks that rise above the thallus.

As in mosses, liverwort sperms can reach the archegonia only by swimming through water; thus the plants must be wet before fertilization can occur. An egg is fertilized in an archegonium, and the zygote develops into the sporophyte as in mosses, with the young sporophyte embedded in the gametophyte and enclosed by the archegonial wall. A liverwort sporophyte, in addition to its foot, usually has a very short seta and a capsule, within which spore mother cells undergo meiosis to form meiospores. The sporophyte of a liverwort has traces of chlorophyll and thus can manufacture a small amount of food. When the sporophyte is mature, the capsule opens and liberates the spores. When favorable conditions prevail, the spores germinate and grow into new thalli, which then reproduce as described earlier.

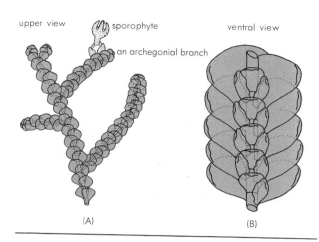

FIG. 24-9.   *Porella*, a leafy liverwort. (A) Upper surface of the gametophyte showing two rows of leaves and an attached sporophyte. (B) Lower surface of the gametophyte showing the ventral row of smaller leaves.

In liverworts, as in mosses, the gametophyte generation forms the conspicuous plant, the sporophyte being little more than a stalked capsule of spores largely parasitic on the gametophyte.

Liverworts	Mosses
1. Two types of gametophytes: a. Foliose (leafy); b. Thallose (strap shaped).	1. One type of gametophyte: Foliose (leafy).
2. Leaves, when present, in rows along the axis: two lateral rows and one ventral row.	2. Leaves appear spirally arranged along the axis.
3. Leaves without midribs.	3. Leaves may have midribs.
4. Sporophytes are small and ephemeral.	4. Sporophytes are relatively large and long lived.
5. Rhizoids are unicellular.	5. Rhizoids are multicellular.
6. Protonemal stage is either absent, or if present, ephemeral.	6. Protonemal stage is long lived.
7. Elaters are the hygroscopic mechanism to aid in spore release from the capsule.	7. The peristome is the hygroscopic mechanism that aids in spore release from the capsule.

TABLE 24-1   Some general differences between liverworts and mosses.

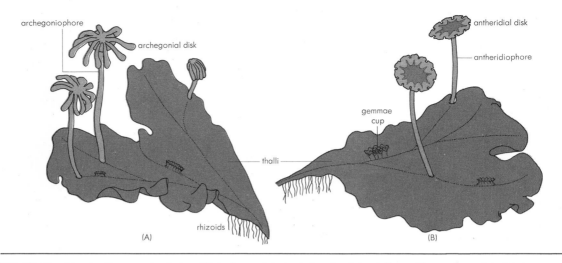

FIG. 24-10. *Marchantia* gametophytes. (A) Archegonial plant showing lobed, finger-like archegonial disk borne on stalk or archegoniophore. (B) Antheridial plant showing antheridial disk borne on stalk on antheriodiophore. Gemmae cups containing femmae are also present.

Representative Members *Marchantia* (Fig. 24-10) is a common, well-known liverwort. The plant is dioecious, and the gametangia are borne on short stalks that grow upward from the upper surfaces of the thalli. Antheridia are embedded in disc-shaped structures (Figs. 24-10 and 24-11) surmounting the stalks of the male thalli; the antheridia open onto the upper surfaces of these disks. The female plants produce stalks with smaller disks (Fig. 24-10) which bear marginal rays like the ribs of an umbrella; the archegonia develop on the undersides of the rays (Fig. 24-12). Sperms reach the archegonia by swimming through water when the plants are wet or are pelted by rain drops, and fertilization of an egg occurs within an archegonium. The small sporophyte is attached by its foot to the disc tissue of the female stalk, from which it absorbs food and water. The mature sporophytes, which are barely visible to the naked eye, occupy a pendulous position under the ribs (Fig. 24-12). Slender threadlike cells called **elaters** are found

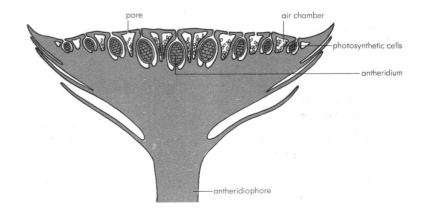

FIG. 24-11. *Marchantia* antheridial disk in longitudinal section showing photosynthetic cells in air chambers and antheridia in sunken cavities.

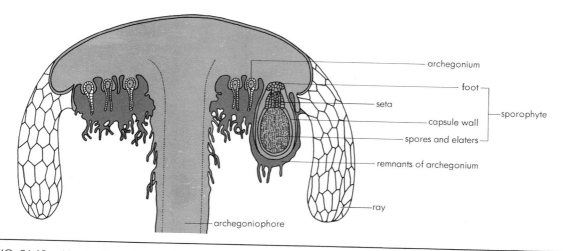

FIG. 24-12. *Marchantia* archegonial disk in longitudinal section, showing archegonia and a sporophyte.

among the spores within the capsule (Fig. 24-12). Elaters undergo twisting movements in response to changes in atmospheric humidity and thus aid in pushing the spores from the capsule. The spores are wind borne for a while and then fall to the ground where they germinate, growing into new thalli. As in dioecious mosses, two types of genetically different but morphologically similar spores are formed, one kind producing male thalli, the other growing into female thalli. The two types of thalli are morphologically similar except for their differing gametangia and the stalks on which these gametangia are borne. The life cycle of *Marchantia* is represented by Fig. 24-6.

In the genus *Riccia,* the thalli (Fig. 24-15) have an internal structure which is similar to that of *Marchantia.* However, the archegonia and antheridia are borne along the base of a furrow that creases the upper surface of the thallus. The sporophyte of *Riccia* is very simple, consisting only of a layer of wall cells that surrounds the mass of spores; foot and seta are absent. *Conoce-*

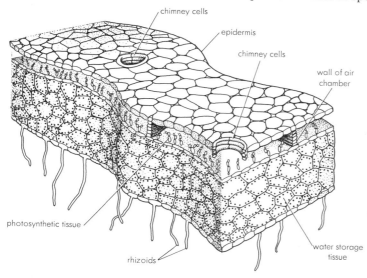

FIG. 24-13. *Marchantia.* Three-dimensional view of the thallus.

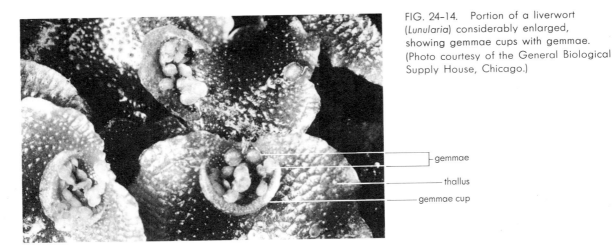

FIG. 24-14. Portion of a liverwort (*Lunularia*) considerably enlarged, showing gemmae cups with gemmae. (Photo courtesy of the General Biological Supply House, Chicago.)

gemmae

thallus

gemmae cup

phalum (Fig. 24-16), is a very common liverwort whose thallose growth form resembles *Marchantia*.

CLASS III—ANTHOCEROTAE (HORNWORTS)   The gametophytes of the Anthocerotae are lobed, dichotomously branched thalli (Fig. 24-17). The gametangia are borne embedded in the surface of the thallus. The sporophyte is elongate, tapered, and grows upward, resembling a horn or antler. The sporophytes of the Anthocerotae, unlike those of other bryophytes, have basal meristems and are indeterminate in growth. Virtually all the aerial portion of the sporophyte is a capsule, and as spores gradually mature at the apex above the meristematic region they are released by progressive and synchronous splitting of the sporophyte wall. The life cycle is similar to that described for other members of this division.

FIG. 24-15. *Riccia*, showing dichotomously-lobed gametophyte.

Relationship with Other Organisms   Little relationship can be shown to exist among the mosses, liverworts, and hornworts at the present time. These three classes are customarily grouped in the division Bryophyta because they all share a similar life cycle which involves regular alternation of a relatively large, free-living gametophyte plant and a smaller, dependent sporophyte plant. The origins of the bryophytes are as obscure as are the relationships among the classes. The earliest known bryophyte fossil is that of a liverwort thallus found in strata of upper Devonian age (about 365 million years ago). This is somewhat later than the earliest occurrence of the structurally more complex vascular plants. Many scientists believe that the bryophytes probably evolved from certain green algae which no longer exist; in addition, there is some evidence that suggests the bryophytes may have developed by reduction from vascular plants. However, there is no evidence that bryophytes gave rise to higher plants. They appear to be a "sideline" of evolution in which the gametophyte generation has come to play the dominant role, this being in contrast to the "mainline" of evolution in land plants in which the sporophyte plays the dominant role. Bryophytes may be regarded as a terminal group of plants which have less obvious adaptations to competitive existence on land than do other embryophytes.

Importance in Nature and in Human Life. Bryophyta play important, though inconspicuous, roles in the cycles of nature. Some of them provide food for herbivorous mammals, birds, and other animals. Water-inhabiting mosses contribute to the filling of ponds and lakes and thus to the building of soil. Extensive mats of terrestrial bryophytes, because of their dense growth, diminish the force of falling rain and absorb large amounts of moisture, thus reducing soil erosion. Some bryophytes that inhabit dry places often serve, along with lichens, as primary colonizers of rock surfaces. They exert a disintegrative action on rocks, thus contributing to the formation of soil and providing a substratum in which higher plants may grow. The direct uses of bryophytes by man are relatively few. Plants of the genus *Sphagnum* called peat mosses are used in a number of ways and are the most important

FIG. 24-16. *Conocephalum*, a thallose liverwort quite similar in appearance to *Marchantia*. It is seen on a rock ledge with some ferns. (Photo by W. R. Kennedy.)

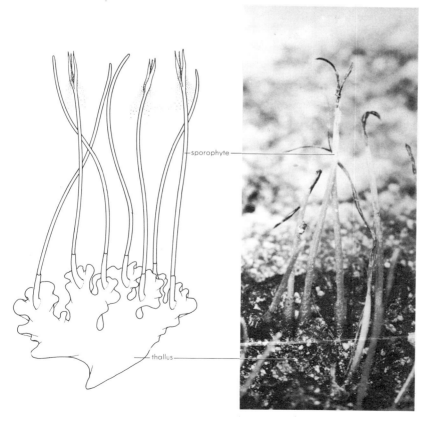

sporophyte

thallus

FIG. 24-17. *Anthoceros* (hornwort). Prostrate, leafy thallus with several mature horn-like sporophytes. Spores are visible in the dehisced terminal portion of the sporophytes. (Photo courtesy of L. E. Crofutt.)

economically of all bryophytes. Peat mosses formerly were commonly used as a packing material in the shipment of china and other fragile objects; as stuffing for upholstery; and as an absorbent substitute for cotton in surgical bandages. They are still commonly used as bedding for domesticated animals, as a source of organic matter to loosen tight, claylike soils, and as packing for cut flowers, grafting scions, and other plant materials that must be protected against drying during shipment. *Sphagnum* leaves contain many large, empty, dead cells that absorb and hold water in large quantities; thus, peat mosses increase the water-holding capacity of soils with which they are mixed and keep plant materials packed in them fresh and moist. Dried, compressed peat dug from peat beds in many parts of the world, is widely used as a fuel.

SUMMARY

1. Plants of the subkingdom Embryophyta have the following common characteristics:

   a. Gametangia, both male (antheridia) and female (archegonia), are multicellular and have sterile wall cells. An antheridium produces numerous sperms, an archegonium contains a single egg. Embryophytes lacking gametangia are thought to be derived by reduction from ancestral forms that had multicellular gametangia.

   b. Multicellular embryos are produced in the archegonia or, when archegonia are lacking, in other parts of the gametophyte. In this way, the embryo receives nourishment and protection from the surrounding tissues. Retention of the embryo is thought to be associated with the transition from an aquatic to a land habitat of plants.

   c. They have heterogamous sexual reproduction.

   d. They have alternation of generations.

2. *Most* members of the Embryophyta have these additional features:

   a. They are chiefly land plants.

   b. They have the vascular tissues xylem and phloem and thus have true roots, stems, and leaves. Bryophyta lack vascular tissues.

   c. They possess a cuticle.

   d. They have chloroplasts that contain pigments similar to those of green algae.

   e. Their sporophytes are dominant, except in Bryophyta.

3. Members of the Bryophyta have the following common characteristics:

   a. They are small in stature, rarely in excess of 20 cm.

   b. They have no vascular tissues.

   c. They have no true roots, stems, or leaves.

   d. Water is necessary for fertilization.

   e. The gametophyte is larger and more complex than the sporophyte and nutritionally independent; the sporophyte is attached to the gametophyte and is wholly or largely dependent on it for food.

   f. Sperms have flagella.

4. The sporophyte of bryophytes consists typically of a foot, seta, and spore-producing capsule. In some species, the sporophyte consists only of a capsule.

5. Bryophyta comprise three major classes: Musci (mosses); Hepaticae (liverworts); and Anthocerotae (hornworts).

6. A true moss plant (leafy shoot) consists of a stemlike axis, bearing rhizoids and leaflike green scales. Antheridia and archegonia are borne at the tips of the shoots, on the same plant or on different plants. Sperms swim to the archegonia in water, a single sperm fertilizing the egg within the archegonium. The zygote develops within the archegonium into the embryo sporophyte, which grows upward from the archegonium. The upper portion of the archegonium may form a hood (calyptra) over the capsule. The sporophyte consists of a foot, seta, and capsule. The capsule produces and liberates spores. Spores germinate on a suitable substratum, a spore forming a branched, green, filamentous protonema; buds borne on the protonema develop into leafy shoots, which then produce antheridia and archegonia. Reduction division occurs within the capsule when spores are formed from spore mother cells. Spores, protonema, leafy shoot, gametangia, and gametes are haploid and constitute the gametophyte generation; the zygote is the first stage of the sporophyte, all cells of which are diploid.

7. Liverworts grow appressed to the substratum (or float on water). A majority of species are "leafy," bearing a superficial resemblance to mosses and some are branched, ribbonlike thalli. The sporophytes of liverworts are smaller and usually simpler in structure than those of mosses. Gametangia of liverworts are embedded in the thalli or are borne on short stalks arising from the thalli. Sperms swim from antheridia to archegonia through water, one sperm fertilizing the single egg in the archegonium. The zygote develops into the sporophyte within the archegonium, the growing sporophyte rupturing the archegonial wall as it enlarges. In many species, elaters occur among the spores and, through their movements, push spores from the capsule. A liverwort sporophyte may consist of foot, stalk, and capsule, or it may consist only of a capsule. As in mosses, the gametophyte is the larger, independent generation, the sporophyte is smaller, less complex morphologically, and wholly or largely dependent on the gametophyte for its food and water.

8. Hornworts resemble thallose liverworts in general appearance but produce elongated sporophytes with basal meristems. As the spores mature at the apex of the growing capsule, the capsule wall splits to release them.

9. The relationships of the bryophytes are obscure. They are regarded as a terminal group that has not given rise to higher types of plants.

10. Bryophyta are important in nature and in human life in these ways: they furnish food for some animals; some species colonize rock surfaces and promote the formation of soil from rocks; they reduce soil erosion;

peat mosses are important for fuel, for packing material, and for the addition of organic matter to soils.

11. Bryophyta grow chiefly in moist, shaded habitats; a few species inhabit dry places, such as bare rock surfaces and a few others are aquatic. Bryophyta are widely distributed on the earth's surface.

SUGGESTED READINGS FOR INTERESTED STUDENTS

1. Bold, H. C., *Morphology of Plants,* 2 ed. Harper & Row, New York, 1967.

2. Conard, H. S., *How to Know the Mosses and Liverworts,* Ed. by H. E. Jaques. Wm. C. Brown, Dubuque, Iowa, 1956.

3. Grout, A. J., *Mosses with a Hand Lens,* 3 ed. Publ. by author, Newfane, Vermont, 1924.

4. Scagel, R. F., et al., *An Evolutionary Survey of the Plant Kingdom,* Ch. 16. Wadsworth, Belmont, Cal., 1965.

5. Smith, G. M., *Cryptogamic Botany,* Vol. II: Bryophytes and Pteridrophytes. McGraw-Hill, New York, 1938.

6. Watson, E. V., *The Structure and Life of Bryophytes,* Hutchinson, London, 1964.

TOPICS AND QUESTIONS FOR STUDY

1. List the characteristic features of Embryophyta, Bryophyta, Musci, Hepaticae, and Anthocerotae.

2. Describe briefly the distribution of Bryophyta.

3. List the ways in which Bryophyta are important in nature and in human life.

4. Describe the structure and life history of a typical moss.

5. Describe alternation of generations in Bryophyta.

6. How might you explain the fact that Bryophyta are small plants?

7. How would you explain the fact that Bryophyta are usually limited to moist habitats?

8. Describe the structure and life history of a liverwort. How do liverworts resemble mosses? How do they differ from mosses?

9. Describe the similarities between bryophytes and thallophytes; the differences between them.

10. Why are rhizoids, axes, and leaflike scales of mosses not considered to be true roots, stems, and leaves?

11. What is the advantage of multicellular gametangia and sporangia over unicellular gametangia and sporangia?

12. What are the advantages of the retention of the embryo sporophyte within the archegonium?

13. Describe briefly the extent of our current knowledge of the origin of the bryophytes; of the relationships of the classes of bryophytes; and of the relationships of bryophytes to vascular plants.

14. How are mosses effective in preventing or reducing soil erosion?

25

VASCULAR EMBRYOPHYTA: PSILOPHYTA (WHISK FERNS)

The vascular Embryophyta include all those plant divisions that characteristically have the vascular tissues xylem and phloem and in which photosynthesis and vegetative propagation are carried out principally by the sporophyte. At present, approximately 262,000 species of vascular embryophytes are known. Of this number, about 11,000 comprise the so-called lower vascular plants which are nonseed bearing and free sporing, that is, plants whose spores are dispersed freely into the surrounding habitat, to give rise later to independent gametophytes. The lower vascular plants include the whisk ferns, horsetails, club mosses, and ferns. The seed-bearing embryophytes, or higher vascular plants, include certain extinct fernlike plants, gymnosperms, and angiosperms.

The Embryophyta as a whole were characterized in the preceding chapter. The vascular Embryophyta are more specifically characterized by the following.

1. The sporophyte generation is the conspicuous phase of the life cycle. In contrast to the gametophyte, the sporophyte is typically auto-

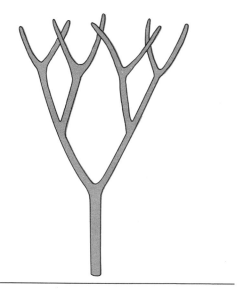

FIG. 25-1. A dichotomous branching system.

trophic and constitutes the major vegetative phase. Only during its embryonic stage is it nutritionally dependent on the preceding gametophyte phase. Familiar vascular plant bodies such as those of ferns, pine trees, rose bushes, and corn are sporophytes. Moreover, the vascular Embryophyta are essentially land plants, and as such, the sporophytes of all have a well developed cuticle that enables them to withstand the drying effects of the terrestrial environment.

2. The gametophyte is a small, inconspicuous structure usually less than 1 centimeter in length and in most cases so small that it can be observed in detail only with a microscope. Among the lower vascular plants, the gametophytes are typically terrestrial or epiphytic, free-living green autotrophs or brownish saprophytes, the latter usually being sustained in part by association with endophytic fungi. Among the higher vascular plants, the gametophyte is not a free-living organism but is a microscopic structure nutritionally and physically supported by the sporophyte. Among the lower vascular plants, the gametophyte generation is relatively long-lived, persisting into early stages of the development of the leafy sporophyte whereas in higher vascular plants the gametophytes are short-lived, persisting only during some or all of the development of the sporophyte embryo.

3. The sporophyte typically has vascular tissue, whereas the gametophyte does not. However, tracheids occur in the gametophyte of extant members of the Psilophyta.

4. Reproduction is typically sexual, but vegetative propagation of the sporophyte is common. Particularly among the lower vascular plants, vegetative propagation often plays a greater role in the formation of new individuals than does sexual reproduction.

DIVISION PSILOPHYTA

General Characteristics   The psilophytes are generally considered to be the earliest evolved, simplest vascular plants. The group flourished in the Devonian period (approximately 400 million years ago) and, with the possible exception of two living genera of questionable affinities, they disappeared from the world flora 350 million years ago. The sporophytes of the extinct Psilophyta consist of horizontal rhizomes with upright aerial stems. Aerial axes are essentially naked and presumed to have been green and photosynthetic. Branching of the stem system is either dichotomous, that is, dividing equally into two parts at each juncture (Fig. 25-1) or is a modified dichotomous branching. A major distinguishing characteristic of the extinct forms of psilophytes is the presence of sporangia borne at the tips of the aerial stems. Furthermore, the members of the group lack roots. Perhaps the best known and most representative of the extinct forms is *Rhynia* (Fig. 25-2). In those plants which are thought to be living members of the Psilophyta, the form of the sporophyte is basically the same as that of the extinct species except for scalelike or small, leafy appendages found on the stem and for sporangia which appear to be terminal on side branches. Psilophytes are **homosporous,** that is, their meiospores are morphologically alike.

FIG. 25-2. *Rhynia.* An extinct psilophyte with leafless, dichotomously-branched, erect axes arising from a creeping rhizome and bearing terminal sporangia.

In the extant genera *Psilotum* and *Tmesipteris* (Figs. 25-3, 25-4 and 25-5), rhizomes bear rhizoids and are permeated with filaments of mycorrhizal fungi. The mycorrhizae of the psilophytes resemble the very common root mycorrhizae of higher plants. Investigations of higher plant mycorrhizae have demonstrated that the vigor and often the survival of the plant is dependent on this fungal association. The abundant, branching filaments of the fungus extend into the soil and greatly increase nutrient and water absorbing capacity. Quite probably the psilophytes are similarly benefited by their mycorrhizae. The aerial stems and leaves, when present, are photosynthetic. The gametophytes (Fig. 25-6) of living Psilophyta are nonphotosynthetic and saprophytic and, like the rhizomes of the sporophytes, are permeated by fungi. The surface tissues of the gametophytes and rhizomes of *Psilotum* are strongly cutinized and are so resistant to decay that even after the

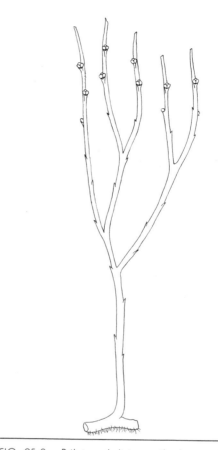

FIG. 25-3. *Psilotum.* A living psilophyte with dichotomously-branched, erect axis arising from a rhizome. Scale-like appendages and tri-lobed sporangia occur at intervals on the stem.

internal tissues have died and rotted away they remain in the soil as hollow "shells." The gametophytes of the extinct psilophytes have not been described.

Reproductive Characteristics   The sexual life cycle of living psilophytes, as in all other vascular plants, is characterized by heteromorphic alternation of generations. The principal events of sexual reproduction, as exemplified by *Psilotum* and *Tmesipteris,* are as follows. The sporangia are lobed bodies produced along the axes or near the leaf bases (Figs. 25-3 and 25-5).

FIG. 25-4. *Psilotum*, a living plant. (Photo by W. R. Kennedy.)

Within the sporangia, spore mother cells undergo meiosis to form haploid meiospores. After germination, each spore gives rise to a small, subterranean, nongreen, saprophytic gametophyte (Fig. 25-6). The gametophyte is an irregularly branched, essentially cylindrical structure which ranges from 1 to 15 millimeters in length and up to 2 millimeters in diameter and is very similar in appearance to a rhizome. A single gametophyte bears both antheridia and archegonia, which are similar to those of the Bryophyta but considerably smaller. Sperms are multiflagellate and swim through water to the archegonium where a single sperm fertilizes the egg. As in the bryophytes, the embryo develops within the archegonium and obtains its food from the surrounding gametophyte tissues. In time the young sporophyte produces photosynthetic, aerial axes and becomes a nutritionally independent plant.

Habitat and Distribution   Psilophytes were apparently distributed widely over the earth between 350 and 410 million years ago, but we have only limited knowledge of the particular kinds of terrestrial habitats they occupied. Available evidence suggests that at least some of them were bog-dwelling plants. The two species of *Psilotum*

FIG. 25-5. *Tmesipteris tannensis* on the left showing one of the two branches of the plant. Inset at right is an enlargement showing bilobed sporangia. (Photo by W. R. Kennedy.)

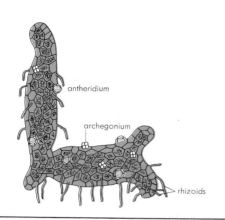

FIG. 25-6. *Psilotum* gametophyte with antheridia and archegonia.

are usually found in moist, rich soils in shaded habitats of the tropics and subtropics of both hemispheres including southeastern United States. The single species of *Tmesipteris* is epiphytic and is restricted in its distribution to Australia, New Zealand, Tasmania, New Caledonia, and the Polynesian Islands.

Representative Members   The best known of the extant Psilophyta is *Psilotum nudum* (Figs. 25-3 and 25-4). The aerial portion of the sporophyte consists of upright, dichotomously branched stems which bear tiny, scalelike appendages. The stem itself is the principal photosynthetic organ, with chlorenchyma just beneath the epidermis. The sporangia are three-lobed and are borne on short stalks in the axils of the upper appendages. *Tmesipteris tannensis* (Fig. 25-5), the only species of the genus, grows as a pendant epiphyte with slender stems and elliptical leaves approximately 1 centimeter in length. In contrast to *Psilotum*, its sporangium is two-lobed. The life cycle of *Psilotum* is shown in Fig. 25-7.

Relationship with Other Organisms   Current studies reveal that the Devonian psilophytes consisted of two groups differing particularly in their sporangia and branching pattern. In the more primitive group (which includes *Rhynia*) sporan-

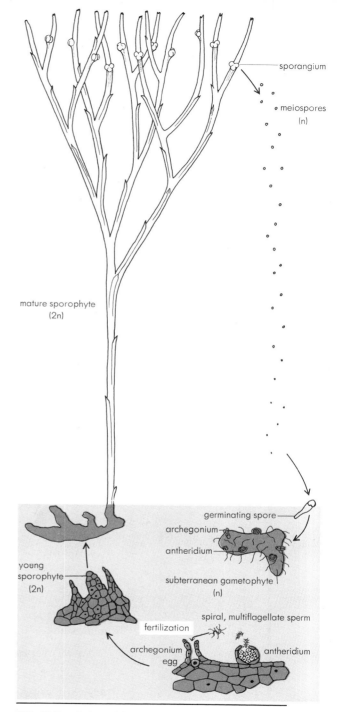

FIG. 25-7. *Psilotum* life cycle. Gametophyte and young sporophyte are enlarged to show detail.

gia occur singly at the tips of branches, and the branching pattern is dichotomous. In the second, more advanced, group sporangia occur in clusters at the tips of aerial branches, and the branching is a modified dichotomous pattern. It is from this latter group that ferns and seed plants are thought to have evolved. However, the lines of descent of these groups are not equally clear or completely known.

It is interesting to note that there are no known fossil forms linking living psilophytes with those of the Devonian; accordingly the putative relationships between living and fossil species are necessarily speculative. Recent studies have suggested the possibility that the living members are more closely related to ferns than to the Devonian psilophytes.

SUMMARY

1.   The two major distinguishing characteristics common to vascular plants are the presence of vascular tissues, xylem and phloem, and a heteromorphic alternation of generations having a dominant sporophyte phase.

2.   The Psilophyta are the most primitive of the vascular plants and, with the possible exception of two genera, are extinct.

3.   The branching pattern of the Psilophyta is basically dichotomous, the sporangia are borne terminally on the stem, and true roots are lacking.

4.   The gametophytes of living species are saprophytic and mycorrhizal.

5.   All psilophytes are believed to be homosporous.

6.   Only two genera of living plants are included in the division Psilophyta—*Psilotum*, with two species, and *Tmesipteris*, with one.

7.   The psilophytes are probably the plants from which ferns and seed plants were derived.

8.   Recent studies have suggested that living psilophytes may actually be ferns.

SUGGESTED READINGS FOR INTERESTED STUDENTS

1.   Andrews, H. N., *Ancient Plants and the World They Lived In.* Comstock, Ithaca, N.Y., 1947.

2.   Bold, H., *Morphology of Plants,* 2 ed. Harper & Row, New York, 1967.

3.   Delevoryas, T., *Morphology and Evolution of Fossil Plants.* Holt, Rinehart and Winston, New York, 1962.

4.   Foster, A. S., and E. M. Gifford, Jr., *Comparative Morphology of Vascular Plants.* Freeman, San Francisco, 1959.

5.   Scagel, R. F., et al., *An Evolutionary Survey of the Plant Kingdom.* Wadsworth, Belmont, Cal., 1965.

6.   Sporne, K. R., *The Morphology of Pteridophytes,* 2 ed. Hutchinson, London, 1966.

TOPICS AND QUESTIONS FOR STUDY

1. Characterize the vascular Embryophyta as a whole.

2. Which plant groups are known as the lower vascular plants? Which are known as the higher vascular plants?

3. List the major distinguishing characteristics of the Psilophyta.

4. What is meant by dichotomous branching?

5. Describe the reproductive cycle of a typical psilophyte, and contrast this with the cycle of a bryophyte.

6. In what parts of the world do the living psilophytes occur?

7. In what ways are the living members structurally different from the fossil forms?

8. Discuss the possible relationships of the Psilophyta to the algae and to other vascular embryophytes.

26

LYCOPODOPHYTA (CLUB MOSSES)

The Lycopodophyta, like the Psilophyta, is a group of plants that reached its greatest development in past geological ages. During the Carboniferous period (345 to 280 million years ago) great forests of giant, 90-foot-tall lycopods as well as herbaceous lycopods and plants of other groups could be found in the numerous swamps that existed on the continents. One such landscape is shown in Fig. 26–1. All the tree lycopods have now been long extinct, and only five herbaceous genera with approximately 1000 species exist today.

General Characteristics The sporophytes of the living lycopods are perennial, herbaceous plants with true roots, stems, and leaves (Figs. 26–2 and 26–3). All lycopods have photosynthetic sporophytes which are nutritionally independent. The photosynthetic pigments are the same as those of green algae, bryophytes and all other Embryophyta. The leaves are usually spirally arranged and quite small, rarely exceeding 1 centimeter in length. Each leaf typically has a single, unbranched vein. Leaves of this type are referred to as **microphylls** and in the Lycopodophyta are

FIG. 26-1. Reconstruction of a Carboniferous landscape showing the variety of arborescent and herbaceous forms. The lycopods are *Lepidodendron,* the two large trees just to the right of center, and *Sigillaria,* the many trees whose leaves are clustered in two or more oval-shaped crowns. True ferns are on the stream bank at the right and arborescent seed ferns are in the right background. The Arthrophyta (jointed stemmed plants) are represented by the *Calamites* with whorled branches on the right stream bank. Other arthrophytes can be seen on the left bank. (Photo courtesy of the Peabody Museum of Natural History, Yale U.)

believed to have originated phylogenetically from small outgrowths (enations) of the stem. As such, these leaves are quite different organs from the more complex leaves of ferns and seed plants. Moreover, the leaf trace, or vascular strand, that enters the microphyll diverges from the vascular cylinder of the stem in the manner shown in Fig. 26-4,A whereas the leaf trace of ferns and seed plants leaves a gap in the vascular cylinder as it departs from the cylinder, as shown in Fig. 26-4,B. The stems and roots of club mosses usually exhibit dichotomous branching, the same primitive type of branching as occurs in the Psilophyta. A few species, however, produce leader stems with lateral branches in a pattern somewhat comparable to the monopodial system of higher plants. The gametophytes may be free-living plants which are either photosynthetic or

saprophytic, or they may reach maturity within the original spore wall, using food absorbed from the parent sporophyte during spore maturation.

Reproductive Characteristics The lycopsid plant just described is part of the sporophyte generation and produces spores in sporangia borne singly on the upper surfaces of specialized leaves called sporophylls (Fig. 26-3,C). The sporophylls of most species are aggregated in elongate or clublike clusters at the tips of the stems (Figs. 26-2,A). It is from these club-shaped clusters of sporophylls, called strobili or cones, that the common name "club moss" is derived. In some species, such as *Lycopodium lucidulum* (Fig. 26-2,B) and *L. selago* (Fig. 26-5), the sporophylls are not clustered in terminal strobili but occur in groups along the stem interrupted by ordinary vegetative leaves. The sporangia produce spore mother cells which undergo meiosis to form haploid meiospores. The spores become wind-borne and later fall to earth where they germinate to produce small gametophyte plants, or they may germinate while still within the sporangium and produce gametophytes endosporically, that is, development of the gametophyte occurs principally within the confines of the spore wall. In some species, only one morphological type of spore is produced, and these spores develop into gametophytes which bear both archegonia and antheridia. Such species are termed **homosporous.** In other species, termed **heterosporous,** two kinds of spores are produced:

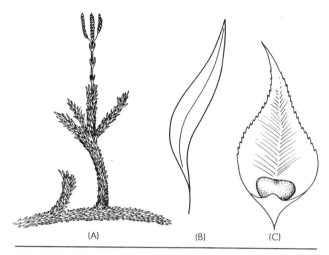

FIG. 26-3. *Lycopodium* or club moss. A. Mature plant with club-shaped strobili borne on upright stems arising from prostrate stem. B. Vegetative leaf. C. Sporophyll bearing sporangium.

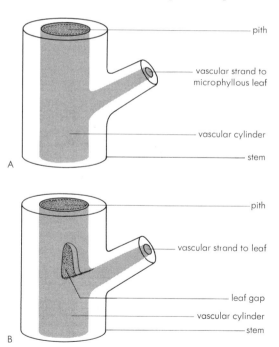

FIG. 26-4. Vascular supply to leaves. A. Vascular strand to microphyllous leaf: no gap in the cylinder. B. Vascular strand to megaphyllous leaf: leaf gap in cylinder.

FIG. 26-5. *Lycopodium selago.* Portion of stem in which the sporophylls are not clustered in terminal strobili but occur in groups along the stem, interspersed among vegetative leaves. Sporangia are visible near the bottom of the photograph. (Courtesy of the General Biological Supply House, Chicago.)

relatively small ones, **microspores,** and larger ones, **megaspores.** These develop, respectively, into male gametophytes **(microgametophytes)** with antheridia and female gametophytes **(megagametophytes)** with archegonia. In both homosporous and heterosporous species, flagellated sperm must swim through water from the antheridia to the archegonia, and a single sperm fertilizes an egg. The zygote begins its growth within the archegonium, forming an embryo that ultimately develops into the mature sporophyte. As in the Psilophyta, the sporophyte generation is larger and structurally more complex than the gametophyte.

Habitat and Distribution   Most lycopods inhabit moist, shaded woodlands, and are especially abundant in the tropics. A few species live partly or wholly submerged in water, and a small group of species is semixerophytic, growing on bark, dry rock surfaces, and in desert regions. The so-called resurrection plant, *Selaginella lepido-*

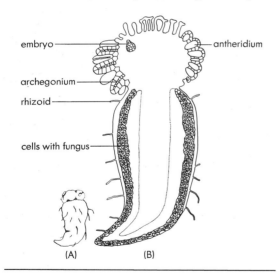

FIG. 26–6.   *Lycopodium* gametophyte. A. External surface of lumpy, subterranean gametophyte. B. Much enlarged longitudinal section of gametophyte showing archegonia and antheridia embedded in the top portion, rhizoids arising at the surface, and cells containing a mycorrhizal fungus.

phylla, is a lycopod found in desert areas of the southwestern United States. When conditions are dry, the leaves turn brown and the branches curl up and inward so that the entire plant becomes spherical and brittle and appears to be dead. When moisture becomes available, the branches rapidly unroll, and the plant resumes its green color, thus being "resurrected" to continue active photosynthetic life.

Representative Members   *Lycopodium* (Figs. 26–2, 26–3, and 26–5) is a genus of plants which are sometimes known as club mosses or ground pines. They are chiefly perennial herbs and are usually terrestrial, although a few are epiphytic. Some have creeping stems with erect, unbranched, or monopodially branched axes; some have erect, dichotomously branched stems; and others are epiphytic with pendulous, dichotomous branches. Adventitious roots arise along the entire length of the prostrate stems of the creeping species, but in species with erect or pendulous stems these roots arise only at the base of the axis. The small, spirally arranged or opposite leaves superficially resemble the leaflike scales of bryophytes, and give *Lycopodium* shoots their mosslike appearance; however, the plants themselves are usually much larger than true mosses. Certain leaves, the sporophylls, bear sporangia on their upper surfaces or in their axils. In those species having creeping stems, the sporophylls are most often aggregated into clublike strobili at the apices of the erect axes (Fig. 26–3), and the sporophylls are smaller than the vegetative leaves, are paler in color, and have distinctive dentate margins. In species such as *L. selago* (Fig. 26–5) with erect axes upcurving from an imperceptible, horizontal stem, the sporophylls resemble the vegetative leaves and occur intermixed with them. *Lycopodium* is homosporous, and when the sporangium walls open at maturity the microscopic spores are dispersed by wind. If a spore is carried to a favorable habitat it germinates and produces a small gametophyte (Fig. 26–6). Depending on the species, the gametophyte shape

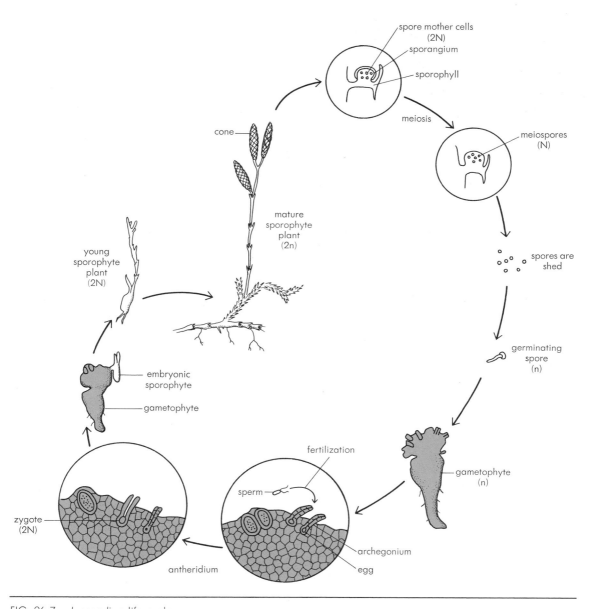

FIG. 26-7. *Lycopodium* life cycle.

FIG. 26-8. *Selaginella.* Rhizophores growing down from semiprostrate leafy stem. (Photo by W. R. Kennedy.)

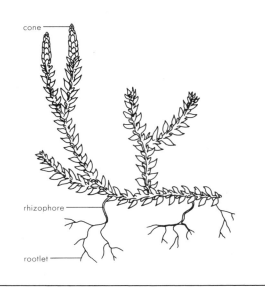

cone

rhizophore

rootlet

FIG. 26-9. *Selaginella.* Small cones are located at the tips of the leafy branches. Leafless axes (rhizophores) grow to the soil and form subterranean rootlets.

may be irregular, oval, or carrot shaped. It rarely exceeds 2 cm in any dimension and may be a green, photosynthetic plant that lives on the surface of the ground, or it may be nongreen and wholly or partly subterranean. In the latter case, it is at least partially heterotrophic, taking food from the soil through mutualistic relationship with a mycorrhizal fungus. The lower portion of a *Lycopodium* gametophyte bears rhizoids, the upper portion archegonia and antheridia. At maturity and in the presence of water, the antheridia liberate sperms which swim to and enter the archegonia. A single sperm fertilizes the egg, and the zygote develops into a small embryo within the archegonium. Until it has grown sufficiently to develop its own green leaves, this embryo is nutritionally dependent on the gametophyte. The embryo also forms a rhizome and roots, and the young sporophyte then begins an independent existence, while the gametophyte from which it developed decays and disappears. The life cycle of *Lycopodium* is shown in Fig. 26-7.

Selaginella is a genus whose members are commonly called spike mosses (Fig. 26-8). *Selaginella* plants are similar in general structure and appearance to *Lycopodium* but differ from the latter in their usually smaller size and more delicate form, in their heterosporous reproduction, and in other features. Although a few species grow erect, and one is a vine, most species have a prostrate growth habit. The stems branch dichotomously and bear tiny leaves that are usually arranged in four longitudinal rows. Many species bear peculiar colorless, unbranched, leafless axes that originate from the leafy axis and grow straight down toward the ground. These structures are known as **rhizophores** and are thought to be adventitious roots. Upon contacting the ground, their tips branch and give rise to subterranean rootlets. Selaginella bears small terminal cones (Fig. 26-9). The uppermost sporophylls in a cone bear sporangia (**microsporangia**) which produce numerous tiny spores (**microspores**). The lower sporophylls of the cone bear sporangia (**megasporangia**), each of which contains four

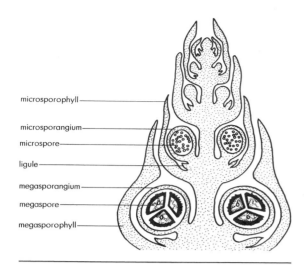

microsporophyll

microsporangium

microspore

ligule

megasporangium

megaspore

megasporophyll

FIG. 26-10. Diagram of a longitudinal section through a *Selaginella* cone, showing upper microsporophylls with microsporangia containing many small microspores, and lower megasporophylls with megasporangia containing four large megaspores (only three are visible).

large spores (megaspores) (Fig. 26-10). The two types of sporophylls are called **microsporophylls** and **megasporophylls,** respectively. While still in the surrounding megasporangium, each megaspore germinates forming a megagametophyte within the spore wall. The megagametophyte consists of a mass of food-storing cells and several archegonia. Some of the cells of this gametophyte may contain chlorophyll and carry on photosynthesis. As a megagametophyte grows, it exerts pressure that ruptures the megaspore wall, exposing its upper portion (Fig. 26-11). Like the megaspore, a microspore begins development endosporically forming a microgametophyte within the spore wall and within the microsporangium. The male gametophyte (Fig. 26-11) consists of a single prothallial cell and an antheridium made up of jacket cells which enclose the developing sperms. None of the cells of a microgametophyte has chlorophyll, and the entire structure is dependent on food previously absorbed from the parent sporophyte. When the microsporangial walls are mature, they rupture and liberate the microspores with their enclosed, growing micro-

gametophytes. Some of the microspores fall or are carried by wind to the vicinity of the megasporangia, which by this time contain mature megagametophytes. In the presence of water, the microspore walls open, and the enclosed antheridia liberate sperms that swim to and into the archegonia. The zygote produced begins to divide, growing into a tiny embryo that is attached to the female gametophyte, which in turn is partly enclosed by the megaspore wall. The embryo lacks chlorophyll and derives its food from the female gametophyte which had earlier obtained most or all of its food from the parent sporophyte. The embryo produces a root, a stem and two

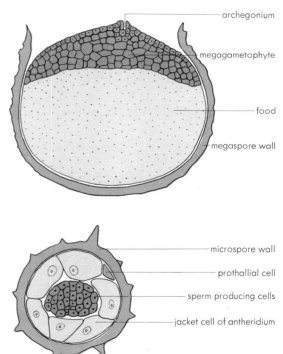

archegonium

megagametophyte

food

megaspore wall

microspore wall

prothallial cell

sperm producing cells

jacket cell of antheridium

FIG. 26-11. *Selaginella* gametophytes, shown at a stage when they are still within the spore wall. *Above:* Section through a megaspore showing the internal female gametophyte or megagametophyte cells with an archegonium at the top and stored food below. *Below:* Section through a microspore showing a single prothallial cell and one antheridium composed of several jacket cells enclosing the sperm-producing cells.

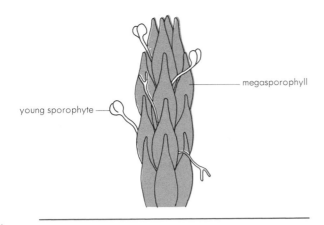

young sporophyte ⎯

megasporophyll ⎯

FIG. 26-12. *Selaginella* cone with young sporophytes. Portion of a cone with young sporophytes growing out from the megagametophytes in the megaspores which are, in turn, in the megasporangia borne in the axils of the megasporophylls. (After Lyon)

cotyledons; the young sporophyte (Fig. 26–12) then develops chlorophyll and begins an independent existence, ultimately becoming a mature sporophyte of the type described.

Selaginella is particularly noteworthy because in its heterospory and in the development of its gametophyte, it closely parallels features found among the seed plants. Such features are: the presence of two kinds of sporophylls, sporangia, spores, and gametophytes; small gametophytes wholly or partly dependent on sporophytic tissues for food; development of the gametophytes within the spore which, in turn, is retained within the sporangium; and development of the embryo (partly at least) within the megaspore wall. The megaspore of *Selaginella* with its enclosed gametophyte and embryo is something like a primitive seed might have been. In attempting to decipher some of the steps in the evolution of the seed, one is interested to see that here in *Selaginella* are found features that perhaps existed in those now extinct heterosporous plant lines that may have given rise to seed plants.

Relationship with Other Organisms   Unlike all the other vascular plants which are presumed to have evolved from the Psilophyta, the lycopods evolved independently in a distinct line of their own. They are thought to have evolved from simple plants that existed contemporaneously with the psilophytes of the Devonian. These ancient progenitors had lateral sporangia and naked or spiny stems that branched dichotomously. Although some of the extinct lycopods produced seedlike structures, there is no evidence that lycopods are in any way related to seed plants.

Importance in Nature and in Human Life   Living species of Lycopodophyta have little economic value. Several species are used for manufacture of Christmas decorations and wreaths, and a few species, especially of *Selaginella,* are sometimes used as ornamentals in greenhouses and gardens. Arboreal lycopod species of the Carboniferous period are of greater economic importance than the living species because their carbonized remains form a large proportion of the earth's coal deposits.

SUMMARY   1. The division Lycopodophyta reached its greatest development during the Carboniferous period (345 to 280 million years ago) and is presently represented in the earth's flora by only five genera and approximately 1000 species.

2. The sporophyte of lycopods, like that of the psilophytes, is the dominant, more complex generation, and the gametophyte is small and relatively simple in structure.

3. Lycopodophyta sporophytes have the following characteristics.

a. They possess the vascular tissues xylem and phloem.

b. They have true roots, stems, and leaves.

c. Their leaves are small, each with single vein, and are arranged spirally or in rows on the stem.

d. The sporangia are borne on sporophylls which are either grouped in clublike cones (strobili) or mixed with the vegetative leaves along the stems.

e. Roots of mature plants are always adventitious.

4. The sporophytes of all Lycopodophyta possess chlorophyll and are autotrophic. The gametophytes, however, depending on the species, are either autotrophic or heterotrophic. Among the homosporous species, heterotrophic gametophytes lack chlorophyll, are subterranean, and rely on mycorrhizal associations for successful development. In heterosporous species, the gametophytes depend largely or entirely on food manufactured by the parent sporophyte and stored in the megaspore or microspore.

5. The life cycle of a homosporous lycopod (for example, *Lycopodium*) is as follows. The sporophyte bears sporangia, within which numerous spore mother cells are produced, each of which gives rise to four, haploid meiospores. A spore germinates, usually on the soil, forming a small gametophyte that bears both antheridia and archegonia. At maturity, sperms swim through water from the antheridia to the archegonia, one sperm fertilizing the single egg in an archegonium. The diploid zygote begins its development into an embryo within the archegonium. The growing embryo pushes its way out of the archegonium and ultimately forms a mature, green, independent sporophyte.

6. The life cycle of a heterosporous lycopod (for example, *Selaginella*) is as follows. The sporophyte bears strobili with microsporophylls above and megasporophylls below. A microsporangium produces numerous microspore mother cells and microspores whereas a megasporangium produces a single megaspore mother cell and four megaspores. Each spore gives rise to a gametophyte within the spore wall (endosporically). A microgametophyte bears one antheridium, which forms several sperms; a megagametophyte bears several archegonia, each with a single egg. A sperm swims through water from a microgametophyte to a megagametophyte, fertilizing an egg in an archegonium. For a time, the embryo sporophyte, megagametophyte, and megaspore wall form a unit resembling the seeds of higher plants. This falls to the ground, the embryo sporophyte roots in the soil, and eventually grows into an independent, mature sporophyte.

7. Most living species of Lycopodophyta inhabit moist, shaded forests. They are especially numerous in humid, tropical areas. A few species are aquatic, and some inhabit desert regions.

8. Various members of the Lycopodophyta have a number of advanced characteristics, namely, the aggregation of sporophylls into strobili, heterospory, and the development of seedlike structures resulting from retention of the female gametophyte and young embryonic sporophyte within the megaspore wall.

9. Lycopodophyta are thought to have evolved from simple Devonian plants contemporaneous with, but unrelated to, the Psilophyta. The ancestral plants bore lateral sporangia on naked or spiny, dichotomous branches. Although relatively complex forms are known from past times, the lycopods seem not to have given rise to more advanced groups of plants.

10. Living species of Lycopodophyta are of little economic significance. Species now extinct, which formed extensive forests during the Carboniferous period, contributed substantially to the world's coal deposits.

SUGGESTED READINGS FOR INTERESTED STUDENTS

1. Andrews, H. N., *Ancient Plants and the World They Lived In.* Comstock, Ithaca, N.Y., 1947.

2. Bold, H., *Morphology of Plants,* 2 ed. Harper & Row, New York, 1967.

3. Delevoryas, T., *Morphology and Evolution of Fossil Plants.* Holt, Rinehart and Winston, New York, 1962.

4. Foster, A. S., and E. M. Gifford, Jr., *Comparative Morphology of Vascular Plants.* Freeman, San Francisco, 1959.

5. Scagel, R. F., et al., *An Evolutionary Survey of the Plant Kingdom.* Wadsworth, Belmont, Cal., 1965.

6. Sporne, K. R., *The Morphology of Pteridophytes,* 2 ed. Hutchinson, London, 1966.

TOPICS AND QUESTIONS FOR STUDY

1. List the distinguishing characteristics of: the Embryophyta as a whole, the vascular Embryophyta, and the Lycopodophyta.

2. Compare the Lycopodophyta and Psilophyta for their differences and similarities.

3. What is the structural nature of the leaves of the Lycopodophyta?

4. Describe the structure of a *Lycopodium* sporophyte, of a *Lycopodium* gametophyte.

5. Outline the life cycle of *Lycopodium.*

6. Describe the structure of a *Selaginella* sporophyte, of a gametophyte.

7. Outline the life cycle of *Selaginella.*

8. List the differences between *Lycopodium* and *Selaginella.*

9. List the resemblances between *Selaginella* and the seed plants.

10. Describe briefly the economic importance of the Lycopodophyta.

11. Describe the distribution of the living species of Lycopodophyta.

12. List three ways in which you might distinguish between true mosses and club mosses.

27

DIVISION ARTHROPHYTA (HORSETAILS)

The Arthrophyta, like the Psilophyta and Lycopodophyta, is a relict group. Arthrophytes were contemporaries of the ancient Paleozoic lycopods. From the Devonian to the end of the Paleozoic many types existed, including large forest trees, shrubs, and herbs. With the passage of time, however, they underwent a drastic decline, and only the single herbaceous genus *Equisetum* survives. Twenty-five species of *Equisetum* are known. They show a great variation in size and have a relatively wide distribution while still retaining a remarkable resemblance to their Paleozoic relatives.

General Characteristics Like other vascular embryophytes, the sporophyte generation is dominant and produces true roots, stems, and leaves. The plant body of living species consists of a usually extensive, underground rhizome system from which the aerial shoots arise. The aerial stems may be branched or unbranched. Both rhizomes and aerial shoots have a striking, jointed

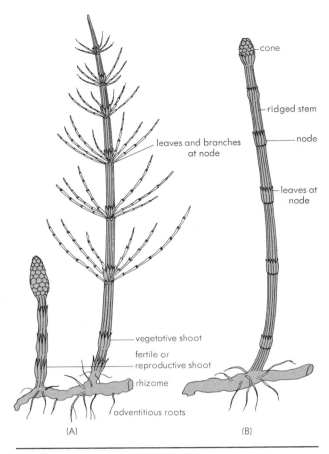

FIG. 27–1. *Equisetum arvense* (A) and *Equisetum hyemale*. (B) two common species of arthrophytes.

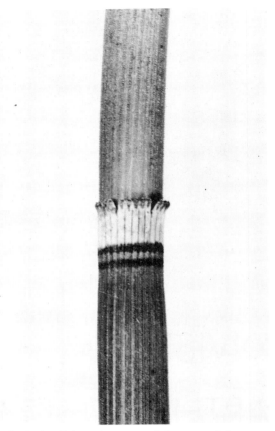

FIG. 27–2. Enlarged section of the stem of *Equisetum hyemale* showing the longitudinal ridges and a sheath of scale-like leaves. (Photo by W. R. Kennedy.)

appearance that is due to the development of well-defined nodes and internodes, the former with whorled leaves and branches (Figs. 27–1 and 27–2). The external surface of the stem usually has conspicuous longitudinal ridges, and internally the stems are hollow except in the nodal regions. The leaves of living species are reduced to small scales. When they are young, the scalelike leaves are photosynthetic, but as they mature they become brown and papery and frequently fall off. In *Equisetum,* most of the photosynthesis is carried out in the erect, green stems. The tissues of living species are impregnated with silica, giving them a rough and harsh feel, and the tissues

of extinct species appear to have been similarly silicified.

Reproductive Characteristics   The sporophyte plants described above produce ovoid cones or strobili composed of umbrella-shaped sporangiophores attached to a central axis (Fig. 27–3). The sporangiophores bear elongated sporangia on their lower surfaces, and within them spore mother cells undergo meiosis. At maturity the axis of the strobilus elongates, separating the heads of the sporangiophores slightly to expose the sporangia (Fig. 27–4). The sporangial walls split longitudinally, the spores are dislodged and fall

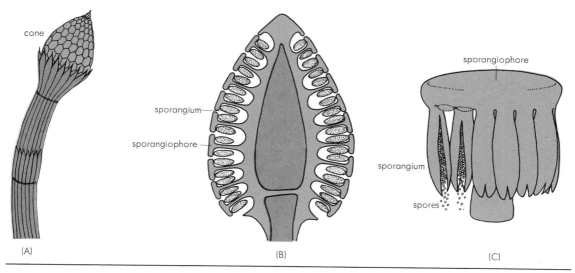

(A)   (B)   (C)

FIG. 27-3.   The cone of *Equisetum* diagrammatically shown. A. Stem with terminal cone. B. Longitudinal section of cone showing its central axis to which are attached sporangiophores, each of which bears sporangia. C. A single sporangiophore shown enlarged with its sporangia.

FIG. 27-4.   Cones (strobili) of *Equisetum*. The cones of *E. arvense* in succeeding stages of maturation. The cone at the right is immature and the sporangiophores are close-packed. As the cone matures, its axis elongates, separating the sporangiophores and exposing the sporangia as seen in the cone at the left. (Photo by W. R. Kennedy.)

to the ground. Shedding and dispersal of the spores is aided by the hygroscopic movement of tiny appendages called elaters which are attached to one end of each spore and coil and uncoil in response to changes in atmospheric humidity (Fig. 27-5). The spores germinate on moist soil to produce small, green, photosynthetic gametophytes (Fig. 27-6). All living species of the Arthrophyta are homosporous, and their gametophytes commonly, but not always, bear both archegonia and antheridia. Sperms swim through water to the

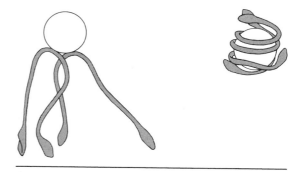

FIG. 27-5.   *Equisetum* spores showing ribbon-like elaters in uncoiled and coiled positions.

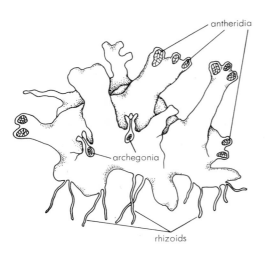

FIG. 27–6. The gametophyte of *Equisetum* showing the antheridia and archegonia and the commonly characteristic, erect photosynthetic lobes growing from the prostrate cushion-like portion.

FIG. 27–7. *Equisetum hyemale. Left:* Without cone. *Right:* With cone. (Photo by W. R. Kennedy.)

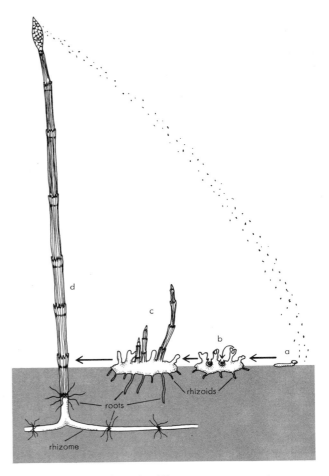

FIG. 27–8. Life cycle of *Equisetum.* a. germinating spore; b. gametophyte with antheridia and archegonia. Fertilization as indicated by arrow; c. young sporophyte shoots and roots on old gametophyte; d. mature sporophyte after several years. Independent of the gametophyte.

FIG. 27-9.   Carboniferous swamp. The trees at right with jointed trunks are *Calamites*, an arthrophyte genus. The small plants in the foreground are sphenophylls, small, vine-like arthrophytes. Courtesy of Field Museum of Natural History.

archegonia, one sperm fertilizing the single egg in an archegonium. The zygote develops into a multicellular embryo within the archegonium. Soon after, the growing embryo emerges from the archegonium and ultimately grows into a mature sporophyte.

Very commonly the plants also reproduce by means of vegetative propagation of the sporophyte. During each growing season the perennial rhizome produces many new aerial shoots, and extensive populations of many hundreds of shoots may develop in this way.

Equisetum can be found from the tropics to the cool areas of temperate zones, occurring everywhere except Australia, New Zealand, and Antarctica. Most species of *Equisetum* thrive in moist habitats, such as creek banks, bottomlands, and humid forests, but some species grow in such dry sites as railroad embankments. The dependence of these plants on water for sperm to swim from antheridia to archegonia, as well as for germination of the spores, is responsible in part for their more frequent growth in moist environments. Once established, the plants ordinarily maintain themselves year after year by vegetative propagation.

Representative Members   *Equisetum,* the only living arthrophyte genus, derives its name from the fact that the erect shoots of the branching

FIG. 27–10.   Left. *Calamites* fossil embedded in rock. Note the whorled leaves. Right. *Sphenophyllum,* another fossil genus with whorled leaves. (Courtesy of Dr. Henry N. Andrews, Jr.)

species resemble superficially the tails of horses (Latin: *equus*, horse and *seta*, bristle) (Figs. 27–1,A). Other, typically nonbranching species (Fig. 27–1,B) are referred to as "pipes" or "scouring rushes." The shoot system of *Equisetum* consists of a creeping, underground rhizome, from which arise the jointed, ridged stems. In branching species, branches as well as leaves arise in whorls at the nodes; such species are unique among the vascular embryophyta in that branches do not arise in the axils of leaves but between adjacent leaves of a whorl. In most *Equisetum* species, the shoots are herbaceous and rarely exceed 4 feet in height, but a few are shrubby, and one South American species is a vine that may reach lengths of more than 30 feet. The life cycle of *Equisetum hyemale* is shown in Fig. 27–8.

A well-known fossil genus, *Calamites*, consisted of large trees that reached heights from 20 to 30 meters (Fig. 27–9). Leaves of one species of *Calamites* are shown in Fig. 27–10, left. *Equisetum* is not descended from *Calamites*, but the

superficial resemblance is striking. *Sphenophyllum*, another fossil genus with whorled leaves, is shown in Fig. 27–10, right.

Relationship with Other Organisms   The origin of the Arthrophyta is speculative. Present botanical opinion holds that they may have been derived from that group of Devonian psilophytes that had single, terminal sporangia.

Importance in Nature and in Human Life   Living species of horsetails have virtually no economic value. Ecologically they appear to be of only minor importance. Because of their rough texture, the stems have been used as abrasive material for scouring pots, pans, and floors (hence the name "scouring rushes") and were used in this way by early European settlers of North America. In contrast, however, the Arthrophyta of the Paleozoic era play a major role in the economy of the modern world, for their carbonized remains constitute a significant portion of our coal deposits.

SUMMARY

1. The Arthrophyta (horsetails) have the following characteristics.

   a. True roots, stems, and leaves with vascular tissues.

   b. The sporophyte consists of a shoot system of horizontal rhizomes and stems, both of which are hollow, jointed in appearance, with distinct nodes and internodes, generally longitudinally ridged, and are commonly impregnated with silica.

   c. Leaves are borne in whorls at the nodes of the erect shoots and the rhizome.

   d. Branches occur in whorls at the nodes of erect shoots.

   e. Sporangia are borne on sporangiophores that form cylindrical or ovoid cones.

2. The sporophyte is the dominant generation and is autotrophic. In the living species, the main organ of photosynthesis is the stem, the leaves being nonphotosynthetic and reduced to small scales.

3. In sexual reproduction, as known in the living species, the sporophyte produces spores which germinate on soil, forming small, often branched gametophytes that are autotrophic and that bear archegonia and antheridia. Sperms swim through water to archegonia, which they enter, one sperm fertilizing an egg. The zygote forms an embryo that is dependent briefly on the gametophyte for food. The embryo grows into a mature autotrophic sporophyte.

4. In asexual reproduction, new aerial shoots are formed by the rhizome which is perennial.

5. Living species are homosporous.

6. Living horsetails are widely distributed over the earth's surface, principally in moist habitats. Some of the extinct species were also widely distributed.

7. The first plants resembling Arthrophytes occur in strata of lower Devonian age. They most probably originated from vascular plants with simple psilophytic features. They reached their greatest development during the time from the Devonian period to the end of the Paleozoic. All are extinct save for the single genus *Equisetum* with about 25 species.

8. Living horsetails have negligible economic value; they are occasionally used as abrasives for scouring purposes. By contrast, horsetails of the Paleozoic era are of considerable economic value because their carbonized remains form much of the world's coal deposits.

9. Some species of *Equisetum* have only one type of shoot which serves both vegetatively for photosynthesis and reproductively as the bearer of cones. Other species have two kinds of shoots, those which are green and serve only in a vegetative capacity and those which are nongreen (commonly pink or tan) and serve only in reproduction.

10. A well-known fossil genus is *Calamites*, most members of which were large trees.

SUGGESTED READINGS FOR INTERESTED STUDENTS

1. Andrews, H. N., Jr., *Studies in Paleobotany*. Wiley, New York, 1961.

2. Bold, H. C., *Morphology of Plants,* 2 ed. Harper & Row, New York, 1967.

3. Delevoryas, T., *Morphology and Evolution of Fossil Plants*. Holt, Rinehart and Winston, New York, 1962.

4. Foster, A. S., and E. M. Gifford, Jr., *Comparative Morphology of Vascular Plants*. Freeman, San Francisco, 1959.

5. Scagel, R. F., et al., *An Evolutionary Survey of the Plant Kingdom*. Wadsworth, Belmont, Cal., 1965.

TOPICS AND QUESTIONS FOR STUDY

1. List the distinguishing characteristics of the Arthrophyta. What similarities exist between Arthrophyta and Lycopodophyta? What differences?

2. In what geological period of the earth's history did Arthrophyta reach their greatest development?

3. What is the present status of the Arthrophyta in the earth's flora?

4. Describe the structure of *Equisetum* sporophytes and gametophytes.

5. Describe the life history of *Equisetum*. Where in the life cycle does the haploid chromosome number change to the diploid number? The diploid number to the haploid number?

28

PTEROPHYTA (FERNS)

Ferns are the most highly evolved and the most successful of the free-sporing plants. Their success may be measured by their large number of species (about 10,000) and their wide variety of habitats. The major features of the fern life cycle are basically the same as those of other free-sporing plants described in preceding chapters. Ferns are characterized by the presence of **megaphylls,** (Fig. 26–4,B) usually large, structurally complex leaves having many veins. This leaf type may have originated phylogenetically by the reduction of a complex branch system. Free-sporing vascular plants typically have rhizomes, but, unlike the psilophytes, lycopods, and arthrophytes which have slender, erect stems growing from the rhizome, the fern has leaves growing from the rhizome. As a result, the above-ground portion of the plant body consists only of leaves held erect by relatively sturdy petioles. The majority of ferns are perennial herbs whose sporophytes are maintained year after year by the production of new leaves from the persistent rhizomes.

General Characteristics   The familiar fern plant is a sporophyte which consists of an underground stem (rhizome) that produces adventitious roots

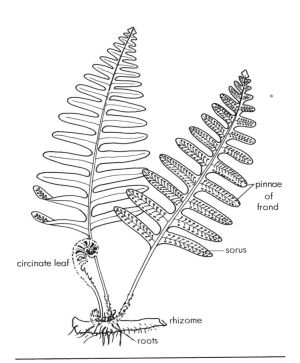

FIG. 28-1. *Polypodium* or polypody fern with rhizome bearing two mature leaves or fronds and one immature, circinately coiled leaf. The frond blade is dissected into many small leaflets or pinnae which bear sori on their lower surface.

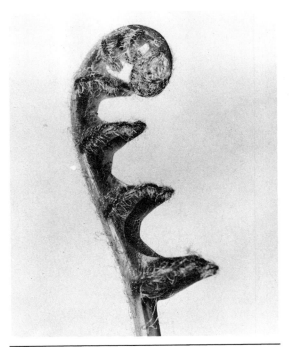

FIG. 28-2. The fiddlehead, or circinately coiled tip of the early growth stage of a fern leaf. (Photo courtesy of W. R. Kennedy.)

and large leaves called **fronds.** The frond consists of a petiole and blade. Typically, the blade is dissected into many small leaflets termed **pinnae** which are borne on a central stalk, the **rachis** (Fig. 28-1). In early growth stages, all the parts of the frond are closely coiled much as in a watch spring. In this form the juvenile leaf is often referred to as a **crozier** or "fiddlehead," which it supposedly resembles (Fig. 28-2). Growth and enlargement result in an uncoiling from the base of the frond to its apex and from the rachis to the margin or tips of the pinnae. Leaves having this coiled form are termed **circinate.** Primary xylem and primary phloem occur in all organs of the plant; secondary tissues, however, are absent because ferns typically lack a vascular cambium. A major anatomical characteristic of ferns and seed plants is the presence of leaf gaps in their vascular cylinders. (See page 413 and Fig. 26–4,B.)

Leaf gaps are found in plants with megaphylls and are absent in those with microphylls. This correlation of leaf type with the presence or absence of leaf gaps is an interesting anatomical feature which appears to be related to the evolution of the two leaf types. The typical fern rhizome elongates horizontally at or just below the soil surface. It bears adventitious roots and produces new leaves near its growing tip. Older parts of the rhizome die and decay away so that a living specimen seldom includes organs more than a few seasons old. This process, together with branch formation at the tip of the rhizome, often results in formation of large, clonal populations of plants that are genetically alike. A few tropical ferns have upright stems and large leaves and are termed "tree ferns" (Fig. 28-3). Sporangia are borne on the undersides of leaves which, according to the species, may be green and photosynthe-

FIG. 28-3. Tree fern in Castleton Gardens, Jamaica. (Courtesy Dr. H. E. Balbach.)

tic or nongreen. Regardless of their other functions, these fertile, sporangia-bearing leaves are classified morphologically as sporophylls. Most fern species are homosporous, but several aquatic species are heterosporous.

Reproductive Characteristics The sporangia of ferns may be borne singly on the sporophylls but are more often produced in tight clusters called **sori.** Often, a sorus is covered and protected during sporangium maturation by a flap of tissue, the **indusium** (Figs. 28-4 and 28-5). In most sorus-producing ferns, a single sporangium consists of a short stalk and a terminal capsule (Fig. 28-6). Within the capsule, spore mother cells undergo meiosis to produce from 16 to 64 meiospores. Commonly a ring of specialized cells called the **annulus** extends up and partly around the capsule from one side of its place of attachment to the stalk. The cells of the annulus are distinguished by thickened inner and lateral walls and thin outer walls. When the spores are mature the annulus cells die, and as the watery protoplasm evaporates, the outer walls are pulled inward (Fig. 28-7,A), shortening the outerside of the annulus and pulling the thick lateral walls toward

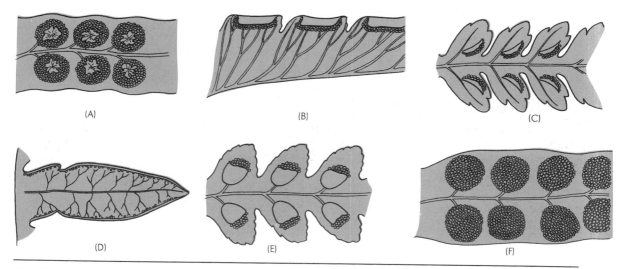

FIG. 28-4. Fern sori and examples of indusia. A. Christmas fern (*Polystichum acrostichoides*). B. Maidenhair fern (*Adiatum pedatum*). C. Lady fern (*Athyrium filix-femina*). D. Bracken fern (*Pteridium aquilinum*). E. Bulblet fern (*Cystopteris bulbifera*). F. Common polypody (*Polypodium virginianum*).

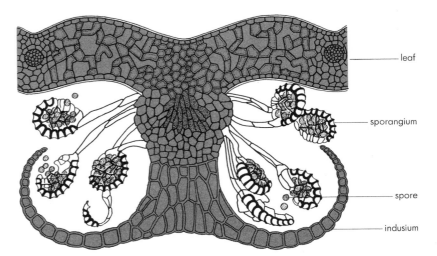

FIG. 28-5.   Cross section of a fern leaf and sorus. The numerous sporangia are covered by the membranous indusium. (After Kny)

leaf

sporangium

spore

indusium

one another. As this happens, the annulus straightens outward or even bends somewhat in the reverse direction, rupturing the sides of the sporangium and releasing some of the spores (Fig. 28-7,B). Many of the remaining spores are carried

back within the terminal portion of the capsule near the tip of the recurved annulus. When water loss from the annulus cells becomes so great that the attraction of the water molecules for the cell walls is overcome, a bubble develops in each cell,

FIG. 28-6.   Left. Fern sporangium with capsule ringed by the hygroscopic annulus and lip cells specialized to rupture the sporangium for spore release. FIG. 28-7.   Right. Fern sporangium in successive stages of spore discharge. A. Initial rupture at the lip cells due to shrinkage of the outside of the annulus. B. Top of capsule is drawn back by the drawstring-like shortening of the annulus. Most of the spores are still in the capsule. C. Tension on the annulus is released and the capsule recoils to its original position, catapulting the spores into the air.

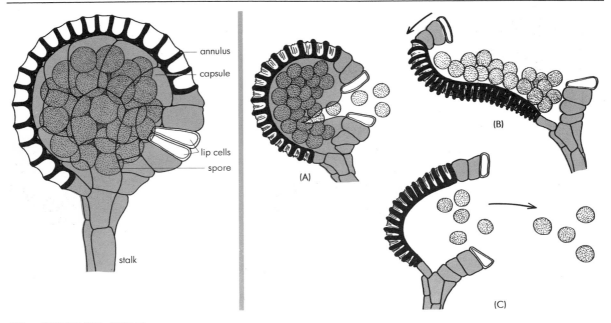

annulus

capsule

lip cells

spore

stalk

(A)

(B)

(C)

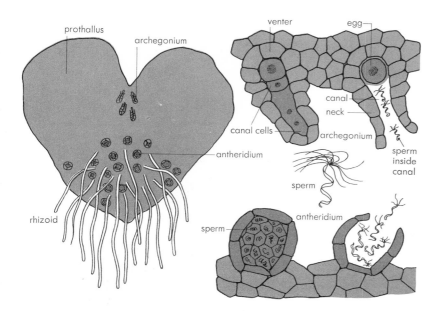

FIG. 28–8. Fern gametophyte (prothallus) with archegonia, antheridia, and rhizoids.

allowing the walls to resume their original shape. The instantaneous release of tension permits the more rigid, lateral walls of the annulus suddenly and forcibly to snap forward, catapulting the spores into the air (Fig. 28–7,C). Ferns which bear larger, isolated sporangia (not clustered in sori) commonly have less specialized annuli which simply rupture the capsule wall, allowing the spores to fall out. These larger sporangia usually produce more spore mother cells and contain larger numbers of meiospores at maturity than do the smaller, more elaborate sporangia.

On reaching a suitable substratum, such as rich, moist, shaded soil, a spore germinates, forming a short filament of cells that soon grows to form a flattened, heart-shaped gametophyte called a **prothallus** (Fig. 28–8). A typical prothallus is approximately ½ cm or less across, is photosynthetic, and is attached to the substratum by rhizoids that grow from its under surface near the pointed end of the "heart." A single prothallus may bear both antheridia and archegonia (Fig. 28–8) or may be functionally only male or female. The antheridia are usually scattered among the bases of the rhizoids on the lower surface, and

the archegonia are borne near the notch of the "heart." When the gametangia and gametes are mature and when water is available, coiled, flagellated sperms (Fig. 28–8) are released from the antheridia and swim to the archegonia. The archegonia are bowling pin-shaped, as in the lower

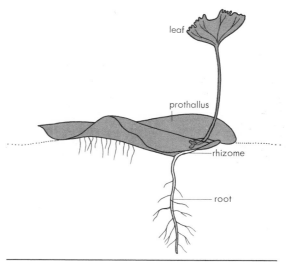

FIG. 28–9. Young fern sporophyte growing out of old gametophyte.

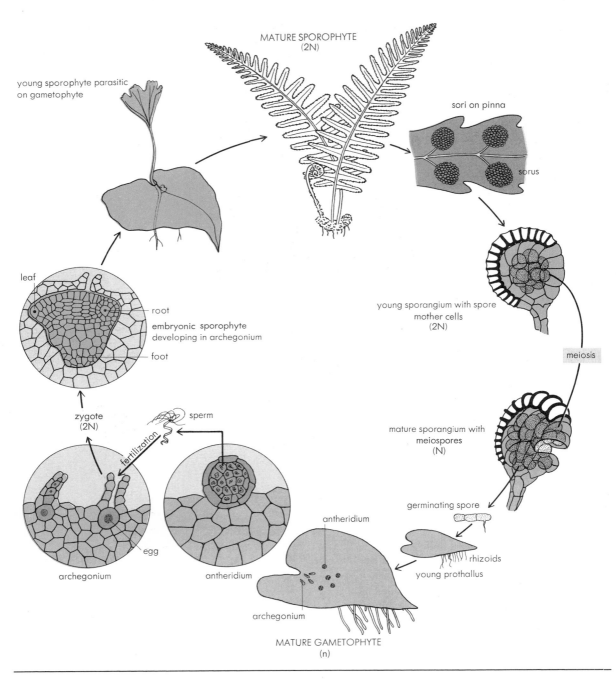

MATURE SPOROPHYTE
(2N)

young sporophyte parasitic
on gametophyte

sori on pinna

sorus

young sporangium with spore
mother cells
(2N)

meiosis

leaf

root

embryonic sporophyte
developing in archegonium

foot

mature sporangium with
meiospores
(N)

zygote
(2N)

sperm

fertilization

germinating spore

egg

antheridium

rhizoids

archegonium

antheridium

archegonium

young prothallus

MATURE GAMETOPHYTE
(n)

FIG. 28–10.   The sexual life cycle of a typical homosporous fern.

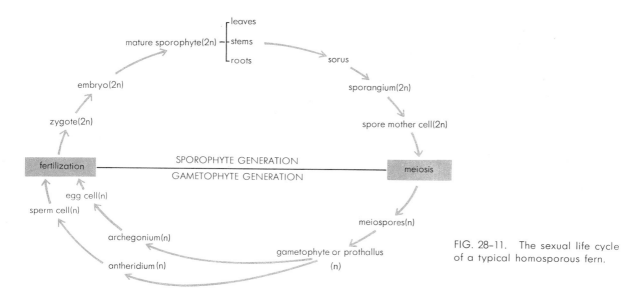

FIG. 28-11. The sexual life cycle of a typical homosporous fern.

vascular plants and mosses, and a single egg is produced in the venter (Fig. 28-8). Sperms swim down the neck canal of the archegonium and one of them fertilizes the egg. The zygote divides within the venter to form an embryo which for a brief period is dependent on the prothallus for its nutrition; continued growth soon results in development of a primordial rhizome which produces a root and foliage leaf (Fig. 28-9). The first foliage leaf is usually dichotomously lobed and veined; however, subsequently formed leaves resemble more and more closely the shape of frond

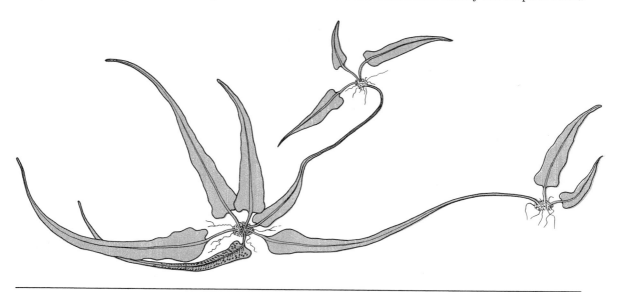

FIG. 28-12. Walking fern (*Asplenium rhizophyllum*). Note new plants developing from tips of leaves that have touched the soil.

FIG. 28-13. Christmas fern (*Polystichum acrostichoides*) shown in winter, growing in the leaf litter of a forest in Illinois. (Photo by W. R. Kennedy.)

FIG. 28-14. Cinnamon fern (*Osmunda cinnamamea*), (Photo by W. R. Kennedy.)

that is characteristic for the species until, ultimately, the mature form is achieved. The fern life cycle is shown in Fig. 28-10.

Although the cycle described above is typical for most ferns, a few have subterranean gametophytes that resemble small tubers. Such prothallia lack chlorophyll and obtain food through mycorrhizal association with fungi which digest and absorb organic matter from the soil. A few ferns are aquatic, and, unlike terrestrial forms, they are heterosporous, producing male and female gametophytes that are extremely minute.

Many ferns are able to reproduce vegetatively. Branching of the rhizome and subsequent isolation of the branch tips by death of the older portions result in production of clones of individuals, as described above. One common fern of North America, the bulblet fern (*Cystopteris bulbifera*), produces small, bulblike growths from the undersides of the fronds that break away and grow into new plants. The walking fern *Asplenium rhizophyllum* (Fig. 28-12) produces new plants from the tips of the elongated leaves when they touch the soil.

Habitat and Distribution   Ferns are widely distributed on the earth's surface, especially in the warmer parts of the temperate zones and in humid, tropical regions. Many ferns are poorly adapted to withstand drought and characteristically grow in moist, shaded sites. The flagellated sperm must swim in water to reach the archegonia, and this factor also tends to limit the plants to habitats that are at least periodically wet. Many tropical ferns are epiphytes and grow suspended from the limbs of trees, and a few species are aquatic and float on the surface of ponds and streams.

Representative Members   Ferns are best observed in their natural habitats, the most common of which is the floor of a deciduous hardwood forest. In mature, moist forests of eastern or far western United States, it is not uncommon to be able to find 15 or 20 species during only half a

FIG. 28–15. Boston fern (*Nephrolepis exaltata*) on the left and Maidenhair fern (*Adiantum capillus-veneris*) on the upper right, both growing on a rocky ledge. (Photo by W. R. Kennedy.)

day's walk. Since many species are evergreen, one can find ferns even in winter months, although, if prostrated by frost, they may have to be cleared of a blanket of dead leaves or snow. The evergreen, hollylike leaflets of *Polystichum acrostichoides* (Fig. 28–13) make it a popular Yuletide decoration and is the basis of its common name, Christmas fern. The commonest fern of eastern and central United States is the bracken fern, *Pteridium aquilinum* which typically grows in extensive colonies of knee-high plants bearing reflexed, almost horizontal leaves. Other well-known species include the cinnamon fern (*Osmunda cinnamomea*) (Fig. 28–14) and the Boston fern (*Nephrolepis exaltata*) and the Maidenhair fern (*Adiantum*) (Fig. 28–15).

Relationship with Other Organisms Ferns are believed to have evolved from psilophytic ancestors. Several quite distinct fern groups exist today and little is known of their interrelationships. Some extant fern families are very ancient, dating back to the Carboniferous and Permian periods of the Paleozoic; others date back to the Mesozoic. In the late Paleozoic and Mesozoic

there lived an important group, the Pteridosperms, that had fernlike foliage but, unlike true ferns, they bore seeds. They are not related to the true ferns, but because their leaves are so fernlike and because they bore seeds, they are referred to as "seed ferns." Impressions of fernlike foliage are so abundant in rocks and coal seams of the Carboniferous period that it has been called the "Age of Ferns."

Importance in Nature and in Human Life The Pterophyta of today are of relatively little importance in nature and in man's economy. Although a few are eaten by wild animals and some are even listed as possible emergency food for man, their contribution is insignificant when compared to the value of flowering plants. A number of species are cultivated for the unsurpassed beauty and grace of their fronds, and the dead and partially degraded root and rhizome systems of a few are widely used as potting media. In contrast to the living forms which are of little importance, the ferns of the Carboniferous period, especially large arborescent forms, contributed significantly to the formation of coal beds.

SUMMARY

1. Ferns share with the psilophytes, lycopods, and arthrophytes the same major life cycle features—a dominant sporophyte phase and an inconspicuous, but independent, gametophyte phase.

2. The leaves (fronds) of ferns are megaphylls, as are those of seed plants.

3. All vascular, free-sporing plants have a rhizome which is perennial. In psilophytes, lycopods and arthorphytes, the rhizome produces erect stems which bear leaves, but in most ferns the rhizome produces leaves which are held erect by petioles.

4. There are about 10,000 species of ferns, and in comparison to the other free-sporing plants, ferns show the greatest amount of variation. They are most abundant in moist, shady places.

5. A typical fern produces an underground stem (rhizome), with adventitious roots and large fronds.

6. Fronds are usually pinnately compound with a petiole, rachis, and pinnae.

7. In most species, fronds serve both vegetative and reproductive functions; in some the sporangia are borne on special, nonphotosynthetic sporophylls.

8. Sporangia are often borne in sori, which may be covered by protective indusia. The stalked capsules of the sporangia are opened by special cells with differentially thickened walls that constitute the annulus.

9. Spores from the capsule usually produce photosynthetic, heart-shaped gametophytes called prothallia. Prothallia bear archegonia and antheridia on their undersides, and sperms must swim in water to reach the eggs.

10. The embryo is briefly parasitic on the prothallus.

11. Many ferns reproduce vegetatively by formation of clones from rhizome branches and by other means.

12. Ferns are believed to have evolved from the Psilophyta, and are hypothesized to share common ancestry with many groups of seed plants including the conifers and flowering plants.

13. Ferns are of relatively little economic importance, although extinct forms contributed importantly to coal formation.

SUGGESTED READINGS FOR INTERESTED STUDENTS

1. Andrews, H. N., *Ancient Plants and the World They Lived In.* Comstock, Ithaca, N.Y., 1947.

2. Bold, H., *Morphology of Plants,* 2 ed. Harper & Row, New York, 1967.

3. Cobb, Boughton, *A Field Guide to the Ferns.* Houghton-Mifflin, Boston, Mass., 1963.

4. Delevoryas, T., *Morphology and Evolution of Fossil Plants.* Holt, Rinehart and Winston, New York, 1962.

5. Foster, A. S., and E. M. Gifford, Jr., *Comparative Morphology of Vascular Plants.* Freeman, San Francisco, 1959.

6. Scagel, R. F., et al., *An Evolutionary Survey of the Plant Kingdom.* Wadsworth, Belmont, Cal., 1965.

7. Sporne, K. R., *The Morphology of Pteridophytes,* 2 ed. Hutchinson, London, 1966.

8. Wherry, E. T., *Guide to Eastern Ferns,* 2 ed. Science Press, Lancaster, Pa., 1942.

TOPICS AND QUESTIONS FOR STUDY

1. Describe the structure of a typical fern plant.
2. Describe the life cycle of a fern, indicating the points at which chromosome numbers change.
3. Draw a fern gametophyte showing the rhizoids and gametangia.
4. Describe the structure of a fern sporangium and the action of the annulus in spore dispersal.
5. What is a sorus? An indusium?
6. Describe three ways ferns may reproduce vegetatively.
7. List the economic uses of ferns.
8. What are the supposed evolutionary relationships of ferns?
9. List the important ways in which the life cycle of a moss differs from that of a fern.
10. In what ways are the life cycles of mosses and ferns similar?
11. Compare the sporophyte of a fern with that of *Lycopodium* and of *Equisetum*.

29

CONIFEROPHYTA, CYCADOPHYTA, AND GINKGOPHYTA (GYMNOSPERMS)

General Characteristics The living gymnosperms are relics of the past. Although some of them are more abundant than flowering plants in certain regions of the world, as a group they consist of only about 725 species compared to the more than 250,000 species of flowering plants. In the Mesozoic period, these plants were far more numerous and probably dominated the world landscape. In one system of classification, they are grouped into several divisions of which we will discuss three: Coniferophyta, Cycadophyta, and Ginkgophyta; of these, the Conifero-phyta comprise the vast majority of the living species. Little relationship exists among these divisions but all the plants exhibit one characteristic in common, namely, they produce "naked" seeds. Such seeds are borne on the surfaces of stalks or scales rather than being enclosed in a fruit as is the case in flowering plants. The term gymnosperm is based on this seed production characteristic, the name being derived from the Greek words *gymnos*, naked, and *sperma*, seed.

Living gymnosperms are woody plants and most are trees. The conifers (Figs. 29–1 and 29–2) and *Ginkgo* (Fig. 29–20) are much-branched trees with slender twigs; the cycads (Figs. 29–18 and 29–19), depending on their age, are shrub or tree-like in stature and consist of a stout, usually unbranched trunk bearing a crown of large, pinnate leaves much in the manner of a palm tree. All have cambial tissue forming secondary xylem and phloem, the xylem lacking vessels and consisting chiefly of tracheids. The conducting elements of the phloem are sieve cells which are structurally less complex than sieve-tube members and which also lack companion cells as are found with sieve-tube members. The leaves

of most conifers and cycads remain attached to the stem and are photosynthetically active for at least two growing seasons; the leaves of ginkgo and certain conifers such as larch are deciduous. Conifer and cycad leaves are typically leathery and stiff and specialized to resist water loss. Leaves of gymnosperms vary enormously in size and shape. Conifer leaves are needlelike or scale-like and range between 2 millimeters and 20 centimeters in length (Fig. 29–4); those of the cycads are frondlike and often 2 meters long or more; ginkgo leaves are fan-shaped, commonly notched, and about 10 centimeters long (Fig. 29–21).

FIG. 29–1. (Left). Douglas fir (*Pseudotsuga menziesii*). FIG. 29–2. (Right). Scots pine (*Pinus sylvestris*) seen in early summer with the new growth on the ends of the branches showing strong negative geotropism. (Photos by W. R. Kennedy.)

FIG. 29-3. Two newly emerged young seed cones of pine prior to pollination in early springtime. Scales are separated or opened out for reception of the pollen. (Photo by W. R. Kennedy.)

Gymnosperms are heterosporous, producing microspores and megaspores that develop into microgametophytes and megagametophytes, respectively. The gametophytes are very small and are nutritionally dependent on the sporophytes. The microgametophyte develops endosporically to produce the pollen grain, and the megagametophyte develops within the megasporangium (nucellus) of the ovule. Transport of sperms to the eggs does not depend on water; rather, this is accomplished by wind and by growth of pollen tubes into the ovules which contain the megagametophytes and eggs. All living gymnosperms produce true seeds containing embryonic sporophytes. The embryo is embedded within the food-rich megagametophyte, which, in turn, is surrounded by the nucellar tissue and protective

FIG. 29-4. Pine seed cone a few weeks after pollination. Scales have grown together and closed the cone. (Photo by W. R. Kennedy.)

integument (seed coat). This entire complex of tissues and structures is termed the seed.

Reproductive Characteristics Reproduction in gymnosperms is principally by seeds formed during sexual reproduction and rarely by vegetative propagation as is common among the flowering plants. Although there are significant differences among cycads, conifers, and ginkgo, the reproductive process of the pine (genus *Pinus*, Coniferophyta) is representative.

FIG. 29-5. Pine seed cone one year after pollination and at about the time of fertilization. (Photo by W. R. Kennedy.)

FIG. 29-6. (Above). Pine seed cone in shedding stage. Depending on the species of pine, this stage is reached in the fall or the next spring following fertilization. (Photo by W. R. Kennedy.) FIG. 29-7. (Right). Developmental stages of the seed cone of pine. A. Young cone in Spring, at time of pollination. B. Young cone a few weeks after pollination. C. Cone one year after pollination and at about the time of fertilization. D. Mature cone in stage of shedding seeds, about two years after pollination.

Pine trees produce two kinds of cones: **pollen cones** (Fig. 29-10), which generally develop on the lower branches of the tree and which are usually rather small and somewhat soft in texture; and **seed cones** (Figs. 29-3; 29-4, 29-5, 29-6, and 29-7), which are usually borne in the upper part of the tree and are larger than pollen cones (sometimes reaching a length of nearly ½ meter) and which become hard and woodlike at maturity. Pine trees are monoecious; that is, a single tree bears both pollen cones and seed cones. A seed cone bears many spirally arranged **ovuliferous scales** (seed cone scales) on a central axis (Fig. 29-8), each scale bearing two megasporangia or ovules on its upper surface. Because a scale represents a reduced branch system rather than being a sporangium-bearing leaf (megasporophyll), it is referred to as a cone scale to denote this distinction.

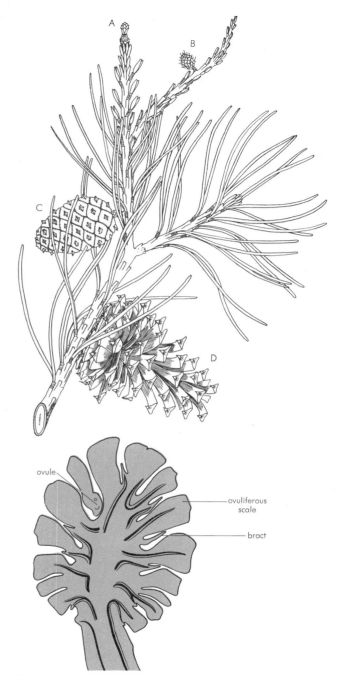

FIG. 29-8. Diagrammatic longitudinal section of young seed cone.

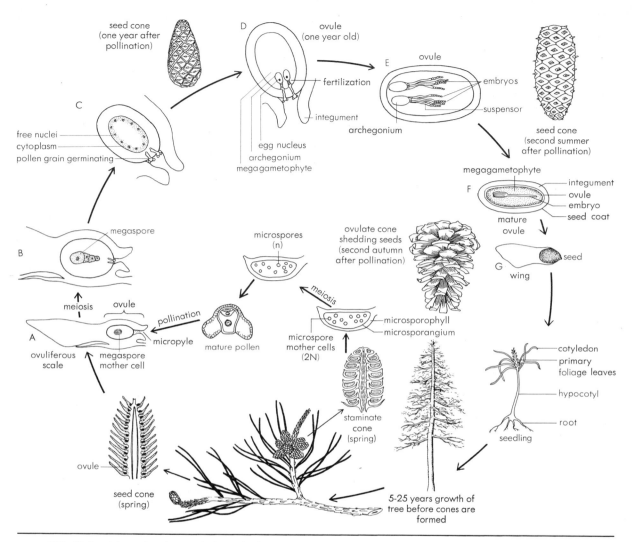

FIG. 29-9.   Life cycle of pine, A through H illustrating the stages of development in the ovules of the ovulate cone from the spore mother cell in A to the mature seed in G.

A salient feature of pine is the length of its reproductive cycle which spans two growing seasons and during which time the seed cone takes on three distinctly different forms (Figs. 29–3, 29–4, 29–5, 29–6, and 29–7) which are related to pollination, fertilization, and seed shedding. During the first season (spring) of this cycle, pollination occurs, and the young seed cone is small, soft, and green, with its scales slightly separated (Figs.

29–3 and 29–7,A); thus it is receptive to pollen grains which fall down between the scales and lodge near the ovules. In the ensuing summer, autumn, and winter months, the cone scales harden and become drawn together to form a compact, closed cone (Figs. 29–5 and 29–7,C) now containing the pollen. Fertilization takes place during the following summer, or approximately 12 to 13 months after pollination, and seeds subsequently develop during this second summer. In the autumn, when the seeds are mature, the scales become separated and recurved (Figs. 29-6 and 29-7,D), thus allowing the seeds to be shed. In some species the cones do not open for yet another year.

Stages in the development of the megagametophyte on a cone scale are shown in Fig. 29-9. A young ovule (Fig. 29-9,A) consists of a megasporangium (nucellus) bearing a single megaspore mother cell and enclosed by an integument. At one end, the integument forms a small pore or micropyle through which the pollen tube will enter. Pollination occurs when the female is in the stage shown in Fig. 29-9,A. During the first year of the reproductive cycle, the spore mother cell undergoes meiosis forming four megaspores (Fig. 29-9,B), three of which disintegrate while the remaining one develops into the female gametophyte within the nucellus (Fig. 29-9,C). The development of the female gametophyte is not completed until the spring following pollination, that is, about a year later. The mature megagametophyte consists of a mass of storage tissue and usually two or three egg-bearing archegonia enclosed by the nucellus (Fig. 29-9,D). Early during this second summer of the reproductive cycle fertilization takes place.

A pollen cone consists of a slender axis that bears many spirally arranged microsporophylls (Fig. 29-11), each consisting of a short stalk and two microsporangia (pollen sacs) within which numerous pollen grains develop following the reduction division of microspore mother cells. The pollen grain contains the microgametophyte and consists of only a few cells. The development of the microgametophyte from the microspore is shown in Fig. 29-12. The microspore (Fig. 29-12, A) protoplast divides twice (Figs. 29-12,B and C), one product of each division becoming prothallial cells which appear to be vestigial and to have no function and the other product being the antheridial cell (Fig. 29-12,C). The antheridial cell divides to form a generative cell and a tube cell, and the pollen grain is ready to be shed (Fig.

FIG. 29-10. A cluster of pollen (microsporangiate) cones of pine. (Photo by W. R. Kennedy.)

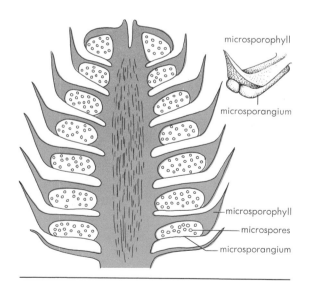

FIG. 29-11. Microsporangiate (pollen) cone of pine in median longitudinal section, shown diagrammatically. One microsporophyll bearing two microsporangia (pollen sacs) is shown on the right.

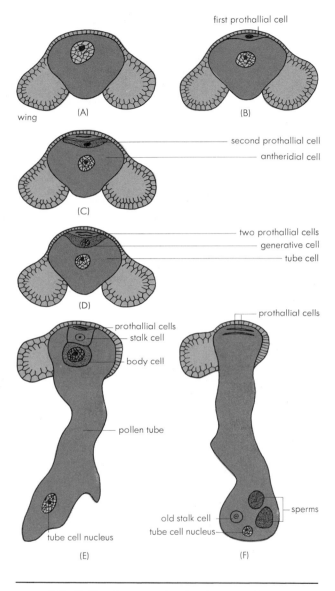

first prothallial cell

wing (A)

(B)

second prothallial cell
antheridial cell

(C)

two prothallial cells
generative cell
tube cell

(D)

prothallial cells

prothallial cells
stalk cell

body cell

pollen tube

tube cell nucleus

(E)

old stalk cell
tube cell nucleus

sperms

(F)

FIG. 29-12. Stages in the development of pine micro-gametophyte. A. Microspore. B, C. Stages in development of pollen grain from a microspore. D. Pollen grain (the stage at which the pollen is shed). E. Nearly mature microgametophyte. F. Mature microgametophyte.

29-12,D). Wind dispersal of the pollen is facilitated by the two balloonlike wings on its surface. During pollination the grains are transported from the microsporangia (pollen sacs) to the ovules at the bases of the seed-cone scales. Pollen which lodges near the small pore or micropyle of an ovule tends to adhere to a drop of sticky liquid which has been exuded from the nucellus (Fig. 29-9,A). As this liquid dries, the pollen grains are drawn into the micropyle until they reach the nucellus. The grain then germinates, and the tube cell grows to form the pollen tube that partially penetrates the nucellus. The following spring the generative cell divides to form a stalk cell and a body cell (Fig. 29-12,E) and then the body cell divides to form two sperm nuclei (Fig. 29-12,F). Upon reaching the vicinity of an archegonium, the pollen tube discharges the sperm nuclei into the egg cell, and one sperm nucleus fuses with the egg nucleus forming a zygote which develops into an embryo. The other sperm nucleus disintegrates. Since two or more archegonia occur in a megagametophyte and since each archegonium contains an egg, two or more eggs may be fertilized. Each zygote thus formed may begin to develop into an embryo, although usually only one embryo survives. Hence a mature pine seed ordinarily contains only one embryo (young sporophyte). A mature embryo (Fig. 29-13) consists of a hypocotyl, several cotyledons, and a shoot apex. In a mature seed (Fig. 29-14), the embryo is embedded in the storage tissue of the gametophyte, which is surrounded by a rather tough seed coat developed from the integument of the ovule. A wing develops with the seed, and this facilitates dispersal by wind. When the seeds are mature, the cone scales shrink and separate, and the seeds fall from the cones. After germination, the embryo grows into a seedling (Fig. 29-15) that ultimately becomes a pine tree, or mature sporophyte.

The life cycle of a pine tree (Fig. 29-16) has several conspicuous features that deserve special emphasis.

a. The gametophytes are very small, lack chlorophyll and are nutritionally dependent on the sporophyte.

b. Pine is wind pollinated. Sperm is carried to the egg by the growth of a portion (pollen tube) of the male gametophyte into the female gametophyte. Thus, water is not necessary for fertilization.

c. The female gametophyte remains within the megasporangium, within which fertilization and embryo development occur. The megasporangium, the enclosed megagametophyte and embryo, and the surrounding, matured integument or seed coat constitute a pine seed.

d. The storage tissue of a pine seed is a part of the megagametophyte, *not* the result of a triple nuclear fusion, as in flowering plants.

Reproduction in other conifers is essentially similar to that of pines, although minor differences occur in some genera.

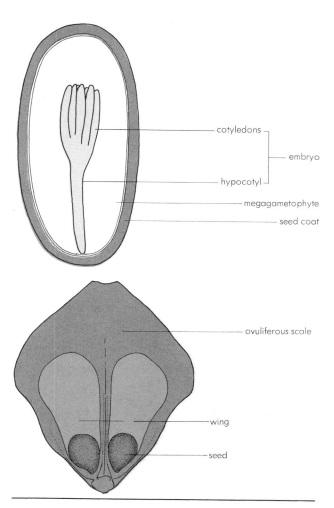

FIG. 29-15. Young pine seedlings showing the numerous cotyledons. On the plant at the right, the cotyledons have not yet lost the seed coat. (Photo by W. R. Kennedy.)

FIG. 29-13. (Above). Longitudinal section of pine seed.
FIG. 29-14. (Below). Single ovuliferous cone scale with two seeds each with a wing.

Representative Members *Coniferophyta*—Plants in the division Coniferophyta are widely distributed on earth and are well known for their ornamental and economic value. Because of their abundance and ecological importance, they have been called the dominant forest makers of the world. In addition to the pines, they include spruces, firs, larches, junipers, yews, hemlocks, cypresses, and many other groups. In the Conifer-

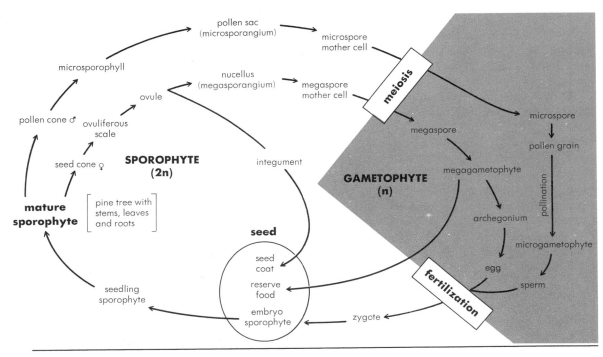

FIG. 29-16. Diagrammatic representation of pine life cycle.

ophyta we find both the largest and the oldest living land organisms, the former being the redwoods (Fig. 29-17) which can reach heights of more than 365 feet, with stem diameters of more than 10 meters and the latter being the bristlecone pines, some living specimens of which are known to be about 5000 years old. The coniferophytes display great variety of seed cone structure. Seed cones of pine usually require two years or more to reach maturity and are hard and persistent objects. Reproduction in other conifers is essentially similar to that of pines, although certain differences do exist. For example, hemlock, fir, spruce, and larch have an interval of only a few weeks between pollination and fertilization, and their seeds ripen in the same season in which pollination takes place. Also, the seed cones of fir and bald cypress fall apart at maturity to release the seeds. The cones of junipers have only a few scales which become fleshy as the cone develops, producing a fructification that resem-

bles a berry with several small, hard seeds. The "cone" of yew is reduced to a single, exposed seed borne at the tip of the cone vestige, with a red, fleshy collar partially enclosing the seed at its base.

Cycadophyta—During the Mesozoic era the distribution of cycads was worldwide, but today there are only nine living genera with approximately 65 species, and they are found only in tropical and subtropical regions. The majority are restricted to Mexico and the West Indies in the Northern Hemisphere and to Australia and South Africa in the Southern Hemisphere. One genus, *Zamia* (Fig. 29-19) has species native to southern Florida. The plants are slow growing; some species may be 1000 years old when only 5 or 6 feet in height. Cycads are dioecious plants with pollen cones and seed cones produced on different individuals. The cones are often massive, and this is true of pollen as well as seed cones. In the cycad seed cone, the ovules are borne on modified

FIG. 29-17.   Redwoods in Jedediah Smith Grove, Cal.
(Rapho Guillumette Photo.)

FIG. 29-18.   A species of *Cycas*, a cycad. (Photo by
W. R. Kennedy.)

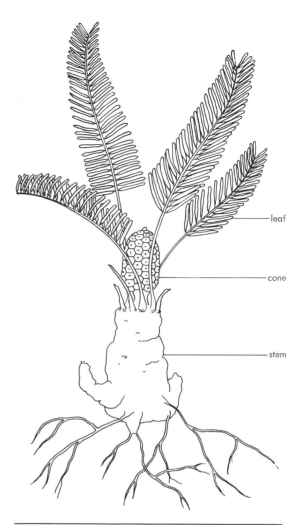

FIG. 29-19.   *Zamia*, a cycad, showing short, tuberous
stem, basal roots, crown of leaves and a seed cone.

leaves (megasporophylls) and not ovuliferous
scales (modified branches) as in the conifers.
Reproduction of cycads is similar to that of conifers except that the sperm cells have cilia and
are released from the pollen tube along with fluid
in which they swim to reach the egg of an archegonium. Two species of cycads are shown in Figs.
29-18 and 29-19.

Ginkgophyta—This division is represented
today by the single species *Ginkgo biloba*, the

FIG. 29-20. (*Left*) Maidenhair, or Japanese fan tree (*Ginkgo biloba*). Photo above shows branch of *Ginkgo* showing characteristic long and short shoots. (Photos by W. R. Kennedy.)

maidenhair tree or ginkgo (Fig. 29-20). Ginkgo is aptly described as a "living fossil"; specimens of essentially identical structure are found in the fossil record as far back as the early Jurassic. The species is believed to be now extinct in the wild state, having been preserved since ancient times as a cultivated plant in Oriental monasteries. Ginkgo trees have branching stems, which bear fan-shaped, often notched leaves (Figs. 29-21 and 29-22). The species is dioecious, some individuals producing pollen, others the seeds. The ovules are borne in pairs at the ends of stalks; usually only one of a pair develops into a mature seed, the outer wall of which becomes fleshy at maturity. As in cycads and conifers, pollination is by wind. The details of sexual reproduction are similar to those of pine, but, like the cycads, ginkgo sperms are ciliated and able to swim from the pollen tube to the egg of an archegonium.

Relationship with Other Organisms   Gymnosperms are thought to have evolved from progymnospermous lines that arose from the psilo-

phytes. Within these lines it can be shown that conifers and cycads have probably been distinct from each other since the Carboniferous period and that the seed fern line was probably ancestral to the cycads. There is no evidence that any of the living groups of gymnosperms are related to the other great group of seed-bearing plants, the Anthophyta or flowering plants.

Importance in Nature and in Human Life   The conifers are exceedingly important in nature and

FIG. 29-21.   Seed "cones" and leaves of *Ginkgo*. (Photo by W. R. Kennedy.)

in man's economy. Vast forests of coniferous trees in many parts of the world are effective in checking soil erosion and are important in providing shelter and edible seeds for many wild animals. The world's important softwoods, such as pine, cedar, redwood, spruce, fir, and Douglas fir, are products of coniferous species. These woods are especially valuable in construction work and in the manufacture of paper pulp. When these woods are distilled, they give off vapors from which are derived wood gas, wood tar, wood alcohol, and other industrially valuable products. Aromatic compounds, such as oil of cedar and oil of pine (turpentine), are important ingredients in medicines, paints, incense, and perfumes. Resins from conifers are particularly valuable in varnishes and paints. Amber, used in jewelry and pipe stems, is the fossilized resin of an extinct Baltic pine. Hemlock bark is an important source of tannins used in the tanning of hides to form leather and in the manufacture of some kinds of ink. The seeds of some pines, such as the piñon pine of the southwestern United States, are eaten by human beings. Many species of conifers are widely used in ornamental planting. Ginkgo has become an important ornamental plant in North America. The trees are graceful, free of disease, hardy, and are less susceptible to damage from smog and other urban air pollutants than most other species which can be grown in temperate

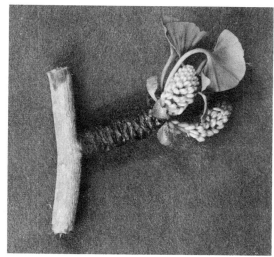

FIG. 29–22. Pollen "cones" and leaves of *Ginkgo*. (Photo by W. R. Kennedy.)

regions. However, the fleshy portion of the berrylike seeds contains quantities of butyric acid and smells disagreeably like rancid butter, so that care should be taken to plant only male trees in most urban areas. The Cycadophyta have very little economic value. They are today uncommon plants even within their areas of natural occurrence. The seeds of some species are edible, and a few are cultivated in warm areas of the country as ornamental plants.

SUMMARY   1.   Gymnosperms are plants which bear their seeds exposed on the surfaces of ovuliferous structures.

2.   The gymnosperms are woody plants which produce secondary xylem and phloem; the xylem lacks vessels and is comprised principally of tracheids; the conducting elements of the phloem are sieve cells.

3.   Gymnosperm leaves are usually stiff and leathery and are specialized for water retention; most gymnosperms are evergreen.

4.   Gymnosperms are heterosporous organisms; both microsporangia and megasporangia are produced on modified leaves or stems which are aggregated into cones.

5.   Microspores develop endosporically to become pollen grains.

6.   Megaspores develop into female gametophytes within the megasporangia of the ovules.

7. Pollen grains are borne by the wind to the ovules. In pine, pollen adheres to liquid exuded from the micropyle of the ovule, and, as the liquid evaporates, the grain is drawn through the micropyle to the nucellus.

8. The megagametophyte is a multicellular structure which is packed with food and which produces two or more archegonia.

9. In pine, the sperm is transported to the egg by growth of the pollen tube through the nucellar tissue to the archegonium of the female gametophyte.

10. After fertilization, the zygote grows into an embryo sporophyte. The embryo, the megagametophyte with stored food, and the nucellus and integument tissues collectively constitute a seed.

11. The division Coniferophyta includes most of the well-known gymnosperms, including pines, firs, spruces, larches, junipers, hemlocks, and others, in addition to their extinct relatives.

12. The division Cycadophyta includes nine living genera of cycads, all of which are tropical or subtropical, plus their extinct relatives.

13. *Ginkgo biloba,* the maidenhair tree, is the sole surviving species of the division Ginkgophyta.

14. The sperms of both the cycadophytes and ginkgophytes are flagellated and motile.

15. The divisions of gymnospermous plants are distantly derived from simpler vascular plants possibly related to psilophytes and are not closely related to one another; nor are they closely related to the flowering plants.

16. Conifers are of great economic value; they are major constituents of the earth's forests. They produce much of man's wood and paper pulp in addition to numerous other products, and they are extensively grown as ornamentals.

17. Neither the cycads nor ginkgo are economically very important, although ginkgo is becoming increasingly popular as an ornamental tree in urban areas because of its ability to withstand air pollution.

SUGGESTED READINGS FOR INTERESTED STUDENTS

1. Chamberlain, C. J., *Gymnosperms: Structure and Evolution.* Reprinted by Dover Publications, New York, 1966.

2. Ferguson, C. W., "Bristlecone pine: science and esthetics." *Science,* Vol. 159, No. 3817, pp. 839–846, 1968.

3. Grosvenor, M. B., "World's tallest tree discovered." *National Geographic,* Vol. 126, No. 1, pp. 1–9, 1964.

4. Scagel, R. F., et al., *An Evolutionary Survey of the Plant Kingdom.* Wadsworth, Belmont, Cal., 1965.

5. Schulman, Edmund, "Bristlecone pine, oldest known living thing." *National Geographic,* Vol. 113, No. 3, pp. 355–372, 1958.

6. Sporne, K. R., *The Morphology of Gymnosperms.* Hutchinson University Library, London, 1965.

7. Zahl, P. A., "Finding the Mt. Everest of all living things." *National Geographic,* Vol. 126, No. 1, pp. 10–51, 1964.

TOPICS AND QUESTIONS FOR STUDY

1. What is the meaning of the word "gymnosperm?"
2. Contrast the wood of gymnosperms with that of angiosperms.
3. What is a seed? How do the seeds of gymnosperms differ from those of angiosperms?
4. Diagram the megagametophyte and microgametophyte of pine and label the parts.
5. Sketch the sequence of cellular events proceeding from the microspore to the mature male gametophyte.
6. Make a list of the gymnospermous plants in some area known to you; of what division or divisions are they members?
7. Compare the diameter of the largest coniferophytes to the length of your laboratory.
8. Compare the divisions of gymnosperms with respect to their leaf forms, branching habits, distribution, and ovule-bearing structures.
9. Make a list of the objects you have used today that were derived wholly or in part from gymnosperms.

30

ANTHOPHYTA (FLOWERING PLANTS)

The flowering plants or Anthophyta (from the Greek *anthos,* meaning flower) comprise the largest division of vascular plants, with approximately 250,000 species. Since they have been described in detail in earlier chapters, this chapter will present only a summary of their salient features and a comparison of certain of these with those of other vascular plants.

General Characteristics   The Anthophyta (flowering plants) have long been known as the angiosperms. This term is derived from the Greek root words *angeion,* vessel or container, and *sperma,* seed, and reflects the fact that anthophytes mature their seeds within the closed structure of the fruit. This condition is in contrast to that of the other seed-bearing plants, the gymnosperms, which bear exposed or "naked" seeds. Angiosperms and gymnosperms share numerous characteristics; for example, all are heterosporous, producing microspores and megaspores which develop, respectively, into microgametophytes and megagametophytes. The gametophytes are small (usually microscopic) and nutritionally dependent on the sporophytes; transportation of the sperms to the eggs is accomplished through pollination and growth of pollen tubes to the female gametophytes; all produce seeds; their sporophytes are large and autotrophic except for a few parasitic and saprophytic species of Anthophyta; and active vascular cambia are common. In contrast to these points of similarity, the angiosperms differ in several important respects from the gymnosperms.

1. The reproductive structures of anthophytes are flowers rather than cones.

2. In the Anthophyta, pollination is commonly accomplished through the activities of insects (although, less commonly, they are pollinated by other animals, wind, or water, whereas gymnosperms are pollinated exclusively by wind.

3. The pollen of angiosperms is deposited on the floral stigmas, and the pollen tubes must grow through the tissues of the styles and ovary walls to reach the enclosed ovules. In gymnosperms, pollen is deposited directly on the exposed ovules.

4. Angiosperm megagametophytes lack archegonia whereas gymnosperm megagametophytes produce archegonia.

5. Angiosperms are characterized by the process of double fertilization, wherein one sperm from the male gametophyte fuses with the egg to form the zygote and the other sperm fuses with polar nuclei to produce the primary endosperm nucleus.

6. The endosperm of angiosperms is usually triploid (occasionally of even higher ploidy level) and is a food storage tissue unique to anthophyte seeds. Storage of food in gymnosperm seeds is a function of the haploid, megagametophyte tissue.

7. The xylem of most angiosperms has vessel members and vessels whereas the conducting cells of most gymnospermous wood are tracheids.

8. The phloem of angiosperms characteristically includes sieve tubes made up of sieve-tube members, and these are associated with companion cells. The conducting cells of the phloem of gymnosperms are sieve cells which are structurally less complex than sieve tube members and lack companion cells.

Reproductive Characteristics   Since the details of reproduction of the Anthophyta have been described in Chapter 15, this section will merely relate these details to alternation of generations (Figs. 30–7 and 30–8).

The typical leafy green plant—the shrub, tree, or herb, such as the rose bush, apple tree or corn plant—is the sporophyte. The flower of the sporophyte houses the gametophytes which, as in the gymnosperms, have become highly reduced microscopic structures. They are nutritionally dependent on the sporophyte, and they lack antheridia and archegonia.

DEVELOPMENT OF THE MALE GAMETOPHYTE The stamens of the flower are the microsporophylls, and the anthers are the microsporangia. Each anther consists of two pollen sacs, which, in turn are two chambered, so that the entire anther consists of four pollen chambers (Fig. 30–1). The pollen is the male gametophyte. The following sequence of events occurs in the development of the pollen. Diploid microspore mother cells are produced in the pollen chamber. Each undergoes meiosis to form four haploid microspores. These separate from each other and each acquires a characteristic shape and surface ornamentation. The nucleus of the microspore undergoes mitosis, following which the microspore consists of a tube cell within which floats a smaller generative cell. This two-celled structure is the **pollen grain**—the young male gametophyte, and in this stage it is shed from the plant by the dehiscence of the anther. The pollen is carried by the wind, insects, or birds to a flower's pistil which houses the female gametophyte. Upon reaching the stigmatic surface of the pistil of the same flower or of another flower, the pollen grain germinates by producing a long, slender protrusion called the **pollen tube.** This tube grows out of the pollen grain through a thin place **(germination pore)** in the wall of the grain and penetrates

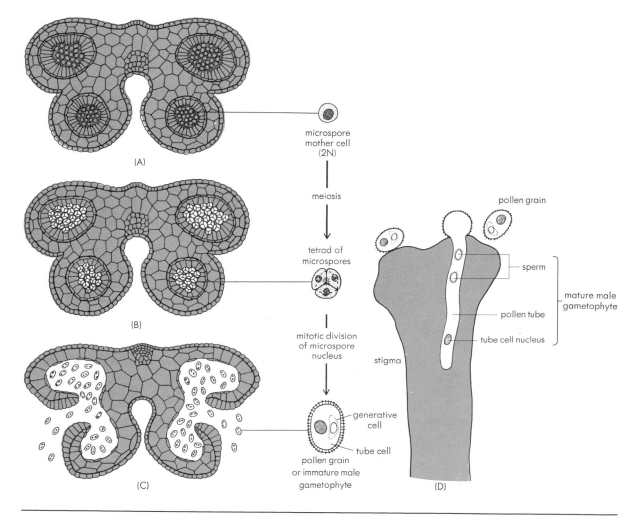

FIG. 30-1. The anther and the development of the male gametophyte. A through C, cross sections of the anther showing it in successive stages of development. A. Young anther containing microspore mother cells. B. Older anther containing haploid microspores formed by the meiotic division of the microspore mother cells. C. Mature dehisced anther shedding pollen grains. D. Stigma of pistil with pollen grains, one of which is now mature, having produced two sperm nuclei and a pollen tube that carries them through the tissues of the pistil to the egg.

the tissue of the stigma and style. At the same time the tube is developing, the generative cell undergoes a single mitotic division forming two sperm cells. The germinated pollen grain with its two sperm cells is now the mature male gametophyte.

DEVELOPMENT OF THE FEMALE GAMETOPHYTE
The carpels (making up the pistil) of the flower are the megasporophylls, and each encloses megasporangia or ovules. Within each ovule one megaspore mother cell is produced (Fig. 30-3). The megaspore mother cell undergoes meiosis to

form four haploid megaspores (Figs. 30-3, 4). Three of these degenerate and the fourth remaining functional megaspore gives rise to the female gametophyte, which in angiosperms is called the **embryo sac.** The functional megaspore enlarges greatly, its wall becoming the embryo sac wall. Its cytoplasmic mass and nucleus both enlarge. By a series of successive nuclear divisions, eight nuclei are formed within the embryo sac. Of these eight, three come to lie in the sac at the micropylar end of the ovule, three at the opposite end of the sac, and two remain in the center (Figs. 30-3, 4). The three nuclei at the micropylar end become invested by membranes thus forming cells, the central one being the **egg cell** and the two adjacent ones being **synergid cells.** Membranous walls also form around the three nuclei at the opposite end of the sac to form cells known as the **antipodal cells.** The nuclei remaining in the center of the sac are called **polar nuclei** and are not invested by membranes. This eight-nucleate embryo sac (Fig. 30-5) is the mature female gametophyte generation. In a few species, however, nuclei numbering other than eight do occur. Usually only the two polar nuclei and the egg cell are involved in reproduction. The remaining cells are interpreted as vestigial structures, or "evolutionary holdovers."

FERTILIZATION   The pollen tube tip enters the micropyle of the ovule and breaks through the embryo sac wall discharging the two sperm cells into the sac. One sperm fertilizes the egg to produce the zygote, the first cell of the sporophyte, and the second sperm unites with the two polar nuclei in a triple fusion. These two nuclear fusions constitute **"double fertilization,"** a phenomenon unique to the angiosperms. The triploid nucleus (formed by the two polar nuclei and the sperm nucleus) forms the primary endosperm nucleus which divides to form endosperm tissue that nourishes the developing embryo and often, later, the germinating seed.

DEVELOPMENT OF THE SEED   The seed, when fully formed, consists of an immature sporophyte

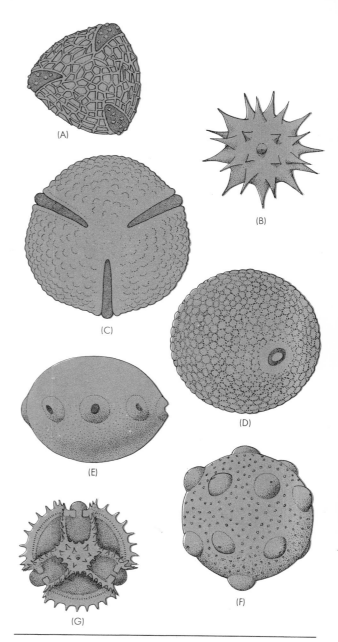

FIG. 30-2.   Angiosperm pollen grains showing examples of shapes and surface ornamentation. (A) *Salix fragilis* (willow), a dicot. (B) *Helianthus annus* (sunflower), a dicot. (C) *Fagus grandifolia* (beech), a dicot. (D) *Phleum pratense* (timothy grass), a monocot. (E) *Juglans nigra* (walnut), a dicot. (F) *Liquidambar styraciflua* (sweet gum), a dicot. (G) *Taraxacum officinale* (dandelion), a dicot.

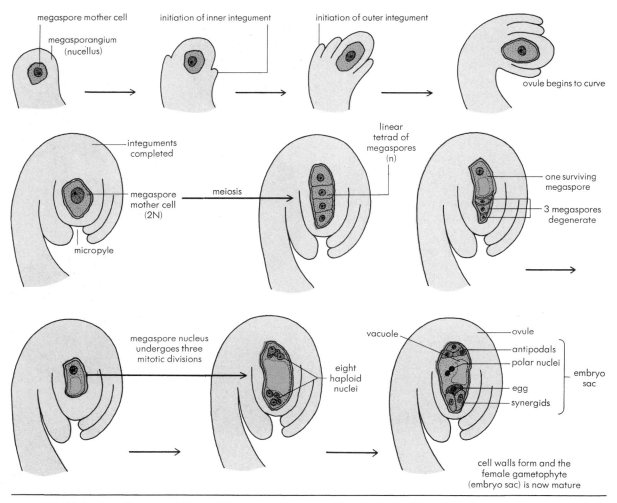

FIG. 30-3. Development of the ovule and the female gametophyte of flowering plants. Longitudinal sections illustrating the development of the ovule from the megasporangium (or nucellus), and the development of the female gametophyte (or embryo sac) from one megaspore formed by meiosis of the megaspore mother cell.

plant—the embryo—which may or may not be accompanied by a quantity of stored food—the endosperm—and surrounded by a protective coat. In the formation of a seed, the development of the endosperm begins immediately after fertilization, while the division of the zygote is delayed for varying lengths of time, from hours to weeks, depending on the species. In the early stages of seed formation, the embryo appears as a simple organ constructed of a stalklike suspensor and

an embryo proper surrounded by the endosperm (Fig. 30-6). Later, the embryo proper becomes differentiated into an embryonic axis composed of an immature shoot and root and bears one or two cotyledons. As development progresses, the cotyledons, or embryonic leaves (one in the case of monocotyledons and two in the case of dicotyledons), digest and absorb a portion of the endosperm. If the process of absorption of the endosperm by the cotyledons occurs during seed

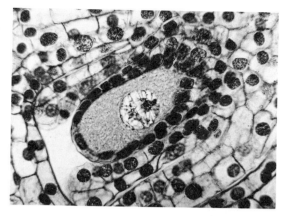

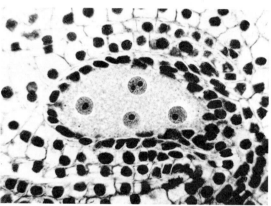

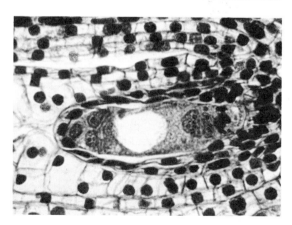

FIG. 30-4. Developmental stages of *Lilium* female gametophyte. (top) Ovule showing large diploid megaspore mother cell. (center) Ovule showing four haploid megasore nuclei. (bottom) Ovule showing 8-nucleate stage.

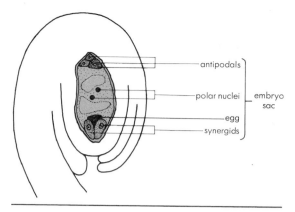

FIG. 30-5. Mature ovule in longitudinal section showing the female gametophyte (embryo sac).

development while the seed is still in the ovary of the flower, then the cotyledons themselves become the main food storage organs of the seed at its maturity. If the process of absorption of the endosperm by the cotyledon(s) occurs during seed germination when the seed is in the ground, the cotyledons serve as digestive organs, secreting enzymes and absorbing the food of the endosperm while the seed is germinating. There are some plants, mostly dicots, in which no endosperm is left at all when the seed reaches maturity. For a full discussion of seed structure and germination, refer to Chapter 2.

ASEXUAL REPRODUCTION   In addition to the usual reproduction by seeds, which involves completion of the entire sexual cycle, many angiosperm sporophytes have the ability to reproduce vegetatively. Very commonly this involves production of adventitious shoots from the root system, or from runners or underground stems (rhizomes). Less common asexual reproductive bodies are exemplified by the aerial bulblets produced by some onions and lilies, the tubers of potatoes and Jerusalem artichokes, the cormels of gladiolus, the plantlets which are produced by leaves of bryophyllum (Fig. 30-9) and some water lilies, and the asexual embryos produced within the seeds of many citrus fruits and dandelions.

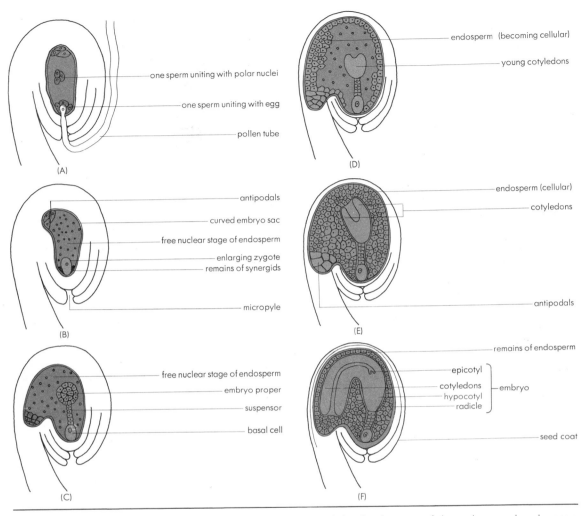

FIG. 30-6.   Sequence of stages showing double fertilization and the development of the embryo and endosperm. (Based on *Capsella*.)

These and other devices permit the establishment of clonal populations by plants with genotypes which are particularly well suited for the specific situation in which the original sporophyte grew.

Habitat and Distribution   Anthophytes are found in great diversity in all terrestrial habitats, and many have become secondarily adapted for survival in water or as epiphytes. Their very great adaptive potential, their development of unusually efficient conductive systems for both metabolites and water, and the remarkable integration of their life cycles with those of animals for efficient pollination, dispersal, and sporophyte establishment has permitted them to become the dominant plant forms over a majority of the land surfaces of the earth.

Representative Members   Most of the familiar plants we see, eat, and use in daily life are an-

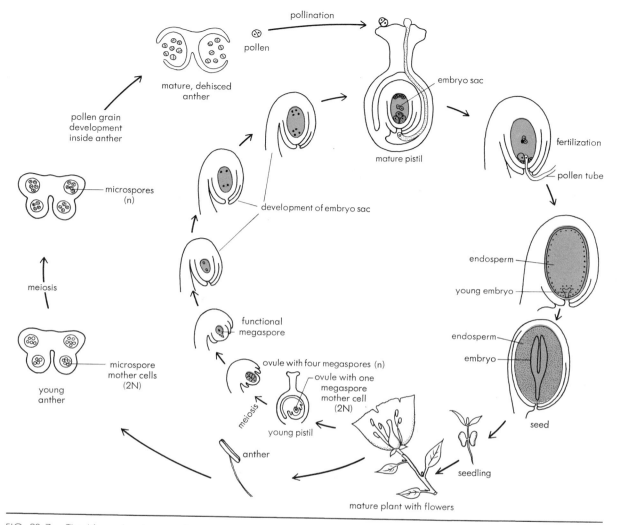

FIG. 30-7. The life cycle of an angiosperm.

giosperms. Many examples have been cited above and in other chapters of the text. The division is subdivided into two great classes, the Monocotyledonae and the Dicotyledonae. As their name implies, the monocotyledons have a single cotyledon in their embryos; in addition, they have floral parts typically in threes, produce pollen grains which have only a single germinal pore, usually lack cambium and thus secondary tissues, have scattered vascular bundles, and commonly bear narrow, elongated leaves with parallel main veins. The dicotyledons have two cotyledons in their embryos, have flower parts most commonly in fives or fours, produce pollen grains with three or more germinal pores, usually have vascular cambia which produce cylinders of secondary xylem and phloem, and commonly have broad leaves with net venation. For these comparisons, see Fig. 30–10. The monocotyledons include about 3000 genera and 50,000 species, the principal

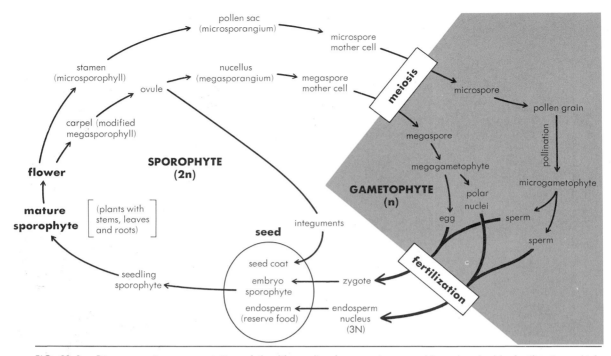

FIG. 30-8. Diagrammatic representation of the life cycle of an angiosperm. Note the double fertilization which occurs only in angiosperms.

orders of which are represented by cattails, grasses, palms, lilies, irises, amaryllises, spiderworts, bananas, and orchids. The dicotyledons, with about 9500 genera and 200,000 known species, are exemplified by magnolias, buttercups, roses, maples, walnuts, oaks, willows, legumes, sunflowers, tomatoes, poppies, mustards, geraniums, phloxes, carnations, cacti, mints, and snapdragons. Of these two classes, the dicotyledons probably appeared first, while the monocotyledons evolved from dicotyledons at an early state of anthophyte history.

Relationship with Other Organisms   The relationships and ancestry of the Anthophyta have been much debated for many years. They appear in the fossil record at the beginning of the Cre-

FIG. 30-9. Leaf of bryophyllum showing numerous small plantlets along the margin. These fall off the leaf and upon contacting the ground, each is capable of producing a bryophyllum plant. (Photo by W. R. Kennedy.)

taceous period, approximately 125,000,000 years ago, and even in these early deposits they occur in such diversity as to provide no clue about primitive forms or progenitors. At the present time, most investigators agree that their unique carpel is a modified megasporophyll which bears the ovules on its upper surface and which has, through gradual processes of evolutionary change, become folded and sealed along the margins in such a way as to place the ovules on the inside (Fig. 30–11). This interpretation of the anthophyte carpel, and the suggested manner of its evolution, has been strengthened by discovery of folded but unfused carpels in groups related

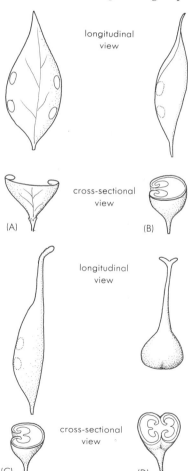

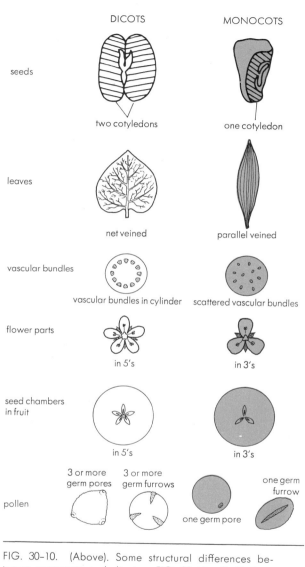

FIG. 30-10. (Above). Some structural differences between monocots and dicots. FIG. 30–11. (*Left*). Suggested sequence in the evolution of the pistil. (A) Primitive, leaf-like carpel with marginal ovules. (B) Carpel partially folded along its midrib. (C) Carpel margins fused, thus enclosing the ovules and forming a simple pistil. (D) Compound pistil made of two fused carpels.

to the magnolia family, one of the least specialized groups of flowering plants. Such a structure resembles the less-specialized megasporophylls of the cycads and extinct seed-bearing fernlike plants. The flower of the angiosperms is believed to be a short, specialized shoot, the leaf units of which have been modified as floral organs.

Importance in Nature and in Human Life   As indicated above, the Anthophyta are today the dominant and most diverse members of the plant kingdom. Their evolution and explosive diversification was probably responsible for extinction of some of the plant groups known today only as fossils, and for reduction in importance of most other divisions of vascular embryophytes. At the same time, however, the abundant food supplies presented by their nectar, fruits, and seeds, and by the foliage of herbaceous forms stimulated the development of insect groups involved in pollination, as well as those that feed on plants, and permitted the diversification and rise to dominance of warm-blooded animals which must have rich and abundant food supplies to maintain proper body function. The most important family of plants for man and other mammals is the grass family. All civilizations have been closely linked to development of cultivated grasses which produce abundant seeds—in Asia rice, in Europe wheat, and in America maize—and this dependence is still absolute. In addition, the angiosperms provide us directly with virtually all other vegetable foods and indirectly with virtually all meat and edible animal products save those derived from fish. They also furnish clothing, medicines, ornamentals, and building and industrial materials.

SUMMARY   1.   The Anthophyta is the largest division of vascular plants, with approximately 250,000 species.

2.   The plants are commonly known as angiosperms for the character of bearing seeds enclosed in fruits. The divisional name Anthophyta means flowering plants.

3.   Anthophytes resemble gymnosperms in gross structure, life-cycle characteristics, and seed production, but they differ significantly in
   a. Bearing flowers
   b. Insect pollination
   c. Germination of the pollen grains some distance from the ovules
   d. Simpler megagametophytes which lack archegonia
   e. Double fertilization
   f. Triploid endosperm, the food-storage tissue of the seed
   g. Production of vessels
   h. Production of more complex phloem conducting cells, the sieve-tube members which are associated with companion cells

4.   The sexual cycle of anthophytes resembles that of other embryophytes but is distinguished by the complexity of the sporophyte generation and extreme reduction of the gametophyte generation.

5.   Numerous asexual means are utilized by angiosperms to produce identical progeny that are particularly well suited for the specific situations in which they grow.

6. The Anthophyta are today the dominant land plants of the earth.

7. The two classes, Monocotyledonae and Dicotyledonae, are distinguished by differences of cotyledon number, flower structure, pollen type, anatomy, and leaf structure.

8. The Anthophyta are believed to be derived from ancestors which resembled the seed-bearing ferns and cycads. This hypothesis is based in part on our interpretation of carpel structure.

9. The flower is interpreted as a short shoot in which the leaf units have been modified as floral organs.

10. The Anthophyta are the most important plants on earth. They have influenced the evolution of both insects and mammals and are used by man in many ways.

11. The grass family provides much of the food for animals and man, and the cultivated grasses are intimately linked to the development of human civilizations.

SUGGESTED READINGS FOR INTERESTED STUDENTS

1. Benson, L., *Plant Classification*. Heath, Boston, 1957.
2. de Wit, H. C. D., *Plants of the World, The Higher Plants,* Vol. I. Dutton, New York, 1966.
3. Eames, A. J., *Morphology of the Angiosperms*. McGraw-Hill, New York, 1961.
4. Porter, C. L., *Taxonomy of Flowering Plants*, 2 ed. Freeman, San Francisco, 1967.
5. Scagel, R. F., et al., *An Evolutionary Survey of the Plant Kingdom*. Wadsworth, Belmont, Cal., 1965.

TOPICS AND QUESTIONS FOR STUDY

1. Compare the Anthophyta and Coniferophyta for significant points of similarity and difference.

2. Drawing on your knowledge of other plant divisions, list the unique features of the anthophyte life cycle; of the sporophyte; of the gametophyte generation.

3. What is the meaning of the terms: angiosperm, double fertilization, endosperm, insect pollination and flower?

4. Compare the monocotyledons and dicotyledons, listing as many points of difference as you can.

5. List ten monocotyledons and ten dicotyledons.

6. To what plants are the Anthophyta possibly related?

7. Discuss the importance of the Anthophyta to insects; to mammals; to man.

8. Make a list of all the items you have seen, eaten, or used today that are in no way associated with angiosperms.

9. With what elements of the anthophyte life cycle is the gametophyte of a moss comparable? Of a fern prothallus? Of a pine tree?

31

THE EVOLUTION
OF PLANTS

Two of the most readily demonstrated aspects of the physical and biological world are change and diversity. Geologists have evidence indicating that over the past five billion years the earth has cooled, the seas developed, and the land masses formed during the process of creation of the physical earth we know today. Furthermore, the seas, the land areas, and even the atmosphere have not remained constant since their development but have undergone changes throughout the history of earth. Mountain ranges have risen and subsequently been leveled by erosion and glacia-

tion; land bridges between some of the continents have appeared and subsided again into the sea; volcanos have burst into fiery activity and become quiescent; the sea has invaded the land and receded, leaving behind identifiable remains and sediments; the continents themselves seem to have broken from some primordial land mass and drifted apart. We see that these processes of change continue at the present time: earthquakes, sometimes vast and devastating, signify sudden shifts in position of the earth's crust; volcanos erupting on the ocean floor build islands where no visible land existed before; and the atmospheric changes inflicted by modern man have become a matter of international concern. The different events of the past have led to physical diversity which further influences both the physical and biological worlds. For example, mountain ranges modify the effects of insolation, rainfall, and temperature, and different rock strata influence the natures of soils developed from them. Similar change and diversity is also characteristic for the biological world. Fossil remains of organisms of the past show them to have been different from those of today, and organic diversity is everywhere apparent, ranging from the array of individual characteristics which distinguish one student from another to the vast differences that distinguish elephants from mosquitos and mushrooms from orchids.

It is evident that the physical and biological diversity we now find on earth is related to and developed from that of the past. The processes of change that have led to the present are termed **evolution; inorganic evolution** embraces all those transformations that nonliving things—rocks, oceans, mountain ranges—have undergone; **organic evolution** includes the continuous series of changes associated with genetic and physiological adaptation of living organisms to earth environments and by means of which living things have achieved modern diversity and complexity. The concept of organic evolution has greatly influenced all fields of biological science, and it is today both the point of departure for and the subject of investigation of many phases of biological research. The basic tenet of organic evolution is that the first organisms to appear on the earth were simple in structure and form and that the more complex plants and animals of the past and present developed from these by gradual modification through long periods of time. Although the discussion in this chapter is concerned principally with plant evolution, similar processes have accompanied the evolutionary development of the animal kingdom. Also, it should be remembered that the evolution of the plant and animal king-

doms and of the earth itself are concurrent phenomena, each interacting with and having complex influences on the others.

EVIDENCES OF ORGANIC EVOLUTION

The evidence that has led biologists to accept evolution as a demonstrated fact is of several kinds and has been derived from many kinds of studies of plants and animals. The most significant evidence comes from: (1) the study of fossils; (2) observations of the comparative morphology of living organisms; (3) investigations of the geographical distribution of organism kinds; and from (4) genetic and (5) biochemical studies.

Evidence from Plant Fossils   When plants die their bodies are ordinarily decomposed, resulting in eradication of all traces of the dead tissues. However, under special circumstances, dead plants or plant parts may be deposited in places where the normal processes of decomposition are greatly retarded or prohibited. One such place, for example, is at the bottom of a lake or pond of mineral-charged, acid water. Under appropriate conditions, such plant remains may be covered with sediments that later become rock, and the plant parts may be preserved in the rock as fossils (Fig. 31-1). The tissue may be petrified

FIG. 31-1. Leaf compression fossil of a fern showing sporangia on leaf margin.

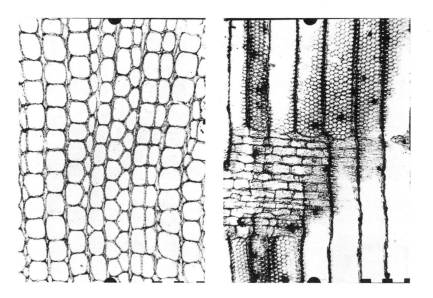

FIG. 31–2. Petrified wood of an ancient seed fern, *Callistophyton poroxyloides*. *Left:* Transverse section showing tracheids. *Right:* Radial section showing a portion of a vascular ray and pits in the tracheid walls. (From Delevoryas and Morgan. *Paleontographica*, 1954.)

by gradual replacement of the organic substance with mineral salts; such **petrifactions** often contain remarkable reproductions of the cellular detail, as in the fossil xylem shown in Fig. 31–2. The tissue may be squashed and reduced under pressure of the developing rock formation to a carbon **compression,** as in coal (Fig. 31–1). Cavities in the original tissue may become filled with fine sediment that hardens to form a **cast,** or the impression of the surface of the plant part may be preserved as a **mold.** Certain parts that are made principally of very stable organic compounds, such as cuticles and spore or pollen walls, may simply persist more or less in their orginal condition for hundreds of millions of years. Such preserved, fossil materials constitute the **fossil record.**

The study of plant fossils, **paleobotany,** shows that different kinds of plants occur in the various layers of rock that constitute the earth's crust. Since the rock layers were formed at different times, lower layers having been deposited before those which lie above them, it is possible to relate the fossils to certain time periods and to study the chronology of plant kinds. Paleobotanical study has shown that, in addition to the occur-

rence of different kinds of plants at different times, older rock strata contain simpler plants and more recent strata contain more complex ones. Thus, only algae and bacteria are found in very old rocks formed more than 600 million years ago, and flowering plant remains first appear in rocks only approximately 125 million years old. Rocks of intermediate age contain fossils of plants of intermediate complexity. In the fossil record, algae appear before vascular plants, lower vascular plants before seed plants, and gymnosperms before angiosperms. Assuming that the known fossils represent a fairly accurate, if incomplete, record of the kinds of organisms that existed on earth at different periods, this can only be interpreted to mean that simple plants of earlier times preceded more complex plants of later times. The fossil record thus provides clear evidence of change through time and of sequential appearance of ever more complex plant kinds.

Evidence from Comparative Morphology of Living Organisms   One of the most striking aspects of the modern flora is that variety of form is not random but that organisms are morphologically clustered. This is the basis for taxonomic classification and provides additional evidence to support organic evolution. Every plant (or animal) species provides examples of this morphological clustering. Each individual of a species is more similar to other individuals of that same species than it is to any individual of another species. Different species of the same genus are more similar to one another than they are to any species of other genera, and similar morphological relationships hold for the genera of a family, families of an order, and so on. We can easily demonstrate the actual relationship of many populations of species by examining genealogies which show that the individuals comprising a discrete population have common parents, grandparents, and so forth. Records of the development of different varieties of cultivated plants within historical times show that groups of organisms comparable to natural varieties or subspecies have been derived from common ancestral types by selection along different breeding lines. It is certain that, within a species, morphological similarity is the result of common ancestry. Genealogical records do not provide similar evidence for common ancestry of different genera of a family, different families of an order, and so on because such records extend over only a very short period of time. However, common ancestry provides a more plausible explanation for morphological resemblance of members of taxonomic groups than does the possibility of chance development of such resemblance among groups descended from wholly unrelated ancestors.

Evidence from Geographical Distribution

The major areas of the world each have species and assemblages of species (floras) characteristic for themselves. The ranges of species, of genera, and often of higher taxa are limited. This limitation cannot be explained wholly on the basis of preferred habitat availability. Exotic species introduced to a new area often find acceptable habitats and flourish as if they were elements of the native flora. (Well-known examples of such species in North America include the introduced orchard grass, timothy grass, Queen-Anne's-lace, water hyacinth, dandelion, field daisy, and Japanese honeysuckle.) Conversely, similar habitats in different parts of the world are often occupied by very different species of plants. A related phenomenon is the frequent occurrence of closely related plant species and genera within given areas. Many studies of plant distribution have led plant geographers to the conclusion that these distributional phenomena are related to plant evolution in the following way: if areas of plant occupancy are separated by barriers—such as high mountain ranges, large bodies of water, or intervening areas of unfavorable climate over which the plants cannot pass—the plants in these isolated areas tend to develop along separate lines so that the floras gradually become more and more distinct. At the same time, divergent evolution within a geographic area over a long period of time often results in accumulation of many related species and genera. In general, the longer the period of isolation of one region from another, the greater is the degree of difference among the plants of the two regions, and the larger is the number of related species in each region. Examples of distinctive plant groups evolved in different areas of the world include the cacti (family Cactaceae) of the American deserts, the cactuslike spurges (family Euphorbiaceae) of the African deserts, the ragweeds (genus *Ambrosia*) and sunflowers (genus *Helianthus*) of North America, and the gum trees (genus *Eucalyptus*) of Australia. Examples of long-isolated lands with very characteristic and limited floras include the Hawaiian and the Galapagos islands.

Genetic Evidence

The ability of organisms to interbreed within a species reflects the essential genetic identity bestowed by their common ancestry. Genetic similarity may also be demonstrated among species of genera and among genera of families by the phenomena of interspecific and intergeneric hybridization. Production of such hybrid organisms demands that the eggs and sperms involved be sufficiently similar genetically to permit formation of viable zygotes capable of developing into functioning organisms. Such hybrids are very well known in the plant kingdom, where their production has become an essential aspect of development of "improved" ornamental and crop plants. Just as genetic similarity within a species is related to common ancestry, genetic similarity within genera and families is related to common ancestry. The probability of the alternative—that is, the simultaneous, independent development of compatible gene systems with thousands of genes similarly aligned on similar chromosomes for all the generations of all the species between which hybridization is possible—is so remote as to be inconceivable, and there is no evidence that this has ever happened. It is easily demonstrated that organisms that are closely related genetically (that is, have recent common ancestry) are also very similar morphologically. Degree of morphological similarity can, thus, be used as a rough index of degree of genetic similarity and degree of common ancestry.

Genetic evidence of evolution is also found in studies of mutation and population genetics. Experimental populations of plants and animals observed in the laboratory show that new characteristics can develop as the result of mutation, spontaneous or induced genetic change. The spread of a new, mutant characteristic through succeeding generations of the population by means of interbreeding changes the nature of the population. Such a change is a small-scale example of evolution. In our everyday lives, similar mutational change has been demonstrated by the development of disease organisms resistant to widely used drugs, and development of insect strains resistant to insecticides. In plant domestication, man has used all these genetically important devices to modify organisms to better suit them to his needs and wants.

Evidence from Comparative Biochemistry   Just as assessment of morphological similarity can be used to estimate the degree of genetic similarity

and the degree of evolutionary divergence, studies of chemical similarity can provide important data. Perhaps the widest use of chemical criteria in the past has been at the higher taxonomic levels; for example, the types of pigments and stored foods are major diagnostic characteristics used in determining divisional affinities among algae. However, as chemists have broadened their knowledge of many kinds of compounds and have developed new tools for chemical analysis and comparison, such data have become increasingly useful in providing information about relationships at lower taxonomic levels. It is not uncommon today for evolutionary studies at the levels of the family, genus, or species to include information about seed proteins, oils, flavonoid and terpenoid substances, and other chemical groups which vary from organism to organism and from race to race. Although it might be expected that certain kinds of chemical studies would be extraordinarily useful in assessing genetic affinity, particularly those involving the chemistry of the genes themselves and of their primary products, it must be remembered that such data are still difficult to obtain and evaluate. In the final analysis, all data from the fields of paleobotany, morphology, plant geography, genetics, and biochemistry must be compatibly accommodated in any evolutionary scheme.

CAUSES OF ORGANIC EVOLUTION

The Theory of Darwin   The theory of organic evolution proposed by Charles Darwin in 1859 in his book, *On the Origin of Species by Natural Selection,* is now well known throughout the world. It is fair to say that no other work has had so profound an effect on biological science. It must be pointed out, however, that although Darwin's name is more intimately associated with the theory of organic evolution than that of any other individual, the concept is as old as philosophical thought. Darwin's justly famous position results not from his development of the idea but from his clear and carefully documented exposition of it. He compelled recognition of the importance of organic evolution for solution of real problems in all areas of biological endeavor. Darwin's theory on the origin of species is based on his observations of the effects which the following attributes had on living organisms: overproduction, competition, variation, and survival of the fittest.

OVERPRODUCTION   Organisms are prodigal in their reproduction and have the capacity to produce far more offspring than can possibly survive in the space available. This principle is recognized as fact by all biologists and is easily demonstrated. A single annual ragweed plant can produce as many as 180,000 seeds, a single orchid fruit may contain 1,000,000 seeds, a single pigweed may form 2,000,000 seeds, and a single puffball may release as many as 7,000,000,000 spores. Obviously, neither the space nor the necessary nutrients are available for growth of the enormous numbers of offspring of which a population is capable; too many offspring are produced under natural conditions for all to develop.

COMPETITION   The production of many more progeny than a given area can support results in intense competition for available space and nutrients, competition which occurs both among the progeny of particular parents and among organisms of different species. Competition acts as a natural check on the numbers of individuals of a given species that can utilize the available habitats and also results in the establishment of equilibria among the species growing in a particular region. Because of competition of progeny, only a small percentage of the potential number will survive to maturity.

VARIATION   The progeny of a mating pair vary. This is especially obvious when we know the parents and progeny well and are experienced observers of individual peculiarities, as with the children of Aunt Eunice and Uncle Robert or the pups of Walt Disney's Lady and Tramp. It is,

in fact, discernable when any parent-progeny group is examined closely, even in sunflowers, daffodils, or bacteria. This variation results in part from the total genetic difference which distinguishes the two parents from other members of the same species, in part from differential mixing of the parental characteristics in the progeny, and in part from spontaneously developed differences in the gametes. Perceptable variability within a population is enhanced by the fact that only a few of the possible progeny actually develop.

SURVIVAL OF THE FITTEST   Among the multitude of variable progeny possible for any species population, some will be better suited to compete successfully, while others will be less well able to exploit available habitats. The latter will be selectively eliminated or their reproductive effectiveness reduced. The result will be "natural selection" of the more favorably endowed to pass their genes and gene combinations to the next generation.

Darwin saw that the result of these basic attributes of life would be a tendency for survival of ever better adapted organisms in any breeding line. Those organisms with favorable characteristics, allowing them best to compete and reproduce in an area, would produce more offspring which would also vary and compete, and the process of improvement and change would continue indefinitely. These processes could result in development of new species in two ways: (1) a given reproductive line could gradually change or evolve through time until the resulting population was so different from the original that it would have become a different species; or (2) different portions of an original population might be subjected to different kinds of selective pressures, adaptive changes could differ for each portion, and the result could be the development of two or more derivative species from the original population. Carried to its ultimate extension, one might hypothesize that Darwin's concept of evolution would permit all terrestrial life to have been developed, over a very long period of time, from a single or limited starting population.

Darwin could not explain the mechanism of inheritance, but the rediscovery of Mendel's work in genetics and the subsequent elaboration of the significance of chromosomes and particulate genes enabled Hugo de Vries many years later to develop the mutation theory to explain the mechanics of evolution.

The Mutation Theory   The Dutch botanist Hugo de Vries spent considerable time prior to 1901 studying the nature of character inheritance in the evening primrose, *Oenothera lamarkiana*. While recording genealogies and carefully studying various progeny lines, de Vries noted that parents of known types derived from pure-breeding lines occasionally produced aberrant progeny with characteristics that could not have been predicted, either from study of the parents and their genealogies, or from study of their other progeny. Most importantly, these new types "bred true"; that is, they passed the new characteristics to their progeny, and the new characteristics were continued indefinitely in the breeding lines thus established. Such sudden, distinct changes of genotype de Vries called **mutations,** and the organisms possessing mutations were termed **mutants.** From his observations, de Vries formulated his mutation theory of evolution, the essential point of which was that new species are developed by means of the accumulation of sudden modifications of considerable magnitude (mutations) that render the mutants distinct from their progenitors from the instant of their origin. Thus, de Vries offered what is essentially a modification of the theory of Darwin, differing only by believing that evolutionary changes are not gradual developments but rather abrupt steps effected at the moment of zygote formation.

The terms mutant and mutation are still used and are applied to changes in genetic make-up, although in general they apply to much smaller changes than those observed by de Vries. It is now known that a peculiarity of the meiotic chromosomal pairing in the plants he was studying did indeed lead to sudden expression of scores of accumulated mutations, but this phenomenon is not at all widespread and is definitely an exception to the manner in which most mutations are expressed.

THE MODERN INTERPRETATION   During this century biologists have learned a great deal about the mechanism of character inheritance and about the nature of genes and their actions. This information has generally supported the theories of Darwin and de Vries but has provided better understanding of how the process of **speciation,** the formation of new species, actually occurs. It has been demonstrated that new genes develop by mutation of existing, parental genes into new forms. These new genes normally represent new alleles which can act in concert with already available alleles and with other genes characteristic for the group. These new gene forms provide the basis for species variability. If they are favorable in their effects, they are spread throughout a breeding population by *outcrossing,* which is the interbreeding of two different individuals to form progeny, and by *recombination,* which is the mixing of parental genes through passage of different chromosomes, chromosome segments, and gene groupings to different gametes. The majority of mutations will be of no value or will engender unfavorable characteristics so that they will be eliminated from the population by the death of the mutant or by its reduced breeding capabilities. A few, however, will be favorable in their effects and will be passed to succeeding generations.

It is popularly believed that mutation is a rare and infrequent event, but modern genetic studies show that mutation is quite common at the level of the **genome,** the total gene compliment of an individual. Although the likelihood of mutation of any particular gene during a single meiosis is very slight (on the order of 1:100,000) the total number of genes comprising the genome of any gamete is so great that the probability of a gamete incorporating a mutation is relatively high (on the order of 50:50). Thus the chance that any given individual formed by union of two gametes will carry at least one mutant gene approaches 75:100. In any large, interbreeding population there will ordinarily be a fairly large number of mutant individuals vying for both space and breeding opportunity, and contributing new genes to the **gene pool** of the population. Favorable mutations (alleles) will tend to become increasingly abundant in a population through time as their possessors outsurvive and outbreed their competitors.

The effect of the processes described will be evolutionary change through change of gene frequency in a population. Because the survival of a particular variant is usually linked to strong competition and selection factors of the environment, the tendency will be toward better and more complex integration of the population with its environment, a process we perceive as adaptive evolution. It must be pointed out, however, that the mutation process is random and the nature of a mutation is not determined by the "need" of the individual. Indeed, the mutations occur during or prior to gamete formation, before any derivative individual exits. Adaptation of a population is, therefore, a direct function not of mutation need but of the kinds of mutations available, and if suitable mutants do not by chance occur, adverse circumstances will bring the population to extinction.

If a population ranges so greatly that individuals in widely separated areas are unable to interbreed as readily as they may with their neighbors, two phenomena may influence subsequent evolutionary events. First, different chance mutations will tend to occur and accumulate in different subpopulations on a purely random basis. Second, different ecological pressures acting on different subpopulations will tend to favor survival of different mutant kinds. For instance, in a species which ranges from Florida to Maine and from the Atlantic Ocean to the Great Plains in North America, subpopulations will be subjected to the selective influences of different climates, soil types, moisture conditions, grazing pressures, summer and winter extremes of temperature, lengths of growing season, and so on. Over a long

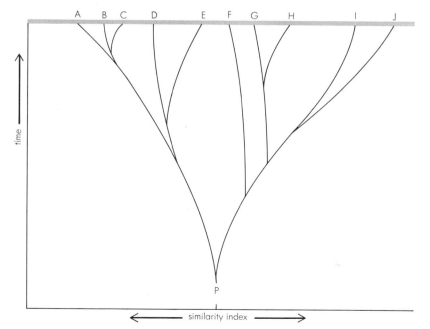

FIG. 31–3. Evolutionary relationships of hypothetical taxa A through J, derived from progenitor P. The line at the top of the diagram represents the present time. Note that the degree of similarity, as represented by the distance any given taxon or group of taxa is removed from any other, accurately reflects the evolutionary affinities except for E and F, a case of convergent evolution, and for F and G, a case of parallel evolution.

period of time, different subpopulations may become so uniquely modified physiologically and genetically that their members will no longer be able to interbreed in normal fashion when brought together; that is, they will have become reproductively isolated from one another. At this point, each such reproductively isolated derivative group may be recognized as a new and distinct species. Reproductive isolation may be accomplished in various ways, including geographic separation of populations, development of physical and physiological barriers to gamete exchange, development in angiosperms of different flower colors and forms that influence behavior of pollen-carrying insects, maturation of sex cells at different times, and development of incompatible chromosome and gene systems that prevent gamete formation or breeding ability in hybrids.

With reflection, it will be obvious that **divergent evolution** (Fig. 31-3) as described above requires the death and extinction of intermediate forms and populations. As we go back through time, the different branches of the evolutionary tree we presently see as distinct species, genera, and families, and even divisions and kingdoms, gradually merge and intermingle in one great continuum proceeding from the primordial life forms. Sudden extinction of entire evolutionary lines—such as the dinosaur, dodo bird, American chestnut, and the stand of prairie orchid that once stood where the new parking lot was built—are likened to what, from the standpoints of the lines involved, are catastrophic and overwhelming modifications of the environment. The gradual extinction of groups or kinds by simple death of parents which thereby removes progenitor and intermediate genotypes and the gradual replacement of one population by the ascendency of another which is better adapted are normal and inescapable results of the evolutionary process.

THE ORIGIN AND EVOLUTION OF PLANTS

Since the earliest recognizable plant fossils are those of morphologically simple algae and bacteria and since the fossils from later periods in the earth's history give ample evidence of increasing structural complexity, it is reasonable to suppose that the earliest plants were at least as simple in their structure as the simplest living thallophytes. Most algae and bacteria decompose rapidly after death and are not ordinarily preserved. Thus the fossil records of these organisms are incomplete and no unmistakable evidence concerning the first living plants has been derived from the record of the rocks.

Recent speculations about the origin of living things suggest that the first organisms were aquatic heterotrophs living in a world devoid of free atmospheric oxygen and in waters containing simple nutrient compounds spontaneously formed from available minerals and gasses. These organisms probably obtained their energy by means of anaerobic respiration, as a result of which carbon dioxide was released. They may have resembled present-day bacteria, which still require a moist medium containing dissolved nutrients. The gradual accumulation of carbon dioxide in the water and in the air set the stage for the next major evolutionary event—the appearance of autotrophic, photosynthetic organisms. Oxygen, released by autotrophs, was slowly accumulated in the evironment and led to the evolution of aerobic respiration. The earliest green plants were probably algae, the oldest green plants in the fossil record, and, morphologically, the simplest of green plants. The blue-greens may have been among the first to appear, for fossils of what seem to be blue-green algae have been found in very ancient rocks (more than two billion years old). Furthermore, blue-green algae are very similar to many bacteria in their structure. Coincident with, or following the appearance of blue-green algae, there may have developed primitive types of animals, probably microscopic and unicellular, like the bacteria and blue-green algae themselves and later other more complex types of algae. The appearance of green plants was the beginning of a great forward movement in the plant world, for it established a mode of nutrition that was to become dominant among plants and initiated lines of development destined to lead through the ages to the almost infinitely varied flora of modern times.

The Family Tree of the Plant Kingdom

As a result of numerous investigations, principally on the structure and reproduction of fossil and of living plants, botanists have reached tentative conclusions concerning the probable path of evolution in the plant kingdom. These conclusions are presented in generalized form in Fig. 20-2. This family tree of the plant world should be regarded as an expression of opinion concerning plant evolution, an opinion based on modern interpretation of plant relationships. Numerous other phylogenetic arrangements have been made in the past and have been altered as new facts about plants have been unearthed; so it is with the present arrangement, which doubtless will undergo changes in the future.

Certain generalizations may be derived from a study of the phylogenetic tree. Most striking of these perhaps is the fact that the course of evolution cannot be represented by a straight line along which various groups of plants may be placed; it is only adequately shown by a branching system of lines, similar in positional relationships to the branches of a tree and hence the popular designation of "family tree" for a scheme of phylogeny. Another feature of evolution clearly illustrated by a phylogenetic tree is the fact that not all the groups of plants that have appeared in succession along a main evolutionary line have survived to the present time. Some of these organisms (for example, the euglenoids) have lived through a large section of geological time; others (for example, some seed ferns) arose from earlier groups, led to the development of later and more complex types of plants, and then became extinct.

Evolutionary Changes in the Plant Kingdom

Our brief survey of living and extinct plant groups has indicated that numerous, striking evolutionary changes have occurred in plants during their long residence on the earth. The more obvious and more significant of these evolutionary transformations have been discussed in earlier chapters but are presented again at this point for emphasis and summary, as follows:

1. The transformation of unicellular plants into colonial and multicellular plants, with increase in size and complexity of external and internal structure.

2. The transition from simple, undifferentiated protoplasts to highly specialized protoplasts with nuclei, plastids, and other organelles.

3. The origin and evolution of sexual reproduction, possibly from some type of asexual reproduction.

4. The evolution of a terrestrial from an aquatic mode of life.

5. The differentiation of vascular, strengthening, storage, and other types of tissues that have made possible successful adaptation to land conditions.

6. The progressive differentiation of vascular plant organs into distinctly vegetative and distinctly reproductive structures termed cones and flowers.

7. The development of seeds as a result of the retention of gametophytes and young sporophytes within sporangial walls.

8. The decrease in size and complexity of the gametophyte generation and the corresponding rise of the sporophyte.

9. The release from dependence on water for fertilization through the development of pollen tubes in the seed plants.

10. The development in angiosperms of a new tissue, the polyploid endosperm, which nourishes the developing embryo.

The most conspicuous tendency in the evolution of plants has been an increase in structural complexity and specialization. This **progressive evolution** has likewise been the principal evolutionary trend in the animal kingdom. Although the course of evolution in both plants and animals has thus been primarily upward, evolutionary changes have not been exclusively progressive, nor have they proceeded at a constant rate. There are many examples among both plants and ani-

FIG. 31-4. Convergent evolution illustrated by the similarities of a cactus (family *Cactaceae*, left) and a spurge (family *Euphorbiaceae*, right). Although these two plants are not at all closely related ancestrally, adaptation to similar life conditions has led to development of vegetative bodies which are closely similar in appearance.

mals of evolutionary transformations leading toward decreased complexity and simplification from structurally more complex ancestors. Examples of such **retrogressive evolution** are common in the plant kingdom: the development of structurally simplified types of flowers from more elaborate, more complex flowers (for example, the evolution of grass flowers from lily-like ancestors), the reduction of sexual structures and activity in certain fungi, the morphological degeneracy accompanying a transition from an autotrophic to a parasitic mode of life in such flowering plants as beechdrops and dodder. Although evolutionary changes of a retrogressive nature have been rather common in certain groups of plants, such changes have been merely sidetracks along the trunk line of progressive evolution and have not appreciably altered the directions of evolutionary advance in the plant kingdom as a whole.

Although we tend to picture the general course of evolutionary change as a complex system in which different evolutionary lines originate and diverge from ancestral forms to become increas-ingly different and distinct, two types of evolutionary development do not fit this generalization, namely, **parallel** and **convergent evolution.** Both of these are probably less common than divergent evolution but must be recognized and sought if our evolutionary interpretations are to reflect evolutionary fact.

Parallel evolution (Fig. 31-3) is followed when two distinct lines originate and proceed in parallel fashion for long periods of time. The resulting taxa may be very similar in appearance and general nature in spite of the fact that they have been long isolated. Since we tend to equate increasing degree of difference with increasing length of time since common ancestry, such cases confuse the overall picture. At the present time, parallel evolution is usually difficult or impossible to detect at the lower taxonomic levels.

Convergent evolution (Figs. 31-3 and 31-4) occurs when the members of very different and widely separated evolutionary lines evolve in such a way as to become increasingly similar. Usually, such convergence is associated with similar selective pressures exerted on the lines by similar environmental circumstances. Such convergence is apparent in numerous groups of plants and may occur in both progressive and retrogressive transformations. Examples include the development of similar plant bodies by the unrelated cacti and spurges in response to evolution in desert environments (Fig. 31-4) and the development of similar body forms and physiological processes in the reduction of the unrelated parasitic and saprophytic dodders, beechdrops, and pinedrops from autotrophic ancestors. Such convergent evolution is usually more readily detected than parallel evolution because the similarities developed tend to be superficial modifications of form, while basic differences in reproductive structures and body chemistry are retained. Convergent evolution is ordinarily a confusing complication in our understanding of evolutionary relationships only when the groups in question are poorly known.

SUMMARY
1. Physical and biological diversity of the earth have been achieved by processes of inorganic and organic evolution.

2. Evolution has been continuing since the formation of the earth and is going on in the present geological period.

3. The basic tenet of organic evolution is that the first organisms to appear on earth were simple in structure and form and that more complex organisms have developed gradually from these.

4. Evidence of organic evolution has accrued from:

    a. Studies of fossils which show that different kinds of organisms have occupied the earth in different times and that simpler organisms preceded more complex ones.

    b. Comparative morphology, which shows that organisms are clustered morphologically, this clustering being a reflection of common ancestry of similar groups.

    c. Geographical distribution of related taxa in limited regions of the world.

    d. Genetic studies that demonstrate genetic similarity of morphologically similar organisms which could only result from common ancestry.

    e. Studies of comparative biochemistry which show groupings similar to those demonstrated by comparative studies of morphology and genetics.

5. The causes of organic evolution include overproduction of progeny, resulting in competition among them for space and nutrients, and differential survival of favored progeny types because of competition and environmental pressures.

6. The above phenomena were convincingly expounded by Charles Darwin in his book *On the Origin of Species by Natural Selection,* published in 1859.

7. The source of variation was perceived by Hugo de Vries to be mutation, heritable changes in genotype.

8. Modern work in the fields of evolution and speciation have offered convincing proof that mutational changes are the basic sources of variation, that new alleles are disseminated through a population and among different genomes by outcrossing and recombination.

9. Favorable mutations are preserved, thus changing the nature of a population in the process of evolution.

10. Different changes in different portions of a population's range may result in the establishment of different evolutionary tendencies. Such subpopulations may eventually become reproductively isolated one from another and be recognizable as new, derived species.

11. Reproductive isolation may result from spatial isolation; development of physical and physiological barriers to gamete exchange; development of floral peculiarities that selectively influence the behavior of

pollen carriers; development of differences in time of sex-cell maturation; development of incompatible gene systems that prohibit hybrid formation or reduce the survival or reproductive potential of hybrids.

12. Development of new populations and species is intimately linked to the probability of extinction of progenitor populations and competitors.

13. The earliest living organisms were probably heterotrophic anaerobes. Photosynthetic organisms appeared later and liberated oxygen as a by-product of photosynthesis; the accumulation of oxygen in the atmosphere made possible the life forms we know best today.

14. The unfavorable habitat afforded by exposed land surfaces demanded significant modifications for survival, and the diversity of growth form among land-inhabiting plants is striking.

15. The major evolutionary changes in the plant kingdom are listed on page 475.

16. Although evolution is pictured as progressive, certain trends are interpreted as retrogressive; such changes include simplification through reduction in complexity of form and physiology.

17. Parallel evolution preserves early similarities through inordinately long periods of time; convergent evolution, often stimulated by strong selective pressures, tends to make different evolutionary lines progressively more similar.

SUGGESTED READINGS FOR INTERESTED STUDENTS

1. Delevoryas, Theodore, *Morphology and Evolution of Fossil Plants*. Holt, Rinehart and Winston, New York, 1962.

2. Merrell, David J., *Evolution and Genetics*. Holt, Rinehart and Winston, New York, 1962.

3. Ross, Herbert H., *A Synthesis of Evolutionary Theory*. Prentice-Hall, Englewood Cliffs, N.J., 1962.

4. Solbrig, Otto T., *Evolution and Systematics*. The Macmillan Co., New York, 1966.

5. Stebbins, G. L., *Processes of Organic Evolution*. Prentice-Hall, Englewood Cliffs, N.J., 1966.

6. Volpe, Peter E., *Understanding Evolution*. Wm. C. Brown, Dubuque, Iowa, 1967.

7. Wallace, Bruce, and A. M. Srb., *Adaptation*. Prentice-Hall, Englewood Cliffs, N.J., 1961.

TOPICS AND QUESTIONS FOR STUDY

1. Distinguish between inorganic evolution and organic evolution.

2. Describe the early steps in the evolution of plants.

3. Is organic evolution a theory or a fact?

4. Describe the evidences in support of organic evolution. Can you cite any evidence that might disprove evolution?

5. Summarize the major evolutionary changes that have taken place in the plant kingdom.

6. Distinguish among progressive, retrogressive, parallel, and convergent evolution.

7. Summarize and evaluate the several theories that attempt to explain the causes of evolution.

8. What is the modern view concerning the causes of evolution?

9. Many plants that inhabit desert regions have reduced leaves, heavy layers of cutin on their leaves and stems, and extensive development of water storage tissue. How would Darwin explain the evolution of these plants? How would de Vries?

32

ECOLOGY AND DISTRIBUTION OF PLANTS

Plants are dynamic organisms that, like animals, possess the fundamental protoplasmic property of irritability and that are, therefore, affected in many ways by the continually shifting factors of their surroundings. The study of living organisms in relation to their environment is called **ecology.** Although the following discussion deals primarily with plants, it should be kept in mind that animal populations form integral parts of biotic associations. **Plant ecology** is a branch of botany that endeavors to determine the effects of environmental influences on such things as the form and activities of individual plants and plant parts, the migration and distribution of plant species, and the formation and distribution of plant communities.

Ecology attempts also, through application of its body of knowledge, to give practical aid to the science of conservation of natural resources. Thus, it contributes to control of floods and soil erosion, to reforestation, and to restoration of wild animal life and natural vegetation, all of which are fundamentally ecological problems.

Ecology is one of the most expansive and intricate fields of biology. It involves the consideration of exceedingly complex factors and relationships, and its searching and discriminating study requires extensive field experience and a broad background in taxonomy, plant physiology, chemistry, geography, geology, meteorology, and soil science.

According to many ecologists, the basic vegetational unit is the **community,** a group of plants living together in a particular environment or habitat. Communities vary greatly in area. For example, a grassland or forest community may cover thousands of acres whereas a lichen or moss growing on a rock may form a community that covers less than a square inch. Within a community, the organisms have mutual relationships among themselves and their environment. The characteristics of a community are influenced to a considerable degree by three intracommunity relationships: **competition** for various factors such as light, water, and nutrients, which are usually in limited supply; **stratification,** the layering that results from differences in the size of mature plants, for example, the trees, shrubs, and herbs of a forest community; and **dependence** of some species on the community structure for their survival, as illustrated by herbs that grow only in dense shade and by epiphytes that grow on tree trunks and branches.

One of the most striking features of plant life is the fact that different kinds of plants grow only in certain places and under specific kinds of environmental conditions. Black willows, for example, grow principally along the banks of streams and the margins of lakes; cattails thrive only in swamps or in the marshy borders of lakes or in moist ditches; sunflowers are plants of open, sunny, moderately dry regions; and cacti are typically inhabitants of arid and semiarid areas. Each species and its distribution pattern represent an intricate adjustment among genetically controlled morphological and physiological tolerance limits and the selective forces of the environment. A species is eliminated from a particular habitat if any one of the environmental factors exceeds the physiological tolerance limits to which that species is genetically adapted.

Some species grow and reproduce in only a few areas where the environmental factors comprising each habitat are quite similar; these species, such as California redwood, some ferns, and many herbs, have narrow tolerance ranges. Other species are much more widely distributed and thus grow in a diversity of habitats. Widely distributed species such as big bluestem grass, ponderosa pine, and quaking aspen are commonly spoken of as species having wide tolerance to variations in factors such as light intensity, soil moisture, soil acidity, and temperature. Experimental data show that the individuals of a given widespread species often constitute genetically distinct populations that are physiologically adapted to slightly different habitats. Such populations are called **ecotypes.** The recognition of ecotypes and ecotypic variation is an important part of ecology because it helps explain how the populations of a species can grow and reproduce in quite different habitats. Ecotypes of some species are known to be adapted to differences in soil, photoperiod, temperature, moisture, and combinations of these factors.

FACTORS THAT INFLUENCE PLANT DISTRIBUTION

The factors that have been, or are, important in determining the distribution of different kinds of plants may be classified into two major categories: factors of the past and contempory factors.

Factors of the Past The distribution of plants on the earth is in part a result of major geological transformations in the earth's history. Many features of plant distribution defy explanations based on present-day conditions; they can be explained only on the basis of long-term climatic and geological phenomena of past ages. Examples include isolated oceanic islands, such as those of Hawaii, which have floras that are very different from floras in other parts of the world;

the great similarities between the plants of the more southerly islands of the West Indies and those of northern South America; the occurrence of entirely different species of plants in the climatically similar desert regions of the southwestern United States and of South Africa and the fact that certain species that grow in the high New England mountains also grow in the far north of Canada and Greenland but not in central and southern Canada. Among the important geological events that have influenced the distribution of plants have been the upthrust of high mountain ranges, the emergence and subsidence of land masses and their shorelines, and the advance and retreat of glaciers. Geological phenomena, together with associated changes in climate, have resulted in the formation of **barriers** and **highways** that have restricted or facilitated the dispersal of various species of plants. Frequently these geological and climatic changes have caused the extinction of species in certain regions. In the study of plant distribution, particularly over rather large areas, a knowledge of the geological and climatic history of these areas is therefore a prerequisite to an interpretation of the observed facts of present-day distribution.

Contemporary Factors   These factors, which at the present time are affecting the daily growth, reactions, and distribution of living plants, may be separated into four categories.

a. *Climatic factors*—those that act on plants through the atmosphere: temperature, precipitation, light, wind, and humidity.

b. *Edaphic factors*—those that act on plants through soils: soil moisture, soil air, soil temperature, soil reaction, and soil nutrients.

c. *Biotic factors*—those that involve relations with other kinds of plants and with animals.

d. *Fire*

In the following discussion of factors influencing plant distribution, emphasis will be placed on the contemporary ecological factors.

Climatic Factors   TEMPERATURE   The climatic factors that are most influential in affecting the distribution of plants are temperature and precipitation. Different species have different ranges of temperature limits within which they can survive and flower. Thus, many temperate zone trees and shrubs have a wide tolerance of temperature extremes and are able to endure high summer and low winter temperatures, whereas woody plants from the tropics are killed when the temperatures to which they are exposed approach the freezing point of water. In most plants, the minimum and maximum temperatures through which active physiological processes continue are in the vicinity of 35°F to 110°F, respectively. Certain algae grow and reproduce in snowbanks at temperatures lower than 35°F, and certain other algae live in 170°F water in hot springs. Temperature variations influence the rates of all physiological processes and may even affect them qualitatively. The production of flowers and the formation of seeds in many species of plants are likewise directly influenced by temperature conditions of the environment. Accordingly, temperature may be a factor in determining survival or extinction of plants within a given area, in part through direct effects on vegetative processes, in part through its effects on reproduction. For example, mistletoe, which is sensitive to low temperatures, grows in Illinois only in the extreme southern part of the state. Following very mild winters, mistletoe plants may extend their range northward. Severe winters kill the plants that have begun to grow in more northerly districts after mild winters, and thus fix the northern limit of the mistletoe at the extreme southern end of the state.

PRECIPITATION   Precipitation is the moisture that falls to earth in the form of rain, snow, sleet, and hail. Only a portion of this moisture enters soils and becomes available to plants; the rest runs off the surface into streams and is evaporated, or it enters the soil and moves down to the water table. The distribution of plants is greatly affected by the amount of available soil moisture, some species surviving in regions of 4 to 6 inches of annual precipitation while others grow only where 60 to 80 inches occur. Seasonal distribution of precipitation is usually more important than the total amount. The vegetation will be more luxuriant in an area where much of the total precipitation occurs in summer than in another area where much of an even higher total precipitation occurs in winter and the summer has one or more dry spells. The ecological importance of soil moisture will be discussed in greater detail in the section on edaphic factors.

LIGHT   Light influences the growth and distribution of plants through its effects on photosynthesis, transpiration, enzyme action, the production of flowers, soil temperatures, rate of water absorption, and numerous other processes. Light is ordinarily less important than temperature and moisture in influencing the distribution of plants over wide regions, but within limited areas, as for example, on a hillside, a forest floor, or in a deep ravine, it is an exceedingly important factor. Just as various species of plants are physiologically adapted to different ranges of temperature and soil moisture, so are they adapted to different ranges of light intensity and duration. Many plants thrive in diffuse light that has only 5 to 25 percent of the intensity of full sunlight; these plants include many species of ferns, mosses, and late spring- and summer-blooming woodland wildflowers, such as lady-slipper orchids, hydrophyllums, geraniums, and the seedlings of numerous forest tree species. Other species grow best and produce abundant seed only in open areas such as grasslands, pasture, and cutover forest land; prominent among them are big bluestem grass, Indian grass, many composites such as sunflowers, rosin weeds, asters, and many species of the milkweed, spurge, and legume families. Shade tolerance or intolerance of a species results largely from its relative efficiency of photosynthesis at low light levels.

Light exerts an important effect on plant distribution through its influence on flowering. Some plants are adjusted to a long-day photoperiod and will flower only in high latitudes (for example, northern Alaska, Canada, southern Argentina) where the days are very long in summer. Other species are short-day plants and will flower only under the short-day conditions of low latitudes or in the spring or fall seasons of midlatitudes. A third group of plants is day-neutral, flowering in response to factors other than day length. Short-day plants are seldom able to flower when grown in high latitudes; conversely, long-day plants of high latitudes usually do not flower when they grow under the short-day conditions of lower latitudes. Photoperiod also influences leaf fall and the seasonal activity of cambium in many tree species. Thus, light duration exerts great influence on the reproduction, distribution, and growth of many plants.

WIND   At high mountain elevations and similarly exposed positions, strong winds may exert marked mechanical effects on plants, bending and twisting them grotesquely. High wind velocity, coupled with low winter temperatures and consequent difficulty of water absorption, is a factor that sets the upper limit (timber line) at which trees are able to grow and is thus important ecologically. The major physiological effect of wind on plants is to increase their rates of transpiration. Plants are able to grow successfully only so long as they can balance their water income with water outgo; if transpiration exceeds absorption for a prolonged period, wilting and death are inevitable. Plants vary greatly in the degree to which they can maintain this balance; those species that are most sensitive to the drying effects of winds and that are unable to increase their rate of water absorption are less likely to survive than species that are less susceptible to wind action and that are able to absorb water more effectively. Winds may also influence the distribution of plants through their effects on the soil in which plants are growing. High winds cause shifting of light soils and thus prevent many kinds of plants from becoming established in such substrata. Ordinarily, only perennials with deep,

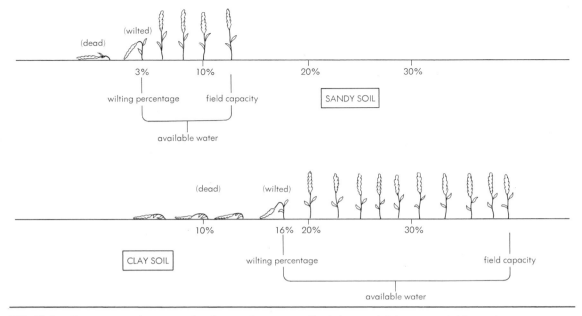

FIG. 32–1.   Comparison of amount of soil water (given as a % of dry weight) that is available to plants growing in sandy soil versus those growing in a clay soil. Note that although sandy soil has less available water than clay soil, it also has a much lower wilting percentage, plants being able, in this example, to extract water when it is down to 3%, versus 16% in a clay soil.

much-branched roots and with well-developed underground rhizomes, or stolons, grow successfully on sand dunes and other types of shifting soils.

Winds are important along sea coasts, where they not only affect transpiration rates but also produce salt spray from the ocean. Species have different salt spray tolerance limits, and thus there are zones of vegetation along coastal areas; grasses are frequently found nearest the shore, followed by shrub and finally forest communities.

HUMIDITY   The amount of water vapor in the air has a profound effect on the rates both of evaporation from the soil and of transpiration. The combination of high temperatures, winds, low precipitation, and low humidity results in very sparse vegetation in some desert areas whereas regions that have higher precipitation and higher humidity support much more luxuriant vegetation.

The presentation thus far would indicate that these factors act independently of each other when, in reality, they usually operate together. **Factor interaction** can best be illustrated in such physiological processes as transpiration and photosynthesis, the rates of which depend in part on available soil moisture, air temperature, humidity, wind, and light intensity.

Edaphic Factors   SOIL MOISTURE   Edaphic factors are those that act on plants through the soil. Of these, soil moisture is of prime importance. Available soil moisture is influenced by many conditions; for example, size and nature of soil particles, rate at which water infiltrates the soil, internal drainage characteristics, amount and distribution of precipitation, and the kinds of plants occupying the site. Water-holding capacity of a soil is largely dependent on soil particle size. Soils with high sand content hold much less water than do soils high in silt and clay because the total surface area and interparticle space is greater in a silt or clay soil. Organic content also increases water-holding capacity of soils. This helps to explain why sandy soils even in regions of adequate precipitation often support desertlike vegetation (Fig. 32-1). Not all the water held within a soil is available to plants. The available water is only that portion between **field capacity,** which is the maximum amount of water the soil can hold against the force of gravity, and **permanent wilting percentage,** which is the water left in the soil at the time plants become permanently wilted. This available water is held in the capillary pore spaces in the soil and is frequently called **capillary water.** For most temperate region plants, permanent wilting percentage occurs at about 15 atmospheres; that is, the plants can remove water in sufficient quantities to replace transpirational losses until the water is held with forces equal to 15 atmospheres. Some of the remaining water may be absorbed by roots but not rapidly enough to prevent permanent wilting. Desert plants, however, and those plants that grow in soils with high soluble salt content can sometimes remove water until forces in excess of 100 atmospheres are developed. This is an important adaptation mechanism that permits these plants to grow in habitats where soil water is held by forces that are beyond the water-absorbing limit of most plants.

The combination of temperature, precipitation, and available soil moisture plays the major role in determining the broad features of plant distribution on the earth's surface. Thus, the most luxuriant vegetation occurs in those regions in which temperatures and available soil moisture are high throughout the year, as in the tropical forests of southeastern Asia, central Africa, and South America. If temperatures are high but soil moisture is not readily available, vegetation is sparse, as in the desert areas of Mexico, southwestern United States, and northern Africa. In northern Alaska, northern Canada, and Greenland, precipitation is adequate but temperatures are low. These conditions limit the vegetation to

lichens and mosses, short grasses, sedges, and dwarf shrubs. Within a rather small area having topographic relief, considerable differences can be found in temperature, humidity, soil moisture, and soil drainage so that exposed ridges with thin soils support only scrub forests of oak whereas moist ravine slopes that are cooler and soils that hold more water support a more luxuriant forest. This again shows the importance of factor interaction. The relationships between plant growth and the available-water content of soils are so striking that plants may be grouped into four categories: **xerophytes** (Fig. 32-13), which survive and live under conditions of scanty available soil moisture (examples: cacti and agaves); **hydrophytes** (Fig. 32-2), which live partly or wholly in water (example: water lilies); **mesophytes** (Fig. 32-11), which grow in soils with moderate supplies of available moisture (example: elms, corn, wheat, petunias, and maples); and **halophytes,** which grow in soils that may contain abundant water but that have high concentrations of soluble salts (examples: greasewood and shadscale).

SOIL AIR   The air content of soils is of great importance, particularly in root growth and seed germination. Actively growing roots require oxygen in considerable quantities for their respiration and usually become stunted or otherwise abnormal when the oxygen content of the soil is reduced. The roots of most mesophytes and xerophytes are especially sensitive to oxygen deficiencies in soils, whereas the roots of most species of hydrophytes are able to grow in apparently normal fashion even when the oxygen supply of the substratum is very low. The oxygen content of soils is also an important factor in seed germination because germinating seeds respire rapidly and ordinarily require large amounts of oxygen. Again, hydrophytes are somewhat of an exception to this generalization because many of them (for example, water lilies and cattails) have seeds that are able to germinate in very low oxygen concentrations, which would inhibit the sprouting of seeds of most other plants. The oxygen

FIG. 32–2. Hydrophytes (*Above.*) Water-lilies (*Victoria* and *Nymphaea*). (*Right.*) Water hyacinth (*Eichornia crassipes*). (Photo by W. R. Kennedy.)

content of the soil air is important also in the activities of bacteria, fungi, worms, and other soil organisms that require oxygen for their respiration. Carbon dioxide content in some soils may attain levels that are toxic to plants. This is especially true of soils that remain flooded for periods of time.

SOIL TEMPERATURE   Soil temperatures are an edaphic factor of importance in the ecological relationships of plants, particularly when temperatures are low, for low temperatures reduce the rate of absorption of water and solutes and the growth of roots. One of the reasons why many kinds of evergreen trees cannot be successfully grown in those parts of the middle latitudes with only moderately cold winters is the fact that air temperatures on winter days are frequently high enough to promote rather rapid transpiration, while soil temperatures are sufficiently low to retard water absorption. In such circumstances, evergreen trees frequently grow very slowly or die as a result of an excess of water outgo over water income. Soil temperatures are affected by air temperatures, the intensity of sunlight, the angle at which sunlight strikes the soil, the daily duration of sunlight, the amount of moisture in the soil, and by other factors.

SOIL REACTION   Another edaphic factor that influences the growth and distribution of plants is the reaction of the soil, that is, its degree of acidity or alkalinity. The principal importance of this factor probably lies in its effect on the solubility and, therefore, the availability of various soil nutrients.

SOIL NUTRIENTS   The nature and availability of the soil solutes is fundamentally important from the standpoint of plant nutrition. Only when all the essential elements are present can green plants grow in normal fashion. Although all green plants apparently require approximately the same ions for normal development, different species require them in varying quantities; thus, certain soils support the growth of some species of plants better than others.

Biotic Factors   The growth and development of all living organisms are influenced by the activities of other living organisms, as well as by climatic and edaphic factors. These biotic relationships are the most complex in the myriad ecological phenomena of living organisms. Not only do various species of plants affect the development of other species, but there are also intimate interrelations between plants and animals. Thus, any ecological investigation that concentrates on plants and neglects the relations of those plants with animals can present only an incomplete analysis. Similarly, an animal ecologist who fails to consider plants in his studies can see only a limited portion of nature's canvas.

COMPETITION   Individual plants of the same species and plants of different species compete for soil moisture, soil nutrients, light, and space for shoot and root development so long as the supply does not meet or exceed the requirements of the individuals. Usually, competition for one or several of these factors is most pronounced between individuals of the same species. One of the reasons why weeds are undesirable in cropland is that they absorb considerable quantities of water and thus deplete the soil moisture that might be absorbed by the cultivated plants with which weeds compete. Weeds compete with cultivated plants also for soil nutrients, for space, and for light. Morphological features, such as depth of root systems, number of root branches, and development of water storage tissues, and physiological characteristics, such as rate of transpiration, rate of water absorption and rate of growth, are factors that determine what species of plants will survive under a given set of environmental conditions and what species will succumb. The natural competition among different species and among individuals of the same species is an important factor in checking the growth of populations. Charles Darwin recognized this significant feature of competition and incorporated it into his natural selection theory of evolution.

PARASITISM   Parasitism is a biotic relationship that influences strikingly the development and distribution of plants. Serious infections by virulent fungous parasites may interfere with photosynthetic activity and thus indirectly reduce the numbers and impair the quality of seeds produced, a result that in turn retards the efficiency with which the infected plants propagate themselves. Toxic substances produced by disease parasites may also impair or damage the physiological and reproductive processes of plants. Especially serious parasites, such as the chestnut blight fungus and the Dutch elm disease fungus, have changed the community composition of numerous forests in the eastern United States by destroying all their host plants. Moreover, it seems probable that such parasitically induced changes in biotic communities have been of regular occurrence over a long period of geologic time. The availability of suitable hosts also determines the abundance and distribution of the parasitic species.

SYMBIOSIS   Akin to parasitic relationships are symbiotic relationships. The term symbiosis merely means "living together" and in this broad sense may be applied to all intimate relations among living organisms, including parasitism and **mutualism.** Mutualism is synonymous with the more restricted meaning of symbiosis, referring to a biotic relation in which the organisms live together more commonly than they live apart and in which this relationship seems to be mutually beneficial. Mutualistic relationships are numerous; lichens, for example, are regarded as symbiotic associations of algae and fungi, in which the fungi receive food from the algae and the algae possibly receive water, mineral nutrients, and protection from the surrounding hyphae. The nitrogen-fixing bacteria that inhabit nodules of leguminous roots live apparently in a symbiotic relationship of mutual benefit with their hosts. These bacteria convert nitrogen of the air into nitrogenous compounds in the soil, which ultimately become a source of nitrate for higher plants, and, in turn, the bacteria receive food from the roots in which they live.

EPIPHYTES   Another interesting biotic relationship is seen in the growth of **epiphytes** (Figs. 32-3 and 32-14) on other plants. Epiphytes are hitchhikers of the plant world; they grow on the limbs of trees and other plants, on wires and wire poles, and roofs of buildings, particularly in warm, humid regions. Most epiphytes are chlorophyllous and manufacture their own food and thus do not deplete the food reserves of the plants on which they grow. They obtain carbon dioxide and some moisture from the humid air, and their roots absorb some moisture and nutrients from the wind-borne debris that collects about them and in the crevices of the bark over which they grow. Many species of orchids, mosses, ferns, lichens, and members of the pineapple family are epiphytes. Though most epiphytes do not take food from the bodies of the plants on which they grow, they may constitute a source of injury, for they shade the leaves of their supporting plants and frequently cause limbs to break and fall because of their weight.

INTERRELATIONSHIPS OF PLANTS AND ANIMALS
The broadest and most inclusive of the various approaches in ecology is that which treats the community and its environment as an in-

FIG. 32-3. *Tillandsia usneoides* (Spanish moss), an epiphyte growing on the branches of trees. *Tillandsia* is a member of the pineapple family.

teracting, functional unit or **ecosystem.** Many studies at this level are concerned with the mutual relationships and exchange of materials within an ecological system. The principal components of an ecosystem may be conveniently classified as follows: (1) **abiotic components,** which include the physical and chemical factors of the nonliving environment, (2) **producers,** or autotrophic organisms, (3) **consumers,** chiefly animals that ingest other organisms, and (4) **decomposers,** those heterotrophic organisms such as bacteria and fungi that utilize organic compounds, eventually releasing simpler substances that can be used again by producers and thus be recycled. The most important abiotic factor is the energy which enters the ecosystem in the form of sunlight. Of this energy, autotrophic plants are able to utilize only 1 or 2 percent, the remainder leaving the system as heat and reflected light. The relatively low amount of available energy for maintenance of the ecosystem is related to such factors as cloud and earth surface reflectance and to the relatively low efficiency of the photosynthetic process. Under ideal conditions green plants utilize only approximately 8 percent of the total sunlight which reaches their chloroplasts, and the overall utilization is diminished to approximately 2 percent by the effects of night periods, shading, winter, drought, senescence of leaves, and so forth. The protoplasm which can be supported in any area is dependent on the interrelationships between energy input and its utilization as influenced by other abiotic (water availability, mineral nutrition, fire, and so forth) and biotic (shading, cropping, and foraging) factors. Autotrophic plants, the producers, form the base within the ecosystem, since all animals depend directly or indirectly on green plants for food. Animals, the consumers, may be divided into primary consumers or **herbivores**—such as cows, rabbits, mice, grasshoppers and aphids—all of which derive nourishment (energy) directly from plants, and **carnivores**—such as foxes, hawks, and dragonflies—each of which obtains its food wholly or largely from herbivores. The nutritional

relationships among plants and animals are often extremely complex and constitute an important field of ecological research. Ecosystem studies may emphasize the investigation of energy transfer from one food level **(trophic level)** to one or more higher levels, for example, from producers to herbivores to carnivores. Other ecosystem studies may focus on the growth of organisms in each trophic level and attempt to relate growth rates to various biotic and abiotic factors. In general, the number of organisms decreases while the average size of the individuals increases at successively higher trophic levels. The intricate nutritional relationships among organisms within an ecosystem are sometimes called **food chains** or **food webs.** Food webs may be traced wherever animals and plants live: in rivers, lakes, oceans, deserts, grasslands, deciduous forests (Fig. 32-4), and all other aggregations of plants and animals. Man is, of course, the terminal link in many food chains, for he directly consumes various plant products, and he eats also the flesh of cattle, hogs, birds, fish, crabs, oysters, deer and other animals, which in turn obtained their nourishment and built up their tissues at the expense of plants or smaller animals or both.

The complexity of biotic relationships that exists within the food chain of a forest ecosystem and the tremendous imbalance that can occur within such an ecosystem can be illustrated with the following example. In a spruce forest, as a result of severe windstorms, most of the woodpeckers normally resident there disappeared. The disappearance of the woodpeckers, which feed on bark beetles, removed a natural check on these insects, so that they multiplied rapidly and attacked the spruce trees. The dead trees, killed by the beetle infestation, then burned as a result of a lightning strike. The destruction of the forest by this fire exposed the soil to the erosive effects of heavy rains with the results that the top soil was washed away. This, in turn, caused streams down the valley to become silted. As a result, these streams swept over their banks and inundated rich farm lands and towns hundreds of miles away.

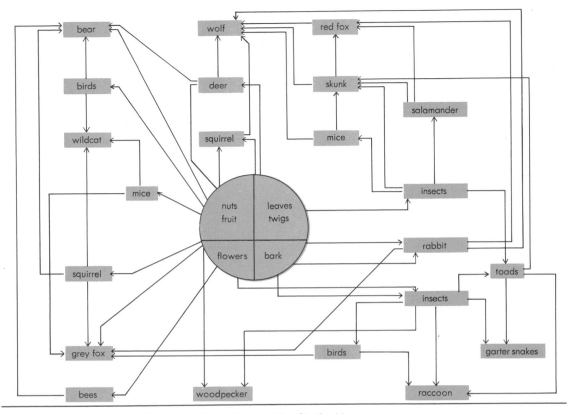

FIG. 32-4. Food web in an Illinois deciduous forest. (After Shelford.)

Another example of complex biotic relationships may be found in the overgrazing of considerable areas by deer on the north rim of the Grand Canyon in Arizona. At various times, government hunters, in order to protect livestock herds, killed many of the mountain lions in this forest, and sportsmen on occasion have been permitted to hunt these lions in the forest. As a result, many lions, which prey on deer, were killed, and the removal of this natural check on deer resulted in enormous increases in the deer population in this area. This population increase taxed the natural feeding resources of the forest beyond its limits to provide feed, and thousands of deer starved. Furthermore, the excessive grazing by the increased deer population killed many plants and led to widespread soil erosion. The study of food

webs is intriguing and economically valuable, since the restoration and maintenance of wild life depends on knowledge of the feeding habits and nutritional relationships among animals and plants.

The decomposers (saprobes and saprophytes), which attack the complex substances that constitute the bodies of plants and animals and their wastes, form an integral part of the ecosystem, for the decay process releases water, carbon dioxide, ammonia, nitrates, and other substances. The carbon dioxide is used again in photosynthesis while other end products of decomposition are the source of essential elements absorbed by green plants. The complex transformations involved in the cycling of carbon and nitrogen are presented in Fig. 32–5. The amounts of nutrients and the time required for their cycling are aspects of some ecosystem studies.

Animals are important biotically as carriers of many kinds of seeds, as has been pointed out in an earlier chapter. Birds eat many types of fruits and seeds; some of the seeds pass through their digestive tracts and are distributed with their feces. Many mammals also eat fruits and seeds and thus aid in seed dissemination. Animals with furry coats frequently carry the spiny or barbed seeds and fruits of cocklebur, beggar-ticks, and other kinds of plants for great distances, and thus unwittingly (sometimes probably wittingly if they have picked up seeds or fruits with large, sharp spines!) distribute plants over considerable areas.

The presence or absence of flower-pollinating insects is an important biotic factor influencing the distribution of plants, for most species of angiosperms are insect pollinated and are therefore dependent on pollinating insects for their production of seeds. Fluctuations of insect populations thus affect the seed crop of many plants and thus influence the degree to which plants may propagate themselves.

Fire Whether it is the result of lightning, of volcanic activity, or of human carelessness, fire destroys thousands of acres of forest and shrub vegetation annually, kills wild animals of these areas, alters the chemical and physical properties of soils, and thus exerts profound and extensive ecological effects. Fire is one of the major factors that destroys stable communities and thus leads to ecological succession. (See the following section of this chapter.) Fire is an important factor in maintaining particular kinds of vegetation,

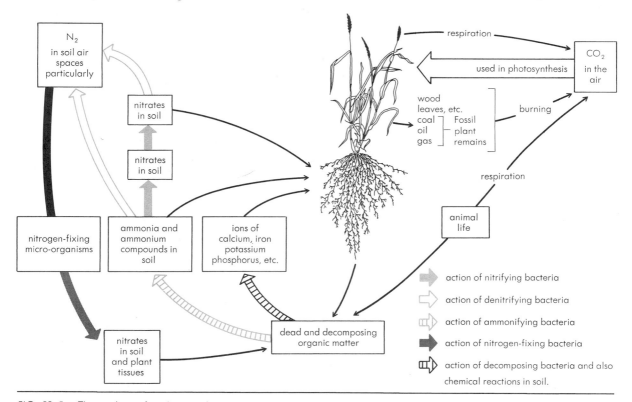

FIG. 32-5.   The cycling of carbon and nitrogen in nature.

such as the low evergreen shrub communities (chaparral) that cover lower slopes of many mountains in California. Fire is also an important factor in maintaining the general boundary between forest and grassland in regions of Illinois, Wisconsin, Iowa, and other states. With the elimination of most fires, open groves of trees become closed forest communities. Moreover, forest species are then able to invade more or less unbroken grassland. Carefully controlled burning is used to maintain pine forests in the coastal plain of the south Atlantic states where the economic return from pines is greater and more rapid than the return from deciduous forests.

PLANT SUCCESSION AND CLIMAX VEGETATION

Plant communities are constantly changing; at times these changes result in replacement of one community type by another on the same site; such sequential changes are termed **succession.** Plant succession is frequently a slow process and thus cannot be readily observed unless one repeatedly visits the same area over a period of years. Succession is very evident in abandoned pasture and cultivated lands (Fig. 32-6) and in burned or lumbered forests. Such conditions as these exemplify **secondary succession,** since the previously established community has been destroyed and replaced by species which constitute a different community. **Primary succession,** on the other hand, involves the establishment of plants on substrata that have not previously supported vegetation, for example, on bare rocks, on newly formed river islands, and on the new substrata provided by volcanic activity, glacial recession, and the natural filling in of lakes.

High in importance among the numerous causes of succession are the modifications of a habitat by the plant community, thereby making that habitat more suitable for another, dissimilar community. One such modification is increased amount of shade. The succession of communities from grasses and other herbaceous plants to co-

FIG. 32-6. Loblolly pine becoming established in a field of broom-sedge grass, an early stage of secondary succession on abandoned farm land in the Piedmont of North Carolina.

niferous forests to forests of deciduous trees is strongly influenced by the shade tolerance of different species. As was mentioned earlier, the shade tolerance of different species is closely associated with relative photosynthetic efficiency under reduced light. This efficiency largely determines whether seedlings of a given species will survive in shaded conditions, such as those on a forest floor. Thus, knowledge of photosynthetic efficiency for certain species during the course of succession contributes much to our understanding of why certain species replace other species. Another community-induced modification is the accumulation of plant debris on and in the soil. Incorporation of plant debris produces significant changes in the soil's organic content, nutrient content, reaction, and water-holding capacity. Other causes of succession include climatic changes, changes in land surface by erosion, and changes resulting from different life cycle patterns, for example, increasing dominance of perennial plants in areas where chiefly annual plants have become established. Similar habitats within a region frequently support similar plant communities and, in turn, have similar patterns of succession whereas communities and successional patterns in different habitats are usually different.

In general, there is a tendency for succession to proceed toward a type of community that is somewhat more mesic (adapted to medium amounts of available moisture) than the earlier successional stages; for example, succession on bare, dry rocks and on the margins of lakes both lead toward communities that have more intermediate moisture requirements than either extreme. In most undisturbed areas, succession continues until a relatively stable community, the **climax community,** ultimately becomes established. It will maintain itself with little change so long as there are no major biotic or abiotic alterations in the immediate environment. When a major environmental change occurs that destroys the climax vegetation or throws it out of equilibrium with the factors of the environment, the climax community may be replaced by another type of climax community that may maintain itself under the changed environmental conditions, or the original climax type may become re-established as the original environmental conditions are restored. The destruction of a climax forest by lumbering or by burning usually sets back the succession of communities a number of stages; succession must proceed again before the climax vegetation is re-established. The climax community (Fig. 32-7) is characterized largely by the ability of its species to reproduce within the established community and to utilize the resources of the environment to the maximum degree. Although directional community changes or succession are quite universal in occurrence, they are not always clear-cut or operative in the same relative proportions.

Many of our forest management practices are based on a knowledge that succession occurs and that sometimes forest types within the successional sequence are of greater economic value than are the climax forest types, especially where time is an important factor. In the southeastern

FIG. 32-7. Climax deciduous forest, Warren Woods, Michigan. The dominant trees, American beech and sugar maple, cast a dense shade on the forest floor, the reduced light limiting the growth of most plants and giving the characteristic open appearance. Seedlings and saplings of beech and maple are, however, tolerant of the shady environment and will perpetuate this climax community. (Photo by W. R. Kennedy.)

United States, pines can be harvested for pulp every 15 to 30 years, whereas it would take much longer for deciduous forest trees to reach a comparable size and market value.

Man has been a major factor in bringing about environmental changes of such magnitude that some climax associations have been largely or completely destroyed. Forest fires that often result from human carelessness, overgrazing by domesticated animals, wasteful lumbering methods, and unrestricted hunting are examples of the destructive forces loosed by man on plant communities. Much of the grassland vegetation of the Great Plains has been destroyed by overgrazing and unsuited agricultural methods; the consequences are appalling soil erosion, lost grazing land, dust storms, and unprofitable agriculture. Much of the so-called "sagebrush desert" of the western United States was originally grassland; the climax grasses have now largely disappeared, and only sound scientific management of such lands will ensure the succession that will lead to restoration of the climax grass associations. The descriptions of the large, natural assemblages of plants that follow are essentially descriptions of these assemblages as they existed 75 to 150 years ago. Man's greed and wastefulness have destroyed many of the original features. Bison no longer roam the rolling grassland of the Great Plains, and the antelope has virtually disappeared from this grassland formation; mountain goats and mountain sheep are extinct in many parts of the coniferous forest formation; the northern white pine is gone from many of the areas in which it was originally a dominant species; the prairie community has all but disappeared from the central United States because of agricultural development; the redwoods of California might now be virtually extinct were it not for the valiant efforts of government conservation agencies and private organizations dedicated to the cause of conserving our dwindling natural biological resources.

PLANT FORMATIONS

The constantly changing panorama of vegetation is one of the most striking features seen in traveling across the continent (Fig. 32-8). If one travels from California to Maine, one passes through the scrubby chaparral of the California coast ranges to the pines and fir of the Sierra Nevada, through the sagebrush and shadscale of the cold desert of the Great Basin to the coniferous forests of the Rocky Mountains, across eastern Colorado where the forests give way to grassland that extends as far as Missouri and Illinois, to the broadleaf forests of Indiana and Ohio, to the Maine forests of pine, hemlock, birch, and maple. Ac-

companying these differing vegetational types are characteristic and distinct animal inhabitants: jack rabbits, prairie dogs, and ground-nesting birds of the Great Plains; bears, deer, and timber wolves of the forested areas; and lizards, desert coyote, and kangaroo rats of desert areas.

These plant formations are the largest vegetational units; when considered with their characteristic faunas, they are termed **biomes.** The concept of the biome emphasizes the interrelations of plants and animals and thus forms an important basis for the study of ecological problems.

The general nature and extent of formations are determined by many factors, some of which were described earlier in this chapter: temperature, precipitation, available soil moisture and other soil factors, barriers, biotic factors, and past geologic and climatic history. A formation is a large natural assemblage of plants, in which the dominant species have a characteristic growth form, that is, tree, shrub, or herb. Although plant formations have a similar appearance throughout, there are usually floristic variations in different parts of the formation resulting in part from climatic, geologic, and topographic differences; therefore, major subdivisions or **associations** can be recognized. For example, we can recognize oak-hickory, beech-maple, and mixed mesophytic associations within the eastern deciduous forest. The Rocky Mountain coniferous forests may be similarly subdivided into spruce-fir, ponderosa pine and Douglas fir associations.

It should be emphasized that plant formations and their constituent plant associations are usually not sharply delimited but merge gradually into each other. The transition zones between overlapping communities are termed **ecotones.** Studies of ecotones usually show that there are environmental gradients that coincide with the vegetational gradients and that the ecotones contain vegetational as well as environmental characteristics of both adjacent communities. Eco-

FIG. 32-8. Map of the major plant formations of North America; regions based on information from Braun, Oosting, Porsild, Rowe, and Shantz and Zon.

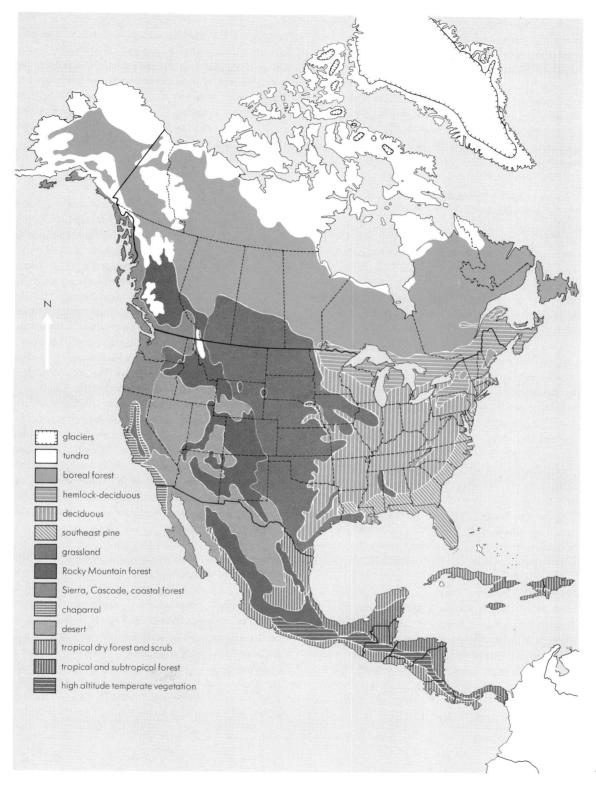

glaciers	
tundra	
boreal forest	
hemlock-deciduous	
deciduous	
southeast pine	
grassland	
Rocky Mountain forest	
Sierra, Cascade, coastal forest	
chaparral	
desert	
tropical dry forest and scrub	
tropical and subtropical forest	
high altitude temperate vegetation	

N

tones are prominent in Wisconsin, Illinois, and Missouri where grassland and deciduous forest meet, in Northern Canada between arctic tundra and coniferous forest, and in Colorado and Wyoming where grassland comes in contact with coniferous forests of the mountains. Ecotones can also be seen in the zonation of communities along a river, bog, or lake margin, and numerous other locations.

MAJOR PLANT FORMATIONS OF NORTH AMERICA

Tundra   Plant ecologists recognize at least two types of tundra: **arctic tundra,** which begins at the tree limit and extends northward to the permanent ice of arctic regions, and **alpine tundra,** which occurs above the tree line in high mountains of lower latitudes. Arctic tundra is found in northern Alaska and Canada, and is characterized by short, cool summers during which the soil may thaw to a depth of only a few feet or less; by summers with very long days or continuous light; and by vegetation composed of grasses, sedges, dwarf shrubs (for example, rhododendron, blueberry, and willow), and many lichens and mosses. Most shrubs over one foot in height are restricted to areas of winter snow cover.

Alpine tundra (Fig. 32-9), such as that found in the Rocky Mountains, Sierra Nevada, and a few of the higher New England mountains, differs from arctic tundra by having warmer soil temperatures in summer, a different photoperiodic regime throughout the year, and, frequently, more wind and snow.

Coniferous Forest   While the predominant trees of this formation are gymnosperms, they are frequently associated with deciduous, hardwood species. The northern or boreal forests, which form a wide belt extending from Alaska to New England, consist principally of spruce, fir, and birch (Fig. 32-10). Boreal forest is also characterized by short, cool summers and long, cold winters with much snow. Coniferous forests of spruce, fir, Douglas fir, and pine also predominate as climax and subclimax vegetation in the mountains of western North America. Because of the low light levels and acid soils within these forests, relatively few herbs and shrubs become established. Pine is one of the dominant species of the extensive subclimax forests in the Gulf states and coastal plain of the southeastern United States. Coniferous forests also occur in the mountains of tropical America.

Deciduous Forest   This formation covers much of the United States east of the Mississippi River. Forest composition is quite variable as would be expected in such a large geographic area with considerable ranges in temperature, precipitation, soils, and topography. The major plant associations within the formation are usually named according to the predominant tree species comprising the various associations; for example, the oak-hickory associations in the drier, western areas and the beech-maple associations on glacial soils in the Great Lakes region (Fig. 32-7). On the moist but well-drained slopes of the Allegheny, Cumberland, and Great Smoky mountains are found mixed mesophytic associations that include basswood, buckeye, hemlock, magnolia, maple, oak, and others (Fig. 32-11). **Stratification,** the development of tree, shrub, and herb layers, is usually quite evident in deciduous forests. This formation is also characterized by spectacular seasonal changes in vegetation as a result of the annual loss of leaves.

Grassland   Grassland is characterized by the dominance of grasses and broad-leaved herbs (Fig. 32-12). It extends north from Texas and New Mexico into southern Canada and from the Rocky Mountains to the deciduous forests in the east: its continuity is broken only by forests along rivers and streams. Near the Rocky Mountains, where precipitation is lower, short and medium grasses such as buffalo grass, grama grasses, and western wheat grass predominate, while in Oklahoma, eastern Kansas, Nebraska, Iowa, and Illinois, tall

FIG. 32-9. Alpine tundra at 12,000 feet elevation in Rocky Mountain National Park, Colorado. Most of the plants are smaller than 6 inches.

FIG. 32-10. Coniferous forest of spruce and fir at 10,300 feet elevation in the Medicine Bow Mountains, Wyoming.

FIG. 32-11. Mixed mesophytic forest in the Great Smokey Mountains. Dominant species include basswood, buckeye, hemlock and sugar maple.

FIG. 32-12. Grassland. (Courtesy U.S. Department of the Interior.)

grasses such as big bluestem, Indian grass, slough grass, and little bluestem predominate. Herbs belonging to the legume and composite families are also of common occurrence. The soils that develop in relation to grassland vegetation with moderate precipitation produce the richest soils from the standpoint of nutrient and organic content and are today our most valuable agricultural lands. Agricultural exploitation has resulted in the near elimination of grassland communities in Illinois, Iowa, and westward to the areas of Kansas, Nebraska, and the Dakotas where grazing lands replace cultivated crops.

Desert   This formation occurs in central and western regions of northern Mexico and in parts of Arizona, New Mexico, southern California, and adjacent states. Deserts in North America, as in

FIG. 32-13. Xerophytes. Joshua trees (*Yucca brevifofia*) and other desert plants in the Mohave desert of California.

other continents, are confined to areas of low precipitation and high evaporation; consequently, plant cover is frequently sparse. Following the usually brief periods of rain, short-lived, colorful annual plants spring into bloom, produce seeds, and die. The dominant shrubby plants of warm, southern deserts include cacti, yuccas, agaves, creosote bush, and mesquite (Fig. 32-13). Northern desert areas, such as those in Utah and Nevada, have low winter temperatures—much lower than in southern deserts. The dominant shrubs of this so-called cold desert include sagebrush, shadscale, and greasewood. Numerous structural modifications help protect desert plants from excessive water loss, for example, reduction in leaf size and number, loss of leaves during the dry season, complete absence of leaves in some species, sunken stomata, thick cuticles, densely hairy or oily surfaces, and extensive root systems.

Tropical Rain Forest   In North America, tropical rain forest is limited to continuously warm and moist regions of southern Mexico and Central America and to areas within the West Indies. This formation typically includes a large number of broad-leaved evergreen tree species representing numerous families of flowering plants. These trees grow rapidly and attain great heights, and many have broad supporting buttresses extending from their bases. Epiphytic plants and climbing vines are also common in tropical rain forest (Fig. 32-14). Stratification within the forest is pronounced and, because of the optimal conditions for growth, plant succession is rapid.

ECOLOGY AND CONSERVATION

The conservation of natural resources in an effective manner may be regarded as a practical application of ecological facts and principles. Conservation programs—which are carried on by various agencies of the United States government and of state governments, by private commercial firms such as lumber companies, by trade associations, by professional scientific organizations,

FIG. 32-14. Tropical rain forest in Java. Notice the numerous epiphytes.

and by civic groups—are usually planned and executed by trained ecologists. These programs have several objectives: restoration of grassland in areas in which the grass associations have been destroyed; reduction and prevention of soil erosion; increase of populations of deer, mountain sheep, antelope, wild birds, fish, and other animals; reforestation of lands from which trees have been removed or burned; control of diseases of forest trees; regulation of water resources to prevent destructive floods and to conserve water for irrigation and the generation of water power; control of weeds; and improvement and maintenance of recreational areas for the citizens of our country. A knowledge of the growth habits, reproduction, water and nutrient requirements, light and temperature relations, and other features of grasses is essential for a conservationist whose job is to restore grasses in their original environments and to ensure their continued growth and productivity. The soil conservationist must also have a knowledge of the chemical and physical properties of soils and of such meteorological phenomena as rainfall, snowfall, wind action, and annual temperature variations. A forester, who is essentially a tree ecologist, must possess information concerning the identification of trees, their growth habits, their moisture, nutrient, light, and temperature requirements, their insect and fungous parasites, their reproductive peculiarities, their susceptibility to fire, the structure and physiology of their seeds, and their potential yield of economically valuable lumber. A wildlife ecologist must possess knowledge gained by years of study of the habits of wild animals and of the relations between animals and plants; he must be familiar with the feeding habits and food sources of animals, with their reproductive cycles and behavior, and with their migrations, diseases, and enemies. Farm advisers and agronomists also are ecologists in a sense and must have information pertaining to crop ecology if their work is to be effective.

Thus, ecology, in addition to its purely scientific value, possesses immeasurable practical significance. As public awareness of the need for conservation practices increases, the demand for thoroughly trained ecologists grows. The future will doubtless bring about an expansion in ecological investigations and applications.

SUMMARY

1. Ecology is the study of the relations of plants and animals with their environments.

2. A community is a group of plants living together in a particular environment or habitat.

3. A widespread species may consist of several ecotypes, that is, populations of individual plants physiologically adapted to different habitats within the range of the species. Ecotypic variation is important in understanding the distribution patterns of many species.

4. The distribution of species into various habitats results from the interaction of their genetically controlled physiological tolerance limits and natural selective forces represented by the environment.

5. The present distribution of plants is related to the long-term climatic and geological phenomena of past ages.

6. The contemporary factors of plant distribution may be divided into four categories: climatic factors, edaphic factors, biotic factors, and fire.

7. Climatic factors are those operative through the atmosphere: precipitation, temperature, light, wind, and humidity.

8. The combination of precipitation and temperature is fundamentally important in determining the distribution of the general vegetation of the earth.

9. Different species of plants are variously affected by differences in temperature, moisture, and light.

10. Temperature affects the rate of physiological processes, reproduction, and the survival or death of plants.

11. Moisture availability to plants is determined by the annual amount of precipitation, the monthly distribution of precipitation, and various soil factors.

12.   Light affects photosynthesis, transpiration, flowering, and other activities of plants.

13.   Winds exert mechanical effects on plants and influence transpiration.

14.   Edaphic factors are those operative through the soil: soil moisture, soil nutrients, soil reaction, soil temperature, soil air, and soil structure.

15.   On the basis of availability of moisture in the soils in which they grow, plants may be classified into four types: xerophytes, hydrophytes, mesophytes, and halophytes.

16.   Normal plant growth requires readily available moisture and the essential nutrient elements from soils.

17.   Soil temperatures influence the rate of absorption by roots and the rate of root growth.

18.   Oxygen in the soil air is essential for the normal respiration of roots and of many soil organisms and for the germination of seeds.

19.   Ecosystem studies attempt to determine the nature and extent of materials and energy exchange among the component trophic levels, that is, producers, consumers, and decomposers.

20.   Plant community changes that are relatively rapid and directional are termed succession. Both primary and secondary succession are recognized.

21.   Succession usually proceeds toward a relatively stable climax community that is in equilibrium with its environment.

22.   The largest spatial communities are called plant formations; each is characterized by a given growth form, that is, tree, shrub, or herb. Formations are subdivided into associations.

23.   Plant formations and their characteristic faunas are collectively termed biomes.

24.   The major plant formations of North America are: arctic and alpine tundra, coniferous forest, deciduous forest, grassland, desert, and tropical rain forest.

25.   Overgrazing, destructive lumbering, agricultural operations, and fires may destroy climax associations. Man has thus been a major factor in altering the biomes and their associations.

26.   The objectives of conservation agencies are the protection of natural resources and their restoration, wherever they have been destroyed. Sound conservation practices are based on ecological facts and principles.

SUGGESTED READINGS FOR INTERESTED STUDENTS

1.   Billings, W. D., *Plants and the Ecosystem.* Wadsworth, Belmont, Cal., 1964.

2.   Buchsbaum, Ralph, and Mildred, *Basic Ecology.* Boxwood Press, Pittsburgh, Pa., 1957.

3. Kormondy, Edward J., Ed., *Readings in Ecology*. Prentice-Hall, Englewood Cliffs, N.J., 1965.

4. Odum, Eugene P., *Ecology*. Holt, Rinehart and Winston, New York, 1963.

5. Phillipson, John, *Ecological Energetics*. The Institute of Biology's *Studies in Biology*, No. 1, St. Martin's Press. New York, 1966.

TOPICS AND QUESTIONS FOR STUDY

1. Define ecology and describe its scope.

2. What subjects should be studied by persons planning careers in ecological work?

3. What is a plant community and what are some of its characteristics?

4. What is the importance of ecotypic variation in understanding the distribution of some species?

5. Name the major climatic factors that influence the distribution of plants, and describe their effects on plants.

6. Describe the effects of soil factors on plant growth and distribution.

7. Explain how geographical and geological factors influence plant distribution.

8. Distinguish among hydrophytes, mesophytes, xerophytes, and halophytes, and name some specific plants as examples of each.

9. What is competition? What is its importance in plant distribution? Name some familiar plants in your area that are successful competitors.

10. What is the importance of competition in evolution?

11. What is a weed? Why are weeds undesirable?

12. May a species of plant be regarded as weedy in one area and as a desirable plant in another region?

13. How have parasites affected the distribution of plants?

14. Define mutualism, and describe some examples of this phenomenon.

15. Distinguish among producers, consumers, and decomposers.

16. What is a food web? Trace out some familiar food web.

17. What is the position of man in food webs? Does man ever form a link in a food web? Explain.

18. Why is the study of food webs important in a practical way?

19. Describe the ways in which animals influence plants.

20. Distinguish among parasites, saprophytes, and epiphytes.

21. What is meant by plant succession? Climax community?

22. What is the difference between primary and secondary succession?

23. What is a plant formation? A biome?

24. What is the relation of an association to a formation?

25. Name the plant formations of North America. What are some of their characteristics? Their important plants?

26. How would you account for the fact that plant formations are not uniform throughout?

27. Describe some of the changes that man has produced in North American biomes.

28. What steps would you take to reverse these changes and to restore these biomes?

29. Name as many specific organizations as you can that are engaged in conservation work.

30. Name and describe briefly the objectives of conservation practices and agencies.

31. Using specific examples, explain how ecological facts and principles are essential to the work of conservationists.

33

PLANTS
AND MAN

Throughout this book, attention has been called to the relationships of plants to human life as sources of food, oxygen, fuel, and other products. These relationships, for the most part, have been mentioned secondarily and incidentally to the discussion of the structure, physiology, and reproduction of various plant groups, and no organized account of the principles underlying the effects of plants on human life has been presented. In the treatment of various lower groups, such as bacteria, fungi, and algae, emphasis was on the influences of these plants on human existence. In this chapter, the major emphasis will be on the significance of seed plants in contemporary life.

The study of the effects of plants on human life is called **economic botany,** a phase of plant study that crosses into such other fields of human knowledge as history, geography, sociology, chemistry, archeology, economics, and anthropology. Some botanists argue against the use of the term economic botany, since, they aver, all plants have significance in human life. For example, some of the oxygen you are breathing in as you read this sentence may have been put into the air as a result of the photosynthesis of some moss or liverwort or fern with no direct economic use, and some of the food you have eaten today owes its synthesis in part to the activities of soil bacteria involved in maintaining soil fertility. Accordingly, one may regard all plants as having some economic significance; however, when we speak of economic botany, we usually refer to the study of the more readily apparent and more direct involvements of plants in our lives.

The effects that seed plants exert on human life may be separated into two categories: **harmful effects** and **beneficial effects.**

HARMFUL EFFECTS OF SEED PLANTS ON HUMAN LIFE

The benefits that seed plants exert in behalf of man far outweight their harmful effects; nevertheless, harmful effects are sufficiently important to deserve emphasis. Seed plants influence man disadvantageously chiefly in the following ways.

Weeds　　As indicated in earlier chapters, many seed plants are weeds that compete with man's field, garden, and orchard crops for space, light, water, and soil nutrients and that, if their growth is not checked, contribute to a reduction in yield or even to the death of man's cultivated crop plants and lawns. Because weeds, which tend to dominate the noncultivated flora of urban areas, habitation sites, and so on, are unsightly and troublesome, they also detract from the general aesthetic experience of man. It should be noted, however, that man's disturbance of natural vegetation systems has created conditions conducive to the invasion of weeds.

Poisonous Plants　　Some species of seed plants synthesize and store in their tissues substances that are poisonous to man and to his domesticated animals. Such plants as deadly nightshade, loco weed, henbane, Jimson weed, death camas, and poison hemlock are responsible for various

types of poisoning in man and in his useful animals. The poisoning may have a superficial but irritating effect, or, if the plant tissue is eaten, it may produce serious illness or death of human beings, and of swine, sheep, cattle, and horses.

Allergenic Plants　　Some wind-pollinated flowers, such as those of ragweeds, some grasses, and various trees, liberate into the air large quantities of wind-borne pollen grains that, in contact with the human respiratory system, induce the physiological reactions known as hayfever or asthma. Although hayfever is rarely fatal in itself, it produces symptoms that bring discomfort and lowered efficiency to persons who are susceptible to the pollens and may contribute to the development of more serious respiratory problems. Other types of allergies in man result from eating certain plant foods. Reaction to poison ivy is probably the most widespread and common allergenic response in North America.

Narcotic Plants　　Some plants, such as opium poppy, common hemp or marijuana, morning glory, and the coca plant, store in their tissues organic substances that, when eaten or smoked by human beings, induce physiological and mental aberrations that commonly lead to physical, intellectual, and moral degeneracy and thus produce grave social problems in human life. An interesting feature of certain narcotics is that, in minute and carefully controlled quantities, they may have beneficial medicinal effects in relieving pain, inducing local anaesthesia, and quieting hysteria.

Plants with Harmful Mechanical Effects　　Some species of plants produce fruits with hard, spiny bristles or other types of outgrowths that may cause injury or death in domesticated animals that eat them or come in contact with them. Thus, cattle and sheep sometimes eat the bristly fruits of porcupine grass or may, as they browse on range grasses, inadvertently eat fruits of the buffalo bur (Fig. 33-1); the hard spines of these fruits

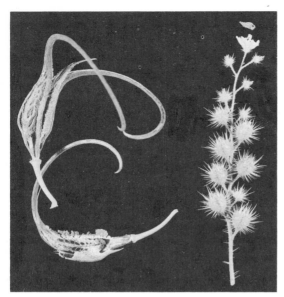

FIG. 33-1. Fruits harmful to grazing animals. *Left:* Unicorn plant. *Right:* Buffalo burr.

may puncture the intestines of these animals and thus may lead to infections that cause death. The tough, spiny fruits of the unicorn plant (Fig. 33-1) sometimes become embedded in the noses or mouths of grazing animals and may result in the establishment of fatal infections in those wounds.

Parasitic Seed Plants   As indicated earlier, mistletoes and dodders parasitize many species of autotrophic seed plants, robbing them of food, decreasing their growth, and often resulting in their death.

BENEFICIAL EFFECTS OF SEED PLANTS ON HUMAN LIFE

The beneficial effects of seed plants in human life may be subdivided into two categories: **indirect effects** and **direct effects.** The indirect effects involve the growth habits or general physiological behavior of seed plants. They include such phenomena as prevention or reduction of soil erosion by vegetation, provision of food and shelter for wild animals, maintenance of the atmospheric oxygen supply through photosynthesis, and the effects of masses of plants in breaking the force of winds and in influencing atmospheric humidity and temperature. The direct effects involve the products that are formed by seed plants and that are immediately useful to man. In this chapter, only these directly beneficial effects will be considered, for many of the indirectly beneficial effects have been previously described.

The major groups of seed plant products that are directly useful to man are the following.

Foods   The complete dependence of human beings and of all other animals on the food synthesized by green plants has received such emphasis in earlier chapters that little additional comment is required. Our cereals (corn, wheat, rice, barley, oats, and rye) are man's basic food plants. They, together with legumes, vegetables, fruits, and nuts, are all products of flowering plants. The edible flesh of cattle, swine, poultry, fish, molluscs, and other groups of animals is produced at the expense of cereal grains, grasses, legumes, algae, and other plants on which these animals feed.

Fibers   Fibers are elongated cells, or tightly cohering groups of cells, that are used principally in the weaving of cloth fabrics and in the manufacture of rope, string, thread, nets, and bags. Some fibers, after physical and chemical alteration, are used in the production of rayon, paper, cellulose lacquers, and cellophane. The most valuable plant fibers are cotton, flax (linen), jute, Indian hemp, Manila hemp, sisal hemp, and ramie.

Wood and Wood Derivatives   The major direct uses of wood as structural and decorative material have been described in Chapter 11 and are sufficiently familiar that they do not require further discussion. Other important uses include the many economically valuable products derived from woods that have been subjected to various physical and chemical treatments: charcoal, wood alcohol, wood gas, acetate of lime, acetic acid, wood tars and resins, rayon, paper, cardboard, and tannins.

Drugs Although many of the plant drugs used by mankind in earlier periods of history have been supplanted by synthetic drugs produced by organic chemists and although many plant drugs formerly thought to possess curative properties have been proved worthless, there are still many kinds of medicinal substances of plant origin that are extremely valuable in modern medicine. Among these are digitalis, a valuable drug in certain types of heart disease; ephedrine, an important ingredient in nasal sprays; cascara and senna, laxatives; morphine, effective in easing pain; cocaine, used in local anaesthesia; and balsams, soothing and healing agents.

Beverages The study of the history of beverage plants indicates that the human civilizations that arose in different parts of the world developed their own characteristic beverages. Thus, tea was the beverage of eastern Asia, cocoa (or cacao) of the civilizations of Mexico and Central America, and coffee of northeastern Africa and Arabia. These beverages are used by man, partly because they contain mildly stimulating alkaloids, such as caffeine, partly because of their pleasing flavors and aromas. Only one of the world's important beverages has any appreciable food value, namely cocoa, which is also used in the form of chocolate as a nutritious food.

Gums and Related Substances These substances are natural derivatives of cellulose and other carbohydrates and are mucilaginous or sticky when wet. Gums swell and dissolve in water, forming viscous liquids used in the manufacture of mucilages and other adhesives and are used also as binders in medicinal pills, as stabilizing agents that keep solid particles in suspension in liquids such as certain inks; as soothing agents for inflamed mucous membranes (many cough drops and syrups contain plant gums), and

as stiffening agents in ice creams, meringues, candies, and other confections.

Essential Oils Essential oils are odoriferous substances that are generally regarded as waste products of metabolism and that occur widely in plant tissues. They are not true oils, but they commonly have an oily texture, and unlike the true oils, they evaporate rapidly when they are exposed to air. Essential oils are extracted from the tissues in which they develop and are used by man in many ways. Essential oils from flowers of jasmine, carnation, lavender, roses, and many other plants give pleasing odors to perfumes, soaps, deodorants, cosmetics, and incense. Oil of camphor is used in medicinal preparations, in cosmetics, and in the manufacture of celluloid. Oil of citronella is a common ingredient in cheap soaps and perfumes. The characteristic odors and flavors of such flavoring ingredients as peppermint, cinnamon, nutmeg, anise, ginger, and cloves are attributable to essential oils. Oil of turpentine, from pine wood, is important as a paint solvent.

Resins Resins are substances that develop in some plants as a result of the partial or complete oxidation of essential oils. Some resins are sticky, viscous liquids, whereas others are hard, brittle solids. Resins of some species are nearly colorless; others range from pale yellow through shades of orange, red, and brown to black. Some are clear, others are turbid. Resins frequently resemble gums superficially but differ from them in their origin and chemical nature, and in their solubility; resins are insoluble in water but dissolve readily in alcohol and other organic solvents whereas gums dissolve in water and are insoluble in alcohol. Resins dissolved in organic solvents are called varnishes; when the solution is spread out in a thin film, the solvent evaporates, leaving a hard, protective layer of resin. Many resins, such as Canada balsam, balsam of Peru, and benzoin, have useful medicinal properties and are utilized in soothing ointments and in cough medicines. Some resins are used as perfume fixatives to retard the rate of evaporation of the essential oils responsible for the aroma and thus prolong perfume fragrance; others are ingredients of incense and tobacco flavorings. Rosin, a distillation residue of turpentine resin, is used in the manufacture of linoleum, oil cloth, printer's ink, roofing compounds, and paper sizing.

Tannins   These are organic compounds of bitter taste that occur in many plant tissues and are usually regarded as metabolic waste products, since they tend to accumulate in dead or physiologically inactive tissues, such as heartwood, cork, and old leaves. Tannins are extracted commercially from bark (mangrove, hemlock, chestnut oak), from wood (quebracho), from leaves (sumac), and from other plant parts. They react with proteins of animal skins in such manner that the skins are preserved and made soft and pliable (leather). In the absence of this tanning treatment, skins soon become hard, brittle, and unsuited for the manufacture of shoes, bags, belts, and other leather objects. Tannins are also used in the manufacture of certain inks, forming blue-black or green-black substances in the presence of soluble iron compounds.

Cork   Cork, from the outer bark of a Mediterranean oak, in addition to its familiar use in bottle stoppers, is employed for various other purposes: insulation against sound and against temperature changes, engine gaskets, flooring, insoles of shoes.

Dyes   Dyes extracted from the tissues of seed plants have been used for thousands of years for the coloring of fabrics and skins, and for personal adornment. Within the past 100 years, many natural dyes have been supplanted by synthetic preparations so that the economic importance of plant dyes has diminished. Nevertheless, a few plant dyes have persisted as important commodities in world trade, largely because they possess certain qualities not supplied by synthetic dyes. For example, one of the best and most nearly

permanent black dyes available is logwood, derived from a tropical American tree and used in dyeing fine fabrics and in the staining of biological tissues. Indigo, a deep blue dye from plants, is unrivaled in the permanency of its color and it still an important natural dye. Fustic, from a tropical American tree, furnishes important yellow, olive, and brown colors still used in the dyeing industry. Several plant dyes are commercially valuable in the coloring of foods and beverages, since they are odorless, tasteless, and without adverse physiological effects on human beings. Dyes of this type are saffron, a yellow dye used in coloring foods and medicines; annato, a yellowish-orange dye utilized in coloring butter, cheese, and other food products; and chlorophyll, the abundant green pigment of plants, used in coloring foods and beverages.

Fatty Oils and Related Substances   These are true oils and fats, synthesized by plants and commonly stored in seeds, fruits, and other parts as reserve foods. Many of these oils, for example, olive, soybean, corn, and cottonseed oil, are important foods in human diets. They are used as cooking oils, in the manufacture of oleomargarine, salad oils, and vegetable shortenings and in the canning of fish and meats. Some fatty oils, such as linseed oil and tung oil, dry rapidly when exposed to air, hardening to form durable films; such drying oils are widely used in the manufacture of paints, linoleum, and printer's ink. Coconut oil, olive oil, and African palm oil are used in the manufacture of soaps. Oilcloth, artificial leather, putty, glycerine, nitroglycerin, and lubricants are other important products of fatty oils.

Plant fats, which are chemically related to oils but which differ from them in their solidity at room temperatures, include cocoa butter, an important ingredient of cosmetics, confections, and medicinal ointments, and nutmeg butter, used in medicines and candies.

Plant waxes are chemically related to fats and are harvested chiefly from the epidermal layers of leaves and fruits, where they sometimes occur in considerable quantities. Most valuable of the plant waxes is carnauba wax, from the leaves of a Brazilian palm. This wax is widely employed in the manufacture of candles and certain polishes. A wax that is well known in the United States, although of minor commercial value, is the aromatic bayberry wax, derived from the fruits of a small shrub native to the northeastern states; bayberry wax is used in the manufacture of candles.

Latex Products Latex, a viscous, milky juice of unknown physiological significance, occurs in several hundred species of flowering plants. The latex of some species contains organic substances that harden when exposed to air or chemical treatment to form pliable or elastic solids. Most familiar and most valuable of these is rubber, which, because of its elasticity, pliability, and resilience, is used in hundreds of products of great economic importance: tires, inner tubes, hose, mattresses, shock absorbers, drug and surgical appliances, and many others. Most of the world's natural rubber is a product of the Pará or Brazil rubber tree (Fig. 33-2), which is a native of the Amazon basin and which is widely cultivated in the East Indies, Malaya, and Africa. Another latex product of economic value is gutta-percha, from several species of Asiatic trees; gutta-percha differs from rubber in that it is only slightly elastic; it is resilient and pliable, however, and finds important uses in the insulation of marine and other kinds of cables, in the manufacture of golf balls, surgical splints and apparatus, and in dentistry for temporary fillings, dentures, and molds. Another latex product, chicle, chiefly from southern Mexico, Central America, and Venezuela, is the basis of chewing gum.

Miscellaneous Products Among other economically valuable plant products are substances that are smoked and chewed by man for their stimulatory action or their fancied production of relief from nervous tension. Tobacco, of course, is the principal plant product smoked; a native of tropi-

FIG. 33-2. Trunk of Para rubber tree, showing tapping cuts and flowing latex.

cal America, tobacco has reached all areas of the earth inhabited by man, and its cultivation and processing are major industries. Chicle, mentioned in the preceding section, is the major ingredient of chewing gum, one of the world's favorite masticatories. Chewing gum possesses no food value; its use supposedly relaxes nervous tension, stimulates the flow of saliva, and may partially clean the teeth; its use is innocuous, except for its violation of auditory and visual sensibilities. The peoples of the Orient chew betel nuts, the seeds of a palm native to Ceylon and Malaya. The chewing of betel nuts provides a mild physiological stimulation and a feeling of mental well-being; the principal objection to its use is the brownish or maroon discoloration that it imparts to the teeth of the user. In many parts of tropical Africa, the natives chew cola nuts, since they contain caffeine and produce a stimulation comparable with that of coffee.

THE ORIGINS OF CULTIVATED PLANTS

Man obtains many useful products from plants growing in their wild state; among such products are chicle, most resins and gums, balata, most woods, many tannins, and some drugs. Most of man's valuable plant products, however, are derived from plants cultivated in gardens, vineyards, fields, and orchards. Obviously these cultivated plants have had their origins in wild plants that have been domesticated through the centuries of their use by mankind.

Botanists have found the study of the origins of these cultivated plants an extremely interesting one, which has shed much light on purely botanical questions and which has had ramifications in the study of human migrations, of archeology, of anthropology, and of other fields of knowledge. In their investigations of the origin of cultivated plants, botanists have attempted to answer two basic questions: how long has man cultivated various species of economic plants, and where on the earth's surface did those useful plants originate?

The answers to these questions have come from several types of studies and from various kinds of evidence, among which the following have been especially important.

Archeological Evidence   This refers to the evidence derived from the study of past civilizations, such as the Egyptian, the Babylonian, the Aztec, the Mayan, and the Incan. The excavation of ancient cities, the study of ancient sculptures, mosaics, and paintings, and the opening of tombs of long-defunct royal personages have provided much information about the plants cultivated by these civilizations and about their agricultural practices. The study of such archeological remains and of seeds and plant fragments found in them have contributed to our knowledge of the origins of cultivated plants, from the geographical and time viewpoints.

Manuscripts   Translation of manuscripts from various periods of human history has revealed much about the agricultural practices and the kinds of plants cultivated by ancient and medieval peoples. Ships' logs, diaries, and travel records written by various explorers of the fifteenth and sixteenth centuries contain descriptions of the economic plants and agricultural practices of the Americas. Similarly, written records of fifteenth- and sixteenth-century explorations of Asia and the islands adjacent to southeastern Asia reveal much about the native cultivated plants of the Orient.

Origins of Plant Names   The names of many cultivated plants are sources of information about the time and places of origin of these plants. Thus, the words avocado, chocolate, and tomato are derived from Aztec words, maize from a Caribbean Indian word, mango from a Malayan word, sugar from a Sanskrit word, and alfalfa from an Arabic word. These philological evidences are useful in the study of plant origins.

Distribution of Cultivated Plants   Most species of plants appear to be of relatively limited distribution on the earth's surface. Thus, when we find a plant cultivated over a wide geographical area, we may reasonably conclude that this plant has been cultivated for a long time by man and that it has been carried by human migrations through the long period of its cultivation. Maize, for example, was cultivated from Argentina to the St. Lawrence river valley shortly after (and probably before) the discovery of America, and, by the beginning of the Christian era, wheat was cultivated from Europe and North Africa across Asia Minor as far east as India. Thus, both maize and wheat are apparently of great antiquity of cultivation.

Wild Ancestors   Some of our valuable cultivated plants have never been found in a wild state and bear little or no resemblance to any known wild plant species. The absence of a wild ancestor is interpreted as indicating a very ancient history of cultivation. Presumably, during many centuries of cultivation such species may have become so changed that they no longer resemble their wild ancestor or the wild ancestor may have become extinct. Thus, the absence of wild ancestors of maize, is regarded as evidence of the great antiquity of its cultivation.

Radioactive Carbon Studies   Carbon-14, an unstable, radioactive form of carbon, occurs in the earth's atmosphere as a result of the bombardment of nitrogen-14 by cosmic rays. These carbon-14 atoms combine with oxygen to form radioactive carbon dioxide, which becomes mixed in the atmosphere with ordinary carbon dioxide in a constant proportion. In their photosynthesis, green plants utilize some carbon-14 in building carbohydrates, and thus all green plant bodies have a fixed proportion of organic compounds containing this radioactive carbon; about 1/trillionth of a gram of carbon-14 occurs with each gram of ordinary, nonradioactive carbon in living plants. When a plant dies, it is no longer utilizing carbon dioxide and thus no longer incorporates carbon-14 into its tissues. Since carbon-14 is unstable, it loses its radioactivity slowly and becomes transformed into nonradioactive carbon. As plant remains (for example, corn cobs and old seeds) age, their proportion of carbon-14 accordingly decreases; the older the plant remains, the lower is the proportion of carbon-14 in them. Thus, physicists, knowing the proportion of carbon-14 in living plant tissues and knowing the rate of carbon-14 disappearance in dead tissues, can estimate the approximate age of any plant fragment, up to about 40,000 years, by determining the amount of carbon-14 in its substance. This method of dating plant remains from ancient tombs and city sites is furnishing valuable evidence of the age of certain cultivated plants.

THE ORIGINS OF SPECIFIC CULTIVATED PLANTS

Utilizing the above-described evidences, botanists have reached some conclusions concerning the general geographical areas of origin of important cultivated plants and their relative ages of cultivation. These conclusions are summarized in Table 33–1. There the term Old World refers to Asia, Europe, and Africa; the term New World refers to the Americas (Figs. 33-3 and 33-4).

These lists, which are not complete but which include man's most important cultivated plants, indicate three major conclusions concerning the origin of cultivated plants:

1. The number of important cultivated plant species of Old World origin is appreciably larger than the number of cultivated species of New World origin. This may be explained by man's longer residence in the Old World; the human species originated in the Old World and there carried on agriculture for many centuries before some of its members migrated to the New World. Thus, mankind has had a much longer period of time in the Old World in which to domesticate native plant species of that portion of the earth.

2. Man's most important cultivated plants (for example, wheat, corn, barley, date, kidney bean, soybean, and rice) are his most ancient cultivated plants; those plants that have come into cultivation since the beginning of the Christian era, both in the Old and New Worlds, are for the most part secondary in importance.

3. There is not a single species of important cultivated plant that is common in origin both to the Old World and the New World. This indicates that the first human beings who migrated from the Old World to the New must have been wandering, nomadic hunters, rather than cultivators of plants, for we know that whenever an agricultural people migrates, it takes with it the seeds of its most important crops. Had these first migrants to the New World cultivated plants, they would inevitably have carried seeds of those plants with them, and thus we might have expected to find some cultivated species common to both the Old World and the New. There are some *genera* of cultivated plants common to both Old World and New, for example, grape, cotton, strawberry, and chestnut; but the *species* of these genera are different in the Old and New Worlds. Table 33–1 shows the breakdown of Old and New World plants.

Plants of Old World Origin

A. Plants cultivated for at least 4000 years, possibly longer:

almond	fig	peach
apple	flax	pear
apricot	grape (some types)	rice
banana	hemp	sorghum
barley	mango	soybean
cabbage	millet	watermelon
date	olive	wheat
eggplant	onion	

B. Plants cultivated for at least 2000 years, probably longer:

alfalfa	chestnut	pepper (black)
asparagus	citrus fruits	plum
beet	cotton (some types)	poppy
breadfruit	lettuce	radish
carrot	nutmeg	rye
celery	oats	sugar cane
cherry	pea	tea
		English walnut

C. Plants cultivated for less than 2000 years:

artichoke	gooseberry	parsnip
buckwheat	muskmelon	raspberry
coffee	okra	rhubarb
currant	parsley	strawberry (some types)

Plants of New World Origin

A. Plants of unknown antiquity of cultivation, certainly over 2000 years and probably more than 4000 years:

cacao (cocoa)	kidney bean	sweet potato
corn	maté	tobacco

B. Plants of more recent cultivation, some since the beginning of the Christian era, others before the Christian era:

avocado	pineapple	rubber
cassava	potato	squash
cotton (some types)	pumpkin	tomato
peanut	red peppers	vanilla

TABLE 33-1   Plant Origins

FIG. 33–3.   Important food plants of Old World origin. (Photo courtesy of the Field Museum of Natural History.)

FIG. 33–4.   Important food plants of New World origin. (Photo courtesy of the Field Museum of Natural History.)

THE FUTURE OF PLANT EXPLOITATION

Although the study of economic botany indicates that the dependence of man on plants increases as his civilization becomes more complex, the basic dependence of modern man on plants is the same as the basic dependence of primitive man, namely, on plants as the source of his foods. The major problem that now faces man in many parts of the world, for example, in Japan, China, and India, is the basic problem of securing enough food. The advances of medical science in the past century have greatly reduced infant mortality and have significantly lengthened the human life span, so that the world's human population is now increasing at a more rapid rate than at any other time in human history. The world's agriculture, as it is now carried on, will soon be inadequate to provide enough food for the human race. Thus, man, if he is to survive, must greatly increase food production by plants. Already economists, botanists, statesmen, biochemists, horticulturists, agronomists, and others are giving consideration to possible methods of increasing the world's food supply. The experiments, observations, and plans of these men indicate that increasing the world's food will involve many different approaches: more effective means of increasing and maintaining soil fertility; more effective methods of soil conservation; increasing the productivity of crop plants by breeding and selection to develop new and better plant varieties; the extension of irrigation projects to bring into agricultural use millions of acres of desert land that now receive insufficient water for crop culture; the breeding of improved types of forage plants and of superior types of meat-producing animals; the increased utilization of food products of the sea, not only of fish and other marine animals but also the direct use of marine algae as sources of human food. It has been estimated that the total amount of photosynthesis carried on by marine algae may be ten times greater than the total photosynthetic activity of all land plants. If this is true, then man may well look to the plants of the sea as a rich, abundant, relatively untapped source of foodstuffs. In some parts of the world, for example, Japan and China, algae of the sea have for many years been important items in the human diet. These various methods of increasing the world's food supply will require the efforts of many kinds of plant scientists and thus will offer numerous opportunities in research and in production to young men and women in the plant sciences.

SUMMARY

1.   Economic botany is the study of the effects of plants on human life.

2.   Some seed plants exert harmful effects on human life; among seed plants that exert such effects are weeds, poisonous plants, allergenic plants, narcotic plants, parasitic plants, and plants that cause physical injuries to domesticated animals.

3.   Indirect beneficial effects of seed plants on human life include the prevention of soil erosion, the provision of food and shelter for wild animals, maintenance of atmospheric oxygen supply, and the influencing of atmospheric humidity and temperature.

4.   Direct beneficial effects of seed plants on human life are found in their products that are useful to man: fibers, wood, drugs, beverages, gums, resins, cork, essential oils, tannins, dyes, fats, latex products, and tobacco.

5. Man's most valuable plants are cultivated plants, which have been derived from wild plants.

6. Evidences used to determine the place of origin and length of cultivation of plants are derived from the study of archeology, of manuscripts, of plant names, of the distribution of cultivated plants, of the presence or absence of wild ancestors, and of radioactive carbon content of plant tissues.

7. The number of important cultivated plants of Old World origin is larger than the number of cultivated plants of New World origin.

8. Man's most important cultivated plants have been under cultivation for at least 4000 years.

9. There is not a single species of important cultivated plant common in origin to both Old and New Worlds.

10. An exceedingly important problem of man in the next few decades will be the need to increase the world's food supply

SUGGESTED READINGS FOR INTERESTED STUDENTS

1. Anderson, Edgar, *Plants, Man, and Life*. Little, Brown, Boston, 1952.
2. Baker, H. G., *Plants and Civilization*. Wadsworth, Belmont, Cal., 1965.
3. Fitzpatrick, Frederick, L., *Our Plant Resources*. Holt, Rinehart and Winston, New York, 1964.
4. Hill, A. F., *Economic Botany*, 2 ed. McGraw-Hill, New York, 1952.
5. Kingsbury, J. M., *Poisonous Plants of the United States and Canada*, Prentice-Hall, Englewood Cliffs, N.J., 1964.
6. Kingsbury, J. M., *Deadly Harvest*. Holt, Rinehart and Winston, New York, 1965.
7. Schery, Robert W., *Plants for Man*. Prentice-Hall, Englewood Cliffs, N.J., 1952.

TOPICS AND QUESTIONS FOR STUDY

1. Assume that all plant products except foods, fibers, and wood, were withdrawn from human use. What changes in our twentieth-century civilization would immediately follow? Would appear more slowly?

2. Make lists of the kinds of plant products that you believe were used by
   a. Europeans during the tenth century A.D.
   b. American Indians, before the discovery of America by Columbus.
   c. Americans of the thirteen colonies in 1775.
   d. Americans in the year 1850.
   Compare these with a list of plant products which Americans use now.

3. Make a list of plant products that are less extensively used now than they were 100 years ago, and account for the decline in their use.

4. List as many ways as you can in which plant taxonomy may be regarded as "economic botany." Do the same for plant physiology, plant morphology, plant genetics, plant ecology.

5. Name the principal groups of plant products and their economic uses.

6. Make a list of economically valuable plants that are native to the Old World (Europe, Asia, and Africa).

7. How would you account for the fact that most of our economic plants are natives of the Old World?

8. List the economically valuable plants that are native to the Americas.

9. List and describe the evidences used to determine the geographical origin and length of cultivation of economic plants.

10. Assume that you and a small group of your friends are to be transported to an uninhabited island in the South Pacific to live and that you will be permitted to take seeds of 12 species of plants with you. State which ones you would select and your reasons for your selection.

11. The world's most important rubber-producing plant, the Pará rubber tree, is a native of Brazil, but most of the world's supply of Pará rubber comes from plantations in Sumatra and Malaya. What factors are responsible for this situation?

12. Although certain countries of the American tropics possess vast forests of hardwood trees, they import softwood lumber in considerable quantities from the United States. How would you explain this?

13. Describe the economic and social differences among people engaged in exploiting these differing types of plant resources in the United States: grasslands, forest, orchards, truck gardens, and grain cultivation.

GLOSSARY

GLOSSARY

Important technical terms, such as names of structures and processes, used in the text are included in this glossary. Excluded are names of individual plants and of plant groups.

Abscission: separation of leaves and other plant parts by the dissolution or separation of the cells of an abscission layer.

Abscission layer: layer of cells that disintegrates and thus separates a leaf or other structure from the plant; separation layer.

Active transport: absorption of ions as a result of expenditure of energy by living protoplasm and usually against a concentration gradient; ion accumulation.

Active water absorption: the osmotic uptake of water by living cells whose osmotic concentration has been raised by ion accumulation; process responsible for guttation and root pressure.

Adenine: one of the nitrogenous bases found in DNA and RNA.

Adenosine triphosphate (ATP): the high energy molecule involved in metabolic reactions which require additional energy before they will proceed at an adequate rate.

Adsorption: the adhesion in very thin layers of a substance to the surface of a solid particle with which it is in contact; the particles that adsorb other materials are chiefly colloidal.

Adventitious bud: a bud that develops in some place other than the axil of a leaf or the tip of a stem.

Adventitious roots: roots that do not arise from a hypocotyl, primary root, or one of its branches, but that arise from stems, leaves, etc.

Aeciospores: binucleate spores produced in cup-shaped aecia of some rust fungi.

Aerobe: an organism that lives in air containing oxygen.

Aerobic respiration: respiration in the presence of free, gaseous oxygen.

Aggregate fruit: cluster of fruits developed from the ovaries of a single flower.

Alkaloid: a nitrogenous organic substance of alkaline (basic) reaction, usually bitter in taste and often poisonous to animals.

Alleles: any of the forms of a given gene.

Alternate: describing the condition in which a single leaf or bud occurs at a node.

Alternation of generations: the alternation of a spore-producing phase and a gamete-producing phase in the sexual life cycle of a plant.

Amino acids: organic, nitrogenous acids from which protein molecules are constructed.

Ammonification: formation of ammonia following the decomposition of proteinaceous substances by ammonifying bacteria.

Amyloplast: colorless plastid which forms starch.

Anaerobe: an organism that lives in the absence of gaseous oxygen.

Anaerobic respiration (see Aerobic respiration): respiration in the absence of free oxygen, or in reduced concentrations of free oxygen.

Anaphase: a stage in mitosis in which the newly separated chromatids (daughter chromosomes) move toward opposite ends of the spindle.

Angiosperm: a plant having its seeds enclosed in an ovary, as in the flowering plants (Anthophyta).

Anion: a negatively charged ionic particle.

Anisogamy: a type of sexual reproduction involving union of two motile gametes of dissimilar size.

Annual: a plant that completes its life cycle and dies within one year.

Annulus: a row of specialized cells in the wall of a fern sporangium; contraction of the annulus causes rupture of the sporangium and dispersal of spores.

Anther: pollen-bearing part of a stamen.

Antheridium: a structure that produces sperms.

Anthocyanins: blue, red, and purple pigments of plants; water soluble, as contrasted with plastid pigments.

Antibiotics: drugs that are obtained from living organisms (chiefly bacteria and true fungi) and that destroy pathogenic organisms, chiefly bacteria.

Anticodon: the triplet of nitrogenous bases complementary to a codon. Example—the mRNA codon CAG has the tRNA anticodon GUC.

Antipodals: three small ephemeral cells within the embryo sac in an ovule.

Antiseptic: a substance that inhibits growth and activities of bacteria and other microorganisms.

Apical dominance: the inhibitory influence of terminal buds upon lateral buds.

Apical meristem: a small mass of cells, characterized by cell duplication activity, situated at the tip of a stem or root.

Archegonium: a multicellular egg-producing gametangium.

Ascocarp: in sac fungi, a structure that produces asci.

Ascogonium: the female gametangium of sac fungi.

Ascospore: a spore produced by sac fungi in asci.

Ascus: a saclike structure within which ascospores are formed.

Asexual: referring to any type of reproduction that is independent of sexual processes.

Association: an assemblage of plants, usually dominated by a few species and representing a major subdivision of a plant formation.

ATP: adenosine triphosphate. See definition.

Autotrophic: referring to a plant that is able to manufacture its own food.

Auxins: a class of growth-regulating compounds.

Avena test: a test for auxin activity, based on the response of living oat (*Avena*) coleoptiles to the growth-regulating compound; a type of bioassay.

Axil: the upper angle between a twig or leaf stalk and the axis from which it grows.

Axillary bud: a bud borne in the axil of a leaf.

Bactericide: any agent used to kill bacteria.

Bacteriostasis: prevention of the growth of bacteria.

Bark: in woody plants, the aggregation of tissues outside the cambium.

Basidiocarp: a fungal fruiting body which bears basidia.

Basidiospores: the spores of basidiomycetes, produced in basidia.

Basidium: a club-shaped spore-producing structure of the basidiomycetes.

Biennial: a plant that produces seeds during the second year of its life, then dies.

Bilateral symmetry: the condition of having distinct and similar right and left sides, as in flowers of sweet pea or snapdragon.

Binomial system: a system of naming organisms; a scientific name consists usually of two words, the first that of a genus, the second that of a species.

Bioassay: a technique using living tissue to measure activity of a growth regulating substance; see *Avena* test.

Biome: a large, natural assemblage of associated plants and animals, extending over large regions of the earth's surface.

Bisexual: describing an organism that produces both eggs and sperms, and a flower that bears both stamens and pistil(s).

Blade: the expanded portion of a leaf.

Bract: a modified leaf associated with a flower or inflorescence.

Branch gap: an interruption in the vascular tissue of a stem at the point where a branch trace arises.

Branch trace: vascular tissue that runs from a stem into a branch.

Bud: on a stem, a terminal or axillary structure consisting of a small mass of meristematic tissue, covered wholly or in part by overlapping leaves.

Bud scale: a specialized protective leaf of a bud.

Bud scar: a scar left on a twig by the falling away of a bud or a group of bud scales.

Budding: a process of grafting in which the scion is a single bud; also, asexual reproduction of yeasts.

Bulb: a short, usually globose underground stem,

bearing many fleshy, food-storing scale leaves; essentially a subterranean bud.

Bundle scars: scars left in leaf scars at the time of leaf fall by the breaking of vascular bundles passing from stem into a petiole.

Bundle sheath: one or more layers of cells surrounding a vascular bundle.

Callus: a tissue of thin-walled cells developed on wound surfaces.

Calorie: a large Calorie (kilogram-calorie) is the amount of heat energy required to raise the temperature of 1 kilogram of water 1° Centigrade; a small calorie is the amount of heat energy required to raise the temperature of 1 gram of water 1°C.

Calyptra: in the sporophyte of a moss, a sheath that covers the capsule and that consists of the upper portion of an archegonium.

Calyx: collective term for the sepals of a flower.

Cambium: layer of meristematic cells between xylem and phloem tissues; same as vascular cambium. See also cork cambium.

Capillarity: the tendency of water to be held between closely approximated surfaces or to climb in tubes of small diameter, due to surface effects associated with curvature of the meniscus. Smaller capillaries result in menisci which are more curved, and water rise in them is higher.

Capillary water: water retained in the spaces among, and on the surfaces of, soil particles after drainage.

Capsule: a simple, dehiscent, dry fruit composed of two or more carpels; also, the spore case of a moss or liverwort; and a slimy outer wall layer of bacteria.

Carbohydrases: enzymes that digest carbohydrates.

Carbohydrate: a group of foods composed of carbon, hydrogen, and oxygen, with the hydrogen and oxygen in the ratio of 2 to 1.

Carotenoids: a class of chemical compounds that includes the carotenes and xanthophylls.

Carpel: a modified megasporophyll that bears and encloses ovules.

Carpogonium: female gametangium of a red alga.

Caruncle: a spongy structure at one end of a seed such as a castor bean.

Catalyst: a substance that regulates the speed of a chemical reaction without being used up in the reaction.

Cation: a positively charged ionic particle.

Cell: the unit of structure of plants and animals; the essential feature of a cell is its living protoplasm, surrounded in plant cells by a wall.

Cell plate: a thin partition formed between daughter nuclei in a cell undergoing cytokinesis.

Cell sap: the liquid in the vacuoles of plant cells.

Cellular totipotentiality: the inherent capacity of a living cell to express all the characteristics of the whole plant.

Cellulose: a complex carbohydrate forming the major part of the cell walls of most plants.

Central cylinder: same as vascular cylinder.

Centromere: the constricted portion of a chromosome to which, in mitosis, the chromosomal fiber is attached.

Chemosynthesis: a process of food manufacture in certain bacteria, which utilizes energy derived from chemical reactions, such as the oxidation of sulfur, ammonia, etc.

Chlorophyll: a green pigment that occurs chiefly in chloroplasts and is involved in photosynthesis.

Chloroplast: specialized cytoplasmic body containing chlorophyll.

Chlorosis: failure of chlorophyll development because of nutritional disturbance, such as lack of iron or magnesium, or because of disease.

Chromatid: a chromosome half, formed by a longitudinal duplication of a chromosome.

Chromatin: deeply staining nuclear material of which hereditary determiners are composed.

Chromoplast: yellowish or red cytoplasmic body containing carotene and xanthophyll.

Chromosomal fiber: in mitosis, a minute strand that connects a chromosome with the spindle apparatus.

Chromosomes: nuclear bodies of definite structure and number formed from chromatin and bearing hereditary determiners, or genes.

Cilium: short, protoplasmic extrusion that propels certain types of unicellular organisms, gametes, and zoospores through water. See Flagellum.

Circinnate: spirally coiled in the manner of a watch spring, as the juvenile leaves of most ferns.

Cisternae: membrane-bound, usually flattened vesicles found in the cytoplasm.

Citric acid cycle: the cyclic phase of oxidative respiration, in which pyruvate from glycolysis is transformed to hydrogen and carbon dioxide; also known as the Krebs cycle or the tricarboxylic acid cycle.

Clay: complex, colloidal, inorganic fraction of soil, consisting largely of alumino-silicates; clay particles are usually negatively charged and absorb positively charged ions.

Climax community: a relatively permanent community that maintains itself with little change in a given region so long as there are no major changes in environmental conditions.

Codon: a single triplet of nitrogenous bases coding for a specific amino acid.

Coenocyte: a cell with several to many nuclei.

Coenzymes: the nonprotein portions of certain enzymes.

Colchicine: an alkaloid, which, when applied to plants, may cause polyploidy.

Collenchyma: a strengthening tissue, composed of cells with walls usually thickened at the angles of the walls.

Colloid: a state of subdivision or dispersion in which the particles of the dispersed substance are of super-molecular size and in which the particles do not diffuse (or diffuse with difficulty) through membranes. Colloidal systems are usually more stable than emulsions or suspensions, are usually electrically charged, and are usually turbid.

Colony: a group of similar organisms living together in close association; more specifically, a group of associated unicellular organisms among which there are no marked structural differences and little or no division of labor.

Community: a group of plants living together in a particular environment.

Companion cells: elongated cells adjoining sieve tubes in phloem tissue of most plants.

Complete flower: a flower that bears 4 types of floral organs: sepals, petals, stamens, and carpels.

Compound leaf: a leaf, the blade of which is subdivided into several distinct parts.

Compound middle lamella: a collective term for the middle lamella and the primary walls of two adjacent cells.

Conceptacle: in certain algae, a cavity within which antheridia or oogonia are produced.

Cone: a specialized branch bearing an aggregation of sporophylls or ovuliferous scales.

Conidiophore: a hypha that produces conidia.

Conidium: an asexual reproductive structure (regarded by some as a one-celled sporangium) in fungi; usually produced in chains by the terminal portions of hyphae of some fungi.

Coniferous: having cones.

Conjugation: a type of isogamous sexual reproduction in which a gamete moves to another gamete through a specially developed connecting tube.

Contact movements: turgor movements, chiefly of leaves and floral parts, that result from contact simuli.

Convergent evolution: evolution of unrelated or distantly related groups of organisms along similar lines, resulting in the development of similar traits or features in the unrelated groups.

Cork: a suberized tissue formed on the stem and root surfaces (sometimes on other parts) chiefly of woody plants from the cork cambium.

Cork cambium: a meristematic tissue that is formed in woody plants usually from certain cells of the cortex and that produces cork cells and phelloderm cells.

Corm: a short, often globose, upright, underground stem that stores food; differs from a bulb in that the latter consists chiefly of fleshy storage leaves growing from a small stem, whereas a corm is chiefly stem tissue.

Corolla: collectively, the petals of a flower.

Correlation: the mutual interaction of plant parts and processes.

Cortex: primary tissue lying between the epidermis and stele of a stem or root.

Cotyledon: a food-digesting and food-storing part of an embryo; also known as seed leaf.

Cristae: internal membrane extensions in mitochondria.

Cross-pollination: the transfer of pollen from a stamen to the stigma of a flower on another plant.

Crossing over: the exchange of matching segments of two homologous chromatids.

Crozier: the young fern leaf in its coiled condition; a fiddlehead.

Cuticle: waxy layer formed on outer walls of epidermal cells.

Cutin: waxy substance that is very impermeable to water; the cuticle is composed of cutin.

Cutting: a portion of a stem or leaf used in vegetative propagation as a result of formation of adventitious roots on the cutting.

Cytochrome: a class of proteinaceous pigments important in the final stages of oxidative respiration and production of ATP.

Cytokinesis: cytoplasmic division by cell plate formation, usually following mitosis or nuclear division.

Cytoplasm: all the protoplasm in a cell, except the nucleus.

Cytosine: one of the nitrogenous bases found in DNA and RNA.

Deciduous: referring to plant parts that fall off within a year of the time of their production; refers also to plants that lose their leaves regularly each year, as opposed to evergreens, the leaves of which persist for more than one year.

Dedifferentiation: the process by which matured cells, chiefly parenchyma cells, revert to a meristematic condition.

Deficiency disease: a disease resulting from lack of one or more essential elements.

Dehiscent: splitting along definite seams at maturity.

Denitrification: conversion of nitrogenous compounds in soil into gaseous nitrogen by denitrifying bacteria.

Deoxyribose nucleic acid (DNA): the material that bears the genetic information of each cell; the principal constituent of chromatin.

Deoxyribose: a 5-carbon sugar that is one of the components of DNA.

Determinate growth: cessation of terminal meristem activity following production of a limited number of lateral organs.

Dichotomous: a type of branching in plants in which the main axis or stem forks repeatedly into two branches.

Dicotyledonous: having two cotyledons in an embryo.

Dictyosomes: small, flattened stacks of net-like cisternae found in the cytoplasm; collectively the golgi apparatus.

Differentially permeable: referring to membranes that allow certain substances to pass through and that retard or prevent the passage of others.

Differentiation: modification of cells, tissues, or organs for the performance of definite functions; maturation.

Diffuse-porous wood: a type of wood in which the vessels are more or less uniform in size and distribution throughout each growth ring.

Diffuse (fibrous) root system: a root system in which there is no single main root larger than other roots.

Diffusion: the spreading of a substance throughout available space from high to low concentrations of that substance, as a result of molecular motion.

Digestion: the transformation of insoluble or complex foods into soluble or simpler substances, through the action of enzymes.

Dihybrid cross: a cross between organisms differing in two characters.

Dikaryon: in some fungi, a pair of compatible nuclei maintained without fusion within a given cell.

Dioecious: having the male and female gametangia, or staminate and pistillate flowers on separate plants.

Diploid: referring to the double chromosome number, characteristic of the sporophyte generation in plants.

Disbudding: the removal of buds from a plant to control branching or to produce larger flowers from remaining buds.

Disjunction: the separation and migration to opposite poles of the members of a pair of homologous chromosomes in anaphase I of meiosis.

DNA: see Deoxyribose nucleic acid.

Dominance: a genetic principle, established by Mendel, that when two contrasting characters are brought together in a hybrid as the result of a cross, one character (dominant) may mask the other (recessive).

Dormancy: a period of reduced physiological activity occurring in seeds, buds, etc.; resting period.

Dormins: a class of plant hormones believed to be responsible for induction of many dormancy phenomena, including leaf abscission.

Double fertilization: in flowering plants, the fusion of one sperm with an egg, of a second sperm with two polar nuclei, in an embryo sac.

Ecology: the study of living organisms in relation to their environment and each other.

Ecosystem: the community and its environment treated as an interacting, functional unit.

Ecotone: the transition zone between two overlapping communities.

Ecotype: a genetically distinct population, physiologically adapted to a particular habitat.

Ectoplast: see Plasma membrane.

Ectotrophic: feeding on the surface, as a fungus living on the surface of a host.

Edaphic: referring to the soil.

Egg: female gamete.

Elaters: hygroscopic structures that are produced in the sporophytes of liverworts and on the spores of horsetails and that aid in spore dispersal.

Elaioplast: a colorless plastid which forms oil.

Embryo: a young sporophytic plant, before the beginning of its rapid growth; the "germ" of a seed.

Embryo sac: the female gametophyte of an angiosperm—a structure within an angiosperm ovule in which the egg is fertilized; an embryo begins its development within an embryo sac.

Endocarp: inner layer of fruit wall.

Endodermis: the innermost layer of cortical cells; most conspicuous in roots.

Endoplasmic reticulum: an extensive system of cytoplasmic membranes within the protoplast.

Endosperm: a food storage tissue in angiosperm seeds; it results from the fusion of a sperm with two polar nuclei and is thus triploid.

Endotrophic: feeding internally, as a fungus living inside the tissues of a host.

Entire margin: the smooth margin of a leaf blade, lacking both teeth and lobes.

Enzyme: an organic proteinaceous catalyst, manufactured by living protoplasm, and controlling digestion and other physiological processes.

Epicotyl: the portion of an embryo axis above the attachment of the cotyledons; the growing apex of the epicotyl forms the young stem of a plant.

Epidermis: the surface layer of leaves and other soft plant parts.

Epigyny: a condition in which the ovary is embedded in the receptacle, so that the other floral parts seem to arise from the top of the ovary.

Epiphyte: a plant that gains physical support from another plant, or from poles, wires, and other objects.

Ergastic substances: the nonprotoplasmic components of the protoplast; for example, crystals and oil droplets.

Essential elements: chemical elements necessary for the normal growth and development of plants.

Essential oils: widely distributed organic compounds in plants, having an oily texture and pronounced odors; thought to be metabolic wastes.

Etiolation: a condition involving abnormal stem elongation, failure of normal leaf development, and absence of chlorophyll, and characterizing plants grown in the absence of light.

Evergreen: having green leaves throughout the entire year.

Evolution: the continuing series of genetic changes that occur within populations through time.

Exocarp: outermost layer of a fruit wall.

Facultative parasite: see Parasite.

Family: a taxonomic category ranking between genera and an order; a family is a group of related genera.

Fascicular cambium: cambium situated within a vascular bundle.

Fat: a kind of food, which is insoluble in water and is made up of carbon, hydrogen, and oxygen, with proportionately less oxygen than in carbohydrates.

Fermentation: decomposition of organic substances by living organisms in the absence of free oxygen, or in the presence of limited amounts of oxygen. See Anaerobic respiration.

Fertilization: an essential feature of sexual reproduction, the fusion of one gamete with another.

Fiber: an elongated, tapering, thick-walled strengthening cell occurring in various plant parts.

Field capacity: the maximum amount of water the soil can hold against the force of gravity.

Filament: the stalk of a stamen, with an anther at its apex; also, a threadlike row of cells.

Fission: asexual reproduction in which a one-celled organism divides into two one-celled organisms.

Flagellum: a protoplasmic extrusion the movements of which propel unicellular organisms, zoospores, etc., through water; a flagellum is similar to a cilium (which see) but is longer.

Florigen: a name given to a hypothetical substance believed to be associated with flower initiation.

Flower: the characteristic reproductive structure of angiosperms, interpreted morphologically as a specialized branch system.

Flower bud: a bud that grows into a flower.

Food: an organic substance that furnishes energy for vital processes or is transformed into living protoplasm and cell walls.

Food web: the nutritional relationships among organisms within an ecosystem; food chain.

Foot: in mosses, liverworts, ferns, and other plant groups, a portion of a young sporophyte that attaches the sporophyte to the gametophyte and often absorbs food from the latter.

Formation: a large natural assemblage of plants, such as tundra or coniferous forest.

Fossil: the imprint or remains of an organism in the earth's crust.

Fragmentation: a type of asexual reproduction involving the separation of several- to many-celled pieces from a multicellular organism.

Free energy: that molecular energy which is available to do work; in diffusion, the energy that moves molecules from place to place.

Fruit: a matured ovary, or cluster of matured ovaries.

Fruit scar: the scar left on a twig after separation of the fruit.

Fucoxanthin: a brown, xanthophyll pigment found in brown algae.

Funiculus: stalk that attaches an ovule to the inner portions of an ovary.

Gametangium: a structure bearing gametes.

Gamete: a cell that fuses with another cell in sexual reproduction—usually an egg with a sperm.

Gametophyte: the gamete-producing phase in alternation of generations, characterized by the haploid chromosome number. See Sporophyte.

Gel: jellylike colloidal system.

Gemma: an asexual or vegetative outgrowth of a parent body, capable of growing into a new individual directly, as in liverworts.

Gene: a hereditary determiner, located on a chromosome.

Gene pool: all the genes of an interbreeding population.

Generative cell: the cell that, upon division, forms sperms in a pollen tube.

Genome: the gene complement of an organism.

Genotype: the genetic constitution of an organism.

Genus: a group of closely related species.

Germination: the sprouting of a seed, spore, zygote, or other reproductive body.

Gibberellins: a class of growth-regulating compounds.

Gill: flattened, spore-producing plates on underside of mushroom caps.

Girdling: the removal of a ring of bark from a portion of a stem.

Glucose: a 6-carbon sugar; also called grape sugar.

Glycolysis: an early stage in respiration in which pyruvic acid is produced from a sugar.

Grafting: the joining of two plant parts, usually stems, so that their tissues grow together.

Grana: small, chlorophyll-bearing bodies found in chloroplasts.

Gravitational water: water that moves downward through soil as a result of the earth's gravitational force upon it.

Ground meristem: meristematic tissue that develops into pith and cortex.

Growth layer: a layer of secondary xylem or phloem produced (ordinarily) in a single growing season.

Growth ring: a growth layer seen in cross section.

Guanine: one of the nitrogenous bases found in DNA and RNA.

Guard cells: paired epidermal chlorophyllous cells that enclose stomata.

Guttation: the exudation of liquid water from plants.

Gymnosperm: a plant having its seeds not enclosed in an ovary, as in the pines and their relatives (e.g., Coniferophyta).

Halophyte: a plant that grows in alkali soils or salt marshes.

Haploid: referring to the single chromosome number, characteristic of the gametophyte generation.

Hardening: the treatment of plants in such a manner as to increase their hardiness.

Hardiness: the ability of plants to withstand low temperatures.

Hardwood. the wood on angiosperms.

Haustorium: in parasitic plants, rootlike structure that penetrates host tissues and cells and absorbs food from them.

Heartwood: the inner growth layers that are non-conducting and contain no living cells; heartwood is usually darker than sapwood.

Hemicellulose: the non-cellulosic, carbohydrate constituents of cell walls.

Herb: a plant that does not develop much woody tissue and thus remains soft and succulent.

Herbaceous: describing an herb (which see).

Herbivorous: describing animals that eat plants.

Heredity: the tendency of an organism to resemble its parents.

Heterocyst: a cell in an algal filament that separates from other cells, causing the filament to separate into hormogonia (which see).

Heteroecism: in rust fungi, the completion of the life cycle upon two kinds of host plants.

Heterogametes: gametes that differ in size, structure, and behavior.

Heterogamy: sexual reproduction by gametes differing in size, structure, and behavior.

Heterosis: hybrid vigor; a type of increased vigor that often occurs in an organism that is the off-spring of parents of different inbred lines, varieties, or species.

Heterosporous: producing spores of two types.

Heterothallic: describing a sexual condition in which an individual produces only one kind of gamete; used chiefly in reference to algae and fungi.

Heterotrophic: referring to organisms that are unable to make their food and are thus parasites or saprophytes.

Heterozygous: referring to a condition in which the members of a gene pair are dissimilar.

Hilum: scar on a seed coat, marking the place of attachment of the seed stalk to the seed.

Holdfast: basal portion of a thallus that anchors it to a solid object in water.

Homologous chromosomes: the members of a chromosome pair.

Homosporous: producing spores of a single type.

Homothallic: describing a sexual condition in which an individual produces two kinds of gametes. See Heterothallic.

Homozygous: referring to a gene pair in which both genes are identical. See Heterozygous.

Hormogonia: reproductive segments of algal filaments.

Hormones: organic substances that are produced by living organisms and that regulate various growth and developmental processes.

Host: a plant or animal that affords nourishment to a parasite.

Humus: in soils, dark-colored organic matter resulting from the decomposition of plants and consisting chiefly of cellulose and lignin derivatives.

Hybrid: a plant or animal that is the offspring of parents differing in one or more traits; also used for the offspring resulting from a cross between two species.

Hybrid vigor: see Heterosis.

Hybridization: the production of hybrids by interbreeding parents of different types or species.

Hydathode: epidermal glands, through which drops of water are exuded.

Hydrolysis: transformation of a compound into a simpler compound, involving the uptake of water; digestion is a process of hydrolysis.

Hydrophyte: a plant that lives in water or exceedingly wet soils.

Hydroponics: the growth of plants in aqueous solutions of nutrient chemicals.

Hypertrophy: an abnormally large growth, resulting usually from a disease.

Hypha: a fungous filament.

Hypocotyl: the portion of an embryo axis below the attachment of the cotyledons; the root meristem is situated at the tip of the hypocotyl.

Hypogyny: a condition in which the ovary of a flower surmounts a receptacle, and in which the sepals, petals, and stamens are attached below the ovary.

Imbibition: the process by which solid (chiefly colloidal) particles absorb liquids and swell.

Imperfect flower: a flower that bears stamens or carpels but not both.

Inbreeding: breeding of closely related individuals or races; used in plant breeding to obtain homozygous condition.

Incomplete dominance: in inheritance, a condition in which neither member of a pair of contrasting characters masks the other.

Incomplete flower: a flower that lacks one or more of the four kinds of floral organs. See Complete flower.

Independent assortment: a genetic principle, established by Mendel, that the factors (genes) representing two or more contrasting pairs of characteristics are segregated to gametes independently of each other in meiosis, following which the gametes combine at random with each other.

Indeterminate growth: the continued production of lateral organs through the activity of a terminal meristem.

Indoleacetic acid: an organic compound belonging to the auxin class of growth-regulating substances.

Inducers: substances which activate portions of the DNA message to trigger production of needed proteins.

Indusium: the membranous cover of a fern sorus.

Inferior ovary: See Epigyny.

Inflorescence: a flower cluster.

Insectivorous: insect-eating or insect-digesting.

Integument: the coat of an ovule.

Interfascicular cambium: cambium situated between vascular bundles.

Internode: the length of stem between two successive nodes.

Interphase: the condition of a nucleus not undergoing mitosis.

Inulin: a white, complex carbohydrate very similar to starch.

Ion: an electrified particle formed by the dissociation of molecules of certain substances called electrolytes.

Ion accumulation: absorption of ions against a concentration gradient as a result of expenditure of energy by living cells. See Active transport.

Irritability: the ability of living protoplasm to receive stimuli and to react to them.

Isogametes: gametes that are alike in size, structure, and often in behavior.

Isogamy: sexual reproduction by isogametes.

Karyogamy: the fusion of two nuclei.

Karyokinesis: nuclear division; see Mitosis.

Knot: the buried base of a branch in a larger branch or tree trunk.

Lamellae: membranaceous, flattened vesicles or sacs, small stacks of which constitute grana.

Lamina: the expanded portion or blade of the leaf.

Lateral bud: an axillary bud.

Lateral meristem: usually cylindrical sheets of meristematic tissue along the length of root or shoot, concerned with secondary growth.

Leaching: the removal of solutes from soil by flowing or percolating water.

Leaf: A plant organ, typically expanded and attached to a stem at a node, serving principally for photosynthesis.

Leaf axil: the upper angle between a leaf petiole and the stem from which it grows.

Leaf bud: a bud that develops into a leafy shoot and does not produce flowers.

Leaf gap: a break in the vascular cylinder, caused by the branching of vascular tissue from the cylinder into a leaf.

Leaf primordium: an outgrowth that develops from the growing point of a bud and grows into a leaf.

Leaf scar: a scar left on a twig following the fall of a leaf.

Leaf trace: a branch of the vascular tissues of a stem, extending out into leaves.

Leaflet: one of the several blades of a compound leaf.

Lenticel: in woody stems (and other plant parts), a pore through which exchange of gases occurs; in woody stems, lenticels occur in bark.

Leucoplast: a colorless plastid involved in the formation of starch in many types of plant cells.

Lignification: impregnation of cell walls with lignin.

Lignin: an organic substance associated with cellulose in the cell walls, especially xylem, of many plants.

Linkage: the tendency for certain genes to remain together in inheritance because of their location on the same chromosome.

Locule: one of the cavities of an ovary.

Macronutrients: those essential elements required in relatively large quantities by plants.

Maturation: process of becoming mature; see Differentiation.

Megagametophyte: a female gametophyte resulting from the growth of a megaspore and producing female gametes or eggs.

Megasporangium: a sporangium that produces megaspores.

Megaspore: a spore, produced within a megasporangium, and forming a megagametophyte.

Megasporophyll: a leaf, or similar structure, which bears a megasporangium.

Meiosis: reduction division; a process in the sexual cycle by means of which chromosome numbers are reduced one half.

Meiospore: a spore developed from a cell which is a product of meiosis.

Meristem: a mass of growing cells, capable of frequent cell division.

Meristematic tissue: a tissue, the cells of which are capable of frequent division and which is thus responsible for the first phase of growth.

Mesocarp: middle layer of a fruit wall.

Mesophyll: the chlorophyllous leaf tissues between the epidermal layers.

Mesophytes: plants that are intermediate between hydrophytes and xerophytes—that is, that grow in soils containing moderate amounts of available moisture.

Messenger RNA: the RNA that carries coded information from the nucleus to the ribosomes where it mediates assembly of amino acids; mRNA.

Metabolism: the sum total of the chemical transformations occurring in the body of a living organism.

Metaphase: the stage in mitosis at which the chromosomes lie at the equator of the spindle.

Micelles: the solid particles dispersed in a colloidal system.

Microfibrils: aggregations of chainlike cellulose molecules into ultramicroscopic fibrils.

Microgametophyte: a male gametophyte resulting from the growth and development of a microspore.

Micronutrients: those essential elements required in only minute amounts by plants.

Micropyle: the minute opening in the integument of an ovule or seed, through which a pollen tube grows to reach the female gametophyte.

Microsporangium: a sporangium that produces microspores.

Microspore: a spore that grows into a male gametophyte.

Microsporophyll: a leaf, or similar structure, which bears microsporangia.

Microtubule: a submicroscopic, proteinaceous tubule found within the cytoplasm.

Middle lamella: the thin layer of intercellular cementing substance, composed chiefly of calcium pectate.

Mitochondria: granular or rod-shaped cytoplasmic bodies, functioning as centers of respiratory activity.

Mitosis: a process of nuclear division involving the duplication of chromosomes, the formation of a spindle, and the separation of chromosome halves to two daughter nuclei. Mitosis is usually, but not always, followed by cytokinesis (which see).

Mixed bud: a bud that produces both flowers and vegetative shoots.

Monocotyledonous: having one cotyledon in an embryo.

Monoecious: having staminate and pistillate flowers, or male and female gametangia, on the same plant.

Monohybrid cross: a cross between parents differing in a single character.

Mother cell: a cell that through cell division gives rise to new cells (daughter cells).

Mulch: material, such as straw, leaves, or paper, spread on a soil to retard water loss and weed growth, or to protect roots against cold, or to improve structure and fertility of the soil.

Mutation: a sudden, heritable change produced in the offspring of a parent organism as a result of an alteration in a gene or chromosome, or of an increase in chromosome number; also, the process by which such changes occur.

Mutualism: a form of symbiosis in which both organisms benefit.

Mycelium: the mass of hyphae forming the body of a true fungus.

Mycorrhiza: a symbiotic association of a fungus with the roots of higher plants.

Naked bud: a bud that is not protected by bud scales.

Nastic movements: growth movements of flattened organs, such as leaves and petals, as a result of differences in growth of cells on upper and lower surfaces of these organs.

Natural (self) pruning: the natural abscission of branches and twigs of woody plants.

Natural selection: the process that tends to cause "survival of the fittest" (survival of the organisms with the most advantageous variations for a given environment); an important feature of Darwin's theory of the causes of evolution.

Neck: the tapering portion of an archegonium; a sperm enters an archegonium through a canal extending lengthwise through the neck.

Nectary: a floral gland that secretes nectar, a sweetish liquid that insects obtain from flowers; rarely, nectaries occur on other parts.

Net venation: a scheme of vein arrangement in leaves, in which the veins branch frequently, forming a network.

Nitrification: the conversion of ammonia and ammonium compounds into nitrites and nitrates through bacterial action in soils.

Nitrogen fixation: the conversion of atmospheric, gaseous nitrogen into nitrogen compounds in soils or plant roots by certain bacteria and blue-green algae.

Node: a point on a stem from which a leaf and bud arise.

Nodule: on the roots of certain plants, an enlargement within which nitrogen-fixing bacteria live.

Nucellus: the megasporangium of an ovule, located inside the integument and enclosing the megagametophyte.

Nuclear envelope: the perforated limiting boundary of the nucleus, composed of two juxtaposed membranes and the intervening perinuclear space.

Nuclear membrane: a double membrane that surrounds the nuclear contents.

Nucleolus: a small, usually spherical body found within the nucleus of most kinds of cells.

Nucleotide: structural units of which nucleic acids are composed, each consisting of a sugar, a phosphate group, and a nitrogenous base.

Nucleus: a usually spherical or ovoid protoplasmic body found in most cells and considered as a directive center of many protoplasmic activities, including the transmission of hereditary charecteristics.

Obligate parasite: see Parasite.

Oil: a fatty substance that is liquid at room temperatures.

Ontogeny: the life history, or development, of an individual, as opposed to that (phylogeny) of the race.

Oogamy: a type of sexual reproduction involving a larger, non-motile egg and a smaller, motile sperm.

Oogonium: the female gametangium in certain thallophytes; an oogonium is one-celled and produces one or more eggs.

Operculum: the lid covering a moss capsule.

Opposite: bearing two leaves or two buds at a node on opposite sides of a stem.

Organ: one of the major parts of a plant body—leaf, stem, root. An organ is composed of tissues.

Organic matter (in soils): materials derived from the decomposition of dead organisms and of their wastes.

Organism: a living plant or animal.

Osmosis: the diffusion of water through a differentially permeable membrane from a region of high water concentration to a region of lower water concentration.

Osmotic concentration: the concentration of osmotically active particles in a solution.

Osmotic potential: a lowering of the free energy of water in the presence of solutes, relative to that of pure water at the same temperature; this represents the maximum osmotic effect that can be exerted by the water molecules when the solution is in an osmotic (membrane) system.

Osmotic pressure: the maximum pressure that can be developed in a solution that is separated from pure water by a rigid membrane permeable only to water.

Ovary: the basal, enlarged portion of a pistil, within which seeds develop.

Ovule: a structure consisting of a female gametophyte, nucellus, and integuments, which develops after fertilization into a seed.

Palisade tissue: a leaf tissue composed of long, cylindrical chlorophyllous cells.

Palmately veined: a type of net venation in which the main veins of a leaf blade branch out from the apex of the petiole like the fingers of a hand.

Parallel evolution: evolution in a similar direction in different groups of organisms.

Parallel venation: a type of leaf venation, in which the principal veins are parallel with each other and to the longitudinal axis of the leaf.

Parasite: a heterotrophic organism that derives its food from the living tissues of another organism; a facultative parasite is one that can obtain its food parasitically or saprophytically; an obligate parasite can obtain food only from the living tissues of a host.

Parenchyma: a tissue composed of thin-walled, often isodiametric cells, which often store food or perform other functions and which usually retain meristematic potentialities.

Parthenocarpy: the development of a fruit without pollination.

Parthenogenesis: the development of an egg into a new individual without fertilization by a sperm.

Passive transport: movement of solute molecules by diffusion.

Passive water absorption: the principal means of water uptake in a plant, initiated by the evaporation and subsequent loss of water from the plant's aerial parts.

Pasteurization: treatment of substances with moderately high temperatures for brief periods to kill certain bacteria.

Pathogen: an organism that causes a disease in another organism.

Pectic substances: complex organic compounds found chiefly in the middle lamella.

Peduncle: the stalk of a solitary flower, or the main stalk of an inflorescence.

Perennial: a plant that lives for more than two years.

Perfect flower: a flower that bears both stamens and carpels.

Perforation plate: the end wall of a vessel member where one or more perforations occurs.

Perianth: the floral envelope, i.e., calyx and corolla.

Pericarp: the wall of a ripened ovary (fruit).

Pericycle: in roots and some stems, a layer (or layers) of cells immediately outside the phloem and inside the endodermis.

Periderm: a collective name for cork, cork cambium, and phelloderm, a tissue found on the inner surface of the cork cambium.

Perigyny: a condition in flowers in which the petals and stamens are usually fused with the calyx and in which the pistil is seated in a concave receptacle.

Peristome: a ring of teeth surrounding the opening of a moss capsule and by its hygroscopic movements scattering the spores.

Permanent wilting percentage: the amount of water in the soil at the time plants become permanently wilted.

Petal: one of the structural units of a corolla.

Petiole: a leaf stalk.

Phellem: cork.

Phelloderm: a secondary tissue produced by the cork cambium and found on the inner surface of the cork cambium; cork parenchyma.

Phellogen: the lateral meristem which produces the periderm; also called the cork cambium.

Phenotype: the external, visible appearance of an organism.

Phloem: a complex tissue that, in flowering plants, consists chiefly of sieve tube members, companion cells, parenchyma, and fibers; the chief function of phloem is food conduction.

Photolysis: a photochemical process that cleaves water molecules into [H] and [OH] fragments.

Photoperiod: the relative duration of night and day to which plants are exposed.

Photosynthesis: the fundamental process of food manufacture in nature.

Phototropism: a growth movement induced by the stimulus of light.

Phylogeny: the history of a plant or animal group in relation to other groups; the study of "family trees." See Ontogeny.

Phytochrome: a photosensitive protein pigment that influences flowering, germination, and other physiological processes.

Pigment: a colored compound, such as chlorophyll.

Pileus: the umbrellalike cap of a mushroom.

Pinnae: the primary subdivisions of a fern frond.

Pinnately veined: a type of net venation in which the secondary veins branch out in parallel fashion from the single midrib of a leaf blade.

Pistil: the ovule-producing part of a flower, consisting of a carpel (simple pistil) or of two or more partly or wholly fused carpels (compound pistil).

Pit: a recess or thin place in the secondary wall of a cell.

Pit-pair: two complementary pits of adjacent cells.

Pith: parenchyma tissue occupying the central portion of a stem inside the xylem.

Placenta: a small mass of ovary tissue to which a seed stalk is attached.

Placentation: the arrangement of placentae within an ovary.

Plant formation: see Formation.

Plasma membrane: the membrane delimiting the outer surface of the protoplast.

Plasmodesmata: fine protoplasmic connections between cells.

Plasmodium: the naked protoplasmic mass of a slime fungus.

Plasmogamy: the fusion of two protoplasts.

Plasmolysis: shrinkage of protoplasm due to water loss.

Plastids: cytoplasmic bodies involved in food synthesis, storage, etc.

Polar nuclei: the (two) nuclei that fuse with a sperm within the embryo sac to form a triploid endosperm nucleus.

Pollen grains: young male gametophytes of seed plants.

Pollen tube: a tube that is formed by a pollen grain and that transports sperms to the eggs in ovules. A pollen grain and its mature tube are a male (micro-) gametophyte.

Pollination: the transfer of pollen grains from a stamen or microsporophyll to a stigma or ovule.

Polyploid: having more than two sets of chromosomes.

Polysome: a chainlike aggregation of ribosomes.

Preprophase band: a transitory, peripheral band of microtubules that appears in the cytoplasm just prior to prophase.

Primary root: the root that develops directly from the hypocotyl of an embryo.

Primary tissue: tissue developed by an apical meristem during growth in length.

Primary wall: cell wall layer lying next to middle lamella, or intercellular layer.

Primordium: the rudiment or beginning of a part.

Procambium: meristematic tissue from which primary phloem and primary xylem are derived.

Progressive evolution: evolution from simple toward more complex and more highly specialized structures.

Promeristem: the distal, least-determined portion of an apical meristem.

Prophase: an early stage in mitosis in which the chromosomes became distinct and in which the nuclear membrane disappears.

Protective layer: a layer of suberized cells formed beneath the abscission layer.

Proteins: complex, organic, nitrogenous substances, built up from amino acids and constituting the major portion of the organic materials in living protoplasm.

Prothallus (prothallium): the gametophyte of ferns and similar plants.

Protoderm: meristematic tissue formed by a terminal meristem and developing into epidermis.

Protonema: a branching filament forming an early stage in the gametophyte generation of a moss.

Protoplasm: the living substance in the cells of plants and animals.

Protoplast: the living component of a single cell.

Pycnia: flask-shaped spore-producing structures of certain rust fungi.

Pycniospores: small, haploid spores produced by pycnia.

Pyrenoid: centers of starch formation on certain chloroplasts, especially of algae.

Quiescence: a rest period caused by external conditions unfavorable to germination or growth.

Rachis: the continuation of the petiole of a frond or leaf that bears the pinnae or leaflets.

Radial section: a section of a stem or root cut longitudinally on a radius.

Radial symmetry: a type of floral symmetry in which the flower may be separated into two approximately equal halves by a longitudinal cut in any plane passing through the center of the flower; that is, a flower built upon a wheel plan, rather than on a right-and-left plan. *Example:* rose.

Radicle: the lower portion of the hypocotyl that grows into the primary root of a seedling; the root primordium of an embryo.

Raphe: the ridge formed by the fusion of the seed stalk with the seed coat.

Ray: the corolla of a marginal flower of a composite inflorescence; also, a vascular ray.

Receptacle: the terminal portion of a pedicel (or peduncle) upon which the floral parts are borne; also, the inflated tips of certain brown algae within which gametangia are borne.

Recessive: one of a pair of contrasting characters that is masked, when both are present, by the other, or dominant, character; also refers to the genes determining such characters.

Repressors: substances which inactivate portions of the DNA message to stop protein production.

Reproduction: the formation of offspring.

Resins: sticky to brittle plant products derived from essential oils and often possessing marked odors; used in varnishes, incense, medicines, etc.

Respiration: chemical oxidative processes whereby living protoplasm breaks down certain organic substances with the release of energy that is used in growth, movements, etc.

Retrogressive evolution: evolution from a structurally complex or specialized condition toward a simpler, less specialized condition.

Rhizoid: in some fungi, mosses, liverworts, etc., hairlike appendages that penetrate the soil or other substratum, anchoring the plant and absorbing water and other substances.

Rhizome: a horizontal underground stem, often enlarged by food storage.

Rhizosphere: the thin envelope of soil immediately surrounding and contacting the growing tips of roots.

Ribose nucleic acid (RNA): a nucleic acid found in the nucleus and cytoplasm; plays a major role in protein synthesis.

Ribose: a 5-carbon sugar; one of the components of RNA.

Ribosomal RNA: RNA that functions as a structural component of the ribosome.

Ribosomes: minute cytoplasmic bodies that function as centers of synthesis of cytoplasmic proteins.

Ring-porous wood: wood in which the pores (vessels) of one part of a growth ring are distinctly different in size or number (or both) from those in the other part of the ring.

RNA: see Ribonucleic acid.

Root: a plant organ, commonly below ground, comprising that portion of the plant axis which serves typically to anchor the plant and for absorption of water and nutrients.

Root cap: a thimblelike mass of cells that fits over the apical meristem of a root and protects it.

Root hair: an absorptive extension from a root epidermal cell.

Root pressure: a pressure developed in roots as a result of active water absorption.

Root system: the total mass of roots of a single plant.

Runner: a stem that grows horizontally over the surface of the soil, often developing new plants at its nodes.

Saprophyte: a heterotrophic plant that derives its food from nonliving organic matter.

Sapwood: the young, physiologically active wood of a tree, consisting in part of living cells and comprising the usually light-colored, outermost growth layers.

Scarification: mechanical breaking of the seed coat to promote germination.

Scion: a detached shoot used in grafting; the shoot that receives a scion is called the stock.

Sclereid: a thick-walled, often slightly elongated or irregularly shaped sclerenchyma cell.

Sclerenchyma: a tissue composed of thick-walled, elongated cells (fibers) or shorter cells (sclereids).

Secondary root: a branch of a primary root.

Secondary tissues: tissues arising from a lateral or secondary meristem such as the cambium or cork cambium, and increasing the diameter of a stem or root.

Secondary wall: the cell wall layer deposited by protoplasm upon the primary wall layer, after cell enlargement is completed.

Seed: the characteristic reproductive structure of seed plants, consisting of an embryo, enclosed by a seed coat, and a food storage tissue. In some species, the storage tissue is absorbed by the embryo before the seed reaches maturity.

Seed scarification: cutting or scratching a seed coat to facilitate the entry of water or oxygen.

Segregation: a genetic principle, established by Mendel, that the factors (or genes) of a pair are separated from each other in reduction division.

Selection: the process of isolating and preserving certain individuals or characters from a group of individuals or characters.

Self-fertility: a condition in which sexual reproduction occurs as a result of the fusion of eggs and sperms produced by the same individual.

Self-pollination: the transfer of pollen from the stamen to the stigma of the same flower, or of another flower on the same plant.

Self-sterility: a condition in which sexual reproduction cannot be achieved by the fusion of eggs and sperms produced by the same individual.

Semipermeable: same as differentially permeable (which see).

Sepals: the divisions of a calyx; the outermost floral organs.

Separation layer: see Abscission layer.

Sessile: lacking a stalk.

Seta: in mosses and liverworts, the stalk that supports the capsule of the sporophyte.

Sex chromosomes: chromosomes that determine sex.

Sex linkage: the occurrence on sex chromosomes of genes that determine characters other than sex.

Sexual: a type of reproduction in which both fertilization and meiosis are involved.

Shoot: a stem with its leaves.

Shrub: a woody plant with several stems arising from the root system.

Sieve area: a generally discrete cluster of sieve pores.

Sieve cell: a phloem-conducting cell with perforations not restricted to end walls; does not occur in series or tubes.

Sieve plate: the perforated wall or wall portion of a sieve tube member.

Sieve pore: an opening in the end wall of a sieve tube member.

Sieve tube: a series of sieve tube members arranged in end-to-end fashion.

Sieve tube member: one cell of a sieve tube; sieve tube members usually have their sieve areas on the end walls.

Simple fruit: a fruit developed from the single ovary of a flower.

Sleep movements: turgor movements of plants initiated by changes in light intensity.

Softwood: the wood of gymnosperms; a wood lacking wood fibers.

Soil solution: the water, with dissolved substances, in the soil.

Sol: a liquid colloidal system.

Solute: a dissolved substance.

Solvent: the substance in which a solute is dissolved.

Soredia: asexual reproductive structures of some lichens; each soredium consists of a small mass of fungal mycelium and a few associated algal cells.

Sorus: a cluster of sporangia on a fern sporophyte.

Speciation: the evolutionary formation of new species.

Species: usually the smallest unit in the classification of organisms; a group of individuals of the same ancestry, of nearly identical structure and behavior, and of relative stability in nature; the individuals of a species ordinarily interbreed freely and maintain themselves and their characteristics in nature.

Sperm: male gamete.

Sphaerosomes: small, cytoplasmic granules to 1 micron in diameter, containing lipids and proteins.

Spindle: the ovoid mass of fine fibrils (spindle fibers) formed in a cell during mitosis.

Spongy tissue: a leaf tissue composed of loosely packed, chlorophyllous cells of diverse form.

Sporangiophore: a structure that bears one or more sporangia.

Sporangium: a spore case.

Spore: an asexual reproductive structure, commonly unicellular and usually produced in a sporangium.

Spore mother cell: a cell that, by cell divisions, produces typically four spores.

Sporophore: a spore-bearing structure, for example, a mushroom.

Sporophyll: a spore-bearing leaf.

Sporophyte: the spore-producing phase in alternation of generations, characterized by the diploid chromosome number.

Springwood: the xylem of a growth layer formed in the early part of a growing season and consisting typically of cells that are larger than those formed later in the season.

Stamen: pollen-producing structure of a flower; a modified microsporophyll.

Starch: white, complex, water-insoluble carbohydrate that is a common storage food in plants.

Stem: a plant organ, commonly above ground, comprising that portion of the plant axis to which leaves and reproductive parts are attached.

Stem pressure: the positive pressure produced under certain conditions in the stems of some plants (for example, maple) and responsible for the exudation of sap from their stems.

Sterilization: the reduction or loss of sexual structures or processes in an individual or race; also, the destruction of bacteria, spores, etc. through the use of light, high temperature, etc.

Stigma: the part of a pistil, usually the apex, that receives pollen and upon which pollen grains germinate.

Stimulus: an environmental factor or change that induces a reaction in a living organism.

Stipe: a stalk, as the stalk of a mushroom, or a brown alga.

Stipule: one of a pair of small appendages borne at the base of a leaf in many species of plants.

Stock: in a graft, the basal portion of a stem, upon which a scion is grafted; also, a stem, or a race or group of genetically similar organisms.

Stolon: a runner (which see).

Stoma: a pore, controlled by guard cells, in the epidermis of a leaf, or other plant parts.

Stone cells: thick-walled, isodiametric, sclerenchyma cells.

Stratification: the layering that results from differences in size of mature plants in a community.

Strobilus: a conelike collection of sporophylls borne on a stem axis.

Stroma: a mass of hyphae bearing reproductive structures.

Style: in flowers, a cylindrical structure that rises from the top of an ovary and through which pollen tubes grow.

Suberin: a fatty, waterproof substance deposited in the walls of certain types of cells, such as cork cells.

Succession: the orderly sequence of differing types of vegetation in a given region.

Sucrose: cane sugar.

Summerwood: the xylem of a growth layer formed late in the growing season and consisting of cells smaller than those of springwood.

Superior ovary: an ovary borne above the points of origin of sepals and petals from a receptacle.

Suspension: a dispersion system in which particles of a solid are distributed in a liquid; e.g., soil particles in water.

Suspensor: a structure in the embryo sporophyte of higher plants, which attaches or forces the embryo into food storage tissue.

Synapsis: the pairing of homologous chromosomes in meiosis.

Synergids: two small cells lying near the egg at micropylar end of the embryo sac in an ovule.

Tangential section: a section of a cylindrical organ, such as a stem, cut lengthwise and at right angles to a radius of the organ.

Tannin: a bitter, astringent, organic substance found in certain plant tissues, such as bark, heartwood, and others.

Tap root system: a root system in which there is a primary root distinctly larger and more conspicuous than any of its branches. Contrast diffuse root system.

Taxon (pl. Taxa): any of the various taxonomic groups, such as a family, genus, or species.

Telia: rust fungus pustules containing teliospores.

Teliospores: dark-colored spores produced in telia; "winter spores."

Telophase: the final stage in mitosis in which the two sets of chromosomes are organized into daughter nuclei, and processes leading to the formation of a cell plate separating the daughter nuclei are initiated.

Tendril: a slender, coiling structure that aids in the support of plant stems; a tendril may be a modified stem, leaf, leaflet, or stipule.

Terminal bud: the bud located at the apex of a stem or twig.

Testa: seed coat, developed from the integument(s) of an ovule.

Tetrad: a group of four cells (usually spores) produced by two divisions of a mother cell.

Tetraploid: having four sets of chromosomes, that is, four times the haploid number.

Thallus: a simple plant body with relatively little cellular differentiation and lacking true roots, stems, and leaves; characteristic of algae, fungi, liverworts, etc.

Thymine: one of the nitrogenous bases found in DNA.

Tissue: an aggregation of cells, usually of similar structure, that perform the same or related functions.

Tonoplast: vacuolar membrane.

Toxin: poisonous secretion of a living organism.

Trace elements: see Micronutrients.

Tracheid: a type of nonperforate conducting and strengthening cell in xylem tissue, of elongated, tapering form and with pitted walls.

Transcription: transfer of coded information from DNA to RNA.

Transduction: transfer of genetic information from one bacterial strain to another by a viral carrier (bacteriophage).

Transfer RNA: the RNA molecules that bring specific amino acids to the ribosomes for protein synthesis; tRNA.

Transformation: change in the genetic constitution of a bacterial strain that has resulted from incorporation of DNA which has diffused through the culture medium from bacteria of another strain.

Translation: assembly of tRNA-borne amino acids into protein molecules in sequences determined by the genetic code as transcribed to mRNA.

Translocation: the conduction of materials within a plant.

Transpiration: the diffusion of water vapor from aerial parts of plants, chiefly through leaf stomata.

Transverse section: a section of a stem or other part cut at right angles to its longitudinal axis.

Tree: a woody, perennial plant with a single main stem (trunk) that rises some distance aboveground before it branches.

Triploid: having three sets of chromosomes, that is, three times the haploid number.

Tropic level: any given position within a food web.

Tropism: a blending movement of a cylindrical organ or other cylindrical structure, caused by differences in growth rate in different parts of the organ and induced by external stimuli.

Trunk: the single main stem of a tree.

Tube nucleus: one of the nuclei in a pollen tube, influencing the growth and behavior of the tube.

Tuber: enlarged, fleshy, underground stem, commonly borne at the end of a rhizome.

Tundra: a plant formation (or biome) of subarctic regions, which has permanently frozen subsoil and a low vegetation of lichens, dwarf hardy herbs, and shrubs.

Turgidity: state of being plump or swollen as a result of internal water pressure.

Turgor: the pressure exerted by the cell contents against the cell wall.

Turgor movements: plant movements resulting from changes of water pressure in certain tissues.

Turgor pressure: pressure developed by water present in plant cells.

Twiner: a plant that climbs by the twining movements of its stems about a support.

Tylosis: a growth from a parenchyma cell through a pit into the cavity of a xylem vessel or tracheid.

Unisexual: describing an organism that produces eggs or sperms, but not both, or a flower that bears stamens or pistils, but not both.

Unit character: a genetic principle, established by Mendel, that the various characters making up an individual are controlled in inheritance by independent determining factors.

Uracil: one of the nitrogenous bases found in RNA.

Uredia: rust fungus pustules containing urediospores.

Urediospores: reddish spores produced in uredia; "summer spores."

Vacuole: a cavity within the protoplasm containing a watery solution of sugars and other substances.

Variation: in an organism, difference in structural or physiological characters from those typical or common in the species to which the organism belongs.

Vascular bundle: a strand of conducting and strengthening tissues (xylem and phloem) in a plant organ.

Vascular cambium: the lateral meristem which produces secondary xylem and phloem.

Vascular cylinder: the central column of conducting and storage tissues of the plant axis, delimited externally by the endodermis; the central cylinder.

Vascular ray: a ribbonlike aggregate of cells extending radially in stems through the xylem and the phloem.

Vegetative reproduction: asexual reproduction by a root, stem, leaf, or some other primarily vegetative part of a plant body.

Vein: one of the vascular bundles of a leaf, petal, or other plant part.

Venation: the arrangement of the vascular bundles in a leaf.

Venter: the enlarged base of an archegonium within which an egg develops.

Vernalization: the brief exposure to low temperatures required by some plants in order to induce flower formation.

Vessel: a conducting tube in xylem tissue.

Vessel member: at maturity, a perforate, nonliving xylem cell; one segment of a vessel.

Viability: the ability to live and grow; applied usually to seeds and spores.

Vitamin: organic substances synthesized by plants and necessary in minute quantities for certain respiratory and developmental processes.

Whorl: a circle of parts, such as leaves.

Whorled: having several parts arranged in a circle at the same level; commonly applied to the condition in which three or more leaves occur at a node.

Wood: technically, xylem; popularly, the xylem of trees and shrubs.

Xerophyte: a plant that grows in soils with scanty water supply, or in soils in which water is absorbed only with difficulty.

Xylem: a complex plant vascular tissue, composed of such cells as tracheids, vessel members, wood fibers, ray cells, and parenchyma cells; wood.

Zoospores: spores that are enabled to swim by movements of cilia or flagella.

Zygote: a fertilized egg; a cell arising from the fusion of gametes.

INDEX

INDEX